Eating Words

Eating Words

A Norton Anthology of

Food Writing

Edited by

Sandra M. Gilbert & Roger J. Porter

With a Foreword by Ruth Reichl

W. W. NORTON & COMPANY

Independent Publishers Since 1923

NEW YORK • LONDON

For information about special discounts for bulk purchases, please contact
W. W. Norton Special Sales at specialsales@wwnorton.com or 800-233-4830

Manufacturing by RR Donnelley Westford
Book design by Brooke Koven
Production manager: Julia Druskin

Library of Congress Cataloging-in-Publication Data

Eating words : a Norton anthology of food writing / edited by
Sandra M. Gilbert & Roger J. Porter ; with a
foreword by Ruth Reichl.
pages cm
Includes bibliographical references and index.
ISBN 978-0-393-23984-3 (hardcover)
1. Gastronomy—History—Sources. 2. Food in literature. 3. Food writing.
I. Gilbert, Sandra M. II. Porter, Roger J., 1936–
TX631.E376 2015
641.01′3—dc23
2015017219

W. W. Norton & Company, Inc.
500 Fifth Avenue, New York, N.Y. 10110
www.wwnorton.com

W. W. Norton & Company Ltd.
Castle House, 75/76 Wells Street, W1T 3QT

1 2 3 4 5 6 7 8 9 0

To the memory of Robert Reynolds,
food guru, inspired teacher, and gastro-wit.
And to Vitaly and Kimberly Paley,
whose great restaurant, Paley's Place,
as been the site of enduring memories.

—RJP

In memory of my beloved grandfather,
Amedeé Mortola, a consummate artist of the kitchen,
and my husband, Elliot L. Gilbert,
cook of a lifetime.

—SMG

ACKNOWLEDGMENTS

WE are grateful to many people who helped make this book happen. In particular, we both want to thank our agent, Ellen Levine, and her assistant Alexa Stark, and, with the same fervor, our editor, Jill Bialosky, and her assistants Rebecca Schulz and Angie Shih. All did much to guide us through the complexities of anthologizing while encouraging our travels in the delicious realm of the culinary imagination.

In addition, Sandra Gilbert wants to thank both the Camargo Foundation and the Bogliasco Foundation for homes-away-from-home during which she could meditate on meals, menus, Brillat-Savarin, and other kitchen philosophies. And just as passionately, she wants to thank all those in her life who help her cook and think, especially her longtime collaborator, Susan Gubar, her traveling companion, Albert Magid, and her amazingly gastronomic children, daughters-in-law, and grandchildren: Roger Gilbert, Gina Campbell, Kathy Gilbert-O'Neil, Robin Gilbert-O'Neil, Susanna Gilbert, Val Gilbert, Aaron Gilbert-O'Neil, Stefan Gilbert-O'Neil, and Sophia Gilbert.

Roger Porter wants to thank Jennifer Ash for her constant interest and subtle ear. And he is grateful for research and travel support given by Reed College.

In addition, we both want to express our gratitude to Ruth Reichl for giving our book such a wonderful foreword, and want to thank our editorial assistant, Jeffrey Scott Blevins, for his energy, perseverance, and dedication to this project. Merely assembling (and getting permissions for) all the words in *Eating Words* would not have been possible without his intelligence and diligence.

Finally, we both want to say how much we've enjoyed working together on this book. Our collaboration has given us each personal delight and intellectual excitement as well as the culinary pleasure of many shared meals.

CONTENTS

II•‒ AT THE FAMILY HEARTH:
Memory, Identity, Ethnicity

III•— HUNGER GAMES:
The Delight and Dread of Eating

IV•– KITCHEN PRACTICES:
Chefs, Cooks, and Tools of the Trade

V•— CULTURAL TALES AND TABLES:
Our Diverse Gastronomic Ways

VI•– FOOD POLITICS:
Disputes Over the Menu

VII•— READING FOOD WRITING:
The Language of Taste

FOREWORD

Ruth Reichl

ASK MOST modern American food writers why they've chosen food as their subject, and you're likely to get a quote from Mary Frances Fisher. It comes from the introduction to *The Art of Eating*.

People ask me: Why do you write about food, and eating and drinking? Why don't you write about the struggle for power and security, and about love, the way others do?

They ask it accusingly, as if I were somehow gross, unfaithful to the honor of my craft.

The easiest answer is to say that, like most other humans, I am hungry. But there is more than that. It seems to me that our three basic needs, for food and security and love, are so mixed and mingled and entwined that we cannot straightly think of one without the others. So it happens that when I write of hunger I am really writing about love and the hunger for it, and warmth and the love of it and the hunger for it . . . and it is all one.

I used to quote that myself when I was trying to explain why I write about food. Now I wonder what possessed me to do that. They are lovely sentiments. They are also an apology.

Over the many years that I knew Mary Frances Fisher she often told me, "I am not a food writer." Indeed, if you read between the lines you realize that she was a bit embarrassed by her passion. And so in this famous passage she insists that food is not her true subject. "I am really," she promises, "writing about bigger things. . . ."

To understand why Fisher considered food too small a subject, why she worried about being "unfaithful to her craft," it helps to read her words in the context of her time. Food and cooking do not exist in a vacuum, and the way people write about what they eat always reflects the society in which they live. For that reason the changing language of food can be extremely revealing.

Consider, for example, the first piece of food writing that ever moved me.

"When you wake up in the morning, Pooh," said Piglet at last, "what's the first thing you say to yourself?"

"What's for breakfast?" said Pooh. "What do you say, Piglet?"

"I say, I wonder what's going to happen exciting today," said Piglet.

Pooh nodded thoughtfully. "It's the same thing," he said.

I must have been six when I first read those words, and they hit me with such force that I stopped to read them a second time. They were so different from the fairy tales to which I was accustomed. The others were also about food, but they contained witches who wanted to cook you, wolves who wanted to eat you, or apples that turned out to be poisoned. In Pooh's tale, food was your friend, and as someone who has always liked to eat I appreciated that. It wasn't until I grew up that I began to wonder why this particular story was so different from the ones that came before.

Alan Alexander Milne wrote *Winnie-the-Pooh* in 1926, and if you look at the England of the time, his attitude toward food becomes completely clear. The First World War had ended, the middle class was rising, and the entire country was beginning to liberate itself from the confines of a rigid Victorian culture that made the enjoyment of food almost impossible for almost everyone.

For poor people there had never been enough. The wealthy, on the other hand, suffered from the opposite extreme: there was too much of everything. Guests at a formal Victorian dinner were forced to wrangle with thirty-one different pieces of flatware, each with a specific purpose. Even those sitting down to lesser meals found themselves confronted by two large knives, a tablespoon for soup, three large forks, and a small silver fish knife and fork. Using the wrong utensil would instantly label one as an uneducated lout who did not belong in polite company.

You were meant to know when to use each fork and knife, and in what order to drink the liquids that filled the many glasses surrounding your plate. You needed to know that the large plate in front of you was for meat and the crescent one for salad, and that they were to be used at the same time. Should you end up with an unused implement at meal's end, your social life was over.

This wasn't dinner: it was an exam. And that was precisely its purpose: in the Victorian era food was a means of keeping the classes separate and preventing social mobility. It's easy to understand how a roly-poly little bear who considered eating a happy adventure turned into a national hero. *Winnie-the-Pooh* may be a children's book, but those few little lines about breakfast offer us a window into a rapidly changing society.

The truth is that you can enter history at almost any point and find out a great deal merely by listening to writers describing their meals.

Here's the Greek poet Philoxenus, around the year 400 BC—as quoted in *The Classical Cookbook*—telling his lover about a great feast he has just attended.

> A casserole full of a noble eel with a look of the conger about him,
> Honey glazed shrimps besides, my love,
> Squid sprinkled with sea-salt,
> Baby birds in flaky pastry,
> And a baked tuna, Gods! What a huge one, fresh from the fire
>   and the pan and the carving knife,
> Enough steaks from its tender belly to delight us both as long as
>   we might care to stay and munch.

Clearly these were happy eaters, people who enjoyed simple food and consumed it without a lot of fuss. Archestratus, who lived around the same time, was kind enough to leave us his recipe for preparing hare: "... bring the roast meat in and serve it to everyone while they are drinking: hot, simply sprinkled with salt, taking it from the spit while still a little rare."

Move forward a few centuries and you instantly see how much things had changed. Marcus Gavius Apicius was the great epicure of the first century. Of a mousse containing minced fish, eggs, oil, pepper, and rue, pressed into a pan and topped with a sea anemone before being steamed, he noted happily: "At table no one will know what he is eating."

And that, of course, was the point: by the time of Apicius, food was no longer simply roasted and sprinkled with salt. The Greek world had grown larger, and along with it, Greek appetites. When Alexander the Great went off on his journeys of conquest, he took botanists with him. It had the same explosive effect as the journey of Christopher Columbus: it changed the way the world ate. Just as Columbus introduced tomatoes to Italy, potatoes to Ireland, and chiles to India, Alexander returned bearing the hitherto unknown citrus, peaches, pistachios, and peacocks. All you need to do is read descriptions of the food to understand how profoundly Greek life had changed.

A similar cultural shift took place in Islamic society. Writers of the time tell us that Mohammad Mohammad would eat just about anything (except lizards, which he loathed), and that his followers did not presume to eat more elaborately than the Prophet. During his lifetime, food in the world of Islam was extremely simple. But as the center of the Muslim universe moved east a deeply epicurean tradition developed around "poems of the table."

At first these poems were simply meant to be recited during banquets, but they soon evolved into something much more complicated. The invitations to one famous banquet given by the caliph instructed each guest to memorize a famous poem praising a particular dish. As the meal progressed each guest stood to recite his poem. As he did so, the cooks rushed off to prepare the dish in the exact manner described in the poem.

The chefs were, apparently, unfazed; at the banquet describe by Al-Masudi in *Meadows of Gold*, the only poem that stumped the chefs was one in praise of asparagus. It was out of season; they had to send runners off to Damascus, and by the time the runners returned the banquet was over.

Reading the description of these feasts tells you more than any history book about the transformation of Islamic society. Clearly it no longer resembled the one in which Mohammad sat in the desert eating the simple dishes that were put before him.

The sheer unself-consciousness of these historical food writings is extremely appealing. The portraits they paint are almost accidental, but that does not reduce their power. This anthology offers a short but telling romp through the edible history of the world, beginning with the Bible and coming right up to the present day.

But fiction writers use food in an entirely different manner. They know there is no more effective means of telegraphing class, caste, and character. Put your heroine to bed with a couple of cream puffs, and people instantly make assumptions. Have her pop a pizza into the microwave for her kid's dinner, and we understand exactly who she is. To fiction writers and to poets as well, food is a marvelous tool, a quick verbal shortcut that can say a great deal in a very few words. Melville and Proust and Chekhov, and poets such as William Carlos Williams and Seamus Heaney—their selections in this book demonstrate how they have used food to devastating effect.

But writing about food does more than merely reflect culture and act in the service of art; it also has the ability to transform society. Nobody has ever recognized this so clearly as the French, who captured the haute cuisine high ground early on by writing about their food, publicizing their food, and using it as a kind of marketing strategy. They gave their food a national identity and sent it off to conquer the world.

The earliest French cookbook was the *Cuisinier français*. Published in 1651, the book proudly staked its claim to national identity. Plenty of previous cookbooks had been published in Europe—from the English Robert May's *The Accomplisht Cook* of 1588 to the Italian *Il Trinciante* (*The Carver*) of 1581—but none of them was stamped with a nationality.

The *Cuisinier français* was to have an enormous influence on cooking throughout the Western world. The English translation, which was published two years after the French version, remained in print for almost two hundred years. By then the French had claimed the language of cooking so effectively that we're still under its influence. Flip through any American cookbook (or walk through any supermarket), and you'll be stunned by how many of our foods have French names.

But we Americans have been slow to adopt the language of food. Even our best-loved national dishes—hamburgers, French fries, and pizza come immediately to mind—pay tribute to other tongues. Where are the American words?

Which brings us back to Ms. Fisher and her reluctant embrace of food writing. In her time, food was not considered a respectable subject. It was relegated to what were then called "the women's pages" of the newspaper. As recently as the seventies, Jacques Pépin, who was studying for a PhD in philosophy and literature at Columbia, proposed writing a doctoral thesis on the history of French food presented in the context of French literature. His adviser turned him down flat. "Cuisine," he pontificated, "is not a serious art form. It's far too trivial for academic study."

But as this book proves, things were about to change. Much of the wonderful writing you will find here was written in the past thirty years by people who took it extremely seriously. What does this say about our own society?

At first it might seem that this reflects a more benign attitude toward food. Look again; much of this writing, whether it is on culture, politics, or identity, reflects a deep malaise about what is taking place at our table. And with good reason: there has never been a time in human history when a population was so profoundly disconnected from its food supply. America was once an agrarian society, but the modern industrialization of food and farming has made us increasingly dependent upon others for our sustenance. We no longer grow our own food, and every year we rely more heavily on others to prepare what we consume. We now eat out so often that many people consider cooking an endangered art.

And yet the less we cook, the more we read about food; it as if we are desperate to reconnect in the only way we can. As a result, we are living in the golden age of food writing. I'm fairly certain that if Mary Frances Fisher were alive today, she would no longer feel the need to apologize. She might even be willing to call herself a food writer. And I'm sure that she would understand that in the modern world, food writing has become as necessary as food itself.

Introduction

A TOAST TO TASTE

AN ABC OF FOOD WRITING

"FOOD AND cooking," proclaimed the theologian and cookbook writer Robert Farrar Capon in 1989, "are not low subjects." Rather, he added, they are "among the richest subjects in the world. Every day of our lives, they preoccupy, delight, and refresh us." Indeed, he concluded, "Food, like all the other triumphs of human nature, is evidence of civilization." Composing a preface to the second edition of his best-selling *The Supper of the Lamb*, Capon was riding the crest of a wave of food writing that gathered strength throughout the twentieth century and into the twenty-first, and has turned into a tsunami of food memoirs ("foodoirs"), chef's bios, cookbooks, gourmet magazines, and culinary essays.

Capon's modern and modernist precursors, as we'll see in this anthology, include such notable figures as Alice B. Toklas and Ernest Hemingway, M.F.K. Fisher and A. J. Liebling. His contemporaries and descendants are equally distinguished: Calvin Trillin, Anthony Bourdain, Adam Gopnik, Michael Pollan—and on and on, as our table of contents reveals. And we might also number among them the writers of food films (*Babette's Feast, Like Water for Chocolate, Ratatouille, Big Night, Julie & Julia*) and food television shows (*Iron Chef, Molto Mario, Bizarre Foods, No Reservations*) along with the matriarch of such gastronomic "infotainment," the great Julia Child herself. But we might also include the authors of a little brightly colored cardboard children's book (aimed presumably at a preschool readership) titled *My Foodie ABC: A Little Gourmet's Guide.*

"Foodie: a person with an avid interest in the latest food fads." "Gourmet: A gourmet is a person who has sharp and refined tastes and is an expert in the art of food." Along with definitions of "chanterelles," "dragon fruit," "farmer's market," "jicama," and "locavore," these are just a few of the bits of wisdom that *My Foodie ABC* seeks to impart to hungry little cosmopolites. If they're watching *Iron Chef* or *Top Chef* as mom reads to them, so much the better. But with-it though they are, their fascination with food dates back not just to the chorus so famously sung in the sixties musical *Oliver!*—"Food, glorious food!"—but to much writing intended for what one critic has lately called "voracious children": *Charlie and the Chocolate Factory, Raggedy Ann and Andy in Cookie Land, Little House on the Prairie, Alice in Wonderland*, and, needless to say, such fairy tales as "Hansel and Gretel" and "Snow White." Children love rivers of ice cream, gingerbread houses, little cakes that say "Eat me," and even sometimes (to their sorrow) poisoned apples.

Can it be that, when we brood on food, glorious food, we are all children? We long for its deliciousness, fear it, taste it in our dreams, dream of its pleasures, and always, always write about it. For food evokes words; we enjoy speaking about food and taste almost as much as we enjoy eating itself. Indeed we can hardly eat without talking about it. *Eating words* may have been, after all, our earliest words. Consider the forbidden fruit in Eden! Consider also the secrets of fire stolen by the culture hero Prometheus, who made cooking possible! This collection of food writings focuses on contemporary "eating words" but finds its origins in biblical and classical times. We represent a passage from the Old Testament to dramatize the culinary choices and taboos that have always marked eating practices in cultures around the world. Just as ancient Jews were urged to forgo meat with milk and to renounce pork, Hindus were taught to abrogate beef, Muslims to renounce alcohol and pork, and Zoroastrians to subsist on raw vegetables. But similarly, classical Greeks were taught by Socrates and his disciple Plato to reject the *material* pleasures of eating. In the *Gorgias*, Plato reports Socrates declaring that "the art of cookery" is as low as "the art of rhetoric." It is to this view that Father Capon, the Episcopalian priest cum cookbook writer, responds when he insists that food and cooking are not "low subjects."

Historically, however, writers about food have been ambivalent. Cooks, usually women, have until the twentieth century been sequestered in kitchens, sometimes structures entirely separated from aristocratic households, sometimes basement bastions below bourgeois homes, and sometimes humble hearths in peasant cottages. Food itself, while a source of delight, also reminds us—as Plato noted—of our materiality. As human beings we both *have* and *are* bodies, and the food that enters so pleasurably between our lips exits, more degradingly, as excrement. Along with the great French gastronome Jean Anthelme Brillat-Savarin, we may extoll its spiritual pleasures—its insubstantial "taste." But, like Plato, we must concede its appeal to our animal nature. And although food writing has from the start been generically diverse, as we shall see throughout this anthology, such ambivalence toward eating and cooking has given the vast literature of gastronomy a special flavor. From the start—in Western culture going back to biblical and classical writers, and in, say, Chinese society to comparable early texts—this writing has been sometimes separately and sometimes simultaneously instructive, mythical, celebratory, and political. From the twentieth century onward, though, such writing has been perhaps even more mainstream than these specific categories suggest, for food has in the last century or so become central to the literary genres that we hold in the highest esteem—the novel, the poem, and (especially as it appears on film and video) the drama.

A LITTLE HISTORY OF FOOD WRITING

WRITTEN RECIPES for dishes as quotidian as bread or as exotic as the Byzantine *monokythron* (meaning "one-pot meal") began to appear centuries ago. The biblical book of Ezekiel offers relatively vague instructions for a sort of sprouted grain bread that was to sustain the Israelites during a siege of Jerusalem: "Take thou . . . wheat, and barley, and beans, and lentiles, and millet, and fitches, and put them in one vessel, and make thee bread thereof." Hopefully, this would sustain countless victims of the Roman siege. The far more specific recipe for the *monokythron* is also more elaborate, calling for (among other ingredients) "four hearts of cabbage . . . a salted neck of swordfish; a middle cut of carp; . . . a slice of salt sturgeon; fourteen eggs and some Cretan cheese" along with "a bit of Vlach cheese and a pint of olive oil, a handful of pepper, twelve little heads of garlic and fifteen chub mackerels." Presumably this would feed many hungry courtiers.

Even while collections of recipes explained culinary practices to literate cooks (of whom there can't have been that many until quite recently), physicians and moralists enjoined diners to watch what they ate. Beyond the food taboos outlined in religious texts from many cultures and the generalized aversion to the materiality of digestion itself expressed by Plato, clerics around the world often preached the virtues of abstinence while denouncing the fleshly pleasures of the table. Some writers, like Petronius in his *Satyricon*, satirized the vulgar excesses of the nouveau riche. Others, like Horace and Plutarch (and countless Hindu and Buddhist thinkers), decried the slaughter of animals for food, exclaiming, as Plutarch does in our selection here, that "I rather wonder both by what accident and in what state of soul or mind the first man who did so, touched his mouth to gore and brought his lips to the flesh of a dead creature."

Even among ordinary, non-philosophical folk, fasting has as long a history as feasting: Jews abstain from eating on Yom Kippur; Catholics reject luxurious foods during Lent and for centuries renounced meat on Fridays; Muslims fast daily, from sunrise to sunset, throughout the month-long observance of Ramadan; Hindus similarly fast during a number of religious festivals. And of course Puritan thinkers regularly and vehemently denounced gluttony (which they often associated with Catholicism); warned one writer, "Be very careful and circumspect in taking thy food, bridle thine appetite." That the delights of the table were temptations to be avoided by all good Christians was a view that persisted in Anglo-American society well into the early twentieth century. In such classic novels as *Oliver Twist* and *Jane Eyre* the young protagonists are scolded for their hunger, and even Miss Temple, Jane's kindly teacher, is rebuked by the hypocritical clergyman Brocklehurst when she offers her charges a lunch of bread and cheese after their breakfast has been burned. "Oh, madam," intones the (personally well-fed) preacher, "when you put bread and cheese, instead of burnt porridge, into these children's mouths, you may indeed feed their vile bodies, but you little think how you starve their immortal souls!"

"Dost thou think, because thou art virtuous, there shall be no more cakes and ale?" "Yes, by Saint Anne, and ginger shall be hot i' the mouth too!" With these famous words, Shakespeare's Sir Toby Belch and his sidekick Sir Andrew Aguecheek rebuke the puritanical Malvolio in *Twelfth Night*. While Malvolio, a bourgeois steward in a grand household, represents the culture of fasting, these two raffish aristocrats yearn to celebrate feasting. And such celebratory feasting has its roots not just in the desire for culinary pleasure but also in myth, magic, and metaphor. For the origin of food has often been attributed to the divine interventions of the gods. Such fire-bringers as Prometheus, in Greek culture, have long been extolled as culture heroes who enabled humble peasants to transform the raw to the cooked. At the same time, foods themselves have often been incarnated as gods. The Aztecs worshipped corn, a sacrificial lordly being who gave himself up to the kettle to be cooked yet was eternal. Christians, for their part, worshipped a mystical rabbi who claimed that his flesh would be their bread, his blood their wine. And countless fairy tales, along with theological works, extol the virtues, charms, and claims of enchanted or enchanting victuals.

Some of the foods they depict may have been what have been called "entheogens," substances containing consciousness-transforming chemicals—for instance, peyote and magic mushrooms. Some foods are imaginatively portrayed as seductive but dangerous, like the gingerbread house in "Hansel and Gretel," to go back to children's literature. Others, as in our selection from Rabelais, inspire extravagant cases of fabulous gluttony. And others are love potions, poisons, strengthening medicinal drinks, as well as lotus roots that lead to lassitude and wines that foster joy. From Homer to the Brothers Grimm, from Virgil to Hans Christian Andersen, from the Child Ballads to the verses of the Romantic poet John Keats and, more recently, the tales for children of Johnny Gruelle and Roald Dahl, writers have focused on foods that are, as Coleridge put it in "Kubla Khan," "honey-dew" and "the milk of Paradise."

Starting in the eighteenth century and on into the nineteenth and twentieth centuries, however, authors working in the new, more realistic genre of the novel began to turn their attention from culinary magic and mystery to everyday reality. The food for which Oliver Twist and Jane Eyre yearn is quotidian food, daily bread: Oliver wants more porridge; Jane savors seed cake. And such ordinary food plays a central, celebratory role in famous works that precede or descend from the books in which Oliver and Jane star. Published in the mid-eighteenth century, Fielding's *Tom Jones*, for instance, features a famous literary seduction in which two lovers supping at a tavern slurp and suck and lick their way through a meal into bed. Published in the early twentieth century, Virginia Woolf's *To the Lighthouse* dramatizes a festive dinner party whose centerpiece is a savory casserole of *boeuf en daube*—a classic French beef stew. The narrator stresses not so much the succulent dish itself as the way it brings the diners together in a culinary communion of delight, momentarily obliterating any conflicts or strains among them.

Modern food writers, arguably, have been influenced by such seemingly ordinary fare. When William Carlos Williams wrote a notoriously plaintive verse note to his sleeping wife, explaining that he had gobbled up the plums she was keeping in the icebox for breakfast because they were "so sweet and so cold," he initiated an entire new mode of food writing, one that would continue to celebrate in lyrical verse and prose the very essence of daily eating. And when the Beat poet Allen Ginsberg explored "A Supermarket in California," through which he was guided by his great spiritual precursor Walt Whitman (as Dante had been guided by Virgil), the magic of the daily had been confirmed. Declared Ginsberg, in one of his finest poems,

> I saw you, Walt Whitman, childless, lonely old grubber, poking
> among the meats in the refrigerator and eyeing the grocery boys.
>
> I heard you asking questions of each: Who killed the pork chops?
> What price bananas? Are you my Angel?

Here, perhaps, began the sorts of eating words that are so central today: words that consider economy ("What price bananas?") along with mystery ("Are you my Angel?"), politics as well as pleasure.

READING EATING WORDS TODAY

WHAT ARE THE pleasures that so many of us currently gain from reading about food? And what are the pleasures inherent in writing about food? Both activities, to begin with, speak to the significance that eating has for us—our gastronomic appetite, our cultural memories of the table, the symbolic value we assign to the most primal of our physical needs. And since the title of our anthology—*Eating Words*—implies a powerful nexus of food and language, what is that relation? Food of course has always brought people together, starting with the way fire served to cook, protect, and encourage people to share common ground; and in Woolf's novel, for instance, a marvel of cooking both produces and celebrates a life-enhancing moment. As in *To the Lighthouse*, much food writing speaks precisely to the ways participating in a meal creates a sense of ensemble, provoking spirited talk—nowadays often talk about food itself, the very meal being consumed, and other memorable meals. When we read about such occasions we frequently have an almost Pavlovian response: "Now that *boeuf* reminds me of a little

bistro where, in Burgundy, I once had . . ." And if others chime in, each topping the others' gastronomic travelogues, we join a circle of knowledge and
shared tastes.

Reading about food in and of itself, outside of narrative structures, can
also be an undeniably sensuous experience. It's not merely that certain foods,
such as oysters, chocolate, snake blood, bull's testicles, and hot peppers are
regarded as aphrodisiacs; any food writing can be seductive. No wonder critics have come to speak of "food porn." Gorgeous food photography may start
the juices flowing, but so do accounts of oysters by M.F.K. Fisher and Seamus Heaney, along with (among other texts we include) Walter Benjamin's
meditation on figs, Austin Clarke's celebration of souse, and Ray Gonzalez's
ode to *menudo*. Given such textual pleasures, we might wonder whether
food reading is a mode of sublimation, a substitute for the real thing, or
conversely a doubling of pleasure, spice and condiment to the enticing ingredient or the steaming platter.

To be sure, for some people the consumption of food can be troubling.
For sufferers from a range of physical illnesses (diabetes, celiac disease,
other allergies, gout) eating can actually be dangerous. To victims of such
psychological disorders as anorexia and bulimia, the pleasures of the table
may appear toxic. Even those possessed of healthy appetites may fear obesity or cringe at the thought of animal slaughter. And from Upton Sinclair
to Eric Schlosser and Michael Pollan, American polemicists have savagely
critiqued the food industry for its brutal butchery practices and unsani-
tary locations. Our section on the politics of food includes angry texts by
these writers along with meditations by such thoughtful locavores as Carlo
Petrini, Wendell Berry, and Barbara Kingsolver, all figures who consider the
possibilities of sensitive agriculture and mindful eating. Perhaps we read the
utopian imaginings of some of these thinkers in order to assuage the anxieties aroused by so many dystopian diatribes.

In the face of such culinary cultural complexity, it can be a relief to
counter the gastronomic superego with sentences that celebrate the joys of
feasting and the pleasures of the palate. Feeling guilty about eating? Read
A. J. Liebling's mouthwatering menus and get a reprieve. Think *you're* being
indulgent? Turn to Julia Child's relish in *sole meunière* and experience digestive delight. Nothing sparks an appetite like a saucy restaurant review by
Jonathan Gold, or will pique your gastronomic curiosity like the narrative of
French president Mitterand's last meal of Armagnac-soaked ortolans. Want

a vicariously dangerous but risk-free experience? Join Diane Ackerman as she flirts with death during a meal of fugu, the sometimes deadly Japanese fish.

Another reason we can't get our fill of food writing is that its stories are at once enticingly familiar and oddly unexpected, tales sometimes nostalgically evoking childhood and sometimes vibrant with surprise. Food recollections like those recounted by writers from Proust to Fisher, Clarke, and Lorde frequently send us in search of our own memories. As we read we may often anticipate a moment when the writer has his or her gastro-epiphany, reminiscence shading into a revelation that changes everything. Consuming food is our earliest source of satisfaction, and we satisfy desire with repetition. Yet, like Chang-rae Lee, who nervously scoops out the weird flesh of a sea urchin, we must learn to expand our taste and open ourselves to experimentation. We read about food to satisfy both impulses: reiteration and renewal.

These days there is much heated discussion of matters culinary; add food to the classic "big three" subjects—religion, politics, and sex. No one any longer cautions children, as some Victorian parents did, against talking about food in polite company. It's not only a permissible topic, it's encouraged, expected, and assumed. Everywhere you look, someone is advising you to try your hand in the kitchen (mothers no longer discourage sons from the stove), introducing you to celebrity chefs, even showing videos of fearless gastronomes scarfing deep-fried scorpions and loin of kangaroo. Food blogging is a growth industry, the Food Network is a mega-channel, food tourism is on the march, and numerous universities now have Food Studies programs (Slow Food in Italy has its own gastro-university). While one might question the reliability of Yelp and Zagat as they turn amateur diners into would-be pros, the popularity of these venues certainly implies that Every Diner has become an expert: nothing more than the possession of presumptuous taste buds seems to justify authority.

Why, more than ever, do so many writers turn to food? Some pundits believe that today we are obsessed with visual and literary representations of food because literal cooking is becoming a lost art. As Michael Pollan has argued, the rise of the Food Network "has, paradoxically, coincided with the rise of fast food, home-meal replacements and the decline and fall of everyday home cooking." Do we in fact prefer the simulacrum of cooking to the real thing? The proliferation of gourmet food stores and trendy kitchenware shops would seem to suggest that despite (or perhaps because of) all the culinary TV shows and restaurants out there, people are still practicing knife skills and demonstrating skillet proficiency. What is certainly true, however, is that in or out of the kitchen, at the table and even in the bedroom, people are reading about, looking at, and thinking about food. Some people even get competitive at the stove, so that for them the kitchen may have replaced the boudoir as a site of performance anxiety. Certainly any serious bookstore is laden with gastronomic tomes. At Powell's in Portland there are easily several hundred food memoirs, and over three dozen shelves bulging with culinary history. And if we had the space, we could easily triple or quadruple the size of this anthology. Consider, therefore, that the pages ahead of you constitute a delectable set of *hors d'œuvres variés* intended to stimulate your appetite for the increasingly rich menu of food writing.

❧PART ONE❧

Food Writing Through History

From Biblical Taboos to Sinclair's Stockyards

INTRODUCTION

P EOPLE HAVE been thinking and writing about eating as long
as people have been eating and talking—in other words, almost
forever. Worldwide, and deep into history, social scientists and
evolutionary biologists have found that sustained food sharing distinguishes humans from animals. Yes, from ants and bees to wolves and bats,
many creatures divide the spoils of foraging or hunting; but the multiple
and complex patterns of food sharing among humans are unique. We share
within and among families, between generations, between tribes and cultures, and, in various ways, across time. And as we share, we think and talk,
set down rules, preach appropriate practices, invite guests to dine, celebrate
delicacies, decry poison and pollution, remember the pleasures of special
tables, brood on culinary wrongdoing, tell—over and over again—tales of
food: food we loved and hated, food that made us well and food that made
us sick, food that gave grace and food that was sour, bitter, even poisonous.

Writing about food, in fact, must have begun when people started to write
and wanted to advise each other about deliciousness or danger, or simply
record their experiences. Our selection here from the Old Testament of the

western Bible, also known by Jews as the Torah, is one of the sources of the dietary laws observed by many Orthodox Jews, forbidding the consumption of pork and shellfish while stipulating the separation of meat products from dairy foods ("Thou shalt not seethe a kid in his mother's milk"). Comparable food rules and taboos are, of course, observed in many other cultures: devout Hindus don't eat beef, for instance, considering the cow a sacred animal, and many are both teetotalers and vegetarians; Muslims don't eat pork nor do they drink alcohol; many Buddhists eschew spices; Catholics traditionally renounce meat on Fridays and during Lent.

The very existence of such restrictions should remind us that eating itself is a fraught and sometimes perilous act. As such, it invites the kinds of philosophical meditation we see in our excerpt from Plutarch's classical vegetarian tract, attacking the savage bloodshed associated with butchery and "flesh-eating." And thoughts of eating invite, too, the moralizings we encounter in our selections from such writers as Joel Barlow, Louisa May Alcott, and Frederick Douglass. Barlow praises the homely "hasty pudding"—a sort of cornmeal mush—that he associates with American purity, which he sees as the opposite of European corruption. Alcott, for her part, attacks the parsimonious gastronomy practiced by the transcendentalist philosophers (the worst culprit her father, Bronson!) who founded Fruitlands, an early New England vegan commune. And in a piece that has connections with both Barlow's writing and Alcott's, Douglass, remembering his origins as a slave in the American South, describes the "ash cake," a cornbread akin to, but not as comforting as, "hasty pudding," that formed the diet of enchained African-Americans, while inveighing against the laden, decadent tables of the plantation owners.

Because eating is also a supremely pleasurable act, however, it also evokes celebratory invitations and reflections. Here we include appetizing gastronomic verses that the Roman poet Horace and his Renaissance acolyte Ben Jonson addressed to prospective dinner guests, outlining the delights of the table, whether "smallish portions of vegetarian food" (Horace) or "partrich, pheasant, wood-cock" and other "fowle" (Jonson). And in a similar vein, though retrospectively, Dumas extolls the French onion, Thoreau the watermelon, Melville the whale, and Proust—perhaps the most famous of all food memoirists—the modest madeleine, dipped in tea, out of which his entire *Remembrance of Things Past* blossomed.

A more nuanced but equally celebratory view of food is offered in Chekhov's "Oysters," whose protagonist, starving in tsarist Russia, is introduced to the delights of raw shellfish—and has his life saved by that gourmet food. At the same time, because the pleasures of eating can be so compelling, a number of writers satirize the excess that culinary luxury can inspire. Petronius's "Trimalchio's Feast," from his classic *Satyricon*, is perhaps the most notable representation of almost obscenely out-of-control eating in Western literary history; the Roman author dramatizes a dinner party thrown by a nouveau riche citizen that features, among other delectables, a whole roast "wild boar of immense size, wearing a liberty cap upon its head," along with attendant dishes. But the French Renaissance writer Rabelais's account of Pantagruel (the son of Gargantua) and his adventures among the "Gastrolaters"—grotesque fabulous foodies—comes in a close second.

How and why did cooking gain such resonance for us, and what is the nature of culinary "taste" anyway? Byron's *Don Juan* features a cannibal episode that turns on the Romantic poet's sardonic note that "man is a carnivorous production, / And must have meals, at least one meal a day," while Charles Lamb's fanciful "Dissertation upon Roast Pig" comically traces the transformative nature of cooking to an episode in a fancifully imagined ancient China, where a swineherd's son burned down a house in which a litter of piglets had been sequestered. But Jean Anthelme Brillat-Savarin, the French father of transcendental gastronomy whose arguments are here represented in a translation by the great American food writer M.F.K. Fisher, seriously meditates on the nature and meaning of *taste*, the physiological phenomenon experienced in tongue and gullet that lets us enjoy and, says Brillat-Savarin, inspires us to think about our times at the table. Like the other selections included in this opening section of *Eating Words*, his writing introduces us to what will be major themes throughout this volume: pleasure and pain, delight and disgust, memory and morality. That the last of these, morality, is crucial to our understanding of the culture of eating and cooking is, finally, emphasized in our excerpt from Upton Sinclair's superb turn-of-the-century novel/polemic *The Jungle*, which powerfully represents the butchery associated with the "flesh-eating" so loathed by Plutarch in ancient Rome. If Plutarch is the literary ancestor of Sinclair, Sinclair is the spiritual father of such contemporary writers as Michael Pollan and Barbara Kingsolver, whom we'll encounter later in this book.

The Old Testament (c. 538–332 BCE)

PROBABLY COMPLETED, ALONG with the rest of the Pentateuch or Hebrew Torah, between 538 and 332 BCE, the book of *Leviticus* sets down stipulations by which the ancient Israelite priests (the Levites) were to organize both daily life and sacred rituals. In Leviticus 11, which we reprint here, many of the dietary rules of Orthodox Judaism are formulated. Others appear in Deuteronomy 14. All together, these principles govern the practices that have come to be called *kosher* or *kashrut*, meaning "fit" for consumption. For instance, *you may not eat milk with meat; you may not eat pork or shellfish; you may not eat animals from whom the blood hasn't been drained.* (Says Deuteronomy, you must not "seethe a kid in his mother's milk"; says Leviticus, "Whatsoever parteth the hoof, and is clovenfooted, and cheweth the cud, among the beasts, that shall ye eat.") Similar food taboos and precepts can be found in many other cultures. Devout Muslims eat only what is *halal.* Hindus, considering the cow sacred, do not eat beef, and many are strict vegetarians.

Leviticus II

1. And the Lord spake unto Moses and to Aaron, saying unto them,
2. Speak unto the children of Israel, saying, These are the beasts which ye shall eat among all the beasts that are on the earth.
3. Whatsoever parteth the hoof, and is clovenfooted, and cheweth the cud, among the beasts, that shall ye eat.
4. Nevertheless these shall ye not eat of them that chew the cud, or of them that divide the hoof: as the camel, because he cheweth the cud, but divideth not the hoof; he is unclean unto you.
5. And the coney, because he cheweth the cud, but divideth not the hoof; he is unclean unto you.
6. And the hare, because he cheweth the cud, but divideth not the hoof; he is unclean unto you.

7. And the swine, though he divide the hoof, and be clovenfooted, yet he cheweth not the cud; he is unclean to you.

8. Of their flesh shall ye not eat, and their carcase shall ye not touch; they are unclean to you.

9. These shall ye eat of all that are in the waters: whatsoever hath fins and scales in the waters, in the seas, and in the rivers, them shall ye eat.

10. And all that have not fins and scales in the seas, and in the rivers, of all that move in the waters, and of any living thing which is in the waters, they shall be an abomination unto you:

11. They shall be even an abomination unto you; ye shall not eat of their flesh, but ye shall have their carcases in abomination.

12. Whatsoever hath no fins nor scales in the waters, that shall be an abomination unto you.

13. And these are they which ye shall have in abomination among the fowls; they shall not be eaten, they are an abomination: the eagle, and the ossifrage, and the ospray,

14. And the vulture, and the kite after his kind;

15. Every raven after his kind;

16. And the owl, and the night hawk, and the cuckow, and the hawk after his kind,

17. And the little owl, and the cormorant, and the great owl,

18. And the swan, and the pelican, and the gier eagle,

19. And the stork, the heron after her kind, and the lapwing, and the bat.

20. All fowls that creep, going upon all four, shall be an abomination unto you.

21. Yet these may ye eat of every flying creeping thing that goeth upon all four, which have legs above their feet, to leap withal upon the earth;

22. Even these of them ye may eat; the locust after his kind, and the bald locust after his kind, and the beetle after his kind, and the grasshopper after his kind.

23. But all other flying creeping things, which have four feet, shall be an abomination unto you.

24. And for these ye shall be unclean: whosoever toucheth the carcase of them shall be unclean until the even.

25. And whosoever beareth ought of the carcase of them shall wash his clothes, and be unclean until the even.

26. The carcases of every beast which divideth the hoof, and is not clovenfooted, nor cheweth the cud, are unclean unto you: every one that toucheth them shall be unclean.

27. And whatsoever goeth upon his paws, among all manner of beasts that go on all four, those are unclean unto you: whoso toucheth their carcase shall be unclean until the even.

28. And he that beareth the carcase of them shall wash his clothes, and be unclean until the even: they are unclean unto you.

29. These also shall be unclean unto you among the creeping things that creep upon the earth; the weasel, and the mouse, and the tortoise after his kind,

30. And the ferret, and the chameleon, and the lizard, and the snail, and the mole.

31. These are unclean to you among all that creep: whosoever doth touch them, when they be dead, shall be unclean until the even.

32. And upon whatsoever any of them, when they are dead, doth fall, it shall be unclean; whether it be any vessel of wood, or raiment, or skin, or sack, whatsoever vessel it be, wherein any work is done, it must be put into water, and it shall be unclean until the even; so it shall be cleansed.

33. And every earthen vessel, whereinto any of them falleth, whatsoever is in it shall be unclean; and ye shall break it.

34. Of all meat which may be eaten, that on which such water cometh shall be unclean: and all drink that may be drunk in every such vessel shall be unclean.

35. And every thing whereupon any part of their carcase falleth shall be unclean; whether it be oven, or ranges for pots, they shall be broken down: for they are unclean and shall be unclean unto you.

36. Nevertheless a fountain or pit, wherein there is plenty of water, shall be clean: but that which toucheth their carcase shall be unclean.

37. And if any part of their carcase fall upon any sowing seed which is to be sown, it shall be clean.

38. But if any water be put upon the seed, and any part of their carcase fall thereon, it shall be unclean unto you.

39. And if any beast, of which ye may eat, die; he that toucheth the carcase thereof shall be unclean until the even.

40. And he that eateth of the carcase of it shall wash his clothes, and be unclean until the even: he also that beareth the carcase of it shall wash his clothes, and be unclean until the even.

41. And every creeping thing that creepeth upon the earth shall be an abomination; it shall not be eaten.

42. Whatsoever goeth upon the belly, and whatsoever goeth upon all four, or whatsoever hath more feet among all creeping things that creep upon the earth, them ye shall not eat; for they are an abomination.

43. Ye shall not make yourselves abominable with any creeping thing that creepeth, neither shall ye make yourselves unclean with them, that ye should be defiled thereby.

44. For I am the Lord your God: ye shall therefore sanctify yourselves, and ye shall be holy; for I am holy: neither shall ye defile yourselves with any manner of creeping thing that creepeth upon the earth.

45. For I am the Lord that bringeth you up out of the land of Egypt, to be your God: ye shall therefore be holy, for I am holy.

46. This is the law of the beasts, and of the fowl, and of every living creature that moveth in the waters, and of every creature that creepeth upon the earth:

47. To make a difference between the unclean and the clean, and between the beast that may be eaten and the beast that may not be eaten.

🐚

Horace (65–8 BCE)

URBANE AND WITTY, Quintus Horatius Flaccus, known as Horace in English, was among the most prominent poets of Augustan Rome. The cherished son of a "freedman"—a former slave who expended a great deal on his heir's education—he studied in Athens, served as an officer in the army, and then worked as a paid scribe before attaining favor with the emperor and taking possession of the elegant villa at the Sabine farm that he memorialized in some of his best-known verses. His odes, epodes, and satires helped forge his reputation, but his epistles were perhaps his most innovative works: the first ostensibly personal letters to have been composed entirely in verse. In the one we represent here, as in several others, he invites a friend to dinner, suavely proposing a meal marked by the moderation ("smallish helpings of vegetarian food") for which he was also known.

from Epistle 5, To Torquatus: A Cheerful Invitation to Dinner

If you can bear to recline on one of Archias' couches,
and can face smallish helpings of vegetarian food,
I shall look forward, Torquatus, to seeing you here at sunset.
The wine you will drink was bottled in Taurus' second consulate
between Minturnae in the marsh and Petrinum near Sinuessa.
If *you*'ve something better, have it brought, or obey orders.
The hearth is already polished, and you'll find the furniture tidy.
Forget for a while your chancy prospects and the race for profits
and the Moschus case. Tomorrow is Caesar's birthday, and so
we have an excuse for sleeping in. No retribution
if we stretch our pleasant talk into the summer night.

What's the point of money if you haven't the chance to enjoy it?
Someone who scrimps and saves more than he needs, in concern
for his heir, is next door to an idiot; I'll begin
drinking and scattering flowers. Who cares if I'm called
    irresponsible?
Think of the wonders uncorked by wine! It opens secrets,
gives heart to our hopes, pushes the cowardly into battle,
lifts the load from anxious minds, and evokes talents.
Thanks to the bottle's prompting no one is lost for words,
no one who's cramped by poverty fails to find release.

I'm under orders, willing and able, to ensure the following:
there'll be no dirty napkins to make you grimace in disgust,
nor any grubby covers; no tankard or plate
that you can't see your face in; no one to noise abroad what is said
to friends in confidence. Getting the right blend of guests
is so important. I shall have Septicius and Butra along
to meet you, and Sabinus if he's not prevented by a previous
    engagement
and prettier company. There's also room for several shadows.
(But at *over*crowded parties one must beware of the goat.)
Let me know how many you'd like; then drop what you're doing
and trick the client in the hall by slipping out the back.

⍦●

Petronius (27–66)

AN INTIMATE MEMBER of the Emperor Nero's court, a Roman consul,
and a noted arbiter of taste and elegance, Petronius was a satirist whose
comic novel *The Satyricon* includes a famous scene of decadent Roman banqueting. Trimalchio, a wealthy hedonist and a portrait of the nouveau riche
in its most extravagant mode, displays lavish vulgarity in trying to impress
his guests. F. Scott Fitzgerald originally intended to call *The Great Gatsby*
"Trimalchio," a reference to the ostentatious side of the novel's main character. The title *The Satyricon* refers to the satyr, who, as a figure in Dionysus's
retinue, yearns for wine, theater, and phallic sexuality, and is a pursuer of
pleasure in all forms. The narrator is an impoverished student who has been
invited to dinner by Trimalchio, and many have speculated that the protagonist of the work was a caricature of Nero himself.

from *The Satyricon*: Trimalchio's Feast

WE FELT DEEPLY obligated by [our host's] great condescension, and the same slave for whom we had interceded, rushed up to us as we entered the dining-room, and to our astonishment, kissed us thick and fast, voicing his thanks for our kindness. "You'll know in a minute whom you did a favor for," he confided, "the master's wine is the thanks of a grateful butler!" At length we reclined, and slave boys from Alexandria poured water cooled with snow upon our hands, while others following, attended to our feet and removed the hangnails with wonderful dexterity, nor were they silent even during this disagreeable operation, but they all kept singing at their work. I was desirous of finding out whether the whole household could sing, so I ordered a drink; a boy near at hand instantly repeated my order in a singsong voice fully as shrill, and whichever one you accosted did the same. You would not imagine that this was the dining-room of a private gentleman, but rather that it was an exhibition of pantomimes. A very inviting relish was brought on, for by now all the couches were occupied save only that of Trimalchio, for whom, after a new custom, the chief place was reserved.

On the tray stood a donkey made of Corinthian bronze, bearing panniers containing olives, white in one and black in the other. Two platters flanked the figure, on the margins of which were engraved Trimalchio's name and the weight of the silver in each. Dormice sprinkled with poppy-seed and honey were served on little bridges soldered fast to the platter, and hot sausages on a silver gridiron, underneath which were damson plums and pomegranate seeds.

WE were in the midst of these delicacies when, to the sound of music, Trimalchio himself was carried in and bolstered up in a nest of small cushions, which forced a snicker from the less wary. A shaven poll protruded from a scarlet mantle, and around his neck, already muffled with heavy clothing, he had tucked a napkin having a broad purple stripe and a fringe that hung down all around. On the little finger of his left hand he wore a massive gilt ring, and on the first joint of the next finger, a smaller one which seemed to me to be of pure gold, but as a matter of fact it had iron stars soldered on all around it. And then, for fear all of his finery would not be displayed, he bared his right arm, adorned with a golden arm-band and an ivory circlet clasped with a plate of shining metal.

Picking his teeth with a silver quill, "Friends," said he, "it was not convenient for me to come into the dining-room just yet, but for fear my absence should cause you any inconvenience, I gave over my own pleasure: permit me, however, to finish my game." A slave followed with a terebinth table and crystal dice, and I noted one piece of luxury that was superlative; for instead of black and white pieces, he used gold and silver coins. He kept up a continual flow of various coarse expressions. We were still dallying with the relishes when a tray was brought in, on which was a basket containing a wooden hen with her wings rounded and spread out as if she were brooding. Two slaves instantly approached, and to the accompaniment of music, commenced to feel around in the straw. They pulled out some pea-hen's eggs, which they distributed among the diners. Turning his head, Trimalchio saw what was going on. "Friends," he remarked. "I ordered pea-hen's eggs set under the hen, but I'm afraid they're addled, by Hercules I am, let's try them anyhow, and see if they're still fit to suck." We picked up our spoons, each of which weighed not less than half a pound, and punctured the shells, which were made of flour and dough, and as a matter of fact, I very nearly threw mine away for it seemed to me that a chick had formed already, but upon hearing an old experienced guest vow, "There must be something good here," I broke open the shell with my hand and discovered a fine fat fig-pecker, imbedded in a yolk seasoned with pepper.

Having finished his game, Trimalchio was served with a helping of everything and was announcing in a loud voice his willingness to join anyone in a second cup of honied wine, when, to a flourish of music, the relishes were suddenly whisked away by a singing chorus, but a small dish happened to fall to the floor, in the scurry, and a slave picked it up. Seeing this, Trimalchio ordered that the boy be punished by a box on the ear, and made him throw it down again; a janitor followed with his broom and swept the silver dish away among the litter. Next followed two long-haired Ethiopians, carrying small leather bottles, such as are commonly seen in the hands of those who sprinkle sand in the arena, and poured wine upon our hands, for no one offered us water. When complimented upon these elegant extras, the host cried out, "Mars loves a fair fight: and so I ordered each one a separate table: that way these stinking slaves won't make us so hot with their crowding." Some glass bottles carefully sealed with gypsum were brought in at that instant; a label bearing this inscription was fastened to the neck of each one:

OPIMIAN FALERNIAN
ONE HUNDRED YEARS OLD.

While we were studying the labels, Trimalchio clapped his hands and cried, "Ah me! To think that wine lives longer than poor little man. Let's fill 'em up! There's life in wine and this is the real Opimian, you can take my word for that. I offered no such vintage yesterday, though my guests were far more respectable." We were tippling away and extolling all these elegant devices, when a slave brought in a silver skeleton, so contrived that the joints and movable vertebra could be turned in any direction. He threw it down upon the table a time or two, and its mobile articulation caused it to assume grotesque attitudes, whereupon Trimalchio chimed in:

"Poor man is nothing in the scheme of things
And Orcus grips us and to Hades flings
Our bones! This skeleton before us here
Is as important as we ever were!
Let's live then while we may and life is dear."

THE applause was followed by a course which, by its oddity, drew every eye, but it did not come up to our expectations. There was a circular tray around which were displayed the signs of the zodiac, and upon each sign the caterer had placed the food best in keeping with it. Ram's vetches on Aries, a piece of beef on Taurus, kidneys and lamb's fry on Gemini, a crown on Cancer, the womb of an unfarrowed sow on Virgo, an African fig on Leo, on Libra a balance, one pan of which held a tart and the other a cake, a small seafish on Scorpio, a bull's eye on Sagittarius, a sea lobster on Capricornus, a goose on Aquarius and two mullets on Pisces. In the middle lay a piece of cut sod upon which rested a honeycomb with the grass arranged around it. An Egyptian slave passed bread around from a silver oven and in a most discordant voice twisted out a song in the manner of the mime in the musical farce called Laserpitium. Seeing that we were rather depressed at the prospect of busying ourselves with such vile fare, Trimalchio urged us to fall to: "Let us fall to, gentlemen, I beg of you, this is only the sauce!"

WHILE he was speaking, four dancers ran in to the time of the music, and removed the upper part of the tray. Beneath, on what seemed to be another tray, we caught sight of stuffed capons and sows' bellies, and in the middle, a hare equipped with wings to resemble Pegasus. At the corners of the tray we also noted four figures of Marsyas and from their bladders spouted a highly spiced sauce upon fish which were swimming about as if in a tide-race. All of us echoed the applause which was started by the servants, and fell to upon these exquisite delicacies, with a laugh. "Carver," cried Trimalchio, no less delighted with the artifice practiced upon us, and the carver appeared immediately. Timing his strokes to the beat of the music he cut up the meat in such a fashion as to lead you to think that a gladiator was fighting from a chariot to the accompaniment of a water-organ. Every now and then Trimalchio would repeat "Carver, Carver," in a low voice, until I finally came to the conclusion that some joke was meant in repeating a word so frequently, so I did not scruple to question him who reclined above me. As he had often experienced byplay of this sort he explained, "You see that fellow who is carving the meat, don't you? Well, his name is Carver. Whenever Trimalchio says Carver, carve her, by the same word, he both calls and commands!"

At length some slaves came in who spread upon the couches some coverlets upon which were embroidered nets and hunters stalking their game with boar-spears, and all the paraphernalia of the chase. We knew not what to look for next, until a hideous uproar commenced, just outside the dining-room door, and some Spartan hounds commenced to run around the table all of a sudden. A tray followed them, upon which was served a wild boar of immense size, wearing a liberty cap upon its head, and from its tusks hung two little baskets of woven palm fibre, one of which contained Syrian dates, the other, Theban. Around it hung little suckling pigs made from pastry, signifying that this was a brood-sow with her pigs at suck. It turned out that these were souvenirs intended to be taken home. When it came to carving the boar, our old friend Carver, who had carved the capons, did not appear, but in his place a great bearded giant, with bands around his legs, and wearing a short hunting cape in which a design was woven. Drawing his hunting-knife, he plunged it fiercely into the boar's side, and some thrushes flew out of the gash. Fowlers, ready with their rods, caught them in a moment, as they fluttered around the room and Trimalchio ordered one to each guest, remarking, "Notice what fine acorns this forest-bred boar fed on," and as he spoke, some slaves removed the little baskets from the tusks and divided the Syrian and Theban dates equally among the diners.

GETTING a moment to myself, in the meantime, I began to speculate as to why the boar had come with a liberty cap upon his head. After exhausting my invention with a thousand foolish guesses, I made bold to put the riddle which teased me to my old informant. "Why, sure," he replied, "even your slave could explain that; there's no riddle, everything's as plain as day! This boar made his first bow as the last course of yesterday's dinner and was dismissed by the guests, so today he comes back as a freedman!" I damned my stupidity and refrained from asking any more questions for fear I might leave the impression that I had never dined among decent people before. While we were speaking, a handsome boy, crowned with vine leaves and ivy, passed grapes around, in a little basket, and impersonated Bacchus-happy, Bacchus-drunk, and Bacchus-dreaming, reciting, in the meantime, his master's verses, in a shrill voice. Trimalchio turned to him and said, "Dionisus, be thou Liber," whereupon the boy immediately snatched the cap from the boar's head, and put it upon his own. At that Trimalchio added, "You can't deny that my father's middle name was Liber!" We applauded Trimalchio's conceit heartily, and kissed the boy as he went around. Trimalchio retired to the close-stool, after this course, and we, having freedom of action with the tyrant away, began to draw the other guests out. After calling for a bowl of wine, Dama spoke up, "A day's nothing at all: it's night before you can turn around, so you can't do better than to go right to the dining-room from your bed. It's been so cold that I can hardly get warm in a bath, but a hot drink's as good as an overcoat: I've had some long pegs, and between you and me, I'm a bit groggy; the booze has gone to my head."

🐾

Plutarch (46–120)

THE GREAT ROMAN writer is best known for his highly influential *Parallel Lives*, a series of biographical essays of famous Greek and Roman figures, arranged in pairs, including warriors, lawgivers, politicians, writers, and philosophers. Shakespeare based several of his plays on these biographies. Though Plutarch is usually regarded as Roman, and was patronized by the Emperor Hadrian, he was born and spent most of his life in Greece, even serving as a priest at the Temple of Apollo at Delphi. Our text is taken from his *Moralia*, a collection of short pieces on contemporary customs and mores, including meditations on such serious matters as friendship, virtue, and worship. But he could also engage with seemingly lighter though no less important topics. In our selection he asks how we can in good conscience eat living creatures when "real" animals kill to survive while we kill only to dine on a mere "appetizer." Plutarch was an early advocate for vegetarianism, and he bases his position not only on sympathy for hunted beasts, even for farm-raised creatures (he asserts they may be mothers or fathers) but also on the natural deficiencies of human anatomy that is not designed, as is that of great predators, for the tearing, rending, and digesting of flesh.

from *Moralia*: On Eating Meat

CAN YOU REALLY ask what reason Pythagoras had for abstaining from flesh? For my part I rather wonder both by what accident and in what state of soul or mind the first man who did so, touched his mouth to gore and brought his lips to the flesh of a dead creature, he who set forth tables of dead, stale bodies and ventured to call food and nourishment the parts that had a little before bellowed and cried, moved and lived. How could his eyes endure the slaughter when throats were slit and hides flayed and limbs torn from limb? How could his nose endure the stench? . . .

But you who live now, what madness, what frenzy drives you to the pollution of shedding blood, you who have such a superfluity of necessities? Why slander the earth by implying that she cannot support you? Why impiously offend law-giving Demeter and bring shame upon Dionysus, lord of the cultivated vine, the gracious one, as if you did not receive enough from their hands? Are you not ashamed to mingle domestic crops with blood and gore? You call serpents and panthers and lions savage, but you yourselves, by your own foul slaughters, leave them no room to outdo you in cruelty; for their slaughter is their living, yours is a mere appetizer.

It is certainly not lions and wolves that we eat out of self-defence; on the contrary, we ignore these and slaughter harmless, tame creatures without stings or teeth to harm us, creatures that, I swear, Nature appears to have produced for the sake of their beauty and grace. . . .

What a terrible thing it is to look on when the tables of the rich are spread, men who employ cooks and spicers to groom the dead! And it is even more terrible to look on when they are taken away, for more is left than has been eaten. So the beasts died for nothing! There are others who refuse when the dishes are already set before them and will not have them cut into or sliced. Though they bid spare the dead, they did not spare the living.

We declare, then, that it is absurd for them to say that the practice of flesh-eating is based on Nature. For that man is not naturally carnivorous is, in the first place, obvious from the structure of his body. A man's frame is in no way similar to those creatures who were made for flesh-eating: he has no hooked beak or sharp nails or jagged teeth, no strong stomach or warmth of vital fluids able to digest and assimilate a heavy diet of flesh. It is from this very fact, the evenness of our teeth, the smallness of our mouths, the softness of our tongues, our possession of vital fluids too inert to digest meat that Nature disavows our eating of flesh. If you declare that you are naturally designed for such a diet, then first kill for yourself what you want to eat. Do it, however, only through your own resources. . . .

For what sort of dinner is not costly for which a living creature loses its life? Do we hold a life cheap? I do not yet go so far as to say that it may well be the life of your mother or father or some friend or child, as Empedocles declared. Yet it does, at least, possess some perception, hearing, seeing, imagination, intelligence, which last every creature receives from Nature to enable it to acquire what is proper for it and to evade what is not. Do but consider which are the philosophers who serve the better to humanize us: those who bid us eat our children and friends and fathers and wives after their death, or Pythagoras and Empedocles who try to accustom us to act justly toward other creatures also? You ridicule a man who abstains from eating mutton. But are we, they will say, to refrain from laughter when we see you slicing off portions from a dead father or mother and sending them to absent friends and inviting those who are at hand, heaping their plates with flesh.

🐌

François Rabelais (1494–1553)

RABELAIS WAS A French Renaissance humanist who viewed the world as a great carnival of pleasurable subversion. Our selection comes from his best-known work, *Gargantua and Pantagruel*, about father and son giants who have wild adventures, many involving prodigious feats of eating and drinking. Some readers have regarded the text's licentious scenes as satires of excess, while others have viewed them as critiques of puritanical repression, self-deprivation, and authoritarian regulation. In the later parts of the work Rabelais celebrates a swaggering freedom in the open-minded Abbey of Thélème, ruled by the motto "Do What You Will." Here the "Gastrolaters (or Belly-Worshippers)" function as surrogates for Gargantua and Pantagruel themselves, consuming dish after dish after dish—and bloated but never satiated.

from *Gargantua and Pantagruel*: On the Gastrolaters

HOW, AT THE COURT OF THE MASTER OF INGENUITY, PANTAGRUEL DETESTED THE ENGASTRIMYTHES AND THE GASTROLATERS.

AT the court of that great master of ingenuity, Pantagruel observed two sorts of troublesome and too officious apparitors, whom he very much detested. The first were called Engastrimythes; the others, Gastrolaters.

The first pretended to be descended of the ancient race of Eurycles, and for this brought the authority of Aristophanes in his comedy called the Wasps; whence of old they were called Euryclians, as Plato writes, and Plutarch in his book of the Cessation of Oracles. In the holy decrees, 26, qu. 3, they are styled Ventriloqui; and the same name is given them in Ionian by Hippocrates, in his fifth book of Epid., as men who speak from the belly. Sophocles calls them Sternomantes. These were soothsayers, enchanters, cheats, who gulled the mob, and seemed not to speak and give answers from the mouth, but from the belly.

Such a one, about the year of our Lord 1513, was Jacoba Rodogina, an Italian woman of mean extract; from whose belly we, as well as an infinite number of others at Ferrara and elsewhere, have often heard the voice of the evil spirit speak, low, feeble, and small, indeed, but yet very distinct, articulate, and intelligible, when she was sent for out of curiosity by the lords and princes of the Cisalpine Gaul. To remove all manner of doubt, and be assured that this was not a trick, they used to have her stripped stark naked, and caused her mouth and nose to be stopped. This evil spirit would be called Curled-pate, or Cincinnatulo, seeming pleased when any called him by that name, at which he was always ready to answer. If any spoke to him of things past or present, he gave pertinent answers, sometimes to the amazement of the hearers; but if of things to come, then the devil was graveled, and used to lie as fast as a dog can trot. Nay, sometimes he seemed to own his ignorance, instead of an answer letting out a rousing fart, or muttering some words with barbarous and uncouth inflexions, and not to be understood.

As for the Gastrolaters, they stuck close to one another in knots and gangs. Some of them merry, wanton, and soft as so many milk-sops; others louring, grim, dogged, demure, and crabbed; all idle, mortal foes to business, spending half their time in sleeping and the rest in doing nothing, a rent-charge and dead unnecessary weight on the earth, as Hesiod saith; afraid, as we judged, of offending or lessening their paunch. Others were masked, disguised, and so oddly dressed that it would have done you good to have seen them.

There's a saying, and several ancient sages write, that the skill of nature appears wonderful in the pleasure which she seems to have taken in the configuration of sea-shells, so great is their variety in figures, colours, streaks, and inimitable shapes. I protest the variety we perceived in the dresses of the gastrolatrous coquillons was not less. They all owned Gaster for their supreme god, adored him as a god, offered him sacrifices as to their omnipotent deity, owned no other god, served, loved, and honoured him above all things.

You would have thought that the holy apostle spoke of those when he said (Phil. chap. 3), Many walk, of whom I have told you often, and now tell you even weeping, that they are enemies of the cross of Christ: whose end is destruction, whose God is their belly. Pantagruel compared them to the Cyclops Polyphemus, whom Euripides brings in speaking thus: I only sacrifice to myself—not to the gods—and to this belly of mine, the greatest of all the gods.

OF THE RIDICULOUS STATUE MANDUCE; AND HOW AND WHAT THE GASTROLATERS SACRIFICE TO THEIR VENTRIPOTENT GOD.

WHILE we fed our eyes with the sight of the phizzes and actions of these lounging gulligutted Gastrolaters, we on a sudden heard the sound of a musical instrument called a bell; at which all of them placed themselves in rank and file as for some mighty battle, everyone according to his office, degree, and seniority.

In this order they moved towards Master Gaster, after a plump, young, lusty, gorbellied fellow, who on a long staff fairly gilt carried a wooden statue, grossly carved, and as scurvily daubed over with paint; such a one as Plautus, Juvenal, and Pomp. Festus describe it. At Lyons during the Carnival it is called Maschecroute or Gnawcrust; they call'd this Manduce.

It was a monstrous, ridiculous, hideous figure, fit to fright little children; its eyes were bigger than its belly, and its head larger than all the rest of its body; well mouth-cloven however, having a goodly pair of wide, broad jaws, lined with two rows of teeth, upper tier and under tier, which, by the magic of a small twine hid in the hollow part of the golden staff, were made to clash, clatter, and rattle dreadfully one against another; as they do at Metz with St. Clement's dragon.

Coming near the Gastrolaters I saw they were followed by a great number of fat waiters and tenders, laden with baskets, dossers, hampers, dishes, wallets, pots, and kettles. Then, under the conduct of Manduce, and singing I do not know what dithyrambics, crepalocomes, and epenons, opening their baskets and pots, they offered their god:

White hippocras, with
dry toasts.
White bread.
Brown bread.
Carbonadoes, six sorts.
Brawn.
Sweetbreads.
Fricassees, nine sorts.

Monastical brewis.
Gravy soup.
Hotch-pots.
Soft bread.
Household bread.
Capirotadoes.
Cold loins of veal, with
spice.

Zinziberine.
Beatille pies.
Brewis.
Marrow-bones, toast,
and cabbage.
Hashes.

Eternal drink intermixed. Brisk delicate white wine led the van; claret and champagne followed, cool, nay, as cold as the very ice, I say, filled and offered in large silver cups. Then they offered:

Chitterlings, garnished
with mustard.
Sausages.
Neats' tongues.
Hung beef.
Chines and peas.

Hog's haslets.
Scotch collops.
Puddings.
Cervelats.
Bologna sausages.
Hams.

Brawn heads.
Powdered venison,
with turnips.
Pickled olives.

All this associated with sempiternal liquor. Then they housed within his muzzle:

Legs of mutton, with
shallots.
Olias.
Lumber pies, with hot
sauce.
Partridges and young
partridges.
Dwarf-herons.
Teals.
Duckers.
Bitterns.
Shovellers.
Curlews.
Wood-hens.
Coots, with leeks.
Fat kids.

Shoulders of mutton,
with capers.
Sirloins of beef.
Breasts of veal.
Pheasants and pheas-
ant poots.
Peacocks.
Storks.
Woodcocks.
Snipes.
Ortolans.
Turkey cocks,
hen turkeys, and
turkey poots.
Stock-doves, and
wood-culvers.

Pigs, with
wine sauce.
Blackbirds, ousels,
and rails.
Moorhens.
Bustards, and bustard
poots.
Fig-peckers.
Young Guinea
hens.
Ribs of pork, with
onion sauce.
Roast capons, basted
with their own
dripping.
Flamingoes.

Cygnets.

A reinforcement of vinegar intermixed.

Venison pasties.

Lark pies.

Dormice pies.

Cabretto pasties.

Roebuck pasties.

Pigeon pies.

Kid pasties.

Capon pies.

Bacon pies.

Soused hog's feet.

Fried pasty-crust.

Forced capons.

Parmesan cheese.

Red and pale hippocras.

Gold-peaches.

Artichokes.

Dry and wet sweetmeats, seventy-eight sorts.

Boiled hens, and fat capons marinated.

Pullets, with eggs.

Chickens.

Rabbits, and sucking rabbits.

Quails, and young quails.

Pigeons, squabs, and squeakers.

Fieldfares.

Caponets.

Caviare and toast.

Fawns, deer.

Hares, leverets.

Plovers.

Herons, and young herons.

Olives.

Thrushes.

Young sea-ravens.

Geese, goslings.

Queests.

Widgeons.

Mavises.

Grouses.

Turtles.

Doe-coneys.

Hedgehogs.

Snites.

Then large puffs.

Thistle-finches.

Whore's farts.

Fritters.

Cakes, sixteen sorts.

Crisp wafers.

Quince tarts.

Curds and cream.

Whipped cream.

Preserved mirabolans.

Jellies.

Welsh barrapyclids.

Macaroons.

Tarts, twenty sorts.

Lemon cream, raspberry cream, &c.

Comfits, one hundred colours.

Cream wafers.

Cream cheese.

Vinegar brought up the rear to wash the mouth, and for fear of the squinsy; also toasts to scour the grinders.

WHAT THE GASTROLATERS SACRIFICED TO THEIR GOD ON INTERLARDED FISH-DAYS.

Pantagruel did not like this pack of rascally scoundrels with their manifold kitchen sacrifices, and would have been gone had not Epistemon prevailed with him to stay and see the end of the farce. He then asked the skipper what the idle lobcocks used to sacrifice to their gorbellied god on interlarded fish-days. For his first course, said the skipper, they gave him:

Caviare.

Botargoes.

Fresh butter.

Pease soup.

Spinach.

Fresh herrings, full roed.

Salads, a hundred varieties, of cresses, sodden hop-tops, bishop's-cods, celery, chives, rampions, jew's-ears (a sort of mushrooms that sprout out of old elders), sparagus, wood-bind, and a world of others.

Red herrings.

Pillchards.

Anchovies.

Fry of tunny.

Cauliflowers.

Beans.

Salt salmon.

Pickled grigs.

Oysters in the shell.

Then he must drink, or the devil would gripe him at the throat; this, therefore, they take care to prevent, and nothing is wanting. Which being done, they give him lampreys with hippocras sauce:

Gurnards.

Salmon trouts.

Barbels, great and small.

Roaches.

Cockerels.

Minnows.

Skate-fish.

Lamprels.

Jegs.

Pickerels.

Golden carps.

Burbates.

Salmons.

Salmon-peels.

Dolphins.

Barn trouts.

Miller's-thumbs.

Precks.

Bret-fish.

Flounders.

Sea-nettles.

Mullets.

Gudgeons.

Dabs and sandings.

Haddocks.

Carps.

Pikes.

Bottitoes.

Rochets.

Sea-bears.

Thornbacks.

Sleeves.

Sturgeons.

Sheath-fish.

Mackerels.

Maids.

Plaice.

Sharplings.

Tunnies.

Silver eels.

Chevins.

Crayfish.

Pallours.

Shrimps.

Congers.

Porpoises.

Bases.

Shads.

Murenes, a sort of lampreys.

Graylings.

Smys.

Turbots.

Trout, not above a foot long.

Salmons.

Meagers.

Sea-breams.

Halibuts.

Dog's tongue, or kind fool.

Fried oysters.

Cockles.

Prawns.

Smelts.

Rock-fish.

Gracious lords.

Sword-fish.

Soles.

Mussels.

Lobsters.

Great prawns.

Dace.

Bleaks.

Tenches.

Ombres.

Fresh cods.

Dried melwels.

Darefish.

Fausens, and grigs.

Eel-pouts.

Tortoises.

Serpents, i.e. wood-eels.

Dories.

Moor-game.

Perches.

Loaches.

Crab-fish.

Snails and whelks.

Frogs.

If, when he had crammed all this down his guttural trapdoor, he did not immediately make the fish swim again in his paunch, death would pack him off in a trice. Special care is taken to antidote his godship with vine-tree syrup. Then is sacrificed to him haberdines, poor-jack, minglemangled, mis-mashed, &c.

Eggs fried, beaten, buttered, poached, hardened, boiled, broiled, stewed, sliced, roasted in the embers, tossed in the chimney, &c.

Stock-fish.

Green-fish.

Sea-batts.

Cod's sounds.

Sea-pikes.

Which to concoct and digest the more easily, vinegar is multiplied. For the latter part of their sacrifices they offer:

Rice milk, and hasty pudding.

Buttered wheat, and flummery.

Water-gruel, and milk-porridge.

Frumenty and bonny clamber.

Stewed prunes, and baked bullace.

Pistachios, or fistic nuts.

Figs.

Almond butter.

Skirret root.

White-pot.

Raisins.

Dates.

Chestnut and walnuts.

Filberts.

Parsnips.

Artichokes.

Perpetuity of soaking with the whole.

It was none of their fault, I will assure you, if this same god of theirs was not publicly, preciously, and plentifully served in the sacrifices, better yet than Heliogabalus's idol; nay, more than Bel and the Dragon in Babylon, under King Belshazzar. Yet Gaster had the manners to own that he was no god, but a poor, vile, wretched creature. And as King Antigonus, first of the name, when one Hermodotus (as poets will flatter, especially princes) in some of his fustian dubbed him a god, and made the sun adopt him for his son, said to him: My lasanophore (or, in plain English, my groom of the close-stool) can give thee the lie; so Master Gaster very civilly used to send back his bigoted worshippers to his close-stool, to see, smell, taste, philosophize, and examine what kind of divinity they could pick out of his sir-reverence.

❧

Ben Jonson (1572–1637)

A NEAR CONTEMPORARY of Shakespeare, Jonson was the most esteemed comic playwright of his day, famous for *Volpone* and *The Alchemist*. He was also a composer of court masques, and a prolific poet, influenced by classical forms. He frequently translated from the Latin and the ancient Greek, favoring such genres as the epigram and satire. As with "Inviting a Friend to Supper," Jonson wrote poems to specific individuals, often his friends. Here he displays an elegance both of verse form and of gracious social manners. Jonson regularly met at the Mermaid Tavern with a circle of writers who called themselves "the Tribe of Ben."

Inviting a Friend to Supper

To night, grave sir, both my poore house, and I
Doe equally desire your companie:
Not that we thinke us worthy such a ghest,
But that your worth will dignifie our feast,
With those that come; whose grace may make that seeme

Something, which, else, could hope for no esteeme.
It is the faire acceptance, Sir, creates
The entertaynment perfect: not the cates.
Yet shall you have, to rectifie your palate,
An olive, capers, or some better sallade
Ushring the mutton; with a short-leg'd hen,
If we can get her, full of egs, and then,
Limons, and wine for sauce: to these, a coney
Is not to be despair'd of, for our money;
And, though fowle, now, be scarce, yet there are darkes,
The skie not falling, thinke we may have larkes.
Ile tell you more, and lye, so you will come:
Of partrich, pheasant, wood-cock, of which some
May yet be there; and godwit, if we can:
Knat, raile, and ruffe too. How so ere, my man
Shall reade a piece of Virgil, Tacitus,
Livie, or of some better booke to us,
Of which wee'll speake our minds, amidst our meate;
And Ile professe no verses to repeate:
To this, if ought appeare, which I not know of,
That will the pastrie, not my paper, show of.
Digestive cheese, and fruit there sure will bee;
But that, which most doth take my Muse, and mee,
Is a pure cup of rich Canary-wine,
Which is the Mermaids, now, but shall be mine:
Of which had Horace, or Anacreon tasted,
Their lives, as doe their lines, till now had lasted.
Tabacco, Nectar, or the Thespian spring,
Are all but Luthers beere, to this I sing.
Of this we will sup free, but moderately,
And we will have no Pooly', or Parrot by;
Nor shall our cups make any guiltie men:
But, at our parting, we will be, as when
We innocently met. No simple word,
That shall be utter'd at our mirthfull boord,
Shall make us sad next morning: or affright
The libertie, that wee'll enjoy to night.

※

Jonathan Swift (1667–1745)

ONE OF THE most savage ironists of all English authors, Swift undermines the pretensions and easy idealisms human beings display in asserting their supposed dignity and grandeur. He suggests that underlying our noble intentions are behaviors base, vile, and cruel. Appointed dean of St. Patrick's Cathedral in Dublin, Swift became an Irish patriot and champion of Irish freedom from English exploitation. His major work is of course *Gulliver's Travels*, among other things an attack on self-deluding rationality. *A Modest Proposal*, which matter-of-factly advocates dining on infants to solve the famine problem in Ireland, gains its power via a surface of mind-numbing plausibility presented by a speaker whose detailed policy recommendations seem madly rational until we think about their insane implications. The "projector," who proposes the solution, speaks with ostensible tenderness even as he puts forth a plan to breed children for food.

from *A Modest Proposal*

IT IS A melancholy object to those, who walk through this great town, or travel in the country, when they see the streets, the roads and cabbin-doors crowded with beggars of the female sex, followed by three, four, or six children, all in rags, and importuning every passenger for an alms. These mothers instead of being able to work for their honest livelihood, are forced to employ all their time in strolling to beg sustenance for their helpless infants who, as they grow up, either turn thieves for want of work, or leave their dear native country, to fight for the Pretender in Spain, or sell themselves to the Barbadoes.

I think it is agreed by all parties, that this prodigious number of children in the arms, or on the backs, or at the heels of their mothers, and frequently of their fathers, is in the present deplorable state of the kingdom, a very great additional grievance; and therefore whoever could find out a fair, cheap and easy method of making these children sound and useful members of the common-wealth, would deserve so well of the publick, as to have his statue set up for a preserver of the nation.

But my intention is very far from being confined to provide only for the children of professed beggars: it is of a much greater extent, and shall take in the whole number of infants at a certain age, who are born of parents in effect as little able to support them, as those who demand our charity in the streets.

As to my own part, having turned my thoughts for many years, upon this important subject, and maturely weighed the several schemes of other projectors, I have always found them grossly mistaken in their computation. It is true, a child just dropt from its dam, may be supported by her milk, for a solar year, with little other nourishment: at most not above the value of two shillings, which the mother may certainly get, or the value in scraps, by her lawful occupation of begging; and it is exactly at one year old that I propose to provide for them in such a manner, as, instead of being a charge upon their parents, or the parish, or wanting food and raiment for the rest of their lives, they shall, on the contrary, contribute to the feeding, and partly to the cloathing of many thousands.

There is likewise another great advantage in my scheme, that it will prevent those voluntary abortions, and that horrid practice of women murdering their bastard children, alas! too frequent among us, sacrificing the poor innocent babes, I doubt, more to avoid the expence than the shame, which would move tears and pity in the most savage and inhuman breast.

The number of souls in Ireland being usually reckoned one million and a half, of these I calculate there may be about two hundred thousand couple whose wives are breeders; from which number I subtract thirty thousand couple, who are able to maintain their own children (although I apprehend there cannot be so many, under the present distresses of the kingdom); but this being granted, there will remain an hundred and seventy thousand breeders. I again subtract fifty thousand, for those women who miscarry, or whose children die by accident or disease within the year. There only remain an hundred and twenty thousand children of poor parents annually born. The question therefore is, How this number shall be reared, and provided for? which, as I have already said, under the present situation of affairs, is utterly impossible by all the methods hitherto proposed. . . .

I shall now therefore humbly propose my own thoughts, which I hope will not be liable to the least objection.

I have been assured by a very knowing American of my acquaintance in London, that a young healthy child well nursed, is, at a year old, a most delicious nourishing and wholesome food, whether stewed, roasted, baked, or boiled; and I make no doubt that it will equally serve in a fricasie, or a ragoust.

I do therefore humbly offer it to publick consideration, that of the hundred and twenty thousand children, already computed, twenty thousand may be reserved for breed, whereof only one fourth part to be males; which is more than we allow to sheep, black cattle, or swine, and my reason is, that these children are seldom the fruits of marriage, a circumstance not much regarded by our savages, therefore, one male will be sufficient to serve four females. That the remaining hundred thousand may, at a year old, be offered in sale to the persons of quality and fortune, through the kingdom, always advising the mother to let them suck plentifully in the last month, so as to render them plump, and fat for a good table. A child will make two dishes at an entertainment for friends, and when the family dines alone, the fore or hind quarter will make a reasonable dish, and seasoned with a little pepper or salt, will be very good boiled on the fourth day, especially in winter.

I have reckoned upon a medium, that a child just born will weigh 12 pounds, and in a solar year, if tolerably nursed, encreaseth to 28 pounds.

I grant this food will be somewhat dear, and therefore very proper for landlords, who, as they have already devoured most of the parents, seem to have the best title to the children.

Infant's flesh will be in season throughout the year, but more plentiful in March, and a little before and after; for we are told by a grave author, an eminent French physician, that fish being a prolifick dyet, there are more children born in Roman Catholick countries about nine months after Lent than at any other season, therefore, reckoning a year after Lent, the markets will be more glutted than usual, because the number of Popish infants, is at least three to one in this kingdom, and therefore it will have one other collateral advantage, by lessening the number of Papists among us.

I have already computed the charge of nursing a beggar's child (in which list I reckon all cottagers, labourers, and four-fifths of the farmers) to be about two shillings per annum, rags included; and I believe no gentleman would repine to give ten shillings for the carcass of a good fat child, which, as I have said, will make four dishes of excellent nutritive meat, when he hath only some particular friend, or his own family to dine with him. Thus the squire will learn to be a good landlord, and grow popular among his tenants, the mother will have eight shillings net profit, and be fit for work until she produces another child.

Those who are more thrifty (as I must confess the times require) may flay the carcass; the skin of which, artificially dressed, will make admirable gloves for ladies, and summer boots for fine gentlemen.

As to our City of Dublin, shambles may be appointed for this purpose, in the most convenient parts of it, and butchers we may be assured will not be wanting; although I rather recommend buying the children alive, and dressing them hot from the knife, as we do roasting pigs.

A very worthy person, a true lover of his country, and whose virtues I highly esteem, was lately pleased, in discoursing on this matter, to offer a refinement upon my scheme. He said, that many gentlemen of this kingdom, having of late destroyed their deer, he conceived that the want of venison might be well supply'd by the bodies of young lads and maidens, not exceeding fourteen years of age, nor under twelve; so great a number of both sexes in every country being now ready to starve for want of work and service: And these to be disposed of by their parents if alive, or otherwise by their nearest relations. But with due deference to so excellent a friend, and so deserving a patriot, I cannot be altogether in his sentiments; for as to the males, my American acquaintance assured me from frequent experience, that their flesh was generally tough and lean, like that of our school-boys, by continual exercise, and their taste disagreeable, and to fatten them would not answer the charge. Then as to the females, it would, I think, with humble submission, be a loss to the publick, because they soon would become breeders themselves: And besides, it is not improbable that some scrupulous people might be apt to censure such a practice, (although indeed very unjustly) as a little bordering upon cruelty, which, I confess, hath always been with me the strongest objection against any project, how well soever intended. . . .

I have too long digressed, and therefore shall return to my subject. I think the advantages by the proposal which I have made are obvious and many, as well as of the highest importance.

For first, as I have already observed, it would greatly lessen the number of Papists, with whom we are yearly over-run, being the principal breeders of the nation, as well as our most dangerous enemies, and who stay at home on purpose with a design to deliver the kingdom to the Pretender, hoping to take their advantage by the absence of so many good Protestants, who have chosen rather to leave their country, than stay at home and pay tithes against their conscience to an idolatrous Episcopal curate.

Secondly, The poorer tenants will have something valuable of their own, which by law may be made liable to distress, and help to pay their landlord's rent, their corn and cattle being already seized, and money a thing unknown.

Thirdly, Whereas the maintenance of an hundred thousand children, from two years old, and upwards, cannot be computed at less than ten shillings a piece per annum, the nation's stock will be thereby encreased fifty thousand pounds per annum, besides the profit of a new dish, introduced to the tables of all gentlemen of fortune in the kingdom, who have any refinement in taste. And the money will circulate among our selves, the goods being entirely of our own growth and manufacture.

Fourthly, The constant breeders, besides the gain of eight shillings sterling per annum by the sale of their children, will be rid of the charge of maintaining them after the first year.

Fifthly, This food would likewise bring great custom to taverns, where the vintners will certainly be so prudent as to procure the best receipts for dressing it to perfection; and consequently have their houses frequented by all the fine gentlemen, who justly value themselves upon their knowledge in good eating; and a skilful cook, who understands how to oblige his guests, will contrive to make it as expensive as they please.

Sixthly, This would be a great inducement to marriage, which all wise nations have either encouraged by rewards, or enforced by laws and penalties. It would encrease the care and tenderness of mothers towards their children, when they were sure of a settlement for life to the poor babes, provided in some sort by the publick, to their annual profit instead of expence. We should soon see an honest emulation among the married women, which of them could bring the fattest child to the market. Men would become as fond of their wives, during the time of their pregnancy, as they are now of their mares in foal, their cows in calf, or sows when they are ready to farrow; nor offer to beat or kick them (as is too frequent a practice) for fear of a miscarriage.

Many other advantages might be enumerated. For instance, the addition of some thousand carcasses in our exportation of barrel'd beef: the propagation of swine's flesh, and improvement in the art of making good bacon, so much wanted among us by the great destruction of pigs, too frequent at our tables; which are no way comparable in taste or magnificence to a well grown, fat yearling child, which roasted whole will make a considerable figure at a Lord Mayor's feast, or any other publick entertainment. But this, and many others, I omit, being studious of brevity.

Supposing that one thousand families in this city would be constant customers for infants flesh, besides others who might have it at merry meetings, particularly weddings and christenings, I compute that Dublin would take off annually about twenty thousand carcasses; and the rest of the kingdom (where probably they will be sold somewhat cheaper) the remaining eighty thousand.

I can think of no one objection that will possibly be raised against this proposal, unless it should be urged, that the number of people will be thereby much lessened in the kingdom. This I freely own, and it was indeed one principal design in offering it to the world. I desire the reader will observe, that I calculate my remedy for this one individual Kingdom of Ireland, and for no other that ever was, is, or, I think, ever can be upon Earth. Therefore let no man talk to me of other expedients: Of taxing our absentees at five shillings a pound: Of using neither cloaths, nor household furniture, except what is of our own growth and manufacture: Of utterly rejecting the materials and instruments that promote foreign luxury: Of curing the expensiveness of pride, vanity, idleness, and gaming in our women: Of introducing a vein of parsimony, prudence and temperance: Of learning to love our country, wherein we differ even from Laplanders, and the inhabitants of Topinamboo: Of quitting our animosities and factions, nor acting any longer like the Jews, who were murdering one another at the very moment their city was taken: Of being a little cautious not to sell our country and consciences for nothing: Of teaching landlords to have at least one degree of mercy towards their tenants. Lastly, of putting a spirit of honesty, industry, and skill into our shop-keepers, who, if a resolution could now be taken to buy only our native goods, would immediately unite to cheat and exact upon us in the price, the measure, and the goodness, nor could ever yet be brought to make one fair proposal of just dealing, though often and earnestly invited to it. . . .

I profess, in the sincerity of my heart, that I have not the least personal interest in endeavouring to promote this necessary work, having no other motive than the publick good of my country, by advancing our trade, providing for infants, relieving the poor, and giving some pleasure to the rich. I have no children by which I can propose to get a single penny; the youngest being nine years old, and my wife past child-bearing.

🐌

Joel Barlow (1754–1812)

A POET, BUSINESSMAN, and diplomat, Barlow was known in his youth as one of the "Hartford wits"—a group of young poets writing in Connecticut—and later renowned for his ambitious epic *The Vision of Columbus*. Although he espoused some conservative political views, he was also an ardent revolutionary, eagerly supporting both the American and French revolutions, and introducing deist ideas into some of his writings. Today he is mainly remembered for his sardonic yet passionately American *The Hasty Pudding*, which castigates the "vicious rules of art" he associated with Old World foods while celebrating the honest virtues of the Yankee's "abundant feast, / With simples furnished, and with plainness dressed." The "hasty pudding" that is the centerpiece of his poem consists of cornmeal simmered in water for about fifteen minutes. But what seems to be a culinary argument becomes, in any case, a political manifesto, decrying what Barlow considered the fakery and pretentiousness of a regime against which he and his compatriots had rebelled.

from *The Hasty Pudding*:
On the American Kitchen Muse

CANTO II

To mix the food by vicious rules of art,
To kill the stomach and to sink the heart,

To make mankind to social virtue sour,
Cram o'er each dish, and be what they devour;
For this the kitchen muse first framed her book,
Commanding sweat to stream from every cook;
Children no more their antic gambols tried,
And friend to physic wondered why they died.
Not so the Yankee—his abundant feast,
With simples furnished, and with plainness dressed,
A numerous offspring gathers round the board,
And cheers alike the servant and the lord;
Whose well-bought hunger prompts the joyous taste,
And health attends them from the short repast.
While the full pail rewards the milkmaid's toil,
The mother sees the morning cauldron boil;
To stir the pudding next demands their care,
To spread the table and the bowls prepare;
To feed the children, as their portions cool,
And comb their heads, and send them off to school.
Yet may the simplest dish some rules impart,
For nature scorns not all the aids of art.
Ev'n Hasty Pudding, purest of all food,
May still be bad, indifferent, or good,
As sage experience the short process guides,
Or want of skill, or want of care presides:
Whoe'er would form it on the surest plan,
To rear the child and long sustain the man;
To shield the morals while it mends the size,
And all the powers of every food supplies,
Attend the lessons that the muse shall bring.
Suspend your spoons, and listen while I sing.
But since, O man! thy life and health demand
Not food alone, but labor from thy hand,
First in the field, beneath the sun's strong rays,
Ask of thy mother earth the needful maize;
She loves the race that courts her yielding soil,
And gives her bounties to the sons of toil.

When now the ox, obedient to thy call,
Repays the loan that filled the winter stall,
Pursue his traces o'er the furrowed plain,
And plant in measured hills the golden grain.
But when the tender germ begins to shoot,
And the green spire declares the sprouting root,
Then guard your nursling from each greedy foe,
The insidious worm, the all-devouring crow.
A little ashes, sprinkled round the spire,
Soon steeped in rain, will bid the worm retire;
The feathered robber with his hungry maw
Swift flies the field before your man of straw,
A frightful image, such as schoolboys bring
When met to burn the Pope or hang the King.
Thrice in the season, through each verdant row
Wield the strong plowshare and the faithful hoe;
The faithful hoe, a double task that takes,
To till the summer corn, and roast the winter cakes.
Slow springs the blade, while checked by chilling rains,
Ere yet the sun the seat of Cancer gains;
But when his fiercest fires emblaze the land,
Then start the juices, then the roots expand;
Then, like a column of Corinthian mold,
The stalk struts upward, and the leaves unfold;
The busy branches all the ridges fill,
Entwine their arms, and kiss from hill to hill.
Here cease to vex them, all your cares are done;
Leave the last labors to the parent sun;
Beneath his genial smiles the well-dressed field,
When autumn calls, a plenteous crop shall yield.
Now the strong foliage bears the standards high,
And shoots the tall top-gallants to the sky;
The suckling ears their silky fringes bend,
And pregnant grown, their swelling coats distend;
The loaded stalk, while still the burden grows,
O'erhangs the space that runs between the rows;

High as a hop-field waves the silent grove,
A safe retreat for little thefts of love,
When the pledged roasting-ears invite the maid,
To meet her swain beneath the new-formed shade;
His generous hand unloads the cumbrous hill,
And the green spoils her ready basket fill;
Small compensation for the two-fold bliss,
The promised wedding and the present kiss.
Slight depredations these; but now the moon
Calls from his hollow tree the sly raccoon;
And while by night he bears his prize away,
The bolder squirrel labors through the day.
Both thieves alike, but provident of time,
A virtue rare, that almost hides their crime.
Then let them steal the little stores they can,
And fill their granaries from the toils of man;
We've one advantage where they take no part,
With all their wiles they ne'er have found the art
To boil the Hasty Pudding; here we shine
Superior far to tenants of the pine;
This envied boon to man shall still belong,
Unshared by them in substance or in song.
At last the closing season browns the plain,
And ripe October gathers in the grain;
Deep loaded carts the spacious corn-house fill,
The sack distended marches to the mill;
The laboring mill beneath the burden groans,
And showers the future pudding from the stones;
Till the glad housewife greets the powdered gold,
And the new crop exterminates the old.

❦

Jean Anthelme Brillat-Savarin
(1755–1826)

OFTEN REGARDED AS the first serious work of gastronomic criticism, Brillat-Savarin's *The Physiology of Taste* is a formidable yet charming meditation upon appetite, gourmandism, hunger, thirst, obesity, fasting, cooking, and restaurateurs, to name only a few of its topics. Famous for his many aphorisms, such as "The table is the only place where a man is never bored for the first hour," and "The discovery of a new dish does more for human happiness than the discovery of a new star," Brillat-Savarin wrote this large volume from the perspectives of both Enlightenment learning and the French Revolution's Rights of Man. Such rights include entitlement to the sensual pleasure of food and the erudition necessary for the gourmet to understand the psychological and physiological nature of his hedonism. So in our selection—translated and annotated by the great contemporary gastronomer M.F.K. Fisher—Brillat-Savarin insists that knowledge is the key to gastronomical enjoyment.

from *The Physiology of Taste*: On Taste

ANALYSIS OF THE SENSATION OF TASTING

I FEEL, having thus set forth the principles of my theory, that it is certain that taste causes sensations of three different kinds: *direct, complete,* and *reflective.*

The *direct* sensation is the first one felt, produced from the immediate operations of the organs of the mouth, while the body under consideration is still on the fore part of the tongue.

The *complete* sensation is the one made up of this first perception plus the impression which arises when the food leaves its original position, passes to the back of the mouth, and attacks the whole organ with its taste and its aroma.

Finally, the *reflective* sensation is the opinion which one's spirit forms from the impressions which have been transmitted to it by the mouth.

Let us put this theory into action, by seeing what happens to a man who is eating or drinking.

He who eats a peach, for instance, is first of all agreeably struck by the perfume which it exhales; he puts a piece of it into his mouth, and enjoys a sensation of tart freshness which invites him to continue; but it is not until the instant of swallowing, when the mouthful passes under his nasal channel, that the full aroma is revealed to him; and this completes the sensation which a peach can cause. Finally, it is not until it has been swallowed that the man, considering what he has just experienced, will say to himself, "Now there is something really delicious!"

In the same way, in drinking: while the wine is in the mouth, one is agreeably but not completely appreciative of it; it is not until the moment when he has finished swallowing it that a man can truly taste, consider, and discover the bouquet peculiar to each variety; and there must still be a little lapse of time before a real connoisseur can say, "It is good, or passable, or bad. By Jove, here is a Chambertin! Confound it, this is only a Suresnes!"

It can thus be seen that it is in following certain well-studied principles that the true amateurs SIP their wine (*ils le sirotent*), for, as they hesitate after each taste of it, they enjoy the same full pleasure that they might have had if they had drunk the whole glass in one gulp.

The same thing happens, but much more obviously, when the sense of taste must be disagreeably assaulted.

Take, for example, an invalid whose doctor prescribes an enormous glass of that old-fashioned black medicine which was drunk during the reign of Louis XIV.

His sense of smell, faithful guide, warns him of the revolting taste of the horrible fluid; his eyes pop out as if he recognizes real danger; disgust is plainly written on his face; already his stomach heaves. But he is begged to drink, and he stiffens with resolve; he gargles first with a little brandy, holds his nose, and swallows . . .

While the foul brew fills his mouth and coats it, the sensation is confused and tolerable; but, with the last swallow, the aftertastes develop, the nauseating odors become clear, and the patient's every feature expresses a horror which only the fear of death itself could make him endure.

If, on the other hand, it is a matter of some such insipid drink as a glass of water, there is neither taste nor aftertaste; one feels nothing, cares nothing; one has drunk, and that is all there is to it.

ORDER OF THE VARIOUS IMPRESSIONS OF TASTE

TASTE is not as richly endowed as hearing, which can listen to and compare several sounds at the same time: taste is simple in its action, which is to say that it cannot receive impressions from two flavors at once.

But taste can be double, and even multiple, in succession, so that in a single mouthful a second and sometimes a third sensation can be realized; they fade gradually, and are called aftertaste, perfume, or aroma. It is the same way as, when a basic note is sounded, an attentive ear distinguishes in it one or more series of other consonant tones, whose number has not yet been correctly estimated.

Men who eat quickly and without thought do not perceive the taste impressions of this second level, which are the exclusive perquisite of a small number of the chosen few; and it is by means of these impressions that gastronomers can classify, in the order of their excellence, the various substances submitted to their approval.

These fleeting nuances vibrate for a long time in the organ of taste: students of them assume without even realizing it a proper stance for the pronouncement of their verdicts, always with necks stretched and noses twisted up and to the left, as it were to larboard.

PLEASURES CAUSED BY TASTE

LET us now look philosophically for a moment at the joy or sadness which can result from the sense of taste.

First of all we are confronted with the application of that truism unfortunately too well known, that man is much more sensitive to pain than to pleasure.

Obviously our reactions to extremely bitter, acid, or sour substances cause us to suffer deeply painful or grievous sensations. It is even held that hydrocyanic acid kills so quickly only because it causes such intense agony that our vital forces cannot long endure it.

On the other hand, agreeable sensations extend over only a small scale, and if there is a fairly appreciable difference between an insipid flavor and one that stimulates the taste, the space between something called good and something reputed to be excellent is not very great. This is made clearer by the following comparisons: first or positive, a dry hard piece of boiled meat; second or comparative, a slice of veal; third or superlative, a pheasant cooked to perfection.

However, taste as Nature has endowed us with it is still that one of our senses which gives us the greatest joy:

(1) Because the pleasure of eating is the only one which, indulged in moderately, is not followed by regret;

(2) Because it is common to all periods in history, all ages of man, and all social conditions;

(3) Because it recurs of necessity at least once every day, and can be repeated without inconvenience two or three times in that space of hours;

(4) Because it can mingle with all the other pleasures, and even console us for their absence;

(5) Because its sensations are at once more lasting than others and more subject to our will;

(6) Because, finally, in eating we experience a certain special and indefinable well-being, which arises from our instinctive realization that by the very act we perform we are repairing our bodily losses and prolonging our lives.

This will be more thoroughly developed in the chapter which we shall devote especially to *the pleasures of the table*, considered from the point to which our modern civilization has brought them.

THE SUPREMACY OF MAN

WE have been reared with the agreeable belief that, of all the creatures who walk, swim, climb, or fly, man is the one whose sense of taste is the most perfect.

This belief threatens to be overthrown.

Dr. Gall states, backed by I do not know what investigations, that there are animals whose tasting apparatus is more developed and even more perfect than ours.

This doctrine is shocking to hear, and smacks of heresy.

Man, king of all nature by divine right, and for whose benefit the earth has been covered and peopled, must perforce be armed with an organ which can put him in contact with all that is toothsome among his subjects.

The tongue of an animal is comparable in its sensitivity to his intelligence: among fish it is but a movable bone; among birds in general it is a membranous cartilage; in the four-legged world it is often sheathed with scales or roughnesses, and moreover has no power of circular movement.

Man's tongue, on the other hand, by the delicacy of its surfaces and of the various membranes which surround it, proves clearly enough the sublimity of the operations for which it is destined.

What is more, I have discovered at least three movements in it which are unknown to animals, and which I describe as movements of SPICATION, ROTATION, AND VERRITION (from the Latin *verro*, I sweep). The first takes place when the tip of the tongue protrudes between the lips which squeeze it; the second, when it rolls around in the space between the cheeks and the palate; the third, when it catches, by curving itself now up and now down, the particles of food which have stuck in the semicircular moat between the lips and the gums.

Animals are limited in their tastes; some live only upon plants, and others eat nothing but meat; still others nourish themselves solely upon seeds; none of them knows combinations of flavors.

Man, on the other hand, is *omnivorous*; everything edible is prey to his vast hunger, and this brings out, as its immediate result, tasting powers proportionate to the general use which he must make of them. That is to say, man's apparatus of the sense of taste has been brought to a state of rare perfection; and, to convince ourselves thoroughly, let us watch it work.

As soon as an edible body has been put into the mouth, it is seized upon, gases, moisture, and all, without possibility of retreat.

Lips stop whatever might try to escape; the teeth bite and break it; saliva drenches it; the tongue mashes and churns it; a breathlike sucking pushes it toward the gullet; the tongue lifts up to make it slide and slip; the sense of smell appreciates it as it passes the nasal channel, and it is pulled down into the stomach to be submitted to sundry baser transformations without, in this whole metamorphosis, a single atom or drop or particle having been missed by the powers of appreciation of the taste sense.

It is, then, because of this perfection that the real enjoyment of eating is a special prerogative of man.

This pleasure is even contagious; and we transmit it quickly enough to the animals which we have tamed and which in one way or another make up a part of our society, like elephants, dogs, cats, and even parrots.

If some animals have a larger tongue than others, a more developed roof to their mouths, an ampler throat, it is because this tongue, acting as a muscle, must move bulky food; this palate must press and this throat must swallow larger portions than average; but all analogy is opposed to the inference that their sense of taste is proportionately greater than that of other animals.

Moreover, since taste must not be weighed except by the nature of the sensation which it arouses in the center of life, an impression received by an animal cannot be compared with one felt by a man: the latter sensation, at once clearer and more precise, presupposes of necessity a superior quality in the organ which transmits it.

Finally, what is left to be desired of a faculty sensitive to such a degree of perfection that the gourmands of Rome could tell by the flavor whether fish was caught between the city bridges or lower down the river?

And do we not have, in our own days, those gastronomers who pretend to have discovered the special flavor of the leg upon which a sleeping pheasant rests his weight?

And are we not surrounded by gourmets who can tell the latitude under which a wine has ripened just as surely as a pupil of Biot or Arago knows how to predict an eclipse?

What follows from there? Simply that what is Caesar's must be rendered unto him, that man must be proclaimed *the great gourmand of Nature*, and that it must not seem too astonishing that the good doctor Gall does as Homer did, and drowses now and then. . . .

Charles Lamb (1775–1834)

A MAJOR ESSAYIST of the English Romantic period, Lamb is most famous for writing, with his sister Mary, the children's book *Tales from Shakespeare*. He composed his work under the pseudonym of "Elia," a name he adopted as the persona of an aging bachelor. Interested in almost everything, as a critic he writes somewhat associationally, just short of rambling. "A Dissertation upon Roast Pig," from which our selection is taken, is part fantastic anthropology, part history, and part gastronomy. In beginning his "dissertation" with references to an ancient Chinese manuscript and the culinary habits of the Abyssinians, Lamb seems to write with tongue in cheek, even as he shows here, in saucing his pig with "brains, and a dash of mild sage," a kind of cheeky tongue.

from A Dissertation upon Roast Pig

MANKIND, SAYS A Chinese manuscript, which my friend M. was obliging enough to read and explain to me, for the first seventy thousand ages ate their meat raw, clawing or biting it from the living animal, just as they do in Abyssinia to this day. This period is not obscurely hinted at by their great Confucius in the second chapter of his Mundane Mutations, where he designates a kind of golden age by the term Chofang, literally the Cooks' Holiday. The manuscript goes on to say, that the art of roasting, or rather broiling (which I take to be the elder brother) was accidentally discovered in the manner following. The swine-herd, Ho-ti, having gone out into the woods one morning, as his manner was, to collect mast for his hogs, left his cottage in the care of his eldest son Bo-bo, a great lubberly boy, who being fond of playing with fire, as younkers of his age commonly are, let some sparks escape into a bundle of straw, which kindling quickly, spread the conflagration over every part of their poor mansion, till it was reduced to ashes. Together with the cottage (a sorry antediluvian make-shift of a building, you may think it), what was of much more importance, a fine litter of new-farrowed pigs, no less than nine in number, perished. China pigs have been esteemed a luxury all over the East, from the remotest periods that we read of. Bo-bo was in the utmost consternation, as you may think, not so much for the sake of the tenement, which his father and he could easily build up again with a few dry branches, and the labour of an hour or two, at any time, as for the loss of the pigs. While he was thinking what he should say to his father, and wringing his hands over the smoking remnants of one of those untimely sufferers, an odour assailed his nostrils, unlike any scent which he had before experienced. What could it proceed from?—not from the burnt cottage—he had smelt that smell before—indeed this was by no

means the first accident of the kind which had occurred through the negligence of this unlucky young fire-brand. Much less did it resemble that of
any known herb, weed, or flower. A premonitory moistening at the same
time overflowed his nether lip. He knew not what to think. He next stooped
down to feel the pig, if there were any signs of life in it. He burnt his fingers,
and to cool them he applied them in his booby fashion to his mouth. Some
of the crumbs of the scorched skin had come away with his fingers, and for
the first time in his life (in the world's life indeed, for before him no man
had known it) he tasted—*crackling*! Again he felt and fumbled at the pig.
It did not burn him so much now, still he licked his fingers from a sort of
habit. The truth at length broke into his slow understanding, that it was
the pig that smelt so, and the pig that tasted so delicious; and surrendering
himself up to the new-born pleasure, he fell to tearing up whole handfuls
of the scorched skin with the flesh next it, and was cramming it down his
throat in his beastly fashion, when his sire entered amid the smoking rafters,
armed with retributory cudgel, and finding how affairs stood, began to rain
blows upon the young rogue's shoulders, as thick as hail-stones, which Bo-bo
heeded not any more than if they had been flies. The tickling pleasure, which
he experienced in his lower regions, had rendered him quite callous to any
inconveniences he might feel in those remote quarters. His father might lay
on, but he could not beat him from his pig, till he had fairly made an end of
it, when, becoming a little more sensible of his situation, something like the
following dialogue ensued.

"You graceless whelp, what have you got there devouring? Is it not enough
that you have burnt me down three houses with your dog's tricks, and be
hanged to you! but you must be eating fire, and I know not what—what have
you got there, I say?"

"O father, the pig, the pig! do come and taste how nice the burnt pig eats."

The ears of Ho-ti tingled with horror. He cursed his son, and he cursed
himself that ever he should beget a son that should eat burnt pig.

Bo-bo, whose scent was wonderfully sharpened since morning, soon
raked out another pig, and fairly rending it asunder, thrust the lesser half by
main force into the fists of Ho-ti, still shouting out, "Eat, eat, eat the burnt
pig, father, only taste—O Lord!"—with such-like barbarous ejaculations,
cramming all the while as if he would choke.

Ho-ti trembled every joint while he grasped the abominable thing, waver-
ing whether he should not put his son to death for an unnatural young mon-

ster, when the crackling scorching his fingers, as it had done his son's, and applying the same remedy to them, he in his turn tasted some of its flavour, which, make what sour mouths he would for a pretense, proved not altogether displeasing to him. In conclusion (for the manuscript here is a little tedious), both father and son fairly set down to the mess, and never left off till they had dispatched all that remained of the litter.

Bo-bo was strictly enjoined not to let the secret escape, for the neighbours would certainly have stoned them for a couple of abominable wretches, who could think of improving upon the good meat which God had sent them. Nevertheless, strange stories got about. It was observed that Ho-ti's cottage was burnt down now more frequently than ever. Nothing but fires from this time forward. Some would break out in broad day, others in the night-time. As often as the sow farrowed, so sure was the house of Ho-ti to be in a blaze; and Ho-ti himself, which was the more remarkable, instead of chastising his son, seemed to grow more indulgent to him than ever. At length they were watched, the terrible mystery discovered, and father and son summoned to take their trial at Pekin, then an inconsiderable assize town. Evidence was given, the obnoxious food itself produced in court, and verdict about to be pronounced, when the foreman of the jury begged that some of the burnt pig, of which the culprits stood accused, might be handed into the box. He handled it, and they all handled it; and burning their fingers, as Bo-bo and his father had done before them, and nature prompting to each of them the same remedy, against the face of all the facts, and the clearest charge which judge had ever given,—to the surprise of the whole court, townsfolk, strangers, reporters, and all present—without leaving the box, or any manner of consultation whatever, they brought in a simultaneous verdict of Not Guilty.

The judge, who was a shrewd fellow, winked at the manifest iniquity of the decision: and when the court was dismissed, went privily and bought up all the pigs that could be had for love or money. In a few days his lordship's town-house was observed to be on fire. The thing took wing, and now there was nothing to be seen but fire in every direction. Fuel and pigs grew enormously dear all over the district. The insurance-offices one and all shut up shop. People built slighter and slighter every day, until it was feared that the very science of architecture would in no long time be lost to the world. Thus this custom of firing houses continued, till in process of time, says my manuscript, a sage arose, like our Locke, who made a discovery that the flesh of swine, or indeed of any other animal, might be cooked (*burnt*, as they called it) without the necessity of consuming a whole house to dress it. Then first began the rude form of a gridiron. Roasting by the string or spit came in a century or two later, I forget in whose dynasty. By such slow degrees, concludes the manuscript, do the most useful, and seemingly the most obvious, arts make their way among mankind——

Without placing too implicit faith in the account above given, it must be agreed that if a worthy pretext for so dangerous an experiment as setting houses on fire (especially in these days) could be assigned in favour of any culinary object, that pretext and excuse might be found in ROAST PIG.

Of all the delicacies in the whole *mundus edibilis*, I will maintain it to be the most delicate—*princeps obsoniorum*.

I speak not of your grown porkers—things between pig and pork—those hobbydehoys—but a young and tender suckling—under a moon old—guiltless as yet of the sty—with no original speck of the *amor immunditoe*, the hereditary failing of the first parent, yet manifest—his voice as yet not broken, but something between a childish treble and a grumble—the mild forerunner or *proeludium* of a grunt.

He must be roasted. I am not ignorant that our ancestors ate them seethed, or boiled—but what a sacrifice to the exterior tegument!

There is no flavour comparable, I will contend, to that of the crisp, tawny, well-watched, not over-roasted, *crackling*, as it is well called—the very teeth are invited to their share of the pleasure at this banquet in overcoming the coy, brittle resistance—with the adhesive oleaginous—O call it not fat! but an indefinable sweetness growing up to it—the tender blossoming of fat—fat cropped in the bud—taken in the shoot—in the first innocence—the cream and quintessence of the child-pig's yet pure food—the lean, no lean, but a kind of animal manna—or, rather, fat and lean (if it must be so) so blended and running into each other, that both together make but one ambrosian result or common substance.

Behold him, while he is "doing"—it seemeth rather a refreshing warmth, than a scorching heat, that he is so passive to. How equably he twirleth round the string!—Now he is just done. To see the extreme sensibility of that tender age! he hath wept out his pretty eyes—radiant jellies—shooting stars—

See him in the dish, his second cradle, how meek he lieth!—wouldst thou have had this innocent grow up to the grossness and indocility which too often accompany maturer swinehood? Ten to one he would have proved a glutton, a sloven, an obstinate, disagreeable animal—wallowing in all manner of filthy conversation—from these sins he is happily snatched away——

> Ere sin could blight or sorrow fade,
> Death came with timely care—

his memory is odoriferous—no clown curseth, while his stomach half rejecteth, the rank bacon—no coal-heaver bolteth him in reeking sausages—he hath a fair sepulchre in the grateful stomach of the judicious epicure—and for such a tomb might be content to die.

He is the best of sapors. Pine-apple is great. She is indeed almost too transcendent—a delight, if not sinful, yet so like to sinning that really a tender-conscienced person would do well to pause—too ravishing for mortal taste, she woundeth and excoriateth the lips that approach her—like lovers' kisses, she biteth—she is a pleasure bordering on pain from the fierceness and insanity of her relish—but she stoppeth at the palate—she meddleth not with the appetite—and the coarsest hunger might barter her consistently for a mutton-chop.

Pig—let me speak his praise—is no less provocative of the appetite, than he is satisfactory to the criticalness of the censorious palate. The strong man may batten on him, and the weakling refuseth not his mild juices.

Unlike to mankind's mixed characters, a bundle of virtues and vices, inexplicably intertwisted, and not to be unraveled without hazard, he is—good throughout. No part of him is better or worse than another. He helpeth, as far as his little means extend, all around. He is the least envious of banquets. He is all neighbours' fare. . . .

His sauce should be considered. Decidedly, a few bread crumbs, done up with his liver and brains, and a dash of mild sage. But banish, dear Mrs. Cook, I beseech you, the whole onion tribe. Barbecue your whole hogs to your palate, steep them in shallots, stuff them out with plantations of the rank and guilty garlic; you cannot poison them, or make them stronger than they are—but consider, he is a weakling—a flower.

George Gordon, Lord Byron (1788–1824)

A HANDSOME, BROODING young aristocrat with a deformed foot, George Gordon, Lord Byron, awoke to find himself famous in 1812, with the publication of his *Childe Harold's Pilgrimage*, a verse narrative recounting the adventurous travels of a handsome, brooding young aristocrat. Soon Byron became a kind of Regency rock star—perhaps the first modern "celebrity." Women threw themselves at him by the score, but he also had a proclivity for affairs with nubile boys. Though he was athletic (he swam the Hellespont in his twenties), he also had a tendency to overweight, periodically putting himself on radical diets and even purging. His brilliant satirical poem *Don Juan* reworks in witty ottava rima the story of another handsome hero, the lady-killing Don Juan, who here appears as an innocent victim of female lustfulness. Our selection dramatizes an episode of cannibalism in an open boat—called "the custom of the sea"—when Juan and his tutor Pedrillo survive a shipwreck only to find themselves and the crew starving.

from *Don Juan*: The Death of Pedrillo

'T is thus with people in an open boat,
    They live upon the love of life, and bear
More than can be believed, or even thought,
    And stand like rocks the tempest's wear and tear;
And hardship still has been the sailor's lot,
    Since Noah's ark went cruising here and there;
She had a curious crew as well as cargo,
Like the first old Greek privateer, the Argo.

But man is a carnivorous production,
    And must have meals, at least one meal a day;
He cannot live, like woodcocks, upon suction,
    But, like the shark and tiger, must have prey;

Although his anatomical construction
    Bears vegetables, in a grumbling way,
Your labouring people think beyond all question,
Beef, veal, and mutton, better for digestion.

And thus it was with this our hapless crew;
    For on the third day there came on a calm,
And though at first their strength it might renew,
    And lying on their weariness like balm,
Lull'd them like turtles sleeping on the blue
    Of ocean, when they woke they felt a qualm,
And fell all ravenously on their provision,
Instead of hoarding it with due precision.

The consequence was easily foreseen—
    They ate up all they had, and drank their wine,
In spite of all remonstrances, and then
    On what, in fact, next day were they to dine?
They hoped the wind would rise, these foolish men!
    And carry them to shore; these hopes were fine,
But as they had but one oar, and that brittle,
It would have been more wise to save their victual.

The fourth day came, but not a breath of air,
    And Ocean slumber'd like an unwean'd child:
The fifth day, and their boat lay floating there,
    The sea and sky were blue, and clear, and mild—
With their one oar (I wish they had had a pair)
    What could they do? and hunger's rage grew wild:
So Juan's spaniel, spite of his entreating,
Was kill'd and portion'd out for present eating.

On the sixth day they fed upon his hide,
    And Juan, who had still refused, because
The creature was his father's dog that died,
    Now feeling all the vulture in his jaws,
With some remorse received (though first denied)

As a great favour one of the fore-paws,
Which he divided with Pedrillo, who
Devour'd it, longing for the other too.

The seventh day, and no wind—the burning sun
    Blister'd and scorch'd, and, stagnant on the sea,
They lay like carcasses; and hope was none,
    Save in the breeze that came not; savagely
They glared upon each other—all was done,
    Water, and wine, and food,—and you might see
The longings of the cannibal arise
(Although they spoke not) in their wolfish eyes.

At length one whisper'd his companion, who
    Whisper'd another, and thus it went round,
And then into a hoarser murmur grew,
    An ominous, and wild, and desperate sound;
And when his comrade's thought each sufferer knew,
    'T was but his own, suppress'd till now, he found:
And out they spoke of lots for flesh and blood,
And who should die to be his fellow's food.

But ere they came to this, they that day shared
    Some leathern caps, and what remain'd of shoes;
And then they look'd around them and despair'd,
    And none to be the sacrifice would choose;
At length the lots were torn up, and prepared,
    But of materials that much shock the Muse—
Having no paper, for the want of better,
They took by force from Juan Julia's letter.

The lots were made, and mark'd, and mix'd, and handed,
    In silent horror, and their distribution
Lull'd even the savage hunger which demanded,
    Like the Promethean vulture, this pollution;
None in particular had sought or plann'd it,
    'T was nature gnaw'd them to this resolution,

By which none were permitted to be neuter—
And the lot fell on Juan's luckless tutor.

He but requested to be bled to death:
    The surgeon had his instruments, and bled
Pedrillo, and so gently ebb'd his breath,
    You hardly could perceive when he was dead.
He died as born, a Catholic in faith,
    Like most in the belief in which they're bred,
And first a little crucifix he kiss'd,
And then held out his jugular and wrist.

The surgeon, as there was no other fee,
    Had his first choice of morsels for his pains;
But being thirstiest at the moment, he
    Preferr'd a draught from the fast-flowing veins:
Part was divided, part thrown in the sea,
    And such things as the entrails and the brains
Regaled two sharks, who follow'd o'er the billow—
The sailors ate the rest of poor Pedrillo.

The sailors ate him, all save three or four,
    Who were not quite so fond of animal food;
To these was added Juan, who, before
    Refusing his own spaniel, hardly could
Feel now his appetite increased much more;
    'T was not to be expected that he should,
Even in extremity of their disaster,
Dine with them on his pastor and his master.

'T was better that he did not; for, in fact,
    The consequence was awful in the extreme;
For they, who were most ravenous in the act,
    Went raging mad—Lord! How they did blaspheme!
And foam and roll, with strange convulsions rack'd,
    Drinking salt water like a mountain-stream,
Tearing, and grinning, howling, screeching, swearing,
And, with hyaena-laughter, died despairing.

Their numbers were much thinn'd by this infliction,
    And all the rest were thin enough, Heaven knows;
And some of them had lost their recollection,
    Happier than they who still perceived their woes;
But others ponder'd on a new dissection,
    As if not warn'd sufficiently by those
Who had already perish'd, suffering madly,
For having used their appetites so sadly.

And next they thought upon the master's mate,
    As fattest; but he saved himself, because,
Besides being much averse from such a fate,
    There were some other reasons; the first was,
He had been rather indisposed of late;
    And that which chiefly proved his saving clause
Was a small present made to him at Cadiz,
By general subscription of the ladies.

Of poor Pedrillo something still remain'd,
    But was used sparingly,—some were afraid,
And others still their appetites constrain'd,
    Or but at times a little supper made;
All except Juan, who throughout abstain'd,
    Chewing a piece of bamboo and some lead:
At length they caught two boobies and a noddy,
And then they left off eating the dead body.

And if Pedrillo's fate should shocking be,
    Remember Ugolino condescends
To eat the head of his arch-enemy
    The moment after he politely ends
His tale: if foes be food in hell, at sea
    'T is surely fair to dine upon our friends,
When shipwreck's short allowance grows too scanty,
Without being much more horrible than Dante.

John Keats (1795–1821)

ONE OF THE greatest of the British Romantic poets who flourished in the early nineteenth century, John Keats died of consumption when he was just twenty-six. But before his demise—in Rome, where he had gone to escape the damp and cold of an English winter—he had produced a magnificent body of work, including such poems as his "Ode on a Grecian Urn" and "Ode to a Nightingale," written during what has been called the *annus mirabilis* of 1819, when he was already a very sick man. His works are sensuous, even voluptuous, sometimes featuring yearning representations of food and wine, as in "The Eve of St. Agnes," where an impassioned lover feasts his beloved with "lucent syrops" and "spiced dainties," or as in "La Belle Dame sans Merci" ("The Beautiful Lady without Mercy"), our selection here, where a femme fatale lures a wandering knight with aphrodisiac "roots of relish sweet, / And honey wild, and manna-dew," reminding readers that supper can perhaps be more seductive than nourishing.

La Belle Dame sans Merci

O what can ail thee, knight-at-arms,
    Alone and palely loitering?
The sedge has withered from the lake,
    And no birds sing.

O what can ail thee, knight-at-arms,
    So haggard and so woe-begone?
The squirrel's granary is full,
    And the harvest's done.

I see a lily on thy brow,
    With anguish moist and fever-dew,
And on thy cheeks a fading rose
    Fast withereth too.

I met a lady in the meads,
    Full beautiful—a faery's child,
Her hair was long, her foot was light,
    And her eyes were wild.

I made a garland for her head,
    And bracelets too, and fragrant zone;
She looked at me as she did love,
    And made sweet moan

I set her on my pacing steed,
    And nothing else saw all day long,
For sidelong would she bend, and sing
    A faery's song.

She found me roots of relish sweet,
    And honey wild, and manna-dew,
And sure in language strange she said—
    'I love thee true'.

She took me to her Elfin grot,
    And there she wept and sighed full sore,
And there I shut her wild wild eyes
    With kisses four.

And there she lullèd me asleep,
    And there I dreamed—Ah! woe betide!—
The latest dream I ever dreamt
    On the cold hill side.

I saw pale kings and princes too,
    Pale warriors, death-pale were they all;
They cried—'La Belle Dame sans Merci
    Hath thee in thrall!'

I saw their starved lips in the gloam,
    With horrid warning gapèd wide,
And I awoke and found me here,
    On the cold hill's side.

And this is why I sojourn here,
    Alone and palely loitering,
Though the sedge is withered from the lake,
    And no birds sing

Alexandre Dumas (1802–1870)

ALEXANDRE DUMAS, KNOWN as *père* because his son of the same name also became a well-known writer, was one of the most prolific novelists in French literary history. Famed as the author of *The Count of Monte Cristo* and *The Three Musketeers*, among other swashbuckling romances, he was also a playwright, travel writer, and noted gourmet. His *Grand dictionnaire de la cuisine* (*Great Dictionary of Cuisine*), published posthumously, reflects both his passion for cooking and his talents as a storyteller. Encyclopedic in its culinary learning and voluminous in its offerings of recipes, the book is sprinkled with charming anecdotes, like the one featured in our selection here. "My taste for cookery, like that for poetry," he once claimed, "came to me from the heavens."

from *The Great Dictionary of Cuisine*:
The Onion

IN ORDER TO talk knowledgably about a subject, you have to have it right in front of your eyes, so it's a good thing I was led to the town of Roscoff at the very moment when I was starting to write about the word "onion."

In fact even more than ancient Egypt the Cape Armorique recalls that during the battle of the gods against Jupiter, the conquered ones, pursued to the very edge of the continent and seeing they could flee no further, in order to escape the wrath of Jupiter turned themselves into onions. This bulb—so praised in antiquity that even the poets sang of it and the Egyptians revered it—is nowhere else in France found in such profusion.

In some years Roscoff sends up to thirty or forty vessels weighted down with onions bound for England.

It was a man from this region who first thought of speculating in the onion trade; but in order to make the French onion known in England, and to demonstrate its superiority to the British bulb, it was necessary to carry out a resoundingly daring scheme. One day this Roscovite went to find a Monsieur Corbière, author of several novels of the sea, a longtime naval officer, and a native of Roscoff, to inquire of him how to say in English: "L'oignon anglais n'est pas bon."

The person whose translation was sought replied: "The English onion is not good."

"Be kind enough to write that on a piece of paper, monsieur," requested the Roscovite. Monsieur Corbière took out a pen and wrote the requisite sentence. The Roscovite thanked him.

Three days later he was seen leaving for London, in a sloop bursting with onions.

Arriving in the English capital, he went straight for the busiest market, unfurled a sign on which was written in large letters the following maxim: "The English onion is not good." And then, under his sign, he placed a little cart full of French onions.

The English are well known for not tolerating whatsoever that kind of a slander. One of them approached and addressed himself to the foreign vendor; the latter, who had not a word of English, contented himself with the reply: "The English onion is not good."

This response infuriated the Englishman; he drew near the Roscovite and put up both fists. The Roscovite had no idea what the Englishman was trying to say, but certainly perceived he was being threatened. He seized the Englishman by the elbow and spinning him like a top, whirled him around three times. After the third twirl, the Englishman fell down; he got up furiously, and came towards his adversary, who was at the ready.

The Roscovite was almost six feet tall, and powerful as the god Teutatès.

He grabbed the Englishman by the arms, lifted him up and threw him down right on his belly.

It was against all the rules of wrestling: it's necessary that one of the antagonist's shoulders touch the ground in order for him to be declared the loser. The Roscovite thus knew he was in the wrong. "It's true, it's true," he said, motioning with his head that he had erred; and he once again stood his ground, just as the Englishman had.

The Englishman came back at him, and this time the onion merchant grabbed him by his shirt collar and by the skin of his stomach, laying him gently on the ground so that not one but both his shoulders squarely touched the earth. He repeated this movement several times, increasing the violence each time, until the Englishman shouted: "Enough, enough!"

Then the cries, the cheers, and the bravos rang out. When it comes to a display of force the English are the most appreciative people in the world. They wanted to hoist the onion merchant in triumph.

"No, don't, no don't," he screamed, on the defensive. "While you carry me in triumph you are going to pilfer my onions."

There was some truth in what the poor devil said. That very day they bought all his onions, and the night was completely dedicated to carrying him around in triumph.

From that moment on, French onions gained the right to be sold in England.

❧

Henry David Thoreau (1817–1862)

THE CONCORD-BORN TRANSCENDENTALIST is more famous for his writings about life at Walden Pond, his perambulations and excursions in New England, and his arguments justifying civil disobedience and the abolition of slavery, than for food writing. A close associate and friend of Emerson, Bronson Alcott, Margaret Fuller, and Hawthorne among many others, Thoreau celebrated an anti-urban nostalgia that shapes pleasure in the produce of the soil. Here, even as he shows a naturalist's interest in the watermelon and its seasonality, he gives a spiritual significance to the common melon, endowing it with values that express the mysteries of our lives, the "redness and ripeness within."

from *Wild Fruits*: Watermelons

WATERMELONS. THE FIRST are ripe from August seventh to twenty-eighth (though the last is late), and they continue to ripen till they freeze; are in their prime in September.

John Josselyn, an old resident in New England, speaks of the watermelon as one of the plants "proper to the country." He says that it is "of a sad grass-green color, or more rightly sap green; with some yellowness admixed when ripe."

September is come with its profusion of large fruits. Melons and apples seem at once to feed my brain.

How differently we fare now from what we did in winter! We give the butcher no encouragement now, but invite him to take a walk in our garden.

I have no respect for those who cannot raise melons or who avoid them as unwholesome. They should be spending their third winter with Parry in the arctic regions. They seem to have taken in their provisions at the commencement of the cruise, I know now how many years ago, and they deserve to have a monument erected to them of the empty cans which held their preserved meats.

Our diet, like that of the birds, must answer to the season. This is the season of west-looking, watery fruits. In the dog-days we come near to sustaining our lives on watermelon juice alone, like those who have fevers. I know of no more agreeable and nutritious food at this season than bread and butter and melons, and you need not be afraid of eating too much of the latter.

When I am going a-berrying in my boat or other carriage. I frequently carry watermelons for drink. It is the most agreeable and refreshing wine in a convenient cask, and most easily kept cool. Carry these green bottles of wine. When you get to the field you put them in the shade or in water till you want them.

When at home, if you would cool a watermelon which has been lying in the sun, do not put it in water, which keeps the heat in, but cut it open and place it on a cellar bottom or in a draught of air in the shade.

There are various ways in which you can tell if a watermelon is ripe. If you have had your eye on the patch much from the first, and so know the history of each one and which was formed first, you may presume that those will ripen soonest. Or else you may incline to those which lie nearest to the center of the hill or root, as the oldest.

Next, the dull, dead color and want of bloom are as good signs as any Some look green and livid, and have a very fog of bloom on them, like a mildew. These are as green as a leek through and through, and you'll find yourself in a pickle if you open one. Others have a dead dark-greenness, the circulations coming less rapid in their cuticles and their blooming period passed, and these you may safely bet on.

If the vine is quite lively, the death of the quirl at the root of the stem is almost a sure sign. Lest we should not discern it before, this is placed for a sign that there is redness and ripeness within. Of two, otherwise similar, take that which yields the lowest tone when struck with your knuckles, that is, which is hollowest. The old or ripe ones ring bass; the young, tenor or falsetto. Some use the violent method of pressing to hear if they crack within, but this is not to be allowed. Above all no tapping on the vine is to be tolerated, suggestive of a greediness which defeats its own purpose. It is very childish.

One man told me that he couldn't raise melons because his children *would cut them all up*. I think that he convicted himself out of his own mouth. It was evident that he could not raise children in the way they should go and was not fit to be the ruler of a country, according to Confucius's standard. I once, looking by a special providence through the blinds, saw one of his boys astride of my earliest watermelon, which grew near a broken paling, and brandishing a case-knife over it, but I instantly blowed him off with my voice before serious damage was done—and I made such an ado about it as convinced him that he was not in his father's dominions, at any rate. This melon, though it lost some of its bloom then, grew to be a remarkably large and sweet one, though it bore, to the last, a triangular scar of the tap which the thief had designed on it.

The farmer is obliged to hide his melon patch far away in the midst of his corn or potatoes. I sometimes stumble on it in my rambles. I see one today where the watermelons are intermixed with carrots in a carrot bed and so concealed by the general resemblance of the leaves at a little distance.

It is an old saying that you cannot carry two melons under one arm. Indeed, it is difficult to carry one far, it is so slippery. I remember hearing of a lady who had been to visit her friends in Lincoln, and when she was ready to return on foot, they made her the rather onerous present of a watermelon. With this under her arm she tript it glibly through the Walden

Woods, which had a rather bad reputation for goblins and so on in those days. While the wood grew thicker and thicker, and the imaginary dangers greater, the melon did not grow any lighter, though frequently shifted from arm to arm: and at length, it may have been through the agency of one of those mischievous goblins, it slipt from under her arm, and in a moment lay in a dozen pieces in the middle of the Walden road. Quick as thought the trembling traveller gathered up the most luscious and lightest fragments with her handkerchief, and flew rather than ran with them to the peaceful streets of Concord.

If you have any watermelons left when the frosts come, you may put them into your cellar and keep them till Thanksgiving time. I have seen a large patch in the woods frozen quite hard, and when cracked open they had a very handsome crystalline

Watermelons, said to be unknown to the Greeks and Romans. It is said to be one of those fruits of Egypt which the Jewish people regretted in the desert under the name of *abbattichim*.

The English botanists may be said to know nothing about watermelons. The nearest that Gerarde gets to our watermelon is in his chapter on "Citrull Cucumbers," where he says. "The meat or pulp of Cucumner Citrill which is next unto the bark is eaten."

In Spence's *Anecdotes* it is said that Galileo used to compare Ariosto's *Orlando* to a melon field. "You may meet with a very good thing here and there in it, but the whole is of very little value." Montaigne says, quoting Aurelius Victor, "The emperor Dioclesian, having resigned his crown and retired to 'private life,' was some time after solicited to resume his charge, but he announced, 'You would not offer to persuade me to this, had you seen the fine condition of the trees I have planted in my orchard, and the fair melons I have sowed in my garden.'" Gosse, in his *Letters from Alabama*, says of the watermelon, "I am not aware that it is known in England: I have never seen it exposed in the London markets," but it is abundant all over the United States; and in the South:

> The very negroes have their own melon "patches," as well as their peach orchards, and it is no small object of their ambition to raise earlier or finer specimens than their masters. . . . [It] may be considered as the best realization of the French princess's idea of "ice with the chill taken off." . . . A cart-load is brought home from the field nearly every evening, to supply the demand of the family for the next day: for during this torrid weather, very little business

but the eating of watermelons is transacted. If a guest call, the first offering of friendship is a glass of cold water as soon as seated; then there is an immediate shout for watermelons, and each taking his own, several are destroyed before the knife is laid down. The ladies cut the hard part, near the rind, into stars, and other pretty shapes, which they candy as a conserve for winter.

Frederick Douglass (1818–1895)

ONE OF THE first and greatest anti-slavery orators and writers in the nineteenth-century United States, the man who called himself Frederick *Douglass* (when he was freed) knew neither when he was born nor his original name. His mother, he understood, was a black slave; his father, he supposed, was a white master. In three separate autobiographies, he told the tale of the life he led as a slave, growing up first in his grandmother's cabin and then on various plantations, where he was brutalized by white overseers. After his escape to the North, he became the most sought-after African-American orator and memoirist in the country. He supported women's rights and indeed, as he put it, "would unite with anybody to do right and with nobody to do wrong." Our excerpt here, on the comparison between the slave diet and the "luxurious" table of the master, is drawn from his last autobiography, and demonstrates how precise and fierce his memories of slavery's abjection continued to be throughout his lifetime, despite all his successes.

from *My Bondage and My Freedom*: Ash Cake and the Rich Man's Table

AS A GENERAL rule, slaves do not come to the quarters for either breakfast or dinner, but take their "ash cake" with them, and eat it in the field. This was so on the home plantation; probably, because the distance from the quarter to the field, was sometimes two, and even three miles.

The dinner of the slaves consisted of a huge piece of ash cake, and a small piece of pork, or two salt herrings. Not having ovens, nor any suitable cooking utensils, the slaves mixed their meal with a little water, to such thickness that a spoon would stand erect in it; and, after the wood had burned away to coals and ashes, they would place the dough between oak leaves and lay it carefully in the ashes, completely covering it; hence, the bread is called ash cake. The surface of this peculiar bread is covered with ashes, to the depth of a sixteenth part of an inch, and the ashes, certainly, do not make it very grateful to the teeth, nor render it very palatable. The bran, or coarse part of the meal, is baked with the fine, and bright scales run through the bread.

This bread, with its ashes and bran, would disgust and choke a northern man, but it is quite liked by the slaves. They eat it with avidity, and are more concerned about the quantity than about the quality. They are far too scantily provided for, and are worked too steadily, to be much concerned for the quality of their food. The few minutes allowed them at dinner time, after partaking of their coarse repast, are variously spent. Some lie down on the "turning row," and go to sleep; others draw together, and talk; and others are at work with needle and thread, mending their tattered garments. Sometimes you may hear a wild, hoarse laugh arise from a circle, and often a song. Soon, however, the overseer comes dashing through the field. "*Tumble up! Tumble up*, and to *work, work*," is the cry; and, now, from twelve o'clock (mid-day) till dark, the human cattle are in motion, wielding their clumsy hoes; hurried on by no hope of reward, no sense of gratitude, no love of children, no prospect of bettering their condition; nothing, save the dread and terror of the slave-driver's lash. So goes one day, and so comes and goes another.

The close-fisted stinginess that fed the poor slave on coarse corn-meal and tainted meat; that clothed him in crashy tow-linen, and hurried him on to toil through the field, in all weathers, with wind and rain beating through his tattered garments; that scarcely gave even the young slave-mother time to nurse her hungry infant in the fence corner; wholly vanishes on approaching the sacred precincts of the great house, the home of the Lloyds. There the scriptural phrase finds an exact illustration; the highly favored inmates of this mansion are literally arrayed "in purple and fine linen," and fare sumptuously every day! The table groans under the heavy and blood-bought luxuries gathered with pains-taking care, at home and abroad. Fields, forests, rivers and seas, are made tributary here. Immense wealth, and its lavish expenditure, fill the great house with all that can please the eye, or tempt the taste. Here, appetite, not food, is the great *desideratum*. Fish, flesh and fowl, are here in profusion. Chickens, of all breeds; ducks, of all kinds, wild and tame, the common, and the huge Muscovite; Guinea fowls, turkeys, geese, and pea fowls, are in their several pens, fat and fatting for the destined vortex. The graceful swan, the mongrels, the black-necked wild goose; partridges, quails, pheasants and pigeons; choice water fowl, with all their strange varieties, are caught in this huge family net. Beef, veal, mutton and venison, of the most select kinds and quality, roll bounteously to this grand consumer. The teeming riches of the Chesapeake bay, its rock, perch, drums, crocus, trout, oysters, crabs, and terrapin, are drawn hither to adorn the glittering table of the great house. The dairy, too, probably the finest on the Eastern Shore of Maryland—supplied by cattle of the best English stock, imported for the purpose, pours its rich donations of fragrant cheese, golden butter, and delicious cream, to heighten the attraction of the gorgeous, unending round of feasting. Nor are the fruits of the earth forgotten or neglected. The fertile garden, many acres in size, constituting a separate establishment, distinct from the common farm—with its scientific gardener, imported from Scotland, (a Mr. McDermott) with four men under his direction, was not behind, either in the abundance or in the delicacy of its contributions to the same full board. The tender asparagus, the succulent celery, and the delicate cauliflower; egg plants, beets, lettuce, parsnips, peas, and French beans, early and late; radishes, cantelopes, melons of all kinds; the fruits and flowers of all climes and of all descriptions, from the hardy apple of the north, to the lemon and orange of the south, culminated at this point. Baltimore gathered figs, raisins, almonds and juicy grapes from Spain. Wines and brandies from France; teas of various flavor, from China; and rich, aromatic coffee from Java, all conspired to swell the tide of high life, where pride and indolence rolled and lounged in magnificence and satiety.

Behind the tall-backed and elaborately wrought chairs, stand the servants, men and maidens—fifteen in number—discriminately selected, not only with a view to their industry and faithfulness, but with special regard to their personal appearance, their graceful agility and captivating address. Some of these are armed with fans, and are fanning reviving breezes toward the over-heated brows of the alabaster ladies; others watch with eager eye,

and with fawn-like step anticipate and supply, wants before they are sufficiently formed to be announced by word or sign.

These servants constituted a sort of black aristocracy on Col. Lloyd's
plantation. They resembled the field hands in nothing, except in color, and
in this they held the advantage of a velvet-like glossiness, rich and beautiful.
The hair, too, showed the same advantage. The delicate colored maid rustled
in the scarcely worn silk of her young mistress, while the servant men were
equally well attired from the overflowing wardrobe of their young masters;
so that, in dress, as well as in form and feature, in manner and speech, in
tastes and habits, the distance between these favored few, and the sorrow
and hunger-smitten multitudes of the quarter in the field, was immense; and
this is seldom passed over.

Let us now glance at the stables and carriage house, and we shall find the
same evidences of pride and luxurious extravagance. Here are three splen-
did coaches, soft within and lustrous without. Here, too, are gigs, phætons,
barouches, sulkeys and sleighs. Here are saddles and harnesses—beautifully
wrought and silver mounted—kept with every care. In the stable you will
find, kept only for pleasure, full thirty-five horses, or the most approved
blood for speed and beauty. There are two men here constantly employed in
taking care of these horses. One of these men must be always in the stable,
to answer every call from the great house. Over the way from the stable, is a
house built expressly for the hounds—a pack of twenty-five or thirty—whose
fare would have made glad the heart of a dozen slaves. Horses and hounds are
not the only consumers of the slave's toil. There was practiced, at the Lloyds',
a hospitality which would have astonished and charmed any health-seeking
northern divine or merchant, who might have chanced to share it. Viewed
from his own table, and not from the field, the colonel was a model of generous hospitality. His house was, literally, a hotel, for weeks during the summer months. At these times, especially, the air was freighted with the rich
fumes of baking, boiling, roasting and broiling. The odors I shared with the
winds; but the meats were under a more stringent monopoly—except that,
occasionally, I got a cake from Mas' Daniel. In Mas' Daniel I had a friend
at court, from whom I learned many things which my eager curiosity was
excited to know. I always knew when company was expected, and who they
were, although I was an outsider, being the property, not of Col. Lloyd, but
of a servant of the wealthy colonel. On these occasions, all that pride, taste
and money could do, to dazzle and charm, was done.

Who could say that the servants of Col. Lloyd were not well clad and cared for, after witnessing one of his magnificent entertainments? Who could say that they did not seem to glory in being the slaves of such a master? Who, but a fanatic, could get up any sympathy for persons whose every movement was agile, easy and graceful, and who evinced a consciousness of high superiority? And who would ever venture to suspect that Col. Lloyd was subject to the troubles of ordinary mortals? Master and slave seem alike in their glory here? Can it all be seeming? Alas! it may only be a sham at last! This immense wealth; this gilded splendor: this profusion of luxury; this exemption from toil; this life of ease; this sea of plenty; aye, what of it all? Are the pearly gates of happiness and sweet content flung open to such suitors? *far from it!* The poor slave, on his hard, pine plank, but scantily covered with his thin blanket, sleeps more soundly than the feverish voluptuary who reclines upon his feather bed and downy pillow. Food, to the indolent lounger, is poison, not sustenance. Lurking beneath all their dishes are invisible spirits of evil, ready to feed the self-deluded gourmandizers with aches, pains, fierce temper, uncontrolled passions, dyspepsia, rheumatism, lumbago and gout; and of these the Lloyds got their full share.

Herman Melville (1819–1891)

AFTER AN ADVENTUROUS young manhood spent sailing the high seas and exploring Pacific islands, the New York-born Melville turned his hand to writing. His early novels—*Typee, Omoo, Mardi,* and *White Jacket*—achieved some popularity because of their exotic settings and apparently straightforward travel narratives. But though this author's masterpiece, *Moby-Dick, or The Whale,* has become one of the great classics of American literature, it was initially received with confusion by critics, one of whom commented that the style of the work is "disfigured by mad (rather than bad) English." Melville himself knew this would be "a strange sort of book" noting that "blubber is blubber you know; tho' you might get oil out of it . . . and to cook the thing up, one must needs throw in a little fancy." A fierce allegory about obsession, mystery, and whaling, the book is certainly not a conventional travelogue, but rather a mélange of suspense and philosophizing. "The Whale as a Dish," with its musings on the cannibalistic qualities of meat-eating, typifies the writer's daring literary cookery.

from *Moby-Dick*: The Whale as a Dish

THAT MORTAL MAN should feed upon the creature that feeds his lamp, and, like Stubb, eat him by his own light, as you may say; this seems so outlandish a thing that one must needs go a little into the history and philosophy of it.

It is upon record, that three centuries ago the tongue of the Right Whale was esteemed a great delicacy in France, and commanded large prices there. Also, that in Henry VIIIth's time, a certain cook of the court obtained a handsome reward for inventing an admirable sauce to be eaten with barbecued porpoises, which, you remember, are a species of whale. Porpoises, indeed, are to this day considered fine eating. The meat is made into balls about the size of billiard balls, and being well seasoned and spiced might be taken for turtle balls or veal balls. The old monks of Dumfermline were very fond of them. They had a great porpoise grant from the crown.

The fact is, that among his hunters at least, the whale would by all hands be considered a noble dish, were there not so much of him; but when you come to sit down before a meat-pie nearly one hundred feet long, it takes away your appetite. Only the most unprejudiced of men like Stubb, nowadays partake of cooked whales; but the Esquimaux are not so fastidious. We all know they live upon whales, and have rare old vintages of prime old train oil. Zogranda, one of their most famous doctors, recommends strips of blubber for infants, as being exceedingly juicy and nourishing. And this reminds me that certain Englishmen, who long ago were accidentally left in Greenland by a whaling vessel—that these men actually lived for several months on the mouldy scraps of whales which had been left ashore after trying out the blubber. Among the Dutch whalemen these scraps are called "fritters;" which, indeed, they greatly resemble, being brown and crisp, and smelling something like old Amsterdam housewives' dough-nuts or oly-cooks, when fresh. They have such an eatable look that the most self-denying stranger can hardly keep his hands off.

But what further depreciates the whale as a civilized dish, is his exceeding richness. He is the great prize ox of the sea, too fat to be delicately good. Look at his hump, which would be as fine eating as the buffalo's (which is esteemed a rare dish), were it not such a solid pyramid of fat. But the spermaceti itself, how bland and creamy that is; like the transparent, half-jellied, white meat of a cocoanut in the third month of its growth, yet far too rich to supply a substitute for butter. Nevertheless, many whalemen have a method of absorbing it into some other substance, and then partaking of it. In the long try watches of the night it is a common thing for the seamen to dip their ship-biscuit into the huge oil-pots and let them fry there awhile. Many a good supper have I thus made.

In the case of a small Sperm Whale the brains are accounted a fine dish. The casket of the skull is broken into with an axe, and the two plump, whitish lobes being withdrawn (precisely resembling two large puddings), they are then mixed with flour, and cooked into a most delectable mess, in flavor somewhat resembling calves' head, which is quite a dish among some epicures; and every one knows that some young bucks among the epicures, by continually dining upon calves' brains, by and by get to have a little brains of their own, so as to be able to tell a calf's head from their own heads; which, indeed, requires uncommon discrimination. And that is the reason why a young buck with an intelligent looking calf's head before him, is somehow one of the saddest sights you can see. The head looks a sort of reproachfully at him, with an "Et tu Brute!" expression.

It is not, perhaps, entirely because the whale is so excessively unctuous that landsmen seem to regard the eating of him with abhorrence; that appears to result, in some way, from the consideration before mentioned: i.e. that a man should eat a newly murdered thing of the sea, and eat it too by its own light. But no doubt the first man that ever murdered an ox was regarded as a murderer; perhaps he was hung; and if he had been put on his trial by oxen, he certainly would have been; and he certainly deserved it if any murderer does. Go to the meatmarket of a Saturday night and see the crowds of live bipeds staring up at the long rows of dead quadrupeds. Does not that sight take a tooth out of the cannibal's jaw? Cannibals? Who is not a cannibal? I tell you it will be more tolerable for the Fejee that salted down a lean missionary in his cellar against a coming famine; it will be more tolerable for that provident Fejee, I say, in the day of judgment, than for thee, civilized and enlightened gourmand, who nailest geese to the ground and feastest on their bloated livers in thy paté-de-foie-gras.

But Stubb, he eats the whale by its own light, does he? and that is adding insult to injury, is it? Look at your knife-handle, there, my civilized and enlightened gourmand dining off that roast beef, what is that handle made of?—what but the bones of the brother of the very ox you are eating? And what do you pick your teeth with, after devouring that fat goose? With a feather of the same fowl. And with what quill did the Secretary of the Society for the Suppression of Cruelty to Ganders formally indite his circulars? It is only within the last month or two that that society passed a resolution to patronize nothing but steel pens.

Louisa May Alcott (1832–1888)

BEST-KNOWN AS THE author of the endearing and enduringly popular children's classics that began with *Little Women* and continued through *Little Men*, *Jo's Boys*, and other novels, Alcott was also an abolitionist, a feminist, and (under the pseudonym A. M. Barnard) a writer of Gothic romances. The family she so lovingly memorialized in *Little Women* was her own, and her parents were both acolytes of the New England movement known as "transcendentalism," which propounded both self-reliance and self-abnegation, along with idealistic mysticism. When she was still a child, her father, Bronson, joined with a few friends to found Fruitlands, a vegetarian commune governed by the spiritual principles he espoused. Well-intentioned but ignorant of agriculture, the would-be farmers nearly starved, and their dietary rules were especially hard on Louisa's mother, Abby May, the beloved "Marmee" of *Little Women*. "Transcendental Wild Oats" is a sardonic send-up of the sad Fruitlands story.

from Transcendental Wild Oats

THE FURNITURE ARRIVED ..., and was soon bestowed; for the principal property of the community consisted in books. To this rare library was devoted the best room in the house, and the few busts and pictures that still survived many flittings were added to beautify the sanctuary, for here the family was to meet for amusement, instruction, and worship.

Any housewife can imagine the emotions of Sister Hope, when she took possession of a large, dilapidated kitchen, containing an old stove and the peculiar stores out of which food was to be evolved for her little family of eleven. Cakes of maple sugar, dried peas and beans, barley and hominy, meal of all sorts, potatoes, and dried fruit. No milk, butter, cheese, tea, or meat appeared. Even salt was considered a useless luxury and spice entirely forbidden by these lovers of Spartan simplicity. A ten years' experience of vegetarian vagaries had been good training for this new freak, and her sense of the ludicrous supported her through many trying scenes.

Unleavened bread, porridge, and water for breakfast; bread, vegetables, and water for dinner; bread, fruit, and water for supper was the bill of fare ordained by the elders. No teapot profaned that sacred stove, no gory steak cried aloud for vengeance from her chaste gridiron; and only a brave woman's taste, time, and temper were sacrificed on that domestic altar. . . .

Such farming probably was never seen before since Adam delved. The band of brothers began by spading garden and field; but a few days of it lessened their ardor amazingly. Blistered hands and aching backs suggested the expediency of permitting the use of cattle till the workers were better fitted for noble toil by a summer of the new life.

Brother Moses brought a yoke of oxen from his farm,—at least, the philosophers thought so till it was discovered that one of the animals was a cow; and Moses confessed that he "must be let down easy, for he couldn't live on garden sarse entirely."

Great was Dictator Lion's indignation at this lapse from virtue. But time pressed, the work must be done; so the meek cow was permitted to wear the yoke and the recreant brother continued to enjoy forbidden draughts in the barn, which dark proceeding caused the children to regard him as one set apart for destruction.

The sowing was equally peculiar, for, owing to some mistake, the three brethren, who devoted themselves to this graceful task, found when about half through the job that each had been sowing a different sort of grain in the same field; a mistake which caused much perplexity, as it could not be remedied; but, after a long consultation and a good deal of laughter, it was decided to say nothing and see what would come of it.

The garden was planted with a generous supply of useful roots and herbs;

but, as manure was not allowed to profane the virgin soil, few of these vegetable treasures ever came up. Purslane reigned supreme, and the disappointed planters ate it philosophically, deciding that Nature knew what was best for them, and would generously supply their needs, if they could only learn to digest her "sallets" and wild roots.

The orchard was laid out, a little grafting done, new trees and vines set, regardless of the unfit season and entire ignorance of the husbandmen, who honestly believed that in the autumn they would reap a bounteous harvest.

Slowly things got into order, and rapidly rumors of the new experiment went abroad, causing many strange spirits to flock thither, for in those days communities were the fashion and transcendentalism raged wildly. Some came to look on and laugh, some to be supported in poetic idleness, a few to believe sincerely and work heartily. Each member was allowed to mount his favorite hobby and ride it to his heart's content. Very queer were some of the riders, and very rampant some of the hobbies. . . .

Transcendental wild oats were sown broadcast that year, and the fame thereof has not yet ceased in the land; for, futile as this crop seemed to outsiders, it bore an invisible harvest, worth much to those who planted in earnest. As none of the members of this particular community have ever recounted their experiences before, a few of them may not be amiss, since the interest in these attempts has never died out and Fruitlands was the most ideal of all these castles in Spain. . . .

They preached vegetarianism everywhere and resisted all temptations of the flesh, contentedly eating apples and bread at well-spread tables, and much afflicting hospitable hostesses by denouncing their food and taking away their appetites, discussing the "horrors of shambles," the "incorporation of the brute in man," and "on elegant abstinence the sign of a pure soul." But, when the perplexed or offended ladies asked what they should eat, they got in reply a bill of fare consisting of "bowls of sunrise for breakfast," "solar seeds of the sphere," "dishes from Plutarch's chaste table," and other viands equally hard to find in any modern market.

Reform conventions of all sorts were haunted by these brethren, who said many wise things and did many foolish ones. Unfortunately, these wanderings interfered with their harvest at home; but the rule was to do what the spirit moved, so they left their crops to Providence and went a-reaping in wider and, let us hope, more fruitful fields than their own.

Luckily, the earthly providence who watched over Abel Lamb was at hand

to glean the scanty crop yielded by the "uncorrupted land," which, "consecrated to human freedom," had received "the sober culture of devout men."

About the time the grain was ready to house, some call of the Oversoul
wafted all the men away. An easterly storm was coming up and the yellow
stacks were sure to be ruined. Then Sister Hope gathered her forces. Three
little girls, one boy (Timon's son), and herself, harnessed to clothes-baskets
and Russia-linen sheets, were the only teams she could command; but with
these poor appliances the indomitable woman got in the grain and saved
food for her young, with the instinct and energy of a mother-bird with a
brood of hungry nestlings to feed.

🐘

Anton Chekhov (1860–1904)

CHEKHOV, AUTHOR OF *The Cherry Orchard*, *Uncle Vanya*, and *The
Seagull*, is Russia's foremost dramatist and a notable writer of short stories.
He was also a physician, who declared, "Medicine is my lawful wife and literature is my mistress." His plays frequently had their premiere at the Moscow
Art Theatre, which became famous as an avant-garde venue. In this tale, the
eight-year-old protagonist consumes oysters for the first time, but is so hungry he tries to crunch on the shells. He becomes sick, but it is not so clear
whether because he has fantasized the bivalve as a hideous animal with claws
and sharp teeth, or because slurping down the "slippy, damp" creatures has
simply not agreed with him. Is the piece a gentle satire on the boy's capacity
to fictionalize, or on the way his imagination allows him to experiment with
unforeseen pleasures? As in Chekhov's plays, there is no definitive conclusion to this question.

Oysters

I NEED NO great effort of memory to recall, in every detail, the rainy
autumn evening when I stood with my father in one of the more frequented

streets of Moscow, and felt that I was gradually being overcome by a strange illness. I had no pain at all, but my legs were giving way under me, the words stuck in my throat, my head slipped weakly on one side. . . . It seemed as though, in a moment, I must fall down and lose consciousness.

If I had been taken into a hospital at that minute, the doctors would have had to write over my bed: *Fames*, a disease which is not in the manuals of medicine.

Beside me on the pavement stood my father in a shabby summer overcoat and a serge cap, from which a bit of white wadding was sticking out. On his feet he had big heavy galoshes. Afraid, vain man, that people would see that his feet were bare under his galoshes, he had drawn the tops of some old boots up round the calves of his legs.

This poor, foolish, queer creature, whom I loved the more warmly the more ragged and dirty his smart summer overcoat became, had come to Moscow, five months before, to look for a job as copying-clerk. For those five months he had been trudging about Moscow looking for work, and it was only on that day that he had brought himself to go into the street to beg for alms.

Before us was a big house of three storeys, adorned with a blue signboard with the word "Restaurant" on it. My head was drooping feebly backwards and on one side, and I could not help looking upwards at the lighted windows of the restaurant. Human figures were flitting about at the windows. I could see the right side of the orchestrion, two oleographs, hanging lamps. . . . Staring into one window, I saw a patch of white. The patch was motionless, and its rectangular outlines stood out sharply against the dark, brown background. I looked intently and made out of the patch a white placard on the wall. Something was written on it, but what it was, I could not see. . . .

For half an hour I kept my eyes on the placard. Its white attracted my eyes, and, as it were, hypnotized my brain. I tried to read it, but my efforts were in vain.

At last the strange disease got the upper hand.

The rumble of the carriages began to seem like thunder, in the stench of the street I distinguished a thousand smells. The restaurant lights and the lamps dazzled my eyes like lightning. My five senses were overstrained and sensitive beyond the normal. I began to see what I had not seen before.

"Oysters . . ." I made out on the placard.

A strange word! I had lived in the world eight years and three months, but had never come across that word. What did it mean? Surely it was not the name of the restaurant-keeper? But signboards with names on them always hang outside, not on the walls indoors!

"Papa, what does 'oysters' mean?" I asked in a husky voice, making an effort to turn my face towards my father.

My father did not hear. He was keeping a watch on the movements of the crowd, and following every passer-by with his eyes. . . . From his eyes I saw that he wanted to say something to the passers-by, but the fatal word hung like a heavy weight on his trembling lips and could not be flung off. He even took a step after one passer-by and touched him on the sleeve, but when he turned round, he said, "I beg your pardon," was overcome with confusion, and staggered back.

"Papa, what does 'oysters' mean?" I repeated.

"It is an animal . . . that lives in the sea."

I instantly pictured to myself this unknown marine animal. . . . I thought it must be something midway between a fish and a crab. As it was from the sea they made of it, of course, a very nice hot fish soup with savoury pepper and laurel leaves, or broth with vinegar and fricassee of fish and cabbage, or crayfish sauce, or served it cold with horse-radish. . . . I vividly imagined it being brought from the market, quickly cleaned, quickly put in the pot, quickly, quickly, for everyone was hungry . . . awfully hungry! From the kitchen rose the smell of hot fish and crayfish soup.

I felt that this smell was tickling my palate and nostrils, that it was gradually taking possession of my whole body. . . . The restaurant, my father, the white placard, my sleeves were all smelling of it, smelling so strongly that I began to chew. I moved my jaws and swallowed as though I really had a piece of this marine animal in my mouth. . . .

My legs gave way from the blissful sensation I was feeling, and I clutched at my father's arm to keep myself from falling, and leant against his wet summer overcoat. My father was trembling and shivering. He was cold. . . .

"Papa, are oysters a Lenten dish?" I asked.

"They are eaten alive . . ." said my father. "They are in shells like tortoises, but . . . in two halves."

The delicious smell instantly left off affecting me, and the illusion vanished. . . . Now I understood it all!

"How nasty," I whispered, "how nasty!"

So that's what "oysters" meant! I imagined to myself a creature like a frog. A frog sitting in a shell, peeping out from it with big, glittering eyes, and a slimy skin, being brought from the market. . . . The children would all hide while the cook, frowning with an air of disgust, would take the creature by its claw, put it on a plate, and carry it into the dining-room. The grown-ups would take it and eat it, eat it alive with its eyes, its teeth, its legs! While it squeaked and tried to bite their lips. . . .

I frowned, but . . . but why did my teeth move as though I were munching? The creature was loathsome, disgusting, terrible, but I ate it, ate it greedily, afraid of distinguishing its taste or smell. As soon as I had eaten one, I saw the glittering eyes of a second, a third . . . I ate them too. . . . At last I ate the table-napkin, the plate, my father's galoshes, the white placard . . . I ate everything that caught my eye, because I felt that nothing but eating would take away my illness. The oysters had a terrible look in their eyes and were loathsome. I shuddered at the thought of them, but I wanted to eat! To eat!

"Oysters! Give me some oysters!" was the cry that broke from me and I stretched out my hand.

"Help us, gentlemen!" I heard at that moment my father say, in a hollow and shaking voice. "I am ashamed to ask but—my God!—I can bear no more!"

"Oysters!" I cried, pulling my father by the skirts of his coat.

"Do you mean to say you eat oysters? A little chap like you!" I heard laughter close to me.

Two gentlemen in top hats were standing before us, looking into my face and laughing.

"Do you really eat oysters, youngster? That's interesting! How do you eat them?"

I remember that a strong hand dragged me into the lighted restaurant. A minute later there was a crowd round me, watching me with curiosity and amusement. I sat at a table and ate something slimy, salt with a flavour of dampness and mouldiness. I ate greedily without chewing, without looking and trying to discover what I was eating. I fancied that if I opened my eyes I should see glittering eyes, claws, and sharp teeth.

All at once I began biting something hard, there was a sound of a scrunching.

"Ha, ha! He is eating the shells," laughed the crowd. "Little silly, do you suppose you can eat that?"

After that I remember a terrible thirst. I was lying in my bed, and could not sleep for heartburn and the strange taste in my parched mouth. My father was walking up and down, gesticulating with his hands.

"I believe I have caught cold," he was muttering. "I've a feeling in my head as though someone were sitting on it. . . . Perhaps it is because I have not . . . er . . . eaten anything today. . . . I really am a queer, stupid creature. . . . I saw those gentlemen pay ten roubles for the oysters. Why didn't I go up to them and ask them . . . to lend me something? They would have given something."

Towards morning, I fell asleep and dreamt of a frog sitting in a shell, moving its eyes. At midday I was awakened by thirst, and looked for my father: he was still walking up and down and gesticulating.

✢

Marcel Proust (1871–1922)

OFTEN CONSIDERED, ALONG with James Joyce, the foremost novelist of the twentieth century, Proust structures his masterpiece, the seven-volume *Remembrance of Things Past*, around his protagonist's memories. Having decided by the end of the entire sequence to become the writer that in fact we have listened to all along as he tells the story of his boyhood and young manhood, the narrator called Marcel not only remembers his life but also theorizes the very nature of memory. Our selection is the most celebrated discussion of how the sensory experience of food (here the fluted small butter cake known as a madeleine) and drink (the lime-blossom tea) evokes memories and begins the mechanism prompting Marcel to recall and examine his entire early life, for some 3000 pages.

from *Remembrance of Things Past*:
On the Madeleine

MANY YEARS HAD elapsed during which nothing of Combray, save what was comprised in the theatre and the drama of my going to bed there, had any existence for me, when one day in winter, as I came home, my mother, seeing that I was cold, offered me some tea, a thing I did not ordinarily take. I declined at first, and then, for no particular reason, changed my mind. She sent out for one of those short, plump little cakes called 'petites madeleines,' which look as though they had been moulded in the fluted scallop of a pilgrim's shell. And soon, mechanically, weary after a dull day with the prospect of a depressing morrow, I raised to my lips a spoonful of the tea in which I had soaked a morsel of the cake. No sooner had the warm liquid, and the crumbs with it, touched my palate than a shudder ran through my whole body, and I stopped, intent upon the extraordinary changes that were taking place. An exquisite pleasure had invaded my senses, but individual, detached, with no suggestion of its origin. And at once the vicissitudes of life had become indifferent to me, its disasters innocuous, its brevity illusory— this new sensation having had on me the effect which love has of filling me with a precious essence; or rather this essence was not in me, it was myself. I had ceased now to feel mediocre, accidental, mortal. Whence could it have come to me, this all-powerful joy? I was conscious that it was connected with the taste of tea and cake, but that it infinitely transcended those savours, could not, indeed, be of the same nature as theirs. Whence did it come? What did it signify? How could I seize upon and define it?

I drink a second mouthful, in which I find nothing more than in the first, a third, which gives me rather less than the second. It is time to stop; the potion is losing its magic. It is plain that the object of my quest, the truth, lies not in the cup but in myself. The tea has called up in me, but does not itself understand, and can only repeat indefinitely with a gradual loss of strength, the same testimony; which I, too, cannot interpret, though I hope at least to be able to call upon the tea for it again and to find it there presently, intact and at my disposal, for my final enlightenment. I put down my cup and examine my own mind. It is for it to discover the truth. But how? What an abyss of uncertainty whenever the mind feels that some part of it has strayed beyond its own borders; when it, the seeker, is at once the dark region through which it must go seeking, where all its equipment will avail it nothing. Seek? More than that: create. It is face to face with something which does not so far exist, to which it alone can give reality and substance, which it alone can bring into the light of day.

And I begin again to ask myself what it could have been, this unremembered state which brought with it no logical proof of its existence, but only the sense that it was a happy, that it was a real state in whose presence other states of consciousness melted and vanished. I decide to attempt to make it reappear. I retrace my thoughts to the moment at which I drank the first spoonful of tea. I find again the same state, illumined by no fresh light. I compel my mind to make one further effort, to follow and recapture once again the fleeting sensation. And that nothing may interrupt it in its course I shut out every obstacle, every extraneous idea, I stop my ears and inhibit all attention to the sounds which come from the next room. And then, feeling that my mind is growing fatigued without having any success to report, I compel it for a change to enjoy that distraction which I have just denied it, to think of other things, to rest and refresh itself before the supreme attempt. And then for the second time I clear an empty space in front of it. I place in position before my mind's eye the still recent taste of that first mouthful, and I feel something start within me, something that leaves its resting-place and attempts to rise, something that has been embedded like an anchor at a great depth; I do not know yet what it is, but I can feel it mounting slowly; I can measure the resistance, I can hear the echo of great spaces traversed.

Undoubtedly what is thus palpitating in the depths of my being must be the image, the visual memory which, being linked to that taste, has tried to follow it into my conscious mind. But its struggles are too far off, too much confused; scarcely can I perceive the colourless reflection in which are blended the uncapturable whirling medley of radiant hues, and I cannot distinguish its form, cannot invite it, as the one possible interpreter, to translate to me the evidence of its contemporary, its inseparable paramour, the taste of the cake soaked in tea; cannot ask it to inform me what special circumstance is in question, of what period in my past life.

Will it ultimately reach the clear surface of my consciousness, this memory, this old, dead moment which the magnetism of an identical moment has travelled so far to importune, to disturb, to raise up out of the very depths of my being? I cannot tell. Now that I feel nothing, it has stopped, has perhaps gone down again into its darkness, from which who can say whether it will ever rise? Ten times over I must essay the task, must lean down over the abyss. And each time the natural laziness which deters us from every diffi-cult enterprise, every work of importance, has urged me to leave the thing alone, to drink my tea and to think merely of the worries of to-day and of my hopes for to-morrow, which let themselves be pondered over without effort or distress of mind.

And suddenly the memory returns. The taste was that of the little crumb of madeleine which on Sunday morning at Combray (because on those mornings I did not go out before church-time), when I went to say good day to her in her bedroom, my aunt Léonie used to give me, dipping it first in her own cup of real or of lime-flower tea. The sight of the little madeleine had recalled nothing to my mind before I tasted it; perhaps because I had so often seen such things in the interval, without tasting them, on the trays in pastry-cooks' windows, that their image had dissociated itself from those Combray days to take its place among others more recent; perhaps because of those memories, so long abandoned and put out of mind, nothing now survived, everything was scattered; the forms of things, including that of the little scallop-shell of pastry, so richly sensual under its severe, religious folds, were either obliterated or had been so long dormant as to have lost the power of expansion which would have allowed them to resume their place in my consciousness. But when from a long-distant past nothing subsists, after the people are dead, after the things are broken and scattered, still, alone, more fragile, but with more vitality, more unsubstantial, more persistent, more faithful, the smell and taste of things remain poised a long time, like souls, ready to remind us, waiting and hoping for their moment, amid the ruins of all the rest; and bear unfaltering, in the tiny and almost impalpable drop of their essence, the vast structure of recollection.

And once I had recognized the taste of the crumb of madeleine soaked in her decoction of lime-flowers which my aunt used to give me (although I did not yet know and must long postpone the discovery of why this memory made me so happy) immediately the old grey house upon the street, where her room was, rose up like the scenery of a theatre to attach itself to the little pavilion, opening on to the garden, which had been built out behind it for my parents (the isolated panel which until that moment had been all that I could see); and with the house the town, from morning to night and in all weathers, the Square where I was sent before luncheon, the streets along which I used to run errands, the country roads we took when it was fine.

And just as the Japanese amuse themselves by filling a porcelain bowl with water and steeping in it little crumbs of paper which until then are without character or form, but, the moment they become wet, stretch themselves and bend, take on colour and distinctive shape, become flowers or houses or people, permanent and recognizable, so in that moment all the flowers in our garden and in M. Swann's park, and the water-lilies on the Vivonne and the good folk of the village and their little dwellings and the parish church and the whole of Combray and its surroundings, taking their proper shapes and growing solid, sprang into being, town and gardens alike, from my cup of tea.

Upton Sinclair (1878–1968)

A GREAT CRUSADER for civil rights and a continually losing candidate for political office, Sinclair ran on the Democratic ticket but considered himself at heart a Socialist. His most famous work, from which our excerpt is taken, is *The Jungle,* an excoriating attack on the meatpacking industry in Chicago. The novel is based on his firsthand investigation of the abattoirs, and is as much about the brutal methods of slaughter as it is about the exploitation of the packinghouse workers. It was enormously successful and persuasive, resulting in government regulation of the meat industry. In this selection Sinclair concentrates on the actual methods of hog and cattle killing in all their visceral horror. His description of the methods of animal slaughter influenced Eric Schlosser's *Fast Food Nation* as well as many vegetarians, several of whose writings appear in the section of this book titled "Food Politics."

from *The Jungle*: A Visit to the Slaughterhouse

THERE IS OVER a square mile of space in the yards, and more than half of it is occupied by cattle pens; north and south as far as the eye can reach there stretches a sea of pens. And they were all filled—so many cattle no one had ever dreamed existed in the world. Red cattle, black, white, and yellow cattle; old cattle and young cattle; great bellowing bulls and little calves not an hour born; meek-eyed milch cows and fierce, long-horned Texas steers. The sound of them here was as of all the barnyards of the universe; and as for counting them—it would have taken all day simply to count the pens. Here and there ran long alleys, blocked at intervals by gates; and . . . the number of these gates was twenty-five thousand. . . . Here and there about the alleys galloped men upon horseback, booted, and carrying long whips; they were very busy, calling to each other, and to those who were driving the cattle. They were drovers and stock raisers, who had come from far states, and brokers and commission merchants, and buyers for all the big packing houses. . . .

There were two hundred and fifty miles of track within the yards, their guide went on to tell them. They brought about ten thousand head of cattle every day, and as many hogs, and half as many sheep—which meant some eight or ten million live creatures turned into food every year. One stood and watched, and little by little caught the drift of the tide, as it set in the direction of the packing houses. There were groups of cattle being driven to the chutes, which were roadways about fifteen feet wide, raised high above the pens. . . .

"They don't waste anything here," said the guide, and then he laughed and added a witticism, which he was pleased that his unsophisticated friends should take to be his own: "They use everything about the hog except the squeal." In front of Brown's General Office building there grows a tiny plot of grass, and this, you may learn, is the only bit of green thing in Packingtown; likewise this jest about the hog and his squeal, the stock in trade of all the guides, is the one gleam of humor that you will find there.

After they had seen enough of the pens, the party went up the street, to the mass of buildings which occupy the center of the yards. These buildings, made of brick and stained with innumerable layers of Packingtown smoke, were painted all over with advertising signs, from which the visitor realized suddenly that he had come to the home of many of the torments of his life. It was here that they made those products with the wonders of which they pestered him so—by placards that defaced the landscape when he traveled, and by staring advertisements in the newspapers and magazines—by silly little jingles that he could not get out of his mind, and gaudy pictures that lurked for him around every street corner. Here was where they made Brown's Imperial Hams and Bacon, Brown's Dressed Beef, Brown's Excelsior Sausages! Here was the headquarters of Durham's Pure Leaf Lard, of Durham's Breakfast Bacon, Durham's Canned Beef, Potted Ham, Deviled Chicken, Peerless Fertilizer!

Entering one of the Durham buildings, they found a number of other visitors waiting; and before long there came a guide, to escort them through the place. They make a great feature of showing strangers through the packing plants, for it is a good advertisement. . . . They climbed a long series of stairways outside of the building, to the top of its five or six stories. Here was the chute, with its river of hogs, all patiently toiling upward; there was a place for them to rest to cool off, and then through another passageway they went into a room from which there is no returning for hogs.

It was a long, narrow room, with a gallery along it for visitors. At the head there was a great iron wheel, about twenty feet in circumference, with rings here and there along its edge. Upon both sides of this wheel there was a narrow space, into which came the hogs at the end of their journey; in the midst of them stood a great burly Negro, bare-armed and bare-chested. He was resting for the moment, for the wheel had stopped while men were cleaning up. In a minute or two, however, it began slowly to revolve, and then the men upon each side of it sprang to work. They had chains which they fastened about the leg of the nearest hog, and the other end of the chain they hooked into one of the rings upon the wheel. So, as the wheel turned, a hog was suddenly jerked off his feet and borne aloft.

At the same instant the car was assailed by a most terrifying shriek; the visitors started in alarm, the women turned pale and shrank back. The shriek was followed by another, louder and yet more agonizing—for once started upon that journey, the hog never came back; at the top of the wheel he was shunted off upon a trolley, and went sailing down the room. And meantime another was swung up, and then another, and another, until there was a double line of them, each dangling by a foot and kicking in frenzy—and squealing. The uproar was appalling, perilous to the eardrums; one feared there was too much sound for the room to hold—that the walls must give way or the ceiling crack. There were high squeals and low squeals, grunts, and wails of agony; there would come a momentary lull, and then a fresh outburst, louder than ever, surging up to a deafening climax. It was too much for some of the visitors—the men would look at each other, laughing nervously, and the women would stand with hands clenched, and the blood rushing to their faces, and the tears starting in their eyes.

Meantime, heedless of all these things, the men upon the floor were going about their work. Neither squeals of hogs nor tears of visitors made any difference to them; one by one they hooked up the hogs, and one by one with a swift stroke they slit their throats. There was a long line of hogs, with squeals and lifeblood ebbing away together; until at last each started again, and vanished with a splash into a huge vat of boiling water.

It was all so very businesslike that one watched it fascinated. It was porkmaking by machinery, porkmaking by applied mathematics. And yet somehow the most matter-of-fact person could not help thinking of the hogs; they were so innocent, they came so very trustingly; and they were so very human in their protests—and so perfectly within their rights! They had done nothing to deserve it; and it was adding insult to injury, as the thing was done here, swinging them up in this cold-blooded, impersonal way, without a pretense of apology, without the homage of a tear. Now and then a visitor wept, to be sure; but this slaughtering machine ran on, visitors or no visitors. It was like some horrible crime committed in a dungeon, all unseen and unheeded, buried out of sight and of memory. . . . .

The carcass hog was scooped out of the vat by machinery, and then it fell to the second floor, passing on the way through a wonderful machine with numerous scrapers, which adjusted themselves to the size and shape of the animal, and sent it out at the other end with nearly all of its bristles removed. It was then again strung up by machinery, and sent upon another trolley ride; this time passing between two lines of men, who sat upon a raised platform, each doing a certain single thing to the carcass as it came to him. One scraped the outside of a leg; another scraped the inside of the same leg. One with a swift stroke cut the throat; another with two swift strokes severed the head, which fell to the floor and vanished through a hole. Another made a slit down the body; a second opened the body wider; a third with a saw cut the breastbone; a fourth loosened the entrails; a fifth pulled them out—and they also slid through a hole in the floor. There were men to scrape each side and men to scrape the back; there were men to clean the carcass inside, to trim it and wash it. Looking down this room, one saw, creeping slowly, a line of dangling hogs a hundred yards in length; and for every yard there was a man, working as if a demon were after him. At the end of this hog's progress every inch of the carcass had been gone over several times; and then it was rolled into the chilling room, where it stayed for twenty-four hours, and where a stranger might lose himself in a forest of freezing hogs. . . .

Then the party went across the street to where they did the killing of beef—where every hour they turned four or five hundred cattle into meat. Unlike the place they had left, all this work was done on one floor; and instead of there being one line of carcasses which moved to the workmen, there were fifteen or twenty lines, and the men moved from one to another of these. This made a scene of intense activity, a picture of human power wonderful to watch. It was all in one great room, like a circus amphitheater, with a gallery for visitors running over the center.

Along one side of the room ran a narrow gallery, a few feet from the floor; into which gallery the cattle were driven by men with goads which gave them electric shocks. Once crowded in here, the creatures were prisoned, each in a separate pen, by gates that shut, leaving them no room to turn around; and while they stood bellowing and plunging, over the top of the pen there leaned one of the "knockers," armed with a sledge hammer, and watching for a chance to deal a blow. The room echoed with the thuds in quick succession, and the stamping and kicking of the steers. The instant the animal had fallen, the "knocker" passed on to another; while a second man raised a lever, and the side of the pen was raised, and the animal, still kicking and struggling, slid out to the "killing bed." Here a man put shackles about one leg, and pressed another lever, and the body was jerked up into the air. There were fifteen or twenty such pens, and it was a matter of only a couple of minutes to knock fifteen or twenty cattle and roll them out. Then once more the gates were opened, and another lot rushed in; and so out of each pen there rolled a steady stream of carcasses, which the men upon the killing beds had to get out of the way.

The manner in which they did this was something to be seen and never forgotten. They worked with furious intensity, literally upon the run—at a pace with which there is nothing to be compared except a football game. It was all highly specialized labor, each man having his task to do; generally this would consist of only two or three specific cuts, and he would pass down the line of fifteen or twenty carcasses, making these cuts upon each. First there came the "butcher," to bleed them; this meant one swift stroke, so swift that you could not see it—only the flash of the knife; and before you could realize it, the man had darted on to the next line, and a stream of bright red was pouring out upon the floor. This floor was half an inch deep with blood, in spite of the best efforts of men who kept shoveling it through holes; it must have made the floor slippery, but no one could have guessed this by watching the men at work.

The carcass hung for a few minutes to bleed; there was no time lost, however, for there were several hanging in each line, and one was always ready. It was let down to the ground, and there came the "headsman," whose task it was to sever the head, with two or three swift strokes. Then came the "floorsman," to make the first cut in the skin; and then another to finish ripping the skin down the center; and then half a dozen more in swift succession, to finish the skinning. After they were through, the carcass was again swung up; and while a man with a stick examined the skin, to make sure that it had not been cut, and another rolled it up and tumbled it through one of the inevitable holes in the floor, the beef proceeded on its journey. There were men to cut it, and men to split it, and men to gut it and scrape it clean inside. There were some with hose which threw jets of boiling water upon it, and others who removed the feet and added the final touches. In the end, as with the hogs, the finished beef was run into the chilling room, to hang its appointed time.

The visitors were taken there and shown them, all neatly hung in rows, labeled conspicuously with the tags of the government inspectors—and some, which had been killed by a special process, marked with the sign of the kosher rabbi, certifying that it was fit for sale to the orthodox. And then the visitors were taken to the other parts of the building, to see what became of each particle of the waste material that had vanished through the floor; and to the pickling rooms, and the salting rooms, the canning rooms, and the packing rooms, where choice meat was prepared for shipping in refrigerator cars, destined to be eaten in all the four corners of civilization. Afterward they went outside, wandering about among the mazes of buildings in which was done the work auxiliary to this great industry. There was scarcely a thing needed in the business that Durham and Company did not make for themselves. There was a great steam power plant and an electricity plant. There was a barrel factory, and a boiler-repair shop. There was a building to which the grease was piped, and made into soap and lard; and then there was a factory for making lard cans, and another for making soap boxes. There was a building in which the bristles were cleaned and dried, for the making of hair cushions and such things; there was a building where the skins were dried and tanned, there was another where heads and feet were made into glue, and another where bones were made into fertilizer. No tiniest particle of organic matter was wasted in Durham's. Out of the horns of the cattle they made combs, buttons, hairpins, and imitation ivory; out of the shinbones and other big bones they cut knife and toothbrush handles, and mouth-pieces for pipes; out of the hoofs they cut hairpins and buttons, before they made the rest into glue. From such things as feet, knuckles, hide clippings, and sinews came such strange and unlikely products as gelatin, isinglass, and phosphorus, bone black, shoe blacking, and bone oil. They had curled-hair works for the cattle tails, and a "wool pullery" for the sheepskins; they made pepsin from the stomachs of the pigs, and albumen from the blood, and violin strings from the ill-smelling entrails. When there was nothing else to be done with a thing, they first put it into a tank and got out of it all the tallow and grease, and then they made it into fertilizer. All these industries were gathered into buildings near by, connected by galleries and railroads with the main establishment; and it was estimated that they had handled nearly a quarter of a billion of animals since the founding of the plant by the elder Durham a generation and more ago. If you counted with it the other big plants—and they were now really all one—it was . . . the greatest aggre-gation of labor and capital ever gathered in one place. It employed thirty thousand men; it supported directly two hundred and fifty thousand people in its neighborhood, and indirectly it supported half a million. It sent its products to every country in the civilized world, and it furnished the food for no less than thirty million people!

❧ PART TWO ❧

At the Family Hearth

Memory, Identity, Ethnicity

INTRODUCTION

SOME OF the most celebrated culinary writing appears in memoirs, many of them coming-of-age stories that show how, when, and why the author became captivated, indeed often obsessed, by food. A number of these works emphasize the role mothers and grandmothers played in introducing the child to the traditions and the cooking of beloved foods or to the raising and growing of cherished ingredients. Sometimes the experience of enchantment is gradual; sometimes it involves a sudden epiphanic revelation. Many of these memoirs dramatize the renunciation of old and an embrace of new ways of thinking about food. In such stories eating, along with meditation on food, seldom remains simple, but may form the foundation of one's identity.

Ethnicity is central to many of these memoirs, the role of family often embedded in a history and conventions that celebrate a unique food culture, enveloping the young gastronome in something beyond his or her private needs and desires. So this section turns to the culinary traditions of such diverse places as Barbados, Appalachia, China, India, and the Middle East, as well to a range of hyphenated American subcultures (Jewish-, Italian-,

African-, Caribbean-). African-American memoirists, for instance, frequently stress the relation between foodways and a rich sense of their own childhood community. Henry Louis Gates Jr. remembers how his family, resisting a prevalent white racist stereotype of black people smelling bad, celebrated the wonderful aromas of their own stew bubbling on the stove pot, and the delicious "Homemade Ring Bologna" concocted by a "colored handyman" at a local bakery. Ntozake Shange recalls the okra, Hoppin' John, pig's feet, collard greens, and corn bread of her ancestors, and relishes sharing those foods with her appropriately named daughter Savannah. As Shange cooks each dish, she feels an entire heritage rising up within her. Similarly, Audre Lorde describes the tradition of crushing in a mortar spices from the West Indies with the precision and passion learned from her wise Barbadian mother.

These stories dramatize the habits and bonding rituals formed around food within families. Often, as in our selections by Susan Gubar and Elizabeth Ehrlich, their writers gain historical awareness through a return to a community abandoned due to assimilation into mainstream society. Sometimes the stories involve a generational skip: a granddaughter intensely watching as a grandmother takes her back to older ways of making things, while the mother—modern and seduced by laborsaving devices and supermarket ease—resists. So her Nonna entrances young Louise DeSalvo by making bread from scratch, while DeSalvo learns that commercial bread— her mother's choice—is too white; with that perception young Louise is on her way to becoming a serious cook like her grandmother. In a different but related situation, the great food writer Ruth Reichl remembers being appalled by her mother, whom she subsequently names "the Queen of Mold," for her habit of keeping and serving foods long since turned green and vile in the fridge, a practice that eventually forced the rebellious child to search out new cuisines.

At the same time, other writers—for instance Linda Furiya and Diana Abu-Jaber—show that no matter how much immigrant parents' food tastes are shared by the child, they may become a source of embarrassment and conflict when set against American culinary habits. Furiya is chagrined when her mother gives her a traditional Japanese bento-box for her school lunch, even though she loves the delicacies it contains, while Abu-Jaber finds herself humiliated when her Jordanian-American family is chastised for barbecuing chicken on their front lawn, a gross violation of suburban mores.

Despite the pain of this incident Abu-Jaber speaks warmly of her parents (in her account there are certainly comic moments), and the title of her book, *The Language of Baklava*, announces that the Middle Eastern cuisine of their household is a language she has come to speak. Less lovingly, Maxine Hong Kingston tells how her Chinese mother cooked raccoons, skunks, snakes, and turtles, and regaled her daughter with tales of monkey feasts in China, the diners scalping the poor beast and scooping out its brains. Kingston's melancholic conclusion: "I would live on plastic."

Other autobiographical texts stress the palate-development of budding culinary enthusiasts. A. J. Liebling recounts his initiation into the nexus of gastronomy and history that characterized the culture of Paris between the two world wars; while M.F.K. Fisher writes about the ambiguities of her initiation into the painful pleasure she associates with one food, oysters, although later in her marvelous memoir, *The Gastronomical Me*, she was to celebrate her own immersion—like Liebling's—in a European culinary milieu.

Some memoirists single out special dishes that signal family bonds: the pumpernickel bagels of Calvin Trillin's Sunday shopping expeditions with his daughters; the savory Mexican *menudo* that Ray Gonzalez considers a hangover cure; the "food suitcase" crammed with Bengali spices and herbs that Jhumpa Lahiri associates with childhood trips to Calcutta. Still others remember foods served at significant family occasions. Here we have Ehrlich's tale of a Passover dinner with its food rituals and cooking across the generations, and Sandra Gilbert's bittersweet verse about her Jewish mother-in-law's dogged resistance to a succulent Italian artichoke that evoked a culinary world for the Italian-American poet. Despite their differences, all these writers understand gastronomy to be a guide to the remembrance of things past, just as the consumption of a simple madeleine was for the narrator of Marcel Proust's sublime novel, in the famous passage that we include in the first section of this anthology.

🦋

A. J. Liebling (1904–1963)

LIEBLING WAS AN essayist on many subjects, including horse racing, box-
ing, the state of the press, New York street life, war, and food. For several
years he wrote columns for *The New Yorker* on these and numerous other
subjects. As a young man in the 1920s he went to Paris to study literature,
but he really wanted to learn about French culture, especially its restaurants;
that year in Paris led to a lifelong obsession with French food, culminating
in *Between Meals*, a book many regard as the best of all food memoirs. Our
selection from this gastronomical coming-of-age tale, Liebling's account of
his "researches as a feeder," argues that a modest restaurant budget allows for
a more discerning palate and more culinary learning than unlimited funds
can provide (one is forced to make interesting trade-offs and to be more
adventurous). Liebling shows his appreciation for small, humble bistros—
where priests and hookers alike might dine—places that serve the simple but
delectable family cooking the French call *cuisine de grandmère*.

from *Between Meals*: Just Enough Money

IF THE FIRST requisite for writing well about food is a good appetite, the
second is to put in your apprenticeship as a feeder when you have enough
money to pay the check but not enough to produce indifference to the size
of the total. The optimum financial position for a serious apprentice feeder is
to have funds in hand for three more days, with a reasonable, but not certain,
prospect of reinforcements thereafter. The student at the Sorbonne waiting
for his remittance, the newspaperman waiting for his salary, the freelance
writer waiting for a check that he has cause to believe is in the mail—all are
favorably situated to learn. (It goes without saying that it is essential to be in
France.) The man of appetite who will stint himself when he can see three
days ahead has no vocation, and I dismiss from consideration, as manic,
the fellow who will spend the lot on one great feast and then live on fried

potatoes until his next increment; Tuaregs eat that way, but only because they never know when they are going to come by their next sheep. The clear-headed voracious man learns because he tries to compose his meals to obtain an appreciable quantity of pleasure from each. It is from this weighing of delights against their cost that the student eater (particularly if he is a student at the University of Paris) erects the scale of values that will serve him until he dies or has to reside in the Middle West for a long period. The scale is different for each eater, as it is for each writer.

Eating is highly subjective, and the man who accepts say-so in youth will wind up in bad and overtouted restaurants in middle age, ordering what the maître d'hôtel suggests. He will have been guided to them by food-snob publications, and he will fall into the habit of drinking too much before dinner to kill the taste of what he has been told he should like but doesn't. . . .

The reference room where I pursued my own first earnest researches as a feeder without the crippling handicap of affluence was the Restaurant des Beaux-Arts, on the Rue Bonaparte, in 1926–27. I was a student, in a highly generalized way, at the Sorbonne, taking targets of opportunity for study. Eating soon developed into one of my major subjects. The franc was at twenty-six to the dollar, and the researcher, if he had only a certain sum— say, six francs—to spend, soon established for himself whether, for example, a half bottle of Tavel *supérieur*, at three and a half francs, and braised beef heart and yellow turnips, at two and a half, gave him more or less pleasure than a *contre-filet* of beef, at five francs, and a half bottle of *ordinaire*, at one franc. He might find that he liked the heart, with its strong, rich flavor and odd texture, nearly as well as the beef, and that since the Tavel was over-whelmingly better than the cheap wine, he had done well to order the first pair. Or he might find that he so much preferred the generous, sanguine *contre-filet* that he could accept the undistinguished *picrate* instead of the Tavel. As in a bridge tournament, the learner played duplicate hands, mak-ing the opposite choice of fare the next time the problem presented itself. (It was seldom as simple as my example, of course, because a meal usually included at least an hors d'oeuvre and a cheese, and there was a complexity of each to choose from. The arrival, in season, of fresh asparagus or venison further complicated matters. In the first case, the investigator had to decide what course to omit in order to fit the asparagus in, and, in the second, whether to forgo all else in order to afford venison.)

A rich man, faced with this simple sumptuary dilemma, would have ordered both the Tavel *and* the *contre-filet*. He would then never know whether he liked beef heart, or whether an *ordinaire* wouldn't do him as well as something better. (There are people to whom wine is merely an alcoholized sauce, although they may have sensitive palates for meat or pastries.) When one considers the millions of permutations of foods and wines to test, it is easy to see that life is too short for the formulation of dogma. Each eater can but establish a few general principles that are true only for him. Our hypothetical rich *client* might even have ordered a Pommard, because it was listed at a higher price than the Tavel, and because he was more likely to be acquainted with it. He would then never have learned that a good Tavel is better than a fair-to-middling Pommard—better than a fair-to-middling almost anything, in my opinion. In student restaurants, renowned wines like Pommard were apt to be mediocre specimens of their kind, since the customers could never have afforded the going prices of the best growths and years. A man who is rich in his adolescence is almost doomed to be a dilettante at table. This is not because all millionaires are stupid but because they are not impelled to experiment. In learning to eat, as in psychoanalysis, the customer, in order to profit, must be sensible of the cost.

There is small likelihood that a rich man will frequent modest restaurants even at the beginning of his gustatory career; he will patronize restaurants, sometimes good, where the prices are high and the repertory is limited to dishes for which it is conventionally permissible to charge high prices. From this list, he will order the dishes that in his limited experience he has already found agreeable. Later, when his habits are formed, he will distrust the originality that he has never been constrained to develop. A diet based chiefly on game birds and oysters becomes a habit as easily as a diet of jelly doughnuts and hamburgers. It is a better habit, of course, but restrictive just the same. Even in Paris, one can dine in the costly restaurants for years without learning that there are fish other than sole, turbot, salmon (in season), trout, and the Mediterranean *rouget* and *loup de mer*. The fresh herring or sardine *sauce moutarde*; the *colin froid mayonnaise*; the conger eel *en matelote*; the small fresh-water fish of the Seine and the Marne, fried crisp and served *en buisson;* the whiting *en colère* (his tail in his mouth, as if contorted with anger); and even the skate and the *dorade*—all these, except by special and infrequent invitation, are out of the swim. (It is a standing tourist joke to say that the fishermen on the quays of the Seine never catch anything, but in fact they often take home the makings of a nice fish fry, especially in winter. In my hotel on the Square Louvois, I had a room waiter—a Czech naturalized in France—who used to catch hundreds of *goujons* and *ablettes* on his days off. He once brought a shoe box of them to my room to prove that Seine fishing was not pure whimsy.) All the fish I have mentioned have their habitats in humbler restaurants, the only places where the aspirant eater can become familiar with their honest fishy tastes and the decisive modes of accommodation that suit them. Personally, I like tastes that know their own minds. The reason that people who detest fish often tolerate sole is that sole doesn't taste very much like fish, and even this degree of resemblance disappears when it is submerged in the kind of sauce that patrons of Piedmontese restaurants in London and New York think characteristically French. People with the same apathy toward decided flavor relish "South African lobster" tails—frozen as long as the Siberian mammoth—because they don't taste lobstery. ("South African lobsters" are a kind of sea crayfish, or *langouste*, but that would be nothing against them if they were fresh.) They prefer processed cheese because it isn't cheesy, and synthetic vanilla extract because it isn't vanillary. They have made a triumph of the Delicious apple because it doesn't taste like an apple, and of the Golden Delicious because it doesn't taste like anything. In a related field, "dry" (non-beery) beer and "light" (non-Scotchlike) Scotch are more of the same. The standard of perfection for vodka (no color, no taste, no smell) was expounded to me long ago by the then Estonian consul-general in New York, and it accounts perfectly for the drink's rising popularity with those who like their alcohol in conjunction with the reassuring tastes of infancy—tomato juice, orange juice, chicken broth. It is the ideal intoxicant for the drinker who wants no reminder of how hurt Mother would be if she knew what he was doing.

The consistently rich man is also unlikely to make the acquaintance of meat dishes of robust taste—the hot *andouille* and *andouillette*, which are close-packed sausages of smoked tripe, and the *boudin*, or blood pudding, and all its relatives that figure in the pages of Rabelais and on the menus of the market restaurants. He will not meet the *civets*, or dark, winy stews of domestic rabbit and old turkey. A tough old turkey with plenty of character makes the best *civet*, and only in a *civet* is turkey good to eat. Young turkey, like young sheep, calf, spring chicken, and baby lobster, is a pale preliminary phase of its species. The pig, the pigeon, and the goat—as suckling, squab, and kid—are the only animals that are at their best to eat when immature. The first in later life becomes gross through indolence; the second and third grow muscular through overactivity. And the world of tripery is barred to the well-heeled, except for occasional exposure to an expurgated version of *tripes à la mode de Caen*. They have never seen *grasdouble* (tripe cooked with vegetables, principally onions) or *pieds et paquets* (sheep's tripe and calves' feet with salt pork). . . .

Finally, to have done with our rich man, seldom does he see even the simple, well-pounded *bifteck* or the *pot-au-feu* itself—the foundation glory of French cooking. Alexandre Dumas the elder wrote in his *Dictionary of Cuisine*: "French cooking, the first of all cuisines, owes its superiority to the excellence of French bouillon. This excellence derives from a sort of intuition with which I shall not say our cooks but our women of the people are endowed." This bouillon is one of the two end products of the *pot*. The other is the material that has produced it—beef, carrots, parsnips, white turnips, leeks, celery, onions, cloves, garlic, and cracked marrowbones, and, for the dress version, fowl. Served *in* some of the bouillon, this constitutes the dish known as *pot-au-feu*. Dumas is against poultry "unless it is old," but advises that "an old pigeon, a partridge, or a rabbit roasted in advance, a crow in November or December" works wonders. He postulates "seven hours of sustained simmering," with constant attention to the "scum" that forms on the surface and to the water level. ("Think twice before adding water, though if your meat actually rises above the level of the bouillon it is necessary to add boiling water to cover it.") This supervision demands the full-time presence of the cook in the kitchen throughout the day, and the maintenance of the temperature calls for a considerable outlay in fuel. It is one reason that the *pot-au-feu* has declined as a chief element of the working-class diet in France. Women go out to work, and gas costs too much. For a genuinely good *pot-au-feu*, Dumas says, one should take a fresh piece of beef—"a twelve-to-fifteen-pound rump"—and simmer it seven hours in the bouillon of the beef that you simmered seven hours the day before. He does not say what good housekeepers did with the first piece of beef—perhaps cut it into sandwiches for the children's lunch. He regrets that even when he wrote, in 1869, excessive haste was beginning to mar cookery; the demanding ritual of the *pot* itself had been abandoned. This was "a receptacle that never left the fire; day or night," Dumas writes. "A chicken was put into it as a chicken was withdrawn, a piece of beef as a piece was taken out, and a glass of water whenever a cup of broth was removed. Every kind of meat that cooked in this bouillon gained, rather than lost, in flavor." *Pot-au-feu* is so hard to find in chic restaurants nowadays that every Saturday evening there is a mass pilgrimage from the fashionable quarters to Chez Benoit, near the Châtelet—a small but not cheap restaurant that serves it once a week. I have never found a crow in Benoit's *pot*, but all the rest is good.

M.F.K. Fisher (1908–1992)

PERHAPS AMERICA'S MOST celebrated food writer, Mary Frances Kennedy Fisher married young and went with her first husband, Al Fisher, to France, where she quickly became a dedicated gourmet. In Dijon, introduced to French cookery, and then in countless culinary researches afterwards, she learned, as she put it, to "feed hungers" not just for food but for love. Her autobiographical *The Gastronomical Me* was probably the most groundbreaking "foodoir" of the twentieth-century, but it was accompanied by countless other books, including *Consider the Oyster* and *How to Cook a Wolf.* After her marriage with Al Fisher broke up, as she recounts in these stories, she met her true love, Dillwyn Parrish, called "Chexbres" in her writings. As she recounts the poignant events of her life, Fisher's talent for remembering fascinating meals is enriched by her genius for dramatizing the significant personal meanings of such occasions. Here, in her narrative of her encounter with a "First Oyster," she explores the parallels between sexual hunger and culinary desire.

from *The Gastronomical Me*: The First Oyster

THERE WERE ABOUT seventy boarders and twenty-five women, and for morning-recess lunch a pack of day-girls, and most of us ate with the delicacy and appreciation of half-starved animals. It must have been sickening to Mrs. Cheever to see us literally wolfing her well-planned, well-cooked, well-served dishes. For in spite of doing things wholesale, which some gastronomers say is impossible with any finesse, the things we ate at Miss Huntingdon's were savory and interesting.

Mrs. Cheever, for instance, would get a consignment of strange honey from the Torrey pine trees, honey which only a few people in the world were supposed to have eaten. I remember it now with some excitement, as a grainy greenish stuff like some I once ate near Adelboden in the Bernese Alps, but then it was to most of us just something sweet and rather queer to put on hot biscuits. Tinned orange marmalade would have done as well.

At Thanksgiving she would let the Filipinos cover the breakfast tables with dozens of odd, beautiful little beasts they had made from vegetables and fruits and nuts, so that the dining room became for a while amazingly funny to us, and we were allowed to make almost as much noise as we wanted while we ate forbidden things like broiled sausage and played with the crazy toys. The boys would try not to laugh too, and even Mrs. Cheever would incline her queenly topknot less scornfully than usual when spoken to. . . .

Once, for the Christmas Party, she served Eastern oysters, fresh oysters, oysters still in their shells.

Nothing could have been more exotic in the early twenties in Southern California. The climate was still considered tropical, so that shellfish imported alive from the East were part of an oil-magnate's dream, or perhaps something to be served once or twice a year at Victor Hugo's, in a private room with pink candleshades and a canary. And of course any local molluscs were automatically deemed inedible, at least by *nice* people.

The people, that Christmas Party night, were indeed nice. We wore our formals: skirts not less than eight nor more than fifteen inches from the floor, dresses of light but not bright colors and of materials semi-transparent or opaque, neck-lines not more than three inches below the collar bone and sleeves long or elbow-length. We all passed the requirements of the catalog, but with such delectable additions as long chiffon scarves twined about our necks in the best Nita-Naldi-bronchitic manner, or great artificial flowers pinned with holiday abandon on our left shoulders. Two or three of the Seniors had fox furs slung nonchalantly about them, with the puffy tails dangling down over their firmly flattened young breasts in a most fashionable way.

There may even have been a certain amount of timid make-up in honor of

Kris Kringle and the approaching libertinage of Christmas vacation, real or devoutly to be hoped for, but fortunately the dining room was lighted that night by candles only.

Mrs. Cheever had outdone herself, although all we thought then was that the old barn had never looked so pretty. The oblong tables, usually in ranks like dominoes in their box, were pushed into a great horseshoe, with a little table for Miss Huntingdon and Miss Blake and the minister and the president of the trustees in the middle, and a sparkling Christmas tree, and . . . yes! . . . a space for dancing! And there were candles, and the smells of pine branches and hot wax, and place cards all along the outer edge of the horseshoe so that the Freshmen would not sit in one clot and the other groups in theirs.

We marched once around the beautiful room in the flickering odorous candlelight, singing, "God Rest You Merry, Gentlemen" or some such thing to the scrapings of the assistant violin instructor and two other musicians, who in spite of their trousers had been accurately judged unable to arouse unseemly longings in our cloistered hearts.

Then we stood by the chairs marked with our names, and waited for the music to stop and Miss Huntingdon and the minister to ask the blessings in their fluty voices. It was all very exciting.

When I saw that I was to sit between a Senior and a Junior, with not a Freshman in sight, I felt almost uplifted with Christmas joy. It must mean that I was Somebody, to be thus honored, that perhaps I would even be elected to the Altar Guild next semester. . . .

I knew enough not to speak first, but could not help looking sideways at the enormous proud nose of Olmsted, who sat at my left. She was president of the Seniors, and moved about the school in a loose-limbed dreamy way that seemed to me seraphic. Inez, the Junior, was less impressive, but still had her own string of horses in Santa Barbara and could curse with great concentration, so many words that I only recognized *damn* and one or two others. Usually she had no use for me, but tonight she smiled, and the candlelight made her beady eyes look almost friendly.

The grace done with, we pulled our chairs in under the unaccustomed silkiness of our party-dress bottoms with less noise than usual, and the orchestra flung itself into a march. The pantry doors opened, and the dapper little house-boys pranced in, their smooth faces pulled straight and their eyes snapping with excitement.

They put a plate in front of each of us. We all looked hazily at what we saw, and waited with mixed feelings until Miss Huntingdon had picked up her fork (where, I wonder now, did Mrs. Cheever even find one hundred oyster forks in a California boarding school?) before we even thought of eating. I heard Inez mutter under her breath, several more words I did not recognize except as such, and then Olmsted said casually, "How charming! Blue Points!"

There was a quiet buzz . . . we were being extremely well-bred, all of us, for the party . . . and I know now that I was not the only Westerner who was scared shaky at the immediate prospect of eating her first raw oyster, and was putting it off for as long as possible.

I remembered hearing Mother say that it was vulgar as well as extremely unpleasant to do anything with an oyster but swallow it as quickly as possible, without *thinking*, but that the after-taste was rather nice. Of course it was different with tinned oysters in turkey dressing: they could be chewed with impunity, both social and hygienic, for some reason or other. But raw, they must be swallowed whole, and rapidly.

And alive.

With the unreasoning and terrible persnicketiness of a sixteen-year-old I knew that I would be sick if I had to swallow anything in the world alive, but especially a live oyster.

Olmsted picked up one deftly on the prongs of her little fork, tucked it under her enormous nose, and gulped. "Delicious," she murmured.

"Jesus," Inez said softly. "Well, here goes. The honor of the old school. Oi!" And she swallowed noisily. A look of smug surprise crept into her face, and she said in my ear, "Try one, Baby-face. It ain't the heat, it's the humidity. Try one. Slip and go easy." She cackled suddenly, watching me with sly bright eyes.

"Yes, do," Olmsted said.

I laughed lightly, tinklingly, like Helen in *Helen and Warren*, said, "Oh, I *love* Blue Points!" and got one with surprising neatness into my mouth.

At that moment the orchestra began to play, with sexless abandon, a popular number called, I think, "Horses." It sounded funny in Miss Huntingdon's dining room. Olmsted laughed, and said to me, "Come on, Kennedy. Let's start the ball rolling, shall we?"

The fact that she, the most wonderful girl in the whole school, and the most intelligent, and the most revered, should ask me to dance when she knew very well that I was only a Sophomore, was so overwhelming that it made even the dreamlike reality that she had called me Kennedy, instead of Mary Frances, seem unimportant.

The oyster was still in my mouth. I smiled with care, and stood up, reeling at the thought of dancing the first dance of the evening with the senior-class president.

The oyster seemed larger. I knew that I must down it, and was equally sure that I could not. Then, as Olmsted put her thin hand on my shoulder blades, I swallowed once, and felt light and attractive and daring, to know what I had done. We danced stiffly around the room, and as soon as a few other pairs of timid girls came into the cleared space by the tree, headed toward Miss Huntingdon's table.

Miss Huntingdon herself spoke to me by name, and Miss Blake laughed silently so that her black wig bobbled, and cracked her knuckles as she always did when she was having a good time, and the minister and Olmsted made a little joke about Silent Sophomores and Solemn Seniors, and I did not make a sound, and nobody seemed to think it strange. I was dumb with pleasure at my own importance . . . practically the Belle of the Ball I was! . . . and with a dawning gastronomic hunger. Oysters, my delicate taste buds were telling me, oysters are *simply marvelous*! More, more!

I floated on, figuratively at least, in Olmsted's arms. The dance ended with a squeaky but cheerful flourish, and the girls went back to their seats almost as flushed as if they were returning from the arms of the most passionate West Point cadets in white gloves and coats.

The plates had been changed. I felt flattened, dismayed, as only children can about such things.

Olmsted said, "You're a funny kid, Kennedy. Oh, green olives!" when I mumbled how wonderful it had been to dance with her, and Inez murmured in my ear, "Dance with me next, will you, Baby-face? There are a couple of things boys can do I can't, but I can dance with you a damn sight better than that bitch Olmsted."

I nodded gently, and smiled a tight smile at her, and thought that she was the most horrible creature I had ever known. Perhaps I might kill her some day. I was going to be sick.

I pushed back my chair.

"Hey, Baby-face!" The music started with a crash, and Inez put her arms surely about me, and led me with expert grace around and around the Christmas tree, while all the candles fluttered in time with my stomach.

"Why don't you talk?" she asked once. "You have the cutest little ears I ever saw, Baby-face . . . like a pony I had, when I was in Colorado. How do you like the way I dance with you?"

Her arm tightened against my back. She was getting a crush on me, I thought, and here it was only Christmas and I was only a Sophomore! What would it be by April, the big month for them? I felt somewhat flattered, because Inez was a Junior and had those horses in Santa Barbara, but I hated her. My stomach felt better.

Miss Huntingdon was watching me again, while she held her water glass in her white thin fingers as if it had wine in it, or the Holy Communion. She leaned over and said something to Miss Blake, who laughed silently like a gargoyle and cracked her knuckles with delight, not at what Miss Huntingdon was saying but that she was saying anything at all. Perhaps they were talking about me, saying that I was nice and dependable and would be a good Senior president in two more years, or that I had the cutest ears. . . .

"Relax, kid," Inez murmured. "Just pretend . . ."

The pantry door swung shut on a quick flash of gray chiffon and pearls, almost at my elbow, and before I knew it myself I was out of Inez' skillful arms and after it. I had to escape from her; and the delightful taste of oyster in my mouth, my new-born gourmandise, sent me toward an unknown rather than a known sensuality.

The thick door shut out almost all the sound from the flickering, noisy dining room. The coolness of the pantry was shocking, and Mrs. Cheever was even more so. She stood, queenly indeed in her beautiful gray evening dress and her pearls and her snowy hair done in the same lumpy rhythm as Mary of England's, and her face was all soft and formless with weeping.

Tears trickled like colorless blood from her eyes, which had always been so stony and now looked at me without seeing me at all. Her mouth, puckered from years of dyspepsia and disapproval, was loose and tender suddenly, and she sniffed with vulgar abandon.

She stood with one arm laid gently over the scarlet shoulders of the fat old nurse, who was dressed fantastically in the ancient costume of Saint Nicholas. It became her well, for her formless body was as generous as his, and her ninny-simple face, pink-cheeked and sweet, was kind like his and neither male nor female. The ratty white wig sat almost tidily on her head, which looked as if it hardly missed its neat black-ribboned nurse's cap, and beside her on the pantry serving table lay the beard, silky and monstrous, ready to be pulled snug against her chins when it was time to give us all our presents under the Christmas tree.

She looked through me without knowing that I stood staring at her like a paralyzed rabbit. I was terrified, of her the costumed nurse and of Mrs. Cheever so hideously weeping and of all old women.

Mrs. Cheever did not see me either. For the first time I did not feel unattractive in her presence, but rather completely unnecessary. She put out one hand, and for a fearful moment I thought perhaps she was going to kiss me: her face was so tender. Then I saw that she was putting oysters carefully on a big platter that sat before the nurse, and that as she watched the old biddy eat them, tears kept running bloodlessly down her soft ravaged cheeks, while she spoke not a word.

I backed toward the door, hot as fire with shock and the dread confusion of adolescence, and said breathlessly, "Oh, excuse me, Mrs. Cheever! But I . . . that is, *all* the Sophomores . . . on behalf of the Sophomore Class I want to thank you for this beautiful, this *simply marvelous* party! Oysters . . . and . . . and everything . . . It's all *so* nice!"

But Mrs. Cheever did not hear me. She stood with one hand still on the wide red shoulders of the nurse, and with the other she put the oysters left from the Christmas Party on a platter. Her eyes were smeared so that they no longer looked hard and hateful, and as she watched the old woman eat steadily, voluptuously, of the fat cold molluscs, she looked so tender that I turned anxiously toward the sureness and stability of such small passions as lay in the dining room.

The pantry door closed behind me. The orchestra was whipping through "Tales from the Vienna Woods," with the assistant violin instructor doubling on the artificial mocking bird. A flock of little Filipino boys skimmed like monkeys into the candlelight, with great trays of cranberry sauce and salted nuts and white curled celery held above their heads, and I could tell by their faces that whatever they had seen in the pantry was already tucked far back behind their eyes, perhaps forever.

If I could still taste my first oyster, if my tongue still felt fresh and excited, it was perhaps too bad. Although things are different now, I hoped then, suddenly and violently, that I would never see one again.

✒

Austin Clarke (1934–)

A LIVELY AND prolific novelist, short story writer, and memoirist, Austin Clarke was born in Barbados but moved to Canada as a young man. His works have won a number of important prizes, especially the novel *The Polished Hoe*, and he has taught or been a writer in residence at universities in the United States and Canada. His exuberant *Pig Tails 'n Breadfruit*, from which we present an excerpt, is a kind of gastronomic autobiography, complete with meditations on his favorite recipes and composed in Barbadian, the West Indies dialect of his homeland. "I don't eat every day," Clarke once confided to an interviewer. "And I can't cook and sit down and eat by myself. . . . So I would eat if I had friends [over]. That is when I would cook." But the gusto with which he whips up tales of Barbadian cookery and its roots in slavery belies this confession, as he evokes the special pleasures of dishes devised by necessity.

from *Pig Tails 'n Breadfruit*: Souse, but no Black Pudding

SOME PEOPLE DOES live only for Sundays. To go to church. Some people does live only for Fridays. Pay-day. Some people does live for Wednesdays. To attend mid-week church or to go to Mothers Union meetings, or just because Wednesday is soup day.

But with me? Gimme Saturdays any morning. Gimme Saturdays seven days of the week! Saturday, when I was growing up, was the day for making black pudding and souse, the best food in the world. As a young, strapping teenager, the race-horse, as my mother called me, I used to walk across half o' the island o' Barbados: from Paynes Bay in Sin-James parish, where I was living at the time, right up to the Abbey in Christ Church parish, a journey of twelve miles at least. And when you realize that Barbados is twenty-one miles in the longest straightest direction, you *know* how long twelve miles is, out o' twenty-one! Just to get pudding and souse.

Up in the Abbey there was the Kings, a whole family o' girls who could make some o' the sweetest pudding and souse in the whole island. To-besides, one of the King girls was in love with me.

But whether or not you was in love, you still would make sure that the woman you eating pudding and souse from was a clean person—clean enough that you could close your two eyes and eat a piece o' snout, or a piece o' the ear, and not feel funny. Yuh know? From childhood you was taught to-don't eat black pudding and souse from any-and-everybody who makes it, you hear? Some people don't clean the belly and the pig feets clean-clean, yuh!

"Watch what going into your stomach, boy!"

So, from reputation, word o' mouth, and because you know the woman who make the black pudding and souse (she and your mother might be friends), you would track she down to the ends o' the earth, just to "taste her hand" on a Saturday. The reputation of the best makers o' pudding and souse does spread through the whole island, and men does travel from Sin-Lucy parish in the north to Oistin's Town in Christ Church in the south, *just* to taste that woman's hand.

But travelling all that distance to eat black pudding and souse, walking for miles and miles in the damn hot sun if you don't have a bicycle, is not merely to full-up your belly with pig foots and snout and pieces of ear. Eating black pudding and souse on a Saturday is a social event, with certain proto-cols that go with it, certain rites and rituals. For example, if you buying the pudding and souse in a rum shop, you have to buy a rum first. If you buying it from a pudding-and-souse woman, you first have to engage her in conver-sation. Axe she 'bout her thrildren (her children), or her boyfriend if you's the same age as she. And only when them pleasantries are finish, then you can tell she, "Child, gimme some o' this nice pudding and souse!"

In Brooklyn, where there is more Barbadians than the sum total o' Bar-badians living in Barbados, the pudding and souse comes in strict political stripes. Lemme explain what this mean.

Pudding and souse, as you remember, is the national dish o' Barbados. The Barbadian national pastime is talking 'bout politics. And since eating pudding and souse is something that you does do in a rum shop, whilst you're talking—and "talking a lotta shite" as we say, meaning talking about politics, church, women, men and thrildren—it is a case o' night following the day that, whilst sucking on a pig foot, you might be hearing about the Barbadian budget, the latest political scandal in Barbados, hearing who really kill Mark Stokes and drop he in the sea, or if a certain prime minister o' Barbados dead from drugs or from poisoning, or if a woman kill he, in truth. So, eating pudding and souse in a rum shop is a dangerous pastime. . . .

When I was a boy, every Saturday afternoon as God send, around two o'clock, the hottest part of the afternoon, you would see a woman sitting down by the door of the neighbourhood shop, Miss Edwards's Shop, behind a big tray placed on a box. The large cloth covering the tray, and protecting its contents from flies, was made from a flour bag that was bleached for days and days until the red and blue names of the Canadian mill and manufacturer disappeared and the cloth became white as snow.

The woman sat on a smaller box as if it were a throne. She wore a starched and ironed dress that had white flowers in the design, and her white apron was starched and pleated, reaching below her knee. Her hair was combed back severely from her forehead in corn rows and tied tightly with a white ribbon.

This is the black-pudding-and-souse woman. A goddess. A Queen of Hot-Cuisine, Bajan style. The High Priestess o' Souse!

If she didn't have a good reputation throughout the whole neighbourhood, and if she wasn't a woman that pass muster, cleanliness-wise and decency-wise, she could sit for days and days on end offering people black pudding and souse free, and not one soul would take even a half-inch o' pudding or one little piece o' souse from her tray. But the fact that this woman sitting down there, beside the door of the shop, where all the neighbours buy their groceries, in full daylight, in all her starched white and hairgreased majesty, mean that she is somebody important, somebody accepted, somebody clean in the neighbourhood. Her place is secure and sanctified.

The fact that she selling black pudding and souse, and that you happen to have money in your pocket, don't mean that you could fork yourself up to her tray and say, "Gimme five shillings in pudding and souse!" You just do not tell *her* what you want and what you don't want. Oh, no! You would have to take what *she* give you, even though it is your money buying it.

Back there and back then, money didn't do the same kind o' talking that money does do up here in Canada and Amurca. Oh, no! Before money, you have to have the class to go with it; 'cause a lot o' other people in the neighbourhood have class, and more class than you. Oh, yes! So, without class, you have to wait your turn.

"And know your blasted place, boy!" the black-pudding-and-souse woman would tell you. And she would laugh, "Heh-hehhh!" to soften the blow in the reminder.

Imagine a boy going up to this black-pudding-and-souse woman and telling she, "Gimme two shillings in souse. And I want the pig's feet and some of the ear! And three shillings in the black pudding. And I want the white black pudding, not the black black pudding!"

He would have to be born mad!

"What you say?" the black-pudding-and-souse woman would ask he. "You *want*? You want *what*? Look, nigger-man, you will get what *I* decide to sell you. What the hell you mean by 'you want'? You want a lash in your arse! Have manners, boy. I have souse put-by for the lady in the wall house, out the Front Road—one o' my steady customers. And I have to save-back ten shillings in pig's feet for the manager o' the Plantation. And Mistress Yard, out the Front Road, have to have her souse, six shillings' worth, and two yards o' the white black pudding. And you come stanning-up in front o' me, in front my tray, telling *me* you want? You want a lash in you lil black arse! Wait your turn, boy. Know your place! I could maybe spare six cents in souse, and give you a sixpence in black pudding. *Maybe*, if yuh lucky. You want it? Or you don't want it? Speak your damn mind. I busy with my regular customers!" And as she is saying, she is serving other customers. . . .

Now, to find out how black pudding and souse is made, we have to return to the big wooden table in Gertrude's backyard where the dead pig is lying.

The pig head cut off by now, and the blood collected in a pail, because some o' this blood is to be used to make the black pudding. The butcher just handed the four feet, or trotters, to Gertrude, along with pieces o' pork up by the knees, the ham hocks.

For the rest of the morning the woman will work and work, cleaning these parts o' the pig, washing them in lime juice. The biggest job is "to clean the belly"—to wash out, over and over again, all the intestines, which is the part used to make black pudding.

First, you take the intestines and empty them out. Then you clean them clean-clean-clean, and soak them in a bucket with lots o' lime juice and white vinegar. You have to find a way to turn the intestines inside-out in order to clean them even more better still. Then turn-back the insides, outside-in, and wash them some more. And some more, until they really clean.

When you finish cleaning the belly, you have to dry them off and then soak them again in lime juice, a lil salt and a lil white vinegar, and leave them to "draw." "Drawing" means that the salt and lime juice and vinegar going have a chance to work into the belly, so that the taste of "freshness" (since a pig was alive one minute, dead the next and eaten the same day) is drowned and killed.

You now have time to start peeling the sweet potatoes and grating them. You got to cut up the onions, eschalots, cucumber and fresh broad-leaf thyme into lil pieces. Cut up the hot pepper, and please, don't pass your two hands near your eyes! That pepper doesn't make sport. It real hot! Mix in a lil flour with the grated sweet potato to give it some body. Add in some nutmeg or cloves, some sugar, some salt and some hot pepper, and mix up all these ingreasements.

To make black pudding that is black, you would have to add in some blood to give colour to the mixture. But if you have bad nerves, or a weak stomach, forget the blood; you can use food colouring instead. Or just leave the mixture as it is. Black pudding without the blood or food colouring is called white black pudding, or white pudding.

Now get a funnel, and tie the funnel to one end of a clean and dry intestine. Tie-off the other end of the intestine and start stuffing the grated potato mixture into the intestine through the funnel. You ever heard of chitlings? Well, this is how chitlings was born.

When the intestine is full-up with the potato, but not packed too tight, tie-she-off with another piece o' string. Full-up all the intestines with the potato mixture in this way, until all the grated potato been used.

If you have any intestines leff back, you could boil them or fry them by themselves. If you run out o' intestine and have some grated potato mixture leff back, throw all of this in a frying pan with hot lard oil, or olive oil, and my God in heaven!—the consequence o' frying this stuffing is bound to gladden your heart.

Food, like most things, is something that you have to improvise with. You have to use the ingreasements that are available, or that grow in your backyard. We in Barbados, where black pudding and souse was made first in 1752—long before anybody heard o' Trinidad or Jamaica or Sin-Kitts—we uses to grow a lot o' sweet potatoes. So we does stuff the intestines with grated sweet potato.

Down in Guyana, and in some parts o' Trinidad, they never saw a real sweet potato in their lives, unless a uncle or a aunt put one in a envelope or a barrel and post it to Port-of-Spain or Georgetown. But they have rice. So,

Trinidadians and Guyanese does stuff their black pudding with rice. It don't taste too bad. You could eat it. But it ain't Bajan pudding!

Back to our intestines. They now stuffed with the grated potatoes and waiting on a large plate. Put a large—and I mean large—pot or saucepan o' water on the fire, and drop in a bay leaf or two. Bring the water to a boil. Then turn down the heat and take up each stuffed intestine careful, careful, careful in your hand, and lay she down in the water, without splashing the water. Don't cover-down the pot. You need to see what happening inside that pot.

The most important thing to remember not to do, whilst your intestines is boiling, is to talk. Do not talk. Talking is the worst thing you could do, over a pot o' black pudding that cooking.

Do not open your mouth, even to tell your boyfriend or your girlfriend that you love him or her, or to tell your husband that he is a son-of-a-bitch for not helping you clean the belly. Do not utter one word. Because to talk while your black pudding is cooking in a pot, according to the best superstitions and laws o' voodoo of Barbados, is to make the black pudding burst in the pot. The sausage casings going burst and explode, and transform the contents o' this big pot into a pool o' brown porridge.

I just give you a quick lesson in making black pudding. I wouldn't advise you to try your hand in making it, though. It's tummuch work. And too risky.

Souse, on the other hand, is different. It's made from the pig's feet, from the ham hocks, from parts o' the pig head, like the snout and the ears, and from some of the leaner parts of the pig, near the belly. These parts, or "features," are boiled until they are soft. They are either left to cool off in the water in which they were cooked, or are taken out and placed on the counter to cool, or are put in cold water to cool off quickly.

While these pig features cooling off, it's time to make the prickle. The prickle for souse is the mixture in which the features are put to soak and get "soused-up." Hence the name of the dish, souse.

Cut up onions, green onions, cucumber and fresh thyme in a large bowl. Don't slice the cucumber; dice it.

Add salt and pepper to suit your taste. Fresh hot peppers is always better than black pepper shaken from a shaker. Don't forget a touch o' white vinegar, to help the pork draw.

Stir up these ingreasements in a bowl, and taste the prickle to make sure it reach the hotness you like. Expert souse-makers does argue that you *must* pour a lil water in which the features was cooked into the prickle, to give it some body and that nice taste o' pork.

Incidentally, souse made from a pig just killed is more better and tastier than souse made from pork that you buy in a supermarket.

When the pork features cool off, clean them using a lot o' lemon. Rub and rub lemon peth all over them. The cleaning of the features at this stage is the most important part of the preparation of souse.

Cut up the features in bite-size pieces and throw them in the prickle. Stir them round, and cover them down for at least one hour. Two hours is the correct amount of time to leave them sousing-up. The more longer they soak in the prickle, the more better they will be soused-up, and the sweeter your souse going taste.

Some people who pretend they was born in the Wessindies does put up their nose at this way of eating souse cold. They argue that souse got to be served hot and eaten *hot*. But don't mind them. Those unbelievers are Wessindians who was born in Sin-Kitts or the Bahamas. No Guyanese, nor Trinidadian nor Grenadian, would try to mislead you by telling you that souse have to be served hot.

Souse, the real Barbadian souse, *have* to be served and eaten one way only: cold.

Another thing that you might hear from some Wessindians is that anyone who does consume blood in their food, from an animal, have cannibalistic tendencies. Well, I am not going tell you that I like pig blood in my black pudding. Nor am I *not* going tell you that I do not like blood in my black pudding. Historically and culturally speaking, there is two kinds o' black pudding: black pudding that is black and black pudding that is white.

Now that the features soaking, you have time to pour yourself a beer or a rum and soda, or better still, a Bajan rum punch. And whilst you are sipping that rum punch take out the lengths o' black pudding from the pot and lay them on a large platter.

Dip a piece o' paper towel, or even better, a few feathers tied together to make a light brush, in some olive oil, lard oil or any kind o' oil, and brush it over each piece o' black pudding as if you're touching up a water-colour painting. Light and nice. You are going to see the black pudding shine like a first-class Polish sausage.

When you ready to serve, this is how you do it. Get a sharp knife and cut off pieces o' black pudding, about two inches in length. Put a couple of pieces on a plate with a few pieces o' souse, consisting of a pig foot, a piece o' the ear, the snout, and a nice piece from the ham hock. Pour a lil prickle all over the souse, and sprinkle a few pieces of fresh parsley or watercress on the black pudding. You could add some fresh parsley to the souse to make it look pretty, or as North Amurcans would say, to "garnish" it.

There is a special way, ordain in Barbadian culture and history, of eating pudding and souse. You eat it out in the open air, in the hot sun, with the sea breeze blowing in your face and the wind licking your body.

If you don't eat-off all the souse and black pudding the same day it made, then have it for breakfast the next morning. All you have to do is fry the black pudding in a pan with a lil butter; not with too much heat, though. And you can fry-up the souse too. But don't pour in the prickle with the souse when you frying it. (Real Barbadians would know how to cut up pieces of the souse, small-small, mix them in flour, and fry them to make "souse-fritters.")

Serve this meal o' pudding and souse with some fresh bread, but no butter, as you would if you were serving it on Saturday.

So, this is pudding and souse, the food of the gods and of the slaves of Barbados.

Black pudding and souse would have to be the ultimate in slave food. It is made from the parts of the pig that nobody else wanted or had the heart to eat. But regardless, pudding and souse is the sweetest thing handed down by our ancestors, African slaves, to each and every one of us present-day Wessindians.

Perhaps it is a dish that you would have to be born in the particular culture that prepares it for you to understand and appreciate it. If you taste it once, you bound to want to taste it every Saturday for the rest of your life.

A lot o' people does talk about it, but few can make it. In other words, the Biblical saying can be applied to the making of pudding and souse: "Many are called, but few are chosen."

When you meet a woman who does make sweet pudding and souse, you will make sure that you keep her as a friend, as a wife or as a lover for the rest o' your life, the rest o' your born days.

The next time you see a black-pudding-and-souse woman, you tell she, "I would like a lil pudding and souse."

"How you want it?" she going to ask you.

"Man, put it in my hand, man! And don't forget to pour some of the prickle..."

She going cut you a inch o' black pudding that is black and a inch o' black pudding that is white, and place them on a sheet o' brown paper. She going pass the feathers dipped in oil over the black pudding. And you going eat-off these two pieces fast fast because the pudding sweet, oh my God in heaven! It too sweet, in-true! And then the real sport going begin.

"You tekking your souse now, then?" she going axe you.

And with her ladle she going stir up all that sweet prickle, all them ingreasements in her souse-bowl, and she going empty a ladleful in the palm of your hand.

And you going raise your palm to your two lips, with your two eyes closed, to measure in intense concentration the "strength" o' this souse-prickle. You will keep your two eyes closed still, and empty the contents o' your palm into your mouth. You will start to chaw and eat, and all the time you're eating—with your two eyes still closed—you gotta say, "Hem! Ah-hem!" in testimony to the fact that the souse have a sweet fragrance o' pepper, and it blasted hot.

Water will come to your two eyes, and your throat will be cleared.

"Good Jesus Christ in heaven!" as my mother say, "*that* is souse, boy!"

🐘

Audre Lorde (1934–1992)

BORN AND RAISED in New York City, Lorde defined herself as a "black, lesbian, feminist, warrior, poet." Her distinguished works in verse include the collections *Coal* and *The Black Unicorn* while her influential contributions to feminist theory are represented in *The Uses of the Erotic* and *Sister Outsider*. From girlhood a rebel and an activist, Lorde was diagnosed with breast cancer in 1978; after undergoing a mastectomy, she became one of the first public figures who refused to wear a prosthesis, explaining in *The Can-*

cer Journals her choice not to falsify herself. Her brilliant "biomythography," *Zami: A New Spelling of My Name*, chronicles her childhood in Harlem and then her years of coming out as a lesbian in the Village and elsewhere. Significant passages of the book meditate on her relationship with her proud West Indian mother, whose native land was "Carriacou" (Curaçao), a lost place of culinary plenty Lorde describes as "my truly private paradise of blugoe and breadfruit hanging from the trees, of nutmeg and lime and sapodilla, of tonka beans and red and yellow Paradise Plums."

from *Zami*: Spices

WHEN I WAS growing up in my mother's house, there were spices you grated and spices you pounded, and whenever you pounded spice and garlic or other herbs, you used a mortar. Every West Indian woman worth her salt had her own mortar. Now if you lost or broke your mortar, you could, of course, buy another one in the market over on Park Avenue, under the bridge, but those were usually Puerto Rican mortars, and even though they were made out of wood and worked exactly the same way, somehow they were never really as good as West Indian mortars. Now where the best mortars came from I was never really sure, but I knew it must be in the vicinity of that amorphous and mystically perfect place called "home." And whatever came from "home" was bound to be special.

My mother's mortar was an elaborate affair, quite at variance with most of her other possessions, and certainly with her projected public view of herself. It stood, solid and elegant, on a shelf in the kitchen cabinet for as long as I can remember, and I loved it dearly.

The mortar was of a foreign fragrant wood, too dark for cherry and too red for walnut. To my child eyes, the outside was carved in an intricate and most enticing manner. There were rounded plums and oval indeterminate fruit, some long and fluted like a banana, others ovular and end-swollen like a ripe alligator pear. In between these were smaller rounded shapes like cherries, lying in batches against and around each other.

I loved to finger the hard roundness of the carved fruit, and the always surprising termination of the shapes as the carvings stopped at the rim and the bowl sloped abruptly downward, smoothly oval but suddenly businesslike. The heavy sturdiness of this useful wooden object always made me feel secure and somehow full; as if it conjured up from all the many different flavors pounded into the inside wall, visions of delicious feasts both once enjoyed and still to come.

The pestle was long and tapering, fashioned from the same mysterious rose-deep wood, and fitted into the hand almost casually, familiarly. The actual shape reminded me of a summer crook-necked squash uncurled and slightly twisted. It could also have been an avocado, with the neck of the alligator pear elongated and the whole made efficient for pounding, without ever losing the apparent soft firmness and the character of the fruit which the wood suggested. It was slightly bigger at the grinding end than most pestles, and the widened curved end fitted into the bowl of the mortar easily. Long use and years of impact and grinding within the bowl's worn hollow had softened the very surface of the wooden pestle, until a thin layer of split fibers coated the rounded end like a layer of velvet. A layer of the same velvety mashed wood lined the bottom inside the sloping bowl.

My mother did not particularly like to pound spice, and she looked upon the advent of powdered everything as a cook's boon. But there were some certain dishes that called for a particular savory blending of garlic, raw onion, and pepper, and souse was one of them.

For our mother's souse, it didn't matter what kind of meat was used. You could have hearts, or beefends, or even chicken backs and gizzards when we were really poor. It was the pounded-up saucy blend of herb and spice rubbed into the meat before it was left to stand so for a few hours before cooking that made that dish so special and unforgettable. But my mother had some very firm ideas about what she liked best to cook and about which were her favorite dishes, and souse was definitely not one of either.

On the very infrequent occasions that my mother would allow one of us three girls to choose a meal—as opposed to helping to prepare it, which was a daily routine—on those occasions my sisters would usually choose one of those proscribed dishes so dear to our hearts remembered from our relatives' tables, contraband, and so very rare in our house. They might ask for hot dogs, perhaps, smothered in ketchup sauce, or with crusty Boston-baked beans; or american chicken, breaded first and fried crispy the way the southern people did it; or creamed something-or-other that one of my sisters had tasted at school; what-have-you croquettes or anything fritters; or once even a daring outrageous request for slices of fresh watermelon, hawked from the back of a rickety wooden pickup truck with the southern road-dust still on her slatted sides, from which a young bony Black man with a turned-around baseball cap on his head would hang and half-yell, half-yodel—"Wahr—deeeeeee-mayyyyyyy-lawnnnnnnn."

There were many american dishes I longed for too, but on the one or two occasions a year that I got to choose a meal, I would always ask for souse. That way, I knew that I would get to use my mother's mortar, and this in itself was more treat for me than any of the forbidden foods. Besides, if I really wanted hot dogs or anything croquettes badly enough, I could steal some money from my father's pocket and buy them in the school lunch.

"Mother, let's have souse," I'd say, and never even stop to think about it. The anticipated taste of the soft spicy meat had become inseparable in my mind from the tactile pleasures of using my mother's mortar.

"But what makes you think anybody can find time to mash up all that stuff?" My mother would cut her hawk-grey eyes at me from beneath their heavy black brows. "Among-you children never stop to think," and she'd turn back to whatever it was she had been doing. If she had just come from the office with my father, she might be checking the day's receipts, or she might be washing the endless piles of dirty linen that always seemed to issue from rooming-houses.

"Oh, I'll pound the garlic, Mommy!" would be my next line in the script written by some ancient and secret hand, and off I'd go to the cabinet to get down the heavy wooden mortar and pestle.

I took a head of garlic out from the garlic bottle in the icebox, and breaking off ten or twelve cloves from the head, I carefully peeled away the tissue lavender skin, slicing each stripped peg in half lengthwise. I dropped them piece by piece into the capacious waiting bowl of the mortar. Taking a slice from a small onion, I put the rest aside to be used later over the meat, and cutting the slice into quarters, I tossed it into the mortar also. Next came the coarsely ground fresh black pepper, and then a lavish blanketing cover of salt over the whole. Last, if we had any, a few leaves from the top of a head of celery. My mother sometimes added a slice of green pepper, but I did not like the texture of the pepper-skin under the pestle, and preferred to add it along with the sliced onion later on, leaving it all to sit over the seasoned and resting meat.

After all the ingredients were in the bowl of the mortar, I fetched the pestle and placing it into the bowl, slowly rotated the shaft a few times, working it gently down through all the ingredients to mix them. Only then would I lift the pestle, and with one hand firmly pressed around the carved side of the mortar caressing the wooden fruit with my aromatic fingers, I thrust sharply downward, feeling the shifting salt and the hard little pellets of garlic right up through the shaft of the wooden pestle. Up again, down, around, and up—so the rhythm began.

The *thud push rub rotate up* repeated over and over. The muted thump of the pestle on the bed of grinding spice as the salt and pepper absorbed the slowly yielding juices of the garlic and celery leaves.

Thud push rub rotate up. The mingling fragrances rising from the bowl of the mortar.

Thud push rub rotate up. The feeling of the pestle held between my curving fingers, and the mortar's outside rounding like fruit into my palm as I steadied it against my body.

All these transported me into a world of scent and rhythm and movement and sound that grew more and more exciting as the ingredients liquefied.

Sometimes my mother would look over at me with that amused annoyance which passed for tenderness.

"What you think you making there, garlic soup? Enough, go get the meat now." And I would fetch the lamb hearts, for instance, from the icebox and begin to prepare them. Cutting away the hardened veins at the top of the smooth firm muscles, I divided each oval heart into four wedge-shaped pieces, and taking a bit of the spicy mash from the mortar with my fingertips, I rubbed each piece with the savory mix, the pungent smell of garlic and onion and celery enveloping the kitchen.

Calvin Trillin (1935–)

TRILLIN IS ONE of America's great writers on food, famous for a set of works—*American Fried*; *Alice, Let's Eat*; and *Third Helpings*—known as "The Tummy Trilogy." He creates the persona—but it's also true—of an insatiable eater whose hedonism in consuming good but unfancy food is matched only by his pleasure in tracking it down, whether he's searching for the perfect bagel shop in Greenwich Village, the best BBQ joint in Kansas City, or a fabled Cajun shack in the Louisiana bayous. He is inevitably serious about food and hilariously funny at the same time. "Health food makes me sick," he once intoned. As in so many of his writings, here he invokes his two daughters and his late wife, whom he once criticized for being unwilling to eat more than three meals a day. Even as he amusingly discusses the sociology of bagels and their consumption in white-bread America, he attempts to bribe one of his San Francisco-based daughters to return to New York (where he lives) by dangling a lure of great bagels, the kind that California, with its raisin and blueberry varieties, can barely approach.

from *Feeding a Yen*: A Magic Bagel

NOT LONG AFTER the turn of the millennium, I had an extended father-daughter conversation with my older daughter, Abigail, on the way back from a dim sum lunch in Chinatown. Abigail, who was living in San Francisco, had come to New York to present a paper at a conference. As a group of us trooped back toward our house in Greenwich Village, where she'd grown up, Abigail and I happened to be walking together. "Let's get this straight, Abigail," I said, after we'd finished off some topic and had gone along in silence for a few yards. "If I can find those gnarly little dark pumpernickel bagels that we used to get at Tanenbaum's, you'll move back to New York. Right?"

"Absolutely," Abigail said.

There's a great comfort in realizing that a child you've helped rear has grown up with her priorities straight. When I phoned Abigail from the Oakland airport once to ask if she knew of an alternative route to her house in San Francisco—I'd learned of a huge traffic jam on the normal route, toward the Bay Bridge—she said, "Sure. Go south on 880, take 92 west across the bridge to 101, and we'll meet you at Fook Yuen for lunch." Fook Yuen is a dim sum restaurant in Millbrae, about five minutes from the San Francisco airport, and its way with a dumpling has persuaded us that flights in and out of San Francisco are best scheduled in the middle of the day. I report this response to a traffic jam as a way of demonstrating not simply that Abigail always has a fallback career as a taxi dispatcher awaiting her but also that she has the sort of culinary standards that could induce her to switch coasts if the right bagel came along.

But when I mentioned the Chinatown walk exchange to my wife, Alice, she had a different interpretation. She said that Abigail had been speaking ironically. I found it difficult to believe that anybody could be ironic about those bagels. They were almost black. Misshapen. Oniony. Abigail had always adored them. Both of my daughters have always taken bagels seriously. When my younger daughter, Sarah, was a little girl, I revealed in print that she wouldn't go to Chinatown without carrying a bagel—"just in case." At the time that Abigail and I had our conversation about the gnarly black pumpernickel bagel, Sarah was also living in California, in Los Angeles. She seemed perfectly comfortable with the Chinese food there. In fact, when I'd eaten with her at Chinois on Main, in Santa Monica, it occurred to me that her knowledge of the menu was nearly encyclopedic. She had many years before outgrown the need to have a bagel with her at a Chinese restaurant—which was fortunate indeed, because bagels in California were not anywhere near up to her standards.

For a while, I brought along a dozen or two New York bagels for Sarah whenever I went to Southern California, but I finally decided that this policy was counterproductive. "If a person prefers to live in California, which happens to be thousands of miles from her very own family," I told her, "it seems to me appropriate that such a person eat California bagels. I understand that in some places out there if you buy a dozen wheat germ bagels you get your choice of a bee pollen bagel or a ginseng bagel free." Sarah eventually moved back East. I'm not going to make any claims for the role of my bagel-withholding policy in that decision, but the fact remains: she did eventually move back East.

I have previously recorded Abigail's response, at age four or five, when, on a visit to my family in Kansas City, Missouri, she'd worked her way partly through a bagel I can describe, given my affection for my hometown, as an honest effort that had simply fallen way short of the mark, the baker having been put in the position a New York deli cook would have found himself in if asked to turn out a bowl of andouille gumbo. "Daddy," she said, "how come in Kansas City the bagels taste like just round bread?" In other words, she knew the difference between those bagel-shaped objects in the Midwest and the authentic New York item that had been hand-rolled and boiled in a vat and then carefully baked by a member in good standing of the Bakery and Confectionery Workers International Union. I think it might be fair to characterize her as having been a bagel prodigy.

When I was a child, bagel consumption in Kansas City was not widespread.

Bagels were thought of as strictly Jewish food, eaten mainly in New York. In those days, of course, salsa would have been considered strictly Mexican food, if anybody I knew in Kansas City had ever given any consideration to salsa. I doubt if many gentiles in Kansas City had ever heard of a bagel, let alone eaten one. Bagels were available in only two or three stores, one of which was called the New York Bakery. It was only in the real New York that bagels were part of the culture, for both Jews and gentiles. New Yorkers have always talked about picking up freshly baked bagels late at night and being reassured, as they felt the warmth coming through the brown paper bag, that they would be at peace with the world the next morning, at least through breakfast. They've talked about that day in the park when nothing seemed to soothe their crying baby until a grandmotherly woman sitting on a nearby bench, nattering with another senior citizen about Social Security payments or angel food cake recipes or Trotskyism, said that the only thing for a teething infant was a day-old bagel. They've talked about the joy of returning to New York from a long sojourn in a place that was completely without bagels—Indonesia or a tiny town in Montana or some other outpost in the vast patches of the world that New Yorkers tend to think of as the Bagel Barrens.

Roughly corresponding to the time it took our girls to grow up and move to California, bagels had become assimilated. Gefilte fish was still Jewish food, but not bagels. The bagel had gone from a regional ethnic food to an American standard, served at McDonald's and available on supermarket shelves all over the part of America that baked-goods sociologists have long identified with white bread. At one point, I read that, because of a new plant established by one of the firms producing supermarket bagels, the state that led all other American states in turning out bagels was Iowa. A couple of years before Abigail and I discussed pumpernickel bagels on the way back from Chinatown, *The New York Times* had run a piece by Suzanne Hamlin reporting that in places recently introduced to bagels, emergency rooms were seeing an increasing number of bagel-related injuries—cuts, gouges, and severed digits caused by "impatient eaters who try to pry apart frozen bagels with screwdrivers, attempt to cut hard bagels with dull knives and, more than likely, use their palms as cutting boards." There had been no increase in New York bagel injuries.

From the *Times* story, you could draw the conclusion that a lot of Americans were being given access to bagels before they knew how to handle them, in the way that a lot of Americans are said to have access to 9-mm pistols or semiautomatic rifles before they know how to handle them. I suspect any number of New Yorkers responded to the story by saying, in the superior tone customarily used by someone from Minneapolis who's relating the chaos caused in Birmingham by a simple snowstorm, "People there just don't have any experience in such things"—or, as the director of emergency medicine at Bellevue did say to the *Times*, "Those people just aren't ethnically equipped."

Aside from the safety issue, the mainstreaming of formerly ethnic or regional food like bagels must have been confusing for those citizens who grew up before it became common to find Cajun restaurants in upper Midwestern shopping malls and lobster shacks in Amarillo. In the eighties, when it was revealed that eating poppy-seed bagels could result in a false positive on a drug test, I saw one of the perils inherent in everybody's suddenly eating everything, whether ethnically equipped or not. I envisioned an applicant to the FBI academy who seems in the tradition of the bureau: he's a well-set-up young man with a square jaw and a direct gaze. He's almost maddeningly polite. His name is O'Connor. He went to Fordham. He always wears a suit and a white shirt and wing-tipped shoes. His father was in the bureau. His drug test seems to indicate that he's a user.

O'Connor is looking stunned. "I can't understand it," he says. "Maybe it was something I ate."

"Oh, yeah, I'm sure that was it," the tester, a grizzled agent near retirement age, says sarcastically. "We all know how corned beef and cabbage can mess up these results."

"You don't think it could have been those chiles rellenos I had for lunch, do you?" O'Connor says, ignoring the sarcasm. "That pico de gallo that came with them was pretty hot stuff."

"Maybe you can catch on with the Parks Department, O'Connor," the tester says, in a more sympathetic tone. "Or Sanitation. You're a husky lad."

"I can't believe blackened redfish would do it," O'Connor says. "Maybe it was that braised bok choy I had with my squid last night. That's all I've eaten lately, except for the poppy-seed bagels with lox and cream cheese that Father Sweeney served at the Holy Name Society breakfast this morning."

"The dope is making you talk crazy, son," the tester says.

The sad part is that they would have almost certainly been inferior poppy-seed bagels. Provisions for the Holy Name Society breakfast might well have been purchased at the local supermarket or at one of those places that make bagels with weird ingredients—blueberries, say, and cinnamon, and more air than you'd find in a Speaker of the House. O'Connor, not having been raised in the connoisseurship, probably wouldn't have known the difference. Not so my daughters. When they were children, bagels were not only their staple food—the food they clung to in unfamiliar surroundings—but also the food used in important rituals. On Sunday mornings, I often took them to Houston Street, on the Lower East Side. At Russ & Daughters, which is what New Yorkers refer to as an appetizing store, we would buy Nova Scotia salmon. Then we'd go next door to Ben's Dairy to get cream cheese and a delicacy known as baked farmer's cheese with scallions. Then we were at Tanenbaum's, a bakery that was probably best known for a large, dark loaf often referred to as Russian health bread. We were not there for Russian health bread. We were there for Abigail's pumpernickel bagels. Abigail had never exhibited any irony when the subject was pumpernickel bagels. Would Proust have been ironic about the madeleine, particularly if he had fetched up in a place where you couldn't get a decent madeleine if your life depended on it?

"So you think she's just humoring her old dad?" I asked Alice, during our discussion of the bagel conversation I'd had with Abigail on the way back from Chinatown.

"I do."

Alice was probably right. I understood that. Abigail was enjoying California, and she had a job there that she loved. As I've admitted before, my daughters have simply made good on their implicit threat to grow up and lead lives of their own. Parents are supposed to accept that. Still, I decided that I'd look around for those pumpernickel bagels. As my father used to say, "What could it hurt?"

۞

Sandra M. Gilbert (1936–)

COEDITOR OF THIS volume, Gilbert is a feminist theorist, literary critic, essayist, and poet. Her eight collections of verse include *Emily's Bread* and *Kissing the Bread*, whose titles reflect the culinary interests that sometimes surface in her writing, including our selection here. A professor emerita at the University of California, Davis, she has most recently authored *The Culinary Imagination: From Myth to Modernity.*

"No Thank You, I Don't Care for Artichokes,"

decreed my mother-in-law as my husband
passed the platter of inward-turning
soft-skulled Martian baby
heads around the table,

and they were O so shyly slyly
jostling each other with their boiled-
green sardonic gossip
(what was the news they told?)

when he sharply answered, "Mother,
have you *ever*
eaten an artichoke?"
                                    "No,"

she said, majestic, "but I just know
I don't *care* for them, don't
care for them at all"—
for truly, if they weren't Martian,

they were at the least Italian,
from that land of "smelly cheese"
she wouldn't eat, that land of oily
curves and stalks, unnerving pots

of churning *who knows what*,
and she, nice, Jewish, from the Bronx,
had fattened on her Russian-
Jewish mother's *kugel*, kosher

chicken, good rye bread. . . .
Bearded, rosy, magisterial
at forty-five, he laughed,
kept plucking, kept on

licking those narcissistic
leaves, each with its razor point
defending the plump, the tender
secret at the center, each

a greave or plate of edible
armor, so she smiled too,
in the flash of dispute,
knowing he'd give her ice cream later,

all she wanted, as the rich
meal drew to an end
with sweets dished out in the lamplit
circle, to parents, children, grandma—

the chocolate mint she craved,
and rocky road he bought especially
for her, whose knees were just
beginning to crumble from arthritis,

whose heart would pump more creakily
each year, whose baby
fat would sag and sorrow
as her voice weakened, breathing

failed until she too
was gathered into the same
blank center
where her son

at sixty bearded still, still
laughing, magisterial
(though pallid now)
had just a year before

inexplicably settled.

※

Maxine Hong Kingston (1940–)

BORN AND RAISED in a Chinese immigrant family in Stockton, California, Maxine Hong Kingston rocketed to fame with the publication of her best-selling memoir *The Woman Warrior*—a work fascinating for its mixture of apparently realistic autobiography with Chinese myths and tales. This excerpt from the book typifies the author's ambivalent feelings toward her mother and the conventions of her Chinese heritage. She both admired her mother (who was a midwife in China) and yet was often embarrassed by her Old World ways. Here she recalls a cuisine marked by strange and, to the young girl, grotesque foods, one of them (about which she only heard secondhand) involving the cruel treatment of a live monkey in a gastronomic practice some say continues in parts of Asia today. *The Woman Warrior* was followed by several other equally compelling books, most notably *China Men*, which meditates on the life of Kingston's father.

from *The Woman Warrior*: Mother's Cooking

MY MOTHER HAS cooked for us: raccoons, skunks, hawks, city pigeons, wild ducks, wild geese, blackskinned bantams, snakes, garden snails, turtles that crawled about the pantry floor and sometimes escaped under refrigerator or stove, catfish that swam in the bathtub. "The emperor used to eat the peaked hump of purple dromedaries," she would say. "They used chopsticks

made from rhinoceros horn, and they ate ducks' tongues and monkeys' lips."
She boiled the weeds we pulled up in the yard. There was a tender plant with
flowers like white stars hiding under the leaves, which were like the flower
petals but green. I've not been able to find it since growing up. It had no
taste. When I was as tall as the washing machine, I stepped out on the back
porch one night, and some heavy, ruffling, windy, clawed thing dived at me.
Even after getting chanted back to sensibility, I shook when I recalled that
perched everywhere, there were owls with great hunched shoulders and yellow scowls. They were a surprise for my mother from my father. We children
used to hide under the beds with our fingers in our ears to shut out the bird
screams and the thud, thud of the turtles swimming in the boiling water,
their shells hitting the sides of the pot. Once the third aunt who worked at
the laundry ran out and bought us bags of candy to hold over our noses; my
mother was dismembering skunk on the chopping block. I would smell the
rubbery odor through the candy.

In a glass jar on a shelf my mother kept a big brown hand with pointed
claws stewing in alcohol and herbs. She must have brought it from China
because I do not remember a time when I did not have the hand to look at.
She said it was a bear's claw, and for many years I thought bears were hairless.
My mother used the tobacco, leeks, and grasses swimming about the hand to
rub our sprains and bruises.

Just as I would climb up to the shelf to take one look after another at the
hand, I would hear my mother's monkey story. I'd take my fingers out of
my ears and let her monkey words enter my brain. I did not always listen
voluntarily, though. She would begin telling the story, perhaps repeating
it to a homesick villager, and I'd overhear before I had a chance to protect
myself. Then the monkey words would unsettle me; a curtain flapped loose
inside my brain. I have wanted to say, "Stop it. Stop it," but not once did I
say, "Stop it."

"Do you know what people in China eat when they have the money?" my
mother began. "They buy into a monkey feast. The eaters sit around a thick
wood table with a hole in the middle. Boys bring in the monkey at the end of a
pole. Its neck is in a collar at the end of the pole, and it is screaming. Its hands
are tied behind it. They clamp the monkey into the table; the whole table fits
like another collar around its neck. Using a surgeon's saw, the cooks cut a
clean line in a circle at the top of its head. To loosen the bone, they tap with a
tiny hammer and wedge here and there with a silver pick. Then an old woman

reaches out her hand to the monkey's face and up to its scalp, where she tufts some hairs and lifts off the lid of the skull. The eaters spoon out the brains."

Did she say, "You should have seen the faces the monkey made"? Did she say, "The people laughed at the monkey screaming"? It was alive? The curtain flaps closed like merciful black wings.

"Eat! Eat!" my mother would shout at our heads bent over bowls, the blood pudding awobble in the middle of the table.

She had one rule to keep us safe from toadstools and such: "If it tastes good, it's bad for you," she said. "If it tastes bad, it's good for you."

We'd have to face four-and five-day old leftovers until we ate it all. The squid eye would keep appearing at breakfast and dinner until eaten. Sometimes brown masses sat on every dish. I have seen revulsion on the faces of visitors who've caught us at meals.

"Have you eaten yet?" the Chinese greet one another.

"Yes, I have," they answer whether they have or not. "And you?"

I would live on plastic.

❧

Judith Moore (1940–2006)

ONE OF THE most fiercely candid food writers of her time, Moore was perhaps best known for *Fat Girl*, a scathing memoir of her childhood with an icy mother, a tough-minded grandmother, and an eccentric uncle, but she also explores the subject in *Eating My Heart Out*, an equally intense memoir. Born in Oklahoma, Moore gradually migrated westward, living in Olympia, Washington, before she settled in Berkeley, California, where she was a long-distance editor of the *San Diego Reader*. Sometimes almost brutal in their frankness—she described herself as a "short, squat toad of a woman"— her autobiographical narratives lamenting her childhood obesity or confiding a passionate tale of adultery explore the sexual and sensual contexts of eating and cooking in powerful detail. Our selection here, "Sauerkraut and a Pig-Sticking," is both a narrative of farm life and a sensitive remembrance of a little girl's early confrontation with the cruelty of the "food chain."

from *Never Eat Your Heart Out*:
Sauerkraut and a Pig-Sticking

AFTER MY MOTHER divorced my father, she sent me to live with my grand-mother on the ramshackle farm Uncle Carl bought her before he joined the Navy. I stayed there two years, until I was ready to start first grade.

With help from her two hired hands, Bushels and Buckles, my grand-mother grew a two-acre vegetable garden. Bushels and Buckles cultivated the rocky soil with a mule. The mule reluctantly pulled the rusted plow, whose parts were held together by baling wire. One hired hand steered while the other went along behind, holding the plow. The mule didn't have a name. "Mule," they called him, or "Jackass," and while they kicked and beat him, they yelled some of the first filthy language I ever heard. That mule led an awful life. Scars ran along his ribs where his former and present owners had whipped him. He hated humans. When you started toward him, he lifted his hairy upper lip and hissed and brayed, swished his tail and pawed the dirt.

My grandmother grew on her two acres: Country Gentleman sweet corn, collards, early and late English peas, Kentucky Wonder green pole beans, Fordhook limas, slicing and pickling cucumbers, dill, green puller and red Bermuda and yellow storage onions, green cabbages and purple cabbages whose outer leaves turned blue under morning dew, carrots, purple-shoul-dered ivory turnips, Mortgage Lifter tomatoes, bell peppers, beets, potatoes, okra, yellow crookneck squash, muskmelon, Charleston Gray watermelon, pumpkin, and Hubbard squash so heavy I couldn't carry even one and whose spiny, prickly green vines wound with a will of their own, as a snake will, in among rows of onions and turnips and beets. The vines were thick as my wrist and the tendrils that clasped tight around onion tops and cornstalks seemed likely any minute to wind their way around me. They would lace me in a tight bodice that squeezed out my breath. I would turn blue as the huge red cabbage heads turned after rain, and my eyes would pop, and I would be too breathless to scream.

Bushels and Buckles and I hauled cucumbers in zinc milking buckets into the kitchen to my grandmother. We carried peppers, onions, and cabbages. We heaped them onto sideboards and into the deep sink. On the stove, its burners' blue flames turned high, vinegar and cloves and mustard and cel-ery seeds seethed in my grandmother's dented canning kettles. Every wind, those mornings, carried the sharp tinge of vinegar with it. My grandmother took her butcher knife, a knife probably larger in memory than in fact, and chopped the hard green tomatoes, green cabbage, bell peppers into smithereens for the piccalilli relish that Uncle Carl liked to eat with meat loaf and chuck roast and Polish sausage. She lobbed the four-pound cabbages up onto her chopping block. She pulled off the outer leaves, each leaf wide as an opened fan. The leaves had been chewed by cabbage moths. This undressing exposed the cabbage's inner leaves, smooth as a man's newly shaved cheek. Grunting with each whack, my little grandmother went after the heads with her butcher knife, attacking as an angry peasant would attack the head of a despotic king.

When she had the cabbage shredded, she tossed it into her stoneware kraut crocks and mixed the raw cabbage with salt. She kept adding cabbage and salt until the crock was full. With each addition, she'd tamp down the cabbage so that it would be packed tightly into the crocks. When she'd chopped up every head and filled every crock, she'd call for one of the hired hands to shift the crocks into the dark pantry next to the kitchen. That done, she shrouded each crock with clean white cheesecloth, and then, on top of the cheesecloth, she set dinner plates. In warm weather, the cabbage would start to "work" in a few days, ambient bacteria producing lactic acid that brought a vile scum to the top. The kitchen and dining room would take on the sour, treacherous odor of fermenting cabbage, treacherous because that odor veers so near the odors that precede death.

Egyptians, my grandmother told me, lived on kraut while they carried the bricks that built the Great Pyramids. Not until I was an adult did I learn that it was the Chinese, while building the Great Wall, who lived on kraut. Whenever I saw photographs of pyramids or camels at the zoo, Elizabeth Taylor as Cleopatra, or Nasser or Anwar Sadat on television declaring war or signing treaties, what came to mind was the briny harsh rotting odor of cabbage fermenting into kraut.

As summer turned to fall, my grandmother kept careful watch over the last of the bell peppers. Nights when temperatures threatened to go down into the low forties and high thirties, Bushels and Buckles would be sent to cover the pepper plants with sheets, and as soon as the sun came up in the morning, they'd uncover the plants. By the time my grandmother's cabbage had turned to kraut, and all through the kitchen the principal odor was that of fermented cabbage, the green and red bell peppers would be big enough to stuff. She would gather together several dozen peppers and cut off their tops, pull out the seeds and the pithy white linings to which the seeds cling. She'd parboil the peppers, put them out on cookie sheets to cool. Once the peppers cooled, she'd stuff each shell with a handful of the cured kraut. She'd have ready the hot, sterilized quart canning jars; on two burners water in the two canning kettles bubbled, and in a third kettle a pickling brine simmered. Into each jar she'd place one red pepper and two green, or two red and one green, pour in a soup ladle of pickling brine, pop a lid on the filled jar, and then screw on the metal ring. When all that was done and the jars wiped clean, she processed the jars in the canning kettles, seven jars to each kettle.

Anyone looking at the jars of green and red peppers cooling on kitchen counters couldn't but think, How pretty! Cooking turned the red peppers' skins to dark ruby and the green to a severe dark olive. The kraut rose in a mound atop each ruby and green pepper and then dangled down the peppers' ribbed sides in ivory strands. When you jostled one of the jars, the kraut strands drifted in the briny pale ocher suspension like the long hair of underwater swimmers.

My grandmother and Bushels and Buckles waited for what they called a "good hog-sticking day" to butcher the Chester Whites and black-and-white Poland Chinas. Such a day would fall after the first hard frost. You wanted cold weather so that the meat wouldn't spoil; you wanted the flies dead, and a good hard frost killed flies.

The trio, dressed in their oldest clothes, killed and butchered two hogs at a time, probably because that was all they could handle in one day, what with farm chores that couldn't wait—feeding stock and poultry, milking cows, separating milk, raking out the henhouse, gathering eggs.

Bushels and Buckles took a rope and walked down to the muddy pig wallow and noosed one of the two chosen hogs and marched it toward a huge tree between the barn and the house. A rope hung off a branch that grew eight or ten feet off the ground. What kind of tree it was I don't know, but it was a tree tall enough and so generously branched that when in full leaf it cast a wide circumference of shadow beneath it, enough shade to keep grass from growing and to make the bare dirt cool even on hot days.

You couldn't help feeling sorry for the hog, grunting and heaving, as the hired hands, sooty hat brims pulled low over their foreheads so you couldn't see their eyes, prodded and harried it uphill on its short stumpy legs and cloven hooves. Brought to a halt beneath the tree, the hog blinked, batted its long hog eyelashes, and seemed to smile the way hogs do, waiting perhaps to have its ears scratched or to be offered some treat. It might root then with its hoelike snout, snorting up melting hoarfrost.

Bushels or Buckles, I don't remember which, drew his finger across his neck, in imitation of a knife cutting a throat, and made a horrible whickering noise. My grandmother and Bushels and Buckles looked at the smiling hog and laughed, and then my grandmother looked at me and shushed the hands, and said they'd need to get busy.

Bushels and Buckles looped and then tied the rope that swung from the branch around the hog's hind legs and pulled until the three- or four-hundred-pound animal dangled upside down. The limb gave off an awful groan while the men pulled, staggering from the effort. Surprised to find itself upended and no doubt terrified, the hog squeaked and squealed. The high-pitched squeals ascended, between branches, into the blue sky.

Bushels or Buckles thrust a long knife into the hog's throat, cutting, I think now, the jugular vein. The hog gasped. Dark blood poured out, gushed really, onto the dirt and fallen leaves. The muddy trotters twitched for a few seconds, the hog's head drooped and its eyes closed, long lashes fluttering. My grandmother would say, "He gave up the ghost."

Did the mule, hens, roosters, Jerseys and Guernseys, the other Poland Chinas and Chester Whites observe a moment of silence? No. But I remember the scene that way, remember that the normally noisy farm, its animal Muzak always playing, for a moment went silent. I remember every cluck and whinny and moo and oink erased. Not even the dog, shut up in the house while they stuck the hog, barked.

After both hogs were stuck and bled, clots and rivulets of blood soaked my grandmother's and Bushels's and Buckles's clothes. My grandmother's strong arms dripped hog blood from the elbows down onto her hands.

The hogs were cut down and dragged across the ground, their black blood leaving trails on the hard dirt, and put to soak in an old footed bathtub filled with steaming water. Pigs are blanketed with coarse hair, and the hot water helped loosen the skin's hold on the hair. My grandmother used her butcher knife to scrape bristles off the ears and more delicate hairs from lips and snouts. She brought her sharpening stone in her pocket; she honed and rehoned her blade. While my grandmother worked on the head, the hired hands shaved the hog's body until the skin was naked and smooth.

With help from one of the hired hands, my grandmother sawed off each of the four feet. The three of them swore while they worked, and sweated, even in the cold air. With her knife, she sliced away the cartilaginous ears, the lips, and the snout. These she saved for pickling.

What did my grandmother do with the hooves? How did she get the hogs' toenails off? I read now that butchers prise them out with pliers. I don't remember what she did. I do remember that in the kitchen she dropped the hooves, ears, and snouts into pots of boiling water set on the kitchen stove. I remember that while the hooves boiled, they bumped against the kettle.

Late afternoon, hawks—or were they vultures?—wheeled and drifted down to the ground beneath the tree where the last of the summer's flies glutted themselves on hog blood. The birds called to their fellows, their calls in a tenor range and more human than birdlike. They grabbed up bits of the Poland China's black-and-white skin; they flocked around the bathtub, filled then with pink water atop which skin and scum and bristle floated as water lilies float. The birds perched on the tub's edge and dipped down their heads and drank and fed. After the hawks or vultures left, black crows flew in over the downed cornstalks and pecked and cawed. Then they, too, flew away.

Hog-sticking nights, while I got ready for bed, my grandmother and Bushels and Buckles, blood dried on their clothing, worked under the kitchen's dim overhead light. Bugs seethed, circling the bulb. Even with the windows and the back door open, the last flies and moths of the season hitting lazily against the screens, the heat was terrible near the stove. The heat was summer-noon heat. Steam rose from kettles set atop every burner. The heat reddened my grandmother's and the hired hands' faces; sweat streamed from their foreheads, dripped off their chins.

The kitchen resembled a butcher shop where a crazy drunken butcher was in charge. Disassembled hog crowded every surface. Hoofless legs and snoutless, earless heads and slabs of fatback and squares of what would be smoked into bacon were puzzle pieces. I reassembled the hogs in my mind back down through the hours to morning, when they seemed to smile under the tree.

The trio worked quickly, to keep the meat from going bad. They ate hurriedly while they worked, cold biscuit in one hand, and nearby, for the men, a brown bottle of bootleg whiskey they called "medicine," which they sipped from. Bushels, who had a finger missing on one hand, massaged rough salt into hind and front thighs and chops for hams and smoked pork chops.

Buckles chewed a dead cigar stub stuck in one corner of his mouth and pressed gobbets of pink flesh through the meat grinder. The meat dropped into bowls and milk buckets; every big bowl my grandmother owned was heaped with ground hog. It was for sausage, a mixture she seasoned with sage and hot red pepper, then rolled into balls and canned.

I don't remember what my dreams were, those nights. I had nightmares back then from which I'd wake, screaming, in the high four-poster bed, from which I always feared I'd fall.

I remember that the next morning when I walked into the kitchen, they would still be working, their bloody clothes hanging looser and stinking from sweat, Bushels and Buckles still wearing their grubby hats. Because all three would be wearing the clothing they'd started out in the day before, because over twenty-four hours stains had spotted their hands and clothing one atop another like stucco, the world seemed to have stood still while the two hogs turned to meat.

From the door into the kitchen I watched them. They drank coffee and ate with their hands from a plate of cold biscuit and sausage and fried cracklin's. They spoke quietly and coughed dry coughs. They did not look each other steadily in the eye. If Bushels, for instance, happened to catch my grandmother's eye, he looked away quickly, looked down toward his filthy overalls. They moved slowly, as if under a spell. I felt newly afraid of all three of them. They seemed like people from a story who together had done some terrible deed and were waiting, fearful, for a knock at the door. But that probably is not how it was for them. Most likely they were tired; "bone weary," as my grandmother said. They were old, too, the men in their fifties and my grandmother sixty-something and, although she did not know it, only six or seven years away from death.

Glass jars packed with sausage balls and pigs' feet, pigs' ears, snouts, and lips lined the counters. More glass jars stood on newspapers laid out on the linoleum. My grandmother pointed to the plate of cold biscuit stuffed with sausage, told me to get myself dressed and then come back and take myself some food and eat it on the dining-room table. "Spread out a newspaper on that table so you don't get my good cloth greasy," she'd say. So that's what I did.

She'd sleep all that morning and afternoon, my grandmother would, while the jars cooled. I listened to her snores, her long stertorous sighs, and to the pings of the cooling jars. I made myself lunch from the breakfast scraps.

What else I did, I don't know. I must have played with my dolls, undressed and redressed them, must have gone outside and walked in between the white Leghorn hens that ran loose between house and barn. I may have tossed pebbles at them to make them fly up and scatter, something I did when I believed no one was watching. I may have played with the farm dog, a brindled male mutt who regularly ran after the Leghorns with his penis hanging out of its sheath. I didn't much like him. He didn't care anything for humans, and if he had a name I can't remember it.

Finally, my grandmother got up and put on a clean housedress and her rubber boots and went out to check her cows. She cooked dinner, a pan of the hogs' ribs she'd baked in the night and sauerkraut scooped out of the crock and boiled potatoes. I remember the rib's seared fat and the charred rib bone sticking out of either end of stringy meat, and I suspect I refused to eat the ribs.

🦢

Louise DeSalvo (1942–)

IN THE COURSE of a long and successful academic career as a professor at Hunter College and a notable scholar of Virginia Woolf, Louise DeSalvo turned to the writing of memoirs and other personal essays. Her lively books include *Asthma*, *Adultery*, and *On Moving* but perhaps the most compelling concern her Italian-American heritage: *Vertigo* and *Crazy in the Kitchen*. Here, especially in the context of food, she explores the ambiguities so often experienced by those who live, as it were, on the hyphen between cultures. On the one hand, she longs to celebrate her grandmother's Old World bread and rejects her mother's problematic attempts at assimilation into white-bread America; on the other hand, she is repelled by many Old World dishes (fresh-killed chicken, head cheese, snails) while savoring all-American apple pie. Similarly, she confides, she wants to make her own pasta, but she decides that "you can tell how enslaved the women of any country are by the kind of preparation their traditional foods require"—including, obviously, rolling out homemade pasta.

from *Crazy in the Kitchen*

THE BREAD

My grandmother is in the kitchen cutting the Italian bread that she has made. The bread that my grandmother has made is a big bread, a substantial bread, a bread that you can use for dunking, or for open-faced sandwiches, or for scraping the last bit of sauce from a bowl of pasta, or for toasting and eating with jam, or for breaking into soups and stews, or for eating with a little olive oil and a shake of coarse salt, or with a thick slice of slightly under-ripe tomato, or with the juices and seeds of a very ripe tomato and some very green olive oil (*pane e pomarole*).

My grandmother's bread is a good bread, not a fine bread. A bread that will stay fresh, cut side down, on the breadboard for three or four days, depending on the weather. A thick-crusted, coarse-crumbed Italian bread. A peasant bread. A bread that my mother disdains because it is everything that my grandmother is, and everything that my mother, in 1950s suburban New Jersey, is trying very hard not to be.

My grandmother's bread and the pizza she makes from her bread dough—tomato and cheese; garlic and olive oil; onion, sugar, and poppy seeds—are the foods that sustain me throughout my childhood. Without them, I know I would starve, because I hate everything my mother cooks. Hate it, because my mother burns the food that she cooks or puts too much salt in it or forgets to time the chicken and brings it to the table running with blood because she doesn't pay attention or because she is angry at my grandmother, at me, at the world, or because she is depressed and doesn't care about food, doesn't care about anything. Hate it because the ingredients themselves are terrible—gristly meat, bloated bratwurst, fatty sausage, slightly off hamburger gotten for a bargain that she tries to disguise with catsup and Worcestershire sauce. Or hate it (without realizing it then) because I can taste the rage in her food, can hear it in the slamming and banging of the pots and pans in her kitchen, in the clash of metal against metal in her stirring.

The kitchen, when my mother is cooking, is not a place I want to be. And so. No cookie-baking in the kitchen. No rolling out pie dough together. No lessons in how to make sauce.

And my mother's rage—at me for being selfish, at my grandmother for living with us since my grandfather died, at herself for her never-ending sorrow at not being able to create a life that can sustain her in spite of her loving my father, loving us (me and my sister), or so she says to my father, but never to me—scares me, makes me want to hide in a closet or rush from the house. It is a thick, scorching rage that I cannot predict, cannot control, cannot understand, a rage that I can feel against my skin. It is a rage that I do not want to catch from her. Though, of course, I do.

And so. I do not eat my mother's food if I can help it. Do not enter the kitchen when she cooks. Do not help her cook, for she will not let me, and prefers when I am not near her, when no one is near her. Do not help her clear the dishes, do not help her clean after we eat. And I leave the table, leave the kitchen, as soon and as fast as I can after what passes for supper in our house.

My eating my grandmother's bread and my not eating my mother's food is one reason my mother screams at me. (She has others: that I will not play with my sister and so keep her out of my mother's hair; that I sulk; that I answer back; that I have a mind of my own; that I am a burden; that I always have my nose in a book; that I do not love her; that I escape the house as often as I can; that I climb onto the roof from the upstairs bathroom window whenever there is a fight in our house, which is often, and so make a spectacle of myself, and let the neighbors know that despite my mother's superclean floors, her superladylike behavior, and her super-American ways, all is not well in our house.)

My eating my grandmother's bread and my not eating my mother's food is another reason my mother hates my grandmother, her stepmother, not her "real" mother, who died when my mother was a baby. A mother, she laments, who would have loved her, who would have taken care of her, and not resented her, as this woman does, this fake mother of hers, because they are not the same blood. My mother shouts this whenever they fight, which is often.

But I do not know what being the same blood means or why their not being the same blood should divide them. For, at times, when my mother talks to my father about what is happening in the world, she says that all people are created equal, and that the differences among people are only skin deep. But once, when I ask her if she and my grandmother were created equal, she said, no, because my grandmother never showed her any love, because my grandmother is a pain in the ass, because my grandmother drives her crazy.

She says that some people, like my dead grandfather, deserve respect, and others don't. And that my grandmother is one of the ones who don't. And that if I don't shape up, I'll become one of the ones who don't, too.

THE OTHER BREAD

My mother does not eat the bread my grandmother bakes. My mother eats the bread that she buys a few times a week from the Dugan's man, who comes round in his truck to our suburban neighborhood in Ridgefield, New Jersey, where we move after my grandfather dies. This bread, unlike my grandmother's, has preservatives, a long shelf life, my mother says. You can keep this bread for a long, long time without it becoming green-molded. To my mother, this bread is everything that a good bread should be.

The bread my mother buys is white bread, sliced bread, American bread. A bread that my father, my sister, and I eat only under protest or when it is transformed into something else. A bread that my grandmother would never eat, even if she were starving, and she told my mother so the one time she tasted this bread, and she told my mother, too, that she knows what it is to starve, what it is not to have enough food, and that even if she did not have enough food, she would not eat this bread.

My mother thinks that eating this bread will change her, that eating this bread will erase this embarrassment of a stepmother—all black dresses and headscarves and scavenging for dandelions on the neighbors' lawns, and superstitions, and tentacled things stewing in pots, and flurries of flour that ruin my mother's spotless kitchen, and infrequently washed Old World long woolen undergarments—this embarrassment of a stepmother who, my mother swears, never bathes, who treats water as if it is something to pray to, not something to wash in. (When my grandmother sees the amount of water my mother puts into the bathtub when my sister and I bathe, she mutters "Mare Adriatico" in disgust, clucks her tongue, and walks into her darkened bedroom to say the rosary.)

Maybe my mother thinks that if she eats enough of this other bread, she will stop being Italian American and she will become American American. Maybe my mother thinks that if she eats enough of this other bread, people will stop thinking that a relative of my father's, who comes to visit us from Brooklyn once in a while, is a Mafioso, because he's Italian American and has New York license plates on his new black car, and sports a black tie and pointy shoes and a shiny suit and a Borsalino hat tipped way down over his forehead so you can hardly see his eyes. And if you can hardly see his eyes, my mother says, what kind of a man must the neighbors think he is? Maybe my mother remembers the incarcerations, deportations, and lynchings of Italians, the invasion of Italian neighborhoods in Hoboken, New Jersey, during the war when we lived there. Maybe my mother thinks eating this bread will keep us safe.

This bread that my mother buys from the Dugan's man is whiter than my grandmother's bread. It is as white, as soft and as spongy, as the cotton balls I use to take off my nail polish when I am a teenager, as white as the Kotex pads I shove into my underpants.

My mother eats this bread all the time, morning, noon, and night, and she uses it to make us toasted-cheese sandwiches. Two slices of American cheese pulled in shreds from their cellophane wrappers, slapped between two slices of buttered American bread (torn when buttered, because it is so soft) fried in a too hot frying pan while my mother, distracted, walks away to do something else until she smells the butter burning, says "Oh my goodness," returns to the stove, flips the sandwiches, gets distracted again, walks away again, smells the butter burning again, says "Oh my goodness" again, and serves the sandwich to us with lots of catsup on the side to disguise the filthy taste.

After Thanksgiving, my mother uses this bread to make turkey sandwiches with stuffing and gravy and cranberry sauce, the most acceptable use for this bread because then the bread is roasted, which hardens it, and, because the toaster we have is automatic, my mother can't fuck up the toast, unless she shoves it back in for a second round. My mother uses this bread to make French toast, too, what she calls her special Sunday night supper. But because she has never developed the knack of completely beating the egg that coats the bread, her French toast always has little pieces of coagulated egg white hanging off it, which I call snot strings.

Sometimes I pull the snot strings off the bread and hang them out of my nostrils. This I do, not to infuriate my parents, but for my own amusement, to distract myself from the funereal atmosphere of our supper table. But when I do it, my father reprimands me for my bad manners, tells me to respect the food my mother made, says all he wants at the end of a day's work, after taking guff from his bosses and hearing the rat-a-tat-rat of the machines all goddamned day long, is a nice meal, and some goddamned peace and quiet. I ignore him, look at the ceiling, pretend he's not there. He comes after me. I jump up, run away. He chases me around the table, out of the room, up the stairs.

But my sister and I like having this bread in our house because you can do many things with it. You can take a piece of this bread, pull off the crust, smash it down, roll it into a little ball. You can play marbles with this bread. You can pull the middle out of a slice of this bread and hang it over your nose or twirl it around your finger. You can pull the middle out of a slice of this bread and bring it up to your eye and pretend you're Nancy Drew looking for clues to a crime that was committed in your kitchen. You can take circles out of this bread and smash them down into Communion wafers and play "Holy Priest of God" dishing out the body of Christ. (This doesn't get my mother angry; this amuses her. She has no use for Holy Communion, for the Church or its priests, even though she sends us to Catholic grammar school.)

You can also eat this bread with your meal, and sometimes we do, if there is none of my grandmother's bread. But when you eat this bread, it sticks to the roof of your mouth and you have to pry it off with your fingers. Then you get yelled at for your horrible table manners, and are told to leave the table and go up to your room. Which is a good thing. If your father had a hard day at work and is in a lousy mood, or if he was out fighting fires as a volunteer and is exhausted, he'll chase you up the stairs to your room, but you can usually outrun him, slam your bedroom door shut, push your bureau against the door. Then you get blamed for ruining dinner.

My grandmother's bread doesn't stick to the roof of your mouth. Which is why I like it. Which is why my father likes it. That my father likes my grandmother's bread more than he likes my mother's bread makes my mother angry. That my father likes my grandmother's bread means that he's on my grandmother's side (the wrong side) in the ongoing bread war. That we like my grandmother's bread means that there's no hope for this family making it into the big time. It means that we're stuck in the rut of where we came from, that we're satisfied with who we are, and not striving for all that we can be. My mother is striving for all that we can be, here in suburban New Jersey. And she wants us to strive along with her.

꩜

Susan Gubar (1944–)

A WRITER, FEMINIST theorist, literary critic, and distinguished university professor, Gubar first gained acclaim when she coauthored *The Madwoman in the Attic* with Sandra M. Gilbert, a book the collaborators followed with a three-volume sequel, *No Man's Land*, and with their coedited *Norton Anthology of Literature by Women*. But Gubar's recent work has been wide-ranging and eclectic; she has produced studies of cross-racial impersonation (*Racechanges*), of Holocaust literature (*Poetry After Auschwitz*), and of religious motifs (*Judas: A Biography*). Her most recent writings have been electrifying examinations of her current struggle with ovarian cancer: *Memoir of a Debulked Woman* and a series of blogs on "living with cancer" for the Well column of *The New York Times*. In the same memoiristic mode, "Cooking the Kaddish," which we have excerpted here, combines a rich meditation on family history and the Jewish prayer for the dead with a series of recipes that brilliantly evoke the savors of the cultural inheritance that has helped shape her own kitchen.

from Cooking the Kaddish

I NEED TO learn how to say the mourner's Kaddish, just as in years past I needed to teach myself how to make matzo-ball soup and challah, brisket and latkes. The urgency is palpable. . . . Most of my closest friends are, somehow, Catholic or rather Catholic-born and in a rage at the Pope and his bishops. Or they are agnostics unschooled in their parents' Protestantism. They cannot help me. But I did teach myself to make the soup and the bread, the meat and potatoes, and even some jokes so surely I can learn how to recite the prayer. It is only twenty-five lines long when I print out a transliteration from the Web. Certain phrases bring back a familiar and profoundly satisfying rhythm. But when I try to read it aloud, I sound like a dyslexic second-grader. And the first line of my print-out looks a bit different, with the letter "t" appearing where the letter "s" should be: "Yitgaddal v'yitkaddash sh'meh rabbah." Who do I need to mourn? . . .

The second line of the Kaddish reads "B'almah dee-v'ra chiru-teh." It means "in the world which He created according to His will." In no way do I fault my mother for providing me with a Jewish "education"—the word has to be put in quotes—that left me ignorant about Judaism or for not teaching me how to cook Jewish foods. She inhabited a world that had shockingly abrogated her will and wishes, when the Nuremberg laws debarred her from attending a university and later when Hitler's genocidal mania necessitated her, my father's, and my brother's flight from Hamburg to New York. We kids were enrolled in a Reformed temple in Brooklyn where no real learning took place.

Somehow I am finding it easy to remember "Yitgaddal v'yitkaddash sh'meh rabbah." It is "Yit" (not "Yis"), a former student explains on email, because younger congregants follow modern Israeli pronunciation which is Sephardic, not Ashkenazi. But it seems harder to get "B'almah dee-v'ra chiru-teh" into my head so I encourage myself by remembering how many decades ago I learned to make my very first Jewish food and perhaps *the* paradigmatic Jewish food. My mother did not made chicken soup from scratch, though one of my keenest memories of my father's funeral—beyond the closed coffin and my Aunt Rosie exclaiming that I shouldn't have been allowed to wear white shoes—was the bowl of Campbell's chicken soup (add one can of water and heat) that I was given upon returning home from the cemetery. With regard to the prayer, I anticipate other rhythms pulsing ahead, phrases I *do* know, but now "Ba'almah deev'ra chiru-teh" must be learned. It takes time to make soup and apparently it will take time to get "Ba'almah deev'ra chiru-teh" into my thick head.

So here is how I make chicken stock. Since it's a no brainer, I can repeat "Ba'almah deev'ra chiru-teh" as often as necessary.

> Put a whole chicken or a bunch of wings and whatever other parts of the chicken you have on hand into a big pot and cover with water. As you bring to a boil, skim off the foamy crud that rises to the top. Then add a carrot, a stalk or two of celery, an onion, maybe a cut-up parsnip and some parsley, and lower the heat to a simmer, cooking (partly covered) for two or three hours. When you pierce the chicken with a fork and it falls apart, it is done. Strain

through a sieve or colander, pushing the soft veggies down to extract their juices. Take the chicken off the bone, throw out the skin, and put some of the meat in the soup, but save some for a chicken salad or pot pie.

"Ba'almah deev'ra chiru-teh" begins to sink in. My dad used to say, when a poor man eats a chicken, either the man is sick or the chicken is sick. "Vas steht am tisch?" An old Yiddish joke comes to mind, from Elliot Gilbert, alev hascholem. What stands on a table, makes flapping like this with its wings, and sings coo-co-reek-oo? A meshugina. . . .

"Kaddish?" my older daughter Molly asks on the phone. "You're writing about Kaddish? Isn't that a drink?"

She had been bat-mitvahed more than two decades ago in the only synagogue in our college town.

"Oh," she then remembered, as I laughed. "Yitgaddal, yitga-something."

Like mother, like daughter. But I think I've got "Ba'almah deevr'a chiru'teh" down so onward to line three which in my (abundantly ignorant) judgment concludes the opening of the prayer: "v'yamlich malchuteh," meaning "May He establish His Kingdom." I hear the three lines forming a unity because of the rhyming of the last syllable "teh" in "chiru'teh" and "malchuteh." . . . In his astoundingly erudite book *Kaddish*, Leon Wieseltier castigates American Jews like me for "sentimentality" about the mourner's prayer. Instead of rending my clothes, as the orthodox mourner does, I am rendering schmaltz. But schmaltz too has its purposes, in small doses.

After schmaltz collects on the top of the frozen or refrigerated stock, it can easily be removed and tossed, for no substance better clogs the arteries, but set aside two tablespoons since a little cannot do much harm and it provides the glue for the matzo-balls which I never tasted as a child. On Friday nights, Grandma Alice came to prepare German food: stuffed cabbage (savory, not sweet), weisswurst, braised flanken and halibut, boiled potatoes, vinegary cucumber salad, Apfelpfannkuchen. On Sunday evenings, one Mr. Levy arrived with a battered attaché case redolent with the most marvelous smells from a sausage named cervelat and a thinly sliced cured beef that I once later found in Italy where it was called bresaola. Weekdays, canned vegetables and pan-fried chops were devoured so quickly by my parents that my stomach cramped with resistance to and fright at their frantic need to eat. "May He establish His Kingdom" so that there will never again be so many dead and unburied relatives, such fear-filled refugees: "v'yam-lich malchuteh." Jewish food was a novelty sampled at friends' houses or on a rare evening out.

Only in graduate school, after finding Jennie Grossinger's cook book, did I learn to produce something better than the dense billiard balls I had tasted in delis. That book is long gone, but I credit it for the lightness of these matzo-balls.

> Bring the stock to a boil, add slices of celery and carrots, and simmer for half an hour. In a Cuisinart, whiz four egg yolks, a slice of onion, a teaspoon of salt, a dash of cayenne pepper, and two tablespoons of schmaltz. In a large bowl, use an electric mixer to whip four egg whites until quite stiff. Gently fold the yolk mixture into the whites and then gently fold in three-quarters of a cup (or a cup) of matzo-meal. Cover tightly and refrigerate for half an hour while adding salt and pepper and (if needed) a bouillon cube (or boxed stock) to the broth. After running your hands under cold water, shape each one-and-a-half inch ball gently between your palms and gently slip it into the simmering stock. Cover and cook (the about twenty matzo-balls) for three quarters of an hour.

The operative word is gently, a word related to the reiteration of the Kad-dish which some people recite for eleven months and many people recite on every jahrzeit. Sometimes one can make up for lack of tradition or ignorance of tradition through reading and experimenting until Jewish penicillin or ambrosia exalts and sanctifies all who gather together. . . .

In matters of religion and language, it is not possible to compensate for a lack of tradition, and exactly why am I making the effort? Regardless of the cause that inhibits one generation from initiating the next into preserving rituals and costumes, what is not handed down cannot be retrieved. A mor-sel or sound bite may be sampled perhaps, but not retrieved. Like cooking the books, cooking the Kaddish deceives through fabrication. Should I be saying words that I don't understand literally, figuratively, or historically? How can I recite what I don't mean? Why do I suppose that my having taught myself to cook Jewish foods would enable me to teach myself a Jew-ish prayer for the dead, when feasting and mourning represent antithetical activities?

Stiff-necked, stubborn, I summon up people who chant, hum, or whisper mantras of incomprehensible sounds as a way of slowing down time and consciousness, and I determine to learn "B'chay-yechon uv'yo-meychon" while kneading bread, which also slows down time and consciousness. My younger daughter Simone used to call our dinners at home "slow food." While kneading, I will need to mourn my mother's disappearance in old age, her loss of a coherent consciousness, so I Google challah and the Kaddish. On You Tube a mild-mannered man in a sweater-vest lets me hear the rhythm of the line and the last syllable of "B'cháy-ye*chon*" echoed by the ending of "uv'yo-méy*chon*": "during your lifetime and during your days" refers back to "malkhuteh." May God establish His kingdom, the prayer asks, soon so we can see it in our own being, with our own eyes. But the orthodox site on challah starts with five pounds of flour, which sounds extravagant, even nonsensical, to me.

I return to an older recipe to produce not the sweet, soft bread that has gained popularity in Midwestern bakeries, but a braided loaf that has the shellacked look of a traditional challah. During my mother's lifetime, she grieved over many losses, but during her days now she forgets them. Sad as the foggy confusion seems, there is a mitvah to losing loss, or so I hope as I make the dough....

"Uv'chay-yey de-chol beit yisra-el / Ba-agalah uvizman kareev": May God establish His kingdom soon so we can see it in our own being "and during the lifetimes of all the House of Israel, speedily and very soon." My mother will not live to see that apocalyptic time, but she did manage to find the leaven to rise three times, like a punched-down challah: after the suicide of her mother, of her father, and of her husband. Their memory was not a blessing. She kept getting dragged to the house of mourning where she lost her appetite for ceremonial feasting, but felt the pressing need to eat so as to survive. "By the sweat of your face you shall eat bread until you return to the ground, for out of it you were taken; you are dust, and to dust you shall return" (Genesis 3:19). Like my father, my mother slaved at manual labor from dawn to dusk so that during her lifetime, speedily and very soon, her children needed not. Her heart was stricken, as she bought the day-old bread at Ebinger's Bakery and smiled at my father's joke of the newly married man who never found his wife's cooking as good as his mother's until one day she accidently burnt his toast and "Ahha," he exulted, "it tastes just like mama's." ...

How astonishing after such heavy slogging, word by word, that the next seven lines arrive like a piece of cake. Did I, after all, take something away from the Saturday services and Sunday classes at Beth Emeth? Or is it the measured music in my mouth?

> Y'hey sh'mey rabbah m'varach
> L'olam ul'olmey almah-yah.
> Yitbarach, v'yishtabach
> V'yitpa-ar v'yiromam
> V'yisnasseh v'yit-haddar
> V'yit-alleh v'yit-hallal
> Sh'mey de kudshah b'reech hu.

No, not like a piece of cake, since the lines are hefty, weighty—more like the meat of the prayer, its main course, its muscle, its nourishing protein. Here is a prayer I can relish, for it simply prays that we pray; it urges no more than that we should extol the creation and its creator. To memorize its injunction, I take out the brisket that I make at Passover, when God told the liberated to open their mouths to be filled. "Y'hey sh'mey rabbah m'varach / L'olam ul'olmey almah-yah": these core lines feel familiar on my lips maybe because they are generally recited by the entire congregation. I pay dues at the local synagogue so as to support the Jewish community, but the only communal event I regularly share—with my Jewish and non-Jewish meshbocha—is the Seder. . . . At Passover in our dining room, many people use the ritual horseradish as a stinging condiment, its nose- and eye-watering bitterness an accent to the sweetness of the brisket. . . .

Both cooking and the Kaddish deeply invest participants in the satisfactions of repetitive rhythms. When years ago I served what Simone called "slow food" at six p.m. every night, I tried to tempt the girls with healthy versions of fast food or with a succession of spicy international kid-pleasers: hamburgers or tacos, fish and chips, spaghetti and meatballs, chicken wings in oyster sauce, lentils and sausage. The Gothic goop over which they hooted because it made them gag was "the daily stuff," a brew concocted by a child at their pre-school who mixed together everything on his tray, like pasta and Jell-O or chili and pudding. Wary of the eating disorders of adolescents, I enlisted my daughters in the slicing and dicing, repetitive and rhythmic acts as habitual and addictive as memorizing and reciting. Both cooking and reciting organize time in unexceptional but visceral increments. Because the habitual and sometimes addictive patterns of cooking involve physical acts, while those of reciting require mental acts, cooking and reciting the Kaddish go together like fish and chips or meatballs and spaghetti or, for that matter, the girls' favorite dish: latkes and applesauce, although making potato pancakes requires a lot of last-minute work. . . .

Putting the latkes in the oven for twenty minutes gives the exhausted cook time to recover so she can enjoy them with her guests. Also a recovery, the next-to-the-last section of the Kaddish takes full advantage of its penultimate position by relying heavily on earlier structures. A variation on an established theme, "Y'heh sh'lamah rabbah min sh'may" ("May there be abundant peace from heaven") invokes the oracular line "Y'he sh'mey rabbah m'varach" ("May His great name be blessed"). "V'chay-yim alenu v'al kol yisrael" ("and life for us and for all of Israel") returns with a difference to the earlier "Uv-chay-yey de-chol beit yisra-el" ("and during the lifetimes of all the house of Israel"). And then we have a third "V'imru amen." Taken together, "May there be abundant peace from heaven / and life for us and for all of Israel / And say, Amen." . . .

The Kaddish is not a kvetch. It has nothing in common with the joke about the grandma who—shocked that a giant wave has taken away her adorable grandson—beseeches God for his return and then, after a giant wave deposits him back on her blanket (complete with his bathing suit, pail, and shovel), beseeches God again, "What about his little cap?" No, the Kaddish does not bemoan the survivor's grief, request resurrection of the dead, beg for consolation, or inscribe the memory of a particular individual into the book of life. Astringent, it is not a tepid thanksgiving either. The Kaddish is an urgent directive to attain a posture of praise and wonder that concludes with a prayer for universal peace: "O-seh shalom / bimromav / Hu-ya-aseh shalom alenu / V'al kol yisra-el / V'imru Amen." Everyone knows the word "shalom." Many know the lyrics of "Shalom Alenu." Shalom functions as a greeting in Israel where Jewish food consists of falafel, eggplant caviar, humus, pita, tabbouleh, and diced cucumbers and tomatoes. If Jewish food is the food eaten by Jews, almost every cuisine pertains, including the German food my relatives craved, so it seems appropriate to learn the lines "May He who makes peace / in His high places / grant peace upon us / and upon all Israel / and say, Amen" while baking a Linzertorte. More dense than cake, a slice tastes like a cookie. . . .

But to be honest, my own density persists. The writing of this essay has proceeded more quickly than full retention of the prayer. . . . I still need a cheat-sheet which I will now take along with me on my daily walks, for it turns out that walking, like cooking, can keep the words bubbling. Boiling and braising the Kaddish, roasting and frying and baking the Kaddish, I have been struggling to translate the meaning of the phrases I am reciting so it cannot be altogether true that the incomprehensibility of its foreign lexicon is the blessing I seek. I have discovered that the Kaddish does not differentiate between the chosen and the not chosen, nor does it affirm any faith in a spiritual afterlife for the individual psyche or soul. As for male God language, it would be just as absurd if the divine were called "She." Why tamper with a language centuries old? I make peace with Leon Wieseltier when he explains, "Tradition is not reproduced. It is thrown and it is caught. It lives a long time in the air." The prayer I hope to catch is airy, unlike the Linzertorte.

Ruth Reichl (1948–)

REICHL WAS THE restaurant critic for *The New York Times* for five years in the 1990s, where she was perhaps best known for wearing a series of costumes representing women of different personalities and social classes in order to remain anonymous and to test a restaurant's attitudes toward its patrons. She wrote about this practice and her life as a reviewer in the third of her food memoirs, *Garlic and Sapphires: The Secret Life of a Critic in Disguise*. Reichl's contribution to the New York restaurant scene was twofold: to expose gastronomical pretention and to celebrate good, serious cooking in off-the-radar places that did not represent the city's preoccupation with haute cuisine. After her stint at the paper she edited *Gourmet* for over a decade. Here Reichl writes about her mother, who inadvertently started her daughter on a career in food exactly because the mother's horrific taste in food was so disconcerting to the young Ruth. This chapter from Reichl's first memoir, *Tender at the Bone: Growing Up at the Table*, is a kind of reverse mentor narrative, suggesting how she was driven to seek out good food in the face of the maternal culinary practices that inspired her daughter to call her "the Queen of Mold."

from *Tender at the Bone*: The Queen of Mold

MOST MORNINGS I got out of bed and went to the refrigerator to see how my mother was feeling. You could tell instantly just by opening the door. One day in 1960 I found a whole suckling pig staring at me. I jumped back and slammed the door, hard. Then I opened it again. I'd never seen a whole animal in our refrigerator before; even the chickens came in parts. He was surrounded by tiny crab apples ("*lady apples*" my mother corrected me later), and a whole wreath of weird vegetables.

This was not a bad sign: the more odd and interesting things there were in the refrigerator, the happier my mother was likely to be. Still, I was puzzled; the refrigerator in our small kitchen had been almost empty when I went to bed.

"Where did you get all this stuff?" I asked. "The stores aren't open yet."

"Oh," said Mom blithely, patting at her crisp gray hair, "I woke up early and decided to go for a walk. You'd be surprised at what goes on in Manhattan at four a.m. I've been down to the Fulton Fish Market. And I found the most interesting produce store on Bleecker Street."

"It was open?" I asked.

"Well," she admitted, "not really." She walked across the worn linoleum and set a basket of bread on the Formica table. "But I saw someone moving around so I knocked. I've been trying to get ideas for the party."

"Party?" I asked warily. "What party?"

"Your brother has decided to get married," she said casually, as if I should have somehow intuited this in my sleep. "And of course we're going to have a party to celebrate the engagement and meet Shelly's family!"

My brother, I knew, would not welcome this news. He was thirteen years older than I and considered it a minor miracle to have reached the age of twenty-five. "I don't know how I survived her cooking," he said as he was telling me about the years when he and Mom were living alone, after she had divorced his father and was waiting to meet mine. "She's a menace to society."

Bob went to live with his father in Pittsburgh right after I was born, but he always came home for holidays. When he was there he always helped me protect the guests, using tact to keep them from eating the more dangerous items.

I took a more direct approach. "Don't eat that," I ordered my best friend Jeanie as her spoon dipped into one of Mom's more creative lunch dishes. My mother believed in celebrating every holiday: in honor of St. Patrick she was serving bananas with green sour cream.

"I don't mind the color," said Jeanie, a trusting soul whose own mother wouldn't dream of offering you an all-orange Halloween extravaganza complete with milk dyed the color of orange juice. Ida served the sort of perfect lunches that I longed for: neat squares of cream cheese and jelly on white bread, bologna sandwiches, Chef Boyardee straight from the can.

"It's not just food coloring," I said. "The sour cream was green to begin with; the carton's been in the refrigerator for months."

Jeanie quickly put her spoon down and when Mom went into the other room to answer the phone we ducked into the bathroom and flushed our lunches down the toilet.

"That was great, Mim," said Jeanie when Mom returned.

"May we be excused?" is all I said. I wanted to get away from the table before anything else appeared.

"Don't you want dessert?" Mom asked.

"Sure," said Jeanie.

"No!" I said. But Mom had already gone to get the cookies. She returned with some strange black lumps on a plate. Jeanie looked at them dubiously, then politely picked one up.

"Oh, go ahead, eat it," I said, reaching for one myself. "They're just Girl Scout mint cookies. She left them on the radiator so all the chocolate melted off, but they won't kill you."

As we munched our cookies, Mom asked idly, "What do you girls think I should serve for Bob's engagement party?"

"You're not going to have the party here, are you?" I asked.

"No," said Mom. I exhaled. "In the country. We have more room in Wilton. And we need to welcome Shelly into the family properly."

I pictured our small, shabby summer house in the woods. Wilton is only an hour from New York, but in 1960 it was still very rural. My parents had bought the land cheaply and designed the house themselves. Since they couldn't afford an architect, they had miscalculated a bit, and the downstairs bedrooms were very strangely shaped. Dad hardly knew how to hold a hammer, but to save money he had built the house himself with the aid of a carpenter. He was very proud of his handiwork, despite the drooping roof and awkward layout. He was even prouder of our long, rutted, meandering driveway. "I didn't want to cut down a single tree!" he said proudly when people asked why it was so crooked.

I loved the house, but I was slightly embarrassed by its unpainted wooden walls and unconventional character. "Why can't we have the party in a hotel?" I asked. In my mind's eye I saw Shelly's impeccable mother, who seemed to go to the beauty parlor everyday and wore nothing but custom-made clothes. Next to her, Mom, a handsome woman who refused to dye her hair, rarely wore makeup, and had very colorful taste in clothes, looked almost bohemian. Shelly's mother wore an enormous diamond ring on her beautifully manicured finger; my mother didn't even wear a wedding band and her fingernails were short and haphazardly polished.

"Nonsense," said Mom. "It will be *much* nicer to have it at home. So much more intimate. I'd like them to see how we live, find out who we are."

"Great," I said under my breath to Jeanie. "That'll be the end of Bob's engagement. And a couple of the relatives might die, but who worries about little things like that?" . . .

Just thinking about it made me nervous. "I've got to stop this party," I said.

"How?" asked Jeanie.

I didn't know. I had four months to figure it out.

My best hope was that my mother's mood would change before the party took place. That was not unrealistic; my mother's moods were erratic. But March turned into April and April into May and Mom was still buzzing around. The phone rang constantly and she was feeling great. She cut her gray hair very short and actually started wearing nail polish. She lost weight and bought a whole new wardrobe. Then she and Dad took a quick cruise to the Caribbean.

"We booked passage on a United Fruit freighter," she said to her friends, "so much more interesting than a conventional cruise." When asked about the revolutions that were then rocking the islands she had a standard response: "The bomb in the hotel lobby in Haiti made the trip *much* more interesting."

When they returned she threw herself into planning the party. I got up every morning and looked hopefully into the refrigerator. Things kept getting worse. Half a baby goat appeared. Next there was cactus fruit. But the morning I found the box of chocolate-covered grasshoppers I decided it was time to talk to Dad.

"The plans are getting more elaborate," I said ominously.

"Yes?" said Dad politely. Parties didn't much interest him.

"It's going to be a disaster," I announced.

"Your mother gives wonderful parties," my father said loyally. He was remarkably blind to my mother's failings, regularly announcing to the world that she was a great cook. I think he actually believed it. He beamed when someone mentioned my mother's "interesting dishes" and considered it a compliment when they said, "I've never tasted anything quite like that before." And, of course, *he* never got sick.

"Did you know that she's planning it as a benefit for Unicef?" I asked.

"Really?" he said. "Isn't that nice." He had turned back to the editorials.

"Dad!" I said, trying to get him to see how embarrassing this could be. "She's sending notices to the newspapers. She's inviting an awful lot of people. This thing is getting out of control. It's only a month away and she has nothing planned."

"It'll all work out," Dad said vaguely, folding the newspaper into his brief-case. "Your mother is a very smart woman. She has a PhD." And then, as if there was no more to be said, he added, "I'm sure you'll be a big help."

It was hard to get mad at my father, who was as baffled by my mother's moods as I was, and just as helpless before them. They were like the weather: unpredictable, and often unpleasant. Dad, I think, enjoyed her energy, but then, he could always go to the office when he needed to escape. Which is what he did now. Disgusted, I called my brother.

Bob lived uptown in a fancy apartment and had as little to do with my parents as he could decently get away with.

"She's planning to make my engagement party a benefit?" he asked. "You mean she expects Shelly's family to pay to attend?" I hadn't quite considered that aspect, but I could see his point.

"I guess so," I said. "But that's not the part that worries me. Can you imagine Mom cooking for over a hundred people in the middle of summer? What if it's a really hot day?"

Bob groaned.

"Can't you get called away on business?" I asked. "What if you had a conference you had to go to? Wouldn't she have to call the whole thing off?"

Unfortunately my mother was not the least bit fazed when informed that my brother might not be in town. "The party's not for you," she said to Bob, "it's for Shelly's family. They'll come even if you're too rude not to make an appearance."

"But Mom," said Bob, "you can't ask them to buy tickets to the party."

"Why not?" asked Mom. "I think it's just disgusting the way people who have so much forget about those who are less fortunate. How could you possibly object to raising money for underprivileged children in honor of your marriage? I can't believe I have such a selfish, thoughtless son!" And Mom slammed down the phone.

She always managed to do that, always turned your arguments against you. And so there we were, 150 people invited to lunch on the lawn, a representative from Unicef and photographers promised from all the newspapers. In one of her more grandiose moments Mom wrote her old friend Bertrand Russell in Wales and asked him to come speak; fortunately he was nearing his ninetieth birthday and declined. But he did send a hundred copies of his most recent antiwar booklet, a sort of fairy tale printed on gold paper. It was called *History of the World in Epitome* (for use in Martian infant schools) and it was very short. The last page was a picture of a mushroom cloud.

"These will make wonderful favors!" said Mom smugly, pointing out that they were autographed. She was so pleased she sent out a few more invitations.

"What are you going to serve?" I asked.

"Do you have any ideas?" she replied.

"Yes," I said, "hire a caterer."

Mom laughed as if I had made a joke. But she was moved to call and rent some tables and folding chairs, so at least the guests wouldn't be sitting on the ground. I suggested that she hire someone to help cook and serve, but she didn't seem to think that was necessary. "We can do that ourselves," she said blithely. "Can't you get your friends to help?"

"No," I said, "I can't." But I did call Jeanie in the city and ask her to ask her parents if she could come out for the week; she thought my mother was "exciting" and I needed moral support.

As the party approached, things got worse and worse. Mom went on cleaning binges that left the house messier when she was done than when she started, and Jeanie and I went around behind her desperately stuffing things back into closets to create some semblance of order. Mom mowed half the lawn; we mowed the other half. Meanwhile my father, looking apologetic and unhappy, conveniently came up with a big project that kept him in the city.

One morning Mom went to a wholesale food company and came back honking her horn loudly, her car filled to the brim. Jeanie and I rushed out to unload fifty pounds of frozen chicken legs, ten pounds of frozen lump crabmeat, industrial-size cans of tomato and split-pea soup, twenty-five-pound sacks of rice, and two cases of canned, spiced peaches.

"This must be the menu," I said to Jeanie.

"What?" she asked.

"I bet she's going to make that awful quick soup she thinks is so great. You know, it's in all the magazines. You mix a can of tomato soup with a can of split pea soup, add a little sherry, and top it with crabmeat."

"Yuck," said Jeanie.

"Then I guess she's going to cook those millions of chicken legs on top of rice, although how she thinks she's going to cook them all in our little oven I don't know. And the canned spiced peaches can be the vegetable; they're easy because all you have to do is open the can and put them on the plates."

I was surprised (and relieved) when she ordered a giant cake from the local bakery. That left only the hors d'oeuvres; I wondered what she had up her sleeve.

The next day I found out. Jeanie and I were playing croquet, but we put down our mallets when Mom's horn started, and watched the car speed through the trees, leaving billows of dust in its wake. We ran out to see what she had dragged home.

"Horn & Hardart was having a sale!" Mom announced triumphantly, pointing to the boxes around her. They were filled with hundreds of small cartons. It looked promising. "It's almost like getting it catered," I said happily to Jeanie as we toted the boxes inside.

My happiness was short-lived; when I began opening the cartons I found that each contained something different.

"The Automat sells leftovers for almost nothing at the end of the day," said Mom, "so I just took everything they had." She was very pleased with herself.

"What are you going to do with it?" I asked.

"Why, serve it," she said.

"In what?" I asked.

"Big bowls," she said.

"But you don't have anything to put in big bowls," I pointed out. "All you have is hundreds of things to put in little bowls. Look," I began ripping the tops off the cartons, "this one is potato salad. This one is coleslaw. This one is cold macaroni and cheese. Here's a beet salad. Here's some sliced ham. Nothing matches!"

"Don't worry," said Mom, "I'm sure we can make something out of all of this. After all, everything in it is good."

"Yes," I muttered to Jeanie, "and by the time it gets served everything in it will be four days old. It will be a miracle if it's not moldy."

"I think it would be better if it was," said practical Jeanie. "If people see mold they won't eat it."

"Pray for rain," I said.

Unfortunately, when I woke up on the day of the party there was not a cloud in the sky. I pulled the covers over my head and went back to sleep. But not for long. "Nobody sleeps today," Mom announced, inexorably pulling back the covers. "It's party day!"

Some of the food had acquired a thin veneer of mold, but Mom blithely scraped it off and began mixing her terrible Horn & Hardart mush. "It's delicious!" she cried, holding out a spoonful. It wasn't. Fortunately it looked even worse than it tasted.

I thought the chicken legs were a little dubious too; in order to get them all cooked we had started two days earlier, and the refrigerator couldn't hold them all. But they glistened invitingly, and the oven-baked rice looked fine. We spooned the peaches into Mom's big glass bowls, and they looked beautiful.

I wasn't very happy about the soup. Mom had left the crabmeat out of the freezer to defrost for two days, and even she didn't like the way it was smelling. "I think I'll just add a little more sherry." she kept saying as she poured in bottles of the stuff.

"People will get drunk on the soup," I said.

"Fine," she said gaily, "then maybe they'll donate more to Unicef."

My brother arrived, took one look at the rickety chairs on our uneven lawn, and headed straight for the bar. Mom had hired some local high school boys to be bartenders, and they were pouring whiskey as if it were Coke.

"You've got to stay sober," I said to him. "You've got to make sure that nobody in Shelly's family eats the soup. And they should probably watch out for the chicken too."

Bob had another drink.

My memories of the party are mercifully blurred, but a yellowed clipping from the *Norwalk Hour* tells part of the story. My mother looks radiantly into the camera beneath a headline reading WILTON FAMILY HOSTS BENEFIT FOR UNICEF.

A family photograph of me handing a check to a grinning official in front of a sign that says SECURITY COUNCIL in both French and English tells another part of the tale.

But my brother owns the end of the story. Thirty-five years later his children can still make him turn green by asking. "Remember the time Nana Mimi poisoned everyone?"

"Ooh," he moans, "don't remind me. It was awful. First she extorted money from them. Then she gave out those antibomb favors; it was the early sixties, for Christ sake, and these were conservative businessmen and housewives. But the worse thing was the phone calls. They kept coming all night long. Nobody felt good. Twenty-six of them actually ended up in the hospital having their stomachs pumped. What a way to meet the family!"

I missed all that, but I do remember the phone ringing while we were still cleaning up. Mom was still exulting in the photographer's flashbulbs, and saying for what seemed like the forty-seventh time, "Look how much money we raised!" She picked up the receiver.

"Yes?" said Mom brightly. I think she expected it to be another reporter. Then her voice drooped with disappointment.

"Who doesn't feel well?"

There was a long silence. Mom ran her hand through her chic, short coiffure. "Really?" she said, sounding shocked. "All of them?" She slumped a little as her bright red fingernails went from her hair to her mouth. Then her back straightened and her head shot up.

"Nonsense," I heard her say into the phone. "We all feel fine. And we ate *everything.*"

꙰

Ntozake Shange (1948–)

"SPEAKING AMERICAN AIN'T necessarily nourishing," declares Shange in this first chapter of her cookbook/memoir *if I can Cook / you KNow God can*. Throughout her career she has celebrated her roots in African-American culture in poems, plays, and novels, including her famous "choreodrama" *for colored girls who have considered suicide / when the rainbow is enuf*. Born Paulette Williams in New Jersey and educated at Barnard, she changed her name to Ntozake ("she who has her own things," in Xhosa) Shange ("she who walks with lions," in Zulu) as she became increasingly involved in chronicling the lives and achievements of black women. "What'd You People Call That?"—with its sardonic title—eloquently muses on classic soul food recipes: Hoppin' John, pig's tails, chitlins, greens. And tellingly, the book from which it is drawn is dedicated "To Ellie, my mother, who could make a kitchen sing and swing, make it a sacred or profane gathering, a spooky, funny place, a refuge, a hallowed midnight meeting with her daughter."

from *if I can Cook / you KNow God can*: What'd You People Call That?

BLACK-EYED PEAS AND rice or "Hoppin' John," even collard greens and pig's feet, are not so much arbitrary predilections of the "nigra" as they are symbolic defiance; we shall celebrate ourselves on a day of our choosing in honor of those events and souls who are an honor to us. Yes, we eat potato

salad on Independence Day, but a shortage of potatoes up and down Brooklyn's Nostrand Avenue in July will not create the serious consternation and
sadness I saw/experienced one New Year's Eve, when there weren't no chitlins to be found.

Like most American families strewn far and near 'cross the mainland,
many African-American families, like my own, experience trans-cross
Caribbean or Pan-American Highway isolation blues during global/
national holidays. One Christmas and New Year's my parents and siblings
were somewhere 'tween Trinidad, Santo Domingo, and Los Angeles. My
daughter and I were lucky enough to have a highly evolved horizontal family, that is, friends and associates from different bloodlines, but of the same
spirit, reliable, loving, and alone, too, except for us.

Anyway, this one winter I was determined that Savannah, my child,
should have a typical Owens/Williams holiday, even though I was not a gag-
gle of aunts and uncles, cousins, second and third cousins twice removed, or
even relatives from Oklahoma or Carolina. I was just me, Mommy, in one
body and with many memories of not enough room for all the toddlers at
the tables. How could I re-create the smells of okra and rice, Hoppin' John,
baked ham, pig's feet, chitlins, collard greens, and corn bread with syrup
if I was goin'ta feed two people? Well, actually one and a half people. She
woulda counted as a half in the census. But how we are counted in the census is enough to give me a migraine, and I am trying to recount how I tried
to make again my very colored childhood and my very "black" adolescence.

So in all of Clinton-Washington where I could walk with my shopping
cart (I am truly an urban soul), there were no chitlins or pig's feet. I remember standing with a very cold little girl right at the mouth of the C train
entrance. Were we going on a quest at dusk on New Year's Eve or were we
going to be improvisationally nimble and work something out? I was cold,
too, and time was not insignificant. Everything I had to prepare before midnight was goin'ta take all night. Back we went into a small market, sawdust
on the floor, and a zillion island accents pushing my requests up toward the
ceiling. "A pound and a half of pig tails," I say. Savannah murmured "pig
tails" like I'd said Darth Vader was her biological father.

Nevertheless, I left outta there with my pig's tails, my sweet potatoes, collards, cornmeal, rice and peas, a coconut, habañera peppers, olive oil, smoked
turkey wings, okra, tomatoes, corn on the cob, and some day-old bread.
We stopped briefly at a liquor store for some bourbon or brandy, I don't
remember which. All this so a five-year-old colored child, whose mother was

obsessed with the cohesion of her childhood, could pass this on to a little girl, who was falling asleep at the dill pickle barrel, 'midst all Mama's tales about suckin' 'em in the heat of the day and sharin' one pickle with anyone I jumped double Dutch with in St. Louis.

Our biggest obstacle was yet to be tackled, though. The members of our horizontal family we were visiting, thanks to the spirits and the Almighty, were practicing Moslems. Clearly, half of what I had to make was profane, if not blasphemous in the eyes/presence of Allah. What was Elegua, Santeria's trickster spirit, goin'ta do to assist me? Or, would I have to get real colloquial and call on Brer Rabbit or Brer Fox?

As fate would have it, my friends agreed that so long as I kept the windows open and destroyed all utensils and dishes I used for these requisite "homestyle" offerings, it was a go. I'll never forget how cold that kitchen was, nor how quickly my child fell asleep, so that I alone tended the greens, pig's tails, and corn bread. Though I ate alone that New Year's Eve, I knew a calm I must attribute to the satisfaction of my ancestors. I tried to feed us.

PIG'S TAILS BY INSTINCT

OBVIOUSLY, the tails have gotta be washed off, even though the fat seems to reappear endlessly. When they are pink enough to suit you, put them in a large pot full of water. Turn the heat high, get 'em boilin'. Add chopped onion, garlic, and I always use some brown sugar, molasses, or syrup. Not everybody does. Some folks like their pig extremities bitter, others, like me, want 'em sweet. It's up to you. Use a large spoon with a bunch of small holes to scrape off the grayish fats that will cover your tails. You don't need this. Throw it out. Let the tails simmer till the meat falls easily from the bones. Like pig's feet, the bones are soft and suckable, too. Don't forget salt, pepper, vinegar, and any kinda hot sauce when servin' your tails. There's nothin' wrong with puttin' a heap of tails, feet, or pig's ears right next to a good-sized portion of Hoppin' John, either. Somethin' about the two dishes mix on the palate well.

HOPPIN' JOHN (BLACK-EYED PEAS AND RICE)

REALLY, we should have soaked our peas overnight, but no such luck. The alternative is to boil 'em for at least an hour after cleaning them and gettin' rid of runty, funny-lookin' portions of peas. Once again, clear off the grayish foam that's goin'ta rise to the top of your pot. Once the peas look like they are about to swell or split open, empty the water, get half as much long grain rice as peas, mix 'em together, cover with water (two knuckles' deep of female hand). Bring to a boil, then simmer. Now, you can settle for salt and pepper. Or you can be adventurous, get yourself a hammer and split open the coconut we bought and either add the milk or the flesh or both to your peas and rice. Habañera peppers chopped really finely, 'long with green pepper and onion diced ever so neatly. Is it necessary to sauté your onion, garlic, pepper, and such before adding to your peas and rice? Not absolutely. You can get away without all that. Simmer in your heavy kettle with the top on till the water is gone away. You want your peas and rice to be relatively firm. However, there is another school of cookin' that doesn't mix the peas with the rice until they are on the actual plate, in which case the peas have a more fluid quality and the rice is just plain rice. Either way, you've got yourself some Hoppin' John that's certain to bring you good luck and health in the New Year. Yes, mostly West Indians add the coconut, but that probably only upset Charlestonians. Don't take that to heart. Cook your peas and rice to your own likin'.

COLLARD GREENS TO BRING YOU MONEY

WASH 2 large bunches of greens carefully 'cause even to this day in winter critters can hide up in those great green leaves that're goin'ta taste so very good. If you are an anal type, go ahead and wash the greens with suds (a small squirt of dish detergent) and warm water. Rinse thoroughly. Otherwise, an individual leaf check under cold runnin' water should do. Some folks like their greens chopped just so, like rows of a field. If that's the case with you, now is the time to get your best knife out, tuck your thumb under your fingers, and go to town. On the other hand, some just want to tear the leaves up with gleeful abandon. There's nothing wrong with that, either. Add to your greens that are covered with water either 1/4 pound salt pork, bacon, ham hocks, 2–3 smoked turkey wings, 3–4 tablespoons olive oil, canola oil, and the juice of 1 whole lemon, depending on your spiritual proclivities and prohibitions. Bring to a boil, turn down. Let 'em simmer till the greens are the texture you want. Nouveau cuisine greens eaters will have much more sculpted-looking leaves than old-fashioned greens eaters who want the stalks to melt in their mouths along with the leaf of the collard. Again, I add 1/3 cup syrup, or 2 tablespoons honey, or 3 tablespoons molasses to my greens, but you don't have to. My mother thinks I ruin my greens that way, but she can always make her own, you know. Serve with vinegar, salt and pepper, and hot sauce to taste. Serves 6–8.

FRENCH-FRIED CHITLINS

I WAS taught to prepare chitlins by my third and fourth cousins on my mother's side, who lived, of course, in Texas. My father, whose people were Canadian and did not eat chitlins at all, told me my daughter's French-fried Chitlin taste like lobster. Most of the time you spend making these 5 pounds of highfalutin chitlins will be spent cleaning them (even if you bought them "pre-cleaned," remember, the butcher doesn't have to eat them!). You need to scrub, rinse, scrub some more, turn them inside out, and scrub even more. By the time you finish, the pile of guts in front of you will be darn near white and shouldn't really smell at all. Now you are ready to start the fun part. Slice the chitlins into 1/2-inch strips and set them aside. Prepare a thin batter with 1/2 cup flour, 1/2 cup milk, 1/3 bottle of beer—drink the rest—and seasonings to taste (if you forget the cayenne, may God have mercy on your soul!). Heat 2–3 inches of oil or bacon grease—use what you like as long as you don't use oil that has been used to fry fish—until very hot but not burning (360–375 degrees). Dip each strip into the batter, let excess drip down, and fry until golden brown. Only fry one layer at a time and be sure to move the chitlins around in the pot. After patting away excess grease with a paper towel, serve with dirty rice, greens, and corn bread. Or you can just eat them by themselves on a roll like a po'boy.

BUT seriously, and here I ask for a moment of quiet meditation, what did L'Ouverture, Pétion, and Dessalines share for their victory dinner, realizing they were the first African nation, slave-free, in the New World? What did Bolivar crave as independence from Spain became evident? What was the last meal of the defiant Inca Atahualpa before the Spaniards made a public spectacle of his defeat? I only ask these questions because the *New York Times* and the *Washington Post* religiously announce the menu of every Inauguration dinner at the White House every four years. Yet I must imagine, along with the surrealistic folk artists of Le Soleil in Port-au-Prince in their depictions of L'Ouverture's triumph, what a free people chose to celebrate victory. What sated the appetites of slaves no longer slaves. Africans now Haitians, ordinary men made mystical by wont of their taste for freedom? How did we consecrate our newfound liberty? Now this may only be important to me, but it is. It is very important. I need to know how we celebrate our victories, our very survival. What did we want for dinner? What was good enough to commemorate our humanity? We know Haitians are still hungry. Don't we?

🐝

Henry Louis Gates Jr. (1950–)

A UNIVERSITY PROFESSOR at Harvard and director of the Hutchins Center for African & African American Research there, Gates is probably the world's most prominent contemporary scholar of African-American literature. His *The Signifying Monkey* was a groundbreaking book in the field, while his *Norton Anthology of African American Literature*, coedited with Nellie Y. McKay, definitively established a canon of the writings he has done so much to define and promote. A producer of numerous shows for PBS ("Finding Your Roots," "African-American Lives"), he has won such awards as the MacArthur Prize and the National Humanities Medal. In the midst of his busy academic and public career, however, he has also found time to write powerful memoirs about his childhood and youth in West Virginia. *Colored People*, from which our selection is drawn, is an extended autobiographical essay that developed from his search for roots and his passionate attention to the minutiae of family history. Its lively culinary analysis ("white people can't cook") offers another way to think about the pleasures of soul food.

from *Colored People*: Wet Dogs and White People

MAMA WAS PRACTICAL as well as proud. Her attitude was that she and Daddy would provide the best for us, so that no white person could put us down or keep us out for reasons of appearance, color aside. The rest was up to us, once we got in those white places. Like school, which desegregated without a peep in 1955, the year before I started first grade. Otherwise she didn't care to live in white neighborhoods or be around white people.

White people, she said, were *dirty*: They tasted right out of pots on the stove. Only some kind of animal, or the lowest order of trash, would ever taste out of a pot on the stove. Anybody with manners knew that; even colored people without manners knew that. It was *white* people who didn't know that. If you are cooking, Mama would say, and want to check your seasoning, take the big wooden spoon you use for stirring, place some stew or whatever it is in a cup or small bowl, and then, with a separate spoon or fork, have a taste. Tasting right out of a pot was almost as bad as drinking after somebody, on the same side of the cup or glass, or right after them on a Coca-Cola bottle without wiping their lips off real good. "I'd rather go *thirsty* myself," Uncle Raymond would say. By the mid-sixties, he was also given to pronouncing: "I'd rather white people call me a *nigger* than call me black." If he'd had to choose between being called black and drinking out of the same bottle after another human being, I'm not sure what Uncle Raymond would have done.

One thing we always did was smell good, partly because we liked scents, but partly because white people said we smelled bad *naturally*, like we had some sort of odor gene. "Here come you niggers, funking up the place"— even we'd crack that kind of joke a lot. So one thing colored people *had* to do around white people was smell good. And not have ash on our elbows or knees. Crust, we called it. Moisturizing cream was "crust eradicator," and Mama made sure we always brought some when we went over to the swimming pool, so as not to Embarrass the Race.

But it was white people who smelled bad, Mama always said. When they got wet. When they get wet, she said, they smell like dogs.

I do hate the smell of a wet dog, I have to confirm. But I don't think white people smell like that when their hair is wet, and I have done a lot of sniffing of wet-headed white people in my time. At first, as a child, I had a mission to test my mama's hypothesis:

"Hello, my name is Skipper. I'm taking a survey. . . . Could I smell your wet hair?"

Actually, my technique was subtler, though only slightly.

I remember sidling up to my favorite classmate, Linda Hoffman, one day at the swimming pool—which had integrated in that same year, 1955—nostrils flared, trying to breathe in as deeply as I could, prepared for the worst. "What's wrong with you?" she asked, suspiciously. "Uh, rose fever," I said.

She didn't believe me.

And my mother would not have believed the result of my researches, even had I shared them with her. That these doggy-smelling white people should cast olfactory aspersions upon *us* was bitter gall for her.

Yet if the anxiety about stereotype made colored Piedmont a generally sweet-smelling lot, there was a very significant exception, one that pertains to the mystery surrounding one of Piedmont's singular attractions—Dent Davis's Famous Homemade Ring Bologna.

Davis's delectable bologna was dark red, with a tight, crimson, translucent skin, and was sold in rings at Davis's Bakery, downtown on Ashfield Street. Dent was German, or so we believed, and he ran the shop with his two middle-aged daughters. Each had her dark hair in a bun, always "done"—as women, for some reason, still say—and one of them, Matilda, always wore luscious red lipstick. She was not a pretty woman, perhaps, but with her light-beige powdered cheeks, her dark-brown, almost black hair and dark-brown eyes, and that red lipstick, when she stood before the golden and dark-brown breads, cookies, and pastries, or wrapped the blood-red links of her daddy's bologna in white waxed butcher's paper with that deliberate way she had, she was, I was convinced, one of the loveliest creatures on God's green earth.

However delicious our tap water, however delicious our local brand of syrup, none of these delicacies of the Potomac Valley tasted better than fried pieces of Dent's bologna. For Dent Davis had a secret ingredient, whose nature nobody has ever ascertained. And I mean nobody.

Nobody white, that is.

Because all the colored people in Piedmont attributed the special taste and texture to Mr. Boxie, Dent Davis's faithful colored handyman, who had Dent's trust and faith, possessed the keys to his shop and house, and was always on hand, even when Davis locked everyone else out so he could make up a batch of that secret bologna.

What's in that bologna? the colored men would ask Mr. Boxie.

Can't say, he'd reply, with a wry twist of his lips. Can't say.

That nigger knows what's in that bologna, the town—*our* town—would whisper. Wonder if Dent lets him help make it?

The town's concern with Dent's liberality in relation to Mr. Boxie had nothing to do with the fact that Dent Davis was German and Mr. Boxie was colored, and the year was 1955 or so, when the words "civil rights" were about to become current. Boxie was Dent's *man*, so all of that was by-the-by. The town's concern was that Mr. Boxie was the dirtiest, smelliest, sloppiest, most disheveled colored man in all of Piedmont, and maybe the world. Mr. Boxie put the *un* in unkempt. The town said Mr. Boxie was *funky*, long before Motown or James Brown thought of making "funky" mean cool, hip, or "down." No, Mr. Boxie was funky because he smelled bad.

"A whiff of Boxcars," Big Mom, Mama's mama, would say, "would knock even a grown man out." And to think that Mr. Boxie was the chief chef in the making of Piedmont's sole contribution to the world's culinary chef d'oeuvre was more than I—once I had confirmed the rumor's truth beyond the wrought-iron railings of the elementary-school courtyard—could bear.

Tell me it ain't so, Pop, I said to my father. It's so, boy. It was true, then: the funk was what did it. It was a long time before I'd try Dent Davis's bologna again, enriched as I now knew it to be by Mr. Boxie's stench. And I *never* again tried it raw. Fried, however, was another matter. Gas will kill *anything*, Aunt Marguerite said to me one day as I eyed my dinner plate balefully, wanting so much to be able to forget the loathsome origins of this delicacy that she had placed before me. Anything, she insisted. I managed to smile at her between mouthfuls, after the first full swallow stayed down.

WHITE people couldn't cook; everybody knew that. Which made it a puzzle why such an important part of the civil rights movement had to do with integrating restaurants and lunch counters. The food wasn't any good anyway. Principle of the thing, Daddy's buddy Mr. Ozzie Washington would assert. They don't know nothin' about seasoning, my aunt Marguerite would say. I like my food seasoned, she'd add.

If there is a key to unlocking the culinary secrets of the Coleman family, it is that a slab of fatback or a cupful of bacon drippings or a couple of ham hocks and a long simmering time are absolutely essential to a well-cooked vegetable. Cook it till it's *done*, Mama would say. Cook it till it's dead, we'd learn to say much later. When I first tasted a steamed vegetable, I thought it was raw. The Colemans were *serious* about their cooking and their eating. There was none of this eating on the run; meals lasted for hours, with lots of good conversation thrown in. The happiest I ever saw my aunts and uncles in the Coleman family was when they'd slowly eat their savory meals, washing everything down with several glasses of iced tea. Especially at the Family Reunion, or on Christmas Day up at Big Mom's house. "Eating good"— with plenty of fat and cholesterol—was held to be essential to proper health and peace of mind.

There were plenty of Colemans: nine brothers—known as "the boys"— and four sisters, the youngest of whom had died when she was a day or two old. (There's enough niggers in your mother's family, Daddy would remark, to cast a Tarzan movie.)

Sunday in Piedmont was everybody's favorite day, because you could eat yourself silly, starting just after church. Mama didn't go to church on Sundays, except to read out her obituaries. She'd cook while we were at Sunday school. Rarely did the menu vary: fried chicken, mashed potatoes, baked corn (corn pudding), green beans and potatoes (with lots of onions and bacon drippings and a hunk of ham), gravy, rolls, and a salad of iceberg lettuce, fresh tomatoes (grown in Uncle Jim's garden), a sliced boiled egg, scallions, and Wishbone's Italian dressing. We'd eat Mama's Sunday dinners in the middle of the day and keep nibbling for the rest of the afternoon and evening. White people just can't cook good, Aunt Marguerite used to say; that's why they need to hire us.

♣

Elizabeth Ehrlich (1954–)

BORN AND RAISED in Detroit, Ehrlich grew up as a "red diaper baby" in a secular Jewish family. She has worked as a journalist for *Business Week*, written a biography of famous turn-of-the-century investigative reporter Nellie Bly, and taught at the Columbia School of Journalism. Her prize-winning recipe-studded memoir *Miriam's Kitchen* traces her conversion to Orthodox Judaism under the aegis of her mother-in-law Miriam, a Holocaust survivor whose meticulous and loving kosher practices become increasingly compelling to the young wife. Learning to separate dairy cookery and its utensils

from meat-based cuisine and its own utensils, preparing foods for the celebratory Shabbas meal, and even taking a ritual bath in a *mikvah*, Ehrlich
examines and meditates on the traditional customs of observant Jews. If the
world of the men is the synagogue, she shows, the realm of the women is
the kitchen, where time is marked by weekly Sabbath dinners and festive
occasions like Rosh Hashanah and Passover. "The year ebbs and flows," she
writes. "Miriam's cakes work, form, swell and subside, and the universe is
good to us: another cake already on horizon's rim."

from *Miriam's Kitchen*: Passover

IN THE BEGINNING there was Brooklyn, and it was Passover. We had
journeyed east in our Plymouth from Detroit. We brought school books,
and our spring coats. The call of our rich tradition had been heard—*Next
year in New York!*—and heeded. We, the destined ones, would miss an extra
week of school, right after Easter vacation.

We sat at my grandmother's dining room table, on stiff mahogany chairs
upholstered in blood-red velvet. Candle flame flickered, chandelier glowed,
crystal refracted, the dark of evening gently fell. Above the Belgian rug, my
feet dangled in navy blue maryjanes. They weren't as fancy as patent leather,
but you could wear them to school. A wineglass stood at every place, with an
extra goblet for Elijah the prophet, who visits every Seder table. At the head
of the table, my father, impressive in his high, boxy, black skullcap, resembling an Eastern Orthodox bishop, performed the Passover recounting, the
Haggadah, in rapid, rusty, musical Hebrew. . . .

"Let's go, Edward," spurred my grandmother. She had been cooking,
cleaning, and changing dishes for days with my mother's help, and didn't
want the roast chicken to dry up. . . .

My father said when to raise glasses, and when to drink the four draughts
of wine—or grape juice—draughts that a free person, celebrating redemption, can drink. He washed his hands ceremoniously, reciting the proper
blessing. He pointed to a roasted lamb bone, which had been set on fire over
the gas burner earlier that day, displayed as a symbol of the animal sacrifices
practiced by early Hebrews.

Holding out his strong, freckled hands, my father broke matzo, the
unleavened bread baked in speed by the escaping slaves, and we handed

around the crisp pieces. During the eight days of Passover, or Pesach, one may not eat regular bread, or anything prepared with or touched by a leavening agent such as yeast or baking powder. We didn't miss it; the Seder's first matzo wipes bread-hunger from the mind.

Next came the dipping, once and twice. My father dipped parsley, a token of green spring and new beginnings, into the salt water that stands for Israelites' tears. Down the table the dripping sprigs were passed. Raw bits of horseradish root, to recall the bitterness of bondage, were dipped in *haroses,* a sweet, wet gravel of finely chopped apples, raisins, cinnamon, and wine. This *haroses* symbolized the mortar with which the slaves toiled under the cruel sun-god. "We built the pyramids!" I breathlessly discovered. From then on, history was personal.

Green-sprouted horseradish pieces were passed. Brave children, dying of hunger by then, tried the bitter herb, yelped, gulped water. Red-eyed, we fanned our open mouths. The physic worked. They taught their children to remember.

Finally, finally, the festive meal. Fruit salad in dishes of gold-rimmed glass. Invariably fruit, though I don't know why—for spring? There were grapefruits and oranges, chunks of pineapple and peeled apples marinated in lemon and orange juice, strawberries, bananas. I had watched this salad prepared. My father, sitting at the kitchen table with a paring knife, peeled and sectioned the citrus fruit. My mother hulled boxes of strawberries, berries selected each by each. The kitchen table grew juicy with brilliant color.

After the fruit, the hard-boiled egg, the pagan sign of life's renewal, served whole to each person in a bowl of saltwater broth. Under the big spoon grasped in a small fist, the egg skittered dangerously. I supposed it was forbidden to cut the egg with a knife. I never asked. I crumbled matzo over the bowl and rose to the challenge of nailing the slippery egg.

Chicken soup with matzo balls, or *kneydlekh,* as we called them, and toasty soup nuts, bought in a blue-and-gray box in the store, kosher for Passover, to float in the shallow dishes.

Ahhh. Here we breathed deeply, wriggled expectantly in our seats. I wonder at our appetites, the quantities we ate as children. I think we ate it all.

Next issued gefilte fish. It came from the kitchen, on a thin china plate, a thick slab of it, homemade, with a slice of carrot and the detested jellied broth. It was served with *khreyn,* grated horseradish root, flavored with vinegar, sugar, and salt. Outside on the stoop that afternoon, my father had rubbed the pungent root on a hand grater balanced atop an enamel basin. His eyes streamed with the hot smell of it. My sister and brother and I ran up for a sniff, a hilarious scream, pretending to faint and die.

Roast chicken, huge quarters of spring pullets my mother had cleaned and plucked, had *kashered*—made kosher, had massaged, according to my grandmother's direction, with a paste of crushed garlic, paprika, pepper, salt, and sage, had roasted in glass baking pans. Skin side down, covered, skin side up, covered, then the foil off to crisp, roasted certainly for hours until the meat nearly fell off the bone, and velvety chunks of potatoes browned in the drippings.

I cannot picture a vegetable. Perhaps I did give up at some point, or was there none? No, this is all I remember, save for a slice of cucumber pickle and possibly a little more matzo, until the stewed prunes, the sponge cake, the coconut macaroons, the chocolate-covered orange peels, the tea with lemon and sugar, the last bit of matzo eaten as dessert, and the final songs.

After the meal, we opened the door for Elijah, and ran back to the table: a quiver ran through his cup of wine. My father looked innocent. . . .

I N the kitchen next morning there was a lightness and cleanliness, a freshness, and Passover smells. New linen dishtowels hung on the rack. The kitchen table was spread with an ironed cloth. There would be eight days of matzo: matzo with whipped butter and salt, matzo sandwiches, matzo puddings, dumplings, *farfel*, sponge cakes, also egg dishes, and fruit salad, and stewed prunes. How many eggs would be purchased for Passover week? Eggs to boil whole, to mix into chopped liver, to make pancakes fluffy, to fry with onions. Five or six per person, per day? No one can do this anymore, but are we really more healthy for it?

My grandmother rendered chicken skin for the yellow fat, schmaltz. As we gathered round the fragrant stove like so many chubby fledglings, she gave us the cracklings, the *grivnes,* to eat.

She made a giant ginger-scented matzo-meal pancake, round in its iron skillet, half-fried, half-baked, dense, crisp-edged, and two inches high. This *fankukhn,* cut into wedges, lavished with sugar and cinnamon, was one kind of breakfast. She steamed matzos over hot boiling water, spread each limp matzo square with hot chicken fat, sprinkled it with coarse salt, and rolled it up, to be eaten with soft-boiled eggs. She poured boiling water over crumbled matzos and strained the pieces, scrambled them with egg, fried them in oil, and this was matzo *brei*. She poured sweet red wine into hot morning tea. There was a week of such breakfasts, a blissful week of spring.

During the days, we walked with my father and played in the neighborhood park, among spring puddles and sunbursts and chalk hopscotch boards. The only cloud in our sky was that vernal harbinger, the first sighting of the Ice Cream Man. Oh, we would badger my father for tempting wares we knew were not kosher for *Pesach*, or face an early crisis of consciousness. Sometimes we had to leave New York in an incomplete state, having partaken of no Good Humor bar.

The years rolled on, it seems so quickly now. One spring I remember teasing for an ice cream and being stunned when my father said, "O.K." The condition was it must be finished at the playground, before we strolled back within view of grandmother's house.

Was this, just maybe, what set our rites of spring so softly crumbling?

After this, my recollections blur. My father began to skip parts of the Haggadah, and to stumble on the Hebrew from time to time. My grandmother died. The family met in New York for Christmas then, not *Pesach*. Our small Detroit Seders drifted toward English, grew shorter. Teenagers tried for political relevance, dogmatic and sincere.

Gefilte fish came from a jar. We barely noticed when the green apple blossom dishes, our own Passover set, stayed packed up in the basement one time, then forever. When was the last bit of chicken skin crisped in the pan, the last *grivn* eaten?

My father still scoured the oven each spring. My mother made matzo balls. I don't blame my parents. One spring in college, I didn't go home for Passover, though spring break coincided with the full April moon. I wandered the empty campus, an exile from history, and I ate a burger in a bun. The tides were bearing my craft away from the high-church Seders I once loved, and I held the rudder.

AT last the man I would marry brought me home to meet his parents, and they chopped gefilte fish by hand.

For years I was content to eat it, oblivious of the work involved, though I uttered empathic things. Now I am going to watch: Miriam, my mother-in-law, feeding chunks of whitefish and pike through an electric grinder. Long pinkish pulverized strings of mash falling hypnotically into a bowl as the face of the grinder goes round and round.

Father-in-law Jacob places two folding chairs seat to seat, covers this makeshift table with an old towel. On it, he balances a wooden board heaped with ground fish. Pulling up a third chair, he sits. He grasps a sharp-bladed cleaver with both hands, and begins to chop. Ten cuts this way, ten cross-hatched cuts, cleaving the translucent sea-flesh, twelve more this way, the ax-blade again mounding the fish, lifting high, weighing down, a lifetime of fine etched lines in the board, like lines on the palm of a hand.

I offer to help.

"Chop the fish?" Jacob, incredulous.

Miriam makes a face: "For what?"

When I insist, Jacob shrugs, a squint of humor in it. He still opens doors for me, hoists the shopping bags of Miriam's cooked food down their front stairs to my car. The implication of female frailty infuriated me once. Now I treasure Jacob, a good man who embodies his responsibilities, whose sense of duty is a kind of knowledge, one that indeed gives him eerie strength.

Where the fish is concerned, at least, I am about to be humbled. Leaning over the board to chop, my back begins to ache. My shoulder throbs with the up-down pulse of the heavy cleaver. Flying bits of fish stick to my hair, mashed pink fish works crazily to the ends of the board. The board wobbles unsteadily on the chairs. The handle grows sticky and hot.

Surreptitious, I glance at the clock.

"It's too hard for you," comments Miriam, her back to me, at the sink. She is cleaning the grinder with a toothbrush and toothpick, piece by shining piece.

"No problem!" I gasp. I scrape fish away from the edges of the board, pull fish into a mound, scrape, pull. I chop. My two red hands grip the cleaver. My shoulders burn, but pride keeps me chopping a good ten minutes, and it seems like forty-five.

"There!" I proclaim, unable to go on. I work the handle out of my claw.

"Thank you!" exclaims Miriam, wiping her hands. "Hmmm," she adds, examining the fish.

I wash my hands tenderly. Miriam sprinkles sugar on the fish. Jacob, wordlessly, resumes chopping. He had not bothered to sit down meanwhile at all.

"Couldn't you use a food processor?" I say, a bit plaintively, once my pulse slows.

"For the fish?" Jacob allows himself a rare, private smile. "Sure not."

"I tried it once," remarks Miriam, cutting onions into a pot with fish bones, a bay leaf, water, and pepper. She will mix the chopped fish with egg, matzo meal, seasonings, then shape oval patties in her palm with a knife to simmer in the broth. "The one you brought."

Oh, yes, I had forgotten. A gift, back when food processors were new, back when Miriam was still asking, "How should I call you to the family?" for I was neither wife nor fiancée, and her cousins and their children were busy with weddings, *mazel-tovs*, bar mitzvahs, and all the other communal demarcations and progressions. I had other things on my mind. "Friend," I used to answer, resolutely obtuse in the face of Miriam's sharp discomfort and longing. One son, and not a *boychik* either . . . living with a girl (though this was not quite acknowledged), and nothing happening. No grandchildren.

"You can have it, it's downstairs in the box still," she said. The food processor. "The fish didn't come out good." She thinks back. "It didn't—feel."

I watch Jacob and the shimmering fish mass, as it is heaped, divided, broken down, pulled together. The texture has gone way beyond chopped flesh. It grows—gelatinous, sponge-like, it glows and expands, gains mass and presence, substance. In a word, it feels. Jacob is one with his task, his wiry arms rising, falling, his face intent but composed.

"What about a chopping bowl? A hand chopper?" I ask faintly, entranced.

"This would be all right," she admits. "But I don't have the bowl." . . .

FOR many Passovers I sat down to Miriam's dense, miraculous gefilte fish wishing it were not sweet. I dressed it in sharp horseradish, while my husband's family corrected my spotty *Litvakish* Yiddish. Then one year it struck me that I had changed. I liked the fish sweet, and the horseradish sweet, and the red cabbage salad and the carrots sweet.

I guess it is only poetic justice and the debt the universe owed my *bubbe*, who must have been raised on sugar in fish. At an age when I moped around college libraries and worse, she was busy transliterating her husband's food preferences. She longed for more sweetness from time to time.

AND so, I began keeping Passover, and hosting an annual Seder. I get ready for Pesach, little by little, and do a little more each year. Some of it is spring cleaning. I dust and wipe and shake out the rugs, and in a good year, I get to the windows. Then I get rid of improper food, the crumbs and crusts and anything not kosher for Passover: the *hametz*. I line drawers and shelves with new paper, and fit them out with Passover dishes. I scour the sink and clean the oven. I cover the countertops and kitchen table. All for a span of eight days, and then I box up Pesach again for another year. . . .

I thought long about changing dishes. A year came when I took the leap. My parents were visiting; we leapt together. My dad commandeered the wheel and we drove to a distant housewares outlet. I chose dishes, enough for the big multiple-course Seder dinner. I bought pots and pans, cutting boards, paring knife, spatula, outfitting a phantom kitchen.

My mother showed me how to boil my silverware, *kasher* my glasses, make Pesach in fridge and sink, remembering this and that as we went along. We packed up the everyday things. And then, only then, we began to make the Seder.

Everyone cooked. We followed the Brooklyn menu, and we followed Miriam's menu. My mother made chicken soup and matzo balls, and Miriam brought her Passover egg noodles for the soup as well, delicate crepe threads of egg and potato starch. I attempted Miriam's *rabinik*, which means "grated thing," a mystery to my mother until she recognized her mother's potato pudding. We boiled eggs, for serving in salt water, for chasing around the bowl with your spoon. Miriam brought the gefilte fish.

We invited the family. My father's sister, Selina, arrived with a *fankukhn*, in a gift box, tied with gold ribbons. Forty years after perfecting soufflés, she had spent the day destroying *fankukhn* failures and had at last got it, "Sort of," she said.

We went through the rites, Jacob in his thick glasses leading, trying hard to read slow and allow for English. We drank wine and retold the story, as children giggled and showed off. It came time for the entrance of Elijah, whose full glass awaited at the table's heart. Children ran to the door, throwing it open under a starry sky.

"If you want wine, come in now!" a child yelled into the night.

It was our firmest apostate, Aunt Selina, who found herself shocked at the joke. "I was the oldest, I used to have to walk down a long dark hallway alone, to let in Elijah. I was scared," she mused. "Imagine them joking about it."

I remembered my grandmother's hallway, long and dark, remembered Elijah's wine in its tall goblet, shimmering and moving as if invisibly sipped, as my father, straight-faced, jostled the table leg with his knee. There was a glowing solemnity about Passover then. I don't know if it will return. Yet for my children, Passover is not a mausoleum, and I like this, too.

🐘

Diana Abu-Jaber (1960–)

THE JORDANIAN-AMERICAN WRITER, who divides her time between Miami and Portland, Oregon, has written several acclaimed novels (including *Arabian Jazz*, *Crescent*, and *Birds of Paradise*) as well as a memoir about her family's traditions—primarily its foodways—titled *The Language of Baklava*, in which she describes meals made with typical Middle Eastern ingredients cooked in suburban upstate New York as well as in Amman and the deserts of Jordan. A frequent contributor to National Public Radio, the American-born Abu-Jaber has spent considerable time in her father's native Jordan, both as a child and later as the recipient of a Fulbright Fellowship, when she interviewed Jordanian and Palestinian women about their lives and work. In this passage from her memoir she recounts the consternation her family caused in their neighborhood when her father grilled in the *front* yard, a practice not only mystifying to the neighbors but disturbing to practitioners of the great American *backyard* barbecue. Abu-Jaber's childhood emotions veer between shame and pride at this seemingly un-American culinary custom.

from *The Language of Baklava*: A House and a Yard

OUR SPRAWLING NEIGHBORHOOD is filled, in its family rooms and rec rooms and extra bedrooms, with a nation of children. There's Karen, Carl, Lilah, Raymond, Lisa, Donna, Sally, Jamie, the Malcolm twins, and many more all within the first three blocks of the school bus route. Jamie Faraday used to be best friends with Sally Holmes until I appeared in the lunchroom with my bags full of cold roasted chicken kabobs slathered in hummus and wrapped in pita bread. Sally dragged back the seat beside me, plumped her chin onto the heel of her palm, and said, "What you eating?" Down the length of the long linoleum table, I see Jamie abandoned. She lifts her head and I see myself come into focus; her forehead rises with a look almost like recognition. Now Jamie eyes me warily every time she gets on the bus, takes note of Sally seated beside me, and waves with an enraged little flip of the hand. Then she clatters down the aisle far from our seat into exile.

I notice all this but don't completely take it in: I'm trying to get my bearings. Throughout our first year back in the States, I seem to see everything through a glittering mist. I hear the expression *American dream* and I think that, somehow, this quality of mistiness must be what it refers to. The children in the neighborhood are so soft and babyish that they barely seem to have outlines. In other ways they are deliberate, remorseless, and exacting. The politics of the school bus and the rumor mill of the classroom are fierce, filled with intrigue and menace. It all feels so different from the good-times kids I knew in Jordan, with their shared gum, their sharp, brown shins and broken-toothed grins. In America, I learn there is a certain way to dress (hip-huggers, flared jeans), a certain way to wear your hair (gleaming, Prince Valiant bobs), a certain lunchbox to carry (Barbie for girls, G.I. Joe for boys—I am nearly cast out of fourth grade when I show up with a Flintstones box). And there are, it turns out, many things that—under any circumstances—you do not do.

For example, the neighbors don't barbecue in their front yards. That is apparently what the backyard is for. The backyards here are fenced off and guarded—spaces as private as other people's dreams. But our front yard has the better view and has easier access to the front door, which is closer to the kitchen and hence a very practical place for grilling. Also, the front yard will allow us to share food, cross our legs on the plastic lawn chairs, and gossip with the neighbors, as we did in Jordan. We have survived a long, howling, isolated Syracuse winter that hardened into filthy icebergs of decaying snow. By April, Bud is ready to pronounce it spring and set up his hibachi. On the first warmish sunny day, we drag out the picnic table, digging mud furrows through the half-frozen yard. Bud has chicken marinated in olive oil, vine-

gar, rosemary, and a whole head of garlic. Its butter yellow skin hisses and
crackles over the coals, and the aroma fills my head. The beautiful charred
smell of the grill circulates through the spring air and bare tree branches,
still shocked with cold. . . .

WE set the table, bring out bowls of elegant baba ghanouj and sprightly
tabbouleh salad full of bulgur and fresh parsley, a basket of hot bread, and
skewers heavy with onion and tomato wedges to be roasted. We sit, marveling over our good fortune—to live in these rolling green lawns, these creamy
houses, and the bold vaulted sky of our new neighborhood. The chicken is
crusty and redolent with garlic and rosemary. We eat well, shivering just a
bit in our jackets. I have a sense—as I often do when I contemplate this blue
moon-stone sky—of the future. It is a broad, euphoric feeling. Does the rest
of the family feel this way? I don't know for sure, though I imagine they do.
Whenever we all drive home together, Mom asks as we pull in the driveway,
"Who do you suppose lives in this little house?"

We are lost in the food, in the smell of grilling, and in the spring when
there is a powdery sort of sensation sprinkling down the back of my neck
and suddenly I realize a man and a woman are standing at the edge of the
street, just a few feet away, staring at us.

I put down my chicken leg, which has rolled juices and smoke between
my fingers. "Hi!" I call brightly. New neighbors! They look hungry. The
woman starts and blushes, as if she didn't imagine that we could see them.
Her eyes are a pale linen blue, of such crisp clarity that she looks as if she
could X-ray with them.

Bud stands, maître d' of the front lawn. "Welcome. I'm Gus, this is my
wife, Pat—"

The two strangers pull back and lightly bump into each other. I dimly
register the sense that they didn't think Bud could talk.

"We just moved here in November." Bud gestures at the house as if they
might assume we were picnicking on someone else's lawn. "I hope you're
hungry! We've got all this crazy food—shish kabob, baba gha—"

The woman's kerchief white hand flutters up to her throat. There's a pause,
and Bud bends back a little and asks me quietly, "Haddol nawal?" (Are they
Gypsies?") They look marooned and stateless, standing there mute in the
street. But I remember seeing a family of Gypsies once in the old market in

Jordan, with their fringed scarves and spangled earrings and high-voltage expressions. These mild, normal people don't look anything like that—the man in belted beige slacks and tasseled loafers and the woman in a milky, synthetic blouse and culottes. Finally the man clears his throat and says, "Oh no, no, thank you—we . . . we just, um, ate. Um." He blinks. "We, uh . . . we uh . . . we live over there, on Cumberland Drive? We uh . . . well, our neighbors—you know the Tinerkes on Roanoke Circle?"

Bud frowns, trying to process the name. I picture rabbity little Timmy and chinless Bitsy Tinerke sitting in the third seat from the front of the school bus.

"Anyway. Well, see, they live really close by here, too." The man and the woman glance at each other. He puts his hands on his slender snaky hips. "Well, they saw you-all out here eating or burning things or something and then called us to say there might be some kind of—I don't know, exactly— maybe some kind of trouble going on out here? And so we just came on over to check into it—you know, we all like to keep an eye on things—this is a nice neighborhood—and so . . ." His voice trails off; his face is slowly turning an alarming, bruised color.

Bud is still standing there, still frowning, as if this man is speaking in tongues. Then my mother stands and the couple look startled once again. She is nearly six feet tall, with good level shoulders and a long neck and unwavering Cassandra eyes. She also puts her hands on her hips, almost casual. "There's no trouble here," she says in her smooth, leaf-blown voice.

They put up their hands and back away as if she is waving a pistol at them. "No, no, no trouble at all—sorry for the—the misunderstanding. . . . Welcome to the neighborhood!" Then they are gone.

And that's about when I get the feeling that starts somewhere at the center of my chest, as heavy as an iron ingot, a bit like fear or sadness or anger, but none of these exactly; it is simply there, suspended between my ribs. I look up at the neighborhood and the mist has cleared. All the mean, cheaply framed windows are gaping at us, the sky empty as a gasp.

THE next day on the school bus, Jamie climbs on, gives me her hard smile, hesitates, then flounces down on the seat next to me. She tilts her head and parts her lips. I look up in alarm. "Just to let you know," she says in a sweet, burning way.

"Let me know what?"

She crosses one bare leg over the other, and her brilliant white socks bounce with the rocking of the bus. "Well, you know, of course. My parents saw you out there the other night. I heard them talking with the neighbors. They said it was an 'unholy disgrace.' See, okay, the thing is, you better know that in this country nobody eats in the front yard. Really. Nobody." She looks at me solemnly and sadly, her bangs a perfect cylinder above her brows. "If your family doesn't know how to behave, my parents will have to find out about getting you out of this neighborhood."

She squints, pinches her lips together in a narrow, bitten-down way. I can see every pointed pale lash, the pink ridges above her lower lids.

I feel the iron inside of me. It drives through every bit of my body. It vibrates like a bell clapper. I turn away from her and tip my forehead against the frigid pane of glass. There's an echo in my head saying: *She's right.* Shame fills me: I see it in the rain stroking the windows, so bright that it burns holes in the backs of my eyes. When Jamie finally slides out of the seat, I don't even hear her go.

I MOPE, barely speaking, for a solid week, appetiteless, rejecting Bud's lunches of stuffed squash, *shawerma*, kibbeh. Even Mom's peanut butter and Fluff on white bread brings tears to my eyes, and I stuff it in the garbage barrel at the cafeteria.

Mrs. Manarelli asks me what's wrong.

But I have no way of explaining to her that I have awakened from the mist and now our neighborhood looks hard and squat and drudgy. I have no way to explain Jamie Faraday's pink-rimmed eyes and long bulb of a nose. Instead I just mope and shrug and sigh wordless blue shadows. So she slants her head to one side, then swats at my behind and tells me I don't have no sign of a butt at all. And I get indignant and say I do so have signs of a butt. And she says fine, well, okay then, come on inside, I need your help in the kitchen.

The entrance to Mrs. Manarelli's house smells like roasting tomatoes and garlic. She doesn't go in much for opening the window curtains, which she says fades everything, so the whole downstairs is doused in shadow and all the furniture crackles under clear plastic covers. Directly over the couch in the living room is a spotlit, gilt-framed painting of the Last Supper, and here the notes of tomato sauce are so pronounced that you could imagine this is what the apostles are eating. Her husband, Johnny, sits on the couch, ankles crossed on the coffee table, always glaring at what seems to be the same word in the newspaper. The family room smells of red wine, fruit, and chocolate, and I know the bedrooms upstairs smell either of bread when she's baking or of the fresh cedar, lavender, and pine hillsides of another country. Once, in the upstairs bathroom, I was so transported by the scent of rosewater that Mrs. Manarelli found me there a half hour later sitting on the edge of the tub, combing my hair and singing.

We go into the kitchen and there is something shimmering in a gelatin mold on the counter. She instructs me to soak a kitchen towel under the warm-water tap and wipe this along the mold. Then she turns it out onto a pastry board dusted with confectioner's sugar; a puff of sugar blooms in the air. It is so brilliantly white that it reminds me of the nuns speaking of food that removes all sin. Mrs. Manarelli wipes a knife with the hot towel, cuts into the whiteness, and brings me a slice of *panna cotta* gleaming and dewy on a Melmac plate.

She sits beside me at the speckled linoleum table just like our own and says speculatively, "Only men in my life—husband, son . . . why do you suppose that is?"

I blink. I want to dwell on my own problems, but this is a novel idea to me, in our house of mostly girls. I reach for my grandmother's favorite explanation: "Maybe it's because Jesus says so."

"Jesus!" she snorts. Then she sighs and fans herself and looks off at the place where the ceiling meets the wall. "Eat your dessert," she says. *"Jesus."*

The first spoonful of *panna cotta* is so startling, I want to laugh or sing or confess my sins. It tastes of sweetness and cream and even of the tiny early flowers the cows have eaten to make the cream.

I take another bite of *panna cotta* and another. Before long, without even realizing it, I'm talking, telling all, secrets dissolving like *panna cotta* in the mouth. Mrs. Manarelli scrapes her chair in closer, puts her chin on her hand, and watches me talk about grilled chicken and the Gypsy people in loafers and the school bus and how Sally now likes me better than Jamie and how that is my fault and Jamie's cinched smile and how I don't have the right lunchbox or the right pants or shoes or socks and how things are different from Jordan and how I can never remember my sins in confession so I make up new ones and isn't that a sin of a sin and does that mean I am going right to hell, are they going to kick us out of the neighborhood, and can we move back to our apartment in the courtyard with my boyfriend Hisham?

When I have exhausted myself and have scraped up every bit of *panna cotta* on my plate, Mrs. Manarelli goes and stands at the stove as if she is cooking something, but the little red light on her stove isn't on. She is muttering things in different languages, and her voice sounds serrated: I hear angry odds and ends of words. Finally she turns around and says, "There's nobody going to hell around here except for the ones think they aren't gonna go. That's if you ask me. And they damn better not ask or they'll find out a thing or five they don't want to know!"

This comment raises more questions for me than it answers. While I'm mulling this over, she grabs the phone receiver and shakes it like a mace. "What're their names?" she demands. "I got a few choice words for them."

"Who?"

"The Gypsies! The Gypsies and their loafers!"

"Maria Elena Theresa, do not call the neighbors." Her grouchy husband's voice erupts from the living room where he is rattling the newspaper. "We are no longer in Brooklyn, we are in civilization up here now. People don't do that kind of stuff up here."

"Don't tell me what people do!" she shouts back. "The Italians invented civilization!"

"I was Italian five years before you was born," he retorts. "I got a PhD in civilization."

She shakes the receiver a few more times at the wall behind Johnny's head, jaw set at an indignant angle, as if she is still arguing with him. But she seems to concede the argument because she slams the phone back down and turns to the counter. Now Mrs. Manarelli is busying herself with a new plan of attack. She wraps up the *panna cotta* in waxed paper, then cloth napkins, like swaddling a big baby. She puts it in a basket with some cold sliced roast beef, some soft white cheese in a jar, some tender roasted red peppers in oil, tiny black olives, and a crusty round loaf of bread. "We're going out!" she shouts at her husband. Then she says to me, "C'mon, kid."

We walk next door to my house and Mrs. Manarelli knocks loudly, then comes halfway in, yelling up the stairs to my mother. Mom comes down the stairs, patting at her new bouffant hairdo, tall and firm and shiny. Mrs. Manarelli holds up her basket, tells her that she's brought a picnic and doesn't want to eat it at the round, speckled table in the kitchen, she wants to eat it outside. Mom starts laughing. "But it's fifty degrees out—and I just got my hair done!" I admire her long neck and towering hair, all of her descending the foyer stairs like a goddess on a trophy.

"Hoity-toity, Pat," Mrs. Manarelli says, and nudges me. "Now, there's a woman."

Mom stares at us a moment as we stand grinning and wind whipped in the doorway, gives a last, regretful pat to her hairdo, and goes in to put on her parka and collect my sisters. Mrs. Manarelli also looks magnificent. Usually she's plump and hunched up, her hair trapped in a net like a dark fish. But once we go back outdoors, she comes unfurled: Her short brown hair bobs in the wind, her lips are round and scarlet against the whiteness of her skin. She stands straighter, and under her wool church coat the hem of her cotton print dress flails around her knees. It's the end of April and we had the last snowfall four weeks ago, our ill-fated barbecue three weeks ago. The neighborhood windows and doorknobs still stay rimmed with frost an hour after the sun comes out.

The hibachi is stowed away in the garage, but the picnic table floats abandoned on the thawing grass out front, and this, of course, is where Mrs. Manarelli wants to eat. She spreads out a checkered tablecloth, and when we can't get the cloth to stop blowing off the table, we sit on top of it. Mom brings out plates and wineglasses and Kool-Aid for me and my sisters, and there is a look on her face as though we've just told one another a good joke. Her cheeks gleam with the cold, and her high hair unravels in the wind like a ball of yarn. It's so cold that I'm having trouble tasting anything, and Monica says she wants to go back inside and see the rest of her soap opera. (She's only four, but she's already addicted to the high drama of *General Hospital*.) But then Mrs. Manarelli unveils the baby *panna cotta*: It shivers and gleams white as a star. We eat it directly from the waxed paper with plastic spoons.

The neighborhood cars pass, some quickly, some slowly, and we wave at them all with the wave we've seen at Macy's Thanksgiving Day parade, a feathery tilt at the wrist, forearm upright. No one can tell us anything. We are five queens drifting over the suburbs on our own private float.

Linda Furiya (1966–)

RAISED IN A small midwestern farm town, Linda Furiya launched her writing career in San Francisco, with a column that appeared in Japanese-American newspapers; eventually she moved to Beijing where she wrote articles on Chinese food, and later she traveled to Shanghai, where she attended a cooking school before returning to the States. Like so many ethnic Americans, she writes about the complexities of growing up in an American community and feeling alien, given the traditions of her foreign-born parents. When she was a child, she recalls here, her Japanese mother's cooking caused her considerable embarrassment: for her school lunch her mother provided bento boxes with chopsticks and rice balls, inspiring stares and taunts from the girl's classmates. Our selection is from the first of Furiya's two memoirs, *Bento Box in the Heartland: My Japanese Girlhood in Whitebread America.* Her more recent memoir is *How to Cook a Dragon: Living, Loving, and Eating in China.*

from *Bento Box in the Heartland*: Swallowing Fish Bones

MY MOTHER FIRST told me this story when I was six years old, before I knew that the language she spoke was Japanese.

Her personal tale takes place in Tokyo during the 1930s, when she was a young girl. Her neighborhood, she explained, was a jigsaw puzzle of low-story, fragile houses constructed of wood and paper. The homes survived the many earthquakes that shook Japan, yet most burned away like dried leaves when Tokyo was bombed during World War II.

Every day a community of mothers in the neighborhood gathered together to feed their babies a midday meal and to rest from endless household duties and the tongues and ears of nosy in-laws.

While the older women gossiped and watched over the little ones, the younger women made lunch for the babies, who ate softer versions of what their mothers served at their tables—rice, fish, soup, and vegetables.

Often the fishmonger's wife brought a whole fish to broil until the skin charred and cracked on a small outside grill. The mothers slid the flaky, sweet, white meat off the bone with the tap of a chopstick.

Using their fingers to feel for any stray fish bones, they thoroughly mashed, pinched, and poked the tender fish meat before mixing it with rice and moistening it with *dashi* (fish stock). Despite all the care, sometimes a transparent bone, pliable and sharp as a shark's tooth, slipped past scrutiny.

I picture her wearing braids and standing in the distance, quietly observing yet part of the gathering. Now her short hair frames her face like the black slashes of an ink brush. In this story my mother explains how before modern medicine, the mortality rate was high not only for newborns, but even for healthy men, who were struck dead from illnesses that would start as a common cold.

"One day you are in good health, the next . . ." Mom's eyes flicker at this point, like two flints sparking. She snaps her fingers at the swiftness of it all. Back then, mothers needed reassurance that their babies were strong, and eating was an infant's first test of survival. If the baby didn't know how to eat, suck from its mother's nipple, or push out a fish bone, the child wouldn't know how to survive when she grew older. . . .

GROWING up in the only Japanese family in Versailles, Indiana, I quickly learned that I would have to overcome many fish bones. My very first notion of how different we really were struck me among the pastel-colored molded trays and long bleached wood tables of the school cafeteria.

MY elementary school lunchroom was a sweaty, brightly lit place that reeked of hot cooking oil, Pine-Sol, and the yeast from rising bread dough. It was dead quiet when empty, and otherwise it echoed with the sound of children's high-pitched talk and laughter and heavy wood and metal chairs scraping against the tile floor.

I had never eaten a lunch before then without my parents. My two older brothers, Keven and Alvin, ate lunch at school. Mom was a stay-at-home mother. She churned out three meals a day as efficiently as a military mess hall. My father worked second shift at a factory in Columbus, Indiana, where he assembled truck engines. Because he started his shift midafternoon, he ate a hot, filling lunch at home to compensate for his dinner, a cold *bento* box of rice, meat, and vegetables, with a cup of green tea from his thermos.

These lunches with my parents were magnificent feasts made in our tiny kitchen. The size of a hall closet, the small room became alive during lunchtime, like a living, breathing creature, with steam puffing from the electric rice cooker, rattling from the simmering pots, and short clipping notes of Mom chopping with her steady hand guiding her *nakiri bocho* (Japanese vegetable knife).

At the dining room table, Dad and I grazed on cold Japanese appetizers—spicy wilted cabbage pickled in brine with lemon peel, garlic, smashed whole red chili peppers, and kombu (seaweed). Meanwhile, Mom prepared hot dishes—cubes of tofu garnished with ginger and bonito flakes (dried fish shavings). There was salmon fillet, if we could get it, grilled to the color of Turkish apricots on a Japanese wire stove-top contraption; or sirloin, sliced tissue-thin, sautéed with onions, soy sauce, and a dash of rice wine. And there was always a bowl of clear fish broth or cloudy miso soup and steamed white rice.

As I was used to such sumptuous lunches, it wasn't long before the novelty of my school's cafeteria fare wore off and my eyes wandered toward the lunch boxes other children brought from home. From inside the metal containers, they pulled out sandwiches with the crusts cut off, followed by tins of chocolate pudding and homemade cookies.

My best friend, Tracy Martin, was part of the lunch box brigade. Her mother packed the same lunch items every day—a cold hot dog and applesauce. We also ate with Mary, a Coppertoned, baby-faced girl with a Clara Bow haircut, whose mother precut all the food in her lunch box, even her cookies, into bite-size pieces.

I wanted to be a part of this exclusive group, and after much pestering, I was thrilled when my mother relented and agreed to pack my lunches.

When I joined Tracy and Mary at lunchtime, carrying my own lunch box, I studied the girls, who carefully unpacked their containers as if they were unveiling family heirloom jewelry, observing the packed-lunch protocol. I unlocked my lunch box and casually peeked under the lid. My stomach lurched. I expected a classic elementary school lunch of a bologna, cheese, and Miracle Whip sandwich and a bag of Durkee's potato sticks, but all I saw were three round rice balls wrapped in waxed paper. Mom had made me an *obento*, a Japanese-style boxed meal.

I snapped the lunch box lid shut before the other girls caught a glimpse of what was inside. How could this have happened?

"Sandwich?" Mom asked in a genuinely astonished voice when I came home from school that afternoon protesting. "Why go to trouble to make lunch for just plain old sandwich?"

"That's what everyone else brings. That's what I want," I demanded. My desire to emulate my classmates was palpable. My *obento* lunches were a glaring reminder of the ethnic differences between my peers and me.

THE agony of being different from my classmates was intensified the day Scott Leach pointed out the slanted shape of my eyes. Scott had snow-white hair and constantly dug his pinkie finger deep in his ear. One morning as we stood in the milk line, he turned to me and furrowed his eyebrows, pointing at my eyes as if they were insect specimens.

"Why do they look like lines?" he asked with a smirk far more adult than his age.

When the other kids laughed, I knew this wasn't a normal question. My throat tightened as if a fish bone were on the verge of lodging itself in my windpipe. I took a step back, bringing my index finger up to my mouth to shush him, only to witness him pull his own eyes back at the corners to more laughter from the classmates in line. Encouraged by the other children's reaction, Scott pulled his eyes back and tilted his head from side to side.

I stood there like a mannequin. I was filled with helpless, choking anxiety. The spell was broken only when the recess bell rang to go back to class. The incident initiated what became open season for teasing me.

A couple of days later at recess, after I won a round at hopscotch, Susie Sillerhorn, a pinch-nosed blond and known sore loser, announced that she had heard my parents talking "sing-songy" in the grocery store. Susie's pal Donna Underwood joined in by pulling back her eyes until they appeared closed and made pinging nonsense noises. The other girls laughed.

Defiantly, I asked why she was doing that. "You should know what I'm saying. This is how your folks talk," she replied haughtily. I didn't know the name of it then, but the feeling this early interaction left me with was my first feeling of injustice.

Still, I wanted their friendship and to be accepted, so silently, but with deep resentment, I put up with friends who called me Chink and Jap. Some innate self-control wouldn't allow me to give my prosecutors the lesson they probably needed to learn, of knowing they were hurting me. Eventually, though, the resentment, anger, and developing drive for self-preservation gave me the gumption to fight back.

My first stand, albeit lame, was against Tracy, who instantly resorted to calling me Jap when we got into an argument about whose tree swings were better. She watched my reaction with calm, steady eyes. Tracy knew the power behind the word.

Unable to think of anything to say, I spurted out the first thing that came to mind. I called her "pizzahead" because of her Italian ancestry. It was weak, like throwing confetti at an opponent, but it was my first stab at fighting back.

At night, I'd lie awake and fantasize about how to get revenge. I imagined that Dad was an undercover agent on a special assignment, a foreign dignitary from Japan. His cover was a factory job in a small Midwest town. I saw the surprised looks on my friends' faces when they realized we weren't who they thought we were. The meanest ones, including Susie and Donna, begged me to be their best friends. I smiled smugly and shook my head. My family was leaving Versailles and I wouldn't be going to school there anymore, I explained. Then I enjoyed their looks of dismay and confusion, just as they had enjoyed themselves when they teased me. A cavalcade of shiny black Cadillac sedans appeared and whisked us away. I waved at my classmates from the rearview window until they disappeared. I hugged my pillow and twisted my bedsheets so hard, wishing my fantasy would come true.

When I believed it couldn't get any worse, a turning point came one afternoon as I waited to use the playground swings. Raymond Neilley, a chubby boy in JCPenney Huskies jeans, pulled his eyes back in the overused imitation my peers favored.

"Chinky, chinky, Chinese," he sang, doing a little dance. For the first time, blinding fury replaced fear. First of all, I wasn't Chinese. I heard the other kids around me snickering as they encircled us and moved in closer. Dread prickled me like a scratchy blanket on a hot day. My mouth was cottony and my palms were slick. I could feel my heart beat quickly, rushing color to my face. Mom's fish bone story came to mind. It wasn't about swallowing or spitting, I realized, but about fight or flight.

"Shut up, fatso," I said, louder than a whisper. I recognized a flash of fear pass over Raymond's plump face, yet he continued to taunt me.

I raised my voice, making it commanding and deep. "I said shut up, you big ball of . . . lard!" I plucked this word out of a conversation I had overheard at the grocery store. It wasn't the choicest of names, but it had a nice menacing ring to it with high potential to damage, like the kind of mud balls my brothers threw when they fought with the neighborhood kids. Inside each firm handful of wet earth was a surprise, a skin-breaking chunk of gravel.

Raymond's darting eyes confirmed I had hit a raw nerve, filling me with giddy power.

Like a bombardier honing in on a target, I unleashed all the anger that I had pent up during the past weeks, screaming "fatso" and "lard" until the other children, like summer cicadas, joined in on my name-calling. Raymond didn't say anything. He stared and tried to figure out how the tables had turned.

After that the other kids thought twice before they teased me. If they tried, I fought back with everything I could get on them. Crossed eyes, crooked bangs, rotten teeth, dirty fingernails, moles, eyeglasses, and freckles were all fair game.

With the gift of victory, I began to shake the overwhelming need to be like my friends. So what if I played by myself, got the cold-shoulder treatment, or had to deal with whispering behind my back? Nothing, I decided, could be as bad as putting up with the name-calling and the dread of waiting for it to come. I understood now why some boys took a beating instead of accepting daily torment: It was pride. I lost a sense of innocence that first year of school, but from it grew a defined measure of self that would stay with me and emerge during difficult times in my life.

TRACY interrupted my thoughts. "Whatcha bring?" A straw pulled at the corner of her mouth as she sipped grape Kool-Aid from a plastic cup. The fish bone scratched at the back of my throat. I knew what I had to do. I took the apple out of my lunch box with discretion.

"Is that all you have?" Tracy asked.

"No, there's more. I'm just not hungry right now." I avoided her eyes.

Along with the apple, Mom had wrapped in plastic a few cookies among the tightly packed rice balls. The conversation was buzzing around me. I said as little as possible. The apple and cookies stuck in my throat like wet soot, but I ate slowly and purposefully, as if nothing were wrong.

Feigning a stomachache, I left the cafeteria with my lunch box tucked safely under my arm. I looked behind me nervously before I ducked into the girls' restroom.

Huddled in the pewter-gray toilet stall with the medicinal smell of Lysol, I cradled one of the three firmly packed rice balls in my hands. Its seaweed wrapping had the crispness of handmade rice paper. My pounding heart steadied a moment as I imagined Mom shaking salt on the palms of her clean wet hands and then pressing and rotating each ball three or four times until it was uniform. Despite my repeated requests for a sandwich, she persisted with the rice balls. She knew they were my favorite.

Startled by the noise of a toilet flushing in a nearby stall, I took a big bite of the *onigiri*. My teeth ripped through the crunchy seaweed wrapping, through the salty rice, to the surprise center, a buttery chunk of salmon placed precisely in the middle of the rice and seaweed ball. The other rice balls had centers of pickled plum and silky kelp.

It was a secret act that I found empowering and primal, rather than diminishing. I was hungry, and yet there was an odd sense of invincibility, the banishment of fear of what might happen if a teacher walked in on me. I had the sensation that if I left one grain uneaten, something inside me would shrivel up and die. I took big mouthfuls of the rice and chewed as fast as I could until there was no more.

That afternoon, delighted to find my lunch box empty, Mom asked if I enjoyed the rice balls. I told her I did and said nothing else. She continued to make one delicious *obento* after another, and for the remainder of the year I ate cookies and apples with my friends and consumed the rest of my lunch in the stall of the girl's bathroom. The lunch box crowd voted unanimously that my mother packed the lamest lunches in history.

I never told Mom about the fish bones I navigated my first year in school. I also announced that I wanted to eat school lunches again once I got into second grade.

Jhumpa Lahiri (1967–)

BORN IN LONDON to parents from West Bengal, Lahiri came to the States when she was two. She was raised in Rhode Island, and though she writes incisively about the hyphenated lives of Indian-Americans, she considers herself American, noting that "I wasn't born here but I might as well have been." An accomplished fiction writer—her first collection of short stories, *The Interpreter of Maladies*, won a Pulitzer Prize, and her novel *The Namesake* was made into a movie—she has also earned a doctorate in English literature, with a dissertation on Renaissance theater. "Indian Takeout" wistfully evokes the sensory pleasures of the "Food Suitcase" that she remembers from childhood family visits to Calcutta, where her parents would furiously purchase the staples of Bengali cooking (mustard oil, curry leaves, saffron) that they couldn't find in New England. Now, as she notes, such foods are widely available in American supermarkets, yet the food suitcase retains its air of geographic mystery, its aromas of distance.

Indian Takeout

I AM THE daughter of former pirates, of a kind. Our loot included gold, silver, even a few precious gems. Mainly though, it was food, so much that throughout my childhood I was convinced my parents were running the modern equivalent of the ancient spice trade. They didn't exactly plunder this food; they bought it in the bazaars of Calcutta, where my mother was born and to which we returned as a family every couple of years. The destination was Rhode Island, where we lived, and where, back in the Seventies, Indian groceries were next to impossible to come by.

Our treasure chest, something we called the Food Suitcase, was an elegant relic from the Fifties with white stitching and brass latches that fastened shut with satisfying clicks. The inside was lined in peach-colored satin, had shirred lingerie pockets on three sides and was large enough to house a wardrobe for a long journey. Leave it to my parents to convert a vintage portmanteau into a portable pantry. They bought it one Saturday morning at a yard sale in the neighborhood, and I think it's safe to say that it had never been to India before.

Trips to Calcutta let my parents eat again, eat the food of their childhood, the food they had been deprived of as adults. As soon as he hit Indian soil, my father began devouring two or three yellow-skinned mangoes a day, sucking the pits lovingly smooth. My mother breakfasted shamelessly on sticky orange sweets called *jelebis*. It was easy to succumb. I insisted on accompanying each of my meals with the yogurt sold at confectioners in red clay cups, their lids made of paper, and my sister formed an addiction to *Moghlai parathas*, flatbread folded, omelet-style, over mincemeat and egg.

As the end of each visit neared, our focus shifted from eating to shopping. My parents created lists on endless sheets of paper, and my father spent days in the bazaars, haggling and buying by the kilo. He always insisted on packing the goods himself, with the aura of a man possessed: bare-chested, seated cross-legged on the floor, determined, above all, to make everything fit. He bound the Food Suitcase with enough rope to baffle Houdini and locked it up with a little padlock, a scheme that succeeded in intimidating the most assiduous customs inspectors. Into the suitcase went an arsenal of lentils and every conceivable spice, wrapped in layers of cloth ripped from an old sari and stitched into individual packets. In went white poppy seeds, and resin made from date syrup, and as many tins of Ganesh mustard oil as possible. In went Lapchu tea, to be brewed only on special occasions, and sacks of black-skinned Gobindovog rice, so named, it is said, because it's fit for offering to the god Govinda. In went six kinds of *dalmoot,* a salty, crunchy snack mix bought from big glass jars in a tiny store at the corner of Vivekananda Road and Cornwallis Street. In, on occasion, went something fresh, and therefore flagrantly illegal: a bumpy, bright green bitter melon, or bay leaves from my uncle's garden. My parents weren't the only ones willing to flout the law. One year my grandmother secretly tucked *parvals,* a vaguely squashlike vegetable, into the Food Suitcase. My mother wept when she found them.

My parents also bought utensils: bowl-shaped iron *karhais,* which my mother still prefers to ordinary pots and pans, and the areca-nut cracker that's now somewhere in the back of the silverware drawer, and even a *boti,* a large curved blade that sits on the floor in Bengali kitchens and is used instead of handheld knives. The most sensational gadget we ever transported was a *sil-nora,* an ancient food processor of sorts, which consists of a massive clublike pestle and a slab the size, shape and weight of a headstone. Bewildered relatives shook their heads, and airport workers in both hemispheres must have cursed us. For a while my mother actually used it, pounding garlic cloves by hand instead of pressing a button on the Osterizer. Then it turned into a decorative device, propped up on the kitchen counter. It's in the basement now.

The suitcase was full during the trip from Rhode Island to Calcutta too, with gifts for family. People there seldom asked for any food from America: instead they requested the stuff of duty-free, Dunhills or Johnnie Walker. We brought them Corning Ware plates and bowls, which, in their eyes, were exotic alternatives to the broad, gleaming stainless steel dishes they normally used. The only food we packed for ourselves was a big jar of Tang, which my father carried with him at all times and stirred obsessively into the bitter purified water.

In spite of everything we managed to haul back, the first meal we ate after returning from India was always a modest affair. My mother prepared the simplest of things: rice, some quartered potatoes, eggs if she was motivated, all boiled together in a single pot. That first meal was never an occasion to celebrate but rather to mourn, for the people and the city we had, once again, left behind. And so my mother made food to mirror our mood, food for the weary and melancholy. I remember thinking how strangely foreign our own kitchen felt that first night back, with its giant, matching appliances, water we could safely drink straight from the tap and rice which bore no stray stones. Just before we ate, my mother would ask my father to untie the ropes and unlock the suitcase. A few pappadams quickly fried and a drop of mustard oil drizzled over the potatoes would convert our survivalist meal into a delicacy. It was enough, that first lonely evening, not only to satisfy our hunger but to make Calcutta seem not so very far away.

My parents returned last August from their thirteenth visit to India in their thirty-odd years abroad. When I asked my mother what foods they'd brought back she replied, with some sadness. "Nothing, really" My father observed matter-of-factly that most everything was sold here these days. It's true. Saffron and cardamom grace supermarket shelves, even in the small towns of Rhode Island. The world, the culinary world in particular, has shrunk considerably. Still, when my cousin's mother recently visited New York City, she packed several pieces of fried *ruhi,* the everyday fish of Bengal, into her bags. Of course, the Indian markets of Jackson Heights, Queens, were only a subway ride away, but the fish had been sliced, salted and fried in Calcutta. This was what mattered.

Today the Food Suitcase sits in our basement, neglected, smelling of cumin. When I opened it on my last trip home, a few stray lentils rolled around in one corner. Yet the signs were still visible, in the cupboards and the refrigerator, that my parents have not abandoned their pirating ways. You would know as much, were you to visit them yourself, by the six kinds of *dalmoot* my mother would set out with tea and the mustard oil she would offer to drizzle on your potatoes at dinner.

❧ PART THREE ❧

Hunger Games

The Delight and Dread of Eating

INTRODUCTION

"**I** HAVE EATEN / the plums / that were in / the icebox," confesses William Carlos Williams in one of the twentieth century's most influential verses, explaining "they were . . . / so sweet / and so cold." The poem's fame derives in large part from its apparent prosiness and casualness: it takes the form of a late night note written by an erring husband to his provident wife. But its intensity comes, too, from its focus on the delight of eating, the deliciousness of the "so sweet and so cold" stolen fruit. As such a celebration of gustatory pleasure, this tiny text can serve as a model for countless other works produced over centuries of literary wining and dining. In this section of our anthology alone we encounter not just William's plums but Seamus Heaney's oysters that taste of "the salty Pleiades," along with Julia Child's famously life-altering *sole meunière*, Walter Benjamin's seductive figs, Robert Capon's mystical onion, and even, more obscurely, the great avant-garde writer Gertrude Stein's enigmatic "Apple plum, carpet steak, seed clam."

Like Proust's madeleine, these delicacies contain and sustain history, both personal (the *sole meunière*) and public (the oysters) while also embodying the variousness and strangeness of the cosmos itself (the onion). At the same time, in their lusciousness they hint at a danger always implicit in appetite: excess. Benjamin's feelings of "satiety and revulsion" after gobbling half a pound of figs point to the perils of gluttony, omnipresent at the laden table. (For other examples of this problem, from the perspective not of the diner but of the observer, see our selections from Petronius, Rabelais, and Douglass, in Part I.) More radical, and perverse, feelings of revulsion mark the practices of anorexics and bulimics, most often young women who try to control their weight through extreme dieting or even (as in the case of the late Princess Diana) by inducing vomiting or using laxatives.

But the psychological conditions of anorexia and bulimia aren't the only manifestations of gastronomic revulsion. Cross-culturally, as we've seen in Part I, food taboos are almost universal. In our society, we don't generally braise Fido the pup or Felix the cat, as Francine Prose points out, nor do we find the eating of rats, as engaged in by the Chinese and explored by Peter Hessler, in the least appetizing. And as Jeffrey Steingarten notes, we all harbor our own, private food aversions; he writes winningly of how, in order to become a restaurant critic, he had to battle his personal distaste for anchovies, Greek cuisine, and a range of other delicacies. At the same time, and more paradoxically, the very taboo nature of certain foods may give them a culinary glamour that transforms them from poisonous to precious, banned to beloved. Consider, after all, the simultaneously repellent and compelling sea urchin about which Chang-rae Lee writes so elegantly. Or think of the illegal ortolans on whom François Mitterand, the late president of France, feasted for his last earthly meal, or, for that matter, the prized fugu, a potentially deadly fish prepared by skilled chefs at popular restaurants throughout Japan: Michael Paterniti narrates the bizarre story of the ortolan, and Diane Ackerman the (sometimes literally) unnerving tale of the fugu.

In the midst of this often problematic plenty, though, we shouldn't forget that even while voluptuaries indulge at table to the point of indigestion or worse, there are 870 million people worldwide (or one out of every eight) who go hungry every day, and in the United States alone nearly 50 million people (or one out of six) are what is called "food insecure." Campbell McGrath brings us up to date on one sad way that some contemporary Americans appease their hunger—on a steady diet of burritos and Slurpees, at the 7-Eleven. But one of the most severe episodes of starvation in recent history killed countless inmates of the horrifying concentration camps built by the Nazis during the Second World War, and among many prisoners such extreme hunger gave rise to culinary memories and visions of the sort recorded by some women at Theresienstadt and later published in a collection edited by Cara de Silva. We include portions of her introduction to *At Memory's Table* to help dramatize their story, along with one of the centerpiece recipes from the book, Wilhelmina Pächter's almost surrealistically appetizing and extravagant "Cold Stuffed Eggs Pächter," scribbled on a scrap of paper in a cell from which she would only escape through death. Her poignant exclamation—"Let fantasy run free!"—should remind us that even in the most dreadful circumstances, human beings keep on thinking and writing about food.

※

Gertrude Stein (1874–1946)

RAISED IN OAKLAND, California (of which she famously remarked "There's no there there"), Stein settled in Paris as a young woman, living first with her brother Leo and then with her life partner Alice B. Toklas. Her dazzling art collection and brilliant salons at the rue de Fleurus soon made her one of the most famous and influential American expatriates. Always defining herself as a genius, she experimented with radical modes of writing. Though her first book, *Three Lives*, was relatively conventional, as was her best-selling *Autobiography of Alice B. Toklas*, her *Tender Buttons*, from which our selections are drawn, is playful, punning, and enigmatic, but curiously focused on food, with pieces that make it seem almost like a daily menu ("Milk," "Eggs," "Apple," "Roast Beef," "Asparagus") or, as the critic Susan Gubar has put it, like "a mad Mrs. Beeton's." Serendipitously, Stein and Toklas summered for many years in Bilignin par Belley, the hometown of the great gastronome Brillat-Savarin, and, confided Toklas, "enjoyed using the furniture from his house."

from *Tender Buttons*

MILK

A WHITE egg and a colored pan and a cabbage showing settlement, a constant increase.

A cold in a nose, a single cold nose makes an excuse. Two are more necessary.

All the goods are stolen, all the blisters are in the cup.

Cooking, cooking is the recognition between sudden and nearly sudden very little and all large holes.

A real pint, one that is open and closed and in the middle is so bad.

Tender colds, seen eye holders, all work, the best of change, the meaning, the dark red, all this and bitten, really bitten.

Guessing again and golfing again and the best men, the very best men.

APPLE

APPLE plum, carpet steak, seed clam, colored wine, calm seen, cold cream, best shake, potato, potato and no no gold work with pet, a green seen is called bake and change sweet is bready, a little piece please.

A little piece please. Cane again to the presupposed and ready eucalyptus tree, count out sherry and ripe plates and little corners of a kind of ham. This is use.

❧

Wallace Stevens (1879–1955)

A MAJOR AMERICAN modernist, the winner of a Pulitzer Prize, the Bollingen Prize for Poetry, and the National Book Award, Stevens was a lawyer for a Hartford insurance company who wrote verse in his spare time.

His poetry is known for its sensuous surface and its highly aestheticized perspective on human experience. Stevens often seems like a connoisseur perceiving elegance in the world around us, even as he writes poetic meditations on seemingly abstract subjects, such as the status of the imagination and the nature of beauty. In his enigmatic "The Emperor of Ice-Cream" a down-home ice cream social appears to take place at a woman's funeral, as if the worldly pleasure of the dessert were a momentary compensation for death. The muscular roller of cigars, who whips up the "concupiscent curds" of ice cream, becomes an impresario of sweetness and hedonism in the face of inevitable decay.

The Emperor of Ice-Cream

Call the roller of big cigars,
The muscular one, and bid him whip
In kitchen cups concupiscent curds.
Let the wenches dawdle in such dress
As they are used to wear, and let the boys
Bring flowers in last month's newspapers.
Let be be finale of seem.
The only emperor is the emperor of ice-cream.

Take from the dresser of deal
Lacking the three glass knobs, that sheet
On which she embroidered fantails once
And spread it so as to cover her face.
If her horny feet protrude, they come
To show how cold she is, and dumb.
Let the lamp affix its beam.
The only emperor is the emperor of ice-cream.

William Carlos Williams (1883–1963)

A LIFELONG RESIDENT of New Jersey and family physician, Williams was also a major modernist poet, experimenting with imagist techniques and innovative prosody. "No ideas but in things," he proclaimed early and often in his career, emphasizing his commitment to specific details and to realistic, sometimes interestingly photographic representations of the quotidian American life that fascinated him. "The pure products of America go crazy," he wrote in one poem, but in another he celebrated the shine of raindrops on a red wheelbarrow. His influential conversational verse "This Is Just To Say" presents itself as (and may really have been) a midnight note scrawled to his young wife Flossie. Yet because of its simplicity of diction and its careful line breaks it has been widely acclaimed and often studied. The plums in the icebox, wrote Williams wistfully, are "so sweet / and so cold"—a line that evokes both the joy and the sorrow of delicious fruit even while it modestly describes a midnight snack.

This Is Just To Say

I have eaten
the plums
that were in
the icebox

and which
you were probably
saving
for breakfast

Forgive me
they were delicious
so sweet
and so cold

Walter Benjamin (1892–1940)

ONE OF THE great political and social philosophers of the twentieth century, Benjamin was associated with the Frankfurt School in Germany which set forth Marxist theories of literature, society, and culture. A major influence on such important thinkers as the playwright Berthold Brecht, the composer Kurt Weill, and the philosopher Theodor Adorno, Benjamin would seem an unlikely person to be writing on food. But like the French philosopher-theorist Roland Barthes, who also wrote occasional culinary essays, Benjamin saw food as an index of culture. For him each item of food yields lessons in human happiness, despair, and sorrow. As Benjamin regards the subject, culinary illuminations are often as powerful as philosophical revelations.

from *Eating*

FRESH FIGS

No one who has never eaten a food to excess has ever really experienced it, or fully exposed himself to it. Unless you do this, you at best enjoy it, but never come to lust after it, or make the acquaintance of that diversion from the straight and narrow road of the appetite which leads to the primeval forest of greed. For in gluttony two things coincide: the boundlessness of desire and the uniformity of the food that sates it. Gourmandizing means above all else to devour one thing to the last crumb. There is no doubt that it enters more deeply into what you eat than mere enjoyment. For example, when you bite into mortadella as if it were bread, or bury your face in a melon as if it were a pillow, or gorge yourself on caviar out of crackling paper, or, when confronted with the sight of a round Edam cheese, find that the existence of every other food simply vanishes from your mind.—How did I first learn all this? It happened just before I had to make a very difficult decision. A letter had to be posted or torn up. I had carried it around in my pocket for two days, but had not given it a thought for some hours. I then took the noisy narrow-gauge railway up to Secondigliano through the sun-parched landscape. The village lay in still solemnity in the weekday peace and quiet. The only traces of the excitement of the previous Sunday were the poles on which Catherine wheels and rockets had been ignited. Now they stood there bare. Some of them still displayed a sign halfway up with the figure of a saint from Naples or an animal. Women sat in the open barns husking corn. I was walking along in a daze, when I noticed a cart with figs standing in the shade. It was sheer idleness that made me go up to them, sheer extravagance that I bought half a pound for a few soldi. The woman gave me a generous measure. But when the black, blue, bright green, violet, and brown fruit lay in the bowl of the scales, it turned out that she had no paper to wrap them in. The housewives of Secondigliano bring their baskets with them, and she was unprepared for globetrotters. For my part, I was ashamed to abandon the fruit. So I left her with figs stuffed in my trouser pockets and in my jacket, figs in both of my outstretched hands, and figs in my mouth. I couldn't stop eating them and was forced to get rid of the mass of plump fruits as quickly as possible. But that could not be described as eating; it was more like a bath, so powerful was the smell of resin that penetrated all my belongings, clung to my hands and impregnated the air through which I carried my burden. And then, after satiety and revulsion—the final bends in the path—had been surmounted, came the ultimate mountain peak of taste. A vista over an unsuspected landscape of the palate spread out before my eyes—an insipid, undifferentiated, greenish flood of greed that could distinguish nothing but the stringy, fibrous waves of the flesh of the open fruit, the utter transformation of enjoyment into habit, of habit into vice. A hatred of those figs welled up inside me; I was desperate to finish with them, to liberate myself, to rid myself of all this overripe, bursting fruit. I ate it to destroy it. Biting had rediscovered its most ancient purpose. When I pulled the last fig from the depths of my pocket, the letter was stuck to it. Its fate was sealed; it, too, had to succumb to the great purification. I took it and tore it into a thousand pieces.

BORSCHT

IT starts by spreading a mask of steam over your features. Long before your tongue touches the spoon, your eyes have started to water and your nose is dripping with borscht. Long before your insides have gone on the alert and your blood has become a single wave that courses through your body with the foaming aroma, your eyes have drunk in the red abundance in your bowl. They are now blind to everything that is not borscht, or its reflection in the eyes of your table companion. It's sour cream, you think, that gives this soup its rich texture. Perhaps. But I have eaten it in the Moscow winter, and I know one thing: it contains snow, molten red flakes, food from the clouds that is akin to the manna that also fell from the sky one day. And doesn't the warm flow soften the pieces of meat, so that it lies inside you like a ploughed field from which you can easily dig up the weed Sadness by the root? Just leave the vodka next to it, untouched; do not start to cut up the piroshkis. It is then that you will discover the secret of the soup that alone among foods has the ability to satisfy you gently. It gradually pervades you entirely, while with other foods a sudden cry of "Enough!" abruptly causes a shudder to pass through your entire body.

PRANZO CAPRESE

SHE had been the Capri village cocotte, and was now the sixty-year-old mother of little Gennaro, whom she beat when she was drunk. She lived in the ocher-colored house in a vineyard on the steep mountainside. I came looking for my girlfriend, to whom she was renting the house. From Capri came the sound of the clock striking twelve. There was no one to be seen; the garden was empty. I reclimbed the steps I had just come down. Suddenly I could hear the old woman close behind me. She stood in the kitchen door-way dressed in a skirt and blouse, discolored items of clothing which you'd have searched in vain for any stains, so evenly, so uniformly was the dirt spread over them. "Voi cercate la signora. E partita colla piccola." And she was due back shortly. But this was just the start: it was followed by a flood of inviting words uttered in her shrill, high-pitched voice, accompanied by rhythmic movements of her imperious head, which decades previously must have had provocative power. I would have had to be an accomplished gentle-man to decline her offer, and I was not even able to express myself in Italian. So much was comprehensible: it was an invitation to share her midday meal. I now caught sight of her wretched husband inside the cottage, taking some-thing out of a dish with a spoon. She now went up to this dish. Immediately afterward, she reappeared in the doorway with a plate, which she held out to me without interrupting her flow of speech. I found myself bereft of the remnants of my ability to understand Italian. I felt instantly that it was too late for me to take my leave. From amid a cloud of garlic, beans, mutton fat, tomatoes, and onions, there appeared the domineering hand from which I took a tin spoon. I am sure you are thinking that I would have choked on this nauseating swill and that my sole thought would be to vomit it all up again as quickly as possible. How little you would understand of the magic of this food, and how little I understood it myself up to the moment I am describing now. To taste it was of no importance. It was nothing but the decisive yet imperceptible transition between two moments: first between the moment of smelling it, and then of being overwhelmed, utterly bowled over and kneaded, by this food, gripped by it, as if by the hands of the old whore, squeezed, and having the juice rubbed into me—whether the juice of the food or of the woman, I am no longer able to say. The obligation of politeness was satisfied and so was the witch's desire, and I went on up the mountain enriched by the knowledge of Odysseus when he saw his companions transformed into swine.

Ernest Hemingway (1899–1961)

HEMINGWAY WON THE Nobel Prize in 1954 for his novels and short stories, which are among the most important in the history of American literature. But one of his most beloved works is *A Moveable Feast*, the nonfiction account of his life in Paris as a young expatriate writer in the 1920s, including his friendship with such luminaries as Ezra Pound, F. Scott Fitzgerald, and Gertrude Stein. Among the highlights of the work are Hemingway's descriptions of the bars, cafés, and restaurants he frequented, places for long hours of scribbling as well as for eating and drinking. But this author's passionate allegiance to what he called "the romance of food" can be traced back to his earliest writings, like the article we include here, produced for the *Toronto Star* where he worked in his twenties. To readers of other early

Hemingway writings—notably the Nick Adams stories, especially "Big Two-Hearted River"—the hunger for simple camping-out fare so central here will be very familiar.

When You Camp Out, Do It Right

THOUSANDS OF PEOPLE will go into the bush this summer to cut the high cost of living. A man who gets his two weeks' salary while he is on vacation should be able to put those two weeks in fishing and camping and be able to save one week's salary clear. He ought to be able to sleep comfortably every night, to eat well every day, and to return to the city rested and in good condition.

But if he goes into the woods with a frying pan, an ignorance of black flies and mosquitoes, and a great and abiding lack of knowledge about cookery, the chances are that his return will be very different. He will come back with enough mosquito bites to make the back of his neck look like a relief map of the Caucasus. His digestion will be wrecked after a valiant battle to assimilate half-cooked or charred grub. And he won't have had a decent night's sleep while he has been gone.

He will solemnly raise his right hand and inform you that he has joined the grand army of never-agains. The call of the wild may be all right, but it's a dog's life. He's heard the call of the tame with both ears. Waiter, bring him an order of milk toast.

In the first place, he overlooked the insects. Black flies, no-see-ums, deer flies, gnats, and mosquitoes were instituted by the devil to force people to live in cities where he could get at them better. If it weren't for them, everybody would live in the bush, and he would be out of work. It was a rather successful invention.

But there are lots of dopes that will counteract the pests. The simplest perhaps is oil of citronella. Two bits' worth of this oil purchased at any pharmacist's will be enough to last for two weeks in the worst fly- and mosquito-ridden country. Rub a little on the back of your neck, your forehead, and your wrists before you start fishing, and the blacks and skeeters will shun you. The odor of citronella is not offensive to people. It smells like gun oil. But the bugs do hate it.

Oil of pennyroyal and eucalyptol are also much hated by mosquitoes, and with citronella they form the basis for many proprietary preparations. But it is cheaper and better to buy the straight citronella. Put a little on the mosquito netting that covers the front of your pup tent or canoe tent at night, and you won't be bothered.

To be really rested and get any benefit out of a vacation, a man must get a good night's sleep every night. The first requisite for this is to have plenty of cover. It is twice as cold as you expect it will be in the bush four nights out of five, and a good plan is to take just double the bedding that you think you will need. An old quilt that you can wrap up in is as warm as two blankets.

Nearly all outdoor writers rhapsodize over the browse bed. It is all right for the man who knows how to make one and has plenty of time. But in a succession of one-night camps on a canoe trip, all you need is level ground for your tent floor, and you will sleep all right if you have plenty of covers under you. Take twice as much cover as you think that you will need, and then put two-thirds of it under you. You will sleep warm and get your rest.

When it is clear weather, you don't need to pitch your tent if you are only stopping for the night. Drive four stakes at the head of your made-up bed, and drape your mosquito bar over that; then you can sleep like a log and laugh at the mosquitoes.

Outside of insects and bum sleeping, the rock that wrecks most camping trips is cooking. The average tyro's idea of cooking is to fry everything and fry it good and plenty. Now, a frying pan is a most necessary thing to any trip, but you also need the old stew kettle and the folding reflector baker.

A pan of fried trout can't be bettered, and they don't cost any more than ever. But there is a good and a bad way of frying them. The beginner puts his trout and his bacon in and over a brightly burning fire; the bacon curls up and dries into a dry tasteless cinder, and the trout is burned outside while it is still raw inside. He eats them, and it is all right if he is only out for the day and going home to a good meal at night. But if he is going to face more trout and bacon the next morning and other equally well-cooked dishes for the remainder of two weeks, he is on the pathway to nervous dyspepsia.

The proper way to cook is over coals. Have several cans of Crisco or Cotosuet or one of the vegetable shortenings along that are as good as lard and excellent for all kinds of shortening. Put the bacon in and when it is about half-cooked, lay the trout in the hot grease, dipping them in cornmeal first. Then put the bacon on top of the trout, and it will baste the fish as they slowly cook.

The coffee can be boiling at the same time, and in a smaller skillet, pancakes being made that are satisfying the other campers while they are waiting for the trout. With the prepared pancake flours, you take a cupful of pancake flour and add a cup of water. Mix the water and flour, and as soon as the lumps are out, the batter is ready for cooking. Have the skillet hot, and keep it well greased. Drop the batter in, and as soon as it is done on one side, loosen it in the skillet and flip it over. Apple butter, syrup, or cinnamon and sugar go well with the cakes.

While the crowd has taken the edge from its appetite with flapjacks, the trout have been cooked, and they and the bacon are ready to serve. The trout are crisp outside and firm and pink inside, and the bacon is well done—but not too done. If there is anything better than that combination, the writer has yet to taste it in a lifetime devoted largely and studiously to eating.

The stew kettle will cook your dried apricots when they have resumed their pre-dried plumpness after a night of soaking; it will serve to concoct a mulligan in, and it will cook macaroni. When you are not using it, it should be boiling water for the dishes.

In the baker, mere man comes into his own, for he can make a pie that to his bush appetite will have it all over the product that Mother used to make. Men have always believed that there was something mysterious and difficult about making a pie. Here is a great secret. There is nothing to it. We've been kidded for years. Any man of average office intelligence can make at least as good a pie as his wife can.

All there is to a pie is a cup and a half of flour, one-half teaspoonful of salt, one-half cup of lard, and cold water. That combination will make pie crust that will bring tears of joy into your camping partners' eyes. Mix the salt with the flour; work the lard into the flour, and make it up into a good workmanlike dough with cold water. Spread some flour on the back of a box or something flat, and pat the dough around a while. Then roll it out with whatever kind of round bottle you prefer. Put a little more lard on the surface of the sheet of dough, and then slosh a little flour and roll it up. Then roll it out again with the bottle.

Cut out a piece of the rolled-out dough big enough to line a pie tin. I like the kind with holes in the bottom. Then put in your dried apples that have soaked all night and been sweetened, or your apricots, or your blueberries, and then take another sheet of the dough, and drape it gracefully over the top, soldering it down at the edges with your fingers. Cut a couple of slits in the top dough sheet, and prick it a few times with a fork in an artistic manner.

Put it in the baker with a good slow fire for forty-five minutes, and then take it out. If your pals are Frenchmen, they will kiss you. The penalty for knowing how to cook is that the others will make you do all the cooking.

It is all right to talk about roughing it in the woods. But the real woodsman is the man who can be really comfortable in the bush.

❦

Julia Child (1912–2004)

ONE OF THE most important American cookbook writers and food personalities, Child revolutionized the way American women regarded French cuisine with her enormously influential, coauthored work, *Mastering the Art of French Cooking*. She helped demystify the subject with her detailed, lucid, step-by-step instructions, and she followed the book with a highly successful TV cooking show, *The French Chef*. Eventually, the tall, singsongy-voiced Child became a beloved presence and such an icon that after her death her Cambridge, Massachusetts, kitchen was removed in its entirety to the Smithsonian National Museum of American History. Probably no other figure in the American food world has been so revered and lauded. But this brilliant Francophile knew little or nothing about French cuisine until her thirties, and this selection shows her ecstatic introduction to that food via one of its great dishes, *sole meunière*. It is charming to read her saying, at her first meal in France, "What's a shallot?" Well, we all have to start somewhere.

from *My Life in France*: Sole Meunière

THE NORMAN COUNTRYSIDE struck me as quintessentially French, in an indefinable way. The real sights and sounds and smells of this place were so much more particular and interesting than a movie montage or a magazine spread about "France" could ever be. Each little town had a distinct character, though some of them, like Yvetot, were still scarred by gaping bomb holes and knots of barbed wire. We saw hardly any other cars, but there were hundreds of bicyclists, old men driving horses-and-buggies, ladies dressed in black, and little boys in wooden shoes. The telephone poles were of a different size and shape from those in America. The fields were intensely cultivated. There were no billboards. And the occasional pink-and-white stucco villa set at the end of a formal *allée* of trees was both silly and charming. Quite unexpectedly, something about the earthy-smoky smells, the curve of the landscape, and the bright greenness of the cabbage fields reminded us both of China.

Oh, *la belle France*—without knowing it, I was already falling in love!

AT twelve-thirty we flashed into Rouen. We passed the city's ancient and beautiful clock tower, and then its famous cathedral, still pockmarked from battle but magnificent with its stained-glass windows. We rolled to a stop in la Place du Vieux Marché, the square where Joan of Arc had met her fiery fate. There the *Guide Michelin* directed us to Restaurant La Couronne ("The Crown"), which had been built in 1345 in a medieval quarter-timbered house. Paul strode ahead, full of anticipation, but I hung back, concerned that I didn't look chic enough, that I wouldn't be able to communicate, and that the waiters would look down their long Gallic noses at us Yankee tourists.

It was warm inside, and the dining room was a comfortably old-fashioned brown-and-white space, neither humble nor luxurious. At the far end was an enormous fireplace with a rotary spit, on which something was cooking that sent out heavenly aromas. We were greeted by the maître d'hôtel, a slim middle-aged man with dark hair who carried himself with an air of gentle seriousness. Paul spoke to him, and the maître d' smiled and said something back in a familiar way, as if they were old friends. Then he led us to a nice table not far from the fireplace. The other customers were all French, and I noticed that they were treated with exactly the same courtesy as we were. Nobody rolled their eyes at us or stuck their nose in the air. Actually, the staff seemed happy to see us.

As we sat down, I heard two businessmen in gray suits at the next table asking questions of their waiter, an older, dignified man who gesticulated with a menu and answered them at length.

"What are they talking about?" I whispered to Paul.

"The waiter is telling them about the chicken they ordered," he whispered back. "How it was raised, how it will be cooked, what side dishes they can have with it, and which wines would go with it best."

"*Wine?*" I said. "At *lunch?*" I had never drunk much wine other than some $1.19 California Burgundy, and certainly not in the middle of the day.

In France, Paul explained, good cooking was regarded as a combination of national sport and high art, and wine was always served with lunch and dinner. "The trick is moderation," he said.

Suddenly the dining room filled with wonderfully intermixing aromas that I sort of recognized but couldn't name. The first smell was something oniony—"shallots," Paul identified it, "being sautéed in fresh butter." ("What's a shallot?" I asked, sheepishly. "You'll see," he said.) Then came a warm and winy fragrance from the kitchen, which was probably a delicious sauce being reduced on the stove. This was followed by a whiff of something astringent: the salad being tossed in a big ceramic bowl with lemon, wine vinegar, olive oil, and a few shakes of salt and pepper.

My stomach gurgled with hunger.

I couldn't help noticing that the waiters carried themselves with a quiet joy, as if their entire mission in life was to make their customers feel comfortable and well tended. One of them glided up to my elbow. Glancing at the menu, Paul asked him questions in rapid-fire French. The waiter seemed to enjoy the back-and-forth with my husband. Oh, how I itched to be in on their conversation! Instead, I smiled and nodded uncomprehendingly, although I tried to absorb all that was going on around me.

We began our lunch with a half-dozen oysters on the half-shell. I was used to bland oysters from Washington and Massachusetts, which I had never cared much for. But this platter of *portugaises* had a sensational briny flavor and a smooth texture that was entirely new and surprising. The oysters were served with rounds of *pain de seigle*, a pale rye bread, with a spread of unsalted butter. Paul explained that, as with wine, the French have "crus" of butter, special regions that produce individually flavored butters. *Beurre de Charentes* is a full-bodied butter, usually recommended for pastry dough or general cooking; *beurre d'Isigny* is a fine, light table butter. It was that delicious *Isigny* that we spread on our rounds of rye.

Rouen is famous for its duck dishes, but after consulting the waiter Paul had decided to order *sole meunière*. It arrived whole: a large, flat Dover sole that was perfectly browned in a sputtering butter sauce with a sprinkling of chopped parsley on top. The waiter carefully placed the platter in front of us, stepped back, and said: "*Bon appétit!*"

I closed my eyes and inhaled the rising perfume. Then I lifted a forkful of fish to my mouth, took a bite, and chewed slowly. The flesh of the sole was delicate, with a light but distinct taste of the ocean that blended marvelously with the browned butter. I chewed slowly and swallowed. It was a morsel of perfection.

In Pasadena, we used to have broiled mackerel for Friday dinners, codfish balls with egg sauce, "boiled" (poached) salmon on the Fourth of July, and the occasional pan-fried trout when camping in the Sierras. But at La Couronne I experienced fish, and a dining experience, of a higher order than any I'd ever had before.

Along with our meal, we happily downed a whole bottle of Pouilly-Fumé, a wonderfully crisp white wine from the Loire Valley. Another revelation!

Then came *salade verte* laced with a lightly acidic vinaigrette. And I tasted my first real baguette—a crisp brown crust giving way to a slightly chewy, rather loosely textured pale-yellow interior, with a faint reminder of wheat and yeast in the odor and taste. Yum!

We followed our meal with a leisurely dessert of *fromage blanc*, and ended with a strong, dark *café filtre*. The waiter placed before us a cup topped with a metal canister, which contained coffee grounds and boiling water. With some urging by us impatient drinkers, the water eventually filtered down into the cup below. It was fun, and it provided a distinctive dark brew.

Paul paid the bill and chatted with the maître d', telling him how much he looked forward to going back to Paris for the first time in eighteen years. The maître d' smiled as he scribbled something on the back of a card. "*Tiens,*" he said, handing it to me. The Dorin family, who owned La Couronne, also owned a restaurant in Paris, called La Truite, he explained, while Paul translated. On the card he had scribbled a note of introduction for us.

"Mairci, monsoor," I said, with a flash of courage and an accent that sounded bad even to my own ear. The waiter nodded as if it were nothing, and moved off to greet some new customers.

Paul and I floated out the door into the brilliant sunshine and cool air. Our first lunch together in France had been absolute perfection. It was the most exciting meal of my life.

Robert Farrar Capon (1925–2013)

AN EPISCOPAL PRIEST and the author of twenty-seven books, most of them theological but some also memoiristic, Capon gained fame with the publication of his third volume, *The Supper of the Lamb*, from which we draw his lyrical and mystical meditation on the nature of the humble onion. In 1977, after a divorce of which his church superiors disapproved, Capon left the ministry to devote himself to full-time writing, but in his later years served again as a priest and a theologian while continuing to contribute columns on food and wine to *The New York Times* and *Newsday*. But as his discussion of the onion reveals, Capon's culinary writing is also itself religious. About his most celebrated book, the novelist and Christian commentator Frederick Buechner declared that merely "to call *The Supper of the Lamb* a cookbook would be like calling *Moby Dick* a whaling manual."

from *The Supper of the Lamb*: On the Onion

I MUST TEACH you first how to deal with onions.

Select three or four medium-size onions—I have in mind the common, or yellow, onion normally available in the supermarket. The first movement of my recipe is simply a stew; small white onions, while more delicate as a vegetable in their own right, are a nuisance to cut up for inclusion in something else. The labor of peeling is enlarged beyond reason, and the attempt to slice up the small slippery balls you are left with can be painful.

Next take one of the onions (preferably the best-looking), a paring knife, and a cutting board and sit down at the kitchen table. Do not attempt to stand at a counter through these opening measures. In fact, to do it justice, you should arrange to have sixty minutes or so free for this part of the exercise. Admittedly, spending an hour in the society of an onion may be something you have never done before. You feel, perhaps, a certain resistance to the project. Please don't. As I shall show later, a number of highly profitable members of the race have undertaken it before you. Onions are excellent company.

Once you are seated, the first order of business is to address yourself to the onion at hand. (You must firmly resist the temptation to feel silly. If necessary, close the doors so no one will see you; but do not give up out of embarrassment.) You will note, to begin with, that the onion is a *thing*, a being, just as you are. Savor that for a moment. The two of you sit here in mutual confrontation. Together with knife, board, table, and chair, you are the constituents of a *place* in the highest sense of the word. This is a Session, a meeting, a society of things.

You have, you see, already discovered something: The uniqueness, the *placiness*, of place derives not from abstractions like *location*, but from confrontations like man-onion. Erring theologians have strayed to their graves without learning what you have come upon. They have insisted, for example, that heaven is no place because it could not be defined in terms of spatial co-ordinates. They have written off man's eternal habitation as a "state of mind." But look what your onion has done for you: It has given you back the possibility of heaven as a place without encumbering you with the irrelevancy of location.

This meeting between the two of you could be moved to a thousand different latitudes and longitudes and still remain the *session* it started out to be. Indeed, by the motions of the earth, the solar systems, the galaxy, and the universe (if that can be defined), every place—every meeting of matter—becomes a kind of cosmic floating crap game: Location is accidental to its deepest meaning. What really matters is not where we are, but who-what real beings—are with us. In that sense, heaven, where we see God face to face through the risen flesh of Jesus, may well be the placiest of all places, as it is the most *gloriously* material of all meetings. Here, perhaps, we do indeed see only through a glass darkly; we mistake one of the earthly husks of place for the heart of its mattering.

But back to the onion itself. As nearly as possible now, try to look at it as if you had never seen an onion before. Try, in other words, to meet it on its own terms, not to dictate yours to it. You are convinced, of course, that you know what an onion is. You think perhaps that it is a brownish yellow vegetable, basically spherical in shape, composed of fundamentally similar layers. All such prejudices should be abandoned. It is what it is, and your work here is to find it out.

For a start, therefore, notice that your onion has two ends: a lower, now marked only by the blackish gray spot from which the root filaments descended into the earth; and an upper, which terminates (unless your onions are over the hill, or have begun to sprout because you store them under a leaky sink trap) in a withered peak of onion paper. Note once again what you have discovered: an onion is not a sphere in repose. It is a linear thing, a bloom of vectors thrusting upward from base to tip. Stand your onion, therefore, root end down upon the board and see it as the paradigm of life that it is—as one member of the vast living, gravity-defying troop that, across the face of the earth, moves light-and airward as long as the world lasts.

Only now have you the perspective needed to enter the onion itself. Begin with the outermost layer of paper, or onionskin. Be careful. In the ordinary processes of cooking, the outer skin of a sound onion is removed by peeling away the immediately underlying layers of flesh with it. It is a legitimate short cut; the working cook cannot afford the time it takes to loosen only the paper. Here, however, it is not time that matters, but the onion. Work gently then, lifting the skin with the point of your knife so as not to cut or puncture the flesh with it. It is harder than you may have thought. Old onion skins give up easily, but new ones can be stubborn.

Look now at the fall of stripped and flaked skin before you. It is dry. It is, all things considered, one of the driest things is the world. Not dusty dry like potatoes, but smoothly and thinly dry, suggesting not accidental dessication, not the withering due to age or external circumstance, but a fresh and essential dryness. Dryness as an achievement, not as a failure. Elegant dryness. Deliberate dryness. More than that, onion paper is, like the onion itself, directional, vectored, ribbed. (It will, oddly, split as easily across its striations as with them: Its grain has been reduced by dryness to a merely visual quality.) Best of all, though, it is of two colors: the outside, a brownish yellow of no particular brightness; but the inside a soft, burnished, coppery gold, ribbed—especially near the upper end—with an exquisiteness only hinted at on the outside. Accordingly, when you have removed all the paper, turn the fragments inside-up on the board. They are elegant company.

For with their understated display of wealth, they bring you to one of the oldest and most secret things of the world: the sight of what no one but you has ever seen. This quiet gold, and the subtly flattened sheen of greenish yellow white onion that now stands exposed, are virgin land. Like the incredible fit of twin almonds in a shell, they present themselves to you as the animals to Adam: as nameless till seen by man, to be met, known and christened into the city of being. They come as deputies of all the hiddennesses of the world, of all the silent competencies endlessly at work deep down things. And they come to *you*—to you as their priest and voice, for oblation by your heart's astonishment at their great glory.

Only now are you ready for the first cut. Holding the onion vertically, slice it cleanly in half right down the center line, and look at what you have done. You have opened the floodgates of being. First, as to the innards. The mental diagram of sphere within sphere is abolished immediately. *Structurally*, the onion is not a ball, but a nested set of fingers within fingers, each thrust up from the base through the center of the one before it. The outer digits are indeed swollen to roundness by the pressure of the inner, but their sphericity is incidental to the linear motion of flame inthrusting flame.

Next, the colors, The cross-section of each several flame follows a rule: On its inner edge it is white, on its outer, pigmented; the color varying from the palest greenish yellow in the middle flames, to more recognizable onion shades as you proceed outward. The centermost flames of all are frankly and startlingly green; it is they which will finally thrust upward into light. Thus the spectrum of the onion: green through white to green again, and ending all in the brown skin you have peeled away. Life inside death. The forces of being storming the walls of the void. Freshness in the face of the burning, oxidizing world which maderizes all life at last to the color of cut apples and old Sherry.

Next, pressure. Look at the cut surface: moisture. The incredible, utter wetness of onions, of course, you cannot know yet: This is only the first hinted pressing of juice. But the sea within all life has tipped its hand. You have cut open no inanimate thing, but a living tumescent being—a whole that is, as all life is, smaller, simpler than its parts; which holds, as all life does, the pieces of its being in compression. To prove it, try to fit the two halves of the onion back together. It cannot be done. The faces which began as two plane surfaces drawn by a straight blade are now mutually convex, and rock against each other. Put them together on one side and the opposite shows a gap of more than two minutes on a clock face.

Again, pressure. But now pressure toward you. The smell of onion, released by the flowing of its juices. Hardly a discovery, of course—even

the boor knows his onions to that degree. But pause still. Reflect how little
smell there is to a whole onion—how well the noble reek was contained till
now by the encompassing dryness. Reflect, too, how it is the humors and
sauces of being that give the world flavor, how all life came from the sea, and
how, without water, nothing can hold a soul. Reflect finally what a soul the
onion must have, if it boasts such juices. Your eyes will not yet have begun to
water, nor the membranes of your nose to recoil. The onion has only, if you
will, *whispered* to you. Yet you have not mistaken a syllable of its voice, not
strained after a single word. How will you stop your senses when it raises this
stage whisper to a shout?

Now, however, the two halves of the onion lie, cut face up, before you.
With the point of your paring knife, carefully remove the base, or bottom
(or heart) much as you would do to free the leaves of an artichoke or of a head
of lettuce. Take away only as much as will make it possible to lift out, one by
one, the several layers. Then gently pry them out in order, working from the
center to the outside. Arrange them in a line as you do, with matching parts
from the separate halves laid next to each other, making them ascend thus by
twos from the smallest green fingers, through white flames, up to the outer
shells which sit like paired Russian church spires.

Then look. The myth of sphericity is finally dead. The onion, as now displayed, is plainly all vectors, rissers and thrusts. *Tongues of fire.* But the pen-
tecost they mark is that of nature, not grace: the Spirit's first brooding on
the face of the waters. Lift one of the flames; feel its lightness and rigidity,
its crispness and strength. Make proof of its membranes. The inner: thin,
translucent, easily removed; the outer, however, thinner, almost transparent—and so tightly bonded to the flesh that it protests audibly against separation. (You will probably have to break the flesh to free even a small piece.)
The membranes, when in place, give the onion its fire, its sheen, soft within
and brighter without. But when they are removed, the flesh is revealed in a
new light. Given a minute to dry, it acquires a pale crystalline flatness like
nothing on earth. Eggshell is the only word for it; but by comparison to the
stripped flesh of an onion, an eggshell is only as delicate as poured concrete.

Set aside your broken flame now and pick up a fresh one. Clear a little
space on the board. Lay it down on its cut face and slice it lengthwise into
several strips. (You will want to tap it lightly with the edge of the knife first.
There is a hollow crisp sound to be gotten that way—something between a
tock and a *tunk*. It is the sound of health and youth, the audible response of

cellularity when it is properly addressed. Neither solid nor soft, it is the voice of life itself.)

Next take one of the slivers and press it. Here you will need firmness. If you have strong nails, use the back of the one on your middle finger; if not, steamroller the slice with a round pencil. Press and roll it until it yields all the water it will. You have reached the deepest revelation of all.

First, and obviously, the onion is now part of you. It will be for days. For the next two mornings at least, when you wash your hands and face, your meetings with it will be reconvened in more than memory. It has spoken a word with power, and even the echo is not in vain.

But, second, the onion itself is all but gone. The flesh, so crisp and solid, turns out to have been an aqueous house of cards. If you have done pressing well, the little scraps of membrane and cell wall are nearly nonexistent. The whole infolded nest of flames was a blaze of water, a burning bush grown from the soil of the primeval oceans. All life is from the sea.

And God said, Let the waters bring forth abundantly. . . . And God saw that it was good. This juice, this liquor, this rough-and-ready cordial, runs freely now on board and hands and knife. Salt, sweet, and yet so much itself as to speak for no other, it enters the city of being. What you have seen, to be sure, is only the smallest part of its singularity, the merest hint of the stunning act of being that it is, but it is enough perhaps to enable you to proceed, if not with safety, then with caution.

For somehow, beneath this gorgeous paradigm of unnecessary being, lies the Act by which it exists. You have just now reduced it to its parts, shivered it into echoes, and pressed it to a memory, but you have also caught the hint that a thing is more than the sum of all the insubstantialities that comprise it. Hopefully, you will never again argue that the solidities of the world are mere matters of accident, creatures of air and darkness, temporary and meaningless shapes out of nothing. Perhaps now you have seen at least dimly that the uniquenesses of creation are the result of continuous creative support, of effective regard by no mean lover. He likes onions, therefore they are. The fit, the colors, the smell, the tensions, the tastes, the textures, the lines, the shapes are a response, not to some forgotten decree that there may as well be onions as turnips, but to His present delight—His intimate and immediate joy in all you have seen, and in the thousand other wonders you do not even suspect. With Peter, the onion says, Lord, it is good for us to be here. Yes, says God. *Tov. Very* good.

Fair enough then. All life is from sea. It takes water to hold a soul. Living beings are full of juices.

But watch out.

&

Seamus Heaney (1939–2013)

THE WINNER OF the Nobel Prize for literature in 1995 and the unquestioned heir of that other great Irish Nobel Prize winner, William Butler Yeats, Heaney was born in Northern Ireland, the son of a farmer and cattle dealer, and throughout his career wrote incisively and poignantly of the "troubles" that characterized his native region: the battles between Protestant and Catholic, the oppression the British dealt to their Irish subjects, and the long history of such oppression, dating back to the Viking invasions centuries ago. But the soil of his country, its geography and topography, preoccupied Heaney as much as its history. In more than twenty volumes of verse and prose he dissected the roots of memory, elegy, and pastoral, dramatizing the life of his land and his time with urgent eloquence. A worldwide audience responded to his words with passion; his collections of poetry sold briskly and, in addition to the Nobel, he won countless prizes, professorships, and other honors. His passion for language becomes clear in our selection here, where as he contemplates the apparently ordinary act of eating oysters, he prays that the sea tang of these humble mollusks will "quicken" him into "verb, pure verb."

Oysters

> Our shells clacked on the plates.
> My tongue was a filling estuary,
> My palate hung with starlight:
> As I tasted the salty Pleiades
> Orion dipped his foot into the water.

Alive and violated
They lay on their beds of ice:
Bivalves: the split bulb
And philandering sigh of ocean.
Millions of them ripped and shucked and scattered.

We had driven to the coast
Through flowers and limestone
And there we were, toasting friendship,
Laying down a perfect memory
In the cool thatch and crockery.

Over the Alps, packed deep in hay and snow,
The Romans hauled their oysters south to Rome:
I saw damp panniers disgorge
The frond-lipped, brine-stung
Glut of privilege

And was angry that my trust could not repose
In the clear light, like poetry or freedom
Leaning in from the sea. I ate the day
Deliberately, that its tang
Might quicken me all into verb, pure verb.

Erica Jong (1942–)

THE FEMINIST NOVELIST Erica Jong gained renown from the best-selling *Fear of Flying*, an account of the adventures of one Isabella Wing in which she famously coined the phrase "zipless fuck." But before she produced this and numerous other works of fiction, Jong was a poet, whose first collection, *Fruits & Vegetables*, evocatively meditates on apples, bananas, carrots, borscht, and—as here—onions. The brio of this volume predicted the charisma that has marked her other writings. "If a woman wants to be a poet," she noted dryly in one of her early verses, "She must dwell in the house of the tomato."

from *Fruits & Vegetables*: "I Am Thinking of the Onion"

I AM THINKING of the onion again, with its two O mouths, like the gaping holes in nobody. Of the outer skin, pinkish brown, peeled to reveal a greenish sphere, bald as a dead planet, glib as glass, & an odor almost animal. I consider its ability to draw tears, its capacity for self-scrutiny, flaying itself away, layer on layer, in search of its heart which is simply another region of skin, but deeper & greener. I remember Peer Gynt: I consider its sometimes double heart. Then I think of despair when the onion searches its soul & finds only its various skins; & I think of the dried tuft of roots leading nowhere & the parched umbilicus, lopped off in the garden. Not self-righteous like the proletarian potato, nor a siren like the apple. No show-off like the banana. But a modest, self-effacing vegetable, questioning, introspective, peeling itself away, or merely radiating halos like lake ripples. I consider it the eternal outsider, the middle child, the sad analysand of the vegetable kingdom. Glorified only in France (otherwise silent sustainer of soups and stews), unloved for itself alone—no wonder it draws our tears! Then I think again how the outer peel resembles paper, how soul & skin merge into one, how each peeling strips bare a heart which in turn turns skin.

Jeffrey Steingarten (1942–)

ON THE WITTY jacket of Jeffrey Steingarten's The *Man Who Ate Everything* it appears as if a bite-sized hunk of the paper has been chewed out, exposing the cloth boards underneath. But in our selection from that work Steingarten confesses that in fact he once harbored unlikely food phobias he had to overcome in order to arrive at the promise of the book's title. Steingarten has been a food writer at *Vogue* for many years, writing for the women's fashion magazine on food both in and out of fashion. His essays are about cooking, food in traveling, ingredients and recipes, dietary fads, and even the science of gastronomy. An accomplished home cook, he writes as easily about frying potatoes in horse fat as he does about tasting the hand-massaged Japanese beef known as *wagyu*. The French government made him a Chevalier in the Order of Merit for his writing on French food, but Steingarten is equally adept at discoursing on the lowly hot dog, confirming that he is indeed a man who at least *aspires* to eat everything.

from *The Man Who Ate Everything*

STEP ONE was to compose an annotated list.

My Food Phobias

1. Foods I wouldn't touch even if I were starving on a desert island:

None, except maybe insects.   Many cultures find insects highly nutritious and love their crunchy texture. The pre-Hispanic Aztecs roasted worms in a variety of ways and made pressed caviar from mosquito eggs. This proves that no innate human programming keeps me from eating them, too. Objectively, I must look as foolish as those Kalahari Bushmen who face famine every few years because they refuse to eat three-quarters of the 223 animal species around them. I will deal with this phobia when I have polished off the easy ones.

2. Foods I wouldn't touch even if I were starving on a desert island until absolutely everything else runs out:

Kimchi, the national pickle of Korea.   Cabbage, ginger, garlic, and red peppers—I love them all, but not when they are fermented together for many months to become kimchi. Nearly forty-one million South Koreans eat kimchi three times a day. They say "kimchi" instead of "cheese" when someone is taking their picture. I say, "Hold the kimchi."

Anything featuring dill.   What could be more benign than dill?

Swordfish.   This is a favorite among the feed-to-succeed set, who like it grilled to the consistency of running shoes and believe it is good for them. A friend of mine eats swordfish five times a week and denies that he has any food phobias. Who's kidding whom? Returning obsessively to a few foods is the same as being phobic toward all the rest. This may explain the Comfort Food Craze. But the goal of the arts, culinary or otherwise, is not to increase our comfort. That is the goal of an easy chair.

During my own praline period, which lasted for three years, I would order any dessert on the menu containing caramelized hazelnuts and ignore the rest. I grew so obsessive that I almost missed out on the crème brûlée fixation, from which I forcibly wrenched myself only six months ago.

Anchovies.   I met my first anchovy on a pizza in 1962, and it was seven years before I mustered the courage to go near another. I am known to cross the street whenever I see an anchovy coming. Why would anybody consciously choose to eat a tiny, oil-soaked, leathery maroon strip of rank and briny flesh?

Lard.   The very word causes my throat to constrict and beads of sweat to appear on my forehead.

Desserts in Indian restaurants.   The taste and texture of face creams belong in the boudoir, not on the plate. See above.

Also: miso, mocha, chutney, raw sea urchins, and falafel (those hard, dry, fried little balls of ground chickpeas unaccountably enjoyed in Middle Eastern countries).

3. Foods I might eat if I were starving on a desert island but only if the refrigerator were filled with nothing but chutney, sea urchins, and falafel:

Greek food. I have always considered "Greek cuisine" an oxymoron. Nations are like people. Some are good at cooking while others have a talent for music or baseball or manufacturing memory chips. The Greeks are really good at both pre-Socratic philosophy and white statues. They have not been good cooks since the fifth century B.C., when Siracusa on Sicily was the gastronomic capital of the world. Typical of modern-day Greek cuisine are feta cheese and retsina wine. Any country that pickles its national cheese in brine and adulterates its national wine with pine pitch should order dinner at the local Chinese place and save its energies for other things. The British go to Greece just for the food, which says volumes to me. You would probably think twice before buying an Algerian or Russian television set. I thought for ten years before buying my last Greek meal.

Clams. I feel a mild horror about what goes on in the wet darkness between the shells of all bivalves, but clams are the only ones I dislike. Is it their rubbery consistency or their rank subterranean taste, or is the horror deeper than I know?

Blue food (not counting plums and berries). This may be a rational aversion, because I am fairly sure that God meant the color blue mainly for food that has gone bad.

Also: cranberries, kidneys, okra, millet, coffee ice cream, refried beans, and many forms of yogurt.

This had to stop.

STEP TWO was to immerse myself in the scientific literature on human food selection.

By design and by destiny, humans are omnivores. Our teeth and digestive systems are all-purpose and ready for anything. Our genes do not dictate what foods we should find tasty or repulsive. We come into the world with a yen for sweets (newborns can even distinguish among glucose, fructose, lactose, and sucrose) and a weak aversion to bitterness, and after four months develop a fondness for salt. Some people are born particularly sensitive to one taste or odor; others have trouble digesting milk sugar or wheat gluten. A tiny fraction of adults, between 1 and 2 percent, have true (and truly dangerous) food allergies. All human cultures consider fur, paper, and hair inappropriate as food.

And that's about it. Everything else is *learned*. Newborns are not repelled even by the sight and smell of putrefied meat crawling with maggots.

The nifty thing about being omnivores is that we can take nourishment from an endless variety of flora and fauna and easily adapt to a changing world—crop failures, droughts, herd migrations, restaurant closings, and the like. Lions and tigers will starve in a salad bar, as will cows in a steak house, but not us. Unlike cows, who remain well nourished eating only grass, humans *need* a great diversity of foods to stay healthy.

Yet by the age of twelve, we all suffer from a haphazard collection of food aversions ranging from revulsion to indifference. The tricky part about being omnivores is that we are always in danger of poisoning ourselves. Catfish have taste buds on their whiskers, but we are not so lucky. Instead, we are born with a cautious ambivalence toward novel foods, a precarious balance between neophilia and neophobia. Just one bad stomach ache or attack of nausea after dinner is enough to form a potent aversion—even if the food we ate did not actually cause the problem and even if we know it didn't. Hives or rashes may lead us rationally to avoid the food that caused them, but only an upset stomach and nausea will result in a lasting, irrational, lifelong sense of disgust. Otherwise, psychologists know very little about the host of powerful likes and dislikes—let us lump them all under the term "food phobias"—that children carry into adulthood.

By closing ourselves off from the bounties of nature, we become failed omnivores. We let down the omnivore team. God tells us in the Book of Genesis, right after Noah's flood, to eat everything under the sun. Those who ignore his instructions are no better than godless heathens.

The more I contemplated food phobias, the more I became convinced that people who habitually avoid certifiably delicious foods are at least as troubled as people who avoid sex, or take no pleasure from it, except that the latter will probably seek psychiatric help, while food phobics rationalize their problem in the name of genetic inheritance, allergy, vegetarianism, matters of taste, nutrition, food safety, obesity, or a sensitive nature. The varieties of neurotic food avoidance would fill several volumes, but milk is a good place to start.

Overnight, everybody you meet has become lactose intolerant. It is the chic food fear of the moment. But the truth is that very, very few of us are so seriously afflicted that we cannot drink even a whole glass of milk a day without ill effects. I know several people who have given up cheese to avoid lactose. But fermented cheeses contain no lactose! Lactose is the sugar found in milk; 98 percent of it is drained off with the whey (cheese is made from the curds), and the other 2 percent is quickly consumed by lactic-acid bacteria in the act of fermentation.

Three more examples: People rid their diet of salt (and their food of flavor) to avoid high blood pressure and countless imagined ills. But no more than 8 percent of the population is sensitive to salt. Only *saturated* fat, mainly from animals, has ever been shown to cause heart disease or cancer, yet nutrition writers and Nabisco get rich pandering to the fear of eating any fat at all. The hyperactivity syndrome supposedly caused by white sugar has never, ever, been verified—and not for lack of trying. In the famous New Haven study, it was the presence of the parents, not the presence of white sugar, that was causing the problem; most of the kids calmed down when their parents left the room.

I cannot figure out why, but the atmosphere in America today rewards this sort of self-deception. Fear and suspicion of food have become the norm. Convivial dinners have nearly disappeared and with them the sense of festivity and exchange, of community and sacrament. People should be deeply ashamed of the irrational food phobias that keep them from sharing food with each other. Instead, they have become proud and isolated, arrogant and aggressively misinformed.

But not me.

STEP THREE was to choose my weapon. Food phobias can be extinguished in five ways. Which one would work best for me?

Brain surgery. Bilateral lesions made in the basolateral region of the amygdala seem to do the trick in rats and, I think, monkeys—eliminating old aversions, preventing the formation of new ones, and increasing the animals' acceptance of novel foods. But the literature does not report whether having a brain operation also diminishes their ability to, say, follow a recipe. If these experimental animals could talk, would they still be able to? Any volunteers?

Starvation.   As Aristotle claimed and modern science has confirmed, any food tastes better the hungrier you are. But as I recently confessed to my doctor, who warned me to take some pill only on an empty stomach, the last time I had an empty stomach was in 1978. He scribbled "hyperphagia" on my chart, your doctor's name for making a spectacle of yourself at the table. He is a jogger.

Bonbons.   Why not reward myself with a delectable little chocolate every time I successfully polish off an anchovy, a dish of kimchi, or a bowl of miso soup? Parents have used rewards ever since spinach was discovered. Offering children more playtime for eating dark leafy greens may temporarily work. But offering children an extra Milky Way bar in return for eating more spinach has perverse results: the spinach grows more repellent and the Milky Way more desired.

Drug dependence.   Finicky laboratory animals find new foods more palatable after a dose of chlordiazepoxide. According to an old *Physicians' Desk Reference,* this is nothing but Librium, the once-popular tranquilizer, also bottled as Reposans and Sereen.

The label warns you about nausea, depression, and operating heavy machinery. I just said no.

Exposure, plain and simple.   Scientists tell us that aversions fade away when we eat moderate doses of the hated foods at moderate intervals, especially if the food is complex and new to us. (Don't try this with allergies, but don't cheat either: few of us have genuine food allergies.) Exposure works by overcoming our innate neophobia, the omnivore's fear of new foods that balances the biological urge to explore for them. Did you know that babies who are breast-fed will later have less trouble with novel foods than those who are given formula? The variety of flavors that make their way into breast milk from the mother's diet prepares the infant for the culinary surprises that lie ahead. Most parents give up trying novel foods on their weanlings after two or three attempts and then complain to the pediatrician; this may be the most common cause of fussy eaters and finicky adults—of omnivores manqués. *Most babies will accept nearly anything after eight or ten tries.*

Clearly, mere exposure was the only hope for me.

STEP FOUR was to make eight or ten reservations at Korean restaurants, purchase eight or ten anchovies, search the Zagat guide for eight or ten places with the names Parthenon or Olympia (which I believe are required by statute for Greek restaurants), and bring a pot of water to the boil for cooking eight or ten chickpeas. My plan was simplicity itself: every day for the next six months I would eat at least one food that I detested.

Here are some of the results:

Kimchi.   After repeatedly sampling ten of the sixty varieties of kimchi, the national pickle of Korea, kimchi has become my national pickle, too.

Anchovies.   I began relating to anchovies a few months ago in northern Italy, where I ordered *bagna caôda* every day—a sauce of garlic, butter, olive oil, and minced anchovies served piping hot over sweet red and yellow peppers as an antipasto in Piemonte. My phobia crumpled when I understood that the anchovies living in American pizza parlors bear no relation to the sweet, tender anchovies of Spain and Italy, cured in dry sea salt and a bit of pepper. Soon I could tell a good *bagna caôda* from a terrific one. On my next trip to Italy I will seek out those fresh charcoal-grilled anchovies of the Adriatic you always hear about.

Clams.   My first assault on clams was at a diner called Lunch near the end of Long Island, where I consumed an order of fried bellies and an order of fried strips. My aversion increased sharply.

Eight clams and a few weeks later it was *capellini* in white clam sauce at an excellent southern Italian restaurant around the corner from my house. As I would do so often in the future, even at the expense of my popularity, I urged my companions to cast off their food phobias by ordering at least one dish they expected to detest. If they would go along my experiment, I would agree to order *nothing* I liked.

All but one agreed, a slim and lovely dancer who protested that her body tells her precisely what to eat and that I am the last person in the universe fit to interfere with those sacred messages. I replied that the innate wisdom of the body is a complete fiction when it comes to omnivores. Soon I had certain proof that my friend was a major closet food phobic when she spent five minutes painstakingly separating her appetizer into two piles. The pile composed of grilled peppers, fennel, and eggplant sat lonely on the plate until her mortified husband and I polished it off. She was so disoriented by either the meal or my unsparing advice that she ate a large handful of potpourri as we waited for our coats.

As for me, the evening was an unqualified success. The white clam sauce was fresh with herbs and lemon and fresh salt air, and my clam phobia was banished in the twinkling of an eye. There is a lot of banal pasta with clam sauce going around these days. If you have a clam phobia, here are two surefire solutions: Order eight to ten white clam pizzas at Frank Pepe's in New Haven, Connecticut, perhaps the single best pizza in the United States and certainly the best thing of any kind in New Haven, Connecticut. Or try the wonderful recipe for linguine with clams and *gremolata* in the *Chez Panisse Pasta, Pizza & Calzone Cookbook* (Random House) once a week for eight consecutive weeks. It is guaranteed to work miracles.

Greek food.   My wife, who considers herself Greek-food-deprived, was on cloud nine when I invited her to our neighborhood Greek restaurant, widely reviewed as the best in the city. As we walked along the street, she hugged me tight like those women in the TV commercials who have just been given a large diamond "for just being you" and launched into a recitation of the only classical Greek she knows, something about the wrath of Achilles. My own mood brightened when I saw that only one retsina befouled the wine list: the other wines were made from aboriginal Greek grapes in Attica or Macedonia or Samos but fermented in the manner of France or California. The dreaded egg-and-lemon soup was nowhere to be seen, and feta was kept mainly in the closet.

We ordered a multitude of appetizers and three main courses. Only the gluey squid, a tough grape leaf that lodged between my teeth, and the Liquid Smoke with which somebody had drenched the roasted eggplant threatened to arouse my slumbering phobia. The rest, most of it simply grilled with lemon and olive oil, was delicious, and as an added bonus I was launched on what still feels like an endless journey toward the acceptance of okra.

Later that evening, my lovely wife was kept up by an upset stomach, and I was kept up by my wife. She swore never to eat Greek food again.

Lard.   Paula Wolfert's magnificent *The Cooking of South-West France* (Dial Press) beguiled me into loving lard with her recipe for *confit de porc*—half-pound chunks of fresh pork shoulder flavored with thyme, garlic, cloves, and pepper, poached for three hours in a half gallon of barely simmering lard, and mellowed in crocks of congealed lard for up to four months. When you bring the pork back to life and brown it gently in its own fat, the result is completely delicious, savory and aromatic. I had never made the dish myself because, following Wolfert's advice, I had always avoided using commercial lard, those one-pound blocks of slightly rank, preservative-filled fat in your butcher's freezer.

Then, one snowy afternoon, I found myself alone in a room with four pounds of pork, an equal amount of pure white pig's fat, and a few hours to spare. Following Wolfert's simple instructions for rendering lard, I chopped up the fat, put it in a deep pot with a little water and some cloves and cinnamon sticks, popped it into a 225-degree oven, and woke up three hours later. After straining out the solids and spices, I was left with a rich, clear golden elixir that perfumed my kitchen, as it will henceforth perfume my life.

Desserts in Indian restaurants. Eight Indian dinners taught me that not every Indian dessert has the texture and taste of face cream. Far from it. Some have the texture and taste of tennis balls. These are named *gulab jamun*, which the menu described as a "light pastry made with dry milk and honey." *Rasmalai* have the texture of day-old bubble gum and refuse to yield to the action of the teeth. On the brighter side, I often finished my *kulfi*, the traditional Indian ice cream, and would love to revisit carrot *halva*, all caramelized and spicy. But I may already have traveled down this road as far as justice requires.

STEP FIVE, final exam and graduation ceremony.

In just six months, I succeeded in purging myself of nearly all repulsions and preferences, in becoming a more perfect omnivore. This became apparent one day in Paris, France—a city to which my arduous professional duties frequently take me. I was trying a nice new restaurant, and when the waiter brought the menu, I found myself in a state unlike any I had ever attained—call it Zen-like if you wish. Everything on the menu, every appetizer, hot and cold, every salad, every fish and bird and piece of meat, was terrifically alluring, but none more than the others. I had absolutely no way of choosing. Though blissful at the prospect of eating, I was unable to order dinner. I was reminded of the medieval church parable of the ass equidistant between two bales of hay, who, because animals lack free will, starves to death. A man, supposedly, would not.

The Catholic Church was dead wrong. I *would* have starved—if my companion had not saved the day by ordering for both of us. I believe I ate a composed salad with slivers of foie gras, a perfect sole meunière, and sweetbreads. Everything was delicious.

STEP SIX, relearning humility. Just because you have become a perfect omnivore does not mean that you must flaunt it. Intoxicated with my own accomplishment, I began to misbehave, especially at dinner parties. When seated next to an especially finicky eater, I would often amuse myself by going straight for the jugular. Sometimes I began slyly by staring slightly too long at the food remaining on her plate and then inquiring whether she would like to borrow my fork. Sometimes I launched a direct assault by asking how long she had had her terror of bread. Sometimes I tricked her by striking up an abstract conversation about allergies. And then I would sit back and complacently listen to her neurotic jumble of excuses and explanations: advice from a personal trainer, intolerance to wheat gluten, a pathetic faith in Dean Ornish, the exquisite—even painful—sensitivity of her taste buds, hints of childhood abuse. And then I would tell her the truth.

I believe that it is the height of compassion and generosity to practice this brand of tough love on dinner-party neighbors who are less omnivorous than oneself. But the perfect omnivore must always keep in mind that, for one to remain omnivorous, it is an absolute necessity to get invited back.

🦑

Francine Prose (1947–)

NOVELIST AND ESSAYIST Francine Prose has published more than twenty books of fiction along with such nonfiction works as *Anne Frank: The Book, the Life, the Afterlife*; *Reading Like a Writer*, and especially pertinent here, the brief but incisive *Gluttony*, in which she dissects one of the seven deadly sins by analyzing appetite, hunger, and body image. A former president of PEN American Center, she has taught writing and literature at Harvard, Sarah Lawrence, the Iowa Writers' Workshop, and the Bread Loaf Writers' Conference. In our selection, she turns her attention from gastronomic excess to forbidden foods—how and why we make the decision not to eat this meat or that fish. If you've watched either Anthony Bourdain's or Andrew Zimmern's gastronomic travel shows (*No Reservations* and *Bizarre Foods*), you've probably seen those intrepid travelers scarf down piranhas, crickets, and suckling pig brains. Even while she meditates on such exotic fare, Prose wittily notes that for a contemporary American gourmet a taboo meal is more likely to be bologna and Velveeta on Wonder Bread.

from Cocktail Hour at the Snake Blood Bar: On the Persistence of Taboo

NOT LONG AGO, at a dinner party, the conversation turned to the subject of why we generally don't eat household pets or our near-neighbors on the food chain. It was a warm summer evening; we were eating *vitello tonnato* and a tomato-arugula salad.

Almost everyone had heard the story of the formal, diplomatic dinner at which the raw, pulsing brain of a monkey was served from the still-warm monkey skull. And everyone knew of some Chinese restaurant, somewhere, suspected of serving cat meat.

A friend said that there are Cambodian restaurants in Washington, D.C., at which you can order dog meat.

He said that you have to know the code. You must ask for "traditional food."

THE best beef I ever tasted was, perhaps needless to say, in Bombay, at a restaurant gleaming with chrome, chandeliers, and mirrored walls, not far from the central market where cows, in their capacity as manifestations of the divine, were permitted to roam freely and graze at the produce stalls.

The beef on my plate at the G. Restaurant had been considerably less lucky.

Or was it actually buffalo? The menu called it steak. Steak Honolulu, Steak Milan, Steak Peking, Steak Paris, steak prepared in the imagined, unimaginable style of a dozen distant cities where cows were not allowed to wander through the streets, and it was perfectly normal to eat them.

It was not at all normal in India in 1976, where from time to time one read accounts of Muslim butchers lynched by Hindu mobs on the suspicion of selling beef. Beef (or buffalo) was expensive, not illegal, but hard to get, except at the famous G. Restaurant, which drew a chic crowd of Anglo-Indians, Parsis, Goan Christians, liberated Hindus, and especially Bombay film stars.

Always there were a few tourists present, but fewer than one might have expected, considering that every travel guidebook enthusiastically recommended the G. Restaurant as a welcome break from vegetable curry for homesick carnivores. Perhaps most tourists suspected—wrongly, as it turned out—that the guides were describing a cultural rather than a culinary experience.

In fact it was both, and I have never again had a steak as tender and sweet as the G. Restaurant's Steak Marseilles, a plump little pillow of beef done rare and topped with a pleasantly briny sauce that claimed to be anchovies and French butter, but was probably *ghee* (clarified butter) and the omnipresent, desiccated tiny fish oddly named Bombay duck.

Of course it's impossible to gauge how much the atmosphere contributed to the deliciousness of the food: for all the place's glitter and brittle display, the mood of the patrons at the G. Restaurant was furtive and intense, and an aura of the forbidden floated over every banquette. People studied one another in mirrors, their faces bright, flushed, and slightly strained—you would have thought everyone there was engaged in some adulterous tryst.

IT used to be that we knew who we were by the foods we refused to eat, and perhaps some species memory is behind the vehemence with which infants assert their autonomy by flinging dinner across the room, the righteousness with which every sentient American child goes through a phase of vegetarianism.

Claude Lévi-Strauss helped us see food preparation as a profound form of social expression, and Margaret Visser's recent book, *The Rituals of Eat-*

ing, makes it clear that even cannibalistic rites were not the stumbly chaotic bloodfeasts out of *Night of the Living Dead* that we might have imagined. Strict rules governed whose flesh you ate, and how and when you consumed it, mostly depending on your emotional, familial, and tribal ties to the taboo or edible dead.

For centuries, Orthodox Jews and Muslims haven't eaten pork, Christians did eat pork but didn't eat meat on Friday, upper-caste Hindus and some Buddhists ate no meat, especially not beef, and Jains didn't eat anything that had ever possessed a living soul, a category that for some reason included onions and garlic. It may be that food taboos affirm special covenants with God, but they also affirm the covenant with like-minded avoidants and (perhaps most importantly) an essential, unbridgeable distance from the food tastes of the Other.

Not only does the Other blithely and greedily consume what we know is unclean; they would like nothing better than to defile us by making us eat it, too. During the early, horrific wars between Indian Sikhs and Muslims, Sikhs were said to ritually wash down mosques with the blood of freshly slaughtered pigs. During the Inquisition, secretly practicing Marrano Jews pretending to have converted were tested on how far they'd progressed by being forced to eat pork; and it seems, sadly, that the fantastic, medieval idea that Jews bake Passover matzos with the blood of Christian children is, even now, not quite so safely dead (or so far from the surface) as one might reasonably suppose. . . .

One needn't be an anthropologist to make the obvious associations between taboos regarding food and taboos about the body and about sex—specifically about (as they say) exogamous relations with the Other who dines on the forbidden and assimilates the unclean flesh into his or her own body.

If, as they say, we are what we eat, then the same must be true of the Other; our flesh, we imagine, is unlike their flesh, made of different stuff, characterized by different colors, tastes, and smells. I remember reading a story about a girl who grew up in China and, on first encountering a crowd of white people, nearly became sick, so repulsed was she by the sour-milk odor of people whose diet included dairy.

Our ideas about the Other's diet are allied with ideas of exotic sex, with the sexual prowess (or lack of it) of some untrustworthy group or race or tribe. Americans are curious and (in the case of environmentalists) enraged by the Chinese belief in the aphrodisiacal properties of various powdered horns and tusks.

There is a grade-Z exploitation movie currently available in the sleazier and more politically incorrect video stores, a low-budget pseudo-documentary purporting to report on the shocking sexual customs practiced in today's "Orient": a Japanese brothel in which businessmen dress up in diapers and pretend to be infants, the sex-change-operation mill in Sri Lanka, etc. The movie is deeply frightening, though not at all in the way it intends. In one scene, a group of worried (indeed, almost stricken-looking) Taiwanese businessmen are shown quaffing the house drink at a Taipei snake blood bar: vampirizing hapless reptiles to render themselves more amorous. The camera lingers lovingly on the nasty serpentine *kris* with which the bartender makes an incision just below the snake's head, then focuses on his rather hammy fist, squeezing out the blood—drip, drip, not a single drop wasted—into a glass. The bartender is all business, he shows neither pleasure nor disgust; for all the emotion on his face, he could be pulling draft beer from a tap.

Then the camera zooms in on the customer's faces, as if to catch some dreamy, abstracted expression; perhaps they are musing on the pleasure that the snake blood is meant to enhance? The customers (or are they actors?) nervously eye the lens; one gets the impression that this is not where they stop off on their way home to their wives. Meanwhile the sonorous voice-over narration drones solemnly on and on: these men, we hear, share the belief that the blood of certain rare vipers can prolong a single act of intercourse for upwards of seven hours.

A friend told me that he and his wife were taken to such a bar on a business trip to Taipei. Determined to be polite, and also frankly intrigued, my friend drank a shot glass of snake blood. Then the company employee assigned to shepherd him around the city asked him if, now that he was properly fortified, he would like to visit a brothel full of fresh country girls, all fourteen years old or younger.

IT is necessary for us to think that such things happen only in faraway places, where the poor and benighted still observe their arcane food tastes and taboos. If we tolerate food superstitions at all, we insist they be benevolent: we like hearing about the good-luck dishes various ethnic groups cook on New Year's Day.

We do know that there are otherwise apparently sensible Muslims and Jews who *still* atavistically persist in not eating pork, Hindu friends we would never invite for a steak dinner. But most of us in the "rational" West consider ourselves light-years beyond all that. As some strictly macrobiotic neighbors once said disapprovingly of my family: They eat *everything*.

Though, naturally, there are limits.

At the dinner at which our friend explained about "traditional food," another guest said that he knew a Venezuelan artist who for a mere four hundred dollars could arrange to have a cube of fresh human flesh shipped, on ice, direct from Caracas to Manhattan. He waited. There were no takers. Was it because of the expense? The guest with the Venezuelan friend said, Wasn't it interesting that no one wanted to try it? He said that the desire to partake of human flesh is the only desire in human history that civilization has ever successfully eradicated.

But civilization (so-called) has apparently been more widely successful at eradicating other food taboos. Aside from obvious exceptions, like the ban on cannibalism, we have (or we flatter ourselves that we have) evolved beyond the forbidden. We no longer really need diet to affirm our group identity or to encourage us to despise those whose diets are different from our own—we have so many neater ways to set ourselves apart (nationalism, for example), careful methods of differentiation that don't muck about in those fuzzy, gray areas involving individual food preferences and unclean forms of animal life.

No longer deemed politically or spiritually necessary, and finally, just an inconvenience, the Church's ban on eating meat on Fridays has been lifted during our lifetimes. Few of my friends are (in any traditional sense) religious, and, though I realize that many do exist, I myself know few Jews of my generation who, were it not for the taboo on cholesterol, wouldn't happily and guiltlessly dine daily on prosciutto and Canadian bacon.

MY paternal grandparents read a Socialist newspaper and kept a kosher kitchen. My mother's parents ran a small restaurant near the docks in lower Manhattan and served ham and pork to stevedores but never once (that they admitted) tasted it themselves. Their children, my parents, ate lobster, shrimp, and bacon, but never ham and pork; and my brother and I, their children, were clearly made to understand that these distinctions were all about health and not at all about religion.

My father, who was a pathologist, informed us about trichinosis, and seemed to take an almost uncanny pleasure in describing the larvae—or were they worms?—who migrated through your bloodstream and, if they didn't kill you right away, took up residence in your brain and rendered you a helpless, jumping mass of uncontrolled tics and twitches.

Yet no one appeared to worry when my brother and I went through a phase of preferring our bacon underdone, pearly and translucent. Our parents might conceivably have let us eat raw bacon if it meant we at least went off to school with something in our stomachs. No one ever suggested that undercooked bacon could harm us—as opposed to, say, dangerous Chinese-restaurant pork, fried till it was closer in texture to cellulose than protein.

During those years, it seemed, Jews who no longer believed in God learned to believe in trichinosis; fear of parasites supplanted the fear of God and the prohibitions in Leviticus. And now we have even lost our religious faith in the punishment-by-parasite for disobeying the God of our Fathers. We know about meat inspection and how the FDA, inefficient as it is, has rendered the incidence of meat contamination statistically insignificant.

Yet the spirit, if not the letter, of the dietary laws remains. The awful little secret of many mixed marriages is that the Jewish member of the couple is always accusing the Other of lethally undercooking the pork, of not roasting or broiling or frying it, until, as the prudent cookbooks say, it "loses its pink color."

IF taboos no longer speak to our spiritual lives, they do still address issues of longevity and health. Perhaps now that we no longer believe in God or in an afterlife, now that we no longer expect the strict observation of dietary restrictions to assure us a berth in heaven, we must endeavor to do the next best thing—that is, live forever.

It's too drearily familiar to track the changing fortunes of various foods that, through no fault of their own, have lost their reputation as elixirs and been identified as poisons. Many of us hope wanly for the day when butter, cream, and cheese will be discovered to be better for us than their pale and ascetic low-fat equivalents.

Those who have any doubt about the extent to which health concerns and taboos have edged out simple good manners should try serving, at a dinner, anything that includes a minimal, detectable trace of animal fat. Many hosts have had the dismaying experience of seeing perfectly healthy guests (those who have not yet been warned by their doctors that overindulgence may prove fatal) push offending, suspect, or high-cholesterol items off to the edge of their plates, or conceal them under the parsley.

Such guests might do well to meditate on the example of the vegetarian Zen monk who, when asked why he'd unprotestingly eaten beef at a dinner party, replied that the cow was already dead—but his hostess wasn't.

🐒

Diane Ackerman (1948–)

THE AUTHOR OF such ambitious works as *A Natural History of Love*, *An Alchemy of Mind*, and *A Natural History of the Senses*, from which our selection is drawn, Diane Ackerman is a poet and essayist who has become a major contemporary science writer. Inevitably, when she discusses taste, she puts food at the center of her investigation of its qualities. In her book, she includes a thorough study of such topics as food and sex, the craving for chocolate, and human taste buds. For Ackerman eating is always a multifaceted business, and her argument is that the more we're aware of the numerous elements that go into the simple act of putting food in our mouths, the greater our understanding of human behavior—indeed of humanity itself—will be. Her notes on the semi-toxic Japanese fish *fugu* are less sensuous than her other culinary descriptions, perhaps because she does not tell us if she herself ever risked its apparently sensuous delights; but she does see the temptation to eat the potentially fatal *fugu* liver as a metaphor for our flirtation with anxiety, horror, and even near-death experiences.

from *A Natural History of the Senses*: Et Fugu, Brute?

A NATION OF sensation-addicts might dine as chic urbanites do, on rhubarb and raspberry tortes, smoked lobster, and hibiscus-wrapped monkfish, wiped with raspberry butter, baked in a clay oven, and then elevated briefly in mesquite smoke. When I was in college, I didn't eat goldfish or cram into Volkswagens, or chug whole bottles of vodka, but others did, in a neo–Roaring Twenties ennui. Shocking the bourgeoisie has always been the unstated encyclical of college students and artists, and sometimes that includes grossing out society in a display of bizarre eating habits. One of the classic *Monty Python's Flying Circus* sketches shows a chocolate manufacturer being cross-examined by policemen for selling chocolate-covered baby frogs, bones and all ("without the bones, they wouldn't be crunchy!" he whines), as well as insects, and other taboo animals sure to appal western taste buds. I've met field scientists of many persuasions who have eaten native foods like grasshoppers, leeches, or bats stewed in coconut milk, in part to be mannerly, in part out of curiosity, and I think in part to provide a good anecdote when they returned to the States. However, these are just nutritious foods that fall beyond our usual sphere of habit and custom.

We don't always eat foods for their taste, but sometimes for their feel. I once ate a popular duck dish in Amazonian Brazil, *pato no tucupi* (Portuguese for *pato*, "duck" + *no*, "within" + *tucupi*, "extracted juice of manioc") whose main attraction is that it's anesthetic: It makes your mouth as tingly numb as Benzedrine. The numbing ingredient is *jambu* (in Latin, *Spilanthes*), a yellow daisy that grows throughout Brazil and is sometimes used as a cold remedy. The effect was startling—it was as if my lips and whole mouth were vibrating. But many cultures have physically startling foods. I adore hot peppers and other spicy foods, ones that sandblast the mouth. We say "taste," when we describe such a food to someone else, but what we're really talking about is a combination of touch, taste, and the absence of discomfort when the deadening or sandblasting finally stops. The thinnest line divides Szechwan hot-pepper sauce from being thrilling (causing your lips to tingle even after the meal is over), and being sulfurically hot enough to cause a gag response as you eat it. A less extreme example is our liking for crunchy or crisp foods, like carrots, which have little taste but lots of noise and mouth action. One of the most successful foods on earth is Coca-Cola, a combination of intense sweetness, caffeine, and a prickly feeling against the nose that we find refreshing. It was first marketed as a mouthwash in 1888, and at that time contained cocaine, a serious refresher—an ingredient that was dropped in 1903. It is still flavored with extract of coca leaves, but minus the cocaine. Coffee, tea, tobacco, and other stimulants all came into use in the western world in the sixteenth and seventeenth centuries, and quickly percolated around Europe. Fashionable and addictive, they offered diners a real nervous-system jolt, either of narcotic calm or caffeine rush, and, unlike normal foods, they could be taken in doses, depending on how high one wished to get or how addicted one already was.

In Japan, specially licensed chefs prepare the rarest sashimi delicacy: the white flesh of the puffer fish, served raw and arranged in elaborate floral patterns on a platter. Diners pay large sums of money for the carefully prepared dish, which has a light, faintly sweet taste, like raw pompano. It had better be carefully prepared, because, unlike pompano, puffer fish is ferociously poisonous. You wouldn't think a puffer fish would need such chemical armor, since its main form of defense is to swallow great gulps of water and become so bloated it is too large for most predators to swallow. And yet its skin, ovaries, liver, and intestines contain tetrodotoxin, one of the most poisonous chemicals in the world, hundreds of times more lethal than strychnine or cyanide. A shred small enough to fit under one's fingernail could kill an entire family. Unless the poison is completely removed by a deft, experienced chef, the diner will die midmeal. That's the appeal of the dish: eating the possibility of death, a fright your lips spell out as you dine. Yet preparing it is a traditional art form in Japan, with widespread aficionados. The most highly respected *fugu* chefs are the ones who manage to leave in the barest touch of the poison, just enough for the diner's lips to tingle from his brush with mortality but not enough to actually kill him. Of course, a certain number of diners do die every year from eating *fugu*, but that doesn't stop intrepid *fugu*-fanciers. The ultimate *fugu* connoisseur orders chiri, puffer flesh lightly cooked in a broth made of the poisonous livers and intestines. It's not that diners don't understand the bizarre danger of puffer-fish toxin. Ancient Egyptian, Chinese, Japanese, and other cultures all describe *fugu* poisoning in excruciating detail: It first produces dizziness, numbness of the mouth and lips, breathing trouble, cramps, blue lips, a desperate itchiness as of insects crawling all over one's body, vomiting, dilated pupils and then a zombielike sleep, really a kind of neurological paralysis during which the victims are often aware of what's going on around them, and from which they die. But sometimes they wake. If a Japanese man or woman dies of *fugu* poison, the family waits a few days before burying them, just in case they wake up. Every now and then someone poisoned by *fugu* is nearly buried alive, coming to at the last moment to describe in horrifying detail their own funeral and burial, during which, although they desperately tried to cry out or signal that they were still alive, they simply couldn't move.

Though it has a certain Russian-roulette quality to it, eating *fugu* is considered a highly aesthetic experience. That makes one wonder about the condition that we, in chauvinistic shorthand, refer to as "human." Creatures who will one day vanish from the earth in that ultimate subtraction of sensuality that we call death, we spend our lives courting death, fomenting wars, watching sickening horror movies in which maniacs slash and torture their victims, hurrying our own death in fast cars, cigarette smoking, suicide. Death obsesses us, as well it might, but our response to it is so strange. Faced with tornadoes chewing up homes, with dust storms ruining crops, with floods and earthquakes swallowing up whole cities, with ghostly diseases that gnaw at one's bone marrow, cripple, or craze—rampant miseries that need no special bidding, but come freely, giving their horror like alms— you'd think human beings would hold out against the forces of Nature, combine their efforts and become allies, and not create devastations of their own, not add to one another's miseries. Death does such fine work without us. How strange that people, whole countries sometimes, wish to be its willing accomplices.

Our horror films say so much about us and our food obsessions. I don't mean the ones in which maniacal men carting chain saws and razors punish single women for living alone or taking jobs—although those are certainly alarming. I don't mean ghost stories, in which we exhale loudly as order falls from chaos in the closing scenes. And I don't mean scary whodunits, at the end of which the universe seems temporarily less random, violent, and inexplicable. Our real passion, by far, is for the juiciest of horror films in which vile, loathsome beasts, gifted with ferocious strength and cunning, stalk human beings and eat them. It doesn't matter much if the beast is a fast-living "Killer Shrew" or a sullen "Cat People" or an abstract "Wolfen" or a nameless, acid-drooling "Alien." The pattern is always the same. They dominate the genre. We are greedy for their brand of terror.

The plain truth is that we don't seem to have gotten used to being at the top of our food chain. It must bother us a great deal, or we wouldn't keep making movies, generation after generation, with exactly the same scare tactics: The tables are turned and we become fodder. All right, so we may be comfortable at the top of the chain as we walk around Manhattan, but suppose—oh, ultimate horror!—that on other planets *we're* at the bottom of *their* food chain? Then you have the diabolically scary "Aliens," who capture human beings, use them as hosts for their maggotlike young, and actually hang them up on slime gallows in a pantry.

We rush obsessively to movie theaters, sit in the cavelike dark, and confront the horror. We make contact with the beasts and live through it. The next week, or the next summer, we'll do it all over again. And, on the way home, we keep listening for the sound of claws on the pavement, a supernatural panting, a vampiric flutter. We spent our formative years as a technologyless species scared with good reason about lions and bears and snakes and sharks and wolves that could, and frequently did, pursue us. You'd think we'd have gotten over that by now. One look at the cozy slabs of cow in a supermarket case, neatly cut, inked, and wrapped, should tell us to relax. But civilization is a more recent phenomenon than we like to think. Are horror films our version of the magic drawings on cave walls that our ancestors confronted? Are we still confronting them?

Fugu might not seem to have much to do with nuclear disarmament or world peace, but it's a small indicator of our psyches. We find the threat of death arousing. Not all of us, and not all the time. But enough do often enough to keep the rest of us peace-loving sorts on our toes when we'd rather be sitting down calmly to a sumptuous meal with friends.

Cara de Silva (1953–)

A FOOD JOURNALIST, historian of gastronomy, and regular author of a travel column called "A Fork in the Road," de Silva edited the poignant cookbook *In Memory's Kitchen*, a collection of recipes recorded by some starving inhabitants of Terezín (Theresienstadt), a concentration camp in which the women were imprisoned during the Holocaust. A supposedly "model" camp, Terezín was often defined by its Nazi masters as an example of the generosity with which they treated the Jewish inmates: there were concerts, plays, lectures—and even a propaganda film claiming that "The Führer Gives the Jews a Town." But in reality, the prisoners lived (and starved) on watery soup and moldy bread. Reviewing the cookbook Wilhelmina Pächter and her friends compiled in these bitter circumstances, the writer Lore Dickstein declared that the work is itself "an act of defiance and resistance, a means of

identification in a dehumanized world [and] a life force in the face of death."
But the book is also a poignant compendium of Proustian memories. We
include here, along with de Silva's introduction, Pächter's own recipe for her
beloved cold stuffed eggs.

from *In Memory's Kitchen*

INTRODUCTION

NO MATTER HOW many times Anny told the story, its power to affect her
and her listeners never diminished. She was not a person who cried easily;
yet even before she began to speak, her lively brown eyes would be brimful
of tears.

"I remember so well the day the call came," she would say as she brushed
the dampness from her timeworn cheeks, "because it was my past at the
other end of the line. 'Is this Anny Stern?' the woman on the phone asked
me, and when I answered yes, she said, 'Then I have a package for you from
your mother.'"

With those words, a quarter-century-long journey from the Czechoslo-
vak ghetto/concentration camp of Terezín to an apartment building on
Manhattan's East Side came to an end.

Inside the package was a picture taken in 1939 of Anny's mother, Mina
Pächter, and Anny's son, Peter (now called David). His arms are around her
neck, her beautiful gray hair is swept back, and they are both smiling—but
dark circles ring Mina's eyes. There were letters, too—"Every evening I kiss
your picture . . . please, Petřičku, do not forget me," Mina had written to her
grandson. But it was a fragile, hand-sewn copy book that made up the bulk
of the package, its cracked and crumbling pages covered with recipes in a
variety of faltering scripts.

Born out of the abyss, it is a document that can be comprehended only
at the farthest reaches of the mind. Did setting down recipes bring comfort
amid chaos and brutality? Did it bring hope for a future in which someone
might prepare a meal from them again? We cannot know. But certainly the
creation of such a cookbook was an act of psychological resistance, forceful
testimony to the power of food to sustain us, not just physically but spiritually.

Food is who we are in the deepest sense, and not because it is transformed into blood and bone. Our personal gastronomic traditions—what we eat, the foods and foodways we associate with the rituals of childhood, marriage, and parenthood, moments around the table, celebrations—are critical components of our identities. To recall them in desperate circumstances is to reinforce a sense of self and to assist us in our struggle to preserve it. "My mother was already in her seventies at this time," said Anny, "yet this book shows that even in adversity her spirit fought on." And so, too, did the spirits of her friends.

Among their weapons were *Heu und Stroh*, fried noodles topped with raisins, cinnamon, and vanilla cream; *Leberknödel*, liver dumplings with a touch of ginger; *Kletzenbrot*, a rich fruit bread; and *Zenichovy Dort*, or Groom's Cake. There were *Erdäpfel Dalken*, or potato doughnuts; and *Badener Caramell Bonbons*, caramels from Baden Baden—about eighty recipes in all. Some were hallmarks of Central European cookery. A few, like *Billige Echte Jüdische Bobe*, cheap real Jewish coffee cake, were specifically Jewish. And one, written down by Mina, is particularly poignant. For *Gefüllte Eier*, stuffed eggs with a variety of garnishes, the recipe instructs the cook to "Let fantasy run free."

"When first I opened the copybook and saw the handwriting of my mother, I had to close it," said Anny of the day she received the package. "I put it away and only much later did I have the courage to look. My husband and I, we were afraid of it. It was something holy. After all those years, it was like her hand was reaching out to me from long ago."

In a way, it was. Just before Mina died in Theresienstadt, she entrusted the package to a friend, Arthur Buxbaum, an antiques dealer, and asked him to get it to her daughter in Palestine. But because most of Anny's letters hadn't reached Mina during the war, she couldn't provide him with an address.

Unable to honor his friend's deathbed wish, Buxbaum simply kept the package. Then one day in 1960, a cousin told him she was leaving for Israel. Still mindful of his promise, he asked her to take the manuscript along, but by the time she got news of Anny and her husband, George Stern, they had moved to the United States to be near their son.

No one knows exactly what happened after that. A letter found in the package and written in 1960 indicates that just as it had been entrusted first to Buxbaum and then to his cousin, so it was entrusted to someone else to carry to New York. Yet according to Anny, it didn't arrive until almost a decade later.

It was then that a stranger from Ohio arrived at a Manhattan gathering of Czechs and asked if anyone there knew the Sterns. "Yes, I have heard of them," responded one woman. A moment later he had produced the parcel and she had become its final custodian. At last, Mina's deathbed gift to her daughter, her startling *kochbuch*, was to be delivered.

Its contents, written in the elliptical style characteristic of European cookery books, are evidence that the inmates of Terezín thought constantly about eating. "Food, memories of it, missing it, craving it, dreaming of it, in short, the obsession with food colours all the Theresienstadt memoirs," writes Ruth Schwertfeger in *Women of Theresienstadt, Voices from a Concentration Camp.*

Bianca Steiner Brown, the translator of the recipes in this book and herself a former inmate of Terezín, explains it this way: "In order to survive, you had to have an imagination. Fantasies about food were like a fantasy that you have about how the outside is if you are inside. You imagine it not only the way it really is but much stronger than it really is. I was, for instance, a nurse, and I worked at night and I looked out at night—Terezín was a town surrounded by walls, a garrison town. So I looked out at all the beds where the children were, and out of that window I could look into freedom. And you were imagining things, like how it would be to run around in the meadow outside. You knew how it was, but you imagined it even better than it was, and that's how it was with food, also. Talking about it helped you."

Most of us can understand that. Far more disquieting is the idea that people who were undernourished, even starving, not only reminisced about favorite foods but also had discussions, even arguments, about the correct way to prepare dishes they might never be able to eat again.

In fact, such behavior was frequent. Brown remembers women sharing recipes in their bunks late at night. "They would say, 'Do you know such and such a cake?'" she recounts. "'I did it in such and such a way.'"

"The hunger was so enormous that one constantly 'cooked' something that was an unattainable ideal and maybe somehow it was a certain help to survive it all," wrote Jaroslav Budlovsky on a death march from Schwarzheide to Terezín in 1943.

And Susan E. Cernyak-Spatz, professor emeritus at the University of North Carolina and a survivor of Terezín and Auschwitz, describes people in both places as speaking of food so much that there was a camp expression for it. "We called it 'cooking with the mouth,'" she says. "Everybody did it. And people got very upset if they thought you made a dish the wrong way or had the wrong recipe for it." . . .

To a degree that may be unfathomable to Americans at the end of the twentieth century, cooking, both doing it and talking about it, was central to the societies from which many of the women of Terezín, and most European women of the period, came. It was also among the chief activities that defined them as wives and mothers.

Some cooked even in the ghetto, albeit in a limited way. "Theresienstadt really happened after May '42, when all civilians were out and we could move freely and women would try to make some kind of meal while putting rations together," says Cernyak-Spatz.

But a cookbook, even if only imaginatively, offered possibilities for "preparing" foods that were more culturally and psychologically meaningful. While written recipes might not feed the hungers of the body, they might temporarily quell the hungers of the soul.

Possibly, even the book's familiar form brought its authors solace. "It used to be the custom in Europe to make your own written cookbooks," notes Brown. "Probably if I had stayed in Prague and lived the life I left, I would also have started a manuscript cookbook exactly like this one." And the Czech Wilma Iggers, a retired professor of German literature and a Jewish social historian, speaks, too, of the handwritten cookbooks she has from her relatives, from her own Bohemian Jewish background. "It was common," she says. Perhaps the writers of the Terezín cookbook were attempting to preserve this tradition. Perhaps getting the copybook to Anny was important to Mina because it resembled a family manuscript that she might once have given her herself.

But whatever its explicit or implicit functions, Mina's cookbook—and the others—make it clear that half a century after the Holocaust, when we thought we were familiar with all the creative ways in which human beings expressed themselves during the long years of the horror, at least one small genre, the making of cookbooks, has gone largely unnoticed.

In the case of Mina's manuscript—a product of Terezín, where cultural ferment was constant—such a demonstration of the domestic arts must also be seen as part of a larger artistic whole.

This surrealistic camp, positioned by the Nazis as a model ghetto, evidence of the Reich's benevolence toward the Jews, was the ultimate publicity ploy. Designed to distract the world from the final solution and all that preceded it, it was in fact a way station to the killing centers of the East and itself a place where many died.

Paradoxically, Terezín was also a crucible of creativity. Among the multitude of Central Europeans whom the Reich sent to this "Paradise Ghetto" were painters, writers, musicians, intellectuals, composers, designers, and others who were too well known for their removal to less deceptive places to go unremarked.

Many contrived ways to continue their work—because cultural activities fostered the illusion of a model camp, the Nazis generally turned a blind eye to such endeavors. As a consequence, there flourished in this bizarre environment an artistic and intellectual life so fierce, so determined, so vibrant, so fertile as to be almost unimaginable.

Despite overcrowding that created pestilent conditions, and in defiance of raging infections, a high death toll, and hunger—all as constant a presence as fear of the transports—here the flower of Central European Jewry participated in what those at Beit Theresienstadt have called "a revolt of the spirit."

They gave well-attended lectures (Mina Pächter, an art historian, was among the speakers); put on opera performances; composed music; performed cabaret; drew; painted; and attended to the education of the young with a fervor born of determination to keep Jewish life alive (and, for some, of determination to ready the young for a future they hoped they still might have in Palestine). "It was heroic, superhuman, the care given the children," says Cernyak-Spatz. "In the face of death, with the SS looking on, these people tried to persist intellectually and artistically."

The resulting juxtapositions overwhelm the mind. "Today, the milk froze in the pot," wrote Gonda Redlich, who kept a diary throughout his stay in Theresienstadt. "The cold is very dangerous. The children don't undress, and so there are a lot of lice in their quarters. Today, there was a premier performance of *The Bartered Bride*. It was the finest I had ever seen in the ghetto."

This was what some have described as "the special reality" of Terezín, and Mina's *kochbuch*, a testament to a lost world and its flavors, was part of it. . . .

Provisions and the means of getting them varied somewhat over the time of Theresienstadt's existence, but some things appear to have remained more or less constant. Ask a survivor about the fare and you are likely to be told of queuing outdoors for food—often for hours even in inclement weather; of the daily ration of soup, variously described as tasteless to disgusting; of the sauce that some days might have a tiny bit of meat in it; of the loaf of bread that had to last three days; of the margarine, the barley, the turnips; and for the fortunate, the food packages gotten to them by Gentile friends or Jewish organizations on the outside or, earlier on, by family and friends who were still free.

In his memoirs, Norbert Troller, one of the camp's most famous artists, speaks of salads made from weeds; in general no fruits or vegetables were supplied to the population of Theresienstadt.

Cakes were also clever improvisations. Inge Auerbacher, who was a child during her time in the camp, remembers having a palm-sized birthday cake made of mashed potato and a small amount of sugar. And Troller describes a "ghetto torte," saying it was particularly well made by a Mrs. Windholz, whose version "tasted almost exactly like the famous Sachertorte. The recipe was secret;" he writes, "its ingredients . . . bread, coffee, saccharine, a trace of margarine, lots of good wishes, and an electric plate. Very impressive and irresistible."

Though food was sparse and often barely edible, and diseases caused by vitamin deficiencies were a constant problem, to some who went on to Auschwitz, like Chernyak-Spatz or Mina's step-granddaughter Liesel Laufer, conditions seemed not so bad. The camp's cultural life, described by Laufer as marvelous, also compensated for a great deal.

Others experienced the camp differently. "Like everyone else," Troller wrote, "I suffered greatly from hunger, so that I was plagued all through the day with thoughts of the kind of food I had been used to, as compared to the food we received. Until that time I had hardly ever suffered the pangs of hunger—I could fast for one day during Yom Kippur—but here, without any transition, our rations were shortened to such an extent (approximately one-third of the customary calories in their most unappetizing form) that hunger weakened and absorbed (one's) every thought."

But while almost all were hungry, some were more hungry than others. In the early days of Theresienstadt (May 1942), it had become clear to the Council of Jewish Elders, the group forced by the Nazis to run the internal affairs of the camp, that the limited food supplies could not be divided equally. They determined that those who labored at the hardest jobs had to be allotted more to eat than those whose work was less arduous and that children, the hope of the future, also had to be fed more than others.

They decided, too, that the fewest calories—and usually the worst accommodations—would have to go those least likely to survive the ordeal of Terezín, namely, the elderly like Mina Pächter, who had been born in 1872 and was 70 when she arrived in the ghetto. Such people were sacrificed so others might live. "For younger people, Theresienstadt was bearable," says Liesel Laufer. "For older people, it was hell."

One must suppose that Mina passed many sorrowful nights remembering that despite her daughter's entreaties, she had refused to accompany Anny when she left for Palestine late in 1939.

After spending nine months struggling to expedite the emigration of Jews at the Prague Palestine Office under Adolf Eichmann and his staff, it had become increasingly clear to Anny that she and her son now had to leave themselves (her husband was already in Palestine). She pleaded with her mother to come, too, but Mina replied, "You don't move an old tree. Besides, who will do anything to old people?"

She was shortly and tragically to find out who.

How one fared in Theresienstadt depended to a certain extent on how well one could negotiate the system. Norbert Troller, for instance, traded portraits of the cooks and bakers to their subjects for extra food; others schemed to get jobs that permitted them greater access to provisions. But the elderly, writes Zdenek Lederer in *Ghetto Theresienstadt*, "unlike the young workers, had no access to the food stores of the Ghetto, while their debility prevented them from making clandestine contacts with a view to acquiring some food.

"Starving elderly men and women begged for watery soup made from synthetic lentil or pea powder, and dug for food in the garbage heaps rotting in the courtyard of the barracks," he writes. "In the morning, at noon, and before nightfall they patiently queued up for their food clutching saucepans, mugs or tins. They were glad to get a few gulps of hot coffee substitute and greedily ate their scanty meals. Then they continued their aimless pilgrimage, dragging along their emaciated bodies, their hands trembling and their clothes soiled."

"The decision [to reduce their rations] transformed many of the elderly into scavengers and beggars," writes George Berkley in *The Story of Theresienstadt*. "They would . . . pounce on any morsel of food such as a pile of potato skins, food considered fit only for pigs." (This scene was so common that it is frequently depicted by Terezín artists.) As a result of eating the raw peelings, many of the elderly developed severe enteritis and diarrhea, a chronic camp condition but especially common, and especially serious, among the aged.

No one knows for certain to what degree this describes Mina's life in Theresienstadt, but we do know it was extremely hard. (Her family believes she escaped transportation only because she had been given an order of merit from the German Red Cross for her aid to German soldiers passing through Czechoslovakia during World War I.)

By the time she was found in the fall of 1943 by her step-granddaughter Liesel Laufer, who had been sent to Terezín earlier that year, Mina was suffering from protein deficiency, a condition referred to as hunger edema. "An acquaintance of my parents told me where she was, and she was in living quarters that were very bad," says Liesel, now a resident of Israel. "When I came, she was really in a poor state. She was suffering very badly from malnutrition. And I saw that she couldn't take care of herself anymore."

Because she was a nurse, Liesel was able to get Mina into the hospital, where she was able to look after her a little. Hospitalization also meant that Liesel's husband, Ernest Reich, a doctor, could include Mina in his study of the effects of protein deficiency. Along with other patients, she was allotted two spoonfuls of white cheese a day (all that was available) to see what effect that small addition to her regular diet would have on her health. It was of little use.

Mina's fear, expressed in one of her poems, that no good would come to her in Terezín proved warrented. She never got to kiss her grandson again. On Yom Kippur 1944, she died in the ghetto hospital. . . .

"The farther away it is, the worse it seems, this enormous thing that happened to the Jews," said Anny late one afternoon as she clutched the cookbook in her elegant hands. "When you look in the caldron, you can't believe what was in it. Yet here is the story of how the inmates of the camp, living on bread and watery soup and dreaming of the cooking habits of the past, found some consolation in the hope that they might be able to use them again in the future. By sharing these recipes, I am honoring the thoughts of my mother and the others that somewhere and somehow, there must be a better world to live in."

WILHELMINA PÄCHTER,
COLD STUFFED EGGS PÄCHTER

HARD BOIL 10 eggs, cut them in half. Remove yolks and press them through a sieve. Add 5 decagrams butter, 2 anchovies pressed through a sieve, a little mustard, 3–4 drops Maggi [liquid seasoning], 1/8 liter whipped heavy cream, parsley, lemon juice. Now put eggs on a platter. Pour [liquid] aspic over. Before [pouring on the aspic] let fantasy run free and the eggs are garnished with ham, [smoked] salmon, caviar, capers. One can put the eggs into paper cuffs and serve them with hot sliced rolls.

Campbell McGrath (1962–)

THE WINNER OF a MacArthur "genius" award and numerous other prizes, McGrath has published nine collections of verse, many centered on the kind of social issue he addresses in "Capitalism #5," our selection here. As one critic has noted, his poetry "thrives on his dissatisfaction with the world," yet at the same time it is populist, empathic, and accessible. A professor of creative writing at Florida International University and a onetime member of the punk band Men from the Manly Planet, McGrath has compared poems to "little seedlings popping out of the soil," noting that "some are tomato plants, some are oak trees, and some are weeds."

Capitalist Poem #5

I was at the 7-11.
I ate a burrito.
I drank a Slurpee.
I was tired.
It was late, after work washing dishes.

The burrito was good.
I had another.

I did it every day for a week.
I did it every day for a month.

To cook a burrito you tear off the plastic wrapper.
You push button #3 on the microwave.
Burritos are large, small, or medium.
Red or green chili peppers.
Beef or bean or both.
There are 7-11's all across the nation.

On the way out I bought a quart of beer for $1.39.
I was aware of social injustice
In only the vaguest possible way.

Michael Paterniti (1964–)

A FREELANCE JOURNALIST, long time correspondent for the magazine *GQ*, and multiple nominee for the National Magazine Award, Paterniti is best known for his exploration of a remarkable Spanish cheese—Paramo de Guzmán; his *The Telling Room: A Tale of Love, Betrayal, Revenge, and the World's Greatest Piece of Cheese* is part loving chronicle of the cheese maker and his extraordinary product, part memoir of an American seduced by the rhythms of rural life and the folks who live by those rhythms. Paterniti has also written *Driving Mr. Albert: A Trip Across America with Einstein's Brain*, a hilarious true story of a road trip across America with the pathologist who autopsied Einstein in 1955 and removed the great scientist's brain, keeping it stashed in a Tupperware bowl for forty years. A resident of Portland, Maine, Paterniti has also written for *Harper's Magazine, Rolling Stone,* and *The New*

York Times Magazine. In our excerpt from his account of French President François Mitterand's last meal, he imagines himself dining on the same extravagant—indeed, controversial—ingredients.

from The Last Meal

WHAT BROUGHT ME to France in the first place was a story I'd heard about François Mitterrand, the former French president, who earlier had gorged himself on one last orgiastic feast before he'd died. For his last meal, he'd eaten oysters and foie gras and capon—all in copious quantities— the succulent, tender, sweet tastes flooding his parched mouth. And then there was the meal's ultimate course: a small, yellow-throated songbird that was illegal to eat. Rare and seductive, the bird—ortolan—supposedly represented the French soul. And this old man, this ravenous president, had taken it whole—wings, feet, liver, heart. Swallowed it, bones and all. Consumed it beneath a white cloth so that God Himself couldn't witness the barbaric act.

DRIVING south from Paris to Bordeaux, to the region where Mitterland ate his last meal—to re-create it for myself—I wonder what it means to knowingly eat a last meal. It means knowing you're going die, right? It means that you've been living under a long-held delusion that the world is infinite and you are immortal. So it means saying sayonara to everything, including the delusions that sustain you, at the same time that you've gained a deeper feeling about those delusions and how you might have lived with more passion and love and generosity.

And then the most difficult part: You must imagine yourself as a memory, laid out and naked and no longer yourself, no longer you, the remarkable Someone who chose a last meal. Rather, you're just a body full of that meal. So you have to imagine yourself gone—first as a pale figure in the basement of a funeral home, then as the lead in a eulogy about how remarkable you were, and then as a bunch of photographs and stories.

And that's when you must imagine one more time what you most need to eat, what last taste must rise to meet your hunger and thirst and linger awhile on your tongue even as, before dessert, you're lowered into the grave.

THE old president asked that the rest of his family and friends be summoned to Latche and that a meal be prepared for New Year's Eve. He gave a precise account of what would be eaten at the table, a feast for thirty people, for he had decided that afterward, he would not eat again.

"I am fed up with myself," he told a friend.

I've come to a table set with a white cloth. An armada of floating wine goblets, the blinding weaponry of knives and forks and spoons. Two windows, shaded purple, stung by bullets of cold rain, lashed by the hurricane winds of an ocean storm.

The chef is a dark-haired man, fiftyish, with a bowling-ball belly. He stands in front of orange flames in his great stone chimney hung with stewpots, finely orchestrating each octave of taste, occasionally sipping his broths and various chorded concoctions with a miffed expression. In breaking the law to serve ortolan, he gruffly claims that it is his duty, as a Frenchman, to serve the food of his region. He thinks the law against serving ortolan is stupid. And yet he had to call forty of his friends in search of the bird, for there were none to be found and almost everyone feared getting caught, risking fines and possible imprisonment.

But then another man, his forty-first friend, arrived an hour ago with three live ortolans in a small pouch—worth up to a hundred dollars each and each no bigger than a thumb. They're brown-backed, with pinkish bellies, part of the yellowhammer family, and when they fly, they tend to keep low to the ground and, when the wind is high, swoop crazily for lack of weight. In all the world, they're really caught only in the pine forests of the southwestern Landes region of France, by about twenty families who lie in wait for the birds each fall as they fly from Europe to Africa. Once caught—they're literally snatched out of the air in traps called *matoles*—they're locked away in a dark room and fattened on millet; to achieve the same effect, French kings and Roman emperors once blinded the bird with a knife so, lost in the darkness, it would eat twenty-four hours a day.

Back at the chimney, the chef reiterates the menu for Mitterand's last meal, including the last course, as he puts it, "the birdies."

"It takes a culture of very good to appreciate the very good," the chef says, nosing the clear juices of the capon rotating in the fire. "And ortolan is beyond even the very good."

THE president was carried to a reclining chair and table apart from the huge table where the guests sat. He was covered with blankets, seemed gone already. And yet when they brought the oysters—Marennes oysters, his favorite, harvested from the waters of this region—he summoned his energies, rose up in his chair, and begun sucking them, the full flesh of them, from their half shells. He'd habitually eaten a hundred a week throughout his life and had been betrayed by bad oysters before, but, oh no, not these! Hydrogen, nitrogen, phosphorous—a dozen, two dozen, and then, astonishingly, more. He couldn't help it, his ravenous attack. It was brain food, and he seemed to slurp them up against the cancer, let the saltwater juices flow to the back of his throat, change champagne-sweet, and then disappear in a flood before he started on the oyster itself. And that was another sublimity. The delicate tearing of a thing so full of ocean. Better than a paper wafer— heaven. When he was done, he lay back in his chair, oblivious to everyone else in the room, and fell fast asleep.

I BEGIN, too, by eating the Marennes oysters—round, fat, luscious oysters split open and peeled back to show their delicate green lungs. Shimmering pendulums of translucent meat, they weigh more than the heavy, carbuncled shells in which they lie. When you lift the shell to your mouth and suck, it's like the first time your tongue ever touched another tongue. The oysters are cool inside, then warm. Everything becomes heightened and alive. Nibbling turns to hormone-humming mastication. Your mouth swims with sensation: sugary, then salty, then again with Atlantic Ocean sweetness. And you try, as best you can, to prolong it. When they're gone, you taste the ghost of them.

And then the foie gras, smooth and surprisingly buttery, a light-brown pâté swirled with light greens, pinks, and yellows and glittering slightly, tasting not so much of animal but of earth. Accompanied by fresh, rough-crusted, homemade bread and the sweet sauternes (which itself is made from shriveled grapes of noble rot), the foie gras dissolves with the faint, rich sparkle of fresh-picked corn. It doesn't matter that it's fattened goose liver.

The capon is superb—not too gamey or stringy—furiously basted to a high state of tenderness in which the meat falls cleanly from the bone with only the help of gravity. In its mildness, in its hint of olive oil and rosemary, it readies the tongue and its several thousand taste buds for the experience of what's coming next.

And then the wines. Besides the sauternes (a 1995 Les Remparts de Bastor, a 1995 Doisy Daëne), there are simple, full-bodied reds, for that's how Mitterrand liked them, simple and full-bodied: a 1900 Château Lestage Simon, a 1994 Château Poujeaux. They are long, old and dark. Complicated potions of flower and fruit. Faint cherry on a tongue tip, the tingle of tannin along the gums. While one bottle is being imbibed, another is being decanted, and all the while there are certain chemical changes taking place between the wine and its new atmosphere and then finally between the changed wine and the atmosphere of your mouth, until it seems to lift from the tongue, vanished.

WITH each course, the president had rallied from sleep, from his oyster dreams, from fever or arctic chill, not daring to miss the next to come: the foie gras slathered over homemade bread or the capon and then, of course, the wines. But what brought him to full attention was a commotion: Some of the guests were confused when a man at last brought in a large platter of tiny, cooked ortolans laid out in rows. The president closely regarded his guests' dismayed expressions, for it gave him quiet satisfaction—between jabs of pain—to realize that he still had the power to surprise.

The ortolans were offered to the table, but not everyone accepted. Those who did draped large, white cloth napkins over their heads, took the ortolans in their fingertips, and disappeared. The room shortly filled with wet noises and chewing. The bones and intestines turned to paste, swallowed eventually in one gulp. Some reveled in it; others spat it out. When they were through, one by one they reappeared from beneath their hoods, slightly dazed.

The president himself took a long sip of wine, let it play in his mouth. After nearly three dozen oysters and several courses, he seemed insatiable, and there was one bird left. He took the ortolan in his fingers, then dove again beneath the hood, the bony impress of his skull against the white cloth—the guests in silence and the self-pleasing, pornographic slurps of the president filling the room like a dirge.

AFTER the president's second ortolan—he had appeared from beneath the hood, wide-eyed, ecstatic, staring into a dark corner of the room—the guests approached him in groups of two and three and made brief small talk about the affairs of the country or Zola or the weather. They knew this was adieu, and yet they hid their sadness; they acted as if in a month's time he would still be among them.

And what about him? There was nothing left to subtract now. What of the white river that flowed through his childhood, the purple attic full of cornhusks? And then his beautiful books—Dostoyevsky, Voltaire, Camus? How would the world continue without him in it?

He tried to flail one last time against the proof of his death. But then he had no energy left. Just an unhappy body weighted with grapefruit tumors, curving earthward. Everything moving toward the center and one final point of pain. Soon after, he refused food and medicine; death took eight days.

"I'm eaten up inside," he said before he was carried from the room.

Chang-rae Lee (1965–)

A YOUNG BOY'S confusion about whether to try something as odd-looking and strange-tasting as a sea urchin becomes even greater when Chang-rae Lee's mother and father, like the good and bad angels of a morality play whispering temptations and prohibitions in the protagonist's ears, voice their respective warning and encouragement. Lee, an astute describer of the spiny, globular creature usually eaten raw, is a Korean-American novelist who teaches creative writing at Princeton. His first novel, *Native Speaker*, is about Korean immigrants to America, while his second, *A Gesture Life*, centers on a Japanese-American doctor who had treated Korean comfort women during World War II. His characters are frequently torn between their country of origin and their new home, afflicted by problems of assimilation and bifurcated identity. His own ambivalence about cultural assimilation seems to be mirrored by his ambivalence toward a peculiar gastronomic experience.

Sea Urchin

JULY 1980. I'M about to turn fifteen and our family is in Seoul, the first time since we left, twelve years earlier. I don't know if it's different. My parents can't really say. They just repeat the equivalent of "How in the world?" whenever we venture into another part of the city, or meet one of their old friends. "Look at that—how in the world?" "This hot spell, yes, yes—how in the world?" My younger sister is very quiet in the astounding heat. We all are. It's the first time I notice how I stink. You can't help smelling like everything else. And in the heat everything smells of ferment and rot and rankness. In my grandfather's old neighborhood, where the two- and three-room houses stand barely head-high, the smell is staggering. "What's that?" I ask. My cousin says, "Shit."

"Shit? What shit?"

"Yours," he says, laughing. "Mine."

On the wide streets near the city center, there are student demonstrations; my cousin says they're a response to a massacre of citizens by the military down south in Kwangju. After the riot troops clear the avenues, the air is laden with tear gas—"spicy," in the idiom. Whenever we're in a taxi moving through there, I open the window and stick out my tongue, trying to taste the poison, the human repellent. My mother wonders what's wrong with me.

I don't know what's wrong. Or maybe I do. I'm bored. Maybe I'm craving a girl. I can't help staring at them, the ones clearing dishes in their parents' eateries, the uniformed schoolgirls walking hand in hand, the slim young women who work in the Lotte department store, smelling of fried kimchi and L'Air du Temps. They're all stunning to me, even with their bad teeth. I let myself drift near them, hoping for the scantest touch.

But there's nothing. I'm too obviously desperate, utterly hopeless. Instead, it seems, I can eat. I've always liked food, but now I'm bent on trying everything. As it is, the days are made up of meals, formal and impromptu, meals between meals and within meals; the streets are a continuous outdoor buffet of braised crabs, cold buckwheat noodles, shaved ice with sweet red beans on top. In Itaewon, the district near the United States Army base, where you can get anything you want, culinary or otherwise, we stop at a seafood stand for dinner. Basically, it's a tent diner, a long bar with stools, a camp stove and fish tank behind the proprietor, an elderly woman with a low, hoarse voice. The roof is a stretch of blue poly-tarp. My father is excited; it's like the old days. He wants raw fish, but my mother shakes her head. I can see why: in plastic bins of speckled, bloody ice sit semi-alive cockles, abalones, eels, conches, sea cucumbers, porgies, shrimps. "Get something fried," she tells him, not caring what the woman might think. "Get something cooked."

A young couple sitting at the end of the bar order live octopus. The old woman nods and hooks one in the tank. It's fairly small, the size of a hand. She lays it on the board and quickly slices off the head with her cleaver. She chops the tentacles and gathers them up onto a plate, dressing them with sesame oil and a spicy bean sauce. "You have to be careful," my father whispers, "or one of the suction cups can stick inside your throat. You could die." The lovers blithely feed each other the sectioned tentacles, taking sips of *soju* in between. My mother immediately orders a scallion-and-seafood pancake for us, then a spicy cod-head stew; my father murmurs that he still wants something live, fresh. I point to a bin and say that's what I want—those split spiny spheres, like cracked-open meteorites, their rusty centers layered with shiny crenellations. I bend down and smell them, and my eyes almost water from the intense ocean tang. "They're sea urchins," the woman says to my father. "He won't like them." My mother is telling my father he's crazy, that I'll get sick from food poisoning, but he nods to the woman, and she picks up a half and cuts out the soft flesh.

What does it taste like? I'm not sure, because I've never had anything like it. All I know is that it tastes alive, something alive at the undragged bottom of the sea; it tastes the way flesh would taste if flesh were a mineral. And I'm half gagging, though still chewing; it's as if I had another tongue in my mouth, this blind, self-satisfied creature. That night I throw up, my mother scolding us, my father chuckling through his concern. The next day, my uncles joke that they'll take me out for some more, and the suggestion is enough to make me retch again.

But a week later I'm better, and I go back by myself. The woman is there, and so are the sea urchins, glistening in the hot sun. "I know what you want," she says. I sit, my mouth slick with anticipation and revulsion, not yet knowing why.

☙

Peter Hessler (1969–)

EVEN AN OLD China hand like Peter Hessler—who has written three books on that country and received a MacArthur Foundation "genius grant" for reporting on the way China's rapid changes affect ordinary citizens—can have very mixed feelings about its more exotic dishes. Though Hessler spent many years in the country as a Peace Corps volunteer and later as a *New Yorker* correspondent in Beijing, his plunge into rat cuisine at two restaurants specializing in the rodent provoked a decidedly mixed response. The creatures may not have been urban sewer rats—they were raised in a free-range environment on grass or fruits—but they did not bring unmitigated pleasure to Hessler, though he shows himself to be relatively game. His piece is an amusing account of the Chinese culinary temperament and an arch narrative of Chinese attitudes toward Western diners.

from A Rat in My Soup

"DO YOU WANT a big rat or a small rat?" the waitress says.

I'm getting used to making difficult decisions in Luogang. It's a small village in southern China's Guangdong Province, and I came here on a whim, having heard that Luogang has a famous rat restaurant. Upon arrival, however, I discovered that there are actually two celebrated restaurants—the Highest Ranking Wild Flavor Restaurant and the New Eight Sceneries Wild Flavor Food City. Both restaurants specialize in rat. They have the same bamboo and wood decor. They are next door to each other, and their owners are named Zhong and Zhong, respectively. Virtually everybody in Luogang village is named Zhong.

The restaurant Zhongs are not related, and the competition between them is keen. As a foreign journalist, I've been cajoled to such an extent that, in an effort to please both Zhongs, I agreed to eat two lunches, one at each restaurant. But before the taste test can begin, I have to answer the question that's been posed by the waitress at the Highest Ranking Wild Flavor

Restaurant. Her name is Zhong. In Chinese it means "bell." She asks the question again: "Do you want a big rat or a small rat?"

"What's the difference?" I say.

"The big rats eat grass stems, and the small ones eat fruit."

This piece of information does not help much. I try a more direct tack. "Which tastes better?"

"Both of them taste good."

"Which do you recommend?"

"Either one."

I glance at the table next to mine. Two parents, a grandmother, and a little boy are having lunch. The boy is gnawing on a rat drumstick. I can't tell if the drumstick once belonged to a big rat or a small rat. The boy eats quickly. It's a warm afternoon. The sun is shining. I make my decision.

"Small rat," I say.

THE Chinese claim that folks in Guangdong will eat anything. Besides rat, a customer at the Highest Ranking Wild Flavor Restaurant can order turtledove, fox, cat, python, and an assortment of strange-looking local animals whose names do not translate well into English. All of them are kept live in pens at the back of the restaurant, and they are killed only when ordered by a customer. Choosing among them is complicated, and it involves more than exoticism. You do not eat cat simply for the thrill of eating cat. You eat cat because cats have a lively *jingshen*, or spirit, and thus by eating the animal you will improve your spirits. You eat snake to become stronger. You eat deer penis to improve virility. And you eat rat to improve your—well, to be honest, I never knew that there was a reason for rat-eating until I got to Luogang, where every Zhong was quick to explain the benefits of the local specialty.

"It keeps you from going bald," said Zhong Shaocong, the daughter of the owner of the Highest Ranking Wild Flavor Restaurant.

"If you have white hair and eat rat regularly, it will turn black," said Zhong Qingjiang, who owns the New Eight Sceneries Wild Flavor Food City. "And if you're going bald and you eat rat every day your hair will stop falling out. A lot of the parents around here feed rat to a small child who doesn't have much hair, and the hair grows better."

Earlier this year, Luogang opened a "Restaurant Street" in the new Luogang Economic Development Zone, which is designed to draw visitors from the nearby city of Guangzhou. The government invested $1.2 million in the project, which enabled the two rat restaurants to move from their old, cramped quarters in a local park. On March 18, the Highest Ranking Wild Flavor Restaurant began serving customers in a twenty-thousand-square-foot facility that cost $42,000. Six days later, the New Eight Sceneries Wild Flavor Food City opened, with an investment of $54,000. A third restaurant—a massive, airconditioned facility, which is expected to cost $72,000—will open soon. A fourth is in the planning stages.

"Their investment wasn't as much as mine," Deng Ximing, the owner of the third restaurant, told me. "You can see that my place is going to be much nicer. We have air-conditioning, which none of the others have."

It was early morning, and we were watching the workers lay the cement floor of the new restaurant. Deng was the only local restaurateur with a different family name, but he was married to a Zhong. He was in his mid-forties, and he had the fast-talking confidence of a successful entrepreneur. I also noticed that he had a good head of hair. He took great pride in Luogang Village's culinary tradition.

"It's more than a thousand years old," he said. "And it's always been rats from the mountain—we're not eating city rats. The mountain rats are clean, because up there they aren't eating anything dirty. Mostly they eat fruit—oranges, plums, jackfruit. People from the government hygiene department have been here to examine the rats. They took them to the laboratory and checked them out thoroughly to see if they had any diseases, and they found nothing. Not even the slightest problem."

Luogang's Restaurant Street has been a resounding success. Newspapers and television stations have reported extensively on the benefits of the local specialty, and an increasing number of customers are making the half-hour trip from Guangzhou. Both the Highest Ranking Wild Flavor Restaurant and the New Eight Sceneries Wild Flavor Food City serve, on average, three thousand rats every day on the weekend. "Many people come from faraway places," Zhong Qingjiang told me. "They come from Guangzhou, Shenzhen, Hong Kong, Macao. One customer came all the way from America with her son. They were visiting relatives in Luogang, and the family brought them here to eat. She said you couldn't find this kind of food in America."

In America, you would also be hard-pressed to find twelve thousand fruit-fed rats anywhere on any weekend, but this isn't a problem in Luogang. On my first morning in the village, I watched dozens of farmers come down from the hills, looking to get a piece of the rat business. They came on mopeds, on bicycles, on foot; and all of them carried squirming burlap sacks full of rats that had been trapped on their farms.

"Last year I sold my oranges for fifteen cents a pound," a farmer named Zhong Senji told me. "But this year the price has dropped to less than ten cents." Like many other farmers, Zhong decided that the rat business was a lot better than the orange business. Today he had nine rats in his sack, which was weighed by a worker at the Highest Ranking Wild Flavor Restaurant. The bag shook and squeaked on the scale. It weighed in at just under three pounds, and Zhong received the equivalent in yuan of $1.45 per pound, for a total of $3.87. In Lougang, rats are more expensive than pork or chicken. A pound of rat costs nearly twice as much as a pound of beef.

AT the Highest Ranking Wild Flavor Restaurant, I begin with a dish called Simmered Mountain Rat with Black Beans. The menu also includes Mountain Rat Soup, Steamed Mountain Rat, Simmered Mountain Rat, Roasted Mountain Rat, Mountain Rat Curry, and Spicy and Salty Mountain Rat. But the waitress enthusiastically recommended the Simmered Mountain Rat with Black Beans, which arrives in a clay pot.

I eat the beans first. They taste fine. I poke at the rat meat. It's clearly well done, and it's attractively garnished with onions, leeks, and ginger. Nestled in a light sauce are skinny rat thighs, short strips of rat flank, and delicate toylike rat ribs. I start with a thigh, put a chunk of it into my mouth, and reach for a glass of beer. The beer helps.

The restaurant's owner, Zhong Dieqin, comes over and sits down. "What do you think?" she asks.

"I think it tastes good."

"You know it's good for your health."

"I've heard that."

"It's good for your hair and skin," she says. "It's also good for your kidneys."

Earlier this morning, I met a farmer who told me that my brown hair might turn black if I ate enough rat. Then he thought for a moment and said that he wasn't certain if eating rat has the same effect on foreigners that it does on the Chinese—it might do something entirely different to me. The possibility seemed to interest him a great deal.

At the table, Zhong Dieqin watches me intently. The audience also includes much of the restaurant staff. "Are you sure you like it?" asks the owner.

"Yes," I say, tentatively. In fact, it isn't bad. The meat is lean and white, without a hint of gaminess. There's no aftertaste. Gradually, my squeamishness fades, and I try to decide what the meat reminds me of, but nothing comes to mind. It simply tastes like rat.

NEXT door, at the New Eight Sceneries Wild Flavor Food City she asks, "How was the other restaurant?"

"It was fine," I say.

"What did you eat?"

"Simmered Mountain Rat with Black Beans."

"You'll like ours better," she says. "Our cook is better, the service is quicker, and the waitresses are more polite."

I decide to order the Spicy and Salty Mountain Rat. This time, when the waitress asks about size, I respond immediately. "Big rat," I say, pleased with my boldness.

"Come and choose it."

"What?"

"Pick out the rat you want."

In Chinese restaurants, fish and other seafood are traditionally shown live to customers for approval, as a way of guaranteeing freshness. It's not what I expected with rat, but now that the invitation has been made, it's too late to back out. I follow one of the kitchen workers to a shed behind the restaurant, where cages are stacked one on top of the other. Each cage contains more than thirty rats. The shed does not smell good. The worker points at a rat.

"How about this one?" he says.

"Um, sure."

He puts on a leather glove, opens the cage, and picks up the chosen rat. It's about the size of a softball. The rat is calm, perched on the hand of the worker, who keeps a grip on the tail.

"Is it OK?" asks the worker.

"Yes."

"Are you certain?"

The rat gazes at me with beady eyes. I have a strong desire to leave the shed.

"Yes," I say. "It's fine."

Before I go, the worker makes a sudden motion. He flips his wrist, keeps a grip on the tail, and swings his arm quickly. The rat makes a neat arc in the air. There is a soft thud when its head strikes the cement floor. There isn't much blood. The worker grins.

"Oh," I say.

"You can sit back down now," says the worker. "We'll bring it out to you soon."

Less than fifteen minutes later the dish is at my table. This time the chunks of rat are garnished with carrots and leeks. The chef comes out of the kitchen to join the rest of the audience, which consists of the owner, the floor manager, and a cousin of the owner. I take a bite.

"How is it?" the chef asks.

"Good."

"Is it too tough?"

"No," I say. "It's fine."

In truth, I'm trying hard not to taste anything. I lost my appetite in the shed, and now I eat quickly, washing every bite down with beer. I do my best to put on a good show, gnawing on the bones as enthusiastically as possible. When I finish, I sit back and manage a smile. The chef and the others nod with approval.

The owner's cousin says, "Next time you should try the Longfu Soup, because it contains tiger, dragon, and phoenix."

"What do you mean by 'tiger, dragon, and phoenix'?" I ask warily. I don't want to make another trip to the shed.

"It's not real tigers, dragons, and phoenixes," he says. "They're represented by other animals—cat for the tiger, snake for the dragon, and chicken for the phoenix. When you mix them together, there are all kinds of health benefits." He smiles and says, "They taste good, too."

❧PART FOUR☙

Kitchen Practices

Chefs, Cooks, and Tools of the Trade

INTRODUCTION

THE ACCOMPLISHED cook and food writer Betty Fussell has told the tale of how she once bought a bag of live eels in New York's Chinatown, carried them home on the subway, and proceeded to try to kill them in her kitchen. Cleaver whacks and mallet slams didn't work, but then she discovered a solution in *The Encyclopedia of Fish Cookery*, which advised throwing them in a container of coarse kosher salt. It did the job, but skinning was yet to come, followed by severing the heads, slitting the muscular body with poultry shears, and plunging them into a final bath of vinegar and white wine. Now that is a "kitchen practice" in spades.

Not all the selections in this chapter are so laborious or terrifying. But like the famous first direction for Brunswick Stew—"Take a squirrel"— many of the essays and poems we include involve transformation, sometimes brute, sometimes sweet, from raw ingredient to wondrous food. The subject matter ought to be familiar to most readers, since we've all, or almost all, had a bout with a burner. Even when the writers of our excerpts are professional chefs or restaurateurs we can imagine ourselves at least momentarily in their place; indeed, many of us would give our favorite chef's knife to work for an hour at the stovetop of a three-star Michelin, under the tutelage of a master. When Gabrielle Hamilton tells us what Sunday brunch is like at Prune, her East Village hot spot, we more or less know what she's talking about. And when Adrian Searle gives us the inside skinny on Ferran Adrià's elBulli "workshop," though molecular gastronomy may be as remote from our experience as a medieval alchemist's lab, we more or less know what *he's* talking about. Bill Buford, a well-known food writer whose work appears elsewhere in this volume, came close to a Walter Mitty moment when he not only apprenticed at superstar restaurateur Mario Batali's Italian spot Babbo, but also went to Italy to learn butchering from a Tuscan master butcher, working for an entire year just to get one hind quarter of a pig exactly right. As with so much writing of this kind, for a certain reader such pieces represent kitchen practice fantasies, culinary wish fulfillments.

But technique is not the only ingredient in these texts. Several authors either castigate or celebrate specific instruments of the kitchen or the table. Thus John Thorne has nothing but hostility toward the microwave, decrying its perversely unnatural mode of cooking food from the inside out. Even the hallowed food processor, however convenient, feels to him like a machine designed to distance the user from the food itself, an interloper imposing itself between hand and ingredient. At the same time, Bee Wilson, a food historian, sings the praises of the cleaver, celebrating its versatility as a utensil in Chinese cookery. Meanwhile, Norbert Elias, a distinguished sociologist of culture, speaks of the role of the fork in the civilizing process; it's fascinating to learn that before what we define as conventional table cutlery people used their hands to eat but often carried a knife with them and employed it, uncleansed, to spear anything on a plate.

Anthony Bourdain, thanks to his TV programs, has gained fame as a remarkably traveled, endlessly adventurous eater, a man of gusto and exuberance at the table. Almost equally well known is his insider dope about kitchens and their practices (he began his food life as a cook), especially the stinging critique of unsavory ways that he mounted in his best-selling *Kitchen Confidential*. It's helpful to know that Tuesday is the best night to eat out, but it's amusing and possibly shocking to learn that behind that suggestion lies a whole litany of menu booby-traps awaiting a customer foolish enough to venture into a restaurant on Monday night, when terrible leftovers are inevitable. There are other kitchen horrors: ever do the rounds with a health inspector? Roger Porter did, and you'll learn of an inspector playing hardball—destructively dumping a quart of Windex into a pot of soup because it wasn't sufficiently cooled down overnight and he thought it might breed a host of deadly bacilli. Then there's a whole subgenre of tales by writers who disguise themselves as diners or workers in restaurants. Of course such reviewers as Ruth Reichl are known for their crafty camouflages, but the food writer James Villas once pretended to be a waiter and produced an essay describing the guff he had to take from surly customers, along the way singing the praises of unheralded workers in restaurant kitchens, from sous-chefs to dishwashers.

Many writers love to describe the process of cooking—that tale of metamorphosis with its gratifying results. Some poets—like Nancy Willard in "How to Stuff a Pepper"—use the transformative power of language as a parallel to what a cook does in the pot, showing how the ordinary (words, ingredients) become the extraordinary (the completed poem, the finished dish). Like good poetry, good cooking seems a balance between convention and individual talent, accepted rules and the imaginative breaking of rules. The making of a lyric and the making of a soufflé are analogous acts.

Inevitably taking us back to Betty Fussell's eel slaughter, the poet William Dickey writes: "We must eat to live, and we must kill to eat. / The serious cook will always face this problem." And on that note, the great companion to Gertrude Stein and author of the famous *Alice B. Toklas Cook Book* considers that when the cook has to dispatch her own food, all kitchens are what she calls crime scenes. A chapter from her book, titled "Murder in the Kitchen," is a record of Toklas's kitchen killings: a carp annihilated with a knife plunged in its vertebral column, a pigeon smothered when Toklas pressed on its fragile windpipe, a duck murdered in some unspeakable way. Such crime victims have little to do with the supermarket's frozen salmon steaks or plastic-wrapped birds, antiseptically laid out on beds of Styrofoam.

🐘

Alice B. Toklas (1877–1967)

IN WHAT SOMEONE has called "one of the most successful marriages of the twentieth century," the slight, practical-minded San-Francisco-born Alice B. Toklas was "wifey" and the imperious, Oakland-born Gertrude Stein was "hubby." They met and joined their lives in Paris, in 1906, settling in the rue de Fleurus apartment where Stein had been living with her brother, Leo, an address that had already become a Modernist Destination. But theirs was a rather conventional living arrangement. Stein, by mutual consent, was the "genius"; Toklas was the cook, embroiderer, and entertainer of visiting wives, whose eminent husbands supposedly came just to see Stein. But in fact the duo were loving partners, and when Stein died Toklas declared that "I am just a memory of her." Nevertheless, to make money she struck out on her own with the *Alice B. Toklas Cook Book*, a compendium of recipes and recollections that has become as popular as the best-selling *Autobiography of Alice B. Toklas*—a memoir Stein claimed to have ghostwritten for her (although to this day some critics continue to argue that Toklas wrote that book herself too).

from *The Alice B. Toklas Cook Book*: Murder in the Kitchen

COOK-BOOKS HAVE ALWAYS intrigued and seduced me. When I was still a dilettante in the kitchen they held my attention, even the dull ones, from cover to cover, the way crime and murder stories did Gertrude Stein.

When we first began reading Dashiell Hammett, Gertrude Stein remarked that it was his modern note to have disposed of his victims before the story commenced. Goodness knows how many were required to follow as the result of the first crime. And so it is in the kitchen. Murder and sudden death seem as unnatural there as they should be anywhere else. They can't, they can never become acceptable facts. Food is far too pleasant to combine with horror. All the same, facts, even distasteful facts, must be accepted and we shall see how, before any story of cooking begins, crime is inevitable. That is why cooking is not an entirely agreeable pastime. There is too much that must happen in advance of the actual cooking. This doesn't of course apply to food that emerges stainless from deep freeze. But the marketing and cooking I know are French and it was in France, where freezing units are unknown, that in due course I graduated at the stove.

In earlier days, memories of which are scattered among my chapters, if indulgent friends on this or that Sunday evening or party occasion said that the cooking I produced wasn't bad, it neither beguiled nor flattered me into liking or wanting to do it. The only way to learn to cook is to cook, and for me, as for so many others, it suddenly and unexpectedly became a disagreeable necessity to have to do it when war came and Occupation followed. It was in those conditions of rationing and shortage that I learned not only to cook seriously but to buy food in a restricted market and not to take too much time in doing it, since there were so many more important and more amusing things to do. It was at this time, then, that murder in the kitchen began.

The first victim was a lively carp brought to the kitchen in a covered basket from which nothing could escape. The fish man who sold me the carp said he had no time to kill, scale or clean it, nor would he tell me with which of these horrible necessities one began. It wasn't difficult to know which was the most repellent. So quickly to the murder and have it over with. On the docks of Puget Sound I had seen fishermen grasp the tail of a huge salmon and lifting it high bring it down on the dock with enough force to kill it. Obviously I was not a fisherman nor was the kitchen table a dock. Should I not dispatch my first victim with a blow on the head from a heavy mallet? After an appraising glance at the lively fish it was evident he would escape attempts aimed at his head. A heavy sharp knife came to my mind as the classic, the perfect choice, so grasping, with my left hand well covered with a dishcloth, for the teeth might be sharp, the lower jaw of the carp, and the knife in my right, I carefully, deliberately found the base of its vertebral column and plunged the knife in. I let go my grasp and looked to see what had happened. Horror of horrors. The carp was dead, killed, assassinated, murdered in the first, second and third degree. Limp, I fell into a chair, with my hands still unwashed reached for a cigarette, lighted it, and waited for the police to come and take me into custody. After a second cigarette my courage returned and I went to prepare poor Mr Carp for the table.

It was in the market of Palma de Mallorca that our French cook tried to teach me to murder by smothering. There is no reason why this crime should have been committed publicly or that I should have been expected to participate. Jeanne was just showing off. When the crowd of market women who had gathered about her began screaming and gesticulating, I retreated. When we met later to drive back in the carry-all filled with our marketing to Terreno where we had a villa I refused to sympathise with Jeanne. She said the Mallorcans were bloodthirsty, didn't they go to bullfights and pay an advanced price for the meat of the beasts they had seen killed in the ring, didn't they prefer to chop off the heads of innocent pigeons instead of humanely smothering them which was the way to prevent all fowl from bleeding to death and so make them fuller and tastier. Had she not tried to explain this to them, to teach them, to show them how an intelligent humane person went about killing pigeons, but no they didn't want to learn, they preferred their own brutal ways. At lunch when she served the pigeons Jeanne discreetly said nothing. Discussing food which she enjoyed above everything had been discouraged at table. But her fine black eyes were eloquent. If the small-sized pigeons the island produced had not achieved jumbo size, squabs they unquestionably were, and larger and more succulent squabs than those we had eaten at the excellent restaurant at Palma.

Later we went back to Paris and then there was war and after a lifetime there was peace. One day passing the *concierge's loge* he called me and said he had something someone had left for us. He said he would bring it to me, which he did and which I wished he hadn't when I saw what it was, a crate of six white pigeons and a note from a friend saying she had nothing better to offer us from her home in the country, ending with But as Alice is clever she will make something delicious of them. It is certainly a mistake to allow a reputation for cleverness to be born and spread by loving friends. It is so cheaply acquired and so dearly paid for. Six white pigeons to be smothered, to be plucked, to be cleaned and all this to be accomplished before Gertrude Stein returned for she didn't like to see work being done. If only I had the courage the two hours before her return would easily suffice. A large cup of strong black coffee would help. This was before a lovely Brazilian told me that in her country a large cup of black coffee was always served before going to bed to ensure a good night's rest. Not yet having acquired this knowledge the black coffee made me lively and courageous. I carefully found the spot on poor innocent Dove's throat where I was to press and pressed. The realization had never come to me before that one saw with one's fingertips as well as one's eyes. It was a most unpleasant experience, though as I laid out one by one the sweet young corpses there was no denying one could become accustomed to murdering. . . .

The next murder was not of my doing. During six months which we spent in the country we raised Barbary ducks. They are larger than ordinary ducks and are famous for the size of their livers. They do not quack and are not friendly. Down in the Ain everyone shoots. Many of the farmers go off to work in the fields with a gun slung over a shoulder and not infrequently return with a bird or two.

Occasionally a farmer would sell us a pheasant or a partridge. An English friend staying with us, astonished to find farmers shooting, remarked, When everyone shoots no one shoots. Our nearest neighbour had a so-called bird dog, mongrel she certainly was, ruby coat like an Irish setter but her head was flat, her paws too large, her tail too short. We would see Diane on the road, she was not sympathetic. The large iron portals at Bilignin were sometimes left open when Gertrude Stein took the car out for a short while, and one morning Diane, finding them open, came into the court and saw the last of our Barbary ducks, Blanchette, because she was blue-black. Perhaps innocently perhaps not, opinion was divided later, she began to chase Blanchette. She would come running at the poor bewildered duck from a distance, charge upon her, retreat and recommence. The cook, having seen from the kitchen window what was happening, hastened out. The poor duck was on her back and Diane was madly barking and running about. By the time I got to the court the cook was tenderly carrying a limp Blanchette in her arms to the kitchen. Having chased Diane out of the court, I closed the portals and returned to my work in the vegetable garden supposing the episode to be over. Not at all. Presently the cook appeared, her face whiter than her apron. Madame, she said, poor Blanchette is no more. That wretched dog frightened her to death. Her heart was beating so furiously I saw there was but one thing to do. I gave her three tablespoonfuls of *eau-de-vie*, that will give her a good flavour. And then I killed her. How does Madame wish her to be cooked. Surprised at the turn the affair had taken, I answered feebly, With orange sauce.

🦎

Norbert Elias (1897–1990)

THE AUTHOR OF the massive treatise titled *The Civilizing Process* was one of the most influential sociologists of the twentieth century. Born in Germany to Jewish parents, Elias studied medicine and philosophy before turning to sociology. He was deeply involved in the German Zionist movement but fled to Paris after the Nazis gained ascendancy, then settled in London, where, ironically, he was detained for nearly a year in internment camps because he was a German "alien." Eventually, after many difficulties, Elias gained a series of teaching positions both in England (at the University of Leicester) and in Africa (at the University of Ghana), while continuing to draft his magnum opus. That work—one among eighteen volumes that marked his extraordinarily productive and brilliant career—traced the metamorphosis of European courtly culture into the early modern bourgeois society whose table manners he discusses in our selection here.

from *The Civilizing Process*: On the Use of the Fork at Table

WHAT IS THE real use of the fork? It serves to lift food that has been cut up to the mouth. Why do we need a fork for this? Why do we not use our fingers? Because it is "cannibal," as the "Man in the Club-Window," the anonymous author of *The Habits of Good Society*, said in 1859. Why is it "cannibal" to eat with one's fingers? That is not a question; it is self-evidently cannibal, barbaric, uncivilized or whatever else it is called.

But that is precisely the question. Why is it more civilized to eat with a fork?

"Because it is unhygienic to eat with one's fingers." That sounds convincing. To our sensibility it is unhygienic if different people put their fingers into the same dish, because there is a danger of contracting disease through contact with others. Each of us seems to fear that the others are diseased.

But this explanation is not entirely satisfactory. Nowadays we do not eat from common dishes. Everyone puts food into their mouth from their own plate. To pick it up from one's own plate with one's fingers cannot be more "unhygienic" than to put cake, bread, chocolate or anything else into one's mouth with one's own fingers.

So why does one really need a fork? Why is it "barbaric" and "uncivilized" to put food into one's mouth by hand from one's own plate? Because it is distasteful to dirty one's fingers, or at least to be seen in society with dirty fingers. The suppression of eating by hand from one's own plate has very little to do with the danger of illness, the so-called "rational" explanation. In observing our feelings towards the fork ritual, we can see with particular clarity that the first authority in our decision between whether behaviour at table is "civilized" or "uncivilized" is our feeling of distaste. The fork is nothing other than the embodiment of a specific standard of emotions and a specific level of revulsion. Behind the change in eating techniques between the Middle Ages and modern times appears the same process that emerged in the analysis of other incarnations of this kind: a change in the economy of drives and emotions.

Modes of behaviour which in the Middle Ages were not felt to be in the least distasteful have increasingly become surrounded by feelings of distaste. The standard of delicacy finds expression in corresponding social prohibitions. These taboos, so far as can be ascertained, are nothing other than ritualized or institutionalized feelings of displeasure, distaste, disgust, fear or shame, feelings which have been socially nurtured under quite specific conditions and which are constantly reproduced, not solely but mainly because they have become institutionally firmly embedded in a particular ritual, in particular forms of conduct.

The examples show—certainly only in a narrow cross-section and in the relatively randomly selected statements of individuals—how, in a phase of development in which the use of the fork was not yet taken for granted, the feeling of distaste that first formed within a narrow circle was slowly extended. "It is very impolite," says Courtin in 1672, "to touch anything greasy, a sauce or syrup, etc., with your fingers, apart from the fact that it obliges you to commit two or three more improper acts. One is to wipe your hand frequently on your serviette and to soil it like a kitchen cloth, so that those who see you wipe your mouth with it feel nauseated. Another is to wipe your fingers on your bread, which again is very improper. [N.B. The French terms *propre* and *malpropre* used by Courtin and explained in one of his chapters coincide less with the German terms for clean and unclean (*sauber* and *unsauber*) than with the word frequently used earlier, "proper."] The third is to lick them, which is the height of impropriety."

The *Civilité* of 1729 by La Salle, which transmitted the behaviour of the upper class to broader circles, says on one page: "When the fingers are very greasy, wipe them first on a piece of bread." This shows how far from general acceptance, even at this time, was the standard of delicacy that Courtin had already represented decades earlier. On the other hand, La Salle took over fairly literally Courtin's precept that "*Bienséance* does not permit anything greasy, a sauce or a syrup, to be touched with the fingers." And, exactly like Courtin, he mentioned among the ensuing *incivilités* wiping the hands on bread and licking the fingers, as well as soiling the napkin.

It can be seen that manners were here still in the process of formation. The new standard did not appear suddenly. Certain forms of behaviour were placed under prohibition, not because they were unhealthy but because they led to an offensive sight and disagreeable associations; shame at offering such a spectacle, originally absent, and fear of arousing such associations were gradually spread from the standard setting circles to larger circles by numerous authorities and institutions. However, once such feelings had been aroused and firmly established in society by means of certain rituals like that involving the fork, they were constantly reproduced so long as the structure of human relations was not fundamentally altered. The older generation, for whom such a standard of conduct is accepted as a matter of course, urges the children, who do not come into the world already equipped with these feelings and this standard, to control themselves more or less rigorously in accordance with it, and to restrain their drives and inclinations. If children tried to touch something sticky, wet or greasy with their fingers they were told, "You must not do that, people do not do things like that." And the displeasure towards such conduct which is thus aroused by the adult finally arises through habit, without being induced by another person.

To a large extent, however, the conduct and drives of the child are forced even without words into the same mould and in the same direction by the fact that a particular use of knife and fork, for example, is completely established in adult society—that is, by the example of the surrounding world. Since the pressure or coercion of individual adults is allied to the pressure and example of the whole surrounding world, most children, as they grow up, forget or repress relatively early the fact that their feelings of shame and embarrassment, of pleasure and displeasure, were moulded into conformity with a certain standard by external pressure and compulsion. All this appears to them as highly personal, something "inside," implanted in them by nature. While it is still directly visible in the writings of Courtin and La Salle that adults, too, were at first dissuaded from eating with their fingers by consideration for each other, by "politeness," to spare others a distasteful spectacle and themselves the shame of being seen with soiled hands, later it became more and more an inner automatism, the imprint of society on the inner self, the superego, that forbade the individual to eat in any other way than with a fork. The social standard to which the individual was first made to conform from outside by external restraint is finally reproduced more or less smoothly within him or her, through a self-restraint which operates to a certain degree even against his or her conscious wishes.

Thus the socio-historical process of centuries, in the course of which the standard of what is felt to be shameful and offensive has been slowly raised, is reenacted in abbreviated form in the life of the individual human being. If one wished to express recurrent processes of this kind in the form of laws, one could speak, as a parallel to the laws of biogenesis, of a fundamental law of sociogenesis and psychogenesis.

Elizabeth Bishop (1911–1979)

AN INVETERATE TRAVELER and a subtle, elegant poet, Bishop was raised for some years by grandparents in Nova Scotia after her father died and her mother became mentally ill, then moved to the home of other relatives in Massachusetts. As a child she suffered from asthma and was rarely able to attend school, though she read voraciously. Later, after graduating from Vassar, she formed strong friendships with a number of her most famous literary contemporaries, in particular Marianne Moore and Robert Lowell. Throughout much of her life, an inheritance gave her the option of living where she wished, so for fifteen years she settled in Brazil, involved in a passionate romantic relationship with the architect Lota de Macedo Soares. Always scrupulously detailed and brilliantly versified, Bishop's poetry can be incisive, speculative, and sometimes—as in our selection here—charmingly playful. "Lines Written in the Fannie Farmer Cookbook" was really inscribed in a cookbook owned by Bishop's longtime friend, the poet Frank Bidart, who, along with her final partner, Alice Methfessel, became one of her literary executors.

Lines Written in the Fannie Farmer Cookbook

[Given to Frank Bidart]

> You won't become a gourmet* cook
> By studying our Fannie's book—
> Her thoughts on Food & Keeping House
> Are scarcely those of Lévi-Strauss.
> Nevertheless, you'll find, Frank dear,
> The basic elements** are here.
> And if a problem should arise:
> The Soufflé fall before your eyes,
> Or strange things happen to the Rice
> —You know I love to give advice.

> Elizabeth
> Christmas, 1971

* Forbidden word
** Forbidden phrase

> P.S. Fannie should not be underrated;
> She has become sophisticated.
> She's picked up many gourmet* tricks
> Since the edition of '96.
> Elizabeth Bishop

🐜

Ruth Stone (1915–2011)

STONE BEGAN HER career as a poet of youthful delight and verve, but her outlook darkened after the suicide of her beloved second husband, the writer Walter Stone. Left indigent with three young daughters to raise, she traveled from campus to campus for short-term teaching jobs, an itinerant academic, while remaining relatively obscure. Yet her often elegiac, sometimes sardonic, always brilliant verse gained an increasing circle of admirers. At the age of seventy-five, when most professors retire, Stone became a tenured member of the faculty at SUNY-Binghamton, and in her eighties and nineties she began winning major prizes. "Vegetables II" reveals her at her wistful yet comic best, meditating on the kitchen as a "cutting room" where "I go . . . / To eat of death."

Vegetables II

Saturated in the room
The ravaged curry and white wine
Tilt on the sink.
Tomatoes in plastic bag
Send up odors of resentment,
Rotting quietly.
It is the cutting room, the kitchen,
Where I go like an addict
To eat of death.
The eggplant is silent.
We put our heads together.
You are so smooth and cool and purple,
I say, Which of us will it be?

William Dickey (1928–1994)

THE AUTHOR OF fifteen volumes of verse, Dickey spent many years teaching at San Francisco State after studying at Reed College, Harvard University, and the Iowa Writers' Workshop. A poet of steely wit and dazzle, he recalled with delight his days with undergraduate and graduate colleagues from Gary Snyder to W. D. Snodgrass. "Killing to Eat" characteristically mingles a seemingly casual culinary reference to Julia Child with a serious meditation on the food chain of which we all are part as eaters who are sooner or later destined to be eaten. Dickey died of HIV-related problems just a few years after retiring from San Francisco State University.

Killing to Eat

The serious cook really must face up to the task personally . . .
Using a sharp knife or lobster shears, cut straight down 1/2
inch into the back of the lobster, at the point where tail and
chest join, thus severing the spinal cord and killing the lobster
instantly.

JULIA CHILD AND SIMONE BECK,

MASTERING THE ART OF FRENCH COOKING, II

In the kitchen sink, two dozen astonished crayfish
crawl over each other to claw at the stainless steel.
I am a serious cook, and I will kill them.
Preparing a bath of vinegar, vegetables, spices,
I bring it to a boil and plunge them in.
They die instantly. They oblige me
by turning, in three minutes, pure Chinese red.

Later that night I wake, half out of dream,
and reach for the bedside glass that has my Sign,
the Archer, on it. Bewildered, I seem to see
not the Sign but one of the crayfish, resurrected,
climbing the inside of my glass to get in touch.

In the backyard of the house on Nelson Street
there was a chopping block and a Boy Scout hatchet
for killing the Sunday chickens. The hen picked up
out of her flock, the accurate glittering blow.
I watched one of them cut up. Inside, for tomorrow,
a completed egg, then one that was not quite finished,

then a dozen others, smaller to microscopic,
crowding her oviduct.

In our Zodiac there is no Sign
of Hen, or Cow, or Pig. It is full of hunters.
Orion stalks our sky with his Dogs, his Bears.
Underneath them scrabbles the eater, Cancer.

Could there be a kitchen Zodiac, in which
the Sign of the virgin Egg, the reclusive Lobster,
climb up the sky? Where we locate north
by looking for the constellation of the Bruised Calf?
where, after we have uneasily crossed the equator
the constellation of the Southern Fish is rising?

We wake from that dream sweating, nothing resolved.
The galaxy is the shape of an eating mouth.
The Wolf salivates in the vacuum, the Snake engorges.
We must eat to live, and we must kill to eat.

The serious cook will always face this problem.

Dorothy Gilbert (1936–)

A MEDIEVALIST, SCIENCE fiction writer, and poet, Gilbert has translated
major books from the old French of Chrétien de Troyes (*Erec and Enide*) and
Marie de France (*The Lays and Other Works*). Her writings have appeared in
a range of publications, including *The New Yorker* and *Fantasy and Science
Fiction*. The "Cook-Songs" we reprint here are drawn from a fabulous tale
of the planet "Musaeus," whose inhabitants broadcast strange poems into
outer space. Even while they satirize the recipe form with wit and grace, they
suggest exotically appetizing extraplanetary edibles.

Two Cook-Songs from the Planet Musaeus on the Same Subject, by Rival Poets

(1)

Ho, I am going to make
some wips: they will transport you.
In a pot I'll put
pittakaskadiblia; slibs, littacocks, lopples,
lorrops, hibbles, and the pips
of koffatids. Lattapurns
are good too, and chittabubs,
and fillakeens, if you like those.
I use korrafits, though coarse spirits don't like them,
bibberits, rissits, kukkadiffilits,
gillabits, timmabiberits and other tidbits,
bilps, bitterpips and stemmerits,
and pripples—pits, pulp and skin.
Stewed for long hours, they lie
finally, seething in a hot
sweet paste. Wips! Wonderful
wips! No one in this world
makes wips like mine. Ho,
I have done it.

(2)

Ho, I am going to make
small wips to excite you. Chittabubs,
lopsided and brown, sleepy features in corners,
I'll use, and fillakeens,
like heavy flowers; hibbles, like pale creatures
caught in cold seas. Landed, they smell
strangely of sweet roots dug from the loonth,
stored long in sunlight. Dubs also make

a sweet, sleepy taste. Lattapurns,
long dried, and hung in branches,
lorrops and korrafits, all the little fruits
called pittakaskadibblia. Then bibberits
and rissits, bitterpips and stemmerits,
pripples and bilps, pippakiperits and fips—
warm wines, green teas, spices for your delight!

All sizzle in my wips, the best
you'll ever have. Ho,
I have done it.

Roger J. Porter (1936–)

COEDITOR OF THIS volume, an english professor at Reed College and
scholar of autobiography by day and restaurant critic and food writer by
night, Porter has written on food matters in Portland, Oregon, for the past
twenty-five years, and was nominated by the James Beard Foundation for its
annual award in restaurant reviewing. One of Porter's favorite assignments
was distinctly "back of the house," in all its grittiness. Here, reporting on the
job of a restaurant health inspector, he comes to realize that even one degree
of temperature too high in a restaurant's walk-in cooler is no laughing matter.
In the mind of a beady-eyed, computer-assisted examiner, a casual, let alone
deliberate slip-up is in danger of producing nothing less than the bubonic
plague. Whether Porter is doing a "working" dinner or not, he doesn't normally concentrate on matters of sanitation, but his report will inevitably
make you worry—for better or worse—about those nasty microbes.

In Search of Filth: A Day in the Life of a Restaurant Health Inspector

I AM SPENDING the morning with a restaurant health inspector for Multnomah County, Oregon. We are at a well-known downtown Portland restaurant where Randy Howarth, a bureaucrat with a human face, has been in place for an hour, peering under storage shelves, checking the garbage cans, and measuring the temperature of the water in the dishwaters. He has scrutinized the floors, looked suspiciously at bottles of toxic chemicals, and felt the wrappings of storage containers to monitor for cross-contamination. He has noted the cleanliness of the workers' clothing, inspected the restrooms, and like a stern camp counselor, made sure there is no litter, that soiled linen is out of sight, and the stockpot handles are well scrubbed. Happily the ventilation is adequate, the walls are free of grease, and there's no evidence of insects, rodents, cats, or turtles. All seems well. Then disaster!

In the walk-in cooler, a five-gallon plastic drum of yesterday's clam chowder sits, awaiting the lunch service. Howarth whips out a battery of thermometers he always carries with him, and plunges one into the thick mass. 54 degrees—14 over the required maximum temperature—and thus a breeding ground for bacteria. Howarth senses danger: "It's got to go," he announces to the chef, who looks crestfallen. "But the soup is my pride and joy," he moans; "it's even better the second day, and besides, there's a hundred bucks worth in that container." Howarth hauls the drum up to the counter. He is firm: "Dispose of it." Meanwhile he goes off for further inspection: refuse disposal, hand-washing practices, utensil sanitizing. A half-hour later the offending soup remains, but Howarth is not a man to play softball. He picks up a quart of Windex and unceremoniously dumps the entire bottle of the ammonia-laden cleaner into the potage. "Just for insurance."

These days an inspector's job is part dispensing old-time homilies, part employing high-tech apparatus (with his laptop he can compare the results of previous visits). If he finds a can of WD-40 used to oil a bread mixer near some tomatoes, he will deliver an earnest lecture on the subject of proper storage. Too much grease on the counter, and he will sound like a matron out of *Godey's Lady's Book*. There are 100 pages in the Oregon Food Sanitation Rules book, and the regulations govern not only restaurants but food carts, and vending machines. Howarth can quote Food Sanitation Rule 333-156-240, with its instructions regarding the separation of food and toxic materials, though (unless pushed) he is less the enforcing martinet than a gentle figure concerned for both the restaurant's reputation and the public weal. If he finds significant violations, the restaurant receives a return visit in two weeks. If things are not sufficiently attended to, the inspector has the power to shut down the place on the spot.

Inspectors give no pre-visit warnings, and they have carte blanche to go everywhere and look at everything. He begins the tour by washing his hands at the kitchen sink, a practice he repeats, like a uniformed Lady Macbeth, a hundred times a day. He then prowls around a walk-in freezer, tests the waster in the dishwasher with little papers that indicate the levels of disinfectant, noses around the soft drink nozzles ("These fellows look real nice"), measures the space between floor and storage racks (6 inches minimum), and delights in the fact that all the cooks are wearing their hats. He tells me that food must be covered especially well under a fan, where dirt particles can be blown in on the ingredients; that mollusk and crustacean shells may not be reused, however cleanly scrubbed; that the food must be thawed in a microwave, refrigerator, or under running water but never at room temperature. He notes, with a touch of sadness, that a piece of Provimi veal on the counter lies perilously close to a turkey breast. Entering the dining room (it's mid-morning and there are no customers), like a detective hunting for clues he picks up some silverware and scans it for dried-on tomato stains. And like a diamond merchant examining the facets of a stone, he holds a goblet of cut crystal to the light.

Howarth prints out his report for the anxious chef. Six months ago the place was only marginally in compliance, and were it to receive a score of less than 70 at this inspection, a notice would be posted at the entrance stating that it had "failed to comply with acceptable sanitation standards," a virtual death blow to business. But Howarth tells the chef, who stands by like a chastened pupil, that the restaurant has barely squeaked by, and as the inspector leaves to discernible sighs of relief, he promises ominously to return sometime by year's end.

Although Howarth's specialty is food service, he is not restricted to restaurants, of which there are more than two thousand in the Portland area. He is also responsible for snack bars, cafés, theater concession stands, school kitchens, daycare facilities, park picnic sites, and farmers' markets. One of his colleagues has a sub-specialty in bed and breakfasts.

All the inspection records are public, so if your favorite eatery hasn't been up to snuff recently—and as a result you haven't been either—it's possible to check the files to see if there's any danger of salmonella, staphylococcus, or hepatitis. The latter is a restaurant's greatest health hazard; in Portland alone a dozen restaurants are under surveillance for this health problem.

The next place we visit is a mom-and-pop Vietnamese restaurant, the kind of small joint you'd think might be at risk. But the opposite is true at this spotless spot. It has but one tiny violation: not enough paper towels accessible at the food handlers' sinks. Howarth glows with satisfaction throughout the visit. The ice is well stored, the glassware gleams, the leftovers are covered to the max. It's a family business: Grandfather peels carrots, Grandmother chops peppers, Nephew sizzles oil on a meticulously clean stove. Perhaps because each family member has a personal stake in things, cleanliness is not a matter of adherence to regulations but of simple pride. Howard pastes up the sticker of approval as everyone gathers and beams.

I begin to look at things with a different eye. Suddenly the floor underneath the refrigerator seems as important as a rack of lamb, the "potable water system anti-back flow production procedures" as crucial as the burnt sugar topping on a *crème brûlée*. But the dangers of excessive self-consciousness are present as well. If you think too much about all that can and does go amiss—or read your Anthony Bourdain—you'll become a neurotic foodaphobe; imagine Woody Allen as a health inspector and you'll get the picture. As one chef told me, "If the regulations were applied strictly by the book, 99 percent of all restaurants wouldn't last a day."

❧

Nancy Willard (1936–)

A PROLIFIC, PRIZE-WINNING author of children's books, Willard is also a novelist, poet, and essayist. On the creative writing faculty at Vassar for many years, she has also illustrated many of her fantastic tales, and is known for the verve with which she illuminates the extraordinary aspects of the seemingly ordinary. Explaining the dedication to "magic" that shapes her work, she has observed that "most of us grow up and put magic away with other childish things. But I think we can all remember a time when magic was as real to us as science, and the things we couldn't see were as important as the things we could." The enchanting insights of her poetic recipe for "How to Stuff a Pepper" arise from such magic-making.

How to Stuff a Pepper

Now, said the cook, I will teach you
how to stuff a pepper with rice.

Take your pepper green, and gently,
for peppers are shy. No matter which side
you approach, it's always the backside.
Perched on her green buttocks, the pepper sleeps.
In its silk tights, it dreams
of somersaults and parsley,
of the days when the sexes were one.

Slash open the sleeve
as if you were cutting into a paper lantern,
and enter a moon, spilled like a melon,
a fever of pearls,
a conversation of glaciers.
It is a temple built to the worship
of morning light.

I have sat under the great globe
of seeds on the roof of that chamber,
too dazzled to gather the taste I came for.
I have taken the pepper in hand,
smooth and blind, a runt in the rich
evolution of roses and ferns.
You say I have not yet taught you

to stuff a pepper?
Cooking takes time.

Next time we'll consider the rice.

John Thorne (1943–)

THORNE IS ONE of America's more unheralded but astute food writers, who established his reputation with a dogged insistence on honest, straightforward recipes. He is the author of an acclaimed food newsletter "Simple Cooking," along with numerous books, including *Serious Pig* and *Mouth Wide Open*. Armed with a weather eye for the bogus, the self-righteous, and the pretentious, and committed to a simple lifestyle in Maine, Thorne takes positions contrary to those of many celebrity chefs. Here he questions the importance of the food processor and the microwave, exposing what he considers their irrelevance to genuine cooking and arguing that they distance the cook from hands-on involvement with food. He regards the microwave oven as especially perverse because it cooks foods from the inside out rather than, as traditional fire-based methods do, from the outside in.

from *The Outlaw Cook*: Cuisine Mécanique

I FIRST ENCOUNTERED the food processor and the microwave oven in the mid-1970s. This didn't happen on the same day or even in the same week or month, but it did happen in close enough proximity to my own newly acquired self-identity as a food enthusiast for the two machines to become forever firmly linked in my mind. At the time, of course, I didn't think of them as twins, or even near relations, although they were impressive in the same way. Both were on the breaking edge of cooking technology; both were designed to make work shorter and easier. Even so, to me—and to others as well—they initially appeared, as kitchen appliances, exactly opposite in *virtu*. While one was opening whole new culinary horizons, the other was fast becoming the boon tool of the I-hate-to-cook crowd, a hyped-up gadget that did things incredibly fast at the cost of not doing them well.

Upwardly mobile *nouveau cuisinier* that I was quickly becoming, there was simply no question in my mind as to which was which—even though I knew the attraction I felt for the food processor was not universally shared. Debates about its merits still raged in the food magazines, fueled by complaints from those of the culinary old guard who had so far refused to join the stampede.

Not me. I read their opinions with interest, but distantly. I knew that no matter how convincing the case against the machine might be, I *had* to have one. All it had taken was a department-store demonstration: the moment I saw that ball of brioche dough take form and leap up onto the whirring blades, I knew, for me, cooking would never be the same. I couldn't afford an actual Cuisinart—not everyone gets a Volvo in life—but I did purchase their own short-lived bargain-basement brand, the quite adequate Omni-chef.

If you were there then, you'll remember the feeling. The food processor was different from other appliances: it compelled belief. Supper guests actually came into the kitchen after dinner to feed it carrots. It was the next best thing to having Paul Bocuse himself come out with the coffee for introductions and acclaim.

As time went on, most serious cooks gave in and got one; the scoffing now came from somewhere else. The food processor has found such a secure place in our kitchen that it seems hard to believe that fifteen years ago it was the same sort of contempt-generating machine that, until very recently, the microwave oven was for us. Cultural critics of the time coined the phrase "Cuisinart liberal" to convey what was wrong with suburbanite reformers: they adopted all the correct positions without having to pay any of the requisite dues.

They were wrong—cultural critics always are—but they do know how to hurt. The phrase stung because we already knew that our culinary titularies—Elizabeth David, Diana Kennedy, Jane Grigson—didn't own Cuisinarts. Nor did we want them to. The thought of hearing the machine's high-pitched keening in Richard Olney's Provençal kitchen would have filled most of us with genuine grief.

The truth was that we felt that we had come too late to pay our dues. We were only just discovering true French cuisine at the very moment it had started to fade away. Now that its ingredients were available and gifted cooks were coming back home to explain it, few of us could imagine devoting ourselves to the time-consuming, meticulous preparation it demanded.

Many of us were, after all, young professionals whose careers were just then getting into gear.

If the food processor had not been right there, we might have paused, might have asked how the French themselves were managing this. We knew that food and its preparation played a different role in their lives than it did in ours, but our understanding of this was, for all our enthusiasm, essentially shallow.

For centuries, they had been on to a good thing, and now—almost too late—we were being let in on it. At last, what they could buy, we could buy; what they could do, we could, too—but *only* because of this machine. What luck for us it was the very same one that, in Roy Andries de Groot's words, had in France "already brought about the major gastronomic revolution of the past twenty years," the style of cooking that was becoming known as *nouvelle cuisine*.

If Carl Sontheimer, the entrepreneur who adapted and marketed the machine in America, is a genius, it is for knowing that the time was ripe for this machine and exactly which cooks it was ripe *for*: those of us who took our cooking *seriously*. Other manufacturers copied the machine but missed the mark. They colored it pink, softened its formidable lines, and advertised it as another kitchen work-saver, a kind of turbo-blender.

In truth, the food processor is a work-*maker*. The sort of things you are drawn to do with it you wouldn't even think of trying without it: shredding your own rillettes, sieving your own quenelles, hand-mounting your own mayonnaise.

If you had no interest in that sort of thing, a food processor was a mistaken purchase. The Dad who bought one as a surprise for Mom to help her out with the kitchen chores was in for a rude surprise: if Mom didn't own at least one French cookbook, she most likely put the machine away under the counter after the first exploratory spin.

But to the fledgling serious cook, the Cuisinart, dressed in its spotless kitchen whites, presented itself not only as a tool of professional chefs (which it was) but as a professionalizing one, the one essential shortcut to chefdom. We had only to follow instructions to be jumped straight from *commis* to *gros bonnet* . . . at least in our own kitchen. Or so we thought. . . .

The food processor is not an electric knife (which had already been invented, only to prove itself nothing much) but a cutting *machine*. It pushes the cook's hands aside, for it works far too quickly for the body to directly control it. Our responses are simply not fast enough; we learn to count seconds instead.

Set the steel blade in place, fill the container with basil, pine nuts, garlic, and chunks of Parmesan, and switch the motor on. The machine begins to sauce the ingredients so immediately that they seem to flow together; for its operator, there is a genuine sensual delight in the way, so quickly, so smoothly, it pulps the basil, grinds the cheese, and, as the olive oil starts dribbling down the feeding tube, plumps it all into a thick and unctuous cream.

Sensual it truly is, but it is the sensuality of observing, not participating. The food processor does not enhance the cook's experience. Instead, that work is divided between the mind, which directs it, and the machine, which performs it. The body's part is reduced to setting out and—mostly—cleaning up afterward.

In short, no matter what the mind learns, the hand remains as ignorant as ever. And as time passes, the ease by which the machine accomplishes its tasks makes the hands seem awkward when we *do* put them to use. Anyone who has tried to make pesto in a mortar and pestle after years of concocting it in a food processor knows that the experience can quickly turn into one of helpless frustration. The body just does not know how to go about it: the pestle feels clumsy and ineffectual in the hand, and as the minutes tick by and the contents of the mortar refuse to meld into a sauce, one feels increasingly foolish. Although one knows, from having read books, that this is how it was always done, it doesn't *feel* right. It simply takes too long.

No other kitchen appliance makes the body feel so impotent because no other dissolves away so much hands-on kitchen work. A blender may whir at an equally incomprehensible speed, but it remains a gadget, its niche in our cooking small. The food processor, on the other hand, is capable of assuming almost the entire repertoire of kitchen prep.

The cost of this usurpation was not only the loss of kitchen work by which the body had formerly refreshed itself, exercising genuinely demanding skills and shaping work to the tempo of personal rhythms. There were two other unexpected consequences.

The first was that, by strength of example, the food processor began to corrode the meaning of *all* kitchen work. This was true not only of the homes that already had a food processor, for once a kind of kitchen work becomes identified as a tiresome chore by enough cooks, it begins to lie heavy and sullen in the hands of all of them. What could not now be done effortlessly, cleanly, perfectly, became by comparison drudgery, all the more susceptible to replacement by some other, cleverer machine.

The second consequence was one to which we *nouveaux cuisiniers* were especially vulnerable. The product of a wealthy, acquisitive culture that could pick the ingredients of its meals almost at will, we had now been given a machine that allowed us to prepare an almost unlimited number of complex dishes without any kind of physical restraint.

For the same reason, we were equally enticed by any and all new recipes that came our way. The less that cooking comes from hands-on kitchen experience, the harder it is for a cook to gauge the desirability of a newly encountered dish. A cook who makes all chicken broth from scratch will cast a more discriminating eye on a recipe that calls for it than the cook who pours it from the can. The cook who does all her own cutting, chopping, and sieving immediately knows the appropriateness of a new recipe: it must fit the hands.

On the contrary, freed of the necessity of such choices, *our* only way of judging a dish's rightness was becoming the wanton appreciation of the tongue and the riot of culinary fad. Appetite has always had a hard time saying no; it needs guidance we were no longer in a position to provide.

None of this, of course, was the food processor's fault. But just as the automobile changed the landscape of America in ways that no one had expected or prepared for, the food processor shifted the nature of culinary reality ... more slowly for the culture at large, but almost immediately in the micro-culture that was beginning to take food seriously. As it proliferated, it began raising the stakes for all, even for those who did not yet possess one. And it is this effect—in an equally unexpected way—that we have just begun to experience with the microwave.

Unlike the food processor, the microwave has no French ancestry, or even—until relatively recently—any influential food-world friends. It lacks the assertively simple high-tech styling and the haute-cuisine associations that might have provided it with Cuisinart-like cachet. In fact, with its buttons, buzzers, and revolving carousels, the microwave, from the very start, has seemed irredeemably prole—right down to the reason for owning one.

For no matter the culinary arguments voiced in its favor, the only truly compelling reason to own a microwave is still the first: it is the best medium yet devised for the almost instant reheating of cooked food.

Even so, what made the microwave seem irresistible to its original purchasers is not all that different from what made the food processor seem so desirable to us. Both fed a fantasy of participating in a cuisine whose rationale had already evaporated, no matter how delicious its dishes. For the first microwave owners, however, that cuisine was the familiar American supper. With its assistance, a family could dispense with a regular cook and even a common dinnertime—and still sit down to the familiar trinity of meat, starch, and vegetable, courtesy of Swanson's LeMenu, served piping hot on a premium plastic plate—no more the TV-dinner tripart, tinfoil, cafeteria-style serving tray.

The price was the same: the cook was obliged to surrender involvement for convenience. Microwave energy offers no equivalent experience to replace our intuitive understanding of heat; indeed, the body's inability to respond or protect itself means the cooking food must be locked away out of reach. Because microwaves cook food from the inside out, they are unable to provide us with any of radiant heat's familiar, helpful clues. As with the Cuisinart, the cook must count seconds instead.

Food processor, microwave oven . . . the one speeds preparation by removing it from human hands and human time; the other does the same to the actual process of cooking. As the food processor devours the experience of knife and cutting board, whisk and bowl, the other eats away at an even more primal experience: the putting of food to fire.

That we *nouveaux cuisiniers* originally missed the connection is not surprising; we put a very different weight on the meaning of the two types of experience. Our inspiration was, after all, the chef; if there was any experience in cooking that remained crucial to us, it was dexterity before the flame.

What we never expected was that as kitchen experience in its entirety became progressively devalued, the aura that still clung to the stove would also necessarily fade. Unnoticed by us, the image of the chef before his range, sweat dripping down his face as hot fat shimmered in his sauté pan, was undergoing as radical a change for microwave users as the role of scullion had for us.

As more and more cooks began to learn how to use their microwave, the conventional oven was progressively being found too hot, too time-consum-

ing, too wasteful of energy, and, above, all, too *greasy* . . . literally, but figuratively, too, for the description began to embrace as well the meals that it was
used to prepare.

Unlike traditional cuisines, recipe-based cooking has never allowed the
home cook to shape a meal by reworking the same dish from day to day
in response to what her family needs to eat—adding or eliminating meat,
throwing in a smaller or larger proportion of chopped greens or a larger or
smaller handful of rice. The amounts and the ingredients of recipe dishes are
already determined forever by someone else who knows none of the eaters—
or their needs or appetites.

There is something relentless about recipes in this regard: they create a
condition not unlike the air temperature in a large office building, where it
is always too hot in the winter and too cold in the summer—but if no one
is really happy, neither can anyone complain. Recipe cooking likewise gives
us too much; whether in the guise of fattening us up or slimming us down,
somehow things are always being waved in front of our mouths. This is the
purpose of recipes, after all: to arouse appetite. Like central heating, food
writing's only task is to make us "comfortable": it might be establishing a
climate of self-indulgence or self-denial, but it is still busy making us feel
hungry—the only question being what we are to become hungry *for*.

So far as reheating was concerned, of course, no food writing was needed
to get microwave owners to turn the appetite thermostat up. Because of its
original audience, much of pre-packaged microwave food was already laden
with calories. Turning the thermostat down, however, was quite another
matter. Microwave cooking, because it required that all recipes be recast
for its peculiar way of heating, offered a glorious opportunity for cookbook
writers to play not only on their readers' increasingly compulsive need for
cooking to be made easy, but also upon their terror of fat.

The microwave's chief handicap—that it cooks best what is best cooked
inside out—suddenly became a plus. No need to apologize that it can't crisp
the fat when there's no fat to crisp—especially when you can harp on the fact
that it can steam broccoli in its own moisture to tender doneness before the
exterior has a chance to dry out—with not a calorie added or a vitamin lost.

"An odd thing happened a few years ago as I began to cook a great deal
in the microwave oven," writes Barbara Kafka in the introduction to her
Microwave Gourmet Healthstyle Cookbook. "It was less hard to lose weight

when it started to go up, and it was easier to keep it off. . . . After a while, I figured it out. The microwave oven doesn't need fat to cook."

Neither, of course, do many conventional cooking techniques, and those that do don't always add that many calories to the completed dish. But such language sells microwaves—just as it once sold food processors. As Henri Gault (of *Le Nouveau Guide de Gault-Millau*) told Roy Andries de Groot in *Revolutionizing French Cooking*: "Our French *Robot Coupe* [the original Cuisinart] . . . is a precious tool for the easy preparation of the new low-fat, low-starch, low-sugar, yet high-pleasure cuisine. With it, you can emulsify and thicken the sauces . . . with no use whatsoever of butter or flour." All you need is the machine—and some new recipes. . . .

Once, not so long ago, we were allowed some of the evening to cook supper. Even in the seventies, when Pierre Franey began his "60-Minute Gourmet" column for *The New York Times*, to make a complete dinner within an hour seemed quite a feat. Now it seems an extravagance. Today, twenty minutes is more like it: hence the *Times*'s food editor Marian Burros's column, "20-Minute Menus." Corby Kummer's five-minute fish bake will soon be eating into that.

The reason we still believe we possess this free time is that we have been persuaded to externalize the experience of cooking into a series of unwanted chores. Whatever the user of the microwave is doing with his or her freed-up time, it is obviously not *cooking*—and to that very limited extent, he or she has been set free. But for what?

To understand what has really happened to us, imagine attempting to reverse the process. Imagine *wanting* to take a whole afternoon to leisurely prepare supper—without food processor, microwave oven, or cookbook. To live, after all, is to experience things, and every time we mince an onion, lower the flame under a simmering pot, shape the idea and substance of a meal, we actually gain rather than lose lived time. Such minutes are not only full and rich in themselves, but they brush a lasting patina of lived experience onto our memory.

꙰

Adrian Searle (1953–)

THE ART CRITIC for *The Guardian*, Searle was trained as a painter and has also published widely in other papers and journals on contemporary aesthetic trends. Currently a visiting professor at the Royal College of Art in London, he has taught at numerous other institutions and curated a number of important exhibitions. His essay on Ferran Adrià's atelier was written in connection with elBulli's selection as a part of the major German art show *documenta*, although Adrià himself was ambivalent about his role in the project. He has been called "the Dalí of the kitchen," but he noted bemusedly that "artists all over battle all their lives to receive an invitation to display their work at *documenta* and now I, a cook, am asked to go along!"

A Visit to Ferran Adrià's Workshop

SCHLLURK. I AM testing an experimental snack, which fills a clear plastic tube roughly the size of a cigarette. This has been presented to me on a transparent plastic cushion filled with blue anti-freeze gel. The goo in the tube makes a satisfying, noisy slurp as I syphon it up, and whatever it is floods my mouth in a nice, gloopy jet. It's caviar lubricated with egg yolk, and maybe something else, but I can't tell what.

This is cyberfood, an astronaut's snack, part "menu degustation," part kiddy food for adults. It comes along with a cocktail in the form of a solid, perfect cube of translucent jelly; plastic slurpies of consommé or mousse, savoury lollipops and little sweeties in cellophane. All of this is still at the R&D stage, and I'm in the lab in Barcelona with the backroom boys, who are working on the new dishes for Ferran Adrià, Spain's—and possibly the world's—most innovative chef.

Are we ever entirely adult when we eat? Etiquette guards us against our infantile instincts. Cutlery, the stately procession of plates and glasses, the authority of the table-setting and the muted atmosphere all suppress our more animal urges. But when dishes come looking like this, and when each new dish invites you to use your hands and your mouth, your ears and your nose in a new way, it is difficult to know quite how to proceed. Things snap, slurp, come as a wisp of smoke or a cloud of foam. Things that should be hot come cold; liquids arrive as solids or as a kind of plasma; a succession of dishes appear which challenge manners. And why are they waving a canister of CO_2 gas back there in the kitchen?

I am in elBullitaller, Adrià's "workshop" off the Rambla in Barcelona, where Adrià, his brother Albert—who works on the desserts—and a team of talented young chefs develop new dishes for the season at elBulli, Adrià's world-famous restaurant, up the coast near Roses, north of Girona. With its three Michelin stars, elBulli is hard to get to, harder still to get a table at. More than half the bookings have already been made for the six-month season ahead. It isn't far from elBulli, either by boat or up the winding mountain road, to the village of Cadaqués, where Picasso invented Cubism, and where Salvador Dalí lived. Adrià has been dubbed the Dalí of the kitchen, though Dalí's alarming personal habits (not now, thanks, not while I'm eating) should warn you off such comparisons, such hyperbole.

Marcel Duchamp, the father of conceptual art, was a frequent summer visitor to Cadaqués. Once, he described painting not as something visual, but as "olfactory," an art of smells: of oil, resins, varnish and turpentine. If a painter works in a perfumed cloud, Adrià invites you to eat it, drink it, sniff it and smoke it. Adrià has also described his cooking as conceptual. He is trying all sorts of new, techno things this season: atomizer sprays to sweeten or salt your food at the table, and while you're at it, how about spray-on sauces and aerosols of wine or chocolate? He has been working, too, with an odour expert, who has created scents which perfume a little menu to accompany a couple of new dishes. Not so much to scratch'n' sniff, but to be transported as you eat. Oriol Castro, one of the team of talented young chefs who work with Adrià, waves a spray-can around the workshop. One squirt and it turns the space into a conceptual forest—suddenly I smell leaf-mould, lichen, moss, wild fungi. Pffft, and another squirt takes me to the coast—the smells of seaweed, ozone and iodine, wet rocks. These memorious fragrances could be gimmicky and annoying. Instead, they're magical. This is a landscape in a can.

For all the effort and backroom stuff, Adrià is remarkably open about his experiments. His kitchen is an open, collaborative venture. I go through the daily notebooks, like artist's daybooks, with great little drawings, handwritten reflections and diagrams. Here's a Russian salad in the shape of a minimalist grid. A cornet, like a tiny ice-cream cone, comes topped with a cloud of parmesan-tasting froth. The same course is repeated in different forms: served first hot, then cold, first solid, then as liquid. The entry for January 12, for example, has seventeen or eighteen preparations listed, annotated with copious notes and little drawings. The notebooks are deconstructivist manuals, in which the familiar is taken in unexpected directions. It evidences a truly creative process.

Isn't it all a bit complicated? I asked. There's no opposition between simple or complicated, Adrià said, there's only good and bad. Bread is complicated. And gastronomy is not the same thing as hunger. Adrià said he didn't discover his mouth till he was twenty, and then, like a kid, he couldn't stop asking *why* all the time, why food had to be the way it is. Adrià says he is interested in the evolution of his restaurant, rather than having a style. This is the same for artists, surely—the best evolve, leaving their followers to turn their advances into style. This is the difference between innovators like Braque and Picasso, and the later cubists. When the imitators start to take risks, things can go horribly wrong.

But Adrià is the master of such things, because he recognizes the difference between good and bad. Nowadays, we are apt to forget that good and bad exist in art. You can kill a chicken in the name of art, but only if it is edible. "There are limits," he reminds me—"Have you seen the movie *Hannibal*," he asks, "with that brain-scooping bit at the end?" Eugh. "It is all," he insists, "a question of harmony."

I came to Adrià's lab expecting the most subtle combinations and rarest ingredients, the real outer limit of the comestible. Where's that oyster, caviar and foie gras dish he's been working on, where's my Daiquiri, made with almond milk and a hot spume of truffles? But the subject for today's experiment was pork scratchings.

We go to the market, the vast cast-iron Boqueria on the Rambla, to shop. It is the nearest place I know, outside of Hieronymus Bosch, to a Garden of Earthly Delights. It is the best food market I know, anywhere. It leaves you in despair of Britain, the rubbish we fill our trolleys with, the desultory selections, the mean-looking, fluorescent-lit pap in the supermarkets. So what do we buy? A kilo of ham fat (not just any old fat, it must be said), white and glistening in a vacuum pack. Back at base we render the fat in the microwave, crisp the gleaming rind, and produce lots of liquid. We try the scratchings with tofu; we try them with little home-made sesame snaps (but one seed deep, perfectly made, in the lightest web of caramel). We try the pork with whatever is lying about.

In the end, the rendered liquid is whisked up with water, producing a thick froth. We have this insubstantial nimbus with fresh peas, a fried egg. What could be more conventional than ham and peas, ham 'n' eggs? Yet, the peas disappearing in the fog, the egg shining through the cloud like the sun, look beautiful. And yes, the froth tastes sweetly of ham.

Over on the bench, the lads are composing a small dish with all the finesse of someone building a micro-processor by hand. On a little bite-sized plinth of solidified, gelatinized water, they arrange three, fingernail-sized blobs. The first is a concentrated island of Thai ingredients, the second a miniaturized Japan, the third a précis of Mexican cooking. With each mouthful, you savour an entire culinary tradition. Adrià swallows Thailand whole, with a fresh oyster on the side. I follow, quickly mopping up Japan and Mexico, each in turn with an oyster. It isn't so much that the flavours of each country are intense and perfectly balanced, so much as the sudden swerve from one compound of flavours and textures to another disorientates the palette. The sliver of jalapeño chili in the Mexican island of creamed maize, like a mariachi band, blasts through the afterburn of the tiny Mount Fuji of wasabi in Japan. The bones behind my ears begin to sing. The whole thing took fifteen minutes to prepare, a moment to eat, and now I'm drooling as I write about it.

Adrià has the Catalan love of details, and of extremes, but his cooking is also founded in humour and a deep respect for Mediterranean tradition dependent on its local cuisines. The new Basque cooking—exemplified by Arzak—retains the robustness which the climate demands, and the tradition of the tapa, of the *montadito*, is as much an influence as nouvelle cuisine.

It is also a question of dialogues, and openness, rather than hidden kitchens and secret ingredients. elBullitaller remains open to visitors. On my visit, a young chef from the Basque country drops by to say hello. A guy in the corner videos the day's experiments. I'm invited to join meetings, to hang around with a beer, stick my finger in things and have a good sniff about. He gives me a list of his favourite chefs; I give him one of favourite artists. Adrià hangs around in the kitchen. There's constant talk and rifling through a library of cookbooks, and checking out other restaurants. Dishes are scrutinised, notes taken at the table. There is a sense of collaboration, and openness, within the gastronomic community. Like celebrity chefs here,

Adrià has branched out into books, recipe manuals for ten-minute cooking at home. TV programmes and an up-market private catering division. He jets off to cook for euro-ministers and royalty. He's raking it in. Yet Adrià reminds us of Lévi-Strauss's distinction between the raw and the cooked, of what it means to be civilised; and the difference between style and innovation, the good and the bad.

🐘

Patricia Smith (1955–)

POET, PLAYWRIGHT, FICTION writer, and journalist Patricia Smith has earned numerous awards and honors for her lively and enlivening work, including four Poetry Slam contests and a nomination for the National Book Award, among other achievements. Currently a professor of English at CUNY/College of Staten Island, Smith was born in Chicago, and her poignant memories of her father's death in that city from a seemingly random gunshot haunts the evocative recipe for "hot water cornbread" that she offers in "When the Burning Begins." As much a formula for poetry as it is an elegy for a dead parent, Smith's poem has a title that is itself ambiguous: does the corn bread get cooked "when the burning" in the cast iron pan "begins," or does the poem come to life when the burning of grief and rage starts up? Either way, the corn bread itself—a savory, sensual dish central to southern, especially African-American culture and analogous to the "bakes" of Barbados (see our selections from Frederick Douglass and Austin Clarke in this volume)—is here heated with meaning.

When the Burning Begins

for Otis Douglas Smith, my father

> The recipe for hot water cornbread is simple:
> Cornmeal, hot water. Mix till sluggish,

then dollop in a sizzling skillet.
When you smell the burning begin, flip it.
When you smell the burning begin again,
dump it onto a plate. You've got to wait
for the burning and get it just right.

Before the bread cools down,
smear it with sweet salted butter
and smash it with your fingers,
crumple it up in a bowl
of collard greens or buttermilk,
forget that I'm telling you it's the first thing
I ever cooked, that my daddy was laughing
and breathing and no bullet in his head
when he taught me.

Mix it till it looks like quicksand, he'd say.
Till it moves like a slow song sounds.

We'd sit there in the kitchen, licking our fingers
and laughing at my mother,
who was probably scrubbing something with bleach,
or watching *Bonanza,*
or thinking how stupid it was to be burning
that nasty old bread in that cast iron skillet.
When I told her that I'd made my first-ever pan
of hot water cornbread, and that my daddy
had branded it glorious, she sniffed and kept
mopping the floor over and over in the same place.

So here's how you do it:

You take out a bowl, like the one
we had with blue flowers and only one crack,
you put the cornmeal in it.
Then you turn on the hot water and you let it run
while you tell the story about the boy

who kissed your cheek after school
or about how you really want to be a reporter
instead of a teacher or nurse like Mama said,
and the water keeps running while Daddy says
You will be a wonderful writer
and you will be famous someday and when
you get famous, if I wrote you a letter and
sent you some money; would you write about me?

and he is laughing and breathing and no bullet
in his head. So you let the water run into this mix
till it moves like mud moves at the bottom of a river,
which is another thing Daddy said, and even though
I'd never even seen a river,
I knew exactly what he meant.
Then you turn the fire way up under the skillet,
and you pour in this mix
that moves like mud moves at the bottom of a river,
like quicksand, like slow song sounds.

That stuff pops something awful when it first hits
that blazing skillet, and sometimes Daddy and I
would dance to those angry pop sounds,
he'd let me rest my feet on top of his
while we waltzed around the kitchen
and my mother huffed and puffed
on the other side of the door. *When you are famous,*
Daddy asks me, will you write about dancing
in the kitchen with your father?
I say everything I write will be about you,
then you will be famous too. And we dip and swirl
and spin, but then he stops.
And sniffs the air.

The thing you have to remember
about hot water cornbread
is to wait for the burning

so you know when to flip it, and then again
so you know when it's crusty and done.
Then eat it the way we did,
with our fingers,
our feet still tingling from dancing.
But remember that sometimes the burning
takes such a long time,
and in that time,
sometimes,
poems are born.

༝

Anthony Bourdain (1956–)

THE NOTORIOUS BAD boy of the food world, Bourdain is a chef, prolific writer about food explorations around the world, and a TV personality, with a consuming passion for food wherever he finds it. Famous for his exposé of the dark side of kitchen practice in *Kitchen Confidential: Adventures in the Culinary Underbelly*, Bourdain is as likely to write about the drug culture at professional stoves (as a young man he did a considerable amount of restaurant cooking high on heroin, cocaine, and LSD) as about restaurants' use of near-rotting leftovers in a Sunday brunch. His writing is full of verve, highly opinionated judgments, and personal revelations no less frank than his unmasking of restaurant conventions. Known for his food sensationalism, Bourdain has consumed ant eggs, seal eyeballs, and the still-beating heart of a cobra on camera, while also declaring chicken nuggets the worst meal of his life, right up there with Namibian warthog rectum. But sometimes his writing has sweetness, joy, and communal spirit: for nothing makes him happier than sharing a meal that turns strangers into friends, whether in the Mekong Delta or San Sebastián.

from *Kitchen Confidential*:
From Our Kitchen to Your Table

I SAW A sign the other day outside one of those Chinese-Japanese hybrids that are beginning to pop up around town, advertising "Discount Sushi." I can't imagine a better example of Things to Be Wary Of in the food department than bargain sushi. Yet the place had customers. I wonder, had the sign said "Cheap Sushi" or "Old Sushi," if they'd still have eaten there.

Good food and good eating are about risk. Every once in a while an oyster, for instance, will make you sick to your stomach. Does this mean you should stop eating oysters? No way. The more exotic the food, the more adventurous the serious eater, the higher the likelihood of later discomfort. I'm not going to deny myself the pleasures of morcilla sausage, or sashimi or even ropa vieja at the local Cuban joint just because sometimes I feel bad a few hours after I've eaten them.

But there are some general principles I adhere to, things I've seen over the years that remain in my mind and have altered my eating habits. I may be perfectly willing to try the grilled lobster at an open-air barbecue shack in the Caribbean, where the refrigeration is dubious and I can see with my own eyes the flies buzzing around the grill (I mean, how often am I in the Caribbean? I want to make the most of it!), but on home turf, with the daily business of eating in restaurants, there are some definite dos and don'ts I've chosen to live by.

I never order fish on Monday, unless I'm eating at Le Bernardin—a four-star restaurant where I *know* they are buying their fish directly from the source. I know how old most seafood is on Monday—about four to five days old!

You walk into a nice two-star place in Tribeca on a sleepy Monday evening and you see they're running a delicious-sounding special of Yellowfin Tuna, Braised Fennel, Confit Tomatoes and a Saffron Sauce. Why not go for it? Here are the two words that should leap out at you when you navigate the menu: "Monday" and "Special."

Here's how it works: The chef of this fine restaurant orders his fish on Thursday for delivery Friday morning. He's ordering a pretty good amount of it, too, as he's not getting another delivery until Monday morning. All right, *some* seafood purveyors make Saturday deliveries, but the market is closed Friday night. *It's the same fish from Thursday!* The chef is hoping to sell the bulk of that fish—your tuna—on Friday and Saturday nights, when he assumes it will be busy. He's assuming also that if he has a little left on Sunday, he can unload the rest of it then, as seafood salad for brunch, or as a special. Monday? It's merchandizing night, when whatever is left over from the weekend is used up, and hopefully sold for money. Terrible, you say? Why doesn't he throw the left-over tuna out? The guy can get deliveries on *Monday*, right? Sure, he can . . . but what is preventing his seafood purveyor from thinking exactly the same way? The seafood vendor is emptying out *his* refrigerator, too! But the Fulton Street fish market is *open* on Monday morning, you say!! He can get *fresh!* I've been to the Fulton Street market at three o'clock on Monday morning, friends, and believe me, it does *not* inspire confidence. Chances are good that that tuna you're thinking of ordering on Monday night has been kicking around in the restaurant's reach-ins, already cut and held with the mise-en-place on line, commingling with the chicken and the salmon and the lamb chops for four days, the reach-in doors swinging open every few seconds as the line cooks plunge their fists in, blindly feeling around for what they need. These are not optimum refrigeration conditions.

This is why you don't see a lot of codfish or other perishable items as a Sunday or Monday night special—they're not sturdy enough. The chef *knows*. He anticipates the likelihood that he might still have some fish lying around on Monday morning—and he'd like to get money for it without poisoning his customers.

Seafood is a tricky business. Red snapper may cost a chef only $4.95 a pound, but that price includes the bones, the head, the scales and all the stuff that gets cut and thrown away. By the time it's cut, the actual cost of each piece of cleaned fillet costs the chef more than *twice* that amount, and he'd greatly prefer to sell it than toss it in the garbage. If it still smells okay on Monday night—you're eating it.

I don't eat mussels in restaurants unless I know the chef personally, or have seen, with my own eyes, how they store and hold their mussels for service. I love mussels. But in my experience, most cooks are less than scrupulous in their handling of them. More often than not, mussels are allowed to wallow in their own foul-smelling piss in the bottom of a reach-in. *Some* restaurants, I'm sure, have special containers, with convenient slotted bins, which allow the mussels to drain while being held—and maybe, just maybe, the cooks at these places pick carefully through every order, mussel by mussel, making sure that *every* one is healthy and alive before throwing them into a pot. I haven't worked in too many places like that. Mussels are too easy. Line cooks consider mussels a gift; they take two minutes to cook, a few seconds to dump in a bowl, and *ba-da-bing*, one more customer taken care of—now they can concentrate on slicing the damn duck breast. I have had, at a very good Paris brasserie, the misfortune to eat a single bad mussel, one treacherous little guy hidden among an otherwise impeccable group. It slammed me shut like a book, sent me crawling to the bathroom shitting like a mink, clutching my stomach and projectile vomiting. I prayed that night. For many hours. And, as you might assume, I'm the worst kind of atheist. Fortunately, the French have liberal policies on doctor's house calls and affordable health care. But I do not care to repeat that experience. No thank you on the mussels. If I'm hungry for mussels, I'll pick the good-looking ones out of *your* order.

How about seafood on Sunday? Well . . . sometimes, but never if it's an obvious attempt to offload aging stuff, like seafood salad vinaigrette or seafood frittata, on a brunch menu. Brunch menus are an open invitation to the cost-conscious chef, a dumping ground for the odd bits left over from Friday and Saturday nights or for the scraps generated in the normal course of business. You see a fish that would be much better served by quick grilling with a slice of lemon, suddenly all dressed up with vinaigrette? For *en vinaigrette* on the menu, read "preserved" or "disguised."

While we're on brunch, how about hollandaise sauce? Not for me. Bacteria *love* hollandaise. And hollandaise, that delicate emulsion of egg yolks and clarified butter, *must* be held at a temperature not too hot nor too cold, lest it break when spooned over your poached eggs. Unfortunately, this lukewarm holding temperature is also the favorite environment for bacteria to copulate and reproduce in. Nobody I know has *ever* made hollandaise to order. Most likely, the stuff on your eggs was made hours ago and held on station. Equally disturbing is the likelihood that the butter used in the hollandaise is melted table butter, heated, clarified and strained to get out all the bread crumbs and cigarette butts. Butter is expensive, you know. Hollandaise is a veritable petri dish of biohazards. And how long has that Canadian bacon been aging in the walk-in anyway? Remember, brunch is served only once a week—on the weekends. Buzzword here, "Brunch Menu." Translation? "Old, nasty odds and ends, and twelve dollars for two eggs with a free Bloody Mary." One other point about brunch. Cooks hate brunch. A wise chef will deploy his *best* line cooks on Friday and Saturday nights; he'll be reluctant to schedule those same cooks early Sunday morning, especially since they probably went out after work Saturday and got hammered until the wee hours. Worse, brunch is demoralizing to the serious line cook. Nothing makes an aspiring Escoffier feel more like an army commissary cook, or Mel from Mel's Diner, than having to slop out eggs over easy with bacon and eggs Benedict for the Sunday brunch crowd. Brunch is punishment block for the "B" Team cooks, or where the farm team of recent dishwashers learn their chops. Most chefs are off on Sundays, too, so supervision is at a minimum. Consider that before ordering the seafood frittata.

I *will* eat bread in restaurants. Even if I *know* it's probably been recycled off someone else's table. The reuse of bread is an industry-wide practice. I saw a recent new exposé, hidden camera and all, where the anchor was *shocked...* *shocked* to see unused bread returned to the kitchen and then sent right back onto the floor. Bullshit. I'm sure that some restaurants explicitly instruct their Bengali busboys to throw out all that unused bread—which amounts to about 50 percent—and maybe some places actually do it. But when it's busy, and the busboy is crumbing tables, emptying ashtrays, refilling water glasses, making espresso and cappuccino, hustling dirty dishes to the dishwasher, and he sees a basket full of untouched bread, most times he's going to use it. This is a fact of life. This doesn't bother me and shouldn't surprise you. Okay, maybe once in a while some tubercular hillbilly has been coughing and spraying in the general direction of that bread basket, or some tourist who's just returned from a walking tour of the wetlands of West Africa sneezes—you might find that prospect upsetting. But you might just as well avoid air travel, or subways, equally dodgy environments for airborne transmission of disease. Eat the bread.

I *won't* eat in a restaurant with filthy bathrooms. This isn't a hard call. They let you *see* the bathrooms. If the restaurant can't be bothered to replace the puck in the urinal or keep the toilets and floors clean, then just imagine what their refrigeration and work spaces look like. Bathrooms are relatively easy to clean. Kitchens are not. In fact, if you see the chef sitting unshaven at the bar, with a dirty apron on, one finger halfway up his nose, you can assume he's not handling your food any better behind closed doors. Your waiter looks like he just woke up under a bridge? If management allows him to wander out on the floor looking like that, God knows what they're doing to your shrimp!

"Beef Parmentier"? "Shepherd's pie"? "Chili special"? Sounds like leftovers to me. How about swordfish? I like it fine. But my seafood purveyor, when he goes out to dinner, won't eat it. He's seen too many of those three-foot-long parasitic worms that riddle the fish's flesh. You see a few of these babies—and we all do—and you won't be tucking into swordfish anytime soon.

Chilean sea bass? Trendy. Expensive. More than likely frozen. This came as a surprise to me when I visited the market recently. Apparently the great majority of the stuff arrives frozen solid, still on the bone. In fact, as I said earlier, the whole Fulton Street market is not an inspiring sight. Fish is left to sit, un-iced, in leaking crates, in the middle of August, right out in the open. What isn't bought early is sold for cheap later. At 7:00 a.m. the Korean and Chinese buyers, who've been sitting in local bars *waiting* for the market to be near closing, swoop down on the overextended fish-monger and buy up what's left at rock-bottom prices. The next folks to arrive will be the cat-food people. Think about that when you see the "Discount Sushi" sign.

"Saving for well-done" is a time-honored tradition dating back to cuisine's earliest days: meat and fish cost money. Every piece of cut, fabricated food must, ideally, be sold for three or even four times its cost in order for the chef to make his "food cost percent." So what happens when the chef finds a tough, slightly skanky end-cut of sirloin that's been pushed repeatedly to the back of the pile? He can throw it out, but that's a total loss, representing a three-fold loss of what it cost him per pound. He can feed it to the family, which is the same as throwing it out. Or he can "save for well-done"—serve it to some rube who *prefers* to eat his meat or fish incinerated into a flavorless, leathery hunk of carbon, who won't be able to tell if what he's eating is food or flotsam. Ordinarily, a proud chef would hate this customer, hold him in contempt for destroying his fine food. But not in this case. The dumb bastard is *paying for the privilege of eating his garbage!* What's not to like?

Vegetarians, and their Hezbollah-like splinter faction, the vegans, are a persistent irritant to any chef worth a damn. To me, life without veal stock, pork fat, sausage, organ meat, demi-glace or even stinky cheese is a life not worth living. Vegetarians are the enemy of everything good and decent in the human spirit, an affront to all I stand for, the pure enjoyment of food. The body, these waterheads imagine, is a temple that should not be polluted by animal protein. It's healthier, they insist, though every vegetarian waiter I've worked with is brought down by any *rumor* of a cold. Oh, I'll accommodate them, I'll rummage around for *something* to feed them, for a "vege-tarian plate," if called on to do so. Fourteen dollars for a few slices of grilled eggplant and zucchini suits my food cost fine. . . .

Pigs are filthy animals, say some, when explaining why they deny them-selves the delights of pork. Maybe they should visit a chicken ranch. Ameri-ca's favorite menu item is also the most likely to make you ill. Commercially available chickens, for the most part (we're not talking about kosher and expensive free-range birds), are loaded with salmonella. Chickens are dirty. They eat their own feces, are kept packed close together like in a rush-hour subway and when handled in a restaurant situation are most likely to infect other foods or cross-contaminate them. And chicken is boring. Chefs see it as a menu item for people who don't know what they want to eat.

Shrimp? All right, if it looks fresh, smells fresh and the restaurant is busy, guaranteeing turnover of product on a regular basis. But shrimp toast? I'll pass. I walk into a restaurant with a mostly empty dining room, and an unhappy-looking owner staring out the window? I'm not ordering shrimp.

This principle applies to anything on a menu, actually, especially some-thing esoteric and adventurous like, say, bouillabaisse. If a restaurant is known for steak, and doesn't seem to be doing much business, how long do you think those few orders of clams and mussels and lobster and fish have been sitting in the refrigerator, waiting for someone like you to order them? The key is rotation. If the restaurant is busy, and you see bouillabaisse flying out the kitchen doors every few minutes, then it's probably a good bet. But a big and varied menu in a slow, half-empty place? Those less popular items like broiled mackerel and calf liver are kept moldering in a dark corner of the reach-in because they look good on the menu. You might not actually want to eat them. Look at your waiter's face. He knows. It's another reason to be polite to your waiter: he could save your life with a raised eyebrow or a sigh. If he likes you, maybe he'll stop you from ordering a piece of fish he knows is going to hurt you. On the other hand, maybe the chef has ordered him, under pain of death, to move that codfish before it begins to *really* reek. Observe the body language and take note.

Watchwords for fine dining? Tuesday through Saturday. Busy. Turnover. Rotation. Tuesdays and Thursdays are the best nights to order fish in New York. The food that comes in Tuesday is fresh, the station prep is new, and the chef is well rested after a Sunday or a Monday off. It's the real start of the new week, when you've got the goodwill of the kitchen on your side. Fridays and Saturdays, the food is fresh, but it's busy, so the chef and cooks can't pay as much attention to your food as they—and you—might like. And weekend diners are universally viewed with suspicion, even contempt, by both cooks and waiters alike; they're the slackjaws, the rubes, the out-of-towners, the well-done-eating, undertipping, bridge-and-tunnel pretheater hordes, in to see *Cats* or *Les Miz* and never to return. Weekday diners, on the other hand, are the home team—potential regulars, whom all concerned want to make happy. Rested and ready after a day off, the chef is going to put his best foot forward on Tuesday; he's got his best-quality product coming in and he's had a day or two to think of creative things to do with it. He *wants* you to be happy on Tuesday night. On Saturday, he's thinking more about turning over tables and getting through the rush. . . .

Do all these horrifying assertions frighten you? Should you stop eating out? Wipe yourself down with antiseptic towelettes every time you pass a restaurant? No way. Like I said before, your body is *not* a temple, it's an amusement park. Enjoy the ride. Sure, it's a "play you pay" sort of an adventure, but you knew that already, every time you ever ordered a taco or a dirty-water hot dog. If you're willing to risk some slight lower GI distress for one of those Italian sweet sausages at the street fair, or for a slice of pizza you just *know* has been sitting on the board for an hour or two, why not take a chance on the good stuff? All the great developments of classical cuisine, the first guys to eat sweetbreads, to try unpasteurized Stilton, to discover that snails actually taste *good* with enough garlic butter, these were daredevils, innovators and desperados. I don't know who figured out that if you crammed rich food into a goose long enough for its liver to balloon up to more than its normal body weight you'd get something as good as foie gras—I believe it was those kooky Romans—but I'm very grateful for their efforts. Popping raw fish into your face, especially in prerefrigeration days, might have seemed like sheer madness to some, but it turned out to be a pretty good idea. They say that Rasputin used to eat a little arsenic with breakfast every day, building up resistance for the day that an enemy might poison him, and that sounds like good sense to me. Judging from accounts of his death, the Mad Monk wasn't fazed at all by the stuff; it took repeated beatings, a couple of bullets and a long fall off a bridge into a frozen river to finish the job. Perhaps we, as serious diners, should emulate his example. We are, after all, citizens of the world—a world filled with bacteria, some friendly, some not so friendly.

Do we really want to travel in hermetically sealed popemobiles through the rural provinces of France, Mexico and the Far East, eating only in Hard Rock Cafés and McDonald's? Or do we want to eat without fear, tearing into the local stew, the humble taqueria's mystery meat, the sincerely offered gift of a lightly grilled fish head? I know what I want. I want it all. I want to try everything once. I'll give you the benefit of the doubt, Señor Tamale Stand Owner, Sushi-chef-san, Monsieur Bucket-head. What's that feathered game bird hanging on the porch, getting riper by the day, the body nearly ready to drop off? I want some.

I have no wish to die, nor do I have some unhealthy fondness for dysentery. If I *know* you're storing your squid at room temperature next to a cat box, I'll get my squid down the street, thank you very much. I will continue to do my seafood eating on Tuesdays, Wednesdays and Thursdays, because I know better, because I can wait. But if I have one chance at a full-blown dinner of blowfish gizzard—even if I have not been properly introduced to the chef—and I'm in a strange, Far Eastern city and my plane leaves tomorrow? I'm going for it. You only go around once.

Gabrielle Hamilton (1965–)

HAMILTON IS THE celebrated author of *Blood, Bones & Butter: The Inadvertent Education of a Reluctant Chef*, one of the most popular recent food memoirs. She is also the owner and chef of Prune, a small American restaurant in New York's East Village. Her gastronomic vision excludes conceptual or intellectual food, extolling instead "the salty, sweet, starchy, brothy, crispy things one craves when one is actually hungry." Hamilton won James Beard awards in 2011 as Best Chef in New York City and in 2012 for the memoir, in which she describes her difficult and often humiliating early life in a series of unrewarding catering and small restaurant jobs and details the rigors of work as a professional chef while raising two children. Our selection describes the frenetic Sunday brunch at Prune, where impatient diners, spilled pancake batter, and other distractions make kitchen life a headache.

from *Blood, Bones & Butter*: The Brunch Rush

SUNDAY BRUNCH IS like the Indy 500 of services at Prune. There is a roaring thunderous stampede every forty minutes as hordes of hungry, angry, mag-wheeled, tricked-out customers line up at the door, scrape the chairs back, take their seats, blow through their steak and eggs. The line is two-full seatings long at nine-thirty even though we don't open the doors until ten. They are waiting for the go flag. Some have physically harmed the hostess as they sprint to get a table. I once worked the host shift on a Sunday brunch at thirty-eight weeks pregnant—and even my huge belly, my chronic shortness of breath, and my clear proprietary aura (you can just tell when I am in the room that I am not an employee; I exude ownership), even that did not stop the stampede that is Sunday brunch. . . .

That heat in the egg station at brunch has a formidable physical presence. It moves about, undulating, coming at you in waves, some of them, like when you open the oven door, smacking you forcefully enough to tighten the skin on your face and make your eyes swell shut slightly.

Much has been written about facing the shocking heat of a restaurant's set of burners, and in spite of what it may reveal about me, I am the only one I know who likes it. I always feel like I am a contender in a nicely matched bout every time we meet—especially every Sunday—when I enter that station at seven-thirty in the morning and begin my setup. Every time I step in front of those ten burners, in that egregiously tight space, less than twelve inches between the wall I am backed up against and the burning stovetop in front of me, I feel like we are two small-time boxers—me and the heat—meeting in the center of the ring to tap gloves. The fight begins with a little slap, totally manageable, when I put that first large pot of water on to boil, and then increases in ferocity from there when the large cast-iron skillet starts to vaguely shimmer and smoke and sputter, magnifying the already immense power of my opponent—inching up the temperature—as I start to render the pancetta for the carbonara. When the pig urine stench of that excellent pancetta hits me in the nose I am red-eyed and snotty—your nose runs in the heat and in the cold equally as it attempts to regulate your body temperature—and it's only eight o'clock in the morning. That your eyes are already a little swollen and your nose is running and your skin is tight on

your face gives you a Raging Bull kind of feeling—which gets me immediately in the right mindset. The whole crew feels it—that tension before
a fight. The customers lined up outside before we have even turned on the
lights and had our family meal, the total knowledge of what we know is
coming—the relentless, nonstop five-hour beating—and we practically huddle up, poised for the bell, we are scared even, saying in psyched but tense
tones, "Here we go!" as Julie unlocks the door and they flood in, scraping the
chairs, and that milk foamer on the espresso machine rages its monster roar,
and we stand motionless in the kitchen, looking out onto the floor, waiting
for the panic of tickets, tickets, tickets.

It's important not to go down early in your shift. And there are things that
will bring you down: You start your first ticket of the day and by accident
you tip a full gallon of pancake batter over in your reach-in—both wasting a
product you desperately need and now creating a jam in your reach-in because
you can't work with pancake batter all over everything. The expediter does
not stop calling out tickets just because you have a mess in your station. The
orders, all of them at least in part your responsibility because every dish at
brunch comes with eggs, keep pouring in while you hustle to get that glop
cleaned up and your station back on track. The circumstances won't change.
You are always, always going to face forces that can bring you to your knees.
No matter how well set up you are, how early you came in, how tight and
awesome your mise en place is, there will be days, forces, events that just
conspire to fuck you and the struggle to stay up—to not sink down into the
blackest, meanest hole—to stay psychologically up and committed to the
fight, is the hardest, by far, part of the day. The heat, the crush of customers,
the special orders and sauces on sides, the blood-sugar crises—none of it is as
difficult as the struggle to stay in the game, once you have suffered a setback
like dropping a full quart of ranchero sauce, which has cracked open and
exploded in your station all over your clogs and the oven doors.

I like to swear the dirtiest, most vulgar swear words I can think of to get
me through it. It can be very Tourette's Syndrome back there when I am
working that egg station and the expediter has failed to tell me about a sauce
on the side or a well-done poached. I always, to be sure, take the moment
to apologize to everyone around me, to promise them that I am not serious, that nothing is personal—but then I rip it out, jaw tight, and spewing
combinations of the word *fuck* that even David Mamet has not thought to

put together. I have fired people who can't suffer their setbacks and petty failures. If they go down early and spend the rest of their five-hour shift that way, it threatens to sink the whole boat and that can't happen just because you burned your first omelette and had to refire it. You've got to get your GI Jane on.

From too many years of going all day without eating—that freakish thing about restaurant work: Water water everywhere and not a drop to drink—I have blood-sugar issues. And they can feel serious. There are a couple of points in that shift—every single time I work it—that I legitimately fear that the entire brunch service will come to a screeching halt if I don't get some orange juice, iced Ovaltine, and a full quart of ice cold Coca-Cola down my throat in seconds, and in that particular order. In a generous light, I am that boxer in his corner, his trainer squirting Gatorade indiscriminately at his face while the boxer keeps his mouth open like a gasping fish, hoping for the jet stream to get to his throat. But I can, in a less generous light, feel like a dirty glue huffer—shoving my head discreetly and desperately into my cool reach-in—sucking, and I mean sucking, down a quart of chocolatey, malty, milky Ovaltine over a quart of ice—like an addict puts that paper bag of paint fumes over his nose and mouth and pulls that shit into his body with a terrifying force—made more terrifying by the utter calm and clarity and complacency that overtakes you once your hit kicks in and reaches the right places. The Coca-Cola so tannic and sweet and achingly cold that it makes my eyes tear up. And then brunch is back on track.

During the eighth round, close to three o'clock, I get dizzy stupid. I don't even know what I'm cooking. By which I mean, I know what each individual item in front of me is, but I don't know what I'm cooking in the larger picture. Is this the eggs Benedict that picks up with the salmon omelette? Or is this the benny that picks up with oatmeal and lamb sausage? This may seem inane to anyone on the outside, but in my industry, which benny is which matters. You don't just cook food indiscriminately, without phrases, without groupings, and carelessly shove it all to the pass to let the expediter sort out. You have to time your food, according to a system, so that you don't produce a benny that sits in the window waiting for five minutes for a lamb sausage from the guy working the grill station. Five minutes in the life of a cooked egg, unlike a nicely resting piece of meat, is the difference between excellent and bullshit. At three o'clock, with the last pummeling of tickets on the board, I need to be told over and over by the expediter, and probably much to his irritation, which benny is this particular benny. I know all of the strategies and I use them—repeating back the ticket after it's called—"echoing" the expediter, and constantly talking in minutes and seconds with my fellow line cooks:

"I'm two out on benny/carbonara."

"Thirty seconds on huevos/pancake."

"Selling benny/oyster!" We break it down to each other from minutes to seconds to sold! But invariably all I can see by the last round through my red, swollen eyes is the pan and the egg in front of me. I'm just punching and hoping I land one on the guy's jaw.

꩜

Bee Wilson (1974–)

A BRITISH FOOD writer, Wilson came to the subject in an unorthodox way, getting a Ph.D. with a dissertation on French utopian socialism and studying the history of political thought. She has written books on honeybees, and on ways food producers have mislabeled, contaminated, even poisoned the foods they sell. In *Consider the Fork* she considers how and why we use pots and pans, measuring implements, plates, and other objects we take for granted in the kitchen and on the dining room table. Our selection on knives shows her characteristic blend of history, anthropology, and science. She's particularly informative about the Chinese *tou*, or cleaver, from a Western viewpoint an unexpectedly versatile instrument.

from *Consider the Fork*: Knife

KITCHENS ARE PLACES of violence. People get burned, scarred, frozen, and above all, cut. After the mandolin incident, I booked myself into a knife skills course, in a shiny new cooking school on the outskirts of town. Most of the men in the course had been given their enrollment as a present by wives and girlfriends, the assumption being that knives are the sort of thing men have fun with, like train sets or drills. They approached the chopping board with a slight swagger. The women stood more diffidently at first. We had without exception signed up for it ourselves, either as a treat (like yoga) or to get over some terror or anxiety around blades (like a self-defense class). I hoped it would teach me how to dice like a samurai, hack like a butcher, and annihilate an onion at ten paces like the chefs on TV. In fact, most of the course was about safety: how to hold vegetables in a clawlike grip with our thumbs tucked under, keeping knuckles always against the body of the knife so that we couldn't inadvertently baton our thumbs along with our carrots; how to steady the chopping board with a damp cloth; how to store our knives in a magnetic strip or in a plastic sheath. Our terror, it seemed, was justified. The teacher—a capable Swedish woman—warned us of the horrible accidents that ensue when sharp knives are carelessly left in a bowl of sudsy dishwashing detergent. You forget the knives are there, plunge your hand in, and slowly the water turns red, like a scene from *Jaws*.

Culinary knives have always been just a step away from weapons. These are tools designed to break, disfigure, and mutilate, even if all you are cutting is a carrot. Unlike lions, we lack the ability to tear meat from a carcass with our bare teeth; so we invented cutting tools to do the job for us. The knife is the oldest tool in the cook's armory, older than the management of fire by somewhere between 1 million and 2 million years, depending on which anthropologist you believe. Cutting with some implement or other is the most basic way of processing food. Knives do some of the work that feeble human teeth cannot. The earliest examples of stone cutting tools date back 2.6 million years to Ethiopia, where excavations have found both sharpened rocks and bones with cut-marks on them, indicating that raw meat was being hacked from the bone. Already, there was some sophistication in the knife skills on display. Stone Age humans fashioned numerous different cutting devices to suit their needs: archaeologists have identified simple sharp choppers, scrapers (both heavy duty and light duty), and hammerstones and spheroids for beating food. Even at this early stage, man was not randomly slashing at his food but making careful decisions about which cuts to make with which tools.

Unlike cooking, toolmaking is not an exclusively human activity. Chimpanzees and bonobos (another type of ape) have shown themselves capable of hammering rocks against other rocks to make sharp implements. Chimps can use stones to crack nuts and twigs to scoop fruit from a husk. Apes have also hammered stone flakes, but there is no evidence that they passed down toolmaking skills from one individual to another, as hominids did. Moreover, primates seem to be less sensitive to raw materials used than their human counterparts. Right from the beginning, hominid toolmakers were intensely interested in finding the best rocks for cutting, rather than just the most convenient, and were prepared to travel to get them. Which rock would make the sharpest flake? Stone Age toolmakers experimented with granite and quartz, obsidian and flint. Knife manufacturers still search for the best materials for a sharp blade; the difference is that the art of metallurgy, from the Bronze Age onward, has vastly expanded our options. From bronze to iron; from iron to steel; from steel to carbon steel, high-carbon steel, and stainless steel; and on to fancy titanium and laminates. You can now spend vast sums on a Japanese chef's knife, handmade by a master cutler from molybdenum-vanadium-enriched steel. Such a knife can perform feats that would have amazed Stone Age man, swooshing through a pumpkin's hard skin as if it were a soft pear.

In my experience, when you ask chefs what their favorite kitchen gadget is, nine times out of ten, they will say a knife. They say it slightly impatiently, because it's just so obvious: the foundation of every great meal is accurate cutting. A chef without a knife would be like a hairdresser without scissors. Knife work—more than the application of heat—is simply what chefs do: using a sharp edge to convert ingredients into something you can cook with. Different chefs go for different knives: a curved scimitar; a straight French "blooding" knife, designed for use by horsemeat butchers; a pointy German slicer; a cleaver. I met one chef who said he used a large serrated bread knife for absolutely everything. He liked the fact that he didn't have to sharpen it. Others favor tiny parers that dissect food with needle-sharp accuracy. Most rely on the classic chef's knife, either nine-inch or ten-inch, because it's about the right size to cover most needs: long enough for jointing, small enough for filleting. A good chef steels his or her knives several times in a single shift, drawing the blade swiftly to and fro at a 20° angle, to ensure the knife never loses its bite.

The story of knives and food is not only about cutting tools getting ever sharper and stronger, however. It is also about how we manage the alarming violence of these utensils. Our Stone Age ancestors took the materials at their disposal and—so far as we can surmise—made them as sharp as possible. But as the technology of knife making developed through iron and steel, the sharpest knife became something casually lethal. The primary function of a knife is to cut; but the secondary question has always been how to tame the knife's cutting power. The Chinese did it by confining their knife work to the kitchen, reducing food to bite-sized pieces with a massive cleaverlike instrument, out of sight. Europeans did it, first, by creating elaborate rules about the use of the knife at the table—the subtext of all table manners is the fear that the man next to you may pull his knife on you—and second, by inventing "table knives" so blunt and feeble that you would struggle to use them to cut people instead of food.

THERE is a peculiar joy in holding a knife that feels just right for your hand and marveling as it dices an onion, almost without effort on your part. During the knife-skills course, our teacher showed us how to joint a chicken. When separating the legs from the thighs, you look for two little mountain tops; on hitting the right spot, the knife goes through like silk. This only works, however, when the knife is sharp enough to begin with.

Chefs always say that the safest knife is the sharpest one (which is true until you actually have an accident). Among domestic cooks, though, knowledge of how to keep a knife sharp has become a private passion rather than a universal skill. The travelling Victorian knife grinder, who could sharpen a set of knives in a matter of minutes—in exchange for whatever you could pay him, pennies or even a pint of ale—is long gone. He has been replaced by eager knife enthusiasts, who grind their knives not as a job or even out of necessity but for the sheer satisfaction of it, swapping tips in online knife forums. Opinion differs as to which sharpening device is best for achieving the perfect edge, whether a Japanese water stone, a traditional whetstone, an Arkansas stone, or a synthetic aluminium oxide stone. (I know of no real knife enthusiast who would favor the electric sharpener, which is generally excoriated for aggressively oversharpening, and hence ruining, good knives.)

Whichever tool is chosen, the basic principle is always the same. You sharpen a knife by grinding off some of the metal, starting with a coarse abrasive and moving to a finer one until you have the required sharpness. In addition, you may wish to steel your blade each time you use it, running it along a steel rod a few times to realign the edge. Steeling can keep a sharp knife sharp, but it cannot make a blunt knife sharp in the first place. What does it mean for a knife to be sharp? It is a question of angle. You get a sharp edge when two surfaces—known as bevels—come together at a thin V-shaped angle. If you could take a cross section through a sharp knife, you would see that the typical angle for a Western kitchen knife is around 20°, or one-eighteenth of a circle. European knives are generally double-beveled, that is, sharpened on both sides of the blade, resulting in a total angle of 40°. Every time you use your knife, a little of the edge wears away, and the angle is gradually lost. Sharpeners renew the edge by grinding bits of the metal away from both sides of the V to restore the original angle. With heavy use and excessive grinding, the blade gradually diminishes.

In an ideal universe, a knife would be able to achieve an angle of zero—representing infinite sharpness. But some concessions have to be made to reality. Thin-angled knives cut better—like razors—but if they are too thin, they will be too fragile to withstand the act of chopping, which rather defeats the purpose. Whereas Western kitchen knives sharpen at an angle of around 20°, Japanese ones, which are thinner, can sharpen at around 15°. This is one of the reasons so many chefs prefer Japanese knives.

There is much that the community of knife enthusiasts disagree upon. Is the best knife large? There's a theory that heavier knives do more of the work for you. Or small? There's another theory that heavy knives make your muscles ache. Are you better off with a flat edge or a curved one? The enthusiasts also disagree on the best way to test the sharpness of an edge to see if it "bites." Should you use your thumb—thus flaunting how at-one you are with the metal—or is it better to cut into a random vegetable or a ballpoint pen? There's a joke about a man who tested his blade using his tongue: sharp blades taste like metal; really sharp blades taste like blood.

What unites knife enthusiasts is the shared knowledge that having a sharp knife, and mastery of it, is the greatest power you will ever feel in a kitchen.

Shamefully late in my cooking life, I have discovered why most chefs think the knife is the one indispensable tool. You no longer feel anxious around onions or bagels. You look at food and see that you can cut it down to any size you want. Your cooking takes on a new refinement. An accurately chopped onion—tiny dice, with no errant larger chunks—lends a suave luxury to a risotto, because the onion and the grains of rice meld harmoniously. A sharp bread knife creates the possibility of elegantly thin toast. Become the boss of a sharp knife, and you are the boss of the whole kitchen.

This shouldn't really come as a revelation. But proficiency with a knife is now a minority enthusiasm. Even many otherwise accomplished cooks have a rack stocked with dull knives. I know, because I used to be one of them. You can survive perfectly well in the modern kitchen without any survivalist knife skills. When something needs to be really finely chopped or shredded, a food processor will pick up the slack. We are not in the Stone Age (as much as some of the knife enthusiasts would like us to be). Our food system enables us to feed ourselves even when we lack the most rudimentary cutting abilities, never mind the ability to make our own slicing tools. Bread comes pre-sliced, and vegetables can be bought pre-diced. Once, though, effective handling of a knife was a more basic and necessary skill than either reading or writing.

In medieval and Renaissance Europe, you carried your own knife everywhere with you and brought it out at mealtimes when you needed to. Almost everyone had a personal eating knife in a sheath dangling from a belt. The knife at a man's girdle could equally well be used for chopping food or defending himself against enemies. Your knife was as much a garment—like a wristwatch now—as a tool. A knife was a universal possession, often your most treasured one. Like a wizard's wand in *Harry Potter,* the knife was tailored to its owner. Knife handles were made of brass, ivory, rock crystal, glass, and shell; of amber, agate, mother of pearl, or tortoiseshell. They might be carved or engraved with images of babies, apostles, flowers, peasants, feathers, or doves. You would no more eat with another person's knife than you would brush your teeth today with a stranger's toothbrush. You wore your knife so habitually that—as with a watch—you might start to regard it as a part of yourself and forget it was there. A sixth-century text (St. Benedict's Rule) reminded monks to detach their knives from their belts before they went to bed, so they didn't cut themselves in the night.

There was a serious danger of this because knives then, with their daggerlike shape, really were sharp. They needed to be, because they might be called upon to tackle everything from rubbery cheese to a crusty loaf. Aside from clothes, a knife was the one possession every adult needed. It has been often assumed, wrongly, that knives, as violent objects, were exclusively masculine. But women wore them, too. A painting from 1640 by H. H. Kluber depicts a rich Swiss family, preparing to eat a meal of meat, bread, and apples. The daughters of the family have flowers in their hair, and dangling from their red dresses are silvery knives, attached to silken ropes tied around their waists. With a knife this close to your body at all times, you would have been very familiar with its construction.

Sharp knives have a certain anatomy. At the tip of the blade is the point, the spikiest part, good for skewering or piercing. You might use a knife's point to slash pastry, flick seeds from a lemon half, or spear a boiled potato to check if it is done. The main body of the blade—the lower cutting edge— is known as the belly, or the curve. This is the part of a knife that does most of the work, from shredding greens into a fine tangle to slicing meat thinly. Turn it on its side and you can use it to pulverize garlic to a paste with coarse salt: good-bye, garlic press! The opposite end of the blade from the belly, log- ically enough, is the spine, the blunt top edge that does no cutting but adds weight and balance. The thick, sharp part of the blade next to the handle is the heel, good for hefty chopping of hard things like nuts and cabbages. The blade then gives way to the tang, the piece of metal hidden inside the handle that joins the knife and its handle together. A tang may be partial—if it only extends partway into the handle—or it may be full. In many high-end Japanese knives now, there is no tang, the whole knife, handle and all, being formed from a single piece of steel. Where the handle meets the blade is called the return. At the bottom of the handle is the butt—the very end of the knife.

When you start to love knives, you come to appreciate everything from the quality of the rivets on the handle to the line of the heel. These are now fairly arcane thrills, but once, they belonged to everyone. A good knife was an object of pride. As you took it from your waist, the familiar handle, worn and polished from use, would ease nicely into your hand as you sliced your bread, speared your meat, or pared your apple. You knew the value of a sharp knife, because without it you would find it so much harder to eat much of what was on the table. And you knew that sharpness meant steel, which by the sixteenth century was already the metal most valued by knife makers.

THE first metal knives were made of bronze during the Bronze Age (c. 3000–700 BC). They looked similar to modern knives in that as well as a cutting edge, they had a tang and bolster, onto which a handle could be fit- ted. But the cutting edge didn't function well because bronze is a terrible material for blades, too soft to hold a really sharp edge. Proof that bronze does not make good knives is confirmed by the fact that during the Bronze Age, cutting devices continued to be made from stone, which was, in many respects, superior to the newfangled metal.

Iron made better knife metal than bronze. The Iron Age was the first great knife age, when the flint blades that had been in use since the time of the Oldowans finally vanished. As a harder metal, iron could be honed far sharper than bronze. It was a handy metal for forging large, heavy tools. Iron Age smiths made pretty decent axes. For knives, however, iron was not ideal. Although harder than bronze, iron rusts easily, making food taste bad. And iron knives still do not hold the sharpest of edges.

The great step forward was steel, which is still, in one form or other, the material from which almost all sharp knives are made, the exception being the new ceramic knives, which have been described as the biggest innovation in blade material for three millennia. Ceramic knives cut like a dream through soft fish fillets or yielding tomatoes but are far too fragile for heavy chopping. For a blade that is sharp, hard enough, and strong, nothing has yet supplanted steel, which can form and hold a sharp edge better than other metals.

Steel is no more than iron with a tiny proportion of added carbon: around 0.2 percent to 2 percent by weight. But that tiny bit makes all the difference. The carbon in steel is what makes it hard enough to hold a really sharp angle, but not so hard it can't be sharpened. If too much carbon is added, the steel will be brittle and snap under pressure. For most food cutting, 0.75 percent carbon is right: this creates a "sheer steel" capable of being forged into chopping knives with a tough, sharp edge, easy to sharpen, without being easily breakable; the kind of knife that could cut almost anything.

By the eighteenth century, methods of making carbon steel had industrialized, and this marvelous substance was being used to make a range of increasingly specialized tools. The cutlery trade was no longer about making a daggerlike personal possession for a single individual. It was about making a range of knives for highly specific uses: filleting knives, paring knives, pastry knives, all from steel.

These specialized knives were both cause and consequence of European ways of dining. It has often been observed that the French haute cuisine that dominated wealthy European tastes from the eighteenth century on was a cuisine of sauces: béchamel, velouté, espagnole, allemande (the four mother sauces of Carême, later revised as the five mother sauces of Escoffier, who ditched the allemande and added hollandaise and tomato sauce). True, but it was no less a cuisine of specialist knives and precision cutting. The French were not the first to use particular knives for particular tasks. As with much of French cuisine, their multitude of knives can be traced to Italy in the sixteenth century. In 1570, Bartolomeo Scappi, Italian cook to the pope, had myriad kitchen weapons at his disposal: scimitars for dismembering, thick-bladed knives for battering, blunt-ended pasta knives, and cake knives, which were long, thin scrapers. Yet Scappi laid down no exact code about how to use these blades. "Then beat it with knives," Scappi will say, or "cut into slices." Again, he does not formally catalog different cutting techniques. It was the French who, with their passion for Cartesian exactness, made knife work into a system, a rule book, and a religion. The cutlery firm Sabatier first produced carbon steel knives in the town of Thiers in the early 1800s—around the time that gastronomy as a concept was invented, through the writings of Grimod de la Reynière and Joseph Berchoux and the cooking of Carême. The knives and the cuisine went hand in hand. Whereever French chefs traveled, they brought with them a series of strict cuts—mince, chiffonade, julienne—and the knives with which to make them.

French food, no matter how simple, has meticulous knife work behind it. A platter of raw oysters on the half shell at a Parisian restaurant doesn't look like cooking at all, but what makes it a pleasure to eat, apart from freshness, is that someone has skillfully opened each mollusk with an oyster shucker, sliding the knife upward to cut the adductor muscle that holds the shell closed without smashing off any sharp pieces. As for the shallot vinegar with which the oyster are served, someone has had to work like crazy, cutting the shallot into brunoise: tiny 0.25 cm cubes. It is only this prepping that prevents the shallot from being too everwhelming against the bland, saline oysters.

The savory French steak that sits before you so invitingly—whether onglet, pavé, or entrecôte—is the result of French butchery using particular utensils: a massive cleaver for the most brutal bone-hacking work, a delicate butcher's knife for seaming out the more elusive cuts, and perhaps a cutlet basher (*batte à côtelettes*) to flatten the meat a little before it is cooked. The classical French kitchen includes ham knives and cheese knives, knives for julienning, and beak-shaped knives for dealing with chestnuts.

Professional haute cuisine was founded on specialism. The great chef Escoffier, who laid the foundation for all modern French restaurant cooking, organized the kitchen into separate stations for sauces, meats, pastries. Each of these units had its own persnickety knives. In a kitchen organized on Escoffier principles, one person might be given the job of "turning" potatoes into perfect little spheres. For this task, he would use a tournet knife, a small parer with a blade like a bird's beak. This curved blade would be awkward for cutting on a board—the angle is all wrong. Yet that arc is just right for swiping the skin off a handheld round object, following its contours to leave an aesthetically pleasing little globe. A garnish of turned vegetables— so pretty, so whimsical, so unmistakably French—is the direct result of a certain knife, wielded in a certain way, guided by a certain philosophy about what food should be.

Our food is shaped by knives. And our knives are fashioned by that mysterious combination of local resources, technological innovation, and cultural preferences that makes up a cuisine. The French way with knives is not the only way. In the case of China, an entire approach to eating and cooking was founded on a single knife, the *tou,* often referred to as the Chinese cleaver, perhaps the most fearsomely useful knife ever devised.

CUTTING devices divide up into those that have one function and one function only—the Gorgonzola cutter, the arrow-shaped crab knife, the pineapple-slicing device that spirals down into the yellow fruit, removing the woody core and leaving only perfect juicy rings—and those that can be pressed into service for countless jobs: the multitaskers. And not surprisingly, different cooking cultures have produces different multitasker knives.

The Inuit *ulu,* for example, is a fan-shaped blade (similar to an Italian *mezzaluna*) traditionally used by Eskimo women for anything from trimming a child's hair to shaving blocks of ice, as well as chopping fish. The Japanese *santoku* is another multitasker, currently regarded as one of the most desirable all-purpose knives for the home kitchen. It is far lighter than a European chef's knife, with a rounded tip, and often has oval dimples, called divots, along the blade. *Santoku* means "three uses," so named because a *santoku* is equally good at cutting meat, chopping vegetables, and slicing fish.

Perhaps no knife is quite as multifunctional, nor quite as essential to an entire food culture, as the Chinese *tou.* This wondrous blade is often referred to as a "cleaver" because it has the same square-bladed hatchet shape as the cleaver that butchers use to hack through meat bones. The *tou*'s use, however, is that of an all-purpose kitchen knife (for once, "all-purpose" is no exaggeration). For E. N. Anderson, the anthropologist of China, the *tou* exemplifies the principle of "minimax": maximum usage from minimum cost and effort. The idea is a frugal one: the best Chinese kitchen would extract the maximum cooking potential from the minimum number of utensils. The *tou* fits the bill. This big-bladed knife, writes Anderson, is useful for

> splitting firewood, gutting and scaling fish, slicing vegetables, mincing meat, crushing garlic (with the dull side of the blade), cutting one's nails, sharpening pencils, whittling new chopsticks, killing pigs, shaving (it is kept sharp enough, or supposedly is), and settling scores old and new with one's enemies

What makes the *tou* still more versatile is the fact that—unlike the Inuit *ulu*—it gave rise to what is widely considered one of the world's two greatest cuisines (the other being French). From ancient times, the great characteristic of Chinese cookery was the intermingling of flavors through fine chopping. The *tou* made this possible. During the Zhou dynasty (1045–256 BC), when iron was first introduced to China, the art of fine gastronomy was referred to as "*k'o'peng*," namely, to "cut and cook." It was said of the philosopher Confucius (who lived from 551–479 BC) that he would eat no meat that had not been properly cut. By around 200 BC, cookbooks were using many different words for cutting and mincing, suggesting a high level of knife skills (*dao gong*).

A typical *tou* has a blade of around 18 to 28 cm (7 to 11 inches) long. So far, very similar to a European chef's knife. What's dramatically different is the width of the blade: around 10 cm, or 4 inches, nearly twice as wide as the widest point on a chef's knife. And the *tou* is the same width all the way along: no tapering, curving, or pointing. It's a sizable rectangle of steel, but also surprisingly thin and light when you pick it up, much lighter than a French cleaver. It commands you to use it in a different way from a chef's knife. Most European cutting uses a "locomotive" motion, rocking the knife back and forth, following the gradient of the blade. Because of its continuous flatness, a *tou* invites chopping with an up-down motion. The sound of knife work in a Chinese kitchen is louder and more percussive than in a French one: *chop-chop-chop* as opposed to *tap-tap-tap*. But this loudness does not reflect any crudeness of technique. With this single knife, Chinese cooks produce a far wider range of cutting shapes than the dicing, julienning, and so on produced by the many knives of French cuisine. A *tou* can create silken threads (8 cm long and very thin), silver-needle silken threads (even thinner), horse ears (3 cm slices cut on a steep angle), cubes, strips, and slices, to name but a few.

No single inventor set out to devise this exceptional knife, or if someone did, the name is lost. The *tou*—and the entire cuisine it made possible—was a product of circumstances. First, metal. Cast iron was discovered in China around 500 BC. It was cheaper to produce than bronze, which allowed for knives that were large hunks of metal with wooden handles. Above all, the *tou* was the product of a frugal peasant culture. A *tou* could reduce ingredients to small enough pieces that the flavors of all the ingredients in a dish melded together and the pieces would cook very quickly, probably over a portable brazier. It was a thrifty tool that could make the most of scarce fuel: cut everything small, cook it fast, waste nothing. As a piece of technology, it is much smarter than it first looks. In tandem with the wok, it works as a device for extracting the most flavor from the bare minimum of cooking energy. When highly chopped food is stir-fried, more of the surface area is exposed to the oil, becoming crispy-brown and delicious. As with all technology, there is a trade-off: the hard work and skill lavished on prepping the ingredients buys you lightning-fast cooking time. A whole, uncut chicken takes more than an hour to cook in the oven. Even a single chicken breast can take twenty minutes. But *tou*-chopped fragments of chicken can cook in five minutes or less; the time is in the chopping (though this, too, is speedy in the right hands; on YouTube you can watch chef Martin Yan breaking down a chicken in eighteen seconds). Chinese cuisine is extremely varied from region to region: the fiery heat of Sichuan; the black beans and seafood of the Cantonese. What unites Chinese cooks from distant areas is their knife skills and their attachment to this one knife.

The *tou* was at the heart of the way classical Chinese cooking was structured, and still is. Every meal must be balanced between *fan*—which normally means rice but can also apply to other grains or noodles—and *ts'ai*, the vegetables and meat dishes. The *tou* is a more essential component in this meal than any single ingredient, because it is the *tou* that cuts up the *ts'ai* and renders it in multiple different forms. There is an entire spectrum of cutting methods, with words to match. Take a carrot. Will you slice it vertically (*qie*) or horizontally (*pian*)? Or will you chop it (*kan*)? If so, what shape will you choose? Slivers (*si*), small cubes (*ding*), or chunks (*kuai*)? Whichever you adopt, you must stick to it exactly; a cook is judged by the precision of his or her knife strokes. There is a famous story about Lu Hsu, who was a prisoner under Emperor Ming. He was given a bowl of meat stew in his cell and knew at once that his mother had visited, for only she knew how to cut the meat in such perfect squares.

Tous look terrifying. Handled by the right person, however, these threatening blades are delicate instruments and can achieve the same precision in cutting that a French chef needs an array of specialist blades to achieve. In skilled hands, a *tou* can cut ginger as thin as parchment; it can dice vegetables so fine they resemble flying-fish roe. This one knife can prepare an entire banquet, from cutting fragile slivers of scallop and 5 cm lengths of green bean to carving cucumbers to look like lotus flowers.

The *tou* is more than a device for fine dining. In poorer times, expensive ingredients can easily be omitted, so long as the knife work and the flavoring remain constant. The *tou* created a remarkable unity across the classes in Chinese cuisine, in contrast to British cookery, where rich food and poor food tend to operate in opposing spheres (the rich had roast beef, eaten from a tablecloth; the poor had bread and cheese, eaten from hand to mouth). Poor cooks in China might have far less *ts'ai*—far less vegetables and meat— to work with than their rich counterparts; but whatever they have, they will treat just the same. It is the technique, above all, that makes a meal Chinese or not. The Chinese cook takes fish and fowl, vegetable and meat, in all their diverse shapes and renders them geometrically exact and bite-sized.

The *tou*'s greatest power is to save those eating from any knife work. Table knives are viewed as unnecessary and also slightly disgusting in China. To cut food at the table is regarded as a form of butchery. Once the *tou* has done its work, all the eater has to do is pick up the perfectly uniform morsels using chopsticks. The *tou* and the chopsticks work in perfect symbiosis: one chops, the other serves. Again, this is a more frugal way of doing things than the classical French approach, where, despite all that laborious slicing with diverse knives in the kitchen, still further knives are needed to eat the meal.

The *tou* and its uses represent a radically different and alien culture of knives from that of Europe (and thence, America). Where a Chinese master cook used one knife, his French equivalent used many, with widely differing functions: butcher's knives and boning knives, fruit knives and fish knives. Nor was it just a question of implements. The *tou* stood for a whole way of life of cooking and eating, one completely removed from the courtly dining of Europe. There is a vast chasm between a dish of tiny dry-fried slivers of beef, celery, and ginger, done in the Sichuan style, seasoned with chili-bean paste and Shaoxing wine in a careful balance of flavors; and a French steak, bloodied and whole, supplied at the table with a sharp knife for cutting and mustard to add flavor, according to the whim of the diner. The two represent diverse worldviews. It is the gulf between a culture of chopping and one of carving.

❧PART FIVE☙

Cultural Tales and Tables

Our Diverse Gastronomic Ways

INTRODUCTION

WHAT CONSTITUTES a cultural tale of food? Anthropologists would give a staggering variety of answers to such a question, but we'll say simply that any story about food and its relation to social life and social practice will do. The writings we have assembled here examine both the most ordinary ways in which a culture consumes its food and the most extraordinary, even bizarre. In the latter category, consider America's fascination with what is called "competitive eating." Every so often newspapers regale us with stories of how a man with an apparently expanding stomach crammed fifty hamburgers into his maw in fifteen minutes, or of a salubrious slurper who slid eight dozen raw oysters down his gullet in a mere ten minutes (brave man, indeed). Jason Fagone reports with relish on a grilled cheese-eating contest, featuring one sandwich that appears to have an image of the Virgin Mary stamped on the toast, "the culinary version of the Shroud of Turin." Turning to more routine modes of consumption, two writers meditate here on the humble chopstick but turn those simple sticks into cultural signs of the highest significance. Thus the literary critic Roland Barthes compares the Japanese way of gently lifting food into the diner's mouth to the manners of a mother animal delicately picking up its young by the scruff of the neck, and he contrasts this practice with that of Western eaters whose implements gouge, rip, tear, and otherwise savagely attack their food. More generally, Margaret Visser, a historian and anthropologist of everyday life, gives us a brief history of Asian chopstick use, showing how that device dictates a certain way of eating, as diners nimbly pick from a common platter but because of that very communality are practically forbidden to lick or bite their chopstick, or to fish around for a morsel before definitively deciding what piece they desire.

What comprehensive account of cultural tables would omit the most horrifying of all meals—not fried grasshoppers or raw witchetty grubs— but human flesh? Felipe Fernández-Armesto edifies us with the "logic of cannibalism," the need to absorb the soul or the courage of the ingested other, or to take drastic revenge on one's enemies. On a less scarifying note, when Jonathan Gold sings the praises of an L.A. hot dog joint, who could not think of the ballpark frank, the stadium Polish? On an equally quotidian matter, Bill Buford's mordant report of the Food Network's round-the-clock culinary fantasies discusses what is regularly piped into America's hungry homes—involvement with food by proxy, a media substitute for the thing itself. But if we're tired of looking at mere images of the reality, think of Anya von Bremzen, whose émigrée mother spent months replicating in New York not only the crowning dishes of tsarist Russia but also the more poignant concoctions of Soviet cuisine. Unlike the youthful Julie Powell painstakingly struggling to cook her way through Julia Child's *Mastering the Art of French Cooking*, von Bremzen's mother Larisa is to the heritage and the manner born.

Finally, we offer here two essays on the place of culture in food. The French sociologist Luce Giard looks at the role of women in the kitchen, seeing them as crucial nourishers and providers, but at the same time resisting the common sociocultural assumption that women's essence is to be cooks. Rather she shows how culture, politics, and history have placed women in that culinary role. A burden or a joy? Giard wishes to claim the importance of female intelligence, imagination, and memory as crucial ingredients in the cultural story of gastronomy. Similarly, Massimo Montanari, an Italian cultural historian also opposed to culinary essentialism, argues that the phenomenon we call "taste" occurs not on the tongue but in the brain, by which he means that culture, not anatomy, conditions us to receive certain foods with pleasure or to dismiss them with displeasure. Taste, for humans, is a function of education, not just physiology; and it is collective as much as subjective. From the perspective of the culture critic, as these writers show, food is valued according to how society regards it. Inevitably our tables are set as they are because of the tales that have made us who we are.

๑

Curnonsky (Maurice Edmond Sailland) (1872–1956)

THE MAN WHO called himself Curnonsky was born Maurice Edmond Sailland in France, but assumed a Russian-sounding name to lend himself a kind of exotic stature. He looked not unlike James Beard, and like Beard a half-century later he became the most trusted gastronome in his country. He was in fact known as "the Prince of Gastronomy," and it was said that Michelin's famous restaurant guides were due to his early advocacy of the motorcar in French gastro-touring. Curnonsky (whose name means "Why not?" in Latin along with the Russian suffix) was the author of some sixty-five books on food, including a memoir, *Literary and Culinary Memories*, and the classic *Larousse Traditional French Cooking*. Not all of his work was universally admired. Julia Child, for instance, described him as a "dogmatic meatball . . . just a big bag of wind," and indeed he ballooned to such girth that he had to be carried by several friends into his favorite restaurants! In our witty selection Curnonsky aligns political divisions of right, center, and left with various cooking and eating preferences. As one who advocated simple, even rustic foods, he would doubtless place himself on the culinary left.

from *The Almanach of Gourmets*: Gastronomy and Politics

THE UNINITIATED IMAGINE a gourmet as an obese, gout-ridden, and single-minded sexagenarian, who lives only to eat, always stuffing himself, someone who does hardly a stitch of work between meals.

But that's not right at all, and it's important to question such hasty generalizations. There are gourmets of all ages, even of both sexes, and I know several "gourmettes" who can show many men a thing or two.

Among all gourmets, there is only one common trait: an open mind. Their harmless passion demands, in effect, a good stomach and perfectly balanced health, for everyone knows the degree to which health influences character. No doubt the greatest of orators must have proclaimed "A generous heart is always master of the body it inhabits." But between eloquence and reality there is room for some uncertainties. If you suffer from a kidney attack, or even a simple toothache, your view of the world can change to the point where you begin to quarrel even with Divine Commandments, some of which are indeed debatable.

But this is not to suggest that all gourmets have identical ideas about everything, particularly not about cuisine. Ever since I have been around them—and not just recently, since my father and my two grandfathers all enjoyed the good life—I've become convinced that one can categorize both gourmets and politicians in similar fashion.

Just reflect for five minutes, and you will soon and clearly realize that gastronomically speaking there is an extreme right, a right, a center, a left, and an extreme left.

The Extreme Right: The enthusiasts of "Haute Cuisine," a cuisine that is informed, refined, and quite complex, the cooking of which demands a great chef and first-class ingredients; this could be called "diplomatic cuisine," to be served at formal banquets in embassies or palaces, compared to which the cooking served in deluxe hotels is only a parody.

The Right: The defenders of "traditional cuisine," who will accept only wood-burning stoves and slowly simmered dishes, who believe on principle that you eat well only with home-cooked food and in the company of no more than six or eight people, and where the cook is an elderly woman who's been with the family for thirty years. These people have a wine cellar with bottles from before the phylloxera epidemic, brandies selected by their great-grandfather, a kitchen garden, and their own chicken coop.

The Center: The lovers of bourgeois and regional cuisines, who will admit that you can still eat well in restaurants and that everywhere in France there remain good inns and excellent hotels that refrain from fancy sauces, and where butter is still butter. These centrists preserve and hold dear the tastes of France's traditional dishes and local wines. They demand that ingredients keep their original taste, are never blandly watered down nor excessively dressed up.

The Left: The partisans of food without affectation or complications, food good enough so to speak for a quickly prepared snack made with the means at hand. These folks happily content themselves with a nicely turned out omelet, a seared cutlet, a steak cooked to perfection, a rabbit stew, even a slice of ham or sausage. They don't turn away from canned foods, and declare that a good sardine in oil has its charm, while a particular brand of canned green beans can be at least as good as fresh beans.

They seek out small places where the owner himself does the cooking. They love to discover, for example, a simple restaurant run by a man from the provinces who gets his meats and sausages from home. They promote country cooking and its pleasant little regional wines. They are the itinerants of gastronomy, and for them I've invented the neologism: "Gastronomades."

The Extreme Left: Those whimsical folks, restless fellows, innovators, whom Napoleon would have called ideologues. Always questing after original sensations and unfamiliar pleasures, curious about all exotic cuisines, all foreign and colonial dishes, they would love to sample old and new dishes, foods from everywhere.

But what really characterizes them is their love of inventing new recipes. In this group sometimes we also come across personalities who are highly prominent yet a bit unsettling, free spirits all—but with one difference: these anarchists are horrified by *bombes*, a dessert they regard as too traditional and outmoded. In other words this group also has its saints and its martyrs. Some thirty years ago a gastronome of this ilk decreed that peas were of a very ordinary shade of green, so he decided to develop peas that were grass-green. He treated them initially with oxygenated water, in order, he said, to dye them with a fixative followed by a strong dose of green malachite mixed with a few flakes of iron. Satisfied at last with the result, and hungry from his all-night vigils, he ate a full pound of these homemade peas. ... When I went to see him, a week later in the hospital, he was slowly beginning to recover; but owing to his poisoning our researcher barely avoided pushing up the daisies.

Let us not overdramatize this one example. Good cooking, as with many other endeavors, flourishes only by renewing itself and adapting to changing human needs. And it would be unfair of me to reject all new dishes and all innovators, since, for the past thirty years, eminent chefs have honored me by lending my name to a dozen original dishes. In 1928 I even created, along with my friend Marcel Dorin, a vertical skewer that has been adapted by numerous caterers and gourmets.

※

Roland Barthes (1915–1980)

BARTHES WAS A French literary critic interested in the way language and ideologies represent cultural systems and social practices. He was fascinated by the way such systems and practices could be understood through an investigation of objects and behaviors identified with them. The meditation on chopsticks that we include here is taken from his work *Empire of Signs*, which narrates a trip he took to Japan. An unusual travel book, it is concerned less with his voyage than with how the smallest gestures, signs, buildings, and even packaging all "signify" the meaning of Japan. For Barthes chopsticks are eminently interpretable phenomena, telling us not merely about the way Asians eat but how their use distinguishes the East from the West. In his view, all aspects of cuisine, from its preparation to its mode of consumption, allow us to see deeply into the culture for which foodways speak.

from *Empire of Signs*: Chopsticks

AT THE FLOATING market in Bangkok, each vendor sits in a tiny motionless canoe, selling minuscule quantities of food: Seeds, a few eggs, bananas, coconuts, mangoes, pimentos (nor to speak of the Unnameable). From himself to his merchandise, including his vessel, everything is *small*. Occidental food, heaped up, dignified, swollen to the majestic, linked to a certain operation of prestige, always tends toward the heavy, the grand, the abundant, the copious; the Oriental follows the converse movement, and tends toward the infinitesimal: the cucumber's future is not its accumulation or its thickening, but its division, its tenuous dispersal, as this haiku puts it:

> *Cucumber slices*
> *The juice runs*
> *Drawing spider legs*

There is a convergence of the tiny and the esculent: things are not only small in order to be eaten, but are also comestible in order to fulfill their essence, which is smallness. The harmony between Oriental food and chopsticks cannot be merely functional, instrumental; the foodstuffs are cut up so they can be grasped by the sticks, but also the chopsticks exist because the foodstuffs are cut into small pieces; one and the same movement, one and the same form transcends the substance and its utensil: Division.

Chopsticks have other functions besides carrying the food from the plate to the mouth (indeed, that is the least pertinent one, since it is also the function of fingers and forks), and these functions are specifically theirs. First of all, a chopstick—as its shape sufficiently indicates—has a deictic function: it points to the food, designates the fragment, brings into existence by the very gesture of choice, which is the index; but thereby, instead of ingestion following a kind of mechanical sequence, in which one would be limited to swallowing little by little the parts of one and the same dish, the chopstick, designating what it selects (and thus selecting there and then *this* and nor *that*), introduces into the use of food not an order but a caprice, a certain indolence: in any case, an intelligent and no longer mechanical operation. Another function of the two chopsticks together, that of pinching the fragment of food (and no longer of piercing it, as our forks do); to *pinch*, moreover, is too strong a word, too aggressive (the word of sly little girls, of surgeons, of seamstresses, of sensitive natures); for the foodstuff never undergoes a pressure greater than is precisely necessary to raise and carry it; in the gesture of chopsticks, further softened by their substance—wood or lacquer—there is something maternal, the same precisely measured care taken in moving a child: a force (in the operative sense of the word), no longer a pulsion; here we have a whole demeanor with regard to food; this is seen clearly in the cook's long chopsticks, which serve not for eating but for preparing foodstuffs: the instrument never pierces, cuts, or slits, never wounds but only selects, turns, shifts. For the chopsticks (third function), in order to divide, must separate, part, peck, instead of cutting and piercing, in the manner of our implements; they never violate the foodstuff: either they gradually unravel it (in the case of vegetables) or else prod it into separate pieces (in the case of fish, eels), thereby rediscovering the natural fissures of the substance (in this, much closer to the primitive finger than to the knife). Finally, and this is perhaps their loveliest function, the chopsticks *transfer* the food, either crossed like two hands, a support and no longer a pincers, they slide under the clump of rice and raise it to the diner's mouth, or (by an age-old gesture of the whole Orient) they push the alimentary snow from bowl to lips in the manner of a scoop. In all these functions, in all the gestures they imply, chopsticks are the converse of our knife (and of its predatory substitute, the fork): they are the alimentary instrument which refuses to cut, to pierce, to mutilate, to trip (very limited gestures, relegated to the preparation of the food for cooking: the fish seller who skins the still-living eel for us exorcises once and for all, in a preliminary sacrifice, the murder of food); by chopsticks, food becomes no longer a prey to which one does violence (meat, flesh over which one does battle), but a substance harmoniously transferred; they transform the previously divided substance into bird food and rice into a flow of milk; maternal, they tirelessly perform the gesture which creates the mouthful, leaving to our alimentary manners, armed with pikes and knives, that of predation.

Margaret Visser (1940–)

SOUTH AFRICAN-BORN, THE Canadian writer and broadcaster Margaret Visser defines her "subject matter" as the "history, anthropology and mythology of everyday life." In such incisive studies of culinary manners and mores as *Much Depends Upon Dinner*, *The Rituals of Dinner*, and *The Way We Are*, all influential best-sellers, she has analyzed a range of topics, from the history of corn to the distinction between chopsticks and Western cutlery, from the dislike of offal to the legend of the Easter bunny. She divides her time between Toronto, Paris, and the southwest of France, but also taught classics for nearly two decades at York University.

from *The Rituals of Dinner*: Chopsticks

THE ULTIMATELY RESTRICTED—and therefore it may be thought the ultimately delicate—manner of eating with one's hands is to use the thumb and two fingers of the right hand, only the tips of these ideally being allowed to touch the food. This gesture, refined even more by artificially elongating the fingers and further reducing their number, is of course the origin of chopsticks. Once people become accustomed to fingers remaining clean throughout the meal, napkins used for serious cleansing seem not only redundant but down-right nasty. Father João Rodrigues observed in the seventeenth century that the Japanese were "much amazed at our eating with the hands and wiping them on napkins, which then remain covered with food stains, and this causes them both nausea and disgust." Napkins laid on knees are still an "ethnic," Western affectation in China and Japan. There is, however, a tradition of supplying diners several times during the meal with small rough towels wrung out in boiling water, for hand- and face-wiping.

Chopsticks seem to have evolved in the East specifically for use with rice: the staple grain in China was originally millet, which the *Li Chi* insists must be eaten with a spoon, not with chopsticks like rice. Chinese rice is not loose and dry like that chosen by Indians, Arabs, and Africans, who prefer eating it with their hands, but sticky and slightly moist even without sauce; it is easily handled with chopsticks. The earliest word for chopsticks seems to have been *zǐ*, related to the root meaning, "help." This is pronounced, however, like the word for "stop," or "becalm" used of boats. Chinese boatmen are said to have renamed them *kuai-zǐ*," which sounds like "fast fellows," because Chinese think of chopsticks as swift and agile, the very opposite of halting and being becalmed. This is now their Chinese name; "chopsticks" is of course a Western barbarism. In Japanese, chopsticks are called *bashi*, "bridge," because they effect the transition from bowl to mouth.

Chopsticks are thought of as fast, then, and helpful. Meals in China often surprise visitors by the speed with which they are eaten; chopsticks enable the Chinese and Japanese to eat food which is sizzling hot, but because it is often served in small pieces it gets cold if people dawdle. Chopstick-users remain more likely than we are to use their hands as aids in eating—but it is not at all advisable to get them greasy: chopsticks, and especially the lacquered chopsticks common in Japan and Korea, are extremely difficult to manage with slippery fingers. Porcelain spoons are used for soups and the more liquid dishes; children are allowed to use spoons for everything until they are about three or four years old, when chopstick training begins.

Chinese tables are round or square rather than oval or oblong: diners sit equidistant from the dishes of *cài* (meat, fish, and vegetables), all set out in one "course," in the middle. Each diner gets a small bowl for *fàn*, literally, "food," meaning rice. The rice is the substance of the meal; the *cài* is merely relish, unless the occasion is a banquet. The host, or the mother, doles out the rice into the bowls. Each guest must take the filled bowl in two hands: receiving in one hand shows disrespectful indifference. You never eat *cài* before being served rice, because that looks as though you are so greedy and selfish that you would be prepared to eat nothing but meat and vegetables, which are the expensive part of the meal, centrally placed in order to be shared with others.

When the host gives the sign, you may begin to take *cài* with your chopsticks. The gestures used by Chinese, Japanese, and others to do this are fascinating for Westerners. They look accomplished, delicate, precise, and gentle—much more polished than our own behaviour at meals. Roland Barthes in *Empire of Signs* speaks eulogies on the Japanese manipulation of chopsticks: "there is something maternal, the same precisely measured care taken in moving a child . . . the instrument never pierces, cuts, or slits, never wounds but only selects, turns, shifts. For the chopsticks . . . in order to divide, must separate, part, peck, instead of cutting and piercing, in the manner of our implements; they never violate the foodstuff; either they gradually unravel it (in the case of vegetables) or else prod it into separate pieces (in the case of fish, eels) thereby rediscovering the natural fissures of the substance."

A Westerner feels like a brute butcher before this Oriental delicacy. Barthes says that we are "armed with pikes and knives" like predators rather than gentle mothers, our food "a prey to which one does violence." B.Y. Chao tells us that the Chinese are aware in themselves of a sequence of commands: "Await, avoid, attack!" You must pause, think of others, consider which piece you want, then zero in on it. You may have to stretch across the path of another's chopsticks—though Chinese, too, try to restrict themselves to taking from the side of the dish more or less facing them; fellow diners cooperate with each other and are not greatly offended by another's "attack." You should never look too intent on obtaining a particular morsel, however. Chinese children are taught that "the best mannered person does not allow co-diners to be aware of what his or her favorite dishes are by his or her eating pattern."

It is politer to transfer food first to your rice bowl, and eat it from there, than to take it directly from the *cài* dish to your mouth. Chopsticks must never be licked or bitten. Japanese bad manners include *neburi-bashi*: licking chopsticks with the tongue; *mogi-kui*: using your mouth to remove rice sticking to your chopsticks; *komi-bashi*: forcing several things into your mouth with your chopsticks; *utsuri-bashi*: one must not break the rule that a mouthful of rice is to be taken between every two bites of meat, fish, or vegetables; *saguri-bashi*: searching with chopsticks to see if anything you want remains in the dish; *bashi-namari*: hesitation whether to take one thing rather than another; and *sora-bashi*: putting back with the chopsticks food you intended to eat.

Mannerly diners with chopsticks never "fish about" for morsels; they must take the bit they touch first. This means that one begins by eyeing one's target carefully: if you prod it, you must take and eat it. Using chopsticks need in no way mean that people eat food touched by implements which have been in other people's mouths. Yet a very Western distaste for even the thought of touching the food of all with the utensils of each has spread. In 1984, Hu Yaobang, the former Communist Party Secretary, criticized the traditional Chinese way of eating and urged change on sanitary grounds. A good deal of such concern must in fact be a desire to participate in Western prestige as being somehow more ineffably "modern." The admiration of people like Roland Barthes for superior Oriental wisdom seems to be less satisfying than the allure of technological hygiene and "modern" metal instruments. A compromise with "modernity" is the Japanese pre-wrapped, disposable set of wooden chopsticks. But unfortunately there is an ecological price to pay for this, as hundreds of millions of trees are chopped down every year to supply throwaway chopstick wood—in 1987, 20 billion chopsticks were used and discarded in Japan alone.

It has never been acceptable to return bitten morsels of meat, vegetables, or fish to the common dish; but because the bowl of rice is "private territory," a piece of meat or vegetable may be held in chopsticks and bitten, and the rest put down on the rice in the bowl, to be finished later. One must never, in Japan, stick the chopsticks upright in the rice. This is done only when offerings are made by Buddhist mourners for their dead: standing chopsticks are rather like our own taboos about an empty chair at table.

With perfect propriety one lifts the small china bowl in the left hand and sweeps the contents into the mouth with precise, busy movements of the two sticks together, held in the right. Barthes's delicate gestures suddenly become swift and purely efficient; the bowl held under the chopsticks is moved dexterously about so as to prevent food spills. We ourselves are surprised to see this done because we are never allowed to lift dishes containing solid food—and we count soup, unless it is in a cup, as "solid food"—to our lips; we gave up doing this when we agreed that formal politeness involves using our cutlery. The Chinese may be thought of as treating the little bowl like a cross between a teacup and a large spoon, with the chopsticks as "helpers." Table manners always impose difficult restraints: "If you rattle your chopsticks against the bowl," says a Chinese proverb, "you and your descendants will always be poor." Whatever happens, however, at an ordinary meal every single grain of rice in one's bowl must be eaten before dinner is over. Leaving rice is disgusting behaviour, because it shows a lack of knowledge of one's own appetite in the first place, together with greed for meat and vegetables, and no respect for rice—its culture, its history, and the hard work that has been involved in getting it to the table.

Rice is never to be gripped, lifted, and eaten grain by grain, as Western novices in the art of chopstick-handling find themselves doing with so much frustration and so many complaints. "Picking" at one's food is very rude, in fact, for Oriental manners, more than our own, demand demonstrations of delight and pleasure in eating, and inept fiddling with one's chopsticks is apt to be interpreted not merely as a want of competence but as a depressing unwillingness as well. The problem that Westerners experience is often the result of attempts to eat rice with chopsticks from flat plates: the small bowl raised towards the face is far easier to manage with the proper zest. Chinese themselves, given food on a flat plate, prefer to use a porcelain spoon (to stand in for its sister, the bowl). This spoon, like a bowl, has a flat bottom, so that it can be laid down without spilling the contents.

The kind of food we ourselves eat, together with the way we cook and serve it, predisposes us to use knives, forks, and spoons, and our idea of what constitutes a "place setting" also influences our food choices. Oriental food is cut up in the kitchen so that it can be eaten with chopsticks—but also, as Barthes points out, chopsticks came into being because each mouthful is regarded as comestible partly because it is small; being confronted with a large slab of meat on a dish can be a disgusting experience for people from rice-and-chopstick cultures. In addition, rice-growing is a land use which reduces the amount of fuel available, so that meat and vegetables must usually be cooked quickly to save wood. Cutting them up small facilitates stir-frying and other quick-cooking methods.

꿍

Massimo Montanari (1949–)

ONE OF THE world's foremost experts in the growing field of food history and culture, Montanari teaches medieval history at the University of Bologna and is director of the journal *Food & History*. Among his book titles are *Italian Cuisine: A Cultural History* and *Food: A Cultural History*. He is interested in all aspects of food as a sign of class and identity, whether institutional, cultural, or personal. He is as likely to write about the use of the fork and how it replaced hands as a utensil as he is to discourse on how certain foods became identified with particular holidays, or why other foods became markers of bourgeois aspiration. In the present selection Montanari insists that taste is never arbitrary or subjective, but a product of a specific culture that celebrates and promotes it, a private experience whose origins are inevitably collective and communal, historical and geographical.

from *Food Is Culture*: Taste Is a Cultural Product

FOOD IS NEITHER good nor bad in the absolute, though we have been taught to recognize it as such. The organ of taste is not the tongue, but the brain, a culturally (and therefore historically) determined organ through which are transmitted and learned the criteria for evaluations. Therefore, these criteria vary in space and in time. What in one epoch is judged positively, in another can change meaning; what in one locale is considered a tasty morsel, in another can be rejected as disgusting. Definitions of taste belong to the cultural heritage of human society. As there are differing tastes and predilections among different peoples and regions of the world, so do tastes and predilections evolve over the course of centuries.

But how can one presume to reconstruct the "taste" in and of food for eras so distant from our own?

The question in reality hearkens back to two distinct meanings of the term *taste*. One of these is taste understood as flavor, as the individual sensation of the tongue and palate—an experience that is by definition subjective, fleeting, and ineffable. From this point of view the historical experience of food is irretrievably lost. But taste can also mean knowledge (*sapere* vs. *sapore*): it is the sensorial assessment of what is good or bad, pleasing or displeasing. And this evaluation, as we have said, begins in the brain before it reaches the palate.

From this perspective, taste is not in fact subjective and incommunicable, but rather collective and eminently communicative. It is a cultural experience transmitted to us from birth, along with other variables that together define the "values" of a society. Jean-Louis Flandrin coined the expression "structures of taste" as suitable for emphasizing the collective and shared "values" of this experience. And it is clear that this second dimension of the problem, which does not coincide with the first but in large measure conditions it, can be investigated historically by examining the memoirs and the archeological finds constituting the traces that every past society has left behind.

Let us take medieval and Renaissance society. What are we able to learn from the documents surrounding the patterns of taste and food consumption from a thousand or even five hundred years ago? What variants stand out in comparison to today?

To a retrospective investigation moving from today in quest of the medieval, it seems suddenly clear that our concept of cuisine and the system of tastes that seem to us so "naturally" preferable are very different from those that for a long time (and not only in the Middle Ages but as recently as two centuries ago) were judged as good and therefore to be sought out.

Today's Italian and European cuisine has a predominantly analytical character. By that I mean that it tends to differentiate tastes: sweet, salty, bitter, sour, spicy . . . reserving for each of these an autonomous space, either in a specific food or in the sequence of the meal.

Tied to this is the notion that insofar as possible, cuisine must respect the natural flavor of each food component. The quest is for a flavor that is different each time and unique, thanks to its having been maintained as specifically distinct from others. But these simple rules do not constitute a global archetype of an "Ur-cuisine," always extant and consistent unto itself. These rules are the fruit of a minor revolution that took place in France between the seventeenth and eighteenth centuries.

"Cabbage soup should taste of cabbage, leeks of leek, turnips of turnip," Nicola de Bonnfons suggested in his *Letters to Household Managers* (mid-seventeenth century). In appearance it is an innocent enough declaration, disconcerting in its banality, but in fact this notion overturned ways of thinking and eating that had been firmly held for centuries.

Renaissance taste, as well as medieval taste, and going back even further, that of ancient Rome, had indeed developed a model of cuisine based principally on the idea of artifice and on the blending of flavors. Both the preparation of individual foods and their placement within the meal answered to a logic more *synthesizing* than analytical: to bind together more than to separate. This also corresponded to the rules of dietetic science, which considered a "balanced" food as that which contained in itself all the nutritional qualities, each displayed in turn, rendered by perceptibly distinct flavors. The perfect food was considered that in which all the tastes (therefore all the virtues) would be simultaneously present. Specific to this end, the cook was obliged to alter the products, changing their characteristics in a more or less radical fashion.

A typical example of this culture is the sweet-salty taste dynamic characterizing many of the medieval and Renaissance food preparations. Or take the bittersweet, a mixture of sugar and citrus fruits (thanks to two new products brought to Europe by the Arabs), which reinterpreted and refined the old combination of honey and vinegar already typical of Roman cuisine. These tastes have not completely vanished, however, since even today they can be found in more conservative European culinary traditions, as in the Germanic countries and, more generally, those of eastern Europe.

Think of blueberry jam, the pears and apples used as garnishes for meats, and especially for game: that is medieval cuisine. To remain in Italy, recall products like Cremona mustard (chutney) which blends the sharpness of spices with the sweetness of sugar: that is medieval cuisine. Think of casseroles or timbales of macaroni (a pastry crust filled with a salted dough flavored with sweet spices), traditional in various Italian regions and cities. Think of pepper and sugar in *panpepato* (pepper bread) and of other Christmas sweets. To wander further afield, think of the sweet and sour in Chinese cooking, of the honey-crusted pigeon in the Moroccan tradition: that too is medieval cuisine. This cuisine of flavor contrasts is a quest for balance, for a zero degree in which the distances between tastes are cancelled out.

This "structure of taste," strongly correlated with dietetic science, and in some way as well with the philosophy and worldview of each age, has been totally transformed in Europe during the last two centuries—first in France, then in Italy. This structure constitutes the greatest barrier for us to understanding a reality so different from our own.

Another basic characteristic of premodern gastronomy, one that keeps it remote from our own, is the extremely sparing use of fats. The cuisine of half a millennium ago was fundamentally *lean*. To assemble sauces, the inevitable accompaniment to meat and fish, one used above all acidic ingredients such as wine, vinegar, citrus juice, and the juice of sour grapes—ingredients to be bound with soft bread crumbs, liver, almond milk, and eggs.

Fatty sauces, based on oil and butter, are far more familiar to our taste. By that I mean mayonnaise, béchamel, and all the gravies typical of nineteenth- and twentieth-century bourgeois cooking. These are modern creations, dating from the seventeenth century, which have profoundly transformed the taste and appearance of foods.

If we want to propose a contemporary parallel to medieval European cooking, I suggest that we look rather at the sauces of Japanese or Southeast Asian cuisines, which are lean and, to be precise, completely without dairy products or oil.

Cooking techniques follow this tendency to superimpose and to blend flavors, rather than to separate and deconstruct them. Boiling, roasting, frying, stewing, brazing, were obviously differing ways of cooking. But they were also, in many cases, different stages of the same cooking process, superimposed or so to speak "cumulative," like successive phases in the preparation of the same dish. In some cases this might have been to answer practical exigencies: preliminary boiling of meats (a process that remained in use until at least the eighteenth century) also helped to preserve the meats until, with a few finishing touches, they were later worked into more complex dishes. Boiling might also have served to tenderize meats. But, like all gastronomic choices, it all ultimately came down to a matter of taste: by combining various cooking techniques, one could obtain particular flavors and special textures.

One element that was very well known to ancient and medieval sensibilities, so much more accustomed to a *tactile* relationship with foods than our own, lay both in the gustatory approach and in the physical relationship to foods directly handled (literally) without intermediaries, thus reducing to a minimum the use of cutlery. Only the spoon was really necessary—for liquid foods.

The fork appeared either as a form of extreme (and long controversial) refinement of the habits of social etiquette, or as a sheer necessity when approaching foods like piping hot and slippery pasta, which were difficult to manage with the hands. It is no accident that the development of the fork first took place in Italy rather than elsewhere, because it was above all in Italy, and as early as the final centuries of the Middle Ages, that the culture of pasta took on a prominence unknown elsewhere. But for meat-based foods, even well into the modern era, the use of the fork continued to seem unnatural and hygienically debatable.

Finally, our relationship to food was radically transformed by the spread toward mid-nineteenth century of the so-called service à la russe. This was the custom of serving guests a succession of courses preselected and the same for all. "Service à la russe" is the norm today and seems to us somehow obvious.

The model adhered to until then was quite different, rather more like what we still find today in China, in Japan, and in other countries of the world. Courses are served on the table *simultaneously*, and it was up to each guest to choose his food and to sequence dishes according to his own taste. In simple meals there would be one dish; in more complex and prestigious meals, a series of hot (kitchen-prepared) dishes or a cold (buffet) succession of dishes, the number depending on the lavishness of the banquet. In any case it was up to individual dinner guests to choose according to their own *pleasure* and their own *need*—two notions that, as we have seen, premodern dietetic science tended to bring together, interpreting desire as revealing a physiological need.

🐝

Felipe Fernández-Armesto (1950–)

A BRITISH-BORN HISTORIAN who has taught at numerous universities in Europe and the Americas, Fernández-Armesto has also written a history of food, titled *Near a Thousand Tables*, from which our excerpt is taken. His book focuses on the major revolutions in history that change the way humans came to regard food, including the origins of cooking, the inception of herding, the invention of agriculture, and the industrial revolution. Our selection centers on the way a particular consumption of food may be understood as ritual and magic, namely cannibalism. Fernandez-Armesto's account barely touches on the dire circumstances with which we often associate such practices—the horrors of the Donner Party expedition, for example, or those of the survivors of a plane crash in the Andes; rather, he discusses the apparently joyful banqueting on humans reported in early modern travel writings up to accounts as late as the early nineteenth century. His most controversial claim may be that since cannibalism is regarded by its devotees as a way to acquire bodily health, it paradoxically has something in common with veganism!

from *Near a Thousand Tables*: The Logic of Cannibalism

Cannibalism is a problem. In many cases the practice is rooted in ritual and superstition rather than gastronomy, but not always. A French Dominican in the seventeenth century observed that the Caribs had most decided notions of the relative merits of their enemies. As one would expect, the French were delicious, by far the best. This is no surprise, even allowing for nationalism. The English came next, I'm glad to say. The Dutch were dull and stodgy and the Spaniards so

*stringy, they were hardly a meal at all, even boiled. All this
sounds sadly like gluttony.*

—*PATRICK LEIGH FERMOR*

IT WAS OFFICIAL. The anthropophagi, humans who fed on human flesh, really existed. Long fabled, and long supported by hearsay, they were now reported as fact, backed by an incontrovertible weight of eyewitness corroboration from virtually the entire crew of Columbus's second transatlantic expedition. The shipboard physician wrote home with an account of Arawak prisoners, liberated from the man-eaters' power on the island now known as Guadeloupe.

We inquired of the women who were prisoners of the inhabitants what sort of people these islanders were and they answered, "Caribs." As soon as they learned that we abhor such kind of people because of their evil practice of eating human flesh they felt delighted. . . . They told us that the Carib men use them with such cruelty as would scarcely be believed; and that they eat the children which they bear them, only bringing up those whom they have by their native wives. Such of their male enemies as they can take away alive they bring here to their homes to make a feast of them and those who are killed in battle they eat up after the fighting is over. They declare that the flesh of man is so good to eat that nothing can compare with it in the world; and this is quite evident, for of the human bones we found in the houses, everything that could be gnawed had already been gnawed so that nothing remained but what was too tough to eat. In one of the houses we found a man's neck cooking in a pot. . . . When the Caribs take away boys as prisoners of war they remove their sexual organs, fatten them until they grow up and then, when they wish to make a great feast, they kill and eat them, for they say the flesh of women and youngsters is not good to eat. Three boys thus mutilated came fleeing to us when we visited the houses.

On his previous voyage, Columbus had misheard the Arawak word "Cariba," and rendered it "Caniba." The terms "cannibal" and "Caribbean" both derive from the same name.

Many similar accounts followed and as European exploration spread, reports of cannibalism multiplied. The cannibals encountered by Odysseus or reported by Herodotus, Aristotle, Strabo and Pliny gained credibility with each new find. The "Renaissance Discovery of Man" included the discovery of man as man-eater. The earliest editions of Vespucci's *Voyages* were illustrated with woodcuts of cannibal barbecues. The Aztecs, according to a sympathetic observer, who made strenuous efforts to gather his information at first hand, had feasts specially supplied with *slaves* purchased for the purpose and fattened "so that their flesh should be tastier." The bellies of the Chichimeca were a "sepulchre of human flesh." The Tupinamba were said to consume their enemies "down to the last fingernail." Hans Staden's account of his captivity among them in the 1550s was a best-selling spine-chiller and cliff-hanger because of the way the author's own immolation at a cannibal feast kept getting postponed. His description of the cannibal ritual was menacingly memorable. The victim had to endure the women's boasts and tend the fire on which he was to cook. He was slaughtered by a blow which dashed out his brains. Then the women

> scrape his skin thoroughly and make him quite white and stop up his arse with a bit of wood so that nothing may be lost. Then a man . . . cuts off the arms and the legs above the knee. Then four women carry away the severed pieces and run with them round the huts with shouts of joy. . . . The entrails are kept by the women who boil them and make a thick broth called "mingau." This they and the children drink. They devour the bowels and the flesh from the head. The brains, tongue and whatever else is edible is given to the children. When this is done all go home, taking their share with them. . . . I was there and have seen all this with my own eyes.

Toward the end of the century, scenes of human limbs butchered for the grill, or of cannibal women supping blood and biting entrails, enlivened many of Theodore De Bry's popular engravings of scenes from American travels. The seventeenth century produced little that was new in the tradition, for the horror was familiar and no major new cannibal peoples or customs came to light. Eighteenth-century Europeans, however, found their fascination revived, as more cannibals were encountered and philosophy strove to reconcile the practice with the emerging theory of the nobility of savagery. Even in the highly civilized Christian empire of Ethiopia, Europeans imagined specialist vendors of human butcher meat. In the Indian wars of eighteenth-century North America, a soldier of the Massachusetts militia was alarmed to discover that his adversaries roasted their enemies bit by bit "at a most doleful rate." The greatest concentration of new cases arose during the exploration of the South Seas by ever more ambitious voyages. Melanesian cannibalism, of which many stories accumulated in the eighteenth century, seemed more practical than most: no edible organ of a captive foe was untasted, and the bones made good needles for sewing sailcloth. When Captain Cook first met Maoris, they mimed how to pick clean a human bone. His account was doubted by skeptics in Europe, but confirmed at the cost of captives' lives. Fijian cannibalism, in accounts made familiar in Europe by missionaries' reports in the early nineteenth century, seemed to exceed all previously known cases in depravity because of the scale on which it was reported and the routine nature of cannibal repasts, bereft of any culturally extenuating context, "not indulged in from a species of horrid revenge," as Methodists averred in 1836, "but from an absolute preference for human flesh over other food."

Taken one by one, the veracity of all these reports was open to question. Cannibalism can be a useful source of the comfortable horrors which boost sales of an otherwise boring travelogue. In the late Middle Ages and, with diminishing force, in the sixteenth and seventeenth centuries, it was an extremely useful attribute to ascribe to one's enemies; for cannibalism, like buggery and blasphemy, was classed as an offense against natural law. Those who committed it put themselves beyond the law's protection. With impunity, Europeans could attack them, enslave them, forcibly subject them and sequester property from them. Sometimes, the "man-eating myth" was a reciprocal fantasy: white enquirers were surprised to find themselves suspected of cannibalism by "natives" who also regarded it with horror. Raleigh in Guiana was mistaken for a cannibal by his Arawak hosts. The Mani of the Gambia supposed that the apparently insatiable Portuguese demand for slaves was caused by their inordinate anthropophagous appetites. When George Vancouver entertained inhabitants of Dalco Passage to dinner in 1792, they refused his venison on the suspicion that it was human flesh. The Ku Waru of highland New Guinea assumed that their Australian "discoverers" were "people who eat other people. They must have come around here in order to kill us and eat us. People said not to go walking around at night." Allegations of cannibalism should be discounted like any other crime statistic: some of them must be supposed to have been invented and others to have gained horror in the telling.

Nevertheless, the numbers of well-authenticated cases put the general question beyond a peradventure. Cannibalism existed. The reality of cannibalism as a social practice is not in any genuine doubt. To judge from archaeological evidence, moreover, it has been extremely widespread: human bones snapped for marrow seem to lie under the stones of every civilization. And as the tally of observed cases grew, the assumption that cannibalism was an inherently aberrant activity, abnormal or unnatural, became ever harder to sustain.

Of course, many stories concerned rogue cases which have arisen in Western society contrary to the accepted norms: what might be called "criminal" cannibalism, practiced with a conscious commitment to outrage. Here "Demon" barbers double as pie-men. Maniacal tyrants, seeking exquisite extremes of sadism, serve enemies at table with concoctions of the flesh and blood of their wives and children. There are even practitioners of cannibalism for kicks: individuals who get intellectual pleasure from transgressing convention, perverts who get sexual thrills from ingesting flesh. The most bizarre and ghoulish story is of the Rocky Mountain prospector who called himself "Alferd" Packer. In a notorious case in 1874, he split his companions' skulls open while they slept—except for one whom he shot in the back—before robbing their corpses and feeding on their remains: after eighteen years' imprisonment, he was released into a changed world, where he was welcome as a curiosity and even honored as "an old mountaineer." Pilgrims still visit his grave and, with a kind of irony which some find appetizing, the Alferd Packer Memorial Grill at the University of Colorado in Boulder is named after him. Hannibal Lecter has other real-life predecessors, including "Liver-eating Johnson," who targeted Crow Indians in revenge for the murder of his wife in 1847, and Isse Sagawa, "the cannibal of the Bois de Boulogne," who disposed of an unwanted girlfriend by eating her in 1981. In 1991 in Milwaukee, Jeffrey Dahmer, whose tastes comprised gay necrophilia and sadism as well as cannibalism, had a fridge full of human body parts when the police came to call.

Even in the modern history of the Western world, a form of social cannibalism has been recognized, practiced and, for a long time, licensed in law. In the extremities of siege or retreat, the quick feed off the dead. Not infrequently, living victims of shipwrecks and air crashes stay alive on the strength of dead comrades' flesh and sometimes end up, *in extremis*, drawing lots to sacrifice their lives to their comrades' hunger. In the early modern era, the age of long and perilous sea journeys under sail, survival cannibalism became a "socially accepted practice among seamen," the "custom of the sea." In 1710, for instance, survivors of the wreck of the *Nottingham Galley* turned "fierce and barbarous" after nourishing themselves from the corpse of the dead ship's carpenter. Further cases were reported at intervals during the nineteenth century. Géricault included scenes of cannibalism in sketches for the most famous of all images of nautical disaster, *The Raft of the Medusa,* though in this instance the evidence was not conclusive. Fiction strove to exceed fact. Captain Ahab's obsession with Moby Dick was motivated by memories of the demoralizing experiences which followed the lash of the whale's tail: his story was based on the real-life saga of the wreck of the *Essex,* whose men drew lots to determine the order in which they ate each other after a similar incident in 1820. In 1835 the homonymous captain of the capsized *Francis Spaight* was rescued, allegedly "in the act of eating the liver and brains of his apprentice." In 1874 a boat from the abandoned collier *Euxine* was rescued in the Indian Ocean, with the remains of the butchered carcass of a crewman in its locker. Conrad's sinister hero Falk had plenty of real-life counter-parts. In 1884 "the custom of the sea" was at last outlawed when two survivors of the foundering of the yacht *Mignonette* were sentenced, to their genuine surprise, for killing a shipmate for food during twenty-four days without succor in an open boat.

The custom of the sea had its landward parallels, though conventional morality has never been unequivocal about it. In 1752, for instance, a party of deserters from the colonial militia fled New York for French territory; lost on the way, they ran out of provisions. Four or five of them were eaten by the others. In 1823, Alexander Pearce, a convict in Tasmania, admitted killing a comrade for food, not to survive but to satisfy an appetite acquired during an earlier attempted escape, when he alone of eight companions returned alive from the bush. Apart from depraved cases like Alferd Packer's, practical or opportunistic cannibalism accounted for many dead among lost miners and wagoners of the North American frontier in the nineteenth century, satirized by Mark Twain's story of respectable passengers' recourse to cannibalism in a delayed railway journey between St. Louis and Chicago. The most recent recorded instance of this sort occurred in 1972, when an aircraft carrying the Old Christians rugby team from Uruguay crashed in the Andes. The survivors stayed alive by eating those who died.

It has never been enough simply to assert that "eating people is wrong." Being "contrary to nature" does not seem a strong enough sanction when people are really hungry. Any more than sanctions against homosexuality on board ship (or in prison) or onanism when alone . . . and no one ever died from a lack of sex. If it seems abnormal to some, it represents normalcy for others. Cannibalism has always had apologists. Sometimes, as in the case of defenders of the custom of the sea, they appeal to necessity: in other words, they explain cannibalism by representing human flesh as a source of food, ultimately morally indistinguishable from other food sources. In other contexts, the defense is based on cultural relativism and the recognition that, in some cultures, human flesh is more than food: its consumption is justified not because it sustains individual lives, but because it nourishes the community, invokes the gods or harnesses magic.

In the early modern period, when Western thought was obliged to come to terms with social cannibalism, reformers intent on saving "primitives" from exploitation and victimization produced ingenious defenses. Bartolomé de Las Casas, who plagued the conquerors of the New World with denunciations of their injustice, argued that cannibalism was merely a phase of development which virtually all societies went through: he cited convincing evidence of it in the remote past of Greece, Carthage, England, Germany, Ireland and Spain. Jean de Léry, who survived captivity among cannibals in Brazil, thought their sensibilities would be offended to hear of the massacre of St. Bartholomew. Montaigne's essay *On Cannibals* is often cited as an example of how Western self-perceptions were revolutionized by the cultural encounters of the conquest of America and the "Renaissance Discovery of Man." He suggested that the morality of cannibalism was no worse than the cant which enabled Europeans to butcher one another with every conviction of self-righteousness, despite the advantages of Christian education and philosophical tradition. The tortures and burnings which confessional foes inflicted on one another in France "ate men alive" and "I consider it more barbarous to eat a man alive than dead. . . . We are justified in calling these people barbarians by reference to the laws of reason but not in comparison with ourselves, who surpass them in every kind of barbarity." Robinson Crusoe was able to purge Friday of his cannibalism by kindness. His first impulse was to shoot any cannibal he encountered for "inhuman, hellish brutality" but reflection made him realize that "these people do not commit this as a crime; it is not against their own conscience's reproving, or their light reproaching them. . . . They think it no more a crime . . . to eat human flesh than we do to eat mutton."

As knowledge of cannibalism grows, the problems it poses seem increasingly acute. The really interesting question concerns not the reality or even the morality of cannibalism, but its purpose. Is it part of the *histoire de l'alimentation*—a feeding practice designed to supply eaters with protein? Or does it belong to the history of food, as presented in this chapter—a ritual practiced not for a meal but for its meaning, nourishment for more than material effect? The literature on the subject is vast. But though a practical line through it leads to a secure conclusion that cannibals may and sometimes do eat people for simple bodily nourishment—that is not why cannibal practices become enshrined in some cultures. Most cases concern other aims: self-transformation, the appropriation of power, the ritualization of the eater's relationship with the eaten. This puts human flesh on the same level as many other foods which we eat not because we need them to stay alive but because we want them to change us for the better: we want them to give us a share of their virtue. In particular, it aligns the cannibals with their real modern counterparts: those who eat "health" diets for self-improvement or worldly success or moral superiority or enhanced beauty or personal purity. Strangely, cannibals turn out to have a lot in common with vegans. The tradition which links them is the subject of this chapter.

In New Guinea, many former cannibals—and some practicing ones— still alive with memories of their raids and feasts, tell anthropologists that their enemies are "their game." In 1971 a court exonerated Gabusi tribesmen who had eaten the corpse of a neighboring villager on the grounds that it was normal practice in their culture. The fact that cannibalism can be socially functional may coexist with the exploitation of human flesh for food. "Famine cannibalism" is still—or was until recently—a regular feature of life in the islands of the Massim near New Guinea and of some other societies of Southeast Asia and the Pacific. But most peoples who tell ethnographic enquirers that they eat their enemies "for food" seem to have concealed the symbolic and ritual logic underlying the act, like the Papuan Orokaiva, for whom it is a means of "capturing spirits" in compensation for lost warriors. There were no obvious ritual features in the cannibal meals of the Onabasulu: the meat was prepared in the same way as for pig or game, except that intestines were discarded; but they ate no fellow humans except witches—an instance of discrimination which suggests that some other motive than protein acquisition was at work. The Hua of New Guinea eat their own dead to conserve nu, the vital fluids that they believe to be nonrenewable in nature.

The women of the Gimi of the Papuan highlands used to eat their dead men-folk. The practice continued until the 1960s and is still reenacted in mime with dummy corpses. Their explanation recalls the famous story of Alexander and the sages, who ate their honored dead out of respect. "We would not have left a man to rot!" protest the women. "We took pity on him!" "Come to me, so you shall not rot on the ground. Let your body dissolve inside me!" More is at stake in the ritual, however, than the decorous disposal of corpses, or the macabre recollection of sex. According to one theory, this is a classic case of protein substitution: as men have progressively monopolized the diminishing resources of the forests, women supplemented their diet by eating men. Yet, as part of the ritual, men distribute pork rations to the women in proportion to the amount of male flesh consumed. So the men seem to acknowledge the women's generosity: if they had wished to assuage their hunger, they could simply have handed over the pork without inviting the cannibalism. The cannibal feast takes place only after four or five days of collective grieving. It takes place in the men's house, where, in normal circumstances, women are excluded, and where, during the feast, the women are treated as men. The symbolic meaning of the meal therefore seems connected with the fact that women can encompass and include masculinity by bearing a male child: the immolation of dead men in women's bodies is a restoration to the womb, a magical guarantee of the cycle of fertility.

Normally—where it is normal—cannibalism occurs in the context of war. This is not like hunting for food: rather, it is a clash of rival predators. Cannibalism is not usually lightly undertaken even by its most enthusiastic practitioners; and the parts of the victims consumed at cannibal meals are often highly selective and sometimes confined to token morsels, most frequently the heart. The whole business tends to be highly ritualized. Among the Aztecs, ingesting the flesh of a captive in war was a way of possessing his prowess: in a complementary gesture, the captor also donned his victim's flayed skin, with the hands flapping at his wrists like trinkets. Even in Fiji before the coming of Christianity, when cannibalism was practiced on a scale which suggests that some people—the chiefly and warrior elites—were getting a useful dietary supplement from human flesh, the surviving bones are always marked by signs of torture and sacrifice: this distinguishes them from the remains of other animal foods, killed cleanly for speed and efficiency. A visitor in 1847 was told that Chief Ra Udreurdre of the Rakiraki district placed a stone to record each body he ate: there were nine hundred stones. But the very fact that cannibal meals were worthy of such spectacular special commemoration puts them in a category apart from that of ordinary eating. Human meat was the gods' food and cannibalism a form of divine communion. Cannibalism makes sense as part of a pattern of "metaphors symbolizing dominance." Alternatively, it is part of a "mythical charter of society" sustained, again in Fiji, by "an elaborate cycle of exchange of raw women for cooked men."

Cannibals and their critics have always agreed about one thing. Cannibalism is not neutral: it affects the eater. Critics claim the effect is depraving, as on Sinbad's companions who began "to act like gluttonous maniacs" as soon as they tasted cannibal food and "after a few hours of guzzling" became "little better than savages." Cannibals, on the other hand, find it a means of self-improvement. In cannibal logic, cannibalism is a conspicuous instance of a universal fact: food reinterpreted as more than bodily sustenance—the replacement of nutrition by symbolic value or magic power as a reason for eating: the discovery that food has meaning. After cooking, this is, perhaps, the second great revolution in the history of food: second in importance, though, for all we know, its origins may even be more ancient than those of cooking. No people, however hungry, has escaped its effects, for there is now no society which merely eats to live. Everywhere, eating is a culturally transforming—sometimes a magically transforming—act. It has its own alchemy. It transmutes individuals into society and sickness into health. It changes personalities. It can sacralize apparently secular acts. It functions like ritual. It becomes ritual. It can make food divine or diabolic. It can release power. It can create bonds. It can signify revenge or love. It can proclaim identity. A change as revolutionary as any in the history of our species happened when eating stopped being merely practical and became ritual, too. From cannibals to homeopathists and health foodies, eaters target foods which they think will burnish their characters, extend their powers, prolong their lives.

❧

Ray Gonzalez (1952–)

A WELL-RECEIVED POET, short story writer, nature essayist, and memoirist, Gonzalez frequently writes about the difficulties he felt growing up as a Chicano in the Southwest and his discovery of Mexican-American literature. In this passage from *Memory Fever*, his collection of autobiographical vignettes about his early life in Texas, Gonzalez celebrates *menudo*, the great Mexican soup made with tripe (honeycombed beef stomach), and flavored with lime, cilantro, oregano, chili peppers, hominy, and, in some variants, with pig's feet. Gonzalez speaks of this dish with reverence, and its designation as "Mama Menudo" is a nod to maternal comfort and something akin to worship, since the soup provides salvation for both his soul and his stomach.

from *Memory Fever*: Mama Menudo

"¡*MENUDO! ¡MAMA MENUDO!*" You must go to La Paloma Café and wave your pained face over a big steaming bowl of hot, quivering chunks of menudo. It is an emergency. Your soul calls for it, prays to it, waits for the red spirit of the Menudo God to bless you and save you from the big mescal death.

You know menudo is the greatest thing anyone has ever sunk his teeth into. Nothing else comes close. Nothing else forces you to get into your car to drive a couple of miles down Paisano Street on a day when everyone else is in church praying. They listen to the Padre whose church sells menudo in the dining hall after *la misa. Los señores y señoras, sus hijos, los vatos*—they all pray first before thinking of eating menudo.

Not you. Your stomach moves like a dying river, a settling of flowing juices needing fresh slices of cow tripe to rise again and be reborn, putting life back into your existence, the magical source of survival in the desert.

Paisano Street is a wide, empty road of newspapers, trash, old tires, and dust. It is nearly empty of traffic, a Sunday morning in south El Paso looking like an abandoned movie lot, cardboard buildings warping in the heat, the

parking lot behind La Paloma stinking of dog shit, half a dozen empty bottles of Carta Blanca reminding you of last night, the mescal and the limes.

You enter La Paloma because Mama Menudo is waiting, the sweet smell
of a Mexican restaurant dampening your head. You are glad to see the place
is nearly empty. The only other customer is an old Mexican sitting heavily
at the counter, his huge body pressing into the stool, a bright cloud of steam
rising from the bowl of menudo he hugs with thick hands.

You don't care that your favorite booth has a new tear in the old vinyl
seat. None of the springs have popped through yet. It is the right place to sit.

Sylvia, the young waitress, knows what you want. She spots the menudo
gleam in your red eyes and smiles beautifully at you. "*¿Café y un plato de
menudo?*"

"*Si, por favor.*" You smile back, the smell of sizzling chorizo and fresh tortillas sprinkling through your nose, preparing you for the taking of the holy
food, a transcendence you have tried to describe to your friends—a state of
menudo mind you share with your family, and with only a few converted
friends.

Sylvia takes your order and you wait, this period very important, a silent
oath of patience calming your heart to ease the hangover. The old man is
hunched over his bowl. John F. Kennedy smiles at you from his portrait
above the door. The painting of a pigeon, *la paloma*, reflects over the long
mirror that stretches the length of the café.

Sylvia brings the silverware and the revolving cup holder, each container
holding the magic ingredients that are part of the ceremony. You look into
the cup of freshly cut onion, glad to see it is as full as the cups of oregano,
chili piquin, and lemon slices. You set it on the right side of the table, the
place it must always be. As you spread your arms over the table, Sylvia comes
out on cue with the smoking bowl of menudo.

You hear the bells of the church ring down the street as she sets the offering before you. "*Gracias.*" She leaves the bowl to steam into your eyes, knows
you must eat alone, and quickly pours the coffee. You wait for her to leave.

The ritual begins. Two spoons of oregano flake into the bowl. The menudo
is finely cut this morning, thin square strips floating among the *posole*. The
soup is a dark red. You know it is a message from Mama that this mixture
comes from a hot chili. Two spoons of chili piquin follow spoons of onion
bits. The thing looks like a collage of chili, meat fat, jello, and black and
green grains that emerge from the oregano. An innocent, ignorant person
would say it looks like dog vomit and leftover cooking grease! But you love

it and that person will never know the meaning of life, never understand why eating Mama Menudo is wild ecstasy and greedy pleasure—and most of all—it saves your life!

You slurp it like an anteater slurps ants, like a vacuum cleaner slurps dirt, like a monkey eats a banana, like a man slurps himself into sleep to wake up in search of his mama. Your right hand boasts of great skill. It digs spoonfuls of menudo straight into your mouth. The stuff is hot. You sigh as the chunks burn your tongue on their way down your throat. It does not take long. It never can. No one takes his time eating menudo. It is a creation of consumption, a snortling and grinding of the senses. The chili makes your eyes water, your ears pop, and it magically takes away the hangover. Your pupils blossom awake. Your heart beats proudly into the world. Your stomach flips awake like a dog that spots a cat and sprints for it!

It vanishes in a final gulp. A thin film of red grease that looks like blood glitters over the inside of the empty bowl. You touched the coffee only twice. You came up for air once. Your nose runs. You are safe and happy. Something moves inside you. You sit still for a few moments, arms resting quietly on the table. A huge burp tries to leap out of you. You hiss it through your teeth. Sylvia appears a final time to see that everything has fallen into place. At the cash register, you pay the dollar fifty. As she counts the change, you pull your pants higher at the waist and see the old man waddle toward you, his ancient body having accepted grace from Mama Menudo as boldly as you have.

Sylvia gives you the change. As you tip her, the old man stands behind you to pay. You turn to say *"Buenos dias,"* and your eyes are filled with the color he wears on his gray shirt, the red badge of courage. A couple of menudo stains shine on his chest and chin.

"Yes," you cry in your heart, "this man knows." He is one of Mama Menudo's lost sons who has returned. You wait in the morning sun for the old man to step out of La Paloma. Standing by your car, you watch him move slowly down the sidewalk. He pauses at the corner, turns around to face you. He raises his right arm slowly and points a friendly finger at you. He smiles and crosses the street as you climb into your car. Before starting the engine, you look down at your T-shirt. It is a clean white, not a single drop on it. You look at the doorway of La Paloma and something moves in your stomach, tells you to come back to reclaim the red badge of menudo stain and wear it on your chest.

Naomi Shihab Nye (1952–)

RAISED IN BOTH San Antonio, Texas, and Jerusalem, the poet, novelist, short story writer, and children's book author Naomi Shihab Nye is the daughter of a Palestinian father and an American mother. Now based in San Antonio, she considers herself "a wandering poet," though she has also been celebrated as an important poet of the Southwest. In her many volumes of prose and verse, she has written vividly of her Arab-American heritage, often examining (as she does in "Arabic Coffee") the ways in which "our own ancestry sift[s] down to us through small, essential daily tasks."

Arabic Coffee

It was never too strong for us:
make it blacker, Papa,
thick in the bottom,
tell again how the years will gather
in small white cups,
how luck lives in a spot of grounds.
Leaning over the stove, he let it
boil to the top, and down again.
Two times. No sugar in his pot.
And the place where men and women
break off from one another
was not present in that room.
The hundred disappointments,
fire swallowing olive-wood beads
at the warehouse, and the dreams
tucked like pocket handkerchiefs
into each day, took their places
on the table, near the half-empty
dish of corn. And none was

more important than the others,
and all were guests. When
he carried the tray into the room,
high and balanced in his hands,
it was an offering to all of them,
stay, be seated, follow the talk
wherever it goes. The coffee was
the center of the flower.
Like clothes on a line saying
you will live long enough to wear me,
a motion of faith. There is this,
and there is more.

Bill Buford (1954–)

JOURNALIST AND EDITOR Buford is best known for his first book, *Among the Thugs*, a sociological analysis of football hooligans in England, and for his second volume, *Heat: An Amateur's Adventures as Kitchen Slave, Line Cook, Pasta-Maker, and Apprentice to a Dante-Quoting Butcher in Tuscany*. Apprenticing himself to famed chef Mario Batali as "kitchen bitch" in the New York restaurant Babbo, Buford went behind the culinary scenes to report on the experience of professional cookery and then traveled to Tuscany, where he studied the theory and practice of meat preparation in the shop of Dario Cecchini, a renowned butcher. Perhaps the experiences that went into *Heat* make its author an especially savvy critic of culinary culture—including the corporate world that shapes the sometimes problematic cooking celebrated by the Food Network, about which he writes so incisively here.

from TV Dinners

THE FIRST SIGN that I'd been unknowingly affected by cooking shows occurred on a Sunday morning when I realized I was talking to myself. I'd been making toast. "First, we cut our bread," I whispered. "Do you know why?" I stopped what I was doing and looked up. "Let me tell you why." It was eight-thirty. It was also Hour 25 of a seventy-two-hour commitment I'd made to watch continuous food television (sleeping only when the shows began repeating at midnight).

I'd begun the venture on a lark, curious about what I'd discover. This, for instance, is what I had learned about the hazelnut: "They grow on hazel trees. . . . They're super-duper rich." That was from the Food Network's *Everyday Italian*, with Giada De Laurentiis. (The following week, on a show hosted by Sandra Lee, I heard, "Do you know when the first cheesecake was ever documented as being eaten or served? It was in 776, or 776 B.C., by the Greeks at the Olympics. Isn't that pretty cool? Say that at a dinner party and everyone's going to think you're brilliant and well read.") I don't want to sound harsh—this wasn't the History Channel—but, on the evidence, there was a surprisingly strong affinity between preparing food and talking baby talk.

At around Hour 36, a more illuminating sign occurred. It was during a rerun of Bobby Flay's "Throwdown." Flay is a veteran food-television personality. "Throwdown" is his seventh show, and it involves Flay's challenging old hands at their game: making Jamaican jerk chicken with a jerk-chicken diva, say, or taking on Cindy the Chili Queen, whose Cin Chili clearly rocks. Flay is then usually humiliated, and the old hand—Butch the pit master, say, with his secret spice rub—gets pumped beyond reason, the little-guy view of the world is vindicated, and everyone feels good. I set out to prepare some supper, and as I removed a loaf of bread from a paper bag I was struck by an unexpected sound: the dry, crisp noise of the bag being disturbed. I'd never noticed this before. It was loud and crinkly: so utterly brown paper. I shrugged (was it a lack of humidity?) and proceeded to dress a salad, in a bowl next to a candle. I cut up a lemon and squeezed a slice. The fruit, crushed in front of the flickering light, was magically transformed. I squeezed again: juice beaded up and fell in a stream of bright droplets. I squeezed one more time, enjoying what

I now regarded as a citrusy translucence, a candle by lemon light. "Veeeeeery pretty!" I said to no one, feeling sixteen and having a late-night-munchies perception moment. I'd been brainwashed, in a fashion, my senses heightened by this long, uninterrupted session of food television. It wasn't an unpleasant state (apart from the consequences for my salad, now inedible).

I had fallen victim to what is called, by its detractors, "food porn." Its creators usually refer to it as "making beauties"—as in "Hey, Al, let's do a beauty of those pecans." Bob Tuschman, the Food Network's head of programming, had described the concept when I visited him in his office, above the Chelsea Market, in Manhattan. The point is to get very close to what you are filming, so close that you can see an ingredient's "pores" ("You should believe the dish is in your living room"), which then triggers some kind of Neanderthal reflex. "If you're flicking from channel to channel and come upon food that has been shot in this way, you will be hardwired as a human being to stop, look, and bring it back to your cave."

Earlier in the week, I'd watched that same Al—Al Ligouri—film some of those beauty pecans at one of the Food Network's studios. Al worked the jib—a high-powered camera at the end of a twelve-foot arm. The pecans, surrounded by five spotlights, were resting on a bent piece of Plexiglas, for a hundred-per-cent reflection (pecans both in a bowl and somehow below it, like mountains on a placid lake), while Al inched closer and closer ("getting tight"). He then manipulated a knob so that some nuts were in focus, while the ones behind, backlit, receded into an arty blur.

Al has shot a lot of food. ("More diced onions than anyone on the planet.") He is thirty-six and has been behind a food camera for ten years. I'd watched him before, during a taping of *Emeril Live*, starring Emeril Lagasse, the portly Portuguese baker from Fall River, Massachusetts, who was probably more naturally an evangelist than a natural chef and, after years at the Commander's Palace, in New Orleans, had been born again as a Creole kitchen crooner. Lagasse was the first to discover that cooking before a bleachers crowd, primed to respond raucously to theatrical additions of garlic or chili flakes or bacon ("Let's take it up a notch!"), can make for inexplicably compelling television. "The trick," Al had told me, "is to film during the lunch hour and get close-ups of the audience—they're crazy with hunger."

After the pecans, Al shot a cup of milk being measured out. This required three takes and was followed by a "sound pass"—same event, but with a microphone close up to get the acoustic ripples. They would be amplified and edited back into the final version. Milk as waterfall.

"You should talk to Hugh," Al said, pointing to a burly man with a hand-held camera. "Hugh Walsh is the beauty specialist."

Hugh was filming a carrot. . . .

During a break, I asked [him] what he'd been doing with his camera. It had always been moving (if I hadn't been studying it, I wouldn't have noticed): a barely perceptible pan, a slow circle, a gentle back-and-forth.

Hugh was an unlikely beauty specialist: a laconic fifty-one, with what looked like a war reporter's battered face, a man who seemed to know the world and didn't much care for it. . . . "I'm trying to get movement." He paused. He seemed unaccustomed to speech. "It's not like the old days."

In America, the old days probably began on a February morning in 1962, when Julia Child, having been asked to promote *Mastering the Art of French Cooking* on a book show on WGBH, the Boston public TV station, phoned ahead, asking for a hot plate and permission to involve the show's host, P. Albert Duhamel, a Boston College professor, in a demonstration. The professor couldn't cook, and, on live television, Child was going to teach him how to make an omelette—a brazen flourish for a novice food writer. Russell Morash, at WGBH, remembers the call, because Child was so unusually well spoken and patrician in manner. It was as though he'd picked up the phone and found Eleanor Roosevelt on the other end. Child was a "hoot," according to one of the twenty-seven viewers who contacted the station afterward—enough for it to find funding to prepare a three-episode pilot that would eventually become *The French Chef*. . . .

There had been earlier television cooks—James Beard's *I Love to Cook*, Dione Lucas's *To the Queen's Taste*—but they were "experts," something Child never seemed to be, mainly because what she knew had been learned so recently and so late in life. Child's culinary education began after she had moved to Paris, at the age of thirty-six, accompanying her husband, Paul Child, a State Department official, and found herself attending the Cordon Bleu. She ended up mastering the national menu, starting a cooking school, and returning to the States with a bulky rough draft that would change the American kitchen. She never lost that new cook's sense of discovery.

For all the obvious production shortcomings, the show was unlike anything else on television. "You have to remember the early sixties," Morash recalled. "Broadcasting was a medium of mayhem. Assassinations, war, riots. You turned on your set, that's what you saw. But if you changed the channel you could watch a soufflé being made." Child, too, was unlike anything else on television: six-feet-two, virtually hunchbacked, seeming too ungainly for a small screen, with a long, manly face, but one that was also remarkable for its intelligent expressiveness. In it you could see her making connections, finding wonder in the properties of egg whites or the behavior of gelatine, a wonder that was at the heart of what now seems like a natural pedagogical imperative. She made people want to cook, often inspiring them with a single detail. . . .

My seventy-two-hour vigil ended on Monday at midnight, with Rachael Ray's *$40 a Day* (go to a city, eat a lot, spend a little, tip cautiously), the fourth Rachael Ray show I'd watched in ten hours. Rachael Ray is probably the most watched kitchen personality in the history of American television. She is available in other guises, too—in a magazine (*Every Day with Rachael Ray*), as a guide ("Rachael Ray's Tasty Travels"), and as a morning talk-show host—but her core achievement is *30 Minute Meals*, built on the conceit that anyone should be able to cook dinner in the time it takes to watch an episode.

Ray—a likable sales-rep personality, with a me-and-my-mom vocabulary and a smile as instantaneous as a light switch—had been a buyer for Cowan & Lobel, a fancy food store in Albany (previous experience: the candy counter at Macy's), and had come up with thirty-minute evening cooking classes to help move goods during the holiday season. The classes were popular; she wrote a booklet to accompany them, later picked up by a small publisher, and was promoting it on an Albany call-in show when a media consultant, hearing her on his car radio, called Bob Tuschman, who signed her up. Ray was exactly what he had been looking for. . . .

What [special] quality does Ray have . . . ? It is probably more apparent in the early broadcasts. A series on perfect burgers filmed during Ray's first year (the Food Network has done two hundred and fourteen shows on how to make a hamburger) includes a characteristic menu: a "no-muss-and-no-fuss" salad, like coleslaw (Ray has thirteen slaw recipes), followed by some meat dish—during my extended viewing, these tended to include bacon and blue cheese (Ray has eighteen blue-cheese recipes, among them a blue-cheese spaghetti, with a sauce, probably unique in the history of pasta, made from bacon fat, butter, olive oil, chicken stock, and cream swirled together, smothered with blue cheese, and then sprinkled with bacon bits: an intensely flavored creation, even if a little alarming to look at—a viscous dull yellow). On this occasion, many of the ingredients, typically, had been prepared at the supermarket and included sealed bags of pre-sliced cabbage, to facilitate getting everything done before the thirty-minute deadline. The coleslaw would be dressed with soy sauce ("It's kinda like balsamic vinegar is to red-wine vinegar—it's a little bit thicker"), but not before Ray had turned on a burner to heat an oven-top grill: this was for her "awesome" turkey patties ("Yummy!"). Heating the oven-top grill beforehand was a tip. So, too, was the use of a garbage bowl—kept on the counter to save trips to the trash—for vegetable trimmings. In fact, the garbage-bowl tip was offered three times. In between, you heard about Ray's mom ("She watches news a lot—maybe too much") and her baby brother, who had just turned twenty-seven ("which is just not possible"). There was also her dog, her dad, a theory about cabbage and cancer, some giggles—an effortless patter that, for all its lack of weight, was not without a goofy charm.

Today, the patter is no longer so obviously aimless, although Ray still believes that having a garbage bowl, now referred to as a "G.B.," is a good tip—good enough to repeat it on every show, sometimes twice. "Yummy" is "Yum-o" (a branding "trademark" expression; among Ray's kitchen products is a "Yum-o" T-shirt), "delicious" has become "de-lish," and her ingredients are often personified, addressed in some form of the third-person butch: a red pepper is a "buddy," meatballs are "guys," a sandwich is "Sammy." "What makes Rachael Ray so exciting to people," Tuschman told me, "is that she speaks their language, shops at the same places they shop, and uses the same ingredients." Ray wants to be just like us.

The two essential premises of *30 Minute Meals*—no one knows how to cook and everyone is in a hurry—now inform most instructional cooking shows. If you have time to watch a Saturday morning of the Food Network, you will learn that you have time for nothing else. There's urgency even in the names—"Good Food Fast," "Quick Fix Meals," "Semi-Homemade Cooking," "Easy Entertaining," "Good Deal"—and a reassuring friendliness in the ingredients, which, like Rachael's, so uniformly come out of the fridge sealed in plastic wrap that it is impossible not to suspect an executive order. You don't have to know how to cook, just how to shop; and everyone knows how to shop. The appeal of squash is that it's a limited time investment, Robin Miller says on *Quick Fix Meals*, illustrating how to prepare one in under fifteen minutes. Sandra Lee recommends pre-peeled carrots—the ones sold by Dole. (Who has the time to peel carrots?) In the supermarket, you can get your melon already cut up—it's over there by the salad bar. Near the meat section, Dave Lieberman tells us on *Good Deal*, you can buy an already cooked rotisserie chicken. (Who knows how to cook one, anyway?)

I found myself taking stock not of what I'd seen during the preceding seventy-two hours but of what I hadn't. I couldn't recall very many potatoes with dirt on them, or beets with ragged greens, or carrots with soil in their creases, or pieces of meat remotely reminiscent of the animals they were butchered from—hardly anything, it seemed, from the planet Earth. There were hamburgers and bacon, but scarcely any other red animal tissue except skirt steak, probably, it occurs to me now, because of its two unique qualities: its texture and its name. It cooks fast (two minutes on each side, according to Rachael Ray—less, according to Robin Miller), and it sounds like something you might pick up at the Gap.

Forty-five years after the publication of *Mastering the Art of French Cooking*, food television is finally and definitively not Julia Child. But the result divides viewers, sometimes quite passionately, into those who have always regarded Child as a good thing and those who may never have heard of her (or what most Food Network executives describe as food élitists and the rest of the country). Although the detractors, including Bourdain, are a vocal bunch—there is a Web site called the Rachael Ray Sucks Community—the Food Network executives are unfazed. They have nothing to defend, and you guys, you just don't get it. . . .

Ours is a different audience from the one that watched Julia Child. In 1962, "microwave oven" and "fast food" hadn't entered the national lexicon. And restaurants were more expensive. Tim Zagat, the publisher of Zagat Guides, points out that for more than two decades the cost of going to restaurants or getting takeout has risen less than the annual rate of inflation—that it's much less expensive today than at any other moment in our history to pay other people to prepare our dinner. Never in our history as a species have we been so ignorant about our food. And it is revealing about our culture that, in the face of such widespread ignorance about a human being's most essential function—the ability to feed itself—there is now a network broadcasting into ninety million American homes, entertaining people with shows about making coleslaw.

🐾

Jonathan Gold (1955–)

IN THE WORDS of *New Yorker* writer Dana Goodyear, Gold is the "high-low priest" of Los Angeles cuisine, and he schooled himself for that role by eating his way through hundreds of the sprawling city's many ethnic restaurants, some of them (like Hot Dog on a Stick) merely food stands or taco trucks, others starred Michelin venues. A graduate of UCLA, he began writing his "Counter Intelligence" column for *LA Weekly* in 1986, then wrote for the *Los Angeles Times* and, for a period in the 1990s, moved to New York, where he wrote for *Gourmet*. In 2007, he was awarded the only Pulitzer Prize ever given to a food writer. An impassioned Angeleno, he insists that his native city is a place where "a great meal is as likely to come from Koreatown or the three-million-strong Mexican community as it is from Beverly Hills, a city where inspiration is often as close as the cold case of the local Vietnamese deli."

from *Counter Intelligence*: Hot Dog on a Stick

NEW YORK HAS pushcart dogs and the garlic knobelwurst at Katz's deli. Chicago has Vienna franks. Rochester has its white-hots, Cincinnati its chili-sluiced coneys. Sheboygan is famous for grilled brats. Santa Monica . . . Santa Monica is the birthplace of Hot Dog on a Stick.

Frankly, as regional hot dog styles go, Hot Dog on a Stick may not rank with Nathan's Famous in Coney Island or the red-hots served outside Wrigley Field, but no other hot dog stand in the world has a spectacle that comes close to the sight of a mini-skirted Hot Dog on a Stick employee mixing a tankful of cool lemonade on a hot day. Hot Dog on a Stick is yet another gift Southern California has bestowed upon the world.

It would be hard to find a native Angeleno without primal memories of Hot Dog on a Stick: of Cheese-on-a-Stick dribbled on the midway at the long-gone P.O.P., of the smell of clean oil that has emanated from the muddy-red outpost under the Santa Monica Pier for more than fifty years. A summer behind the fryers at Hot Dog on a Stick is almost the archetypal first teenage job, and the garishly costumed employees figure in the teenage iconography as surely as lifeguards or cheerleaders.

The high level of organization and the extremely limited menu—hot dog on a stick, cheese on a stick, fries, lemonade—could almost have been custom designed for the valuable slivers of real estate in the food courts of shopping malls, and at the Westside Pavilion or the Glendale Galleria it sometimes seems as if the Hot Dog on a Stick franchises attract more customers than all of the quickie Chinese and falafel stands combined. One high school senior shimmies to the Spice Girls as she burnishes the kiosk's metal to a high shine, and a second runs the cash register. A third twirls skewered frankfurters and cheese sticks through vats of pale corn batter, then plunges them into specially designed canisters of boiling canola oil.

Even within the skewed universe defined by Johnny Rockets and Tacones, Hot Dog on a Stick has always stood a little bit apart, bathed in the sort of unearthly glow that comes from underneath the lid of a Xerox machine. The high parabolic curve of the Hot Dog on a Stick cap may (or may not) allude to the elongated shape of the stand's principal product; the super-bright graphics may (or may not) derive from the cheerful color scheme of an old-fashioned beach ball.

"The hat seems sort of awkward at first," confesses a veteran Santa Monica dog dipper, "but you really do get used to it after a while."

You can find corn dogs at county fairs, junior high school cafeterias and—in Oldsmobile-size boxes—at the Price Club, but the model served at Hot Dog on a Stick would be instantly distinguishable in a blind taste test, even if you hadn't tried one since you were a teenager.

Institutional corn dogs tend to be on the wan side, but a Hot Dog on a Stick is fried to a deep chestnut-brown that is several degrees past the doneness of its competitors—a full city roast, if you're into coffee metaphors—

and the slight bitter tang of caramelization balances out the inherent high sweetness of toasted corn. The outer crust is smooth and crisp, more complexly flavored than you may remember, speckled with gritty bits of burnt grain that crunch under your teeth. The batter is slippery where it touches the hot dog, slightly rubbery, almost crepelike, resilient as the underskin of a really fresh bagel. The thick turkey hot dog inside seems quite bland, essentially a vehicle for garlic and juice.

This is rude food, resisting the attempts of civilizers far more strenuously than, say, the burrito or the triple-deck cheeseburger, though Vida's Fred Eric can sometimes be seen at chefs' events, meting out bite-size samples of corn dogs as if they were morsels of sautéed foie gras.

The Hot Dog on a Stick we love is a Space Age variation on the classic pig-in-a-blanket, Victorian-era American comfort food retooled to meet the demands of the California beach.

🐘

Anya von Bremzen (1963–)

IN THE COMPANY of her mother, Larisa, an impassioned cook, Moscow-born Anya von Bremzen fled the oppression of the Soviet Union when she was ten years old. After an impoverished stay in the suburbs of Philadelphia, the pair settled in New York, where the young Anya studied piano and, by her mother's side, was introduced to Russian culinary culture. Eventually, when an injury to her wrist impeded her piano work, von Bremzen turned to cookbook writing: she has produced five acclaimed volumes, and is a regular contributor to such major journals as *Saveur* and *Food & Wine*. In 2013 she published *Mastering the Art of Soviet Cooking: A Memoir of Food and Longing*, which recounts the almost Proustian efforts that she and her mother—both, now, wonderful cooks—have made to recapture their inheritance. The seed of the book, she has said, was our selection here, "The Émigrée's Feast," an essay where she describes an ambitious tsarist dinner the two women hosted in, of all unlikely places, the modest section of Queens called Jackson Heights.

The Émigrée's Feast

EIGHT GUESTS IN period costume are expected shortly for a six-course dinner chez Mom, but right now her kitchen looks like a construction site. A tower of dishes teeters in the sink; various appliances drone in unison. Unfazed, Mom cuts scraps of dough into leaf shapes. The dough will decorate a kulebyaka, the magnificent Slavic fish pie that will crown her extravagant, 19th-century-style Russian banquet tonight.

"Why, why, why, didn't you let me serve game?" she says. I point out, for the umpteenth time, that grouse is hard to come by in Jackson Heights, Queens, where Mom has lived for more than two decades in a small one-bedroom apartment.

Angry sighing. "But they—they!—always followed the meat course with a game roast!"

"They" happen to be a noble 19th-century St. Petersburg family whose feasts Mom has been obsessively replicating for quite some time now. Her inspiration comes from a single source: a 1996 book called *High Society Dinners*. Cowritten by Mom's favorite Russian cultural historian, Yuri Lotman, this handsome volume chronicles a year at the table in the house of a powerful statesman named Pavel Durnovo. The menus, culled from Durnovo family archives, are interspersed with family letters and diaries, shopping lists and guest lists, snippets from the period's press, plus plenty of scholarly commentary. The result is a fascinating panorama of aristocratic domesticity in bygone St. Petersburg. Some people cook Julia cover to cover. Mom's grand ambition has been to whisk and sauté her way through an entire year of Russian society gatherings circa 1858. Tonight she'll be showing off the elaborate fruits of her labor to a clutch of Russian émigré intellectuals and artistes, all co-conspirators who share her passion for our home country's food mores.

When my mother, Larisa Frumkin, was growing up in the Soviet Union in the 1940s, the reality of a 19th-century aristocratic banquet was as unattainable as cheese from the moon. Her own favorite childhood treat was sosiski, or frankfurters, and I was hooked on them, too—though Mother claims that the sosiski of my 1970s Brezhnev-era childhood were nothing compared with the true, Stalinist article. Why do those proletarian franks remain the madeleine of every *Homo sovieticus*? Because besides sosiski with canned peas, kotlety (Russian hamburgers), borscht, and a few other simplicities, there was precious little to eat back in the USSR.

Our isolation from the rest of the world during Iron Curtain times—not to mention the sheer imagination required to elevate family meals out of their grinding drabness—go a long way toward explaining why my mother, a retired teacher now in her 70s, became an epicurean archivist-adventuress of the highest order. Dreaming, in and out of the kitchen, has always been Mom's style. Other Muscovite moms served up pirog (savory pie) plain; mine stuffed hers with cheese and tomato paste and insisted on calling it pizza. In her hands, the watery cabbage soup known as shchi was "pot au feu." Back in those days, we hadn't a clue as to what real pizza or pot au feu tasted like, but the words filled us with romantic longing. Mom was a gastronomic Don Quixote.

Eventually, the straitjacket of Soviet life could no longer contain her, and in 1974 we emigrated to America, leaving my father behind. With access to cookbooks and the cornucopia at New York City's food stores, she wasted no time turning her former reveries into tasty reality. Once, on returning from a trip to the Great Pyramids, she served an ancient Egyptian banquet replete with barley bread and a mess of strange greens. Another time, inspired by an exhibition of northern Italian art at the Metropolitan Museum of Art, where she now works as a volunteer lecturer and tour guide, she astounded the show's curator by inviting her to a home-cooked period dinner featuring uncannily perfect edible replicas of 16th-century Lombardian still lifes. But while Mom can swing ancient Egypt and Renaissance Italy with equal panache, her most spirited efforts have been devoted to the Durnovo feasts.

Tonight Mom and I reminisce while decorating the table. Arranging red roses on a cream-colored, antique-looking tablecloth, she recalls the chipped, mismatched dinnerware of her childhood. A momentous household event was the arrival, in the late 1950s, of a real *serviz* (dinner service), a gift from a high-ranking general to my granddad, who was Stalin's chief of naval intelligence for the Baltic region. To Mom, the *serviz* suggested possibilities for entertaining beyond sosiski. She discovered such forbidden literature as a pre-revolutionary edition of Elena Molokhovets's *A Gift to Young Housewives*, a 19th-century kitchen bible in which many of the recipes begin with "Send your maid to the cellar." She salivated over descriptions of live-poached sturgeons and rosy hams in Tolstoy and Chekhov. As the years of corruption, enforced collectivization, and state-induced famine following the 1917 Revolution had wiped out such comestibles, this was the Soviet idea of food porn.

STANDING in her Queens kitchen, brushing the kulebyaka with egg glaze, Mom expounds on the Durnovo lifestyle. Meals at the family's home were relatively restrained, she explains, because excess went out of style after the Napoleonic War of 1812 had ravaged the country. What's more, under the rule of the reformist tsar Alexander II, the mood in the city's aristocratic salons was increasingly nationalistic. Since the 18th century, the Russian aristocracy had spoken and dined French, but by the 1850s, in a reflection of the new Slavophile spirit, à la russe specialties had started appearing on aristocratic menus alongside the usual soupe printanière and poulard à l'estragon.

When Mom embarked on the Durnovo project, she reckoned that the period feasts would be quite doable in New York, given a bit of recipe research and ingredient sleuthing. Then again, there were obstacles. The Durnovos occupied a vast neoclassical mansion on the granite-paved English Embankment, then the poshest address in St. Petersburg. Mom entertains in a cramped apartment whose kitchen is smaller than the Durnovo's cupboard. *They* had serfs setting their tables with heavy silver, fine china, and enough monogrammed linen to blanket Siberia. But Mom wasn't going to be outdone. Repeated raids on the 99-cents store on nearby Roosevelt Avenue have yielded two dinner sets—one silvery, one white and burgundy—bearing convincingly neoclassical patterns. From other Queens tchotchke shops Mom has hauled home such indispensable dinner paraphernalia as soup tureens, crystal goblets, and a fine assortment of candelabra.

Mom's high-society meals always follow the same strict, six-course progression observed in the Durnovo household. Soup gives way to fish—either something au gratin or a Slavic-style fish pie—and then a meat course. Next comes roasted game, followed by a vegetable course and, finally, dessert. Though Mom's menu was to be no exception, its exact composition had the two of us quarreling in the days leading up to tonight's meal.

We were in agreement on only two dishes, both of them 19th-century classics that were popular at the Durnovo table: kulebyaka, that glorious oblong pastry filled with layers of fish, wild mushrooms, and rice (and a subject of delirious odes by Chekhov and Gogol), and also pozharsky cutlets, which were immortalized in the writing of Alexander Pushkin, Russia's national poet. Mom's version of the dish contains freshly ground chicken breast instead of the usual veal. I watch her shape the meat into plump, oval patties, into which she tucks a pat of butter, "for extra succu-lence." Just before dinner, she'll coat them in fine homemade bread crumbs and sauté them.

Beyond these two dishes, our disagreements over the evening's menu roughly mirrored 19th-century Russian debates between Westernizers (Mom) and Slavophiles (me):

Mom: "I will try potage à la tortue."

Me: "Turtle soup? Eeks. What's wrong with borscht?"

Mom: "Nyet. Don't be silly; the Durnovos didn't eat borscht."

Me: "Yeah, and what's this on page 303?"

In the end Mom conceded. She even liked my idea of serving beef boiled in borscht stock as a separate course. "Catherine the Great, after all, adored boiled beef," she said. But the beef constituted a seventh dish, forcing us to eliminate the crucial game course. She grumbled, I hectored, until, finally, the menu took shape: borscht accompanied by teeny pirozhki (pastries) with egg-and-scallion filling; the kulebyaka; the pozharsky cutlets and boiled beef; a vegetable course of turnips braised in málaga wine; and, for dessert, a macédoine en gelée—berries in a quivering black currant-gelatin mold. A lavish zakuski (hors d'oeuvres) spread would precede dinner, and both the meal and its prologue would be washed down with plenty of flavored vod-kas, champagne, and French wines.

After the game-or-meat conundrum, determining the human ingredients for the party was a no-brainer. Ira and Sasha Genis *had* to attend. Sasha, whose Radio Liberty cultural broadcasts are listened to by millions in Rus-sia, is a food scholar himself, a man whose dinners tend to revolve around mushrooms gathered by moonlight in the Siberian woods and rare Latvian lamprey eels. Also among the invitees: the artist Vitaly Komar, renowned for his mock-Stalinist paintings, as well as the documentary-film maker Andrei Zagdansky and his vivacious wife, Toma. A last-minute request by my boy-friend, Barry Yourgrau, a writer, to invite Junzo Sawa, his Tokyo-based literary agent who was in town, left Mom scratching her head. "But the Russo-Japanese relationship was strained in the mid-1800s!" she protested. Then: "Okay, he can play an envoy from a Central Asian colony. An emir or maybe a khan. Here, here, give him this Kirghiz hat."

The true reason, I think, why Mom so relishes her costume dramas is this: as a young girl she earned praise for her roles in student plays and dreams of becoming an actress. Never mind that the Dumovo dinners were catered by professional staff and a cadre of serfs; Mom thrives on being a one-woman show. Shopping, cooking, serving, popping out of the kitchen to perform "high society" hostess duties—to her it's all one big play.

STILL, as dinnertime looms, Mom looks exhausted. Ordering her to rest, Barry and I set up the zakuski buffet in the antechamber—er, Mom's tiny foyer. Out come little plates of smoked herring, caviar, and cheeses. Here are Mom's famous pickles, in which canned Chinese straw mushrooms are married with supermarket Italian dressing, to a surprisingly 19th-century-Russian effect.

"Kvas, don't forget the pitcher of kvas!" Mom yells from the couch. But of course! This fermented peasant drink based on rye bread was much in vogue among St. Petersburg aristocracy 150 years ago.

At long last, and with shocking suddenness, all the guests arrive. Clustered in the foyer, they laugh, kiss, and take snapshots of one another's costumes. Zakuski swiftly devoured, everyone attacks dinner. The guests are floored by the deep flavor of Mom's ruby red borscht. They gasp when she slices open the kulebyaka, filling the room with mushroom-scented steam. Ira and Sasha swear that not even Pushkin tasted pozharsky cutlets this juicy, and Vitaly likens the whole affair to performance art. As for Junzo, his love for Mom's horseradish vodka—"just like wasabi!"—is visibly profound. Tonight's show is a smash hit.

Later, after everyone has finally departed, leaving truckloads of dirty dishes behind, it dawns on me: what will Mom do when she's finally finished with every menu in *High Society Dinners?* Apparently she's already thought of that inevitability. "How about a series of retro-kitsch meals, very Soviet, very Socialist Realist?" she murmurs, nostalgically smacking her lips. I guess that means a lot of sosiski. I wish Mom luck keeping the hordes of hungry Russians away.

Jason Fagone (1979–)

A WIDELY PUBLISHED journalist, Fagone has written for *Slate*, *Wired*, *GQ*, *The Atlantic*, and other venues. His first book, *Horsemen of the Esophagus*, from which our selection is drawn, is a study of the curious American sport of competitive eating, which involves the ingestion of huge numbers of hot dogs, grilled cheese sandwiches, oysters, and other foods by what can only be called gastronomic athletes. The eating contest, he says, is both "an American horror show and an American success story."

from *Horsemen of the Esophagus*: The Passion of the Toast

SHE HAS PICKED a fine day to grace Southern California with Her presence. The sun is shining, the sky is blue. Gulls loop above the Venice Beach boardwalk in jazzy little arcs. The February air is warm, but not warm enough to melt the grilled cheese sandwich through which She has chosen to broadcast her message of peace. Anyway, She's packed inside a plastic box, surrounded by cotton balls, and encased in a frame for protection. Ten years ago the image of the Virgin Mary appeared on a grilled cheese sandwich in the frying pan of Diana Duyser, a Florida jewelry designer. Now, She is here.

The Blessed Virgin, in recent years, has been appearing less and less in crop formations and curvy building glass. She seems to prefer, as holy vehicles, specific kinds of food. She has not seared Herself onto a piece of ahi sushi, or a crepe suzette. She has not arranged Her visage in mosaic form using the grains of a delicate risotto. Instead, She has chosen as vehicles to become flesh a popcorn kernel, a Funyun, and a Rold Gold Honey Mustard pretzel twist—and, here, now, a grilled cheese sandwich. Even deities change with the times. In 2005, Our Lady seems to be a voracious snacker. The Virgin's palate is no longer demure. She's hungry.

This afternoon, when it comes to appetite, the old girl is flat outclassed.

In fifteen minutes, here at Venice Beach, the World Grilled Cheese Eating Championship will be decided. It's an eating contest. Whoever eats the most grilled cheese sandwiches in ten minutes wins $3,500. The prize pot has attracted some of the hungriest people in the world—people who eat under the banner of the International Federation of Competitive Eating, also known as the IFOCE or the Federation. They consider themselves professionals, and athletes. Guys like Eric "Badlands" Booker, a 420-pound subway conductor, rapper, and world champion in the donut, corned beef hash, and cheesecake disciplines. "Hungry" Charles Hardy, who just half an hour ago tattooed the initials "IFOCE" onto his right bicep. Ed "Cookie" Jarvis, a Long Island realtor who embroiders his numerous eating titles onto a gargantuan flowing robe with his portrait airbrushed on the front, flanked by a lightning bolt. Rich and Carlene LeFevre, the First Couple of competitive eating—a pair of sweetly manic retirees from the outskirts of Las Vegas. Carlene is a consistent top-five finisher, and Rich, nicknamed "The Locust," holds records in Spam (6 pounds in 12 minutes), chili (one and a half gallons in 10 minutes), and corny dogs (18½ in 10 minutes).

Even the Locust's accomplishments pale in comparison to America's greatest eater, now sitting in the concrete bleachers, beaming, her ponytail held in place by two star-shaped barrettes. Sonya Thomas. Five feet five, 103 pounds. She calls herself "The Black Widow" because she gleefully devours the males; she may or may not be playing on an Asian stereotype. Her eating titles are so numerous that promoters list them alphabetically: asparagus, baked beans, chicken nuggets, chicken wings, eggs, fruitcake, giant burger, hamburger, jambalaya, Maine lobster, meatballs, oysters, pulled pork, quesadilla, sweet potato casserole, tacos, toasted ravioli, Turducken . . .

"BROTHERS AND SISTERS!"

It's starting. The voice is miked up. It booms from the concrete expanse near the stretch of boardwalk called Muscle Beach, named after an outdoor gym where exhibitionists yank dumbbells. Beyond the gym, toward the beach, is a concrete amphitheater, with bleachers that face the stage and a stage that faces the Pacific. The stage sits directly underneath a giant concrete barbell, looming like a relic of some extinct bodybuilding race. The stage's speakers broadcast the voice, which is saying:

"There are moments in our days when we are suddenly LOST."

Conversations stop. One hundred and fifty curious heads swivel toward the man onstage in the dark blazer and the straw boater hat. This is the contest emcee: George Shea, chairman of the IFOCE, which bills itself as "the governing body of all stomach-centric sport." His hands, clasped together over his crotch, hold a microphone. He looks down and widens his stance dramatically as the opening lament of Moby's "Natural Blues" emerges from the PA system.

"We hum along doing the million things that Americans do, and then suddenly we are STRUCK—"

A woman, excited, screams.

"—and we wonder why. There is no trigger. There is no reason. And yet there it is. Sadness. Isolation. Loss. Why?"

Shea pauses, then answers his question:

"Because the PURSUITS of our lives have OBSCURED our lives, ladies and gentlemen. It is not only the hustle and bustle, the cars, and the kids, the debts and the acquisitions—it is something more."

Often, Shea refers to competitive eating as the country's "fastest-growing sport," and he likes to say, tongue two-thirds in cheek, that eating is now number five in America's heart after baseball, basketball, football, and golf, having surpassed hockey and badminton. Today's contest is just one of a hundred scheduled for 2005, up from about seventy in 2004. Prize pots surge, TV deals dangle . . .

"We cannot SEE!" Shea is saying. "We cannot HEAR! We cannot THINK! And that is why . . . she has come! Amid no fanfare whatsoever!

"A woman!" says Shea. "Grilling a cheese sandwich!"

The music shifts to a gentle adult contemporary track. George Shea bleeds all aggression from his voice.

"Ladies and gentlemen. It is said that pearls are the precipitate of sunlight, slowed and bent by the ocean until it forms a nugget of beauty inside the lowly mollusk. And likewise, this grilled cheese sandwich is the precipitate of the divine spirit"—and here the music shifts again, to a dark minor-key vamp, and Shea's voice skews evil—"captured here on Earth in the most unlikely of places, delivered to us in the image of the Virgin Mary!"

Shea has sensitive features, an aristocratic nose, and neat black hair. Goodlooking, compact. Perfect posture. His voice is melodious but powerful—precise, all syllables enunciated, with the pitch control of a cabaret singer and the gestural excess of a dinner-theater Hamlet.

"It is the bane of our species," he says, "that we are warped most when we know it the least, ladies and gentlemen. It is time to put aside the pursuits that push us through our day, because this change is here today as an athletic and religious experience. TODAY WE HOLD THE GOLDENPALACE .COM WORLD GRILLED CHEESE EATING CHAMPIONSHIP! An all-you-can-eat contest that will stand as an homage, as a recognition, a dramatic illustration of the message delivered [to] us by the Virgin Mary Grilled Cheese Sandwich!"

The music softens. Shea ushers onstage a representative of GoldenPalace .com, Steve Baker. Last November, GoldenPalace.com bought the sandwich for $28,000 on eBay, hoping to use it for promotional stunts like this one. Wearing a grubby sweatshirt, jeans, and two-day stubble, Baker raises the Virgin Mary Grilled Cheese above his head and proclaims:

"The Passion of the Toast lives."

Baker steps down into the crowd, now a sea of limbs holding digicams and angling for a keepsake shot. He parades the sandwich, which Shea calls "the culinary version of the Shroud of Turin," into the digicam throng, and then the sandwich is placed onto an easel, at the side of the stage, to make way for the gurgitators.

❧PART SIX❧

Food Politics

Disputes Over the Menu

INTRODUCTION

I F, A S the old feminist saw would have it, the personal is the political, the culinary—so subject to individual taste, to class, to social precepts—is also intensely political. Though the home kitchen may seem to be a private space, it's also an extension of a public domain in which gastronomic choices are shaped by moral as well as economic pressures. And the restaurant kitchen, perhaps more obviously public, has also, especially in recent years, become a political battleground. Eating, declares the farmer-poet-novelist Wendell Berry, is "an agricultural act, a political act," for what we eat presupposes choices about how (or whether) animals are killed for food, where (and how) fruits and vegetables are grown, and in what ways the foods we eat may (or may not) have been industrially processed.

Of course, culinary controversies are hardly new. As we've seen in our brief introduction to early food writing, eating taboos have long functioned to separate Jews from Christians, Muslims from Hindus, sometimes intensifying religious turmoil. Similarly, gastronomic practices have long been the subject of intense debate, especially the slaughter of domestic animals. "I rather wonder," mused the Platonist philosopher Plutarch in his *Moralia*, "both by what accident and in what state of soul or mind the first man who did so, touched his mouth to gore and brought his lips to the flesh of a dead creature. . . . How could his eyes endure the slaughter . . . ? How could his nose endure the stench?" Horror of the gore and stench made Pythagoras, Plato, Plutarch himself, and Horace—among classical thinkers—into confirmed vegetarians, along with such later figures as Shelley, Tolstoi, Shaw, Kafka, Gandhi, Einstein, and (even) Hitler. More recently, the passions of vegetarians and the more austere vegans (who refuse to eat "anything that's had a mother") have led to polemical writings by the ethicist Peter Singer as well as the novelists J. M. Coetzee and Jonathan Safran Foer, among others. Cookbooks and restaurants too have been shaped by their views. Deborah Madison's famous Greens, in San Francisco, along with her well-received *Greens Cook Book*, exemplify—along with many other eateries and collections of recipes—the real-world results of the political ideals advanced by Plutarch's modern descendants.

But vegetarianism is only one branch of the political philosophy that Wendell Berry represents. Berry himself, for instance—like Barbara Kingsolver and the late David Foster Wallace—is neither vegan nor vegetarian. His views are fueled by distaste for the kind of industrialized "cattle metropolis" that Michael Pollan so powerful describes in our selection here, and also by the horrifying visions of slaughterhouses recorded by writers from Upton Sinclair (in our first section) to Eric Schlosser (in this section). Nor would Berry disagree with Henry Miller's impassioned declaration that "if the bread is bad, the life is bad." Underlying all these arguments is surely Brillat-Savarin's famous assertion that "you are what you eat." If you eat—and have *chosen* to eat—degraded, synthetic commercial food, you yourself are in some sense morally or physically degraded. Though Filippo Tommaso Marinetti's *Futurist Cookbook* was based on problematic politics (the Futurists were essentially fascists), his precepts too implied that not just your physical but also your mental health could be contaminated by bad food: he thought that pasta was making Italians soft! Today, his Italian counterpart Carlo Petrini has become famous as the founder and exponent of the Slow Food Movement. His manifesto is very different from Marinetti's—Marinetti, for instance, celebrated technology, whereas Petrini sees industrial food as the enemy of slow, delicious cooking—yet as careful readers will see, both these writers consider culinary matters central to both individual and social well-being.

Rather than eat Fast Food or heavy pasta, these thinkers would aver, we should eat fresh fruits and vegetables, grass-fed beef, and free-range chickens, while renouncing the processed foods hawked by corporate culture. But, observes Rachel Laudan, there is an element of nostalgia in a wholesale rejection of advances in the cultivation and preservation of food. Our ancestors, she argues, didn't inhabit quite the gastronomic utopias that Berry and Pollan would have us imagine. More troublesome still, declare others in attacking the group one recent writer has called "Pollanites," there's a decided element of elitism in the farm-to-table movement. If you don't, like Kingsolver, inherit a farm in Appalachia, or have the means, like Pollan, to hunt and forage in Northern California—if you're a migrant worker or an inner-city ghetto dweller—you might just be stuck with the junk foods available in your local bodega or on sale at McDonald's and Burger King.

Increasingly, to be sure, activists influenced by thinkers from Berry to Petrini and Pollan have worked to add salads to fast food menus, to plant community gardens (like Alice Waters's "Edible Schoolyard") in urban areas, and to convince shoppers that fruits and vegetables are cheap to buy and easy to cook. Michele Obama has even used the bully pulpit of the White House to enlist Walmart in the fight against childhood obesity. In a society whose tastes and tastings are literally and figuratively flavored by the marketing maneuvers of giant corporations, culinary change may be slow—but perhaps healthier foods are even now simmering on a range of back burners.

Filippo Tommaso Marinetti (1876–1944)

MARINETTI WAS THE founder of the proto-fascist Italian avant-garde movement known as Futurism. During some forty tempestuous years, he passionately propagandized for progress, speed, militarism, and innovative technology. Like Futurist poetry, Futurist cooking was defined as a culinary art that renounced old-fashioned, "soft" foods—especially the pasta so beloved of Italians—in favor of experimental cuisine that in some ways looked forward to Ferran Adrià's "molecular gastronomy." Marinetti preached strange combinations (chicken roasted with a steel bullet in its breast) but he and fellow Futurists also suggested varieties of food that are still defined as healthy—for instance, instead of traditional spaghetti Bolognese (considered too heavy for the tough, fit Italians of the future), a salad of shredded carrots seasoned with lemon juice.

from *The Futurist Cookbook*:
The Manifesto of Futurist Cooking

ITALIAN FUTURISM, FATHER of numerous Futurisms and avant-garde-isms abroad, will not remain a prisoner of those worldwide victories secured 'in twenty years of great artistic and political battles frequently consecrated in blood,' as Benito Mussolini put it. Italian Futurism will face unpopularity again with a programme for the total renewal of food and cooking.

Of all artistic and literary movements Futurism is the only one whose essence is reckless audacity. Twentieth-century painting and twentieth-century literature are in reality two very moderate and practical Futurisms of the right. Attached to tradition, dependent on each other, they prudently only essay the new.

AGAINST PASTA

FUTURISM has been defined by the philosophers as *'mysticism in action'*, by Benedetto Croce as *'anti-historicism'*, by Graca Aranha as *'liberation from aesthetic terror'*. We call it *'the renewal of Italian pride'*, a formula for *'original art-life'*, *'the religion of speed'*, *'mankind straining with all his might towards synthesis'*, *'spiritual hygiene'*, *'a method of infallible creation'*, *'the geometric splendour of speed'*, *'the aesthetics of the machine'*.

Against practicality we Futurists therefore disdain the example and admonition of tradition in order to invent at any cost something *new* which everyone considers crazy.

While recognizing that badly or crudely nourished men have achieved great things in the past, we affirm this truth: men think, dream and act according to what they eat and drink.

Let us consult on this matter our lips, tongue, palate, taste buds, glandular secretions and probe with genius into gastric chemistry.

We Futurists feel that for the male the voluptuousness of love is an abysmal excavator hollowing him out from top to bottom, whereas for the female it works horizontally and fan-wise. The voluptuousness of the palate, however, is for both men and women always an upward movement through the human body. We also feel that we must stop the Italian male from becoming a solid leaden block of blind and opaque density. Instead he should harmonize more and more with the Italian female, a swift spiralling transparency of passion, tenderness, light, will, vitality, heroic constancy. Let us make our Italian bodies agile, ready for the featherweight aluminum trains which will replace the present heavy ones of wood iron steel.

Convinced that in the probable future conflagration those who are most agile, most ready for action, will win, we Futurists have injected agility into world literature with words-in-liberty and simultaneity. We have generated surprises with illogical syntheses and dramas of inanimate objects that have purged the theatre of boredom. Having enlarged sculptural possibility with anti-realism, having created geometric architectonic splendour without decorativism and made cinematography and photography abstract, we will now establish the way of eating best suited to an ever more high speed, airborne life.

Above all we believe necessary:

a) The abolition of pastasciutta, an absurd Italian gastronomic religion.

It may be that a diet of cod, roast beef and steamed pudding is beneficial to the English, cold cuts and cheese to the Dutch and sauerkraut, smoked [salt] pork and sausage to the Germans, but pasta is not beneficial to the Italians. For example it is completely hostile to the vivacious spirit and passionate, generous, intuitive soul of the Neapolitans. If these people have been heroic fighters, inspired artists, awe-inspiring orators, shrewd lawyers, tenacious farmers it was in spite of their voluminous daily plate of pasta. When they eat it they develop that typical ironic and sentimental scepticism which can often cut short their enthusiasm.

A highly intelligent Neapolitan Professor, Signorelli, writes: 'In contrast to bread and rice, pasta is a food which is swallowed, not masticated. Such starchy food should mainly be digested in the mouth by the saliva but in this case the task of transformation is carried out by the pancreas and the liver. This leads to an interrupted equilibrium in these organs. From such disturbances derive lassitude, pessimism, nostalgic inactivity and neutralism.'

AN INVITATION TO CHEMISTRY

PASTASCIUTTA, 40% less nutritious than meat, fish or pulses, ties today's Italians with its tangled threads to Penelope's slow looms and to somnolent old sailing-ships in search of wind. Why let its massive heaviness interfere with the immense network of short long waves which Italian genius has thrown across oceans and continents? Why let it block the path of those landscapes of colour form sound which circumnavigate the world thanks to radio and television? The defenders of pasta are shackled by its ball and chain like convicted lifers or carry its ruins in their stomachs like archaeologists. And remember too that the abolition of pasta will free Italy from expensive foreign grain and promote the Italian rice industry.

b) The abolition of volume and weight in the conception and evaluation of food.

c) The abolition of traditional mixtures in favour of experimentation with new, apparently absurd mixtures, following the advice of Jarro Maincave and other Futurist cooks.

d) The abolition of everyday mediocrity from the pleasures of the palate.

We invite chemistry immediately to take on the task of providing the body with its necessary calories through equivalent nutrients provided free by the State, in powder or pills, albumoid compounds, synthetic fats and vitamins. This way we will achieve a real lowering of the cost of living and of salaries, with a relative reduction in working hours. Today only one workman is needed for two thousand kilowatts. Soon machines will constitute an obedient proletariat of iron steel aluminum at the service of men who are almost totally relieved of manual work. With work reduced to two or three hours, the other hours can be perfected and ennobled though study, the arts, and the anticipation of perfect meals.

In all social classes meals will be less frequent but perfect in their daily provision of equivalent nutrients.

THE perfect meal requires:
1. Originality and harmony in the table setting (crystal, china, décor) extending to the flavours and colours of the foods.
2. Absolute originality in the food.

☙

Henry Miller (1891–1980)

PERHAPS BEST KNOWN for his controversial, erotically explicit novels and quasi-memoirs, Miller was also an essayist and polemicist of considerable stature. For years his most famous books (*The Tropic of Cancer, The Tropic of Capricorn*) were banned as pornographic in the United States, but after the 1960s they were legitimized and became best-sellers. Born in New York City, Miller spent much of his early career as an expatriate in Paris, then lived for many years in Big Sur, on the California coast. He had five wives and numerous lovers, including the lyrical novelist and memoirist Anaïs Nin. As his essay on bread, excerpted here, indicates, he was an energetic social critic whose views on sexual liberation were paralleled by his other analyses of what he considered American puritanism and conformism.

from *Remember to Remember*: The Staff of Life

BREAD: PRIME SYMBOL. Try and find a good loaf. You can travel fifty thousand miles in America without once tasting a piece of good bread. Americans don't care about good bread. They are dying of inanition but they go on eating bread without substance, bread without flavor, bread without vitamins, bread without life. Why? Because the very core of life is contaminated. If they knew what good bread was they would not have such wonderful machines on which they lavish all their time, energy and affection. A plate of false teeth means much more to an American than a loaf of good bread. Here is the sequence: poor bread, bad teeth, indigestion, constipation, halitosis, sexual starvation, disease and accidents, the operating table, artificial limbs, spectacles, baldness, kidney and bladder trouble, neurosis, psychosis, schizophrenia, war and famine. Start with the American loaf of bread so beautifully wrapped in cellophane and you end on the scrap heap at forty-five. The only place to find a good loaf of bread is in the ghettos. Wherever there is a foreign quarter there is apt to be good bread. Wherever there is a Jewish grocer or delicatessen you are almost certain to find an excellent loaf of bread. The dark Russian bread, light in weight, found only rarely on this huge continent, is the best bread of all. No vitamins have been injected into it by laboratory specialists in conformance with the latest food regulations. The Russian just naturally likes good bread, because he also likes caviar and vodka and other good things. Americans are whiskey, gin and beer drinkers who long ago lost their taste for food. And losing that they have also lost their taste for life. For enjoyment. For good conversation. For everything worth while, to put it briefly:

What do I find wrong with America? Everything. I begin at the beginning, with the staff of life: bread. If the bread is bad the whole life is bad. Bad? Rotten, I should say. Like that piece of bread only twenty-four hours old which is good for nothing except perhaps to fill up a hole. Good for target practice maybe. Or shuttlecock and shuffle board. Even soaked in urine it is unpalatable; even perverts shun it. Yet millions are wasted advertising it. Who are the men engaged in this wasteful pursuit? Drunkards and failures for the most part. Men who have prostituted their talents in order to help further the decay and dissolution of our once glorious Republic.

Here is one of the latest widely advertised products: Hollywood Bread. On the red, white and blue cellophane jacket in which it is wrapped, this last word in bread from the American bakeries, it reads as follows:

whole wheat flour, clear wheat flour, water, non-diastatic malt, yeast, salt, honey, caramel, whole rye flour, yeast food, stone ground oatmeal, soya flour, gluten flour, barley flour, sesame seed, and a small quantity of dehydrated (water free) vegetables including celery, lettuce, pumpkin, cabbage, carrots, spinach, parsley, sea kelp, added for flavor only.

The only thing missing from this concoction is powdered diamonds. How does it taste? Much like any other American product. Of course, this is a reducing bread of which one should eat two slices a day three times a day and not ask how it tastes. Grow thin, as in Hollywood, and be thankful it doesn't taste worse. That's the idea. For several days now I have been trying to get a whiff of some of those ingredients—sea kelp especially—which were included "for flavor only." Why they were not added for health too I don't know. Naturally all these delicious-sounding items amount to about one ten-thousandth part of the loaf. And on the second day, stale, flat and unprofitable, this marvelous new bread is no more attractive to the palate or the stomach than any other loaf of American bread. On the second day it is good for replacing a missing tile on the roof. Or to make a scratchboard for the cat. . . .

Outside of the foreign quarters, then, take it for granted that there is no good bread to be had. Every foreign group has introduced into our life some good substantial bread, even the Scandinavians. (Excepting the English, I should add, but then we hardly think of them as foreign, though why we shouldn't I don't know, for when you think of it the English are even less like us than the Poles or Latvians.) In a Jewish restaurant you usually have a basket filled with all kinds of bread from which to choose. In a typical American restaurant, should you ask for rye, whole wheat or any other kind of bread but the insidious, unwholesome, and unpalatable white, you get white bread. If you insist on rye bread you get whole wheat. If you insist on whole wheat you get graham bread. Once in a great while you come upon nut bread; this is always a sheer accident. Raisin bread is a sort of decoy to lure you into eating unpalatable, perfidious and debilitating white bread. When in doubt go to a Jewish restaurant or delicatessen; if necessary, stand up and eat a sandwich made of sour rye, sweet butter, pastrami and pickle. A Jewish sandwich contains more food value than an eighty-five cent meal in the ordinary American restaurant. With a glass of water to wash it down you can walk away feeling fit. . . .

The moment you sit down at a table in the ordinary American restaurant, the moment you begin scanning the menu, the waitress asks you what you wish to drink. (If by chance you should say "cocoa," the whole kitchen would be thrown out of gear.) To this question I usually counter with another: "Do you have anything but white bread?" If the answer is not a flat No, it is: "We have whole wheat," or "We have graham bread." Whereupon I usually mumble under my breath: "You can stick that up your ass!" When she says; "What did you say?" I reply, "Do you have rye bread by any chance?" Then, before she can say no, I launch into an elaborate explanation of the fact that I don't mean by rye bread the ordinary rye bread, which is no better than white, graham, or whole wheat, but a succulent, tasty, dark, sour rye such as the Russians and the Jews serve. At the mention of these two suspect nationalities a scowl spreads over her face. . . .

Today the mailman brought three kinds of bread: Italian bread, a milk loaf, and pumpernickel. (No sour rye, of course, no corn bread.) The bread comes from Monterey, the nearest town, which is fifty miles away. In Monterey there is no Jewish grocer or delicatessen, worse luck. In Monterey there are Mexicans, Portuguese and Filipinos, but who gives a damn what these poor devils eat? The Mexicans have their tortillas, the Portuguese their garlic, and the Filipinos . . . well, among other things they have all our bad habits. Nobody in Monterey has a good slice of bread to eat. Nor in Carmel either, unless it's Robinson Jeffers, and that would be a sacramental bread. Just outside of Carmel lives Edward Weston, the photographer. And that leads me to speak of another kind of bread: photographic bread. Have you ever noticed that even the photographic bread tastes poorly? Have you ever seen a piece of bread photographed by our advertising maniacs which you would like to bite into? I haven't. Edward Weston could undoubtedly make you the most wonderful photographic bread conceivable—*but could you eat it?* The bread you hang on your wall is not the bread you want to eat at table. Even a piece of bread by Man Ray would prove unpalatable, particularly if he just happened to be reading his favorite author, the Marquis de Sade. Sacher Masoch might have made a good bread, if he had lived long enough. It has a Kosher sound, *Sacher Masoch*. But in the long run I have a feeling it would make one morbid and introspective, this Sacher Masoch bread.

I have now found that the only way to eat our most unwholesome, unpalatable and unappetizing American bread, the staff of our unsavory and monotonous life, is to adopt the following procedure. This is a recipe, so please follow instructions to the letter.

To begin with, accept any loaf that is offered you without question, even if it is not wrapped in cellophane, even if it contains no kelp. Throw it in the back of the car with the oil can and the grease rags; if possible, bury it under a sack of coal, *bituminous coal*. As you climb up the road to your home, drop it in the mud a few times and dig your heels into it. If you have a dog with you, let him pee on it now and then. When you get to the house, and after you have prepared the other dishes, take a huge carving knife and rip the loaf from stem to stern. Then take one whole onion, peeled or unpeeled, one carrot, one stalk of celery, one huge piece of garlic, one sliced apple, a herring, a handful of anchovies, a sprig of parsley, and an old toothbrush and shove them into the disemboweled guts of the bread. Over these pour first a thimbleful of kerosene, a dash of Lavoris and just a wee bit of Clorox; then sprinkle guts liberally with the following—molasses, honey, orange marmalade, vanilla, soy bean sauce, tabasco sauce, ketchup and arnica. Over this add a layer of chopped nuts, assorted nuts, of course, a few bay leaves (whole), some marjoram, and a stick of licorice cut into fine pieces. Put the loaf in the oven for ten minutes and serve. If it is still lacking in taste whip up a chili con carne piping hot and mix bread with it until it becomes a thick gruel. If this fails, piss on it and throw it to the dog. But under no circumstances feed it to the birds. The birds of North America are already on the decline, as I pointed out earlier. Their beaks have become dull, their wing-span shortened; they are pining and drooping, moulting in season and out. Above all, they no longer sing as they used to; they make sour notes, they bleat instead of tweeting, and sometimes, when the fogs set in, they have even been heard to cackle and wheeze.

🪰

Gary Snyder (1930–)

ONCE DESCRIBED AS "the Poet Laureate of Deep Ecology," Snyder began his career during the so-called San Francisco Renaissance of the late fifties and sixties, as a member of a literary circle that included Beat poets Allen Ginsberg and Michael McClure. After graduating from Reed College, where he double majored in English and anthropology, he embarked on a long and rich writing career, while supporting himself in a range of jobs— logger, fire-lookout, member of a steam-freighter crew, translator, carpenter, and (for many years) professor of English and creative writing at the University of California, Davis. A passionate student of Zen Buddhism, Snyder traveled between Japan and California for decades, living as a de facto Zen monk. His fascination with ecology prompted his work on the Pulitzer Prize-winning collection *Turtle Island*, and can be traced in some of his culinary poems, including the one we present here.

Steak

Up on the bluff, the steak houses
called "The Embers"—called
"Fireside"
with a smiling Disney cow on the sign
or a stockman's pride—huge
full-color photo of standing Hereford stud
above the very booth
his bloody sliced muscle is
        served in;
        "rare"

The Chamber of Commerce eats there,
the visiting lecturer,
stockmen in Denver suits,
Japanese-American animal nutrition experts
        From Kansas,
        With Buddhist beads;

And down by the tracks
in frozen mud, in the feed lots,
fed surplus grain
(the ripped-off land)
the beeves are standing round—
bred heavy.
Steaming, stamping,
long-lashed, slowly thinking
with the rhythm of their
breathing,
frosty—breezy—
early morning prairie sky.

𕣲

Wendell Berry (1934–)

KENTUCKY NATIVE WENDELL Berry has gained acclaim as a working farmer who is also a poet, novelist, short story writer, and essayist on key agricultural issues. His principled resistance to industrial farming has been broadly influential; his admirers include such advocates of localism as Michael Pollan and Alice Waters. In a number of works, including most recently the prestigious Jefferson Lecture of 2012, he has called attention to the axiom that is at the center of the piece we include here: "Eating is an agricultural act," noting that every culinary choice supports either globalized technological farming or local organic farming that respects the land. *New York Times* writer Mark Bittman has remarked that although Berry is "sometimes described as a modern-day Thoreau . . . I'd call [him] the soul of the real food movement."

from *What Are People For?*:
The Pleasures of Eating

MANY TIMES, AFTER I have finished a lecture on the decline of American farming and rural life, someone in the audience has asked, "What can city people do?"

"Eat responsibly," I have usually answered. Of course, I have tried to explain what I meant, but afterwards I have invariably felt that there was more to be said than I had been able to say. Now I would like to attempt a better explanation.

I begin with the proposition that eating is an agricultural act. Eating ends the annual drama of the food economy that begins with planting and birth. Most eaters, however, are no longer aware that this is true. They think of food as an agricultural product, perhaps, but they do not think of themselves as participants in agriculture. They think of themselves as "consumers." If they think beyond that, they recognize that they are passive consumers. They buy what they want—or what they have been persuaded to want—within the limits of what they can get. They pay, mostly without protest, what they are charged. And they mostly ignore certain critical questions about the quality and the cost of what they are sold: How fresh is it? How pure or clean is it, how free of dangerous chemicals? How far was it transported, and what did transportation add to the cost? How much did manufacturing or packaging or advertising add to the cost? When the food product has been "manufactured" or "processed" or "precooked," how has that affected its quality or nutritional value?

Most urban shoppers would tell you that food is produced on farms. But most of them do not know on what farms, or what kinds of farms, or where the farms are, or what knowledge or skills are involved in farming. They apparently have little doubt that farms will continue to produce, but they do not know how or over what obstacles. For them, then, food is pretty much an abstract idea—something they do not know or imagine—until it appears on the grocery shelf or on the table.

The specialization of production induces specialization of consumption. Patrons of the entertainment industry, for example, entertain themselves less and less and have become more and more passively dependent on commercial suppliers. This is certainly also true of patrons of the food industry, who have tended more and more to be *mere* consumers—passive, uncritical, and dependent. Indeed, this sort of consumption may be said to be one of the chief goals of industrial production. The food industrialists have by now persuaded millions of consumers to prefer food that is already prepared. They will grow, deliver, and cook your food for you and (just like your mother) beg you to eat it. That they do not yet offer to insert it, prechewed, into your mouth is only because they have found no profitable way to do so. We may rest assured that they would be glad to find such a way. The ideal industrial food consumer would be strapped to a table with a tube running from the food factory directly into his or her stomach. (Think of the savings, the efficiency, and the effortlessness of such an arrangement!)

Perhaps I exaggerate, but not by much. The industrial eater is, in fact, one who does not know that eating is an agricultural act, who no longer knows or imagines the connections between eating and the land, and who is therefore necessarily passive and uncritical—in short, a victim. When food, in the minds of eaters, is no longer associated with farming and with the land, then the eaters are suffering a kind of cultural amnesia that is misleading and dangerous. The current version of the "dream home" of the future involves "effortless" shopping from a list of available goods on a television monitor and heating precooked food by remote control. Of course, this implies, and indeed depends on, a perfect ignorance of the history of the food that is consumed. It requires that the citizenry should give up their hereditary and sensible aversion to buying a pig in a poke. It wishes to make the selling of pigs in pokes an honorable and glamorous activity. The dreamer in this dream home will perforce know nothing about the kind or quality of this food, or where it came from, or how it was produced and prepared, or what ingredients, additives, and residues it contains. Unless, that is, the dreamer undertakes a close and constant study of the food industry, in which case he or she might as well wake up and play an active and responsible part in the economy of food.

There is, then, a politics of food that, like any politics, involves our freedom. We still (sometimes) remember that we cannot be free if our minds and voices are controlled by someone else. But we have neglected to understand that neither can we be free if our food and its sources are controlled by someone else. The condition of the passive consumer of food is not a democratic condition. One reason to eat responsibly is to live free.

But, if there is a food politics, there are also a food aesthetics and a food ethics, neither of which is dissociated from politics. Like industrial sex, industrial eating has become a degraded, poor, and paltry thing. Our kitchens and other eating places more and more resemble filling stations, as our homes more and more resemble motels. "Life is not very interesting," we seem to have decided. "Let its satisfactions be minimal, perfunctory, and fast." We hurry through our meals to go to work and hurry through our work in order to "recreate" ourselves in the evenings and on weekends and vacations. And then we hurry, with the greatest possible speed and noise and violence, through our recreation—for what? To eat the billionth hamburger at some fast-food joint hell-bent on increasing the "quality" of our life. And all this is carried out in a remarkable obliviousness of the causes and effects, the possibilities and the purposes of the life of the body in this world.

One will find this obliviousness represented in virgin purity in the advertisements of the food industry, in which the food wears as much makeup as the actors. If one gained one's whole knowledge of food—as some presumably do—from these advertisements, one would not know that the various edibles were ever living creatures, or that they all come from the soil, or that they were produced by work. The passive American consumer, sitting down to a meal of pre-prepared or fast food, confronts a platter covered with inert, anonymous substances that have been processed, dyed, breaded, sauced, gravied, ground, pulped, strained, blended, prettified, and sanitized beyond resemblance to any part of any creature that ever lived. The products of nature and agriculture have been made, to all appearances, the products of industry. Both eater and eaten are thus in exile from biological reality. And the result is a kind of solitude, unprecedented in human experience, in which the eater may think of eating as, first, a purely commercial transaction between him and a supplier, and then as a purely appetitive transaction between him and his food.

And this peculiar specialization of the act of eating is, again, of obvious benefit to the food industry, which has good reason to obscure the connection between food and farming. It would not do for the consumer to know that the hamburger she is eating came from a steer that spent much of its life standing deep in its own excrement in a feedlot, helping to pollute the local streams, or that the calf that yielded the veal cutlet on her plate spent its life in a box in which it did not have room to turn around. And, though her sympathy for the coleslaw might be less tender, she should not be encouraged to meditate on the hygienic and biological implications of mile-square fields of cabbage, for vegetables grown in huge monocultures are dependent on toxic chemicals just as animals in close confinement are dependent on antibiotics and other drugs. . . .

The pleasure of eating should be an *extensive* pleasure, not that of the mere gourmet. People who know the garden in which their vegetables have grown and know that the garden is healthy will remember the beauty of the growing plants, perhaps in the dewy first light of morning when gardens are at their best. Such a memory involves itself with the food and is one of the pleasures of eating. The knowledge of the good health of the garden relieves and frees and comforts the eater. The same goes for eating meat. The thought of the good pasture, and of the calf contentedly grazing, flavors the steak. Some, I know, will think it bloodthirsty or worse to eat a fellow creature you have known all its life. On the contrary, I think, it means that you eat with understanding and with gratitude. A significant part of the pleasure of eating is in one's accurate consciousness of the lives and the world from which food comes. The pleasure of eating, then, may be the best available standard of our health. And this pleasure, I think, is pretty fully available to the urban consumer who will make the necessary effort.

I mentioned earlier the politics, aesthetics, and ethics of food. But to speak of the pleasure of eating is to go beyond those categories. Eating with the fullest pleasure—pleasure, that is, that does not depend on ignorance—is perhaps the profoundest enactment of our connection with the world. In this pleasure we experience and celebrate our dependence and our gratitude, for we are living from mystery, from creatures we did not make and powers we cannot comprehend. When I think of the meaning of food, I always remember these lines by the poet William Carlos Williams, which seem to me merely honest:

> There is nothing to eat,
>   seek it where you will,
>   but of the body of the Lord.
> The blessed plants
>   and the sea, yield it
>   to the imagination
> intact.

❧

Alan Richman (1944–)

ALAN RICHMAN IS a distinguished food writer for the magazine *GQ*, dean of food journalism at the French Culinary Institute, and the most decorated James Beard Award winner of all time—some fourteen food journalism medals. The author of *Fork It Over: The Intrepid Adventures of a Professional Eater*, Richman has also aroused the opprobrium of Anthony Bourdain, who once wrote an essay entitled "Alan Richman Is a Douchebag." The man who provokes such contrary opinions is a smart, knowledgeable, witty, and often authoritative food writer never afraid to assert his prejudices: he called one demolition job on a New York restaurant "Dinner for Schmucks."

For Richman, dining with a vegan is like an anthropologist examining the arcane and exotic habits of an alien people. But, as he reports here, he seems to have been quite amused when a vegan date defined honey as "bee-puke." Bourdain once spoke of "vegetarians and their Hezbollah-like splinter faction, the vegans"; though he might find it painful to concur with his nemesis, Richman probably wouldn't disagree.

from *Fork It Over*: My Beef with Vegans

MY FIRST CONTACT with hard-core veganism occurred in the offices of *GQ*, heretofore never thought of as a breeding ground for countercultural doctrine. An editor who is a fierce vegan sent me a note urging that I repent and "see that meat eating has grim consequences that extend beyond the health of the individual omnivore." I can see why I might not be a vegan icon, considering my predisposition to lurk hungrily in the foyers of butcher shops.

Included with his overture was a guide to veganism ("Think of all the exciting new foods you'll be trying") and a pamphlet entitled "101 Reasons Why I'm a Vegetarian." It was indeed informative. I learned that the combined weight of all the cattle on earth is greater than the combined weight of the entire human population. The solution, as I see it, is to eat more cows.

Vegans do not eat meat, of course. Nor do they admire anyone who does. They are the radical arm of the vegetarian movement, ill-tempered all the time. One of their fundamental tenets, that it is immoral to eat eggs, milk, butter, or any of the fruits of animal labor, makes them seem a few beans short of a burrito. Another of their goals, to put an end to cruelty in commercial slaughterhouses, is compelling enough to make me uncomfortable.

As they lurch between acts of insanity and acts of humanity, vegans seem no better or worse than any of our domestic extremists, the ones I do my best to ignore. What appalls me about them is that they are not content to exorcise pleasure from their own dinner tables. They insist that everybody who enjoys eating join them in their odd brand of masochism.

Not all people who decline to eat meat are like them. Macrobiotics, who share the vegan affinity for food colored unattractive shades of brown, are kindly souls who believe in the Zen principle of not irritating everybody with whom they come in contact. The way I see it, macrobiotics is the art of prolonging life, whereas veganism is the art of making life not worth prolonging. The ovo-lacto-vegetarians we see around all the time are much more tolerable. They are actually happier than most people, since all they eat are giant chocolate-chip cookies.

I've always felt vegans are best avoided, and they have certain attributes that make them easy to identify and evade. First is their grimness. At the vegan restaurant Angelica Kitchen, in New York's East Village, I asked my waitress, an attractive young woman with green fingernails, for some of the best vegan pickup lines tried on her. She replied bluntly, "Vegans aren't funny." Another is their pallor, a minor side effect of existing on a diet that cannot sustain human life. A third is the miso stains on their hemp wear, while the fourth is the terrifying attitude they assume.

I have heard stories, all reputedly true, of the outrages perpetuated by the worst of them. A vegan invited into a home throws open the refrigerator door and announces that children are being poisoned. A vegan served honey by a kindly host denounces it as "bee puke." A Memphis rib joint is spray-painted, the owner warned that his family could be the next to suffer. An Austin, Texas, newspaper columnist receives a death threat after poking fun at them. It would be nice to believe these are the deeds of isolated rogue vegans, but I'm skeptical. I suspect I have just made a list of what vegans consider a good time.

I myself have sat beside vegans, eaten with them, listened to the horror-movie mantra they utter lifelessly to one another upon meeting: "Where did you get your protein?" I have tales to tell, stories that would curdle the very milk vegans forbid their children to drink. The most terrible one is of a beautiful young woman I know who turned vegan and immediately fell for her yoga instructor.

Since vegan women eat nothing and are therefore as skinny as super-models, they are unusually attractive to men, but there is no sense in ordinary men pursuing them. Vegan women all fall hopelessly in love with their yoga instructors. These are spindly yet extraordinary flexible guys who project an irresistible air of serenity and piety. Yoga instructors don't have students; they have harems. . . .

While sitting in Angelica Kitchen, an immensely popular restaurant that must gross more money than Lutèce, I said the three little words I never expected to say in a vegan restaurant. I turned to my friends and announced, "This is delicious." I was eating marinated tofu on mixed-grain bread. The bread was an unhealthy-looking speckled brown, and while I dislike indiscriminate speckles in my food, the bread was fresh, which is not all that common in vegan restaurants. The tofu was doing no harm, which is all I ever ask of that product, the roasted carrots added a sweet crunch, and the parsley-almond pesto was vibrant. Vibrant is another word I never expected to utter in a vegan restaurant. I was almost as pleased with the soup of the day, split-pea that could not have tasted better had a beef bone been used for the stock. In my newly devised four-tier classification of vegan food, I rated both the sandwich and the soup Worth Ordering Again.

I was never quite as satisfied with anything else at Angelica Kitchen. Let me put it more precisely: I hated everything else.

I want to be fair about this. Nobody is more close-minded than me when it comes to vegetarian cuisine, regardless of whether it's vegan, macrobiotic, or vegetarian. I think vegetarian restaurants generally prepare vegetables worse than nonvegetarian restaurants. Vegetarian restaurants have little respect for the individual properties of their ingredients, only a realization that one takes longer to get soft than another. I've always suspected that vegetarian chefs toss their turnips, potatoes, and cabbage into the same pot and follow a one-line recipe that reads: "Turn up the heat."

I find vegetarian restaurants both smug and culinarily unsuccessful. Still, I have always been inclined to allow vegetarians to go about their business without interference from me. But I don't feel quite the same about vegans. What infuriates me about them is their self-righteousness, their insistence that we miscreants give up our enjoyment of food and eat what they eat. I set out to determine if their dogma made any sense at all, if I was mistaken about the inferiority of their cuisine. To do that, I decided to eat at three of the most esteemed vegan restaurants in New York—the aforementioned Angelica Kitchen; the branch of Zen Palate located on Ninth Avenue; and Hangawi, in Midtown.

Angelica Kitchen is something of a vegetarian cliché, with insufficient room between the plain, varnished-wood tables, place settings that include chopsticks for no good reason, a friendly but ineffectual staff that might well have trained on some alien plant world, and all the staples one would expect—carrot juice, sesame sauce, miso soup, mulled apple cider, and the like. Near the entrance is a community help board offering assistance with the essentials of life, such as channeling, massage, and meditation, and a lot of notices promising rewards for the return of lost animals. Vegans seem to lose more than their share of cats.

After Worth Ordering Again, my next vegan gastronomic rating is Just Plain Bad. In that classification I place Angelica Kitchen's three-bean chili, one of those profoundly unsuccessful attempts to make a dish that ordinarily relies on meat taste as though the meat isn't missed. Also Just Plain Bad was the overly spiced, overly smooth hummus served with a lump of cauliflower plopped in it, a carrot-apple juice melding two incompatible flavors, and a translucent fruit-and-gelatin parfait that looked like baby food but would frighten any child who tasted it.

Making my third vegan category, Bad Beyond Belief, was a "daily seasonal special" called Scary, Posh, Baby & Sporty. It had lots of everything, including tofu sour cream, yellowed cauliflower, gnarled radishes, and what seemed to be weeds. On a second visit, my special of "baked ginger tofu triangles with udon noodles in a silky peanut sauce" arrived with sweet potatoes, broccoli, kimchi, mizuna, peanuts, and sesame seeds but without the tofu. In real cooking, unlike vegan cooking, main ingredients seldom if ever are forgotten by the kitchen.

If Angelica Kitchen satisfies the repressed hippie yearnings of the vegan community, then Zen Palate addresses a different psychological need, a longing to connect with the mystical East. The décor of the Ninth Avenue branch is surprisingly trendy, with oversize sconces, sponged walls, and dimmed lights, but any decorative effort is overwhelmed by a drab, indifferent staff. The kitchen is determined to cook food quickly rather than well, and the outerwear of customers is strewn about, making the place look like a suburban rec room on NFL game day.

I ate one dish Worth Ordering Again, a plate of delicate ravioli stuffed with a not unpleasant mixture of soy protein, bamboo shoots, and snow peas and topped with a subdued sesame-wasabi sauce. Very nearly Worth Ordering Again, but I wouldn't, were the "sizzling medallions," which I liked until the monotonous texture of the chewy little orange-flavored wheat-gluten blobs tired me out. Bad Beyond Belief were cardboard-like scallion pancakes with no scallion taste, pan-fried vegetable dumplings filled with a repugnant brown mash, and a dish called Dreamland. I thought Dreamland had promise. It contained deep-fried linguine, black mushrooms, and marinated ginger. This dish severely tested my karma, because after a single bite, I wanted to throw it across the room.

Hangawi, a Korean vegan restaurant, turned out to be so much more admirable than the other two places that I would put it on a totally different spiritual and culinary plane. I didn't love what I ate there, simply because the food suffered mightily from the limitations of the vegan diet, but I did find the cooking impressive.

I approached Hangawi warily, because like most Americans, I find Korean cuisine a little too unconventional, with its emphasis on steaming, marinating, and casseroles that aren't anything like the ones our mothers made. I yanked open the imposing outer door to the restaurant and entered a tiny anteroom. Then I had a choice to make: go forward or flee. To commit to a meal at Hangawi takes courage, for the staff confiscates your shoes, and then there is no escape. On the other hand, the polished wood floor feels really good under stocking feet.

Joining me for this meal was the vegan who fell prey to her yoga instructor. She seemed in a pleasant enough mood, particularly for a vegan, although she complained of not having had sufficient time to enjoy her usual predinner massage. She told me she'd had some really good falafel for lunch. This is how vegans normally begin a meal, by reciting the details of their previous one, a side effect of a near starvation diet. The room, appropriately serene, had polished wood tables, screens, and lots of pots and ceramics. The music was mostly that Eastern-style wailing that sounds like a soprano holding a high note.

As an aperitif, we tasted two drinks she recommended, cold pine-tree juice and hot citron-paste tea. Both were indeed delicious, and both were insanely sweet, which brings me to my fourth category of vegan cuisine: Shockingly Sweet. With no animal fat permitted in the diet and surprisingly few fried foods on menus, vegans seem to obtain almost all their pleasure from sweetness. Much of the food I sampled at Hangawi went directly to the gratification of that craving. The best dish, as it should have been, was a $29.95 plate of wild matsutaki mushrooms grilled over pine needles; the mushrooms had a clean, woodsy, earthy flavor, although I doubt they detoxified me, as promised. Vegans seem to believe that every bite they take has an immediate physiological effect on the body, while we everyday omnivores understand that it takes decades of burgers and fries to really mess us up.

MY DATE WITH A VEGAN

SHE wore a dress with spaghetti straps, quite elegant by vegan standards, in the photo that appeared in the personals section of the *Veggie Singles News*. I wrote to her, suggesting lunch. She responded, recommending Zenith Vegetarian Cuisine, a vegan restaurant in the Hell's Kitchen section of Manhattan. Actually, any restaurant dishing up vegan food is Hell's Kitchen to me.

She looked lovely, head to toe. Well, maybe not her toes, since they were encased in vegan-sanctioned Payless nonleather shoes. She told me she had been on three previous dates with men who had answered her singles ad, and all of them had turned out to be vegetarians, not vegans. I was relieved to learn that there are not as many vegans out there as I had feared.

She told me she was twenty-nine, worked as a corporate travel agent, and lived in Queens with her eight-year-old daughter, who adores Chicken McNuggets. That's as lax a brand of family veganism as I've ever come across. She told me she didn't get along with the first vegetarian because he was too macho and insisted on paying for the meal. "We went out to shoot pool after dinner and I won," she said. "That didn't go over too well." She said she didn't get along with the second man because of his attitude. When they got to the restaurant and she asked him where he wanted to sit, he replied, "On your lap."

I agreed that was an inappropriate comment for vegans and vegetarians alike.

She said he was an Israeli.

I told her that was a pretty typical comment for an Israeli.

Her third date was the most promising, but the budding relationship stalled when he started lecturing her on the breakdown of the American family, how every household needs a man. This is not an approach recommended to anyone attempting to charm a woman who is a single parent.

I wished her the best of luck in future dating endeavors and warned her about the seductive powers of the vegan yoga instructors she was certain to meet. She promised she would ask my advice before she ever went out with a "crazy nut-job yoga instructor."

I had done my duty. If I can save even one woman from one of them, I will have left the vegan world a better place.

As long as there have been vegans, I have looked upon them as persons with whom I would not want to break bread—actually, one bite of the revoltingly dry corn bread at Angelica Kitchen should be enough to make even vegans not want to break bread with vegans.

I have now changed my mind. I had a lovely lunch with the woman who placed her advertisement in the *Veggie Single News* and would eat with her again, as long as she didn't order the "eggplant chips" at Zenith. I had a nice dinner with my friend at Hangawi, but she was my friend before turning to veganism and so we could talk about the old days, before her life centered around tofu.

I'm not even certain any longer that vegans are the worst people who have ever lived. After all, Adolf Hitler was merely a vegetarian.

Rachel Laudan (1944–)

HISTORIAN RACHEL LAUDAN was born and raised on a farm in Wiltshire, a locale she has described as a sort of Arcadia. She has taught at various universities and lived in Mexico and Hawaii, writing about her investigations of the cuisine in those cultures. Her recent work has focused on the falsely sentimental "nostalgia" she sees as shaping the Slow Food Movement; in various influential essays she has argued against the positions taken by Michael Pollan and others whose works she regards as fantasizing about the culinary past. Her latest book is an ambitious volume titled *Cuisine and Empire: Cooking in World History.*

from A Plea for Culinary Modernism

MODERN, FAST, PROCESSED food is a disaster. That, at least, is the message conveyed by newspapers and magazines, on televison cooking programs, and in prizewinning cookbooks. It is a mark of sophistication to bemoan the steel roller mill and supermarket bread while yearning for stone-ground flour and brick ovens; to seek out heirloom apples and pumpkins while despising modern tomatoes and hybrid corn; to be hostile to agronomists who develop high-yielding modern crops and to home economists who invent new recipes for General Mills. We hover between ridicule and shame when we remember how our mothers and grandmothers enthusiastically embraced canned and frozen foods. We nod in agreement when the waiter proclaims that the restaurant showcases the freshest local produce. We shun Wonder Bread and Coca-Cola. Above all, we loathe the great culminating symbol of Culinary Modernism, McDonald's—modern, fast, homogenous, and international.

Like so many of my generation, my culinary style was created by those who scorned industrialized food; Culinary Luddites, we may call them, after the English hand workers of the nineteenth century who abhorred the machines that were destroying their traditional way of life. I learned to cook from the books of Elizabeth David, who urged us to sweep our store cupboards "clean for ever of the cluttering debris of commercial sauce bottles and all synthetic flavorings." I progressed to the Time-Life *Good Cook* series and to *Simple French Food,* in which Richard Olney hoped against hope that "the reins of stubborn habit are strong enough to frustrate the famous industrial revolution for some time to come." I turned to Paula Wolfert to learn more about Mediterranean cooking and was assured that I wouldn't "find a dishonest dish in this book. . . . The food here is real food . . . the real food of real people." Today I rush to the newsstand to pick up *Saveur* with its promise to teach me to "Savor a world of authentic cuisine."

Culinary Luddism involves more than just taste. Since the days of the counterculture, it has also presented itself as a moral and political crusade. Now in Boston, the Oldways Preservation and Exchange Trust works to provide "a scientific basis for the preservation and revitalization of traditional diets." Meanwhile, Slow Food, founded in 1989 to protest the opening of a McDonald's in Rome, is a self-described Greenpeace for Food; its manifesto begins, "We are enslaved by speed and have all succumbed to the same insidious virus: Fast Life, which disrupts our habits, pervades the privacy of our homes and forces us to eat Fast Foods. . . . Slow Food is now the only truly progressive answer." As one of its spokesmen was reported as saying in the *New York Times,* "Our real enemy is the obtuse consumer."

At this point I begin to back off. I want to cry, "Enough!" But why? Why would I, who learned to cook from Culinary Luddites, who grew up in a family that, in Elizabeth David's words, produced their "own home-cured bacon, ham and sausages . . . churned their own butter, fed their chickens and geese, cherished their fruit trees, skinned and cleaned their own hares" (well, to be honest, not the geese and sausages), not rejoice at the growth of Culinary Luddism? Why would I (or anyone else) want to be thought "an obtuse consumer"? Or admit to preferring unreal food for unreal people? Or to savoring inauthentic cuisine?

The answer is not far to seek: because I am a historian. As a historian I cannot accept the account of the past implied by Culinary Luddism, a past sharply divided between good and bad, between the sunny rural days of yore and the grey industrial present. My enthusiasm for the Luddites' kitchen wisdom does not carry over to their history, any more than my response to a stirring political speech inclines me to accept the orator as scholar. The Luddites' fable of disaster, of a fall from grace, smacks more of wishful thinking than of digging through archives. It gains credence not from scholarship but from evocative dichotomies: fresh and natural versus processed and preserved; local versus global; slow versus fast; artisanal and traditional versus urban and industrial; healthful versus contaminated and fatty. History shows, I believe, that the Luddites have things back to front.

That food should be fresh and natural has become an article of faith. It comes as something of a shock to realize that this is a latter-day creed. For our ancestors, natural was something quite nasty. Natural often tasted bad. Fresh meat was rank and tough, fresh milk warm and unmistakably a bodily excretion; fresh fruits (dates and grapes being rare exceptions outside the tropics) were inedibly sour, fresh vegetables bitter. Even today, natural can be a shock when we actually encounter it. When Jacques Pépin offered free-range chickens to friends, they found "the flesh tough and the flavor too strong," prompting him to wonder whether they would really like things the way they naturally used to be.

Natural was unreliable. Fresh fish began to stink, fresh milk soured, eggs went rotten. Everywhere seasons of plenty were followed by seasons of hunger when the days were short, the weather turned cold, or the rain did not fall. Hens stopped laying eggs, cows went dry, fruits and vegetables were not to be found, fish could not be caught in the stormy seas. Natural was usually indigestible. Grains, which supplied from fifty to ninety percent of the calories in most societies, have to be threshed, ground, and cooked to make them edible. Other plants, including the roots and tubers that were the life support of the societies that did not eat grains, are often downright poisonous. Without careful processing, green potatoes, stinging taro, and cassava bitter with prussic acid are not just indigestible, but toxic.

Nor did our ancestors' physiological theories dispose them to the natural. Until about two hundred years ago, from China to Europe, and in Mesoamerica, too, everyone believed that the fires in the belly cooked foodstuffs and turned them into nutrients. That was what digesting was. Cooking foods in effect pre-digested them and made them easier to assimilate. Given a choice, no one would burden the stomach with raw, unprocessed foods.

So to make food tasty, safe, digestible and healthy, our forebears bred, ground, soaked, leached, curdled, fermented, and cooked naturally occurring plants and animals until they were literally beaten into submission. To lower toxin levels, they cooked plants, treated them with clay (the Kaopectate effect), and leached them with water, acid fruits and vinegars, and alkaline lye. They intensively bred maize to the point that it could not reproduce without human help. They created sweet oranges and juicy apples and non-bitter legumes, happily abandoning their more natural but less tasty ancestors. They built granaries for their grain, dried their meat and their fruit, salted and smoked their fish, curdled and fermented their dairy products, and cheerfully used whatever additives and preservatives they could—sugar, salt, oil, vinegar, lye—to make edible foodstuffs. In the twelfth century, the Chinese sage Wu Tzu-mu listed the six foodstuffs essential to life: rice, salt, vinegar, soy sauce, oil, and tea. Four had been unrecognizably transformed from their naturally occurring state. Who could have imagined vinegar as rice that had been fermented to ale and then soured? Or soy sauce as cooked and fermented beans? Or oil as the extract of crushed cabbage seeds? Or bricks of tea as leaves that had been killed by heat, powdered, and compressed? Only salt and rice had any claim to fresh or natural, and even then the latter had been stored for months or years, threshed, and husked.

Processed and preserved foods kept well, were easier to digest, and were delicious: raised white bread instead of chewy wheat porridge; thick, nutritious, heady beer instead of prickly grains of barley; unctuous olive oil instead of a tiny, bitter fruit; soy milk, sauce, and tofu instead of dreary, flatulent soy beans; flexible, fragrant tortillas instead of dry, tough maize; not to mention red wine, blue cheese, sauerkraut, hundred-year-old eggs, Smithfield hams, smoked salmon, yogurt, sugar, chocolate, and fish sauce.

Eating fresh, natural food was regarded with suspicion verging on horror, something to which only the uncivilized, the poor, and the starving resorted. When the compiler of the Confucian classic *Book of Rites* (ca. 200 B.C.) distinguished the first humans—people who had no alternative to wild, uncooked foods—from civilized peoples who took "advantage of the benefits of fire . . . [who] toasted, grilled, boiled, and roasted," he was only repeating a commonplace. When the ancient Greeks took it as a sign of bad times if people were driven to eat greens and root vegetables, they too were rehearsing common wisdom. Happiness was not a verdant Garden of Eden abounding in fresh fruits, but a securely locked storehouse jammed with preserved, processed foods.

Local food was greeted with about as much enthuasiasm as fresh and natural. Local foods were the lot of the poor who could neither escape the tyranny of local climate and biology nor the monotonous, often precarious, diet it afforded. Meanwhile, the rich, in search of a more varied diet, bought, stole, wheedled, robbed, taxed, and ran off with appealing plants and animals, foodstuffs, and culinary techniques from wherever they could find them....

By the standard measures of health and nutrition—life expectancy and height—our ancestors were far worse off than we are. Much of the blame was due to the diet, exacerbated by living conditions and infections which affect the body's ability to use the food that is ingested. No amount of nostalgia for the pastoral foods of the distant past can wish away the fact that our ancestors lived mean, short lives, constantly afflicted with diseases, many of which can be directly attributed to what they did and did not eat.

Historical myths, though, can mislead as much by what they don't say as by what they do. Culinary Luddites typically gloss over the moral problems intrinsic to the labor of producing and preparing food. In 1800, ninety-five percent of the Russian population and eighty percent of the French lived in the country; in other words, they spent their days getting food on the table for themselves and other people. A century later, eighty-eight percent of Russians, eighty-five percent of Greeks, and over fifty percent of the French were still on the land. Traditional societies were aristocratic, made up of the many who toiled to produce, process, preserve, and prepare food, and the few who, supported by the limited surplus, could do other things.

In the great kitchens of the few—royalty, aristocracy, and rich merchants—cooks created elaborate cuisines. The cuisines drove home the power of the mighty few with a symbol that everyone understood: ostentatious shows of more food than the powerful could possibly consume. Feasts were public occasions for the display of power, not private occasions for celebration, for enjoying food for food's sake. The poor were invited to watch, groveling as the rich gorged themselves. Louis xiv was exploiting a tradition going back to the Roman Empire when he encouraged spectators at his feasts. Sometimes, to hammer home the point while amusing the court, the spectators were let loose on the leftovers. "The destruction of so handsome an arrangement served to give another agreeable entertainment to the court," observed a commentator, "by the alacrity and disorder of those who demolished these castles of marzipan, and these mountains of preserved fruit."

Meanwhile, most men were born to a life of labor in the fields, most women to a life of grinding, chopping, and cooking. "Servitude," said my mother as she prepared home-cooked breakfast, dinner, and tea for eight to ten people three hundred and sixty-five days a year. She was right. Churning butter and skinning and cleaning hares, without the option of picking up the phone for a pizza if something goes wrong, is unremitting, unforgiving toil. Perhaps, though, my mother did not realize how much worse her lot might have been. She could at least buy our bread from the bakery. In Mexico, at the same time, women without servants could expect to spend five hours a day—one third of their waking hours—kneeling at the grindstone preparing the dough for the family's tortillas. Not until the 1950s did the invention of the tortilla machine release them from the drudgery.

In the eighteenth and early nineteenth centuries, it looked as if the distinction between gorgers and grovelers would worsen. Between 1575 and 1825 world population had doubled from 500 million to a billion, and it was to double again by 1925. Malthus sounded his dire predictions. The poor, driven by necessity or government mandate, resorted to basic foods that produced bountifully even if they were disliked: maize and sweet potatoes in China and Japan, maize in Italy, Spain, and Romania, potatoes in northern Europe. They eked out an existence on porridges or polentas of oats or maize, on coarse breads of rye or barley bulked out with chaff or even clay and ground bark, and on boiled potatoes; they saw meat only on rare occasions. The privation continued. In Europe, 1840 was a year of hunger, best remembered now as the time of the devastating potato famine of Ireland. Meanwhile, the rich continued to indulge, feasting on white bread, meats, rich fatty sauces, sweet desserts, exotic hothouse-grown pineapples, wine, and tea, coffee, and chocolate drunk from fine china. In 1845, shortly after revolutions had rocked Europe, the British prime minister Benjamin Disraeli described "two nations, between whom there is no intercourse and no sympathy . . . who are formed by a different breeding, are fed by a different food, are ordered by different manners and are not governed by the same laws . . . THE RICH AND THE POOR."

In the nick of time, in the 1880s, the industrialization of food got under way long after the production of other common items of consumption, such as textiles and clothing, had been mechanized. Farmers brought new land into production, utilized reapers and later tractors and combines, spread more fertilizer, and by the 1930s began growing hybrid maize. Steamships and trains brought fresh and canned meats, fruits, vegetables, and milk to the growing towns. Instead of starving, the poor of the industrialized world survived and thrived. In Britain the retail price of food in a typical work-man's budget fell by a third between 1877 and 1887 (though he would still spend seventy-one percent of his income on food and drink). In 1898 in the United States a dollar bought forty-two percent more milk, fifty-one percent more coffee, a third more beef, twice as much sugar, and twice as much flour as in 1872. By the beginning of the twentieth century, the British working class were drinking sugary tea from china teacups and eating white bread spread with jam and margarine, canned meats, canned pineapple, and an orange from the Christmas stocking.

To us, the cheap jam, the margarine, and the starchy diet look pathetic. Yet white bread did not cause the "weakness, indigestion, or nausea" that coarse whole wheat bread did when it supplied most of the calories (not a problem for us since we never consume it in such quantities). Besides, it was easier to detect stretchers such as sawdust in white bread. Margarine and jam made the bread more attractive and easier to swallow. Sugar tasted good, and hot tea in an unheated house in mid-winter provided good cheer. For those for whom fruit had been available, if at all, only from June to October, canned pineapple and a Christmas orange were treats to be relished. For the diners, therefore, the meals were a dream come true, a first step away from a coarse, monotonous diet and the constant threat of hunger, even starvation.

Nor should we think it was only the British, not famed for their cuisine, who were delighted with industrialized foods. Everyone was, whether American, Asian, African, or European. In the first half of the twentieth century, Italians embraced factory-made pasta and canned tomatoes. In the second half of the century, Japanese women welcomed factory-made bread because they could sleep in a little longer instead of having to get up to make rice. Similarly, Mexicans seized on bread as a good food to have on hand when there was no time to prepare tortillas. Working women in India are happy to serve commercially made bread during the week, saving the time-consuming business of making chapatis for the weekend. As supermarkets appeared in Eastern Europe and Russia, housewives rejoiced at the choice and convenience of ready-made goods. For all, Culinary Modernism had provided what was wanted: food that was processed, preservable, industrial, novel, and fast, the food of the elite at a price everyone could afford. Where modern food became available, populations grew taller and stronger, had fewer diseases, and lived longer. Men had choices other than hard agricultural labor, women other than kneeling at the *metate* five hours a day.

So the sunlit past of the Culinary Luddites never existed. So their ethos is based not on history but on a fairy tale. So what? Perhaps we now need this culinary philosophy. Certainly no one would deny that an industrialized food supply has its own problems, problems we hear about every day. Perhaps we *should* eat more fresh, natural, local, artisanal, slow food. Why not create a historical myth to further that end? The past is over and gone. Does it matter if the history is not quite right?

It matters quite a bit, I believe. If we do not understand that most people had no choice but to devote their lives to growing and cooking food, we are incapable of comprehending that the foods of Culinary Modernism—egalitarian, available more or less equally to all, without demanding the disproportionate amount of the resources of time or money that traditional foodstuffs did—allow us unparalleled choices not just of diet but of what to do with our lives. If we urge the Mexican to stay at her *metate*, the farmer to stay at his olive press, the housewife to stay at her stove instead of going to McDonald's, all so that we may eat handmade tortillas, traditionally pressed olive oil, and home-cooked meals, we are assuming the mantle of the aristocrats of old. We are reducing the options of others as we attempt to impose our elite culinary preferences on the rest of the population.

Culinary Luddites are right, though, about two important things. We need to know how to prepare good food, and we need a culinary ethos. As far as good food goes, they've done us all a service by teaching us to how to use the bounty delivered to us (ironically) by the global economy. Their culinary ethos, though, is another matter. Were we able to turn back the clock, as they urge, most of us would be toiling all day in the fields or the kitchen; many of us would be starving. Nostalgia is not what we need. What we need is an ethos that comes to terms with contemporary, industrialized food, not one that dismisses it, an ethos that opens choices for everyone, not one that closes them for many so that a few may enjoy their labor, and an ethos that does not prejudge, but decides case by case when natural is preferable to processed, fresh to preserved, old to new, slow to fast, artisanal to industrial. Such an ethos, and not a timorous Luddism, is what will impel us to create the matchless modern cuisines appropriate to our time.

ॐ

Steven G. Kellman (1947–)

A PROFESSOR OF comparative literature at the University of Texas, San Antonio, Kellman has written or edited numerous volumes, including *The Translingual Imagination* (2000) and *Redemption* (2005), a prize-winning biography of the novelist Henry Roth. Kellman writes literary journalism regularly for a range of newspapers and has been awarded the National Book Critics Circle's Nona Balakian Citation for Excellence in Reviewing. In our selection, he offers a lively history of vegetarianism while explaining with verve and wit why, as a committed vegan, he prefers not to eat what George Bernard Shaw called "the scorched corpses of animals."

from Fish, Flesh, and Foul: The Anti-Vegetarian Animus

GIVING UP FLESH is not nearly as traumatic as giving up the ghost. Although thousands have been martyred for their refusal to eat meat, vegetarians today suffer merely a species of social death. Stop eating what George Bernard Shaw, a recovered carnivore, called "scorched corpses of animals" and you become either the pariah or the cynosure of the dinner party, either barred or badgered over culinary preferences. "Tell me what you eat, and I will tell you who you are," declared the French gourmet Anthelme Brillat-Savarin, not the first or last to demand a full accounting of a stranger's diet. Determined to minimize suffering, I ate my last hamburger almost thirty years ago, but I still am often grilled about who I think I am.

What about the pain you cause to carrots? Do you get enough protein and vitamin B$_{12}$? Are you willing to provide sanctuary to endangered cockroaches? In a dog-eat-dog world, why deny yourself the savor of a wiener? Would you be so self-righteous if you were stranded in the Sierras with the Donners? . . .

VEGETARIANISM has a history, stretching into the Paleolithic mists when, hunting and gathering, *Homo sapiens* distinguished himself from most other hominids by feeding on flesh. Opportunistic organisms, humans eat everything, though the invention of Alka-Seltzer is a caveat that maybe we should not. Yet, according to the Book of Genesis, Adam and Eve never needed flesh and blood to sustain themselves in the Garden of Eden; and Ovid—like Raphael in Milton's *Paradise Lost*—imagined a Golden Age in which butchery would not be a precondition for nutrition. Ambrosia and nectar were sustenance enough for the Greek gods, and in the Homeric "Hymn to Hermes," the messenger of Mount Olympus resisted the temptation to feast on meat, lest it make him mortal. Though it is moot whether Socrates and Plato themselves partook of meat at the banquets they attended, the ideal state imagined in *The Republic* is a vegetopia. Many other ancient writers, including Empedocles, Plotinus, Plutarch, Porphyry, Seneca, and Theophrastus, fixed their canons and appetites against slaughter, and the original Epicurean, Epicurus himself, found pleasure in forgoing flesh. Pythagoras's regimen, which, for obscure reasons, banned beans as well as meat, was so exemplary that for more than two thousand years those who abstained at least from flesh were called Pythagoreans. The word *vegetarian*—from *vegetus*, Latin for sound, whole, vital—was not coined until 1847, at the founding of the Vegetarian Society of the UK in Ramsgate, England. But shadowing this history, like a fungus on a cantaloupe, is a chronicle of animosity—a persistent record of misunderstanding, mistrust, and misbehavior toward those who refuse to consume fish, flesh, or fowl. Vegephobia blights Greek comedies of the third and fourth centuries that satirize Pythagoras, and it persists in belligerent banter by the dinner-party smart-ass intent on discrediting guests who prefer aubergine in tomato to *vitello tonnato*. . . .

"Vegetables are interesting," quipped the humorist Fran Lebowitz, "but lack a sense of purpose when unaccompanied by a good cut of meat." Such cracks are merely obnoxious; ridicule is the tribute that carnivores pay Pythagoreans. More genuinely noxious was the mob of butchers and bakers who rioted in Boston in 1837 when Sylvester Graham, Presbyterian minister and the inventor of an eponymous cracker, preached against the evils of abattoirs and white flour. It is one thing to declare—as the senior George Bush (who advertised his populist tastes by munching publicly on fried pork rinds) did in 1986—one's abhorrence of broccoli. . . . But it is quite another matter to crucify those who feed on crucifers.

In 276 A.D., Mani, founder of the religious movement that bore his name, was tortured and executed by the Sasanian rulers of Persia for trying to convert them to his unorthodox ways, which were meatless. A century later, Timothy, the Patriarch of Alexandria, was so fearful that Manichaeanism might infiltrate Christendom that he exacted taste tests of his clergy; those who refused to eat meat were presumed Manichaean and punished severely. The dualism of the Manichaeans disturbed the early fathers more than their asceticism, but both challenged church dogma and authority, and it was easy to seize on vegetarianism as both a symptom and an assertion of heresy. Despite the best efforts of Augustine, himself a lapsed Manichaean, the doctrine was not entirely eradicated, and when it resurfaced in the eleventh century with the steak-spurning Bogomils, many were in fact burned at the stake. . . .

DESPITE centuries of persecution, vegetarianism has survived. Vegetarians, less vulnerable to heart disease, stroke, cancer, and other ills that flesh eaters are heir to, have thrived. According to the adage, one man's meat is another man's poison, and according to much current research, meat can be toxic to a man or woman. Though a Jewish proverb insists that "meat, not hay, makes the lion roar," many humans whom we lionize have disagreed. Vegetarianism has not impeded the athletic achievements of Hank Aaron, Billie Jean King, Martina Navratilova, Paavo Nurmi, Dave Scott, or Bill Walton. Though Victor Frankenstein's gentle creature ate no flesh, it is also true that Adolf Hitler gave up meat shortly after the suspicious death of his niece Geli Raubal in 1931. Yet so have many finer ethical minds, including Gautama Buddha, Leonardo da Vinci, John Wesley, Percy Bysshe Shelley, Susan B. Anthony, Leo Tolstoy, Mohandas Gandhi, Franz Kafka,

S. Y. Agnon, Albert Schweitzer, and Cesar Chavez. "For the animals, it is an eternal Treblinka," observed Isaac Bashevis Singer, who refused to be complicit in the culinary holocaust. Vincent van Gogh became a vegetarian after visiting a slaughterhouse, and so would many others if meat were less convenient—or were not packaged in savory patties and cutlets that obscure their bloody origins.

"Animals are my friends," explained Shaw, "and I don't eat my friends." Animals are not necessarily my friends, but I do not feast on sentient strangers either. Nor do I exploit them. As a vegan (a word coined in 1944, for a practice that goes back to ancient times), I avoid all animal products, including dairy, eggs, and leather. . . .

"I want there to be no peasant in my realm so poor that he will not have a chicken in his pot every Sunday," proclaimed Henri IV. If the Bourbon monarch's wish had been their command, every subject would have been conscripted as a carnivore. Echoing Henri IV, Herbert Hoover was elected president of the United States in 1928 with the slogan "A chicken in every pot, a car in every garage." . . . Politicians have little to gain and, owing to the corporate clout of those who process and market animal carcasses, much to lose by publicly embracing vegetarianism. Even heavyweight Mike Tyson cannot match the clout of a lobbyist for the Tyson poultry empire. The ritual demand of any national election is that candidates sample the cuisines of the regions and ethnic groups whose support they are seeking, and they score best sharing meat: fajitas, kielbasa, gumbo, pastrami, ribs, fried chicken, prosciutto. The road to the White House is paved with the bones of slaughtered beasts. On the quintessential American holiday, Thanksgiving, any national leader who does not devour a turkey may be thought seditious. . . .

YET vegetarians are not such rare birds. The *Vegetarian Times* estimates that 12.5 million Americans are vegetarians. . . .

In Britain, where the Royal Society for the Prevention of Cruelty to Animals, a model for humane organizations in other countries, was founded in 1824 and where animal rights agitation has a longer and more strident history than anywhere else in the West, vegetarianism is more commonplace. Even in provincial English village pubs. . . .

A 1998 poll found that 7 percent of Britons agreed with the statement: "I am a vegetarian and eat no meat at all." And since the prospect of pestilence tends to concentrate the mind, incidents of mad cow disease, *E. coli,* and salmonella have provided additional incentives to avoid red meat and poultry. The founding of the Carnivores Club in London in 1996, in the midst of the European crisis over British beef, was an act of bravado that defied the patent logic of vegetarianism. So, too, did Auberon Waugh, when, in a 1999 article in the *Daily Telegraph,* he railed against "the vegetarian underground, a worldwide conspiracy of animal sentimentalists working in secret, or under deep cover, using our traditional class and regional animosities to promote its repulsive cause."

"Vegetarian underground" sounds like a mushroom factory, and whatever movement there is to encourage abstention from meat is not nearly as organized or as potent as the culture of carnivorism. Dining on chops is firmly rooted in the patriarchy. "Beefeater" is the name the English apply to the hardy, valiant yeomen of the guard, as if meat were implicit in masculinity. William Cody acquired his manly reputation and his nickname—Buffalo Bill—by slaying thousands of burly beasts. In the sexual ecology of the dinner table, salads are "lady food," unlike steaks and roasts. According to the historian Todd L. Savitt, male slaves in antebellum Virginia were fed twice as much meat as their female counterparts. During World War I, meat was withheld from civilian women in order to provide a steady supply for fighting men. A meat-and-potatoes man is a redundancy, since, echoing cannibalistic cultures in which warriors acquire strength by devouring their foes, males nourish and affirm their virility by consuming flesh. If, like butcher shops, taverns are a man's domain, salad bar is an oxymoron.

Real Men Don't Eat Quiche, announced Bruce Feirstein in a 1982 bestseller that spoofed the culture's paradigm of yahoo machismo. "Real Men," wrote Feirstein, "avoid all members of the wimp food group, including crudités, lemon mousse, crêpes, avocado, capons, chives, shrimp dip, and fruit compote." . . . In the demographics of vegetarianism there is a notable gender gap. Women constitute a disproportionate share of the population of Pythagoreans. In the survey that found Britain 7 percent vegetarian, the figure was 10 percent for women but only 4 percent for men. In a 1997 Roper Poll in which 5 percent of Americans claimed never to eat red meat, the figure was 6 percent for women and only 4 percent for men. A man who chooses ratatouille over ribs risks aspersions over his sexual identity, as though swallowing compote earned one the derogatory epithet "fruit." . . .

For most of European history, meat has been a mark of power and privilege and a rare delicacy for the peasantry. The origins of "pecuniary" in *pecus*, the Latin word for herd, and of "capital" in *capita*, Latin for head (of cattle), are a reminder that meat was long a measure of wealth. Monks renounced flesh, to demonstrate their indifference to worldly advantage, and it was not until the twentieth century, when Colonel Sanders catered to the civilian infantry and even soup kitchens put a chicken in the pot, that the implications of flesh for class were reversed. Now the gentry sups on arugula, while plebeians munch meat loaf. . . .

Standards of decency change, and arbiters of etiquette have since adopted a more decent respect for the opinions of noncarnivorous mankind. "Dieters and teetotalers should never feel it necessary to eat anything that is injurious to their health or contrary to their moral standards," insists Emily Post. "If you are, for example, a vegetarian, you need not feel obliged to taste the roast." And Peggy Post, advising hosts, also counsels toleration: "When you're planning a larger party, you needn't ask each guest about food restrictions, but to be on the safe side, make sure you include some 'neutral' dishes such as a vegetable platter, pasta with meatless sauce, and fresh fruit for dessert. That way, everybody will find something he or she enjoys." If every host was required to read the Posts, vegetarianism would be less a matter of social martyrdom.

Manners were not minded in January 1998, when vegetarianism was put on trial in Amarillo, Texas. Oprah Winfrey was charged with violating the state's food defamation law. During one of her TV shows in April 1996, vegetarian activist Howard Lyman had warned about the spread of mad cow disease into American herds. Oprah replied: "It has just stopped me cold from eating another burger." After her statement was aired, the market for cattle dropped by about $36 million. Instead of a posse, angry ranchers organized a lawsuit. But the not-guilty verdict affirmed the rights of Americans, even in Texas, to avow in public their aversion to beef. . . .

It has long been easy to dismiss vegetarians as tender, feckless folk—like those who with Bronson Alcott created Fruitlands, the meat-free commune in nineteenth-century Massachusetts that lasted only seven months. They seem as quixotic as Esperantists, who plot world peace by evangelizing for a single artificial language. In fact, some Esperantists and vegetarians have been making gentle common cause since 1906, when they formed Tutmonda Esperantista Vegetariana Asocio.

Yet vegetarians today are more assertive. Many are no longer willing to settle for celery or gruel in schools, prisons, and restaurants. Airlines report an increase in requests for special meals. Passengers who reserve vegetarian entrées for their trips often draw envious stares from those nearby, who are forced to sate their appetites with standard fare. Airline food has probably done more than Leo Tolstoy to persuade our neighbors to pass up meat. . . .

BUT if vegetarianism has become more prominent and popular, it has also provoked a new backlash, one that differs from familiar strategies of ridicule and ostracism only in its defensiveness. Like determined smokers who continue to puff long after tobacco has been proved lethal, some meat-eaters protest too much. In *Eat Fat* (1996), for example, Richard Klein attacks what Orwell might call the food police, the voices heard throughout the land that inveigh against pandemic obesity. . . . Jeffrey Steingarten, too, attempts to stigmatize vegetarianism as a derangement. In *The Man Who Ate Everything* (1997), he celebrates his own omnivorousness and declares: "The more I contemplated food phobias, the more I became convinced that people who habitually avoid certifiably delicious foods are at least as troubled as people who avoid sex, or take no pleasure from it, except that the latter will probably seek psychiatric help, while food phobics rationalize their problem in the name of genetic inheritance, allergy, vegetarianism, matters of taste, nutrition, food safety, obesity, or a sensitive nature." Lacking evidence of meat's benefits for physical health, Steingarten and Klein presume that vegetarianism is harmful to mental health. Ignoring the ethical claims of vegetarianism, they can more easily dismiss it as dementia.

Assigned by a muckraking weekly called *Appeal to Reason* to investigate working conditions in the Chicago stockyards, Upton Sinclair was converted to vegetarianism—for merely three years, admittedly—by observing the process by which living animals are transformed into food. "One could not stand and watch very long without becoming philosophical, without beginning to deal in symbols and similes, and to hear the hog squeal of the universe," he wrote in *The Jungle*, the novel that provoked passage of the Pure Food and Drug Act of 1906. But Sinclair, who was more interested in the rights of workers than those of cattle, was disappointed at instigating food reform rather than industrial revolution. "I aimed at the public's heart and by accident I hit it in the stomach," he complained.

Yet the stomach is a more reliable organ. About as virtuous as the penis, the heart can lead us into bloody deeds, but the belly is a moral compass. Haunted by the hog squeal of the world, I will not stomach nourishment that requires processing pigs into pork, calves into veal, and turkeys into drumsticks. Foie gras might be deemed a delicacy, but my conscience is too delicate to countenance any sustenance that is obtained by thrusting a spike down the throat of a living goose. It is an ichthyophagist's self-serving fantasy that, as the StarKist ad contends, Charlie the Tuna yearns to be hooked, canned, and chewed. Kraft Foods would have us believe that the noblest avatar of a cow is the hot dog: "Oh I wish I was an Oscar Mayer wiener, for that is what I'd really like to be," goes the genial jingle, but the reality is much crueler. . . .

Once, in a remote foreign capital, a dinner was held in my honor. To salute my presence in their country, the hosts set out on my plate a whole roast suckling pig. I stared at the unfortunate creature, a victim of brutal culinary customs, and he stared back. Though the pig was the evening's pièce de résistance, I managed to resist. It was better to risk puzzling or antagonizing my benefactors than to bear forever the guilt of slaying a shoat. No human need eat meat, and we most honor our humanity when we do not.

Carlo Petrini (1949–)

THE ITALIAN FOUNDER of the enormously influential Slow Food Movement, Petrini first came to notice through his opposition to the quintessential fast food icon McDonald's when it sought to open a branch near the Spanish Steps in Rome. In 2004 he founded the University of Gastronomic Sciences in Piedmont, seeking to bridge gastronomy and agriculture. In the same way, the Slow Food Movement aims to preserve traditional methods of farming, heirloom seeds and plants, even traditional breeds of livestock; and it has been a major force in combating genetic engineering and pesticides, as well as in alerting consumers to the dangers of factory farms. Through Petrini's assiduous campaigning for its principles, the movement now has chapters worldwide and sponsors a biannual conference in Turin that brings together sympathetic farmers, producers, and food writers.

Slow Food Manifesto

BORN AND NURTURED under the sign of Industrialization, this century first invented the machine and then modeled its lifestyle after it. Speed became our shackles. We fell prey to the same virus: the fast life that fractures our customs and assails us even in our own homes, forcing us to ingest "fast-food."

Homo sapiens must regain wisdom and liberate itself from the "velocity" that is propelling it on the road to extinction. Let us defend ourselves against the universal madness of "the fast life" with tranquil material pleasure.

Against those—or, rather, the vast majority—who confuse efficiency with frenzy, we propose the vaccine of an adequate portion of sensual gourmandise pleasures, to be taken with slow and prolonged enjoyment.

Appropriately, we will start in the kitchen, with Slow Food. To escape the tediousness of "fast-food," let us rediscover the rich varieties and aromas of local cuisines.

In the name of productivity, the "fast life" has changed our lifestyle and now threatens our environment and our land (and city) scapes. Slow Food is the alternative, the avant-garde's riposte.

Real culture is here to be found. First of all, we can begin by cultivating taste, rather than impoverishing it, by stimulating progress, by encouraging international exchange programs, by endorsing worthwhile projects, by advocating historical food culture and by defending old-fashioned food traditions.

Slow Food assures us of a better-quality lifestyle. With a snail purposely chosen as its patron and symbol, it is an idea and a way of life that needs much sure but steady support.

᠀

Barbara Kingsolver (1955–)

A BEST-SELLING NOVELIST whose books include *The Bean Trees, The Poisonwood Bible*, and *The Prodigal Summer*, Kingsolver has always been concerned with the way human communities and natural ecology define our culture. To apply these issues to their own lives, she and her family moved in 2005 to a farm they inherited in Virginia, where they embarked on a year-long experiment: to raise almost all their own food, or at least to obtain from local farmers and neighbors what they could not raise themselves. Becoming passionate locavores, they not only rejected supermarket culture but threw themselves into farm life with all its gratifications and hard work. For a year their soil and their kitchen were the center of their existence. The resulting book, which includes contributions by Kingsolver's husband and teenage daughter, tells how they raised their own chickens, learned about seeds, and evolved into a one-family slow food movement as they sought to preserve heritage crops from extinction. In our selection from *Animal, Vegetable, Miracle: A Year of Food Life,* Kingsolver confronts the age-old problem of killing other beings in order to eat them. Her moral commitment is to raise each animal in the most benign of conditions and to show respect for the creature she has bred and is about to harvest.

from *Animal, Vegetable, Miracle:*
You Can't Run Away on Harvest Day

SEPTEMBER

THE Saturday of Labor Day weekend dawned with a sweet, translucent bite, like a Golden Delicious apple. I always seem to harbor a childlike hope through the berry-stained months of June and July that summer will be for keeps. But then a day comes in early fall to remind me why it should end, after all. In September the quality of daylight shifts toward flirtation. The green berries on the spicebush shrubs along our lane begin to blink red, first one and then another, like faltering but resolute holiday lights. The woods fill with the restless singing of migrant birds warming up to the proposition of flying south. The cool air makes us restless too: jeans and sweater weather, perfect for a hike. Steven and I rose early that morning, looked out the window, looked at each other, and started in on the time-honored marital grumble: Was this *your* idea?

We weren't going on a hike today. Nor would we have the postsummer Saturday luxury of sitting on the porch with a cup of coffee and watching the farm wake up. On the docket instead was a hard day of work we could not postpone. The previous morning we'd sequestered half a dozen roosters and as many tom turkeys in a room of the barn we call "death row." We hold poultry there, clean and comfortable with water but no food, for a twenty-four-hour fast prior to harvest. It makes the processing cleaner and seems to calm the animals also. I could tell you it gives them time to get their emotional affairs in order, if that helps. But they have limited emotional affairs, and no idea what's coming.

We had a lot more of both. Our plan for this gorgeous day was the removal of some of our animals from the world of the living into the realm of food. At five months of age our roosters had put on a good harvest weight, and had lately opened rounds of cockfighting, venting their rising hormonal angst against any moving target, including us. When a rooster flies up at you with his spurs, he leaves marks. Lily now had to arm herself with a length of pipe in order to gather the eggs. Our barnyard wasn't big enough for this much machismo. We would certainly take no pleasure in the chore, but it was high time for the testosterone-reduction program. We sighed at the lovely weather and pulled out our old, bloody sneakers for harvest day.

THERE was probably a time when I thought it euphemistic to speak of "harvesting" animals. Now I don't. We calculate "months to harvest" when planning for the right time to start poultry. We invite friends to "harvest parties," whether we'll be gleaning vegetable or animal. A harvest implies planning, respect, and effort. With animals, both the planning and physical effort are often greater, and respect for the enterprise is substantially more complex. It's a lot less fun than spending an autumn day picking apples off trees, but it's a similar operation on principle and the same word.

Killing is a culturally loaded term, for most of us inextricably tied up with some version of a command that begins, "Thou shalt not." Every faith has it. And for all but perhaps the Jainists of India, that command is absolutely conditional. We know it does not refer to mosquitoes. Who among us has never killed living creatures on purpose? When a child is sick with an infection we rush for the medicine spoon, committing an eager and purposeful streptococcus massacre. We sprinkle boric acid or grab a spray can to rid our kitchens of cockroaches. What we mean by "killing" is to take a life cruelly, as in murder—or else more accidentally as in "Oops, looks like I killed my African violet." Though the results are incomparable, what these different "killings" have in common is needless waste and some presumed measure of regret.

Most of us, if we know even a little about where our food comes from, understand that every bite put into our mouths since infancy (barring the odd rock or marble) was formerly alive. The blunt biological truth is that we animals can only remain alive by eating other life. Plants are inherently more blameless, having been born with the talent of whipping up their own food, peacefully and without noise, out of sunshine, water, and the odd mineral ingredient sucked up through their toes. Strangely enough, it's the animals to which we've assigned some rights, while the saintly plants we maim and behead with moral impunity. Who thinks to beg forgiveness while mowing the lawn?

The moral rules of destroying our fellow biota get even more tangled, the deeper we go. If we draw the okay-to-kill line between "animal" and "plant," and thus exclude meat, fowl, and fish from our diet on moral grounds, we still must live with the fact that every sack of flour and every soybean-based block of tofu came from a field where countless winged and furry lives were extinguished in the plowing, cultivating, and harvest. An estimated 67 million birds die each year from pesticide exposure on U.S. farms. Butterflies, too, are universally killed on contact in larval form by the genetically modified pollen contained in most U.S. corn. Foxes, rabbits, and bobolinks are starved out of their homes or dismembered by the sickle mower. Insects are "controlled" even by organic pesticides; earthworms are cut in half by the plow. Contrary to lore, they won't grow into two; both halves die.

To believe we can live without taking life is delusional. Humans may only cultivate nonviolence in our diets by degree. I've heard a Buddhist monk suggest the *number* of food-caused deaths is minimized in steak dinners, which share one death over many meals, whereas the equation is reversed for a bowl of clams. Others of us have lost heart for eating any steak dinner that's been shoved through the assembly line of feedlot life—however broadly we might share that responsibility. I take my gospel from Wendell Berry, who writes in *What Are People For?*, "I dislike the thought that some animal has been made miserable in order to feed me. If I am going to eat meat, I want it to be from an animal that has lived a pleasant, uncrowded life outdoors, on bountiful pasture, with good water nearby and trees for shade. And I am getting almost as fussy about food plants."

I find myself fundamentally allied with a vegetarian position in every way except one: however selectively, I eat meat. I'm unimpressed by arguments that condemn animal harvest while ignoring, wholesale, the animal killing that underwrites vegetal foods. Uncountable deaths by pesticide and habitat removal—the beetles and bunnies that die collaterally for our bread and veggie-burgers—are lives plumb wasted. Animal harvest is at least not gratuitous, as part of a plan involving labor and recompense. We raise these creatures for a reason. Such premeditation may be presumed unkind, but without it our gentle domestic beasts in their picturesque shapes, colors, and finely tuned purposes would never have had the distinction of existing. To envision a vegan version of civilization, start by erasing from all time the Three Little Pigs, the boy who cried wolf, *Charlotte's Web*, the golden calf, *Tess of the d'Urbervilles*. Next, erase civilization, brought to you by the people who learned to domesticate animals. Finally, rewrite our evolutionary history, since *Homo sapiens* became the species we are by means of regular binges of carnivory. . . .

Believing in the righteousness of a piece of work, alas, is not what gets it done. On harvest day we pulled on our stained shoes, sharpened our knives, lit a fire under the big kettle, and set ourselves to the whole show: mud, blood, and lots of little feathers. There are some things about a chicken harvest that are irrepressibly funny, and one of them is the feathers: in your hair, on the backs of your hands, dangling behind your left shoe the way toilet paper does in slapstick movies. Feathery little white tags end up stuck all over the chopping block and the butchering table like Post-it notes from the chicken hereafter. Sometimes we get through the awful parts on the strength of black comedy, joking about the feathers or our barn's death row and the "dead roosters walking."

But today was not one of those times. Some friends had come over to help us, including a family that had recently lost their teenage son in a drowning accident. Their surviving younger children, Abby and Eli, were among Lily's closest friends. The kids were understandably solemn and the adults measured all our words under the immense weight of grief as we set to work. Lily and Abby went to get the first rooster from the barn while I laid out the knives and spread plastic sheets over our butchering table on the back patio. The guys stoked a fire under our fifty-gallon kettle, an antique brass instrument Steven and I scored at a farm auction.

The girls returned carrying rooster #1 upside down, by the legs. Inversion has the immediate effect of lulling a chicken to sleep, or something near to it. What comes next is quick and final. We set the rooster gently across our big chopping block (a legendary fixture of our backyard, whose bloodstains hold visiting children in thrall), and down comes the ax. All sensation ends with that quick stroke. He must then be held by the legs over a large plastic bucket until all the blood has run out. Farmers who regularly process poultry have more equipment, including banks of "killing cones" or inverted funnels that contain the birds while the processor pierces each neck with a sharp knife, cutting two major arteries and ending brain function. We're not pros, so we have a more rudimentary setup. By lulling and swiftly decapitating my animal, I can make sure my relatively unpracticed handling won't draw out the procedure or cause pain.

What you've heard is true: the rooster will flap his wings hard during this part. If you drop him he'll thrash right across the yard, unpleasantly spewing blood all around, though the body doesn't *run*—it's nothing that well coordinated. His newly detached head silently opens and closes its mouth, down in the bottom of the gut bucket, a world apart from the ruckus. The cause of all these actions is an explosion of massively firing neurons without a brain to supervise them. Most people who claim to be running around like a chicken with its head cut off, really, are not even close. The nearest thing might be the final convulsive seconds of an All Star wrestling match.

For Rooster #1 it was over, and into the big kettle for a quick scald. After a one-minute immersion in 145-degree water, the muscle tissue releases the feathers so they're easier to pluck. "Easier" is relative—every last feather still has to be pulled, carefully enough to avoid tearing the skin. The downy breast feathers come out by handfuls, while the long wing and tail feathers sometimes must be removed individually with pliers. If we were pros we would have an electric scalder and automatic plucker, a fascinating bucket full of rotating rubber fingers that does the job in no time flat. For future harvests we might borrow a friend's equipment, but for today we had a pulley on a tree limb so we could hoist the scalded carcass to shoulder level, suspending it there from a rope so several of us could pluck at once. Lily, Abby, and Eli pulled neck and breast feathers, making necessary observations such as "Gag, look where his head came off," and "Wonder which one of these tube thingies was his windpipe." Most kids need only about ninety seconds to get from *eeew gross* to solid science. A few weeks later Abby would give an award-winning, fully illustrated 4-H presentation entitled "You Can't Run Away on Harvest Day."

Laura and Becky and I answered the kids' questions, and also talked about Mom things while working on back and wing feathers. (Our husbands were on to the next beheading.) Laura and I compared notes on our teenage daughters—relatively new drivers on the narrow country roads between their jobs, friends, and home—and the worries that come with that territory. I was painfully conscious of Becky's quiet, her ache for a teenage son who never even got to acquire a driver's license. The accident that killed Larry could not have been avoided through any amount of worry. We all cultivate illusions of safety that could fall away in the knife edge of one second.

I wondered how we would get through this afternoon, how *she* would get through months and years of living with impossible loss. I wondered if I'd been tactless, inviting these dear friends to an afternoon of ending lives.

And then felt stupid for that thought. People who are grieving walk with death, every waking moment. When the rest of us dread that we'll somehow remind them of death's existence, we are missing their reality. Harvesting turkeys—which this family would soon do on their own farm—was just another kind of work. A rendezvous with death, for them, was waking up each morning without their brother and son.

By early afternoon six roosters had lost their heads, feathers, and viscera, and were chilling on ice. We had six turkeys to go, the hardest piece of our work simply because the animals are larger and heavier. Some of these birds were close to twenty pounds. They would take center stage on our holiday table and those of some of our friends. At least one would be charcuterie—in the garden I had sage, rosemary, garlic, onions, everything we needed for turkey sausage. And the first two roosters we'd harvested would be going on the rotisserie later that afternoon.

And that was the end of a day's work. I hosed down the butcher shop and changed into more civilized attire (happy to see my wedding ring was still on) while everybody else set the big picnic table on our patio with plates and glasses and all the food in the fridge we'd prepared ahead. The meat on the rotisserie smelled really good, helping to move our party's mindset toward the end stages of the "cooking from scratch" proposition. Steven brushed the chicken skin with our house-specialty sweet-and-sour sauce and we uncorked the wine. At dusk we finally sat down to feast on cold bean salad, sliced tomatoes with basil, blue potato salad, and meat that had met this day's dawn by crowing.

Michael Pollan (1955–)

AMONG THE BEST-KNOWN contemporary American writers on food, Michael Pollan is an heir to the counterculture and back-to-the-land movement of the 1960s who has been dubbed "a liberal foodie intellectual." He has written such classics as *The Botany of Desire* and *The Omnivore's Dilemma*. In the former he recounts the myths surrounding apples, tulips, marijuana, and potatoes. In the latter he treats four different modes of food production: the corn-based industrial operation; the large corporate organic model; the small, local self-sufficient farm; and the ways of the hunter-forager. Currently a professor of journalism at the University of California, Berkeley, and a prolific lecturer on gastronomy, agriculture, health, and the environment, Pollan was listed by *Time* in 2010 as one of the world's hundred most influential persons. In our selection, he describes the horrifying circumstances in which beef cattle are currently raised. His report, from *The Omnivore's Dilemma*, implicitly expands on the extract from Upton Sinclair's *The Jungle* included in Part I of this collection. And like Sinclair's powerful writing, Pollan's journalism reveals a mind that is scientific, aesthetic, witty, and sagacious.

from *The Omnivore's Dilemma*: Cattle Metropolis

THE LANDSCAPE THAT corn has made in the American Middle West is unmistakable: It forms a second great American lawn, unfurling through the summer like an absurdly deep-pile carpet of green across the vast lands drained by the Mississippi River. Corn the plant has colonized some 125,000 square miles of the American continent, an area twice the size of New York State; even from outer space you can't miss it. It takes a bit more looking, however, to see some of the other landscapes that corn the commodity has created, in obscure places like Garden City, Kansas. Here in the high plains of western Kansas is where America's first feedlots were built, beginning in the early fifties.

You'll be speeding down one of Finney County's ramrod roads when the empty, dun-colored January prairie suddenly turns black and geometric, an urban grid of steel-fenced rectangles as far as the eye can see—which in Kansas is really far. I say "suddenly" but in fact the swiftly rising odor—an aroma whose Proustian echoes are decidedly more bus station men's room than cows in the country—has been heralding the feedlot's approach for more than a mile. And then it's upon you: Poky Feeders, population, thirty-seven thousand. A sloping subdivision of cattle pens stretches to the horizon, each one home to a hundred or so animals standing dully or lying around in a grayish mud that, it eventually dawns on you, isn't mud at all. The pens line a network of unpaved roads that loop around vast waste lagoons on their way to the feedyard's thunderously beating heart and dominating landmark: a rhythmically chugging feed mill that rises, soaring and silvery in the early morning light, like an industrial cathedral in the midst of a teeming metropolis of meat. As it does twelve hours a day seven days a week, the mill is noisily converting America's river of corn into cattle feed.

I'd traveled to Poky early one January with the slightly improbable notion of visiting one particular resident, though as I nosed my rental car through the feedlot's rolling black sea of bovinity, I began to wonder if this was realistic. I was looking for a young black steer with three white blazes on his face that I'd met the previous fall on a ranch in Vale, South Dakota, five hundred miles due north of here. In fact, the steer I hoped to find belonged to me: I'd purchased him as an eight-month-old calf from the Blair Ranch for $598. I was paying Poky Feeders $1.60 a day for his room and board (all the corn he could eat) and meds.

My interest in this steer was not strictly financial, or even gustatory. No, my primary interest in this animal was educational. I wanted to learn how the industrial food chain transforms bushels of corn into steaks. How do you enlist so unlikely a creature—for the cow is an herbivore by nature—to help dispose of America's corn surplus? By far the biggest portion of a bushel of American commodity corn (about 60 percent of it, or some fifty-four thousand kernels) goes to feeding livestock, and much of that goes to feeding America's 100 million beef cattle—cows and bulls and steers that in times past spent most of their lives grazing on grasses out on the prairie.

America's food animals have undergone a revolution in lifestyle in the years since World War II. At the same time much of America's human population found itself leaving the city for the suburbs, our food animals found themselves traveling in the opposite direction, leaving widely dispersed farms in places like Iowa to live in densely populated new animal cities. These places are so different from farms and ranches that a new term was needed to denote them: CAFO—Confined Animal Feeding Operation. The new animal and human landscapes were both products of government policy. The postwar suburbs would never have been built if not for the interstate highway system, as well as the G.I Bill and federally subsidized mortgages. The urbanization of America's animal population would never have taken place if not for the advent of cheap, federally subsidized corn.

Corn itself profited from the urbanization of livestock twice. As the animals left the farm, more of the farm was left for corn, which rapidly colonized the paddocks and pastures and even the barnyards that had once been the animals' territory. The animals left because the farmers simply couldn't compete with the CAFOs. It cost a farmer more to grow feed corn than it cost a CAFO to buy it, for the simple reason that commodity corn now was routinely sold for less than it cost to grow. Corn profited again as the factory farms expanded, absorbing increasing amounts of its surplus. Corn found its way into the diet of animals that never used to eat very much of it (like cattle) or any corn at all, like the farmed salmon now being bred to tolerate grain. All that excess biomass has to go somewhere.

The economic logic of gathering so many animals together to feed them cheap corn in CAFOs is hard to argue with; it has made meat, which used to be a special occasion in most American homes, so cheap and abundant that many of us now eat it three times a day. Not so compelling is the biological logic behind this cheap meat. Already in their short history CAFOs have produced more than their share of environmental and health problems: polluted water and air, toxic wastes, novel and deadly pathogens.

Raising animals on old-fashioned mixed farms such as the Naylors' used to make simple biological sense: You can feed them the waste products of your crops, and you can feed their waste products to your crops. In fact, when animals live on farms the very idea of waste ceases to exist; what you have instead is a closed ecological loop—what in retrospect you might call a solution. One of the most striking things that animal feedlots do (to paraphrase Wendell Berry) is to take this elegant solution and neatly divide it into two new problems: a fertility problem on the farm (which must be remedied with chemical fertilizers) and a pollution problem on the feedlot (which seldom is remedied at all).

This biological absurdity, characteristic of all CAFOs, is compounded in the cattle feedyard by a second absurdity. Here animals exquisitely adapted by natural selection to live on grass must be adapted by us—at considerable cost to their health, to the health of the land, and ultimately to the health of their eaters—to live on corn, for no other reason than it offers the cheapest calories around and because the great pile must be consumed. This is why I decided to follow the trail of industrial corn through a single steer rather than, say, a chicken or a pig, which can get by just fine on a diet of grain: The short, unhappy life of a corn-fed feedlot steer represents the ultimate triumph of industrial thinking over the logic of evolution.

⁂

Eric Schlosser (1959–)

IT'S PROBABLE THAT no book since *Fast Food Nation: The Dark Side of the All-American Meal* has so awakened America to methods of restrictive animal confinement, assembly line practices at slaughterhouses, the uniformity of mass produced meals at fast food outlets, and the illnesses that accrue from eating such food, laden as it is with fat and cholesterol and given how seductively it has become a mainstay of the national diet. In calling attention to the problematic quality of industrially produced meals, Schlosser sought to publicize a growing national health problem. Not surprisingly when he undertook the research for *Fast Food Nation,* which was on the *New York Times* best-seller list for two years and become a 2006 film with the same title, he was denied access to meatpacking plants and was refused interviews with executives at McDonald's, though he managed to arrange many meetings with workers on the line. As our excerpt shows, thing have not changed greatly from the early days of Upton Sinclair and the Chicago stockyards, so the passionate muckraking continues.

from *Fast Food Nation*: The Worst

SOME OF THE most dangerous jobs in meatpacking today are performed by the late-night cleaning crews. A large proportion of these workers are illegal immigrants. They are considered "independent contractors," employed not by the meatpacking firms but by sanitation companies. They earn hourly wages that are about one-third lower than those of regular production employees. And their work is so hard and so horrendous that words seem inadequate to describe it. The men and women who now clean the nation's slaughterhouses may arguably have the worst job in the United States. "It takes a really dedicated person," a former member of a cleaning crew told me, "or a really desperate person to get the job done."

When a sanitation crew arrives at a meatpacking plant, usually around midnight, it faces a mess of monumental proportions. Three to four thousand cattle, each weighing about a thousand pounds, have been slaughtered there that day. The place has to be clean by sunrise. Some of the workers wear water-resistant clothing; most don't. Their principal cleaning tool is a high-pressure hose that shoots a mixture of water and chlorine heated to about 180 degrees. As the water is sprayed, the plant fills with a thick, heavy fog. Visibility drops to as little as five feet. The conveyor belts and machinery are running. Workers stand on the belts, spraying them, riding them like moving sidewalks, as high as fifteen feet off the ground. Workers climb ladders with hoses and spray the catwalks. They get under tables and conveyer belts, climbing right into the bloody muck, cleaning out grease, fat, manure, leftover scraps of meat.

Glasses and safety goggles fog up. The inside of the plant heats up; temperatures soon exceed 100 degrees. "It's hot, and it's foggy, and you can't see anything," a former sanitation worker said. The crew members can't see or hear each other when the machinery's running. They routinely spray each other with burning hot, chemical-laden water. They are sickened by the fumes. Jesus, a soft-spoken employee of DCS Sanitation Management, Inc., the company that IBP uses in many of its plants, told me that every night on the job he gets terrible headaches. "You feel it in your head," he said. "You feel it in your stomach, like you want to throw up." A friend of his vomits whenever they clean the rendering area. Other workers tease the young man as he retches. Jesus says the stench in rendering is so powerful that it won't wash off; no matter how much soap you use after a shift, the smell comes home with you, seeps from your pores.

One night while Jesus was cleaning, a coworker forgot to turn off a machine, lost two fingers, and went into shock. An ambulance came and took him away, as everyone else continued to clean. He was back at work the following week. "If one hand is no good," the supervisor told him, "use the other." Another sanitation worker lost an arm in a machine. Now he folds towels in the locker room. The scariest job, according to Jesus, is cleaning the vents on the roof of the slaughterhouse. The vents become clogged with grease and dried blood. In the winter, when everything gets icy and the winds pick up, Jesus worries that a sudden gust will blow him off the roof into the darkness.

Although official statistics are not kept, the death rate among slaughterhouse sanitation crews is extraordinarily high. They are the ultimate in disposable workers: illegal, illiterate, impoverished, untrained. The nation's worst job can end in just about the worst way. Sometimes these workers are literally ground up and reduced to nothing.

A brief description of some cleaning-crew accidents over the past decade says more about the work and the danger than any set of statistics. At the Monfort plant in Grand Island, Nebraska, Richard Skala was beheaded by a dehiding machine. Carlos Vincente—an employee of T and G Service Company, a twenty-eight-year-old Guatemalan who'd been in the United States for only a week—was pulled into the cogs of a conveyor belt at an Excel plant in Fort Morgan, Colorado, and torn apart. Lorenzo Marin, Sr., an employee of DCS Sanitation, fell from the top of a skinning machine while cleaning it with a high-pressure hose, struck his head on the concrete floor of an IBP plant in Columbus Junction, Iowa, and died. Another employee of DCS Sanitation, Salvador Hernandez-Gonzalez, had his head crushed by a pork-loin processing machine at an IBP plant in Madison, Nebraska. The same machine had fatally crushed the head of another worker, Ben Barone, a few years earlier. At a National Beef plant in Liberal, Kansas, Homer Stull climbed into a blood-collection tank to clean it, a filthy tank thirty feet high. Stull was overcome by hydrogen sulfide fumes. Two coworkers climbed into the tank and tried to rescue him. All three men died. Eight years earlier, Henry Wolf had been overcome by hydrogen sulfide fumes while cleaning the very same tank; Gary Sanders had tried to rescue him; both men died; and the Occupational Safety and Health Administration (OSHA) later fined National Beef for its negligence. The fine was $480 for each man's death.

꧁

David Foster Wallace (1962–2008)

ONE OF THE most widely read young novelists of the late twentieth and early twenty-first centuries, Wallace also wrote short stories and essays. His fiction is highly innovative, and often very long; for instance, his most renowned work, *Infinite Jest*, bulks to 1100 pages. Affected by a long and severe depression, Wallace hanged himself at age forty-six. During his brief lifetime, he wrote with engaging curiosity about a multitude of subjects, including tennis, travel, conservative talk radio, the porn industry, and state fairs. He loved offbeat venues, and in our selection he visits the annual Maine Lobster Festival, focusing here on the issue of whether lobsters are able to feel pain when plunged into boiling water. Part discussion of animal ethics, part discussion of comparative neuroanatomy, the essay takes no position on the matter, but the "consider" of the title means two things— think about the lobster and be kind to it—and Wallace means for us to take such considerations very seriously.

from Consider the Lobster

A DETAIL SO obvious that most recipes don't even bother to mention it is that each lobster is supposed to be alive when you put it in the kettle. This is part of lobster's modern appeal—it's the freshest food there is. There's no decomposition between harvesting and eating. And not only do lobsters require no cleaning or dressing or plucking, they're relatively easy for vendors to keep alive. They come up alive in the traps, are placed in containers of seawater, and can—so long as the water's aerated and the animals' claws are pegged or banded to keep them from tearing one another up under the stresses of captivity—survive right up until they're boiled. Most of us have been in supermarkets or restaurants that feature tanks of live lobsters, from which you can pick out your supper while it watches you point. And part of the overall spectacle of the Maine Lobster Festival is that you can see actual lobstermen's vessels docking at the wharves along the northeast grounds and unloading fresh-caught product, which is transferred by hand or cart 150 yards to the great clear tanks stacked up around the festival's cooker—which is, as mentioned, billed as the World's Largest Lobster Cooker and can process over 100 lobsters at a time for the Main Eating Tent.

So then here is a question that's all but unavoidable at the World's Largest Lobster Cooker, and may arise in kitchens across the US: Is it all right to boil a sentient creature alive just for our gustatory pleasure? A related set of concerns: Is the previous question irksomely PC or sentimental? What does "all right" even mean in this context? Is the whole thing just a matter of personal choice?

As you may or may not know, a certain well-known group called People for the Ethical Treatment of Animals thinks that the morality of lobster-boiling is not just a matter of individual conscience. In fact, one of the very first things we hear about the MLF . . . well, to set the scene: We're coming in by cab from the almost indescribably odd and rustic Knox County Airport very late on the night before the festival opens, sharing the cab with a wealthy political consultant who lives on Vinalhaven Island in the bay half the year (he's headed for the island ferry in Rockland). The consultant and cabdriver are responding to informal journalistic probes about how people who live in the midcoast region actually view the MLF, as in is the festival just a big-dollar tourist thing or is it something local residents look forward to attending, take genuine civic pride in, etc. The cabdriver (who's in his seventies, one of apparently a whole platoon of retirees the cab company puts on to help with the summer rush, and wears a US-flag lapel pin, and drives in what can only be called a very *deliberate* way) assures us that locals do endorse and enjoy the MLF, although he himself hasn't gone in years, and now come to think of it no one he and his wife know has, either. However, the demilocal consultant's been to recent festivals a couple times (one gets the impression it was at his wife's behest), of which his most vivid impression was that "you have to line up for an ungodly long time to get your lobsters, and meanwhile there are all these ex-flower children coming up and down along the line handling out pamphlets that say the lobsters die in terrible pain and you shouldn't eat them."

And it turns out that the post-hippies of the consultant's recollection were activists from PETA. There were no PETA people in obvious view at the 2003 MLF, but they've been conspicuous at many of the recent festivals. Since at least the mid-1990s, articles in everything from the *Camden Herald* to the *New York Times* have described PETA urging boycotts of the Maine Lobster Festival, often deploying celebrity spokesmen like Mary Tyler Moore for open letters and ads saying stuff like "Lobsters are extraordinarily sensitive" and "To me, eating a lobster is out of the question." More concrete is the oral testimony of Dick, our florid and extremely gregarious rental-car liaison, to the effect that PETA's been around so much during recent years that a kind of brittlely tolerant homeostasis now obtains between the activists and the festival's locals, e.g.: "We had some incidents a couple years ago. One lady took most of her clothes off and painted herself like a lobster, almost got herself arrested. But for the most part they're let alone. [Rapid series of small ambiguous laughs, which with Dick happens a lot.] They do their thing and we do our thing."

This whole interchange takes place on Route 1, 30 July, during a four-mile, 50-minute ride from the airport to the dealership to sign car-rental papers. Several irreproducible segues down the road from the PETA anecdotes, Dick—whose son-in-law happens to be a professional lobsterman and one of the Main Eating Tent's regular suppliers—explains what he and his family feel is the crucial mitigating factor in the whole morality-of-boiling-lobsters-alive issue: "There's a part of the brain in people and animals that lets us feel pain, and lobsters' brains don't have this part."

Besides the fact that it's incorrect in about nine different ways, the main reason Dick's statement is interesting is that its thesis is more or less echoed by the festival's own pronouncement on lobsters and pain, which is part of a Test Your Lobster IQ quiz that appears in the 2003 MLF program courtesy of the Maine Lobster Promotion Council:

> The nervous system of a lobster is very simple, and is in fact most similar to the nervous system of the grasshopper. It is decentralized with no brain. There is no cerebral cortex, which in humans is the area of the brain that gives the experience of pain.

Though it sounds more sophisticated, a lot of the neurology in this latter claim is still either false or fuzzy. The human cerebral cortex is the brain-part that deals with higher faculties like reason, metaphysical self-awareness, language, etc. Pain reception is known to be part of a much older and more primitive system of nociceptors and prostaglandins that are managed by the brain stem and thalamus. On the other hand, it is true that the cerebral cortex is involved in what's variously called suffering, distress, or the emotional experience of pain—i.e., experiencing painful stimuli as unpleasant, very unpleasant, unbearable, and so on.

Before we go any further, let's acknowledge that the questions of whether and how different kinds of animals feel pain, and of whether and why it might be justifiable to inflict pain on them in order to eat them, turn out to be extremely complex and difficult. And comparative neuroanatomy is only part of the problem. Since pain is a totally subjective mental experience, we do not have direct access to anyone or anything's pain but our own; and even just the principles by which we can infer that other human beings experience pain and have a legitimate interest in not feeling pain involve hard-core philosophy—metaphysics, epistemology, value theory, ethics. The fact that even the most highly evolved nonhuman mammals can't use language to communicate with us about their subjective mental experience is only the first layer of additional complication in trying to extend our reasoning about pain and morality to animals. And everything gets progressively more abstract and convolved as we move farther and farther out from the higher-type mammals into cattle and swine and dogs and cats and rodents, and then birds and fish, and finally invertebrates like lobsters.

The more important point here, though, is that the whole animal-cruelty-and-eating issue is not just complex, it's also uncomfortable. It is, at any rate, uncomfortable for me, and for just about everyone I know who enjoys a variety of foods and yet does not want to see herself as cruel or unfeeling. As far as I can tell, my own main way of dealing with this conflict has been to avoid thinking about the whole unpleasant thing. I should add that it appears to me unlikely that many readers of *Gourmet* wish to think about it, either, or to be queried about the morality of their eating habits in the pages of a culinary monthly. Since, however, the assigned subject of this article is what it was like to attend the 2003 MLF, and thus to spend several days in the midst of a great mass of Americans all eating lobster, and thus to be more or less impelled to think hard about lobster and the experience of buying and eating lobster, it turns out that there is no honest way to avoid certain moral questions.

There are several reasons for this. For one thing, it's not just that lobsters get boiled alive, it's that you do it yourself—or at least it's done specifically for you, on-site. As mentioned, the World's Largest Lobster Cooker, which is highlighted as an attraction in the festival's program, is right out there on the MLF's north grounds for everyone to see. Try to imagine a Nebraska Beef Festival at which part of the festivities is watching trucks pull up and the live cattle get driven down the ramp and slaughtered right there on the World's Largest Killing Floor or something—there's no way.

The intimacy of the whole thing is maximized at home, which of course is where most lobster gets prepared and eaten (although note already the semiconscious euphemism "prepared," which in the case of lobster really means killing them right there in our kitchens). The basic scenario is that we come in from the store and make our little preparations like getting the kettle filled and boiling, and then we lift the lobsters out of the bag or whatever retail container they came home in . . . whereupon some uncomfortable things start to happen. However stuporous a lobster is from the trip home, for instance, it tends to come alarmingly to life when placed in boiling water. If you're tilting it from a container into the steaming kettle, the lobster will sometimes try to cling to the container's sides or even to hook its claws over the kettle's rim like a person trying to keep from going over the edge of a roof. And worse is when the lobster's fully immersed. Even if you cover the kettle and turn away, you can usually hear the cover rattling and clanking as the lobster tries to push it off. Or the creature's claws scraping the sides of the kettle as it thrashes around. The lobster, in other words, behaves very much as you or I would behave if we were plunged into boiling water (with the obvious exception of screaming). A blunter way to say this is that the lobster acts as if it's in terrible pain, causing some cooks to leave the kitchen altogether and to take one of those little lightweight plastic oven-timers with them into another room and wait until the whole process is over.

THERE happen to be two main criteria that most ethicists agree on for determining whether a living creature has the capacity to suffer and so has genuine interests that it may or may not be our moral duty to consider. One is how much of the neurological hardware required for pain-experience the animal comes equipped with—nociceptors, prostaglandins, neuronal opioid receptors, etc. The other criterion is whether the animal demonstrates behavior associated with pain. And it takes a lot of intellectual gymnastics and behaviorist hairsplitting not to see struggling, thrashing, and lidclattering as just such pain-behavior. According to marine zoologists, it usually takes lobsters between 35 and 45 seconds to die in boiling water. (No source I could find talks about how long it takes them to die in superheated steam; one rather hopes it's faster.)

There are, of course, other ways to kill your lobster on-site and so achieve maximum freshness. Some cooks' practice is to drive a sharp heavy knife point-first into a spot just above the midpoint between the lobster's eyestalks (more or less where the Third Eye is in human foreheads). This is alleged either to kill the lobster instantly or to render it insensate, and is said at least to eliminate some of the cowardice involved in throwing a creature into boiling water and then fleeing the room. As far as I can tell from talking to proponents of the knife-in-head method, the idea is that it's more violent but ultimately more merciful, plus that a willingness to exert personal agency and accept responsibility for stabbing the lobster's head honors the lobster somehow and entitles one to eat it (there's often a vague sort of Native American spirituality-of-the-hunt flavor to pro-knife arguments). But the problem with the knife method is basic biology: Lobsters' nervous systems operate off not one but several ganglia, a.k.a. nerve bundles, which are sort of wired in series and distributed all along the lobster's underside, from stem to stern. And disabling only the frontal ganglion does not normally result in quick death or unconsciousness.

Another alternative is to put the lobster in cold saltwater and then very slowly bring it up to a full boil. Cooks who advocate this method are going on the analogy to a frog, which can supposedly be kept from jumping out of a boiling pot by heating the water incrementally. In order to save a lot of research-summarizing, I'll simply assure you that the analogy between frogs and lobsters turns out not to hold—plus, if the kettle's water isn't aerated seawater, the immersed lobster suffers from slow suffocation, although usually not decisive enough suffocation to keep it from still thrashing and clattering when the water gets hot enough to kill it. In fact, lobsters boiled incrementally often display a whole bonus set of gruesome, convulsionlike reactions that you don't see in regular boiling.

Ultimately, the only certain virtues of the home-lobotomy and slow-heating methods are comparative, because there are even worse/crueler ways people prepare lobster. Time-thrifty cooks sometimes microwave them alive (usually after poking several vent-holes in the carapace, which is a precaution most shellfish-microwavers learn about the hard way). Live dismemberment, on the other hand, is big in Europe—some chefs cut the lobster in half before cooking; others like to tear off the claws and tail and toss only these parts into the pot.

And there's more unhappy news respecting suffering-criterion number one. Lobsters don't have much in the way of eyesight or hearing, but they do have an exquisite tactile sense, one facilitated by hundreds of thousands of tiny hairs that protrude through their carapace. "Thus it is," in the words of T.M. Prudden's industry classic *About Lobster*, "that although encased in what seems a solid, impenetrable armor, the lobster can receive stimuli and impressions from without as readily as if it possessed a soft and delicate skin." And lobsters do have nociceptors, as well as invertebrate versions of the prostaglandins and major neurotransmitters via which our own brains register pain.

Lobsters do not, on the other hand, appear to have the equipment for making or absorbing natural opioids like endorphins and enkephalins, which are what more advanced nervous systems use to try to handle intense pain. From this fact, though, one could conclude either that lobsters are maybe even *more* vulnerable to pain, since they lack mammalian nervous systems' built-in analgesia, or, instead, that the absence of natural opioids implies an absence of the really intense pain-sensations that natural opioids are designed to mitigate. I for one can detect a marked upswing in mood as I contemplate this latter possibility. It could be that their lack of endorphin/enkephalin hardware means that lobsters' raw subjective experience of pain is so radically different from mammals' that it may not even deserve the term "pain." Perhaps lobsters are more like those frontal-lobotomy patients one reads about who report experiencing pain in a totally different way than you and I. These patients evidently do feel physical pain, neurologically speaking, but don't dislike it—though neither do they like it; it's more that they feel it but don't feel anything *about* it—the point being that the pain is not distressing to them or something they want to get away from. Maybe lobsters, who are also without frontal lobes, are detached from the neurological-registration-of-injury-or-hazard we call pain in just the same way. There is, after all, a difference between (1) pain as a purely neurological event, and (2) actual suffering, which seems crucially to involve an emotional component, an awareness of pain as unpleasant, as something to fear/dislike/want to avoid.

Still, after all the abstract intellection, there remain the facts of the frantically clanking lid, the pathetic clinging to the edge of the pot. Standing at the stove, it is hard to deny in any meaningful way that this is a living creature experiencing pain and wishing to avoid/escape the painful experience. To my lay mind, the lobster's behavior in the kettle appears to be the expression of a *preference*; and it may well be that an ability to form preferences is the decisive criterion for real suffering. The logic of this (preference → suffering) relation may be easiest to see in the negative case. If you cut certain kinds of worms in half, the halves will often keep crawling around and going about their vermiform business as if nothing had happened. When we assert, based on their post-op behavior, that these worms appear not to be suffering, what we're really saying is that there's no sign the worms know anything bad has happened or would *prefer* not to have gotten cut in half.

Lobsters, though, are known to exhibit preferences. Experiments have shown that they can detect changes of only a degree or two in water temperature; one reason for their complex migratory cycles (which can often cover 100-plus miles a year) is to pursue the temperatures they like best. And, as mentioned, they're bottom-dwellers and do not like bright light—if a tank of food-lobsters is out in the sunlight or a store's fluorescence, the lobsters will always congregate in whatever part is darkest. Fairly solitary in the ocean, they also clearly dislike the crowding that's part of their captivity in tanks, since (as also mentioned) one reason why lobster's claws are banded on capture is to keep them from attacking one another under the stress of close-quarter storage.

In any event, at the Festival, standing by the bubbling tanks outside the World's Largest Lobster Cooker, watching the fresh-caught lobsters pile over one another, wave their hobbled claws impotently, huddle in the rear corners, or scrabble frantically back from the glass as you approach, it is difficult not to sense that they're unhappy, or frightened, even if it's some rudimentary version of these feelings . . . and, again, why does rudimentariness even enter into it? Why is a primitive, inarticulate form of suffering less urgent or uncomfortable for the person who's helping to inflict it by paying for the food it results in? I'm not trying to give you a PETA-like screed here—at least I don't think so. I'm trying, rather, to work out and articulate some of the troubling questions that arise amid all the laughter and saltation and community pride of the Maine Lobster Festival. The truth is that if you, the Festival attendee, permit yourself to think that lobsters can suffer and would rather not, the MLF can begin to take on aspects of something like a Roman circus or medieval torture-fest.

Does that comparison seem a bit much? If so, exactly why? Or what about this one: Is it not possible that future generations will regard our own present agribusiness and eating practices in much the same way we now view Nero's entertainments or Aztec sacrifices? My own immediate reaction is that such a comparison is hysterical, extreme—and yet the reason it seems extreme to me appears to be that I believe animals are less morally important than human beings; and when it comes to defending such a belief, even to myself, I have to acknowledge that (a) I have an obvious selfish interest in this belief, since I like to eat certain kinds of animals and want to be able to keep doing it, and (b) I have not succeeded in working out any sort of personal ethical system in which the belief is truly defensible instead of just selfishly convenient.

Given this article's venue and my own lack of culinary sophistication, I'm curious about whether the reader can identify with any of these reactions and acknowledgments and discomforts. I am also concerned not to come off as shrill or preachy when what I really am is confused. Given the (possible) moral status and (very possible) physical suffering of the animals involved, what ethical convictions do gourmets evolve that allow them not just to eat but to savor and enjoy flesh-based viands (since of course refined *enjoyment*, rather than just ingestion, is the whole point of gastronomy)? And for those gourmets who'll have no truck with convictions or rationales and who regard stuff like the previous paragraph as just so much pointless navel-gazing, what makes it feel okay, inside, to dismiss the whole issue out of hand? That is, is their refusal to think about any of this the product of actual thought, or is it just that they don't want to think about it? Do they ever think about their reluctance to think about it? After all, isn't being extra aware and attentive and thoughtful about one's food and its overall context part of what distinguishes a real gourmet? Or is all the gourmet's extra attention and sensibility just supposed to be aesthetic, gustatory?

These last couple queries, though, while sincere, obviously involve much larger and more abstract questions about the connections (if any) between aesthetics and morality, and these questions lead straightaway into such deep and treacherous waters that it's probably best to stop the public discussion right here. There are limits to what even interested persons can ask of each other.

፞ॐ

PETA (People for the Ethical Treatment of Animals, founded 1980)

PEOPLE FOR THE Ethical Treatment of Animals, an animal rights group known by the acronym PETA, has upwards of three million members and a complex reputation. On the one hand, it has been celebrated for spearheading public awareness of abuses in the industrial killing of domesticated animals; for exposing cruel conditions on many breeding farms and for calling attention to the misuse of animals in laboratory experiments for medical research and product testing. On the other hand, PETA has been controversial for its aggressive protests and zealous undercover operations in slaughterhouses and circuses. Some scare tactics—for instance, a comic book for kids titled *Your Mommy Kills Animals*—have brought widespread condemnation. PETA has likened animals killed for food, however humanely, to African-American slaves and to Jews murdered by the Nazis (one campaign spoke of "the Holocaust on your plate"), a position which echoes points made by such vegetarians as Isaac Bashevis Singer and J.M. Coetzee but which has nonetheless offended some civil rights groups.

The Natural Human Diet

WHEN YOU SEE dead animals on the side of the road, are you tempted to stop and snack on them? Does the sight of a dead bird make you salivate? Do you daydream about killing cows with your bare hands and eating them raw? If you answered "no" to these questions, congratulations—like it or not, you're an herbivore.

According to biologists and anthropologists who study our anatomy and our evolutionary history, humans are herbivores who are not well suited to eating meat. Humans lack both the physical characteristics of carnivores and the instinct that drives them to kill animals and devour their raw carcasses.

HUMAN PHYSIOLOGY

ALTHOUGH many humans choose to eat a wide variety of plant and animal foods, earning us the dubious title of "omnivore," we are anatomically herbivorous.

TEETH, JAWS, AND NAILS

HUMANS have short, soft fingernails and pathetically small "canine" teeth. In contrast, carnivores all have sharp claws and large canine teeth capable of tearing flesh.

Carnivores' jaws move only up and down, requiring them to tear chunks of flesh from their prey and swallow them whole. Humans and other herbivores can move their jaws up and down and from side to side, allowing them to grind up fruit and vegetables with their back teeth. Like other herbivores' teeth, human back molars are flat for grinding fibrous plant foods. Carnivores lack these flat molars.

Dr. Richard Leakey, a renowned anthropologist, summarizes, "You can't tear flesh by hand, you can't tear hide by hand. Our anterior teeth are not suited for tearing flesh or hide. We don't have large canine teeth, and we wouldn't have been able to deal with food sources that require those large canines."

STOMACH ACIDITY

CARNIVORES swallow their food whole, relying on their extremely acidic stomach juices to break down flesh and kill the dangerous bacteria in meat that would otherwise sicken or kill them. Our stomach acids are much weaker in comparison because strong acids aren't needed to digest prechewed fruits and vegetables.

INTESTINAL LENGTH

CARNIVORES have short intestinal tracts and colons that allow meat to pass through the animal relatively quickly, before it can rot and cause illness. Humans' intestinal tracts are much longer than those of carnivores of comparable size. Longer intestines allow the body more time to break down fiber and absorb the nutrients from plant-based foods, but they make it dangerous for humans to eat meat. The bacteria in meat have extra time to multiply during the long trip through the digestive system, increasing the risk of food poisoning. Meat actually begins to rot while it makes its way through human intestines, which increases the risk of colon cancer.

HUMAN PSYCHOLOGY

HUMANS also lack the instinct that drives carnivores to kill animals and devour their raw carcasses. While carnivores take pleasure in killing animals and eating their raw flesh, any human who killed an animal with his or her bare hands and ate the raw corpse would be considered deranged. Carnivorous animals are excited by the scent of blood and the thrill of the chase. Most humans, on the other hand, are revolted by the sight of blood, intestines and raw flesh, and cannot tolerate hearing the screams of animals being ripped apart and killed. The bloody reality of eating animals is innately repulsive to us, another indication that we were not designed to eat meat.

IF WE WERE MEANT TO EAT MEAT, WHY IS IT KILLING US?

CARNIVOROUS animals in the wild virtually never suffer from heart disease, cancer, diabetes, strokes, or obesity, ailments that are caused in humans in large part by the consumption of the saturated fat and cholesterol in meat.

FAT AND CHOLESTEROL

STUDIES have shown that even when fed 200 times the amount of animal fat and cholesterol that the average human consumes each day, carnivores do not develop the hardening of the arteries that leads to heart disease and strokes in humans. Researchers have actually found that it is impossible for carnivores to develop hardening of the arteries, no matter how much animal fat they consume.

Human bodies, on the other hand, were not designed to process animal flesh, so all the excess fat and cholesterol from a meat-based diet makes us sick. Heart disease, for example, is the number one killer in America according to the American Heart Association, and medical experts agree that this ailment is largely the result of the consumption of animal products. Meat-eaters have a 50 percent higher risk of developing heart disease than vegetarians!

EXCESS PROTEIN

WE consume twice as much protein as we need when we eat a meat-based diet, and this contributes to osteoporosis and kidney stones. Animal protein raises the acid level in our blood, causing calcium to be excreted from the bones to restore the blood's natural pH balance. This calcium depletion leads to osteoporosis, and the excreted calcium ends up in the kidneys, where it can form kidney stones or even trigger kidney disease.

Consuming animal protein has also been linked to cancer of the colon, breast, prostate, and pancreas. According to Dr. T. Colin Campbell, the director of the Cornell-China-Oxford Project on Nutrition, Health, and the Environment, "In the next ten years, one of the things you're bound to hear is that animal protein . . . is one of the most toxic nutrients of all that can be considered."

Eating meat can also have negative consequences for stamina and sexual potency. One Danish study indicated that "Men peddling on a stationary bicycle until muscle failure lasted an average of 114 minutes on a mixed meat and vegetable diet, 57 minutes on a high-meat diet, and a whopping 167 minutes on a strict vegetarian diet." Besides having increased physical endurance, vegan men are also less likely to suffer from impotence.

FOOD POISONING

SINCE we don't have strong stomach acids like carnivores to kill all the bacteria in meat, dining on animal flesh can also give us food poisoning. According to the USDA, meat is the cause of 70 percent of foodborne illnesses in the United States because it's often contaminated with dangerous bacteria like E.coli, listeria, and campylobacter. Every year in the United

States alone, food poisoning sickens over 75 million people and kills more than 5,000.

Dr. William C. Roberts, M.D., editor of the authoritative *American Journal of Cardiology*, sums it up this way: "[A]lthough we think we are one and we act as if we are one, human beings are not natural carnivores. When we kill animals to eat them, they end up killing us because their flesh, which contains cholesterol and saturated fat, was never intended for human beings, who are natural herbivores."

HUMAN EVOLUTION AND THE RISE OF MEAT-HEAVY DIETS

IF it's so unhealthy and unnatural for humans to eat meat, why did our ancestors sometimes turn to flesh for sustenance?

During most of our evolutionary history, we were largely vegetarian. Plant foods like potatoes made up the bulk of our ancestors' diet. The more frequent addition of modest amounts of meat to the early human diet came with the discovery of fire, which allowed us to lower the risk of being sickened or killed by parasites in meat. This practice did not turn our ancestors into carnivores but rather allowed early humans to survive in periods when plant foods were unavailable.

MODERN HUMANS

UNTIL recently, only the wealthiest people could afford to feed, raise, and slaughter animals for meat; less wealthy and poor people ate mostly plant foods. Consequently, prior to the 20th century, only the rich routinely were plagued with diseases like heart disease and obesity.

Since 1950, the per capita consumption of meat has almost doubled. Now that animal flesh has become relatively cheap and easily available (thanks to the cruel, cost-cutting practices of factory farming), deadly ailments like heart disease, strokes, cancer, and obesity have spread to people across the socio-economic spectrum. And as the Western lifestyle spills over into less developed areas in Asia and Africa, people there, too, have started to suffer and die from the diseases associated with meat-based diets.

❧PART SEVEN❧

Reading Food Writing

The Language of Taste

INTRODUCTION

O NE OF the issues this section addresses is the very one that stands at the heart of the entire anthology: What is the appeal of reading about food? In effect this question is analogous to a related one: What is the attraction of looking at pictures of food instead of eating that food? Hungry lions would probably not salivate at the photo of a zebra, but show a person an image of a sour pickle and the juices will start to flow. Similarly, we might ask what is the attraction—sensuous, intellectual or emotional—in reading about food? We live in a world saturated by food writing (besides the tsunami of restaurant reviews, food blogs, and magazines centered on food and drink, over three thousand cookbooks were published last year), so why are we drawn to this writing? What exactly is so compelling?

Molly O'Neill calls her selection here "Food Porn," and we're all familiar with enticing, seductive, and titillating photos of lavish or sensuously exciting dishes. But if looking at images of food at once draws us towards and distances us from the experience itself, what of reading about food? If a picture is worth a thousand words, how many words does it take to make our taste buds explode with pleasure, or our brains dream of great meals? O'Neill implicitly speaks to this issue when she traces a brief history of food writing, and shows how such literature is at once nostalgic in its ability to summon food memories and as alluring in its voluptuous appeal as a Victoria's Secret catalog. But O'Neill's mission is also high-minded: she sees good food writing as addressing important issues of science, economy, health, culture, and politics, as much as it does the hedonism of the palate.

One of our best writers on food is Adam Gopnik, who takes a similar stance in his book *The Table Comes First*: "There is too much food in most food writing now—too much food and little that goes further." Referring to several of the most eminent, classic authors in the field, he continues: "When [A. J.] Liebling and [M.F.K.] Fisher wrote, they gestured from plate and glass to something bigger, outside the dining room." Gopnik wants food writing to speak to larger issues: to family, to "appetite itself," and to the world outside mere food. This is precisely what he himself does in the selection we've included here. Analyzing why we read cookbooks, he argues that they speak to our fantasy of making recipes come out perfectly, doing what might well be impossible to master; but poignantly he suggests that while we read food writing because of our desire to be like the cookbook's author or a master chef, the process leads to disillusionment when we realize that we cannot triumph in the kitchen merely by following a set of rules. Rather, it takes a lifetime of skill and experience to turn out brilliant meals. For Gopnik, reading about cooking is a plaintive life-lesson in disappointment and frustration.

Betty Fussell emphasizes the relation of food to words, beginning with the observation that eating and speaking both involve the mouth. She argues that food and language inevitably belong together insofar as both activities "are forms of knowledge," teaching us to distinguish what is inside ourselves from what is outside. She notes that food writers often speak of such issues as love and war, and hence discourse about food frequently expands to treat grander themes. Doubling down on this coupling, Terry Eagleton shows how figures of speech connect feasting and writing, whether through metaphors of one activity for the other or through the characterization of literary texts and writing style in terms of food and digestion. Who previously would have thought to link the cliché to fast food?

At its best, then, the food writing we cherish is both sensual and a reminder of our human limitations: its themes are hunger and satiety, yearning and disappointment, indulgence and remorse. It encompasses other dualities as well: comfort and adventure, memories of the past and hopes for the future, delicacy and gluttony. In short, we read about food because it reminds us of our complex cravings, what we've most enjoyed, and what we have been deprived of and might restore in the next meal or, if not at the table, then perhaps on the page, in the very act of reading about eating.

🦖

Betty Fussell (1927–)

ELOQUENT, AWARD-WINNING FOOD writer Betty Fussell began her career as a specialist in Shakespearean and Renaissance literature, teaching at Connecticut College, Rutgers, and Columbia before devoting herself full-time to freelance culinary writing. She has written a number of cookbooks as well as scholarly histories of corn and beef but is perhaps best known for her witty memoir *My Kitchen Wars*, which describes her years as a popular Princeton hostess and the wife of critic Paul Fussell, often hilariously exploring boozy academic dinner parties while bitingly lampooning her onetime husband. Our selection reveals how wide-ranging and thoughtful her approach to gastronomy can be.

Eating My Words

FOOD IS NOT a subject in the way that the great subjects of literature like War, Love, Death, Sex, Power, Betrayal, or Honor are subjects. Neither is food an object, in the way that a Car, a Washing Machine, a Computer, a House are objects—generic commodities that we desire and consume. Rather, food is an action, more primal than speech and more universal than language. And for humans, there's the rub. While everything in the created universe eats, not everything speaks. Wind and water eat stone, night eats day, black holes eat light—silently. We find words to address these actions, but long before we ever arrived on the scene or said a word about it, every link in the terrestrial food chain, as in the cosmic chain, was chomping away and changing one thing into another. It's one of those givens we like to avoid because we don't fancy our table companions or dining conditions. We don't like to be reminded that if dung were not caviar to the dung beetle, the earth would be covered in shit.

Nor do we like to be reminded that we are steak tartare to worms or, if we thwart their slow munch, a grillade to flames. We want to be exempt, special, excused. We don't want to be reminded that in the game preserve staked out for us, we are flesh and blood like our fellow animals, subject to the same feeding frenzies but with inferior teeth. In terms of brains, we may be first among mammals, but we are mammals nonetheless, and as such we cannibalize our mothers in order to live. Each of us, no matter how noble his sentiments at a later stage of development, drinks mother's blood from the time he is a tiny egg clinging hungrily to a uterine wall. Long before speech, the drama of communication begins in the womb and is merely amplified with baby's first intake of breath that ends in a howl, acknowledging in premonitory outrage that life-long separation of the feeder from the fed. From birth on, what comes out of the mouth and what goes in are inextricably mingled because there is only the one orifice for both feeding and speaking, not to mention kissing. Was that a mistake in engineering or a brilliant subversion of human pretense?

Elias Canetti asks whether it wouldn't have been better to have one orifice for food and another for words. "Or does this intimate mixing of all our utterances with the lips, teeth, tongue, throat, all those parts of the mouth that serve the business of eating—does this mixing tell us that language and eating forever belong together, that we can never be nobler and better than we are?" But what if we ask the question another way? Does this intimate mixing of language and eating suggest that both are forms of knowledge and of communication, that ingesting what is outside us with lips, teeth, tongue, and throat is intimately related to excreting from within the cries, sighs, babbles, and prattles that are eventually transformed into words and sentences in the cauldrons of the human mind and imagination? Could we go further and suggest that the lineaments of the mouth lick into shape the very images that the mind of man conceives in his struggle to find sound bites and transmit them? The crunch of teeth biting into an apple shapes the image of the father of mankind, who hungers and thirsts after righteousness with actual lips and throat. Does not this intimate mixing suggest that the human animal is forever a bewildering compound of body parts and spirit sensors, a belcher of hymns, an angel that farts, and that wise eaters and speakers will savor the mixture?

For is not the mouth our primary mediator in distinguishing what is without from what is within, as we suck first our own and then other people's fingers and toes? We learn to see and to say "Mama" out of hunger, for both speaking and eating express similar actions of hungering, desiring, gathering, preserving, communing, laughing, fearing, loving, and dying in the long agon of separation and connection. Even a mouth eating in solitude—and silence—is engaged willy-nilly in discovering and communing with what is outside itself, which its hunger transforms by taking the outside literally in. We eat the world to know it and ourselves. If we fail to distinguish outside from in, we are stamped with a name and a story: Narcissus, hungering to eat himself, imaged in a pool, opened his mouth and drowned.

Eating, like speaking, reconnects through the imagination what reason has learned to disconnect through the senses. In this way, eating is a form of magic. When Shakespeare's Leontes discovers in *The Winter's Tale* that the statue of his Hermione is alive, he exclaims, "If this be magic, let it be an art lawful as eating." Eating, like speaking, mediates between opposite worlds, forging a bridge over the natal chasm between mind and body, images and substances, symbols and things that reason works hard to keep apart. Even as a noun, food suggests the action of ferrying meaning across species, across ontological continents, ensuring that despite the logic of appearances, you *can* turn a sow's ear into a silk purse through the "turn" of trope, or the "transfer" of metaphor, through speaking pictures, or images in action.

Food is always image and icon as well as substance. Semioticians explained decades ago how food, cooking, and eating create a tripartite language of their own through which a culture expresses itself, and this language dances between the literal and the figurative in the way that we usually expect of speech but not always of food. Despite laboratory analyses, mother's milk is never simply the sum of its biochemical or molecular parts, no more than a bottle of milk is. Who's holding the breast or the bottle or the baby, and where? Are mother and baby sitting on the grass in suburban sunshine or are they flat on a canvas surrounded by drapery and haloed cherubs? Are they on a railway platform herded into a cattle car by soldiers in uniform? Food always condenses a happening, a plot, which unfolds like any enacted drama in the spotlit present, surrounded by shadows of the past.

The most ancient originating plots in the Western world, in fact, hinge on the relation of food to language. Before the Madonna there was Eve, and before Eve there was Nin-ti, the Sumerian mother goddess whose story, told in the world's first written language, Sumer, is a food story. After the water god Enki ate eight of Nin-ti's magic plants, the goddess cursed eight of his bodily organs with death, then relented and restored the god to life. Nin-ti's name was a pun, which meant both "rib" and "to make live." In the language of Sumer, Eve's name also meant "rib," but the language and the food got muddled in the transition from Sumer to Hebrew, so that in the Hebrew story the lady Eve was given life by the rib of the man, whose death was caused by the woman's eating of a magic plant. Despite the gender and cultural reversal from mother goddess to father god, the paradox of the human animal remains intact: that which gives him life also kills him, and his tragedy is that he knows it.

Human life is so bound up with food—the sounds, textures, smells, tastes, emotions, ideas, and rituals of the one so meshed with the other—that to take a slice of life at any point is to cut into a full loaf, a pie, a roast, a terrine of meaning. Personal and cultural memories are so integral to eating and speaking that simply to name a food is to invoke the lifetime of a person—and a culture. We don't need Proust's madeleine. We have Twain's cornpone. Even when the nominal subject is a single food, such as coffee or oysters or beans, it is also about place and time and occasion and memory and need, just as it is about politics and economics and trade and war and religion and ceremony. While the first person singular is the instinctive voice in which to express our thoughts and feelings about food, the point of view will be as diverse as the position of the speaker: social critic, gardener, connoisseur, athlete, chef, housewife, farmer, dentist, historian, garbageman, politician, pastor, poet. All walks of life eat, in every corner of the world, whether in Nigeria, Bombay, Austria, Israel, Kyoto, or Iowa. Although attitude and tone of voice may play every key from rhapsodic to obscene, both the particularities of food and the universality of hunger keep the speaker, or writer, rooted in common ground.

Food, like language, forever unites the concrete with the universal, and a writer's attitude toward food will appear in how he manipulates the nervy relation between substance and symbol, jittery with dramatic tension, that dictates the behavior of us all. The materialist asserts the primacy of flesh: "*Erst kommt das Fressen, dann kommt die Moral,*" sings Brecht. The spiritualist denies or subjugates the flesh: "*I need nothing. I feel nothing. I desire nothing*," writes Wole Soyinka in prison on the eleventh day of his fast. The ritualist transforms substance by symbol into rules of purity: Chitrita Banerji tells us that only *luchis*, a kind of fried bread, and cold vegetables may be eaten by the widows of Bengal. The sensualist translates substance and symbol alike into physical sensation: "The gamey taste and smell of ripened cheese is sexual, and provocative; the smell is maternal still, but now it is the smell of cyclical time," writes Paul Schmidt. The satirist mocks symbols by fabricating ridiculous substance: "The correct drink for fried bologna *à la Nutley, Nouveau Jersey*, is a 1927 Nehi Cola," writes Russell Baker.

Writings about food are necessarily as diverse as writings about any part of life and as illuminative of the things that matter because food is connected to everything. Homer, whether speaking of epic wars or journeys, never neglected food and drink. He specified in detail how to roast and salt the joint of meat and how to mix wine with water to invite the gods in. Greek gods ate and drank in the company of man long before Christians turned their God into cooked food to be eaten by men. That changed the nature of the feast, of course, although there was nothing new in gods who existed to be eaten. Think of Prometheus with his eternally gnawed, eternally renewed liver, wherein man's lips and tongue tasted forever the sour of cyclical time, the bitter of eternal hunger, the sweet of immortality, the salt of death.

In imaging the unavoidable and appalling fact that life eats life, the Ancient Maya invented a language in which men and gods were made of the self-same food in an eternal interchange of substance. A literal ear of corn growing in the fields was also the finely shaped head of the sacrificed young corn god with his hair of green leaves. To eat corn was to eat one's mother, father, sister, brother, and ancestor gods. Substance and symbol were so intimately mixed in the mouth of man that life and death were as mingled as body and soul, as eating and speaking. Maya speech wrapped the cosmos in a language of verbal and visual food puns, so that eating and speaking were alike actions of punning. To eat a kernel of corn, the substance of life, was to swallow a drop of blood, a sign of death. The Maya sign, or glyph, for bread abstracted the corn-husk wrapper and the ball of corn dough of an actual tamale, so that both speaker and eater alike shared in the bread's layered meanings of "sacred offering," "sacrificial blood," "something precious," "day." Every kernel of corn condensed the plot of the *Popul Vuh* and its hero, the sacrificed god Hunahpu, whose decapitated head in the calabash tree, after he and his twin brother outwitted the Lords of Death, impregnated Blood Woman who gave birth to man from her body of corn.

> And so then they put into words the creation,
>> The shaping
> Of our first mother
>> And father.
> Only yellow corn
>> And white corn were their bodies.
> Only food were the legs
>> And arms of man.
> Those who were our first fathers
>> Were the original men.
> Only food at the outset
>> Were their bodies.

Nothing else can do for man's mind and imagination what food does because it is the one and only thing that accompanies every single man, Maya, Christian, Muslim, Buddhist, on his journey from cradle to grave. If his first sound is a cry for milk, his last may be a whimper for sugared tea or a spoonful of Jell-O. Sans teeth, tongue, or throat, he still must open the veins of his body to the outside world to sustain life, whether or not he is conscious of that mechanized connection. His final image may not be of the loved face hovering over his bedside at all, but of a wished-for muffin or martini, as real and intense as the griever left behind.

Never underestimate the power of food to summon images and dictate lives in the here and hereafter. Why are the graves in almost every ancient culture stuffed with containers for food and drink to accompany the corpse on its journey between worlds? As in life, so in death, food remains our most faithful attendant on the ferry across the river Styx, giving comfort and sustenance to the frightened soul soon to swallow and be swallowed by a realm where outside and inside have no meaning and where that peculiar mixture of eating and speaking will vanish in the emptying out of appetite and the entering in of silence.

Terry Eagleton (1943–)

FINDING FRESH WAYS to describe taste has always been difficult, and the metaphors used to do the job are relatively meager. But while he is not especially interested in helping restaurant reviewers be more eloquent with their writing, Eagleton does show how much everyday language employs images and terms from eating. He finds "gustatory tropes" everywhere in our speech, and conversely maintains that when we talk about food we're inevitably talking about something else—love, joy, anger, power. Furthermore, he argues, the language we use is charged with emotional significance, as if contemplating food were indistinguishable from a grand passion. As he puts it, "Food looks like an object but is actually a relationship." Eagleton analyzes talk and writing about food as carefully as if he were interpreting a literary text—understandably, since he is one of the foremost literary thinkers in the English-speaking world, having written some forty works of criticism including the highly influential *Literary Theory: An Introduction*.

Edible Écriture

THE LINK BETWEEN eating and writing has a venerable pedigree. Francis Bacon famously observed in his essay "Of Studies" that "some books are to be tasted, others to be swallowed, and some few to be chewed and digested." Literary language can be mouth-filling or subtly flavored, meaty or hard-boiled, spicy or indigestible. Words can nourish or poison, and somewhere beneath this figurative equation lurks the Eucharistic word itself, a body that feeds other bodies, a sign that is also a meal. There are anorexic texts such as Samuel Beckett's, in which discourse is in danger of dwindling to a mere skeleton of itself, and bulimic ones like Gerard Manley Hopkins's, muscle-bound and semiotically overstuffed. The language of Keats is as plump and well-packed as an apple, while less palatable poets such as Swinburne are all froth and ooze. If Dylan Thomas binges on words, Harold Pinter approaches them with the wariness of a man on a diet. Bombast is a kind of verbal flatulence, a swelling which, like the bodies of the famished, conceals a hollowness.

Words issue from the lips as food enters them, though one can always take one's words back by eating them. And writing is a processing of raw speech just as cooking is a transformation of raw materials. One of Roland Barthes's structuralist models, bathetically enough, was a menu: just as a diner selects one item each from the "paradigmatic axes" of starters, entreés and desserts, and then combines them along a "syntagmatic axis" in the actual process of eating, so a literary work chooses items from various repertoires (genres, formal devices, narrative forms) and then goes on to string them together. These are the kind of speculations that send most English critics scrambling for their Helen Gardner. The later, post-structuralist Barthes threw over this model for the delights of semantic indeterminacy, but nothing is more alimentary than the ambiguous. If there is one sure thing about food, it is that it is never just food. Like the post-structuralist text, food is endlessly interpretable, as gift, threat, poison, recompense, barter, seduction, solidarity, suffocation.

Food is just as much materialised emotion as a love lyric, though both can also be substitutes for the genuine article. A sign expresses something but also stands in for its absence, so that a child may be unsure whether receiving nourishment from its mother's hands or breast is a symbol of her affection or a replacement for it. Perhaps a child may rebuff its food because what it really wants is some impossibly immaterial gift of affection, rather as a symbolist poet wants to strip language of its drably functional character and express its very essence. Food looks like an object but is actually a relationship, and the same is true of literary works.

If there is no literary text without an author, neither is there one without a reader. The doctrine of transubstantiation, which states that the bread and wine of the mass become the body and blood of Christ, redescribes physical substances in terms of relationships. A chemist would still identify the consecrated elements as bread and wine, but this for Catholic theology would be as pointless as describing the proferring of a box of chocolates in physiological terms. There is a parallel mystery about writing: why are these little black marks actually meanings? By what strange transfiguration do arbitrary physical inscriptions come to be the medium of spirit, a matter of human address in the way that random tracks in the sand are not?

Language is at once material fact and rhetorical communication, just as eating combines biological necessity with cultural significance.

Hunger-striking is not just refusing food, but a question of not taking it from a specific oppressor, and thus a dialogical affair. Starving here is a message rather than just a physical condition, semiotic as well as somatic. Food is cusped between nature and culture, and so too is language. Nobody will perish without Mars bars, just as nobody ever died of not reading *Paradise Lost*, but food and language of some sort are essential to our survival.

Fast food is like cliché or computerese, an emotionless exchange or purely instrumental form of discourse. Genuine eating combines pleasure, utility and sociality, and so differs from a take-away in much the same way that Proust differs from a bus ticket. Snatching a meal alone bears the same relation to eating in company as talking to yourself does to conversation. It is hardly surprising that a civilisation for which a dialogue of the mind with itself has provided a paradigm of human language should reach its apotheosis in the Big Mac.

Those starved words, gaunt bodies and sterile landscapes of Beckett's dramas may well carry with them a race memory of the Irish famine, a catastrophe that was the slow death of language as well as of one million people. The famine decimated the farm labourers and small tenants, who made up most of the Irish speakers, and using the language in post-famine Ireland rapidly became a symbol of ill-luck. It is possible to read Beckett's meticulously pared-down prose as a satirical smack at the blather and blarney of stage-Irish speech. Beckett hoards his meagre clutch of words like a tight-fisted peasant, ringing pedantic changes on the same few signs or stage properties like someone eking out a scanty diet. There is, perhaps, a Protestant suspicion of superfluity here, in contrast to the extravagant expenditure of a Joyce, the linguistic opulence of J. M. Synge or the verbal gluttony of Brendan Behan.

But all that reckless prodigality may itself have a bearing on food, as a form of compensation in the mind for what is lacking in historical reality. In conditions of colonial backwardness, language is one of the few things you have left; and though even that in Ireland had been put down by the imperial power, words were still a good deal more plentiful than hot dinners. Part of the point of language was to bamboozle the colonialists. The linguistic virtuosity of the Irish writers springs partly from the fact that, like Joseph Conrad and many a modernist émigré, they are inside and outside a language simultaneously. But it is also a form of displacement, whereby you hope to discover in discourse a richness denied to you in reality.

The most celebrated food-text of English literature is the work of an Anglo-Irish patriot who bitterly recommended munching babies as a solution to his country's economic ills. During the Great Famine, this may well have happened; as Swift's fellow Dubliner Oscar Wilde observed, life has a remarkable knack of imitating art. Language in Irish culture, however, is associated less with food than with drink. As drink flows in, so words pour out, each fuelling the other in a self-sustaining process. In fact, apart from the notoriously bibulous trinity of Behan, Flann O'Brien and Patrick Kavanagh, remarkably few Irish writers have been alcoholics—far fewer than American authors, for whom alcohol seems as much of a prerequisite as a typewriter.

There is a fair amount of eating in *Ulysses*, but the novel itself, at least in the view of the critic John Bayley, is impossible to consume, "sunk in its own richness like a plumcake." Bayley misses the point that Joyce's work is deliberately calculated to induce dyspepsia. Modernist art was born at much the same time as mass culture, and one reason for its obscurity is to resist being sucked in as easily as tabloid print. By fragmenting its forms, thickening its textures and garbling its narratives, the modernist text hopes to escape the indignities of instant consumption.

It is significant that our word for the use of a commodity—consumption—is drawn from the guts and the gullet. This modern metaphor has a rather more high-toned ancestor: taste. The 18th-century idea of taste was partly a way of freeing artistic evaluation from too rigid a consensus: taste was subjective, beyond disputation, a je ne sais quoi that refused any total reduction to rules. Just as there was no moral obligation to like rhubarb, so it was not a capital offence to turn up your nose at Rembrandt. Similarly, what food you enjoyed was a private, arbitrary affair—until, that is, you tried ordering in your London club the kind of meal they ate in rural Cork. But this gustatory trope made room for individual freedom only at the risk of trivialising art to the status of a sausage, rather as the modern idea of consumption celebrates individual choice while threatening to drain it of value.

Food is what makes up our bodies, just as words are what constitute our minds; and if body and mind are hard to distinguish, it is no wonder that eating and speaking should continually cross over in metaphorical exchange. Both are in any case media of exchange themselves. There is no more modish topic in contemporary literary theory than the human body. But there has been strikingly little concern with the physical stuff of which bodies are composed, as opposed to an excited interest in their genitalia. The human body is generally agreed to be "constructed," but what starts off that construction for all of us—milk—has been curiously passed over. There has been much critical interest in the famished body of the Western anorexic, but rather little attention to the malnutrition of the Third World. Perhaps such dwindled bodies are too bluntly material a matter for a so-called "materialist" criticism.

One notable exception to this indifference to the politics of starvation is Maud Ellmann's brilliant study *The Hunger Artists*, which concludes with the following reflections: "[Food's] disintegration in the stomach, its assimilation in the blood, its diaphoresis in the epidermis, its metempsychosis in the large intestine; its viscosity in okra, gumbo, oysters; its elasticity in jellies; its deliquescence in blancmanges; its tumescence in the throats of serpents, its slow erosion in the bellies of sharks; its odysseys through pastures, orchards, wheat fields, stock-yards, supermarkets, kitchens, pig troughs, rubbish dumps, disposals; the industries of sowing, hunting, cooking, milling, processing, and canning it; the wizardry of its mutations, ballooning in bread, subsiding in soufflés; raw and cooked, solid and melting, vegetable and mineral, fish, flesh, and fowl, encompassing the whole compendium of living substance: food is the symbol of the passage, the totem of sociality, the epitome of all creative and destructive labour."

Ellmann quite properly makes a meal of it. Her paragraph coils like an intestine, the sense slipping from clause to clause like a morsel down the oesophagus. As these lines track the processing of food, so they in turn process that subject matter, by the cuisinary transformations of style, into a delectable feast.

🐂

Molly O'Neill (1952–)

A WELL-KNOWN COOKBOOK author and writer on food, O'Neill has been a recipe columnist for *The New York Times* and a restaurant reviewer for *Newsday*. The sister of former New York Yankee outfielder Paul O'Neill, she has written a memoir, *Mostly True: A Memoir of Family, Food, and Baseball*, and edited the award-winning *New York Cookbook*. She has also hosted the PBS series *Great Food* and edited the anthology *American Food Writing* for the Library of America. In addition to the ingredients, recipes, preparations, and menus of the American table, she focuses on the connection of food to our relationships, our communities, and our family memories. Here, in her brief account of how food writing has evolved over the centuries, O'Neill moves the narrative of culinary journalism forward to its current moment of obsession with what she calls "food porn": the way the foodie lifestyle and the fantasies embodied in our preoccupation with food have become gastronomic versions of erotic dreams.

from Food Porn

FOOD WRITERS HAVE always walked the dangerous lines between journalism, art, and their role as handmaiden to advertising. But we have not wobbled quite so regularly in nearly a half century as we do today. Food has carried us into the vortex of cool. There, the urge to become part of the story is stronger than the duty to detach and observe and report the story.

ROOTS

TRADITIONALLY, there were several schools of food writing and each served as social arbiter. In the gentlemanly tradition of gastronomic prose, the food writer was a sort of everyman's "Jeeves," the one who knew all. The domestic science branch of food writing was the voice of an über-Mom. The merging of these two sensibilities was part of what created food-writer chic in the final years of the twentieth century.

As early as the 1840s, when food writing first appeared in American newspapers, culinary writers were already established as more than cooking instructors. They were trusted to describe the world, as explorers had in the earliest written accounts of food in America. They were also relied upon to supply guidelines for upward mobility. The first cookbook published in America, known as *American Cookery*, was written in 1796 by Amelia Simmons, presumably a member of the serving class, and gave clear instruction on cooking for the gentry. The cookery writing by abolitionists, ideologues, and dietary religionists also primed the culture to look to food writers for life advice.

That advice began to appear regularly in newspapers in the late 1880s. An enormous wave of immigration had brought people who wanted to live and eat like Americans, and newspaper publishers wanted each of them to read their papers. Women with sights set on the middle class needed instruction in living accordingly, and given the rise of suffrage and increased female literacy, newspapers were happy to oblige. Another social and economic change—the shift from making everything in the home to mass production—was also an incentive to publish food stories. Food, fashion, and fiction that were heart-rending, or inspiring, or an object lesson for gender or class training were as heady as free chocolate to Victorian ladies—and to the advertisers who wanted to reach them.

As nonpartisan commercial journalism grew, so did a code of ethics designed to protect its editorial integrity. Except in women's news. "During the time that women's pages were emerging, journalism was becoming more independent politically, and objectivity was emerging as the dominant journalistic ethic," says David Mindich, a professor of journalism at St. Michael's College. "But the women's pages were not included in the objective mix. Even into the twentieth century, women's pages were not seen as real journalism."

In fact, until the early 1940s, newspaper food writing was generally the province of home economists or reporters who'd failed elsewhere. Then, in the unprecedented prosperity of the postwar era, food began moving up the social scale.

RIPENING

SINCE Pliny, stories about food have located the reader in time and then, by evoking distant lands, exotic flavors, or lives unlived, taken the reader elsewhere.

For almost as long, gastronomic writing has also sought to ease readers' anxieties and to affirm their ambitions. Therefore, the aspirations of those who read food stories influence their style and content.

As the middle class grew after World War II, a reconciliation began between elite cuisine and the meals of everyday people. The concerns of those who cook (traditionally, women) and those who savor but do not cook (traditionally, men) became more similar. The polarization between continental taste (once considered the gold standard of cuisine) and American taste (once thought to be an oxymoron) began to subside.

These changes were reflected in the pages of *Gourmet* magazine and in the food coverage of *The New York Times,* and they suggest that a new audience—if not a nascent mass market—for fine food had taken root.

When *Gourmet* was introduced in 1941 it was conceived not as a food magazine, but as a general interest one. The early *Gourmet* was aimed at a small social elite that could afford to hunt, fish, and travel, and that viewed fine dining much as it did art, theater, or opera: as something one need only appreciate in order to possess. During its first decade, the magazine sounded as if it were written by and for members of "a pre-war London gentleman's club," wrote the food historian Anne Mendelson in an analysis of sixty years of *Gourmet* that appeared in the magazine's September 2001 issue.

The food advice that appeared during the magazine's first decade wasn't aimed at people who cooked; it was crafted for people who considered themselves connoisseurs. But by the 1950s, the magazine began to recognize people outside the old club. Its travel stories became more service-oriented; its recipes more accurate and concise; its tone less pompous and more practical.

As if to balance the shifting class lines of the postwar era, food was romanticized, primarily in nostalgic ways. In fact, according to Mendelson, the most important part of *Gourmet*'s identity in the 1950s was "an intense fixation on the past as the standard of meaning."

But even in the whirl of their purple prose and gossamer tales of edibles gone by, food writers promoted a fundamental shift in the way America began to view dinner in the 1950s. "Food acquired a . . . gloss of snobbery it had hitherto possessed only in certain upper-income groups," writes Nora Ephron in an essay called "The Food Establishment" that appeared in her 1967 book *Wallflower at the Orgy.* "Hostesses were expected to know that iceberg lettuce was déclassé and tuna fish casseroles de trop."

The photographs in *Gourmet* reflected this change. When I was growing up, an elderly neighbor subscribed to the magazine and I remember leafing through it before I could read, studying pictures of quiet streets dappled with light, charming doorways, and wide open, unpopulated vistas. But by the late 1960s, when I perused *Gourmet* while waiting in the orthodontist's office, there was a picture of girls in miniskirts outside a pub in London, and one of a long-haired boy careening around a fountain in Rome on a Vespa. There was a picture of people eating paella—people I wanted to know.

By 1968 good food was no longer remote and rarefied in *Gourmet*; it no longer revolved around a "romantic glorification of the past," wrote Mendelson. Good food was young. It drank. It showed thigh. It probably rubbed elbows with the Beatles. "Food became, for dinner-party conversations in the sixties, what abstract expressionism had been in the fifties," writes Ephron.

This evolution from food-as-fuel to food-as-aesthetic-experience was mirrored—if not urged along—by the food coverage in *The New York Times*.

From the nineteenth century until nearly the middle of the twentieth century, the *Times* published a single weekly column dedicated to food, and its titles, "The Household," "Hints for the Household," and "Timely Hints for the Household" suggested whom the column was written for.

In the late 1930s, however, food information in the *Times* became newsier and appeared under the heading "Food News of the Week." And while most stories maintained a dowdy and dutiful tone, a few suggested that food was social climbing. In 1940 a story by Dr. O. Gentsch, for instance, declared cooking "one of the greatest arts."

The best evidence that food had arrived, however, was the anointing of its own specialist. The term "food writer" first appeared in the *Times* on March 12, 1950. Given the intimate connection between food writing and the food industry, it may be no coincidence that the phrase made its debut in a story by Jane Nickerson about a press trip to the manufacturing plant of Tabasco sauce in Louisiana. Interestingly, Nickerson was the one of the first to apply news-side ethics to the food report.

When Craig Claiborne became food editor at the *Times* in 1957, he continued the trend, banning press trips, free meals, and gifts (other than food samples and cookbooks) for those who wrote in his pages. With an undergraduate degree in journalism and culinary training from École Hôtelière, the venerable Swiss hotel school, Claiborne treated food pages as if they were part of the news report. He also reformatted recipes and lifted them from within stories to an adjacent space, making them easier for aspiring cooks to follow. Many were, in fact, learning to cook from books, cooking classes, and the food section of the paper and, by melding culinary criticism, consumer information, and education, Claiborne became their guide. His authority rested, in part, on his gentlemanly reserve, on the fact that he was the paper's first male food editor. However, his most significant contribution, the four-star restaurant rating system with its protocol of multiple, anonymous visits, was not a result of his gender, but of his training as both a journalist and chef.

Claiborne's tenure at the *Times* spanned nearly thirty years. In 1976 food was broken out into its own section, called "Living," a rubric that suggested both simple sustenance and "really living," as in "the good life."

By then, Claiborne was established as one side of a gastronomic trinity that also included Julia Child, a.k.a. The French Chef on PBS, and James Beard, the cooking teacher, cookbook writer, and impresario.

Between them, they brought journalistic muscle as well as style and joy to the subject. In addition, each personified some of the characteristics that defined food writing until the last decade of the twentieth century; they embodied, in other words, the traits and qualities that lent cachet to culinary expertise. Claiborne's air of impeccability and unflagging curiosity engendered absolute trust in his readers. He also commanded a respect among his colleagues that had not previously existed. Beard's memoirist approach to food writing lent mystique to daily life and created an emotional resonance with readers. Child was a clown who made cooking fun and, week by week, demonstrated the delight of being wholly human and less than perfect.

Not one set out to be a food person. Beard imagined himself in the theater, Child wanted to be a spy, Claiborne had writerly ambitions. Food was Plan B for all of them. Each, therefore, exuded the delight and wonder of the amateur, a feeling that resonated with the counterculture's antiestablishment, anticorporate cosmology. Food was fun and relatively lawless when I started writing about it. The hurdle between being a culinary illiterate and having food savvy was not particularly high. There was plenty of room for idiosyncrasy, but most of all, the writers who shaped my generation—primarily Claiborne, Child, Michael Field, M.F.K. Fisher, Richard Olney, and Elizabeth David—exuded the excitement of discovery.

I wanted to be all of them, with a slice of Woodward and Bernstein on the side. My fantasy was fated. The "foodie stories" (such as a chef profile, a report on an ingredient or cooking technique) had slowly been eclipsing "news" stories (such as a report on famine or food poisoning or a culinary event with news value) for almost forty years. . . .

Led as much by Claiborne's frequent profiles of them in *The New York*

Times Magazine as by the era's idealization of "working-class heroes," American chefs began to be viewed as trailblazers and life-style gurus in the late 1970s. And the celebration of the amateurism of the early Claiborne era began to give way to a celebration of professionalism.

Chefs, and by association food writers, became stars, an image bolstered by the habit of dressing sex up in gourmet drag in food stories. Books such as *Blue Skies, No Candy*, the 1976 novel by Gael Greene, the restaurant critic for *New York Magazine*, that chronicled the awakening of a young woman's appetite for good sex and good food, brought an outlaw aura to food writing. The mystique of food writing received another boost from *Heartburn*, Nora Ephron's 1983 novel whose heroine is a cookbook writer.

But even as the profession came to be seen as a sexy life-style arbiter, food writers had, by the early 1980s, begun to respond to public taste rather than lead it. In part, this was because food became news during the decade and covering news is, by its nature, reactive. Nouvelle Cuisine unseated traditional French cooking, and America finally began to mint its own tastemakers—native-born chefs. In California, New Orleans, New Mexico, Boston, and New York, American cooking was being elevated to "cuisine."

At first, these happenings were reported in excited trumpet blasts—it was so cool to see the small town of Food becoming Food Nation! But as the decade waned, food writing began to sound arch. The detachment was an understandable response to the 1980s ethos: although more and more people were turning gourmet, the conversion had less to do with sensual engagement than it had to do with status and the appearance of living like a sybarite.

The pursuit of lean body mass was, after all, second only to the pursuit of lucre in the early 1980s. Treadmills and Stair-Masters gobbled rare leisure hours, liquid diets were vogue, and both anorexia and bulimia were on the rise. Food writing became voyeuristic, providing windows into a world of unattainable bodies and unimaginable disposable income and time, an unreal world.

There is a fine line between soothing readers' anxiety and becoming the Victoria's Secret of the Fourth Estate.

This world was increasingly attractive to advertisers. *The New York Times* began publishing the first freestanding magazine supplement on food in 1979. The appearance of the advertising-driven insert signaled that food had become a comfortable atmosphere for advertisers such as automobile, liquor, and credit-card companies. Food, in other words was not just food, it was a life-style. And, as the decade progressed, the taste for living high on the food chain trickled into the middle class from the wealthier spheres and spread from both coasts into the nation's center. At the same time, dietary health concerns became more pronounced, everyday life became more frenetic— and fine homemade meals became the stuff of dreams.

Given the dissonance between food fantasies and everyday eating, the birth of food porn was all but unavoidable. Waxing sentimental may have been questionable art, but as a counterpoint to the technological changes that clicked through the culture over the past three decades, nostalgia served an important role. Likewise, first person singular was a reassuringly human voice; it was also a logical extension of the confessional mode that was popularized in the feminism of the 1970s.

Some social analysts believe that citizens of an increasingly violent world watch crime shows to feel safe. Reading food writing offers a similar sort of reassurance. People tell me that they read my cookbooks "like novels," to enter an alternate reality where cooking is slow and leisurely and imbued with a comforting glamour.

The upper middle class is willing to pay dearly for these feelings. By the mid-1990s, it was not uncommon for people to spend much of their disposable income on fancy food and wine, traveling to eat, and building kitchens large enough to accommodate crowds: cooking was becoming a spectator sport.

🐝

Adam Gopnik (1956–)

ONE OF AMERICA'S outstanding essayists, and a dependably brilliant writer for *The New Yorker*, Gopnik has produced hugely popular books on Paris, on raising children in New York City, and most recently a magisterial work on food, *The Table Comes First: Family, France, and the Meaning of Food*. A witty and highly quotable writer, Gopnik meditates in his latest volume on the preoccupation with food that has made gastronomy such a large part of modern life. As he says, our top chefs are "deities" and our favorite restaurants are "places of pilgrimage." Gopnik finds the community *of* the table more important than the dishes *on* that table. In our selection he shows how good cooking is never a matter of simply following recipes, but also always a function of intuition and experience. Mere imitation can never lead to mastery, Gopnik asserts, since you need to know about the very nature of cooking itself, not just lists and quantities of ingredients. His piece is a philosophy of kitchen practice, as much as the writing of his admired precursor Brillat-Savarin.

from What's the Recipe?: Our Hunger for Cookbooks

A MAN AND a woman lie in bed at night in the short hour between kid sleep and parent sleep, turning down page corners as they read. She is leafing through a fashion magazine, he through a cookbook. Why they read these things mystifies even the readers. The closet and the cupboard are both about as full as they're going to get, and though we can credit the fashion reader with at least wanting to know what is in fashion when she sees it, what can the recipe reader possibly be reading for? The shelf of cookbooks long ago overflowed, so that the sad relations and failed hopes (*Monet's Table, A Drizzle of Honey: The Lives and Recipes of Spain's Secret Jews*) now are stacked horizontally, high up. The things he knows how to make that are actually in demand are as fixed as any cocktail pianist's set list, and for a clientele of children every bit as conservative as the barflies around that piano: make Parmesan-crusted chicken—the "Feelings" of food—every night and they would be delighted. Yet the new cookbooks show up in bed, and the corners still go down.

Vicarious pleasure? More like deferred frustration. Anyone who cooks knows that it is in following recipes that one first learns the anticlimax of the actual, the perpetual disappointment of the thing achieved. I learned it as I learned to bake. When I was in my early teens, the sick yearning for sweets that adolescents suffer drove me, in afternoons taken off from school, to bake, which, miraculously, meant just doing what the books said and hoping to get what they promised to yield. I followed the recipes as closely as I could: dense Boston cream pie, Rigó Jancsi slices, *Sacher Torte* with apricot jam between the layers. The potential miracle of the cookbook was immediately apparent: you start with a feeling of greed, find a list of rules, assemble a bunch of ingredients, and then you have something to be greedy about. You begin with the ache and end with the object, where in most of the life of appetites—courtship, marriage—you start with the object and end with the ache.

Yet, if the first thing a cadet cook learns is that words can become tastes, the second is that a space exists between what the rules promise and what the cook gets. It is partly that the steps between—the melted chocolate's gleam, the chastened, improved look of the egg yolks mixed with sugar—are often more satisfying than the finished cake. But the trouble also lies in the same good words that got you going. How do you know when a thing "just begins to boil"? How can you be sure that the milk has scorched but not burned? Or touch something too hot to touch, or tell firm peaks from stiff peaks? How do you define "chopped"? At the same time as I was illicitly baking in the afternoons, I was learning non-recipe main-course cooking at night from my mother, a scientist by day, who had long been off-book, as they say in the theatre, and she would show, not tell: how you softened the onions, made them golden, browned them. This practice got you deeper than the words ever could.

Handed-down wisdom and worked-up information remain the double piers of a cook's life. The recipe book always contains two things: news of how something is made, and assurance that there's a way to make it, with the implicit belief that if I know how it is done I can show you how to do it. The premise of the recipe book is that these two things are naturally balanced; the secret of the recipe book is that they're not. The space between learning the facts about how something is done and learning how to do it always turns out to be large, at times immense. What kids make depends on what moms know: skills, implicit knowledge, inherited craft, buried assumptions, finger know-how that no recipe can sum up. The recipe is a blueprint but also a red herring, a way to do something and a false summing up of a living process that can be handed on only by experience, a knack posing as a knowledge. We say "What's the recipe?" when we mean "How do you do it?" And though we want the answer to be "Like this!" the honest answer is

"Be me!" "What's the recipe?" you ask the weary pro chef, and he gives you a weary-pro-chef look, since the recipe is the totality of the activity, the real work. The recipe is to spend your life cooking.

Yet the cookbooks keep coming, and we continue to turn down their pages: *The Asian Grandmothers Cookbook, The Adaptable Feast*, the ones with disingenuously plain names—*How to Roast a Lamb: New Greek Classic Cooking* (a good one, in fact)—and the ones with elaborately nostalgic premises, like *Dining on the B. & O.: Recipes and Sidelights from a Bygone Age*. Once-familiar things depart from their pages silently, like Minerva's owls. "Yield," for instance, a word that appeared at the top of every recipe in every cookbook that my mother owned—"Yield: six portions," or twelve, or twenty—is gone. Maybe it seemed too cold, too technical. In any case, the recipe no longer yields; it merely serves. "Makes six servings" or "Serves four to six as part of an appetizer" is all you get.

Other good things go. Clarified butter (melted butter with the milk solids skimmed and strained) has vanished—Graham Kerr, the Galloping Gourmet, once used it like holy water—while emulsified butter (melted butter with a little water whisked in), thanks to Thomas Keller's sponsorship, plays an ever-larger role. The cult of the cooking vessel—the wok, the tagine, the Dutch oven, the smoker, the hibachi, the Tibetan kiln or the Inuit ice oven or whatever—seems to be over. Paula Wolfert has a new book devoted to clay-pot cooking, but it feels too ambitious in advance; we have tried too many other modish pots, and know that, like Elvis's and Michael Jackson's chimps, after their hour is done they will live out their years forgotten and alone, on the floor of the closet, alongside the fondue forks and the spice grinder and the George Foreman grill. Even the imagery of cooking has changed. Sometime in the past decade or so, the actual eating line was breached. Now the cooking magazines and the cookbooks are filled with half-devoured dishes and cut-open vegetables. Michael Psilakis's fine Greek cookbook devotes an entire page to a downbeat still-life of torn-off artichoke leaves lying in a pile; the point is not to entice the eater but to ennoble the effort. . . .

The urge to meld identities with the pros is tied to a desire to get something out of a cookbook besides another recipe. For beneath those conscious enthusiasms and trends lies a new and deeper uncertainty in the relation between the recipe book and its reader. In this the Great Age of Disaggregation, all the old forms are being smashed apart and their contents spilled out like piñatas at a birthday party. The cookbook isn't spared. The Internet has broken what once seemed a natural tie, between the recipe and the cookbook, as it has broken the tie between the news story and the newspaper. You can find pretty much any recipe you want online now. If you need a recipe for mustard-shallot sauce or boeuf à la mode, you enter a few search terms, and there it is.

So the old question "What's the recipe for?" gives way to "What's the cookbook for?," which turns it, like everything else these days, toward the memoir, the confessional, the recipe as self-revelation. . . .

ANOTHER answer to the question "What good is the cookbook?" lies in what might be called the grammatical turn: the idea that what the cookbook should supply is the rules, the deep structure—a fixed, underlying grammar that enables you to *use* all the recipes you find. This grammatical turn is available in the popular "Best Recipe" series in *Cook's Illustrated,* and in the "Cook's Bible" of its editor, Christopher Kimball, in which recipes begin with a long disquisition on various approaches, ending with the best (and so brining was born); in Michael Ruhlman's *The Elements of Cooking,* with its allusion to Strunk & White's usage guide; and, most of all, in Mark Bittman's indispensable new classic *How to Cook Everything,* which, though claiming "minimalism" of style, is maximalist in purpose—not a collection of recipes for all occasions but a set of techniques for all time.

You see a progression if you compare the classics of the past century: Escoffier's culinary dictionary, Julia Child's *Mastering the Art of French Cooking,* Julee Rosso and Sheila Lukins's *The New Basics,* and Bittman's recently revised *Everything.* The standard kitchen bible, the book you turn to most often, has evolved from dictionary to encyclopedia, and to anthology and then grammar. Escoffier's book was pure dictionary: quick reminders to clarify a point or make a variation eloquent. Escoffier lists every recipe for tournedos and all its variations. His recipes are summaries, aide-mémoires for cooks who know how to make it already but need to be reminded what's in it. (Is a béarnaise sauce tarragon leaves and stems, or just leaves?) This was the way all cooks cooked once. (In the B. & O. cookbook, one finds this recipe for short ribs: "Put short ribs in a saucepan with one quart of nice stock, with one onion cut fine, steam until nice and tender. Place in roasting pan and put in oven until they are nice and brown." That's it. Everything else is commentary.)

In *Mastering the Art of French Cooking*, as in Waverly Root's *The Food of France*, which came out at around the same time, the turn is encyclopedic: here's all you can find on a particular kind of cooking, which you will master by reading this book. Things are explained, but, as in an encyclopedia, what is assumed is the need for more and deeper information about material already taken to be essential. You get a list not of everything there is but of everything that matters. Julia gives you only the tournedos recipes that count.

You didn't want to master the art of French cooking unless you believed that it was an art uniquely worth mastering. When people did master it, they realized that it wasn't—that no one style of cooking really was adequate to our appetites. So the cookbook as anthology arrived, open to many sources, from American Thanksgiving and Jewish brisket through Italian pasta and French Stroganoff—most successfully in *The New Basics* cookbook, which was the standard for the past generation. The anthology cookbooks assumed curiosity about styles and certainty about methods. In *The New Basics*, the tone is chatty, informal, taking for granted that the readers—women, mostly—know the old basics: what should be in the kitchen, what kinds of machines to use, how to handle a knife.

THE cookbooks of the grammatical turn assume that you don't know how to do the simple things, but that the simple things, mastered, will enable you to do it all. Bittman assumes that you have no idea how to chop an onion, or boil a potato, much less how chopping differs from slicing or from dicing. Each basic step is tenderly detailed. How to Boil Water: "Put water in a pot (usually to about two-thirds full), and turn the heat to high." How to Slice with a Knife: "You still press down, just with a little more precision, and cut into thick or thin slices of fairly uniform size." To sauté: "Put a large skillet on the stove and add the butter or oil. Turn the heat to medium-high. When the butter bubbles or the oil shimmers, add the food you want to sauté." Measuring dry ingredients, you are told to "scoop them up or use a spoon to put them in the cup." And, "Much of cooking is about heat."

This all feels masculine in tone—no pretty side drawings, a systematic progression from recipe to recipe—and seems written mainly for male readers who are either starting to cook for friends or just married and learning that if you don't cook she's not about to. The old *New Basics*, one recalls nostalgically, was exclamatory and feminine. "The celebration continues," reads the blurb, and inside the authors "indulge" and "savor" and "delight"; a warm chicken salad is "perfection when dressed in even more lemon," another chicken salad is "lush and abundant." The authors' perpetual "we" ("We like all our holidays accompanied with a bit of the bubbly"), though meant, in part, to suggest a merry partnership, was generous and inclusive, a "we" that honest-to-God extended to all of their readers.

Bittman never gushes but always gathers up: he has seven ways to vary a chicken kebab; eighteen ideas for pizza toppings; and, the best, an "infinite number of ways to customize" mashed potatoes. He is cautious, and even, post-Pollan, skeptical; while Rosso and Lukins "love" and "crave" their filet of beef, to all of animal flesh Bittman allows no more than "Meat is filling and requires little work to prepare. It's relatively inexpensive and an excellent source of many nutrients. And most people like it." *Most people like it!* Rosso and Lukins would have tossed out any recipe, much less an entire food group, of which no more than that could be said. Lamb is a thing they "fall in love with again every season of the year," and of pork they know that it is "divinely succulent." Bittman thinks that most people like it. His tone is that of Ed Harris in *Apollo 13*: Let's work the problem, people. Want to thicken a sauce? Well, try Plan A: cook it down. Copy that, Houston. Plan A inadequate? Try Plan B: add roux. And so on, ever upward, until you get to the old one, which they knew on the B. & O.: add a little cornstarch. The progressive pattern appeals to men. The implication, slightly illusory, is that there's a neat set of steps from each point to the next, as in a Bill Walsh pass pattern: each pattern on the tree proceeds logically and the quarterback just has to look a little farther upfield.

GRAMMARS teach foreign tongues, and the advantage of Bittman's approach is that it can teach you how to cook. But is learning how to cook from a grammar book—item by item, and by rote—really learning how to cook? Doesn't it miss the social context—the dialogue of generations, the commonality of the family recipe—that makes cooking something more than just assembling calories and nutrients? It's as if someone had written a book called *How to Play Catch*. ("Open your glove so that it faces the person throwing you the ball. As the ball arrives, squeeze the glove shut.") What it would tell you is not that we have figured out how to play catch but that we must now live in a culture without dads. In a world denuded of living examples, we end up with the guy who insists on making Malaysian Shrimp one night and Penne all' Amatriciana the next; it isn't about anything except having learned how it's done. Your grandmother's pound cake may have been like concrete, but it was about a whole history and view of life; it got that tough for a reason. . . .

However we take cookbooks—grammatically or encyclopedically, as storehouses of craft or illusions of knowledge—one can't read them in bed for many years without feeling that there is a conspiracy between readers and writers to obscure the ultimate point. A kind of primal scene of eating hovers over every cookbook, just as a primal scene of sex lurks behind every love story. In cooking, the primal scene, or substance, is salt, sugar, and fat held in maximum solution with starch; add protein as necessary, and finish with caffeine (coffee or chocolate) as desired. That's what, suitably disguised in some decent dimension of dressup, we always end up making. We make béarnaise sauce by whisking a stick of melted butter into a couple of eggs, and, now that we no longer make béarnaise sauce, we make salsa verde by beating a cup of olive oil into a fistful of anchovies. The herbs change; the hope does not. . . .

All appetites have their illusions, which are part of their pleasure. Going back to our own primal scene, that's why the husband turns those pages. The truth is that we don't passively look at the pictures and leap to the results; we actively read the lines and internally act out the jobs. The woman who reads the fashion magazines isn't passively imagining the act of having; she's actively imagining the act of shopping. (And distantly imagining the act of wearing.) She turns down pages not because she wants to look again but because, for that moment, she really intends to buy that—for a decisive imagined moment she did buy it, even if she knows she never will. Reading recipe books is an active practice, too, even if all the action takes place in your mind. We reanimate our passions by imagining the possibilities, and the act of wanting ends up mattering more than the fact of getting. It's not the false hope that it will turn out right that makes us go on with our reading but our being resigned to the knowledge that it won't ever, quite.

The desire to go on desiring, the wanting to want, is what makes you turn the pages—all the while aware that the next Boston cream pie, the sweet-salty-fatty-starchy thing you will turn out tomorrow, will be neither more nor less unsatisfying than last night's was. When you start to cook, as when you begin to live, you think that the point is to improve the technique until you end up with something perfect, and that the reason you haven't been able to break the cycle of desire and disillusion is that you haven't yet mastered the rules. Then you grow up, and you learn that that's the game.

PERMISSIONS

233 "Introduction" from *In Memory's Kitchen: A Legacy from the Women of Terezin* by Cara de Silva, reprinted by permission of Cara De Silva and Rowman & Littlefield Publishers, Inc.

242 "Capitalist Poem #5" by Campbell McGrath: from *Capitalism*, permission of the author.

243 "The Last Meal" by Michael Paterniti: from *Esquire*, permission of the author.

248 "Sea Urchin" by Chang-rae Lee: from *The New Yorker*, permission of the author.

251 From *Strange Stones* by Peter Hessler: "Wild Flavor" by Peter Hessler. First published as "A Rat in My Soup" in *The New Yorker*. Copyright © 2012 by Peter Hessler. Reprinted by permission of the author.

259 Excerpt from pp. 39–40 of *The Alice B. Toklas Cook Book* by Alice B. Toklas. Copyright 1954 by Alice B. Toklas. Copyright renewed 1982 by Edward M. Burns. Forward copyright © 1984 by M. F. K. Fisher. Publisher's note copyright © 1984 by Simon Michael Bessie. Reprinted by permission of HarperCollins Publishers.

263 From *The Civilizing Process* by Norbert Elias: Reprinted by permission of Wiley UK.

267 "Lines Written in the Fannie Farmer Cookbook" from *The Complete Poems 1927–1979* by Elizabeth Bishop. Copyright © 1979, 1983 by Alice Helen Methfessel. Reprinted by permission of Farrar, Straus and Giroux, LLC.

268 "Vegetables II" from *What Love Comes To: New and Selected Poems*. Copyright © 1975, 2008 by Ruth Stone. Reprinted with the permission of The Permissions Company, Inc., on behalf of Copper Canyon Press, www.coppercanyonpress.org.

269 "Killing to Eat" from *Rainbow Grocery* by William Dickey, reprinted by permission of William Dickey and *The Massachusetts Review*.

271 "Two Cook-Songs from the Planet Musaeus on the Same Subject, by Rival Poets" by Dorothy Gilbert, reprinted by permission of Dorothy Gilbert and *Tattoo Highway* journal.

273 "In Search of Filth: A Day in the Life of a Restaurant Health Inspector" by Roger Porter: permission of the author.

276 "How to Stuff a Pepper" from *Carpenter in The Sun* by Nancy Willard. Copyright © 1974 by Nancy Willard. Used by permission of the author in care of the Jean V. Naggar Literary Agency, Inc. (permissions @jvnla.com).

278 "Cuisine Mecanique" by John Thorne © 1992 from *Outlaw Cook* by John